Lecture Notes in Computer Science   9163

Commenced Publication in 1973
Founding and Former Series Editors:
Gerhard Goos, Juris Hartmanis, and Jan van Leeuwen

Editorial Board

More information about this series at http://www.springer.com/series/7407

Lazaros Nalpantidis · Volker Krüger
Jan-Olof Eklundh · Antonios Gasteratos (Eds.)

Computer
Vision Systems

10th International Conference, ICVS 2015
Copenhagen, Denmark, July 6–9, 2015
Proceedings

 Springer

Editors
Lazaros Nalpantidis
Aalborg University
Copenhagen
Denmark

Volker Krüger
Aalborg University
Copenhagen
Denmark

Jan-Olof Eklundh
Royal Institute of Technology - KTH
Stockholm
Sweden

Antonios Gasteratos
Democritus University of Thrace
Xanthi
Greece

ISSN 0302-9743   ISSN 1611-3349   (electronic)
Lecture Notes in Computer Science
ISBN 978-3-319-20903-6   ISBN 978-3-319-20904-3   (eBook)
DOI 10.1007/978-3-319-20904-3

Library of Congress Control Number: 2015942620

LNCS Sublibrary: SL1 – Theoretical Computer Science and General Issues

Springer Cham Heidelberg New York Dordrecht London

Springer International Publishing AG Switzerland is part of Springer Science+Business Media
(www.springer.com)

Preface

Vision is arguably the most important modality for humans to perceive their environment. Naturally, seeing machines have been the dream and goal of generations of scientists and engineers dealing with computer vision. While developments in algorithms and models have been enormous during the last decades, the computer vision community cannot but agree that implementing and deploying vision systems in real environments and applications is always a challenging task. This fact was the motivation behind the conception of the International Conference on Computer Vision Systems (ICVS), as well as the driving force that brought it from its debut at Las Palmas in 1999 to its 10th repetition at Copenhagen in 2015.

ICVS 2015 received 92 submissions, out of which 48 were selected after a double-blind review process. Each paper was reviewed by at least three members of the Program Committee and the authors of accepted submissions were asked to submit their final versions taking into consideration the comments and suggestions of the reviewers. The best paper of the conference was selected by the general and program chairs, after suggestions from the Program Committee. The accepted papers cover a broad spectrum of issues arising in the design and deployment of comprehensive computer vision systems. Among them, the two most represented topics were robot vision and vision systems applications, revealing the interest of the community in deploying vision systems in real conditions.

The pace of the technical program of ICVS 2015 was set by four invited speakers. First, Prof. John K. Tsotsos (York University, Canada) described how computer vision can be motivated by human vision. The second invited speaker, Prof. Henrik I. Christensen (Georgia Institute of Technology, USA), covered state-of-the-art model-based 2D and 3D tracking systems. The talk of Prof. Danica Kragic (Royal Institute of Technology - KTH, Sweden) was about machines that see, act, and interact with their environments. Finally, Dr. Achintya Bhowmik (Intel Corp., USA) talked about the approach of his perceptual computing group to bridging the real and virtual worlds with natural sensing and interactions.

Two tutorials were selected and organized in conjunction with the main conference. Both of them combined talks and active involvement of the audience. The "Tutorial on Commercial Industrial Vision Systems" was organized by Dr. Michael Nielsen, Thomas Sølund, and Carsten Panck Isaksen, while the second tutorial, "An Open-Source Recipe for Teaching/Learning Robotics with a Simulator," was organized by Dr. Renaud Detry and Prof. Peter Corke.

We wish to thank our platinum sponsors, Intel, NVIDIA, and the Obel Family Foundation, our Sponsor, the Danish Technological Institute (DTI), as well as our Supporters, the Department of Mechanical and Manufacturing Engineering of Aalborg University, and Wonderful Copenhagen. Finally, we feel the need to thank the people who made ICVS 2015 happen, our Workshop and Tutorial Chairs Dr. Dima Damen and Dr. Renaud Detry, our Publication Chair Dr. Dimitris Chrysostomou, our Local Chair Dr. Mikkel Rath Pedersen, the 79 members of our Program Committee, as well as all the authors who submitted their work to ICVS 2015.

May 2015

Lazaros Nalpantidis
Volker Krüger
Jan-Olof Eklundh
Antonios Gasteratos

Organization

Conference General Chairs

Lazaros Nalpantidis   Aalborg University, Denmark
Volker Krüger   Aalborg University, Denmark

Program Co-chairs

Jan-Olof Eklundh   Royal Institute of Technology - KTH, Sweden
Antonios Gasteratos   Democritus University of Thrace, Greece

Workshop and Tutorial Chairs

Dima Damen   University of Bristol, UK
Renaud Detry   University of Liege, Belgium

Publication Chair

Dimitris Chrysostomou   Aalborg University, Denmark

Program Committee

Balasundram Amavasai	Procter & Gamble, UK
Michael Arens	Fraunhofer IOSB, Germany
Antonios Argyros	University of Crete, Greece
Kalle Åström	Lund University, Sweden
Stephane Bazeille	Istituto Italiano di Tecnologia, Italy
Sven Behnke	University of Bonn, Germany
Yasemin Bekiroglu	Royal Institute of Technology - KTH, Sweden
Vasileios Belagiannis	Technical University Munich, Germany
Anna Belardinelli	University of Tübingen, Germany
Alexandre Bernardino	Instituto Superior Tecnico, Portugal
Mårten Björkman	Royal Institute of Technology, Sweden
Aaron Bobick	Georgia Institute of Technology, USA
Jeannette Bohg	Max Planck Institute for Intelligent Systems, Germany
Francois Bremond	Inria Sophia Antipolis, France
Andrea Carbone	Lutin Userlab, France
Henrik Christensen	Georgia Institute of Technology, USA
Regis Clouard	GREYC Laboratory, France
Peter Corke	Queensland University of Technology, Australia
James Crowley	Inria Grenoble Rhone-Alpes, France

Georgios Ch. Sirakoulis	Democritus University of Thrace, Greece
Calliope-Louisa Sotiropoulou	University of Pisa, Italy
Joerg Stueckler	Technical University of Munich, Germany
Anastasios Tefas	Aristotle University of Thessaloniki, Greece
Panos Trahanias	University of Crete, Greece
Georgios Triantafyllidis	Aalborg University, Denmark
Efstratios Tsougenis	Hong Kong University of Science and Technology, Hong Kong, SAR China
Marc Van Droogenbroeck	University of Liege, Belgium
Sergio Velastin	Kingston University, UK
David Vernon	University of Skövde, Sweden
Markus Vincze	Vienna University of Technology, Austria
Sebastian Wrede	Bielefeld University, Germany
Zhaozheng Yin	Missouri University, USA
Hongbin Zha	Peking University, China
Michael Zillich	Vienna University of Technology, Austria

Local Chair

| Mikkel Rath Pedersen | Aalborg University, Denmark |

Sponsors

Intel Corp.
Nvidia Corp.
Obel Family Foundation
Danish Technological Institute
Department of Mechanical & Manufacturing Engineering, Aalborg University
Wonderful Copenhagen

Contents

High-Level Vision

Learning and Adaptation

Vision Systems Applications

Biological and Cognitive Vision

Comparison of Statistical Features for Medical Colour Image Classification

Cecilia Di Ruberto, Giuseppe Fodde, and Lorenzo Putzu[✉]

Department of Mathematics and Computer Science, University of Cagliari,
via Ospedale 72, 09124 Cagliari, Italy
{dirubert,giufodde,lorenzo.putzu}@unica.it

Abstract. Analysis of cells and tissues allow the evaluation and diagnosis of a vast number of diseases. Nowadays this analysis is still performed manually, involving numerous drawbacks, in particular the results accuracy heavily depends on the operator skills. Differently, the automated analysis by computer is performed quickly, requires only one image of the sample and provides precise results. In this work we investigate different texture descriptors extracted from colour medical images. We compare and combine these features in order to identify the features set able to properly classify medical images presenting different classification problems. The tested feature sets are based on a generalization of some existent grey scale approaches for feature extraction to colour images. The generalization has been applied to the calculation of Grey-Level Co-Occurrence Matrix, Grey-Level Difference Matrix and Grey-Level Run-Length Matrix. Furthermore, we calculate Grey-Level Run-Length Matrix starting from the Grey-Level Difference Matrix. The resulting feature sets performances have been compared using the Support Vector Machine model. To validate our method we have used three different databases, HistologyDS, Pap-smear and Lymphoma, that present different medical problems and so they represent different classification problems. The obtained experimental results have showed that the features extracted from the generalized Grey-Level Co-Occurrence Matrix perform better than the other set of features, demonstrating also that a combination of features selected from all the feature subsets leads always to better performances.

Keywords: Medical image analysis · Features extraction · Feature selection · Colour texture classification

1 Introduction

Tissue image analysis is a process that allows through various computer assisted methods to evaluate if tissue samples are affected by diseases. Image analysis involves complex algorithms which identify and characterize cellular colour, shape and quantity of the tissue sample using image pattern recognition technology. Tissue image analysis could be used to measure the cancer cells in a biopsy

© Springer International Publishing Switzerland 2015
L. Nalpantidis et al. (Eds.): ICVS 2015, LNCS 9163, pp. 3–13, 2015.
DOI: 10.1007/978-3-319-20904-3_1

of a cancerous tumour taken from a patient and it can significantly reduce uncertainty in characterizing tumours compared to evaluations done by histologists, or improve the prediction rate of recurrence of some cancers. For example, in [1] global features are used to automatically discriminate lymphoma, in [2] image texture informations are used to automatically discriminate polyps in colonscopy images and in [3] wavelet features are used for the detection of tumours in endoscopic images. Although there isn't a specific definition of texture accepted by all, it can be viewed as a global descriptors generated from the repetition of local patterns. Texture is an any and repetitive geometric arrangement of the grey levels of an image. It provides important information about the spatial disposition of the grey levels and the relationship with their neighbourhood. Human visual system determines and recognizes easily different types of textures but although for a human observer it is very simple to associate a surface with a texture, to give a rigorous definition for this is very complex. Typically it is used a qualitative definition to describe textures. It can easily guess that the quantitative analysis of texture passes through statistical and structural relations among the basic elements of what we call just texture. The most important aspect of texture analysis is classification that concerns the search for particular texture among different predefined classes of texture. Classification is carried out using statistical methods that define the descriptors of the texture. Many different methods for managing texture have been developed that are based on the various ways texture can be characterized. Although there are many powerful methods reported in the literature for texture analysis, including the scale-invariant feature transform (SIFT) [4], speeded up robust feature (SURF)[5], histogram of oriented gradients (HOG) [6], local binary patterns (LBP) [7], Gabor filters [8] and others, in this work we focus on improving some of the earliest methods used for the analysis of grey level texture based on statistical approaches, that are: Grey-Level Co-Occurrence Matrix (GLCM), Grey-Level Difference Matrix (GLDM), Grey-Level Run-Length Matrix (GLRLM). Motivated by the wide diffusion of these methods and by the increasing numbers of medical datasets presenting colour images we wished to investigate the possibility to improve the accuracy of these methods using the colour information. Some interesting methods have been presented in order to extend the original implementation of GLCM. In [9] the authors evaluate different values for the distance parameter that influence the matrices computation, in [10] the GLCM descriptors are extracted by calculating the weighted sum of GLCM elements, in [11] the GLCM features are calculated by using the local gradient of the matrix. In [12] to calculate the features, the grey levels and the edge orientation of the image are considered. In [13] the authors propose to use a variable window size by multiple scales to extract descriptors by GLCM. The method in [14] uses the colour gradient to extract from GLCM a statistical features. In [15] various types of GLCM descriptors (classical Haralick features and features from 3D co-occurrence matrix) and grey-level run-length features are extracted. Although the colour information to extract GLCM has already been used by other authors such as [16], one of the goals of this work is to evaluate the performance improvement that can arise from the computation of co-occurrence matrix using the colour information. Another goal of this work is the use of the colour information also for the computation of difference matrix and run-length matrix, assessing their performance improvement for the classification task. The classification accuracy of each feature subsets have been compared using the Support Vector Machine (SVM), that we consider as the best classification model for biomedical application, as showed in [17]. To validate our method we have used three different databases, HistologyDS [18], Pap-smear [19] and Lymphoma [1], that present different medical problems and so they represent different classification problems. So, our main goal is to find a feature set or a combination of features able to properly classify medical images presenting different classification problem. In [20] an exhaustive comparison of colour texture features and classification methods for medical image has been made, but the authors validated their method using only one database dealing with only one medical problem, that consists on discrimination of cells categories in histological images of fish ovary. The rest of the paper is organized as follows. In Sect. 2 we report some background information necessary to introduce the existing methods used. Section 3 shows the approach proposed for the inclusion of colour information to the existent methods. Section 4 present the experimentations realised to asses the classification performances. Finally, in Sect. 5 we present our conclusions and some possible future works.

2   Background

A feature is defined as a function of one or more measurements, specifying some quantifiable property of an object. Features are classified into general features, that are application independent such as colour, texture and shape, and domain-specific features that are application dependent. Moreover, all features can be coarsely classified into low-level features and high-level features. Low-level features can be extracted directly from the original images, whereas high-level feature extraction must be based on low-level features. There are various methods for features extraction and texture classification and the most important are based on statistical approach. In our work we use a statistical approach, evaluating features extracted from: co-occurrence matrix, difference matrices and run-length matrix. The most powerful model for texture analysis was proposed by Haralick [21]. His method involves the creation of the GLCMs from which features that represent some image aspects, can be calculated. A GLCM represents the probability of finding two pixels i and j with distance d and orientation θ and it is denoted with $p_{d,\theta}$. Obviously, the d and θ values can assume different values, but the most used are $d = 1$ and $\theta = [0, 45, 90, 135]$. A GLCM for an image of size N x M with Ng grey levels is a 2D array of size Ng x Ng. Haralick proposed thirteen descriptors that can be extracted from these matrices: *Angular Second Moment, Contrast, Correlation, Variance, Inverse Difference Moment, Sum Average, Sum Variance, Sum Entropy, Entropy, Difference Variance, Difference Entropy, Measure of correlation 1 and 2.* Another useful tool for texture analysis is the Grey Level Difference Matrix (GLDM) [22], that is a particular type of matrix originated by the absolute differences between pairs of grey levels. Actually, the GLDM is defined in a manner very similar to the GLCM, using the same notions of distance and orientation to find the pairs of grey levels. The main difference arises in the construction and dimension of the matrix. In fact the GLDM preserves the size of the original image N x M (and not Ng x Ng), collecting the absolute difference between pairs of pixel values (and not the occurrences of two grey levels). This matrix is used to calculate the histogram $h(d)$ that denotes the number of differences with value d. The histogram is then normalized $h_N(d) = h(d)/N$ with $N = \sum_d h(d)$ in order to compute easily nine descriptors: *Mean, Angular Second Moment, Contrast, Variance, Inverse Difference Moment, Entropy, Product Moment, Cluster Shade* and *Cluster Prominence*. A different tool for texture analysis is based on information of higher order statistics that uses the grey level run-length matrices (GLRLMs) [23]. In this approach the GLRLM contains information on a particular number of equal grey levels (run) in a given direction. So, a run-length matrix is defined as a set of consecutive pixels having the same grey level. The element (i, j) of a run-length matrix specifies the number of times that the image contains a run of length j composed by all pixels with grey level i. The creation of the run-length matrices is very simple and the number of operations to be done is directly proportional to the number of image points. A coarse texture will be characterized by a long run while a finer texture will be characterized by shorter run. Also, the GLRLMs are calculated by considering the main four orientations and for each matrix eleven descriptors can be extracted: *Short Run Emphasis, Long Run Emphasis, Grey Level Non-uniformity, Run Length Non-uniformity, Run Percentage, Low Grey Level Run Emphasis, High Grey Level Run Emphasis, Short Run Low Grey Level Emphasis, Short Run High Grey Level Emphasis, Long Run Low Grey Level Emphasis, Long Run High Grey Level Emphasis.*

3   System Design

In order to extend the classical grey level texture features to colour texture features we start by decomposing the colour image into the three bands RGB (Red, Green and Blue), obtaining three different images, R, G and B. The most intuitive way to take into account colour information for the computation of texture feature is to use the classical implementation and pass to them every time a different colour band. This approach could be very useful thanks to an higher number of significant descriptors extracted and passed to the classifier. An improvement to this approach belongs to the combination of the colour bands in pairs (RG, RB and GB) by using them as input parameters for the matrices computation (see Fig. 1). Combining the bands in pairs means that the occurrences and differences are calculated between two different images and not in the same image. For example, computing a GLCM with two bands M_1 and M_2 means that we calculate the $GLCM(M_1, M_2)$ by storing on each (i, j) the number of occurrences of $i \epsilon M_1$ and $j \epsilon M_2$ having distance=d and orientation=θ. This improvement is necessary in order to take into account not only repeated pattern inside the same colour band, but also the correlation between the colour bands. This should improve not only the accuracy but also the robustness for the classification task. So, we compute from the six matrices (considering the three classical matrices and the three new matrices) the occurrences with $d = 1$ and $\theta = [0, 45, 90, 135]$ for a total of 24 GLCMs and a total number of 312 features. In the same way we compute the 24 GLDMs and a total number of 216 features. Obviously, the GLRLMs can be computed by using the three classical bands only, but in order to consider also repetitive pattern belonging to different colour bands we have decided to extract also run-lengths starting from the difference matrix. This brings to 36 GLRMs considering the three colour

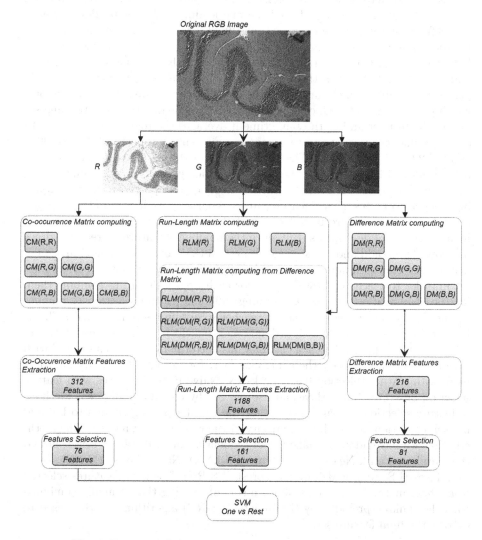

Fig. 1. Diagram of the system for colour medical image analysis.

bands that we have used to compute run-lengths in the four main directions (12 GLRMs) and the 24 GLDMS already computed, that we have used to compute run-length in the four main directions (96 GLRLMs). From all these matrices we have extracted their respective features, for a total of 1188 descriptors (see Fig. 1). Each feature subset extracted has been used to train a Support Vector Machine (SVM), that we consider as the best classification model for biomedical application, as we showed in [17], where different classification model performances have been compared in classification of white blood cells affected by leukaemia. The SVM classifier is trained using the *one VS rest* approach because it is the fastest to create our classification model. During our experimentations we have tested various kernels and parameters and after a process of cross-validation we have selected the one leading to better results. For each kernel function the parameters have been tuned through optimization techniques in order to find the maximum accuracy value. The selected kernel function is the RBF that uses a Gaussian radial basis function, with c parameter equal to $1e3$ and γ equal to $1e2$. Given the variable size of the datasets we have decided to perform the validation of our method using a 5 time repeated stratified holdout, which guarantees that each class is properly represented both in the training set and in the test set and at the same time it averages the roles of each subset. In our experiments training and test sets are represented respectively by the 80 % and the 20 % of the samples. The performances of the classification models have been evaluated by calculating the accuracy, which gives us a good indication of the performance since it considers each class of equal importance. After comparing the performances of each feature subset separately we have decided to create a combination of feature in order to test if the classifier could benefit from a higher number of descriptors. But since the number of features is really high we have decided to add another step to our system that consists of a combination of feature selection techniques. This step is applied separately to each feature subset in order to trace the best features for each approach and to combine them for the classification process. Combining different feature selection techniques means that we have used various approaches to obtain a stronger result. This is because in general all the classification models benefit from the process of feature selection, but in particular each classifier has better performance associated with feature selection based on the same classifier, for example the k-NN improves more with feature selection based on k-NN, Naive Bayes improves with feature selection based on Naive Bayes and so on. So, by combining different methods of feature selection we can be sure that the result is strong enough to be used in each condition and with the majority of the classification models. The methods that we have adopted make use of sequential forward feature selection and they are based on k-Nearest Neighbour (FS-kNN), Naive Bayes (FS-NB), Decision Trees (FS-tree), and Random Forest (FS-RF). Using the features selected from these methods we can establish a sort of ranking that is finally combined with the ranking provided by the ReliefF (FS-Rel) algorithm and then used to extract the final feature set.

4   Experimental Evaluation

The experimentation has been carried out on three of the most famous colour medical image databases, HistologyDS, Pap-smear and Lymphoma, that represent three very different computer vision problems.

HystologyDS (HIS) database [18] is a collection of 20,000 images of histology for the study of fundamental tissues. It is provided in a subset of 2828 images annotated by four fundamental tissues: connective, epithelial, muscular and nervous. Each tissue is captured in a 24-bit RGB image of size 720×480. Some tissue images from HIS database are showed in Fig. 2. The database is available at the following link: http://168.176.61.90/histologyDS/

Pap-smear (PAP) database [19] is a collection of pap-smear images acquired from healthy and cancerous smears coming from the Herlev University Hospital (Denmark). This database is composed by 917 images containing cells, annotated into seven classes, four representing abnormal cells and three representing normal cases. Nevertheless, from the medical diagnosis viewpoint the most important requirement corresponds to the general two-class problem of correct separation between normal from abnormal cells. For this reason in our experiments we have tested only the binary case. Each cell is captured in a 24-bit RGB image without a fixed size that ranges from about 50×50 to about 300×300. Some examples are showed in Fig. 3. The database is available at the following link: http://labs. fme.aegean.gr/decision/downloads

Lymphoma (LYM) database [1] is a collection of tissues affected by the three most common types of lymphoma, chronic lymphocytic leukaemia, follicular lymphoma and mantle cell lymphoma. This slide collection contains significant variation in sectioning and staining and for this reason it is more representative of slides

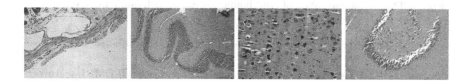

Fig. 2. Four different tissues from HistologyDS database.

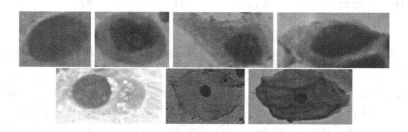

Fig. 3. The seven classes of cells belonging to Pap-smear database: first four abnormal and last three normal.

commonly encountered in a clinical setting. This database contains a collection of 374 slides captured in a 24-bit RGB image of size 1380 × 1040. Some examples are showed in Fig. 4. The database is available at the following link: http://ome. grc.nia.nih.gov/iicbu2008/

As said previously, our aim was to compare all the feature subsets extracted with our approach. So, we have tested the original features subsets separately on each database to asses its classification performance applied on different medical problems. The results are reported in Table 1. As it can be seen the best results have been obtained using the generalised co-occurrence matrix. Even if the performances can be considered good, we decided to create a combination of feature, in order to test if the classifier could benefit from a higher number of descriptors. Then, we have created and tested a bigger feature set combining all the feature subsets extracted (Table 2). But since the number of features is really high, in order to avoid overfitting problems caused by a too complex model, we have used the feature selection step described previously. In order to show the improvements obtained with our feature selection step in Table 2 we present the accuracy values obtained without feature selection (No FS column), with different feature selection technique used separately (from FS-kNN to FS-Rel column) and finally with our feature selection step (Our FS).

Fig. 4. Three different kinds of lymphoma belonging to Lymphoma database.

Table 1. Accuracy values using different feature subsets.

Database	GLCM features	GLDM features	GLRL features	GLDMRL features
HIS	89.65	81.43	76.18	86.67
PAP	93.61	85.36	83.93	89.95
LYM	92.77	79.13	71.87	87.07

Table 2. Accuracy values after feature selection for the single features subsets and for all datasets.

Database	No FS	FS-kNN	FS-NB	FS-tree	FS-RF	FS-Rel	Our FS	Previous Best
HIS	91.17	88.59	89.56	91.27	93.89	89.40	**96**	92.4 [15]
PAP	93.99	90.71	89.29	91.15	94.43	93.99	**96.49**	92.5 [15]
LYM	94.2	80.43	88.62	90	92.23	78.62	**96.8**	85 [1]

It is interesting to see that using some of the feature selection techniques there isn't any improvement, rather the performances are worst than using the whole feature set. On the contrary the performances benefits considerably from our feature selection step. In Table 3 we report a comparison between our results and others present in literature. In particular in [15] the results have been obtained by computing co-occurrence matrices using a multi-scale approach, than the features are extracted with a sub-window approach on the original co-occurrence matrix. In [25] a framework based on the novel and robust Collateral Representative Subspace Projection Modelling has been used. The cell image is first divided into 25 blocks classifying each block separately and then applying a fusion algorithm with a weighted majority voting strategy to decide the final class label of the whole image. In [26] the authors used an unsupervised feature learning framework based on local patches represented by a bag-of-features or a convolutional neural network. In [27] the authors realised an ensemble of features composed of six different local descriptors, including LBP and Rotation invariant LBP, combining them using the Edge approach and the Bag of Features. As it can be seen the proposed approach outperform the results proposed in literature for all the tested databases. In particular we would like to highlight that only few authors have analysed more than one database and that none used all the three databases which contain different histological images. As a consequence it's really difficult to identify an approach able to achieve good classification performances for different medical problems.

Table 3. Comparison of our results with the state of the art.

Database	Nanni [15]	Meng [25]	Arevalo [26]	dos Santos [27]	Our approach
HIS	92.4	-	94.1	92.4	**96**
PAP	92.5	-	-	91.4	**96.49**
LYM	-	92.5	-	-	**96.8**

5   Conclusion

In this work we have proposed a successful combination of statistical texture features in order to classify colour medical images. The feature set has been obtained by generalizing the existent grey scale approaches to colour images, by decomposing the original RGB image in separated bands and then recombining the bands in pairs. This approach has permitted to extract more meaningful descriptors useful for colour texture classification. The resulting feature subset performances has been compared using a Support Vector Machine model. The classification results obtained by testing each feature subset separately on three different databases, HistologyDS, Pap-smear and Lymphoma, have showed that the co-occurrence matrix features extracted using the colour information are the best in recognizing different types of tissues and classify diseases, but also that a combination of features selected from all the feature subsets extracted leads always to better performances. The next step for this work will include the analysis of other colour spaces, in order to investigate which colour space is the most useful for disease discrimination and tissue recognition for different type of medical problems. At the same time we could compare our approach with the recent extensions of LBP descriptors to colour images [24]. Another issue consists in a further reduction of the feature set, by using also PCA and LDA, in order to decrease the training time and being able to apply our approach on bigger databases with other significant medical problems, including the possibility to study different stages of pathology, if present. Further research will be devoted to improve robustness and accuracy of the method in rotation invariant classification task, which is an important issue especially for medical images that can occur in different and uncontrolled rotation angles.

Acknowledgments. This work has been funded by Regione Autonoma della Sardegna (R.A.S.) Project CRP-17615 DENIS: Dataspace Enhancing Next Internet in Sardinia. Lorenzo Putzu gratefully acknowledges Sardinia Regional Government for the financial support of his PhD scholarship (P.O.R. Sardegna F.S.E. Operational Programme of the Autonomous Region of Sardinia, European Social Fund 2007–2013 - Axis IV Human Resources, Objective l.3, Line of Activity l.3.1.).

References

1. Shamir, L., Orlov, N., Eckley, D.M., Macura, T., Goldberg, I.G.: A proposed benchmark suite for biological image analysis. Med. Biol. Eng. Comput. **46**(9), 943–947 (2008)
2. Ameling, S., Wirth, S., Paulus, D., Lacey, G., Vilarino, F.: Texture-based polyp detection in colonoscopy. Bildverarbeitung fr die Medizin, pp. 346–350 (2009)
3. Karkanis, S.A., Iakovidis, D.K., Maroulis, D.E., Karras, D.A., Tzivras, M.: Computer-aided tumor detection in endoscopic video using color wavelet features. IEEE Trans. Inf. Technol. BioMed. **7**(3), 141–152 (2003)
4. Lowe, D.G.: Distinctive image features from scale-invariant keypoints. Int. J. Comput. Vision **60**(2), 91–110 (2004)
5. Bay, H., Tuytelaars, T., Van Gool, L.: SURF:Speeded up robust features. In: Leonardis, A., Bischof, H., Pinz, A. (eds.) ECCV 2006, Part I. LNCS, vol. 3951, pp. 404–417. Springer, Heidelberg (2006)
6. Dalal, N., Triggs, B.: Histograms of oriented gradients for human detection. In: IEEE Computer Society Conference on Conference on Computer Vision and Pattern Recognition (CVPR), vol.1, pp. 886–893 (2005)
7. Ojala, T., Pietikinen, M., Harwood, D.: A comparative study of texture measures with classification based on featured distributions. Pattern Recogn. **29**(1), 51–59 (1996)
8. Jain, A.K., Farrokhnia, F.: Unsupervised texture segmentation using Gabor filters. In: IEEE International Conference on Systems, Man and Cybernetics, pp. 14–19 (1990)
9. Gelzinis, A., Verikas, A., Bacauskiene, M.: Increasing the discrimination power of the co-occurrence matrix-based features. Pattern Recogn. **40**(9), 2367–2372 (2007)

10. Walker, R., Jackway, P., Longstaff, D.: Genetic algorithm optimization of adaptive multi-scale GLCM features. Int. J. Pattern Recogn. Artificial Intell. **17**(1), 17–39 (2003)
11. Chen, S., Chengdong, W., Chen, D., Tan, W.: Scene classification based on gray level-gradient co-occurrence matrix in the neighborhood of interest points. In: IEEE International Conference on Intelligent Computing and Intelligent Systems (ICIS), pp. 482–485 (2009)
12. Mitrea, D., Mitrea, P., Nedevschi, S., Badea, R., Lupsor, M.: Abdominal tumor characterization and recognition using superior-order cooccurrence matrices, based on ultrasound images. Comput. Math. Methods Med. **2012**, 1–7 (2012)
13. Hu, Y.: Unsupervised texture classification by combining multi-scale features and k-means classifier. In: Chinese Conference on Pattern Recognition, pp. 1–5 (2009)
14. Gong, R., Wang, H.: Steganalysis for GIF images based on colors-gradient co-occurrence matrix. Optics Commun. **285**(24), 4961–4965 (2012)
15. Nanni, L., Brahnam, S., Ghidoni, S., Menegatti, E., Barrier, T.: Different Approaches for Extracting Information from the Co-Occurrence Matrix. PLoS One **8**(12) (2013)
16. Benco, M., Hudec, R.: Novel method for color textures features extraction based on GLCM. Radio Eng. **4**(16), 64–67 (2007)
17. Putzu, L., Di Ruberto, C.: Investigation of different classification models to determine the presence of leukemia in peripheral blood image. In: Petrosino, A. (ed.) ICIAP 2013, Part I. LNCS, vol. 8156, pp. 612–621. Springer, Heidelberg (2013)
18. Cruz-Roa, A., Caicedo, J.C.: Visual pattern mining in histology image collections using bag of features. Artificial Intell. Med. **52**(2), 91–106 (2011)
19. Jantzen, J., Dounias, G.: Analysis of Pap-Smear Data. NISIS, 2006: Puerto de la Cruz. Tenerife, Spain (2006)
20. GonzlezRufino, E., Carrin, P., Cernadas, E., FernndezDelgado, M., DomnguezPetit, R.: Exhaustive comparison of colour texture features and classification methods to discriminate cells categories in histological images of fish ovary. Pattern Recogn. **46**(9), 2391–2407 (2013)
21. Haralick, R.M., Shanmugam, K., Dinstein, I.: Textural features for image classification. IEEE Trans. Syst. Man Cybern. **3**(6), 610–621 (1973)
22. Conners, R.W., Harlow, C.A.: A theoretical comparison of texture algorithms. IEEE Trans. Pattern Anal. Mach. Intell. (PAMI) **3**, 204–222 (1980)
23. Tang, X.: Texture information in run-length matrices. IEEE Trans. Image Proces. **7**(11), 1602–1609 (1998)
24. Porebski, A., Vandenbroucke, N., Hamad, D.: LBP histogram selection for supervised color texture classification. In: IEEE International Conference on Image Processing (ICIP), pp. 3239–3243 (2013)
25. Meng, T., Lin, L., Shyu, M., Chen, S.: Histology Image Classification Using Supervised Classification and Multimodal Fusion. In: IEEE International Symposium on Multimedia, pp. 145–152 (2010)
26. Arevalo, J., CruzRoa, A., Arias, V., Romero, E., Gonzlez, F.A.: An unsupervised feature learning framework for basal cell carcinoma image analysis. Artificial Intell. Med. (2015). doi:10.1016/j.artmed.2015.04.004
27. dos Santos, F.L.C., Paci, M., Nanni, L., Brahnam, S., Hyttinen, J.: Computer vision for virus image classification. Biosyst. Eng. (2015). doi:10.1016/j.biosystemseng.2015.01.005

Improving FREAK Descriptor
for Image Classification

Cristina Hilario Gomez[1]([✉]), Kartheek Medathati[2], Pierre Kornprobst[2],
Vittorio Murino[1,3], and Diego Sona[1]

[1] Department of Pattern Analysis and Computer Vision, (PAVIS),
Istituto Italiano di Tecnologia, Genova, Italy
{cristina.hilario,vittorio.murino,diego.sona}@iit.it
[2] Neuromathcomp Project Team, INRIA, Sophia Antipolis, France
{kartheek.medathati,pierre.kornprobst}@inria.fr
[3] Department of Computer Science,
University of Verona, Verona, Italy

Abstract. In this paper we propose a new set of bio-inspired descriptors for image classification based on low-level processing performed by the retina. Taking as a starting point a descriptor called FREAK (Fast Retina Keypoint), we further extend it mimicking the center-surround organization of ganglion receptive fields. To test our approach we compared the performance of the original FREAK and our proposal on the 15 scene categories database. The results show that our approach outperforms the original FREAK for the scene classification task.

Keywords: Bio-inspired descriptor · Binary descriptor · Center-surround ganglion cell organization · FREAK · Scene classification

1 Introduction

Image classification is a challenging task in computer vision which can be accomplished with a number of different approaches. In particular, scene categorization strongly relies on the appropiate image representation. In the literature, the vast majority of the works use descriptors based on visual information and the recognition of the scenes is achieved either based on the global information or the objects in the image [4,6–8]. For example, SIFT [4] and GIST [8] are two of the most used descriptors for scene categorization. Although SIFT was originally proposed for object recognition, it can be used to describe the global features in an image using a bag-of-words (BOW) approach. Under this approach, descriptors are quantized to form a visual codebook. In [4], the authors incorporated spatial information to further improve the BOW model based on SIFT descriptors.

On the other hand, GIST was proposed in [8] as a descriptor based on how humans recognize a scene. Using global information about the scene can significantly improve the classification results. This descriptor, is based on the spatial envelope that represents the most relevant global structure of a scene [7].

L. Nalpantidis et al. (Eds.): ICVS 2015, LNCS 9163, pp. 14–23, 2015.
DOI: 10.1007/978-3-319-20904-3_2

Recently, it has been shown that better performance is achieved when both local and global structures in an image are considered [9,17]. In this regard, Census Transform Histogram (CENTRIST) descriptor has been proposed [17], which is based on local binary patterns (LBP) and captures both kind of information.

An alternative approach is to perform image classification inspired by the human visual system. FREAK (Fast Retina Keypoint) was proposed as a fast keypoint descriptor inspired by the retina [1]. The organization of the retina is imitated, using a circular grid where receptive fields of different sizes are considered. The difference in intensity between pairs of receptive fields is calculated and further codified in a binary vector. In particular, the concentration of receptive fields is higher near the center of the pattern, corresponding to the fovea in the retina. In addition to this, they overlap sampling regions adding redundancy which is also present in the retina and this increases the final descriptor discriminative power. FREAK has been evaluated on a matching task showing high object detection performance. BRISK [5] and DAISY [10] are previous descriptors that also compare pairs of intensities using a circular pattern. Compared to state of the art descriptors, such as SIFT, SURF or BRISK, it outperforms them while being faster and simpler. In a new descriptor called CS-FREAK [14], the original grid is simplified reducing the number of receptive fields, and the neighborhood intensity is encoded improving the matching accuracy. In a different kind of task, FREAK has been applied to action recognition in videos through an extension to the descriptor that encodes motion named as MoFREAK [15].

However, biologically inspired descriptors have mainly been applied to object recognition task [1,5,10]. In [13] a Difference of Gaussian (DoG) filtering which simulates the performance of the retina is applied to texture classification. In this work, we propose a new set of bio-inspired descriptors for the scene categorization task. Using FREAK descriptor as a baseline, we further enrich it imitating models of the retina. Our proposal is to use a grid based on the center-surround organization of the ganglion receptive fields and perform low-level features extraction in order to classify scenes. In particular, we propose to imitate the ON and OFF cell response by calculating Difference of Gaussians (DoG) of different sizes. Moreover, each receptive field in our grid is described with a linear-nonlinear model (LN) which is typically used in retina models.

The rest of the paper is organized as follows. Section. 2 explains the retinal sampling pattern configuration used and describes the construction of each of the descriptors. It also introduces the BOW pipeline used for the classification of the scenes. In Sect. 3 experimental results on the 15 scene categories dataset are reported. Finally, in Sect. 4, conclusions are drawn.

2   Method

In this section we introduce a new set of image descriptors based on the center-surround organization of the ganglion receptive fields. We propose three different binary descriptors each constructed considering different components of ganglion cell response. To start with, the main aspects of FREAK descriptor [1] which are related to our contribution are presented. Next, each of our proposed descriptors are explained in detail. Finally, the bag-of-words approach used for the scene categorization task is introduced.

2.1   Retinal Ganglion Cells Configuration

In FREAK [1], the sampling grid shown in Fig. 1 is proposed. Each circle corresponds to a receptive field of a ganglion cell and its size represents the standard deviation of the Gaussian kernels applied to the underlying sampling point. However, the Gaussian smoothing applied to each receptive field is approximated calculating the mean intensity. They experimentally observed that changing the size of receptive fields with respect to the log-polar pattern improved the performance. In addition to this, overlapping the receptive fields further improved the results. Based on such a sampling grid, they compared the mean intensity of pairs of receptive fields.

In our model, the configuration of the receptive fields is inspired by FREAK but including several changes to constrain it more closely to biology. As in FREAK, we also consider 43 cells organized in 8 different concentric circles, as can be seen in Fig. 1.

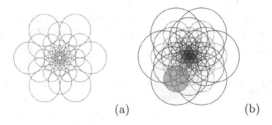

(a)   (b)

Fig. 1. A. Original FREAK sampling pattern. B. Our sampling pattern. In red the center of each receptive field is depicted and in blue the surround. The size of the center corresponds to the size of the cells in the original pattern (Color figure online).

As opposed to FREAK where, for each receptive field (RF) mean averages are calculated, we propose to use a difference of Gaussians (DoG) centered in each cell. Mimicking biology, each RF in our model is composed of a center and a surround. The DoG can be calculated as the subtraction of two Gaussians fitted to each area. More specifically, the radius of the center r_C will be considered as the size of each cell in the original FREAK. The standard deviation of the corresponding Gaussian can be approximated as follows:

$$\sigma_C = \frac{r_C}{3}. \tag{1}$$

Based on the literature [16], the relative surround extent has a wide range across retinal ganglion cells. We have empirically chosen the surround to be double size of the center, since the DoG behaves as an edge detector and this is the functionality we are interested in. Therefore, the standard deviation of the surround can be obtained as follows:

$$\sigma_S/\sigma_C = 2. \tag{2}$$

From this equation, the size of the surround can be obtained replaicing Eq. 2. The formula for the difference of Gaussians (DoG) is the following:

$$K(x,y) = w_C G_{\sigma_C}(x,y) - w_S G_{\sigma_S}(x,y). \tag{3}$$

where w_C and w_S are constants, which determine the type of features estimated by this filtering stage. As before, this parameter presents a high variability depending on the cell type. In our case, the relative surround weight used is $w_S/w_C = 0.9$ based on previous work [16].

2.2   Retinal Inspired Descriptors

Our descriptors will be estimated based on the retinal activity defined by a classical linear-nonlinear (LN) model, where the activity A of a ganglion cell centered at position (x, y) is defined by:

$$A^\varepsilon = N(RF^\varepsilon) \quad \text{where for each cell} \quad RF^\varepsilon = \varepsilon I * K(x,y). \tag{4}$$

I is the still image or stimulus and K is the weighted difference of Gaussians. ON and OFF ganglion cells are simulated by setting the parameter ε to respectively $+1$ or -1. The static nonlinear function N is defined by:

$$N(RF^\varepsilon) = \begin{cases} \dfrac{\alpha}{1 - \lambda(RF^\varepsilon - \beta)/\alpha} & \text{if } RF^\varepsilon < \beta \\ \alpha + \lambda(RF^\varepsilon - \beta) & \text{otherwise} \end{cases} \tag{5}$$

where λ and α represent reduced currents. β is the threshold after which the response of the cells becomes linear. Based on previous authors [16] we used $\lambda = 3$, $\alpha = 1$, $\beta = 0$. Such rectification is a common feature in retinal models [3]. It simulates static nonlinearities observed experimentally in the retina. Our aim with this formula is to imitate the response of a type of ganglion cells.

Based on the LN model, we propose the three binary descriptors depicted in Fig. 2. Each descriptor is constructed considering different components of ganglion cell response. The first component (D_C), just considers the response of the center of each receptive field. The second one (D_S), adds some information about the sign of the DoG. The last one (D_{ONOFF}), calculates the DoG of two population of cells, namely, ON and OFF cells. In the following each of them is explained in detail.

The Center Response. The first component of our descriptors is defined considering the response of the center of the receptive field (RF). For all the cells in our pattern, we blur the center with the corresponding Gaussian kernel $K(x,y)$

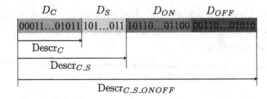

Fig. 2. Illustration of the construction of our descriptors from its components

obtained from Eq. 3, where the surround kernel G_{σ_C} is equal to 0. The activity in the center of the RF is calculated using Eq. 4. The purpose of this component is to mimick the original FREAK by performing the Gaussian smoothing as opposed to the approximation with the mean intensity calculation.

This binary component is constructed by calculating the difference in activity between all pairs of receptive fields.

$$D_C(i,j) = \begin{cases} 1 & \text{if } N(RF_i) - N(RF_j) >= 0, \ \forall i \neq j \\ 0 & \text{otherwise} \end{cases} \tag{6}$$

In the following components of our proposal, the inhibitory effect of surround is taken into account.

The Sign of the Center-Surround Response. This component takes into account the sign of the DoG centered in each of the 43 receptive fields of our model.

$$RF = sign(N(I * K(x,y))). \tag{7}$$

As a result, the binary component is calculated as:

$$D_S(i) = \begin{cases} 1 & \text{if } N(RF_i) >= 0, \ \forall i \\ 0 & \text{otherwise} \end{cases} \tag{8}$$

In this way the contribution of adding some information about the inhibitory surround is evaluated.

The ON and OFF Cell Response. Finally, the responses of both ON and OFF ganglion cells are considered. The activation of the ON cells is calculated from the formula 4, where ε is equal to +1. In a similar way, the activation of the OFF cells is calculated considering ε equal to -1.

The binary component is constructed comparing the activation between pairs of cells. For instance, for ON cells:

$$D_{ON}(i,j) = \begin{cases} 1 & \text{if } N(RF_i) - N(RF_j) >= 0, \ \forall i \neq j \\ 0 & \text{otherwise} \end{cases} \tag{9}$$

The activity of the OFF cells $D_{OFF}(i, j)$ is encoded in an analogous way. In summary, this component, named $D_{ONOFF}(i, j)$, is constructed upon the concatenation of $D_{ON}(i, j)$ and $D_{OFF}(i, j)$.

However, depending on the images used as stimulus, the response of ON and OFF cells can be noisy. As a result the encoded information leds to less discriminative descriptors. Since our aim is to construct sparse descriptors, we implemented a variant of the $D_{ONOFF}(i, j)$ component. In an attempt to reduce noise, the activity of these cell types has been thresholded based on the neighborhood information [6]. For a given image, a pyramid of DoG is calculated corresponding to the 8 different cell sizes in our pattern. The average DoG is used to filter those pairs whose activity difference is above the threshold.

For instance, for the ON cells we consider:

$$D_{ON_{Th}}(i, j) = \begin{cases} 1 & \text{if } N(RF_i) - N(RF_j) >= T, \ \forall i \neq j \\ 0 & \text{otherwise} \end{cases} \tag{10}$$

where T is the average DoG. For the OFF cells, the activity response is thresholded in the same way. As a result, the variant of the ON and OFF cell response, named $D_{ONOFF_{Th}}(i, j)$, is composed of the thresholded ON cell pairs $D_{ON_{Th}}$ and the thresholded OFF cell pairs $D_{OFF_{Th}}$. Therefore, the corresponding descriptor is named $Descr_{C\_S\_ONOFF\_Th}$ and is similar to third descriptor shown in Fig. 2, but considering the thresholded ON and OFF responses. All our descriptors have been tested on the scene classification task. The pipeline used in order to achieve this goal is described in the next section.

2.3   BOW Approach for Scene Categorization

Scene categorization is accomplished using a bag-of-words (BOW) approach. The descriptors are densely extracted from the images using a grid at steps of 5 pixels. Each position of the grid is considered as a keypoint and the sampling grid is situated on top of it. For the original FREAK, the pattern size is 45×45 pixel. Since our sampling grid is slightly bigger because the surround is added to the original pattern, the size of our pattern is 60×60 pixel. As a result we obtain overlapping patches, which has been shown to be efficient for the image categorization task [11].

Regarding the descriptor size, for the original FREAK is 64 bytes because only selected pairs are considered, whereas our descriptors are larger since all the possible pairs are taken into account. We made all of them 512 bytes long, adding padding where necessary. All the descriptors are quantized into visual words by k-means, using as distance metric the Euclidean distance. Spatial pyramid histograms are used as kernels. After the training phase, the final classification is performed using a linear SVM.

3   Performance Evaluation

We evaluated the performance of our descriptors on the 15 scene categories dataset [4], which is an extension to the 8 scene categories provided by [7].

As established in previous works [4], from each class 100 images are used as training and the rest as test. In total, 1500 images have been used for the training set and 2985 for the test set. All the tests have been done using 10 random splits. We used 100 randomly selected images from the training set to form the dictionary. In the Table 1 we can see the mean accuracy of each approach using 600 visual words. The code for FREAK is available in openCV [2] and our descriptors have been implemented based on that code. The BOW approach is based on the VLFeat toolbox [12].

Table 1. Comparison of FREAK and our descriptors for image classification on the 15 scene categories dataset [4].

	FREAK	Descr$_C$	Descr$_{C\_S}$	Descr$_{C\_S\_ONOFF}$	Descr$_{C\_S\_ONOFF\_Th}$
mean	66.42%	67.93%	68.42%	70.37%	72.19%
std	±0.45	±0.70	±0.41	±0.68	±0.6

As a baseline we used the original FREAK, where selected pairs are used retaining the most informative and discriminative ones. Moreover, the more relevant pairs correspond to the outer region of the pattern, suggesting that first the periphery of an object is explored in an attempt to find interesting regions, mimicking the saccadic search. However, the gaussian filtering is approximated calculating the mean intensity inside each receptive field.

In our descriptors we considered all the possible pairs, since the ones selected in [1] are obtained after learning the best pairs from their training data. Experimentally we obtained better results when all the pairs are considered. As is shown in the Table 1, all our descriptors are able to perform better than FREAK. The drawback is that the size of the descriptors is larger and there can be correlations between pairs. In the Table 2 we show preliminary results obtained by reducing the dimensionality of the $Descr_{OnOff_{th}}$, using the same 10 random splits as in Table 1.

Table 2. Effect of PCA dimensionality reduction: PCA applied to the thresholded response of ON and OFF cells Descr$_{C\_S\_ONOFF\_Th}$

Eigenvectors	Descr$_{C\_S\_ONOFF\_Th}$
64	72.11 % ±0.61
128	72.46 % ±0.75
256	72.78 % ±0.70

In this table we can observe that eliminating the less discriminative pairs from the descriptor increases the performance. Best results are obtained when the size is reduced to 256 bytes. In comparison, our approach outperforms the original FREAK even when both methods use the same size of descriptors (i.e. 64 bytes). In addition to this, in all our experiments the scale and orientation normalization is not used, since we are using a dense grid and not a keypoint detector as in the original idea.

The confusion matrix from one run of the $Descr_{C\_S\_ONOFF\_Th}$ descriptor is shown in Fig. 3, where row names are true labels and column names are the predicted ones. The highest confusion happens between category pairs such as inside city/tall building, coast/open country, forest/mountain, bedroom/living room, industrial/store, which has been previously stated by other authors [4,17].

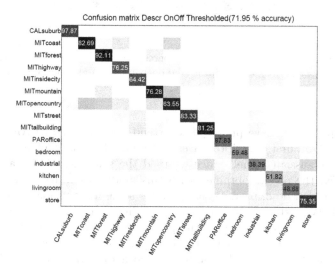

Fig. 3. Confusion matrix showing results obtained using our $Descr_{C\_S\_ONOFF\_Th}$ descriptor on the 15 scene categories dataset [4].

A further analysis of the results is shown in the Fig. 4, where the mean accuracy results obtained with both the original FREAK and our descriptor $Descr_{C\_S\_ONOFF\_Th}$ are plotted. In comparison our descriptor is able to classify better all the classes with the exception of two, namely, tallbuilding and living room. But for all the rest, our proposal outperforms the original FREAK. Overall, our third thresholded descriptor is able to achieve a high accuracy in recognizing natural scene categories, such as forest and coast. However, the results drop for most of the indoor scenes, as can be observed in the graph. There are other works related to scene classification that have reported the same issue. As explained in [9], the main two reasons could be, on the one hand, the lack of a large dataset of indoor scenes to train and test the approaches and, on the other hand, the difficulty in characterizing such scenes, which mainly requires a combination of both local and global image information. Interestingly, store and office images are classified much better with our descriptor than with FREAK, which suggests that our approach is able to better represent the properties of those type of images.

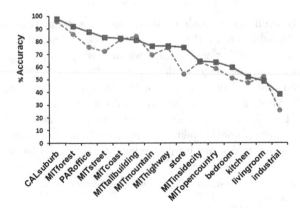

Fig. 4. Comparison of the mean accuracy percentage between FREAK (green curve) and our Descr$_{C\_S\_ONOFF\_Th}$ descriptor (red dashed curve) for each image class (Color figure online).

In this paper, we have proposed to extend the original FREAK in the following way. Our first descriptor, Descr$_C$, blurs the center of each receptive field with a Gaussian kernel. Since we used the same kernel size as the original FREAK, the results obtained with this modification are similiar in both cases. Our second descriptor, Descr$_{C\_S}$, adds some information about the sign of the DoG. We tested the contribution of using both the center response D_C and the DoG sign D_S, improving the performance slightly. Our third descriptor, Descr$_{C\_S\_ONOFF}$, implements the DoG considering two population of cells, namely, ON and OFF cells. In comparison with FREAK (66.42 %) the results obtained with our descriptor are better (70.37 %). Moreover, when the cell activiy is thresholded the classification accuracy is improved. If instead of using the D_{ONOFF} as our third component, we use the tresholded response D_{ONOFF_Th} the accuracy obtained is 72.19 %. In addition to this, PCA dimensionality reduction applied to this descriptor further improves the results, achieving a 72.78 % of correct classifications.

4   Conclusions

The goal of this work was to implement a bio-inspired descriptor, mimicking some functionalities of the visual system. From biology, it is well known that the retina extracts details from images using a Difference of Gaussians (DoG) of different sizes and encodes such differences with action potentials. We have presented a set of modifications to FREAK which are more biologically inspired. As a conclusion it seems that difference of gaussians calculated inside each receptive field, as is done by the visual system, extracts useful information for scene classification task. In the future, other low-level processing performed by the retina could be considered. In relation with this, other organization of the cells can also be tested, since as stated by Alahi et al. [1], changing the size of the receptive fields and their overlap increases the performance. Finally, the dimensionality of our descriptors can be reduced learning the most significant pairs in our model. Potentially, retaining the most significant pairs will further improve the classification results.

Acknowledgement. We thank M. San Biagio for his support in the image classification algorithm. This research received financial support from the 7th Framework Programme for Research of the European Commission, under Grant agreement num 600847: RENVISION project of the Future and Emerging Technologies (FET) programme Neuro-bio-inspired systems (NBIS) FET-Proactive Initiative.

References

1. Alahi, A., Ortiz, R., Vandergheynst, P.: FREAK: fast retina keypoint. In: IEEE Conference on Computer Vision and Pattern Recognition, pp. 510–517 (2012)
2. Bradski, G.: The opencv library. Dr. Dobb's J. Softw. Tools **25**, 120–126 (2000)
3. Chichilnisky, E.J.: A simple white noise analysis of neuronal light responses. Netw.: Comput. Neural Syst. **12**(2), 199–213 (2001)
4. Lazebnik, S., Schmid, C., Ponce, J.: Beyond bags of features: spatial pyramid matching for recognizing natural scene categories. In: IEEE Conference on Computer Vision and Pattern Recognition, vol. 2, pp. 2169–2178. IEEE Computer Society (2006)
5. Leutenegger, S., Chli, M., Siegwart, R.: Brisk: binary robust invariant scalable keypoints. In: ICCV 2011, pp. 2548–2555 (2011)
6. Meng, X., Wang, Z., Wu, L.: Building global image features for scene recognition. Pattern Recogn. **45**(1), 373–380 (2012)
7. Oliva, A., Torralba, A.: Modeling the shape of the scene: a holistic representation of the spatial envelope. Int. J. Comput. Vision **42**(3), 145–175 (2001)
8. Oliva, A., Torralba, A.: Building the gist of a scene: the role of global image features in recognition. Prog. Brain Res. **155**, 23–36 (2006)
9. Quattoni, A., Torralba, A.: Recognizing indoor scenes. In: IEEE Conference on Computer Vision and Pattern Recognition, pp. 413–420 (2009)
10. Tola, E., Lepetit, V., Fua, P.: DAISY: an efficient dense descriptor applied to wide baseline stereo. IEEE Trans. Pattern Anal. Mach. Intell. **32**(5), 815–830 (2010)
11. Tuytelaars, T.: Dense interest points. In: The Twenty-Third IEEE Conference on Computer Vision and Pattern Recognition, CVPR 2010, pp. 2281–2288, San Francisco, CA, USA, 13–18 June 2010 (2010)
12. Vedaldi, A., Fulkerson, B.: VLFeat: an open and portable library of computer vision algorithms (2008). http://www.vlfeat.org/
13. Vu, N.-S., Nguyen, T.P., Garcia, C.: Improving texture categorization with biologically inspired filtering. Image Vis. Comput. **32**, 424–436 (2013)
14. Wang, J., Wang, X., Yang, X., Zhao, A.: CS-FREAK: an improved binary descriptor. In: Tan, T., Ruan, Q., Wang, S., Ma, H., Huang, K. (eds.) IGTA 2014. CCIS, vol. 437, pp. 129–136. Springer, Heidelberg (2014)
15. Whiten, C., Laganiere, R., Bilodeau, G.A.: Efficient action recognition with MoF-REAK. In: Proceedings of the 2013 International Conference on Computer and Robot Vision, pp. 319–325. IEEE Computer Society (2013)
16. Wohrer, A.: Model and large-scale simulator of a biological retina with contrast gain control. Ph.D. thesis, University of Nice Sophia-Antipolis (2008)
17. Wu, J., Rehg, J.M.: Centrist: a visual descriptor for scene categorization. IEEE Trans. Pattern Anal. Mach. Intell. **33**(8), 1489–1501 (2011)

Arabic-Latin Offline Signature Recognition Based on Shape Context Descriptor

Ahmed M. Omar[(⊠)], Nagia M. Ghanem, Mohamed A. Ismail,
and Sahar M. Ghanem

Computer and Systems Engineering Department, Faculty of Engineering,
University of Alexandria, Alexandria 21544, Egypt
{eng.ahmed3omar,nagia.mghanem,drmaismail,
sghanem123}@gmail.com

Abstract. Offline signature recognition is a very difficult task due to normal variability in signatures and the unavailability of dynamic information regarding the pen path. In this paper, a technique for signature recognition is proposed based on shape context that summarizes the global signature features in a rich local descriptor. The proposed system reaches 100 % accuracy but had some scalability problems as a result of the correspondence problem between the queried signature and all the data set signatures. To address the scalability problem of using shape context for signature matching, the proposed method speeds up the matching stage by representing the shape context features as a feature vector and then applies a clustering algorithm to assign signatures to their corresponding classes.

1 Introduction

Offline signature recognition is the process of identifying intelligible handwritten signatures from sources such as documents and images. It is preferred among various biometrics due to its popularity and cost-effectiveness. Offline signature recognition has been used in the context of indexing and retrieving signatures images in large database. However, most of signature recognition techniques that construct global shape representations, e.g. the Fourier descriptors [1], suffer from low accuracies due to the difficulty of extracting global descriptors from real signatures images. These techniques also require high degree of rigidity as any minimal change in the signature can affect the results of the identification process. Offline signature processing remains important since it is required in office automation systems.

Many approaches have been developed for offline signature recognition like:

- Using global, directional and grid features of signatures [2] a support vector machine (SVM) was used to verify and classify the signatures and a classification ratio of 95 % was obtained.
- Using Radon transform, fractal dimension combined with Support Vector Machine [3]. This method obtained a max accuracy of 97 %.
- Based on fuzzy algebraic concepts, a multistage classifier and a combination of global and local features [4]. In this proposed system, two separate phases for

© Springer International Publishing Switzerland 2015
L. Nalpantidis et al. (Eds.): ICVS 2015, LNCS 9163, pp. 24–33, 2015.
DOI: 10.1007/978-3-319-20904-3_3

signature recognition and verification are developed. An accuracy of 98 % can be obtained.

- Using a set of geometric signature features for describing the signature envelope and the interior stroke distribution in polar and Cartesian coordinates [5]. The FRR (False Rejection Rate) reported was 2.12 % and FAR (False Acceptance Rate) was 3.13 %.
- Using a back propagation neural network prototype for the offline signature recognition [6]. The reported FAR was in the ranges of 10–40 % and the FRR in the range of 5–16 %.

On the other hand, there are other techniques that produce better accuracies as they tolerate lower degrees of rigidity. These techniques rely on extracting point features on the contours of the signatures and solving the correspondence problem between these points. However, they are usually computationally expensive and require solving the correspondence problem. Because, they try recover the unknown transformation between the shapes. Shape context is known to fall in this category of techniques and it has been successfully applied in solving many shape matching problems such as plant species identification [7], symbol recognition [8] and visual shape descriptor [9]. Although high accuracies have been reached by using shape context local descriptors, the matching stage requires solving the correspondence problem among the points of the queried shape and the points of every shape in the dataset. This makes shape context impractical for real time applications.

This paper proposes a basic technique that uses shape matching in offline signature recognition that yields perfect results. The technique is then extended to solve the large runtime problem caused by the correspondence problem. The new technique derives a signature representative feature vector from shape context features and then applies a clustering algorithm to assign the queried signature to its corresponding class. This makes the new technique more scalable and reduces the matching time from order of minutes to order of seconds. However, a small loss in accuracies from 100 % to 97 % is sacrificed to improve the performance.

The paper is organized as follows: Sect. 2 discusses the use of shape context in Arabic-Latin signature recognition. In Sect. 3, the general shape context method for signature recognition is detailed. In Sect. 4, the extended scalable method is explained. Experimental results are shown in Sect. 5. Conclusions and future work are discussed in Sect. 6.

2 Arabic–Latin Offline Signature Recognition

Extracting features for Arabic signatures recognition is hard due to the complex shapes and letters combination used in the signatures. This complexity makes it very difficult to automate [10]. But since the proposed technique handles the signatures as images, there is no great difference between Arabic signatures and other signatures and the applied experiments have proven that [4].

Shape context is a feature descriptor used in object recognition. The shape context is intended to be a way of describing shapes. It allows for measuring shape similarity and the recovering of point correspondences. The algorithm succeeded in achieving perfect results. However, it didn't scale up well with large datasets. As a result of this, another extended variant of the technique is presented in this paper. This extended technique aims to enhance the performance of the matching against large signature datasets and preserving a high degree of accuracy.

Shape context is used to accurately capture the structure of the signatures. Furthermore, to avoid solving the computationally expensive point correspondence problem, a single feature vector is derived from shape context features and a clustering algorithm is used to assign signatures to their corresponding classes.

3   Using Shape Context for Signature Recognition

The shape context at a point captures the distribution over relative positions of other shape points and thus summarizes global shape in a rich local descriptor. The steps of using shape contexts to match two signatures P & Q is illustrated in Fig. 2 and works as follows:

1. Use an edge detector to find the edge points of the two signatures P & Q.
2. Randomly select a set of n points that lie on the edges of signature P and another set of n points on signature Q (Figs. 1 and 3).
3. Compute the signature context of each point found in step 2 on both signatures.
4. Match each point from signature P to a point on signature Q.
5. Calculate the "signature distance" between the two signatures.
6. Repeat steps from 2 to 5 for L times (usually L is from 3 to 6) and select the minimum calculated distance between the two signatures and this is considered the distance between the two signatures.

To identify queried signatures in the system, a nearest-neighbor classifier is used to find matching signatures.

3.1   Edge Detection

The Canny edge detection algorithm [11] is used as an edge detection technique. It's known as one of the optimal edge detectors. The reason for using this algorithm is

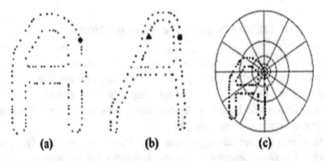

Fig. 1. (a) And (b) are the sampled edge points of the two shapes. (c) The log-polar bins.

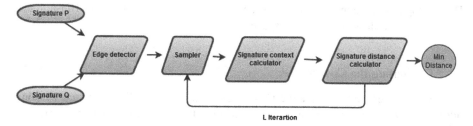

Fig. 2. Signature matching using shape context

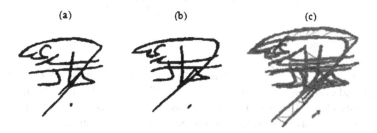

Fig. 3. (a) (b) two signatures (c) An image showing the sampled points within the two signatures and, their matching points using shape context in signatures matching

because of its low error rate, the distance between the edge pixels as found by the detector and the actual edge is to be at a minimum and the fact that it has only one response to a single edge. The Canny edge detection technique smoothes the image to eliminate the noise, it then finds the image radiant to highlight regions with high spatial derivatives. The algorithm then tracks along these regions and suppresses any pixel that is not at maximum (non-maximum suppression). The gradient array is now further reduced by hysteresis. Hysteresis is used to track along the remaining pixels that have not been suppressed. Hysteresis uses two thresholds and if the magnitude is below the first threshold, it is set to zero (made a non-edge). After detecting the edges of the signature, n points are then sampled uniformly from the detected signatures to be used later through the implementation.

3.2   Computing the Signature Context

For each Point P (i) on signature P we consider a set of n-1 vectors originating from a point to all other sampled points on a shape. These vectors represent the configuration of the entire shape relative to the reference point. As n gets larger the representation of the shape becomes more exact. Using the full set of vectors as a signature descriptor is much too detailed since signatures and their sampled representation may vary from one instance to another in a category. Then according to the angle and the length of each vector the points are placed into a circular histogram H_i bin. The histogram has K bins.

This histogram is defined to be the shape context of point P (i). The Bins of the histogram are uniform in log-polar space [12].

3.3   Computing the Cost Matrix

Now we consider another signature Q that has been processed like signature P. Consider C (P, Q) which denotes the cost of matching the two points P (i) and Q (j)

$$C_{ij} = C(p_i, q_j) = \frac{1}{2} \sum_{k=1}^{k} \frac{[h_i(k) - h_j(k)]^2}{h_i(k) + h_j(k)} \tag{1}$$

Where $h_i(k)$ and $h_j(k)$ denote the K-bin normalized histogram at p_i and q_j respectively.

The cost matrix is a matrix that represents the distance between each point on signature P and every point on signature Q having C_{ij} representing the distance between the two points [12]. The cost of matching two signatures can be represented as the summation of the costs of matching all the points on the two signatures.

3.4   Computing the Shape Distance

Each point P (i) in signature P, should be matched with point Q (j) in signature Q. The matching distances between all points in both signatures are represented in a square matrix. To find the minimal cost for matching these two signatures the Hungarian algorithm [13] is used as, this problem can be considered an assignment problem.

The sum of the distances (2) resulting from this assignment problem [12] is considered the distance between the two signatures P & Q the signatures with the minimum distance are then considered a match using the nearest neighbor classifier.

$$H(\pi) = \sum_i C(p_i, q_\pi(i)) \tag{2}$$

Figure 3 shows two signatures (a) and (b) and the result of applying the matching algorithm to both signatures.

4   Extended Signature Context Matching Algorithm

The main disadvantage of using shape context for signature recognition is that, during the matching phase, the cost matrix between the new signature and every signature in the database should be computed. Then the point correspondence problem should be solved. If the database contains n persons with k signatures for every person, these steps are repeated (n*k) times. This makes the algorithm not scalable for larger

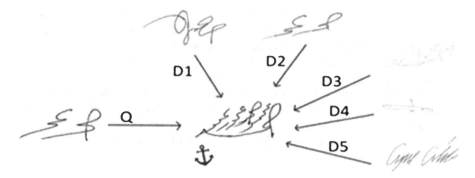

Fig. 4. The anchor signature, $D_{1,2,3}$ feature vectors of the knowledge base, Q queried feature vector

databases. The shape context accurately captures the structure of the signature but it is not readily described by a feature vector, which is the basis of many learning techniques. So, an approach to build a feature vector for each signature image is needed. This approach would enable using several machine learning techniques while keeping the rich information provided by the shape context descriptor [14].

In this approach each signature is represented by a feature vector. This vector consists of the distances calculated by applying shape context matching between this signature and an anchor signature as shown in (Fig. 4). In the matching phase, the new signature is compared to the same anchor signature image using the signature context method and the feature vector is computed in the same way. Then, to determine the output class, K-Medoids algorithm can be used. Using only precomputed feature vectors of a set of representative signatures, instead of using whole signature image comparisons, has the effect of reducing the matching time drastically.

By representative signatures, we assume that in a preprocessing step, a small number of best signatures for each person can be found and used to represent this person in the system. So, if k (usually k is between 8 and 12) signatures are provided for a single person, a smaller set is used as representative signatures for that person (usually this number is between 2 and 5). In a preprocessing step, these representative signatures are chosen as centers for K-Medoids clustering step. Only these representative signatures are used during matching phase. In the following, the steps the extended method of matching using a fixed anchor is explained.

4.1 Training Phase

1. Select an arbitrary signature and use it as an anchor (A)
2. Sample n points from the anchor signature where n can be tuned according to the system requirements. These points are fixed and will not change through the training and matching phase.
3. For each signature (B) in the training set of the classifier

(a) Sample k * n points from the training set signature where k is a constant to sample more points on B to provide a richer set of points while running the assignment process using the Hungarian algorithm [13].

(b) Use shape context matching to match each point in signature A points with the nearest point in the sampled from signature B.

(c) Create the feature vector DB = $[d_1, d_2, d_3, \ldots d_i \ldots d_n]$ where d_i represents the distances between the matched points using the Hungarian algorithm in shape matching.

(d) Store this feature vector in the knowledge base of the classifier.

4.2 Matching Phase

For each queried signature:

1. Sample k*n points from the queried signature
2. Use shape context matching to match each point in the queried signature with the nearest point in the pre-sampled points of the anchor signature
3. Create the feature vector DQ = $[d_1, d_2, d_3, \ldots d_i \ldots d_n]$ where d_i represents the distances between the matched points using the Hungarian algorithm in shape matching
4. The K-Medoids algorithm is used to specify the class of the queried vector DQ.

K-Medoids Algorithm. Knowing the label of the training phase signature vectors we divide the training set as K clusters each assigned to a class (user). A centroid is created from each class and is used to represent the class label. Upon querying a signature its signature vector is generated and the distance between it and all the K centroids are calculated and the signature is assigned to the class having the smallest distance to the centroid.

5 Experimental Results

A dataset of about 698 signatures was collected from 101 different persons with an average of 7 signatures from every user. The dataset was created by merging 509 collected Arabic signatures with 190 Latin signatures from the tobacco dataset [15] (Fig. 5). The signatures were scanned with a precision of 300×500 pixels. 466 signatures were used to train the classifier and the remaining signatures were used to test it. To show the effect of our proposed method, we compare the performance of using the original shape context and the extended (new) proposed method.

Graphs 1 and 2 show the accuracy of running both of the algorithms over the Arabic and Latin signatures separately.

By running the algorithms over the combined dataset (Arabic-Latin), Graph 3 show that the original algorithm can reach 100 % accuracy using about 100 sample points, while the extended (new) algorithm could reach only 97 % due to not using the shape context matching technique upon each calculation.

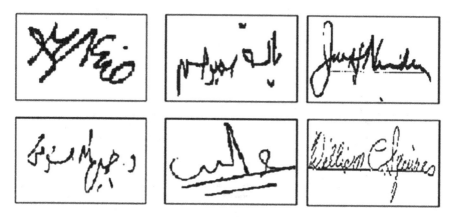

Fig. 5. Samples from the signatures used in testing

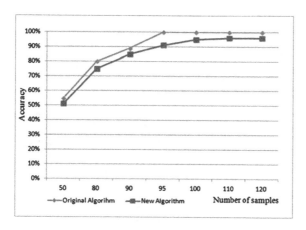

Graph 1. Comparing the two techniques based on accuracy over the Arabic dataset

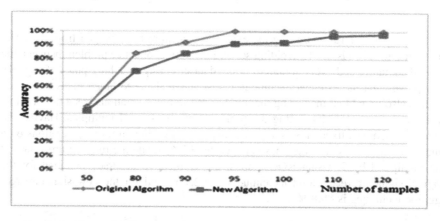

Graph 2. Comparing the two techniques based on accuracy over the Latin dataset

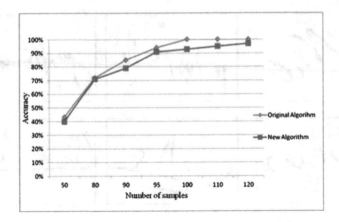

Graph 3. Comparing the two techniques based on accuracy over the combined dataset

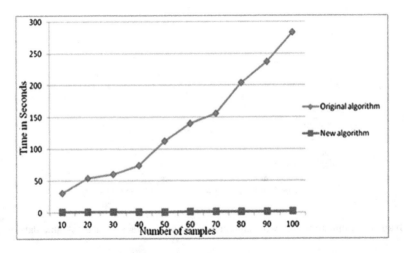

Graph 4. Comparing the two techniques based on time

Meanwhile, the runtime using the extended algorithm has changed from the order of minutes to seconds due to avoiding solving the correspondence problem between the queried signature and every signature in the dataset during matching phase (Graph 4). This proves that the extended technique is fast and scalable to larger datasets.

It is also noted that increasing the number of sampling iterations has a minor effect on the accuracy while increasing the running time by several multiples. Having the number of samples fixed at 80 samples while increasing the number of iterations on a range from 3 to 6 the accuracy has changed by 3.7 % while the running time elapsed had multiplied by 3. Using ROC graphs, the verification accuracy obtained for the original signature recognition technique was 92.1 % and for the new signature recognition technique is 89.8 %.

6 Conclusions and Future Work

A new fast and scalable method for signature recognition is proposed. The new method uses shape context to accurately capture the structure of the signature. To address the computational problem of using shape context for signature matching, the technique derives a global feature vector from the shape context features and then a clustering algorithm is used to assign signatures to their corresponding classes. Experiments show that the matching time was enhanced significantly which made the method scalable for large datasets. Many directions can be considered to extend the work presented in this paper. Using data fusion to improve the results, dealing with imperfect signature images that produce partial signatures and testing with different biometrics and larger datasets should be considered to continue this research.

References

1. Lin, C.C., Chellappa, R.: Classification of partial 2D shapes using Fourier descriptors. IEEE Trans. Pattern Anal. Mach. Intell. **9**(5), 686–690 (1987)
2. Özgündüz, E., Sentürk, T., Elif Karsligil, M.: Off-line signature verification and recognition by support vector machine. In: Eusipco 2005, Anatalya, Turkey, pp. 113–116 (2005)
3. Radmehr, M., Anisheh, S.M., Nikpour, M., Yaseri, A.: Designing an offline method for signature recognition. World Appl. Sci. J. **13**(3), 438–443 (2011)
4. Ismail, M.A., Gad, S.: On-line Arabic signature recognition and verification. Pattern Recogn. **33**(10), 1727–1740 (2000)
5. Ferrer, M., Alonso, J., Travieso, C.: Offline geometric parameters for automatic signature verification using fixed-point arithmetic. IEEE Trans. Pattern Anal. Mach. Intell. **27**(6), 993–997 (2005)
6. Abbas, R.: Back propagation Neural Network Prototype for off line signature verification. Thesis Submitted to RMIT (2003)
7. Mouine, S., Yahiaoui, I., Verroust-Blondet, A.: Advanced shape context for plant species identification using leaf image retrieval. In: Proceedings of the 2nd ACM International Conference on Multimedia Retrieval, Article No. 49 (2012)
8. T. Ha Do and Loria, New Approach for Symbol Recognition Combining Shape Context of Interest Points with Sparse Representation, ICDAR, pp: 265–269 (2013)
9. Penga, S., Kima, D., Leeb, S., Chungc, C.: A visual shape descriptor using sectors and shape context of contour lines. Inf. Sci. **180**(16), 2925–2939 (2010)
10. Hiary, H., et al.: Off-line signature verification system based on dwt and common features extraction. J. Theor. Appl. Inform. Technol. **51**(2) (2013)
11. Canny, J.: A computational approach to edge detection. IEEE Trans. PAMI **8**(6), 679–698 (1986)
12. Belongie, S., Malik, J., Puzicha, J.: Shape matching and object recognition using shape context. IEEE PAMI **24**(4), 509–522 (2002)
13. Taha, H.A.: Operations Research an Introduction, 8th edn. Prentice Hall, Upper Saddle River (2006)
14. Zhang, H., Malik, J.: Learning a discriminative classifier using shape context distances. In: ICVPR 2003, vol. 1 (2003)
15. Du, X., Abd Al Mageed, W., Doermann, D.: Large-scale signature matching using multi-stage hashing. In: ICDAR 2013, pp: 976–980 (2013)

Saliency-Guided Object Candidates Based on Gestalt Principles

Thomas Werner[1,2][(⊠)], Germán Martín-García[2], and Simone Frintrop[2]

[1] Fraunhofer Institut Für Intelligent Analyse- und
Informationssysteme Schloss Birlinghofen, 53757 Sankt Augustin, Germany
thomas.werner@iais.fraunhofer.de
[2] Computer Science Department III, Rheinische Friedrich-Wilhelms Universität,
Römerstr. 164, 53117 Bonn, Germany

Abstract. We present a new method for generating general object candidates for cluttered RGB-D scenes. Starting from an over-segmentation of the image, we build a graph representation and define an object candidate as a subgraph that has maximal internal similarity as well as minimal external similarity. These candidates are created by successively adding segments to a seed segment in a saliency-guided way. Finally, the resulting object candidates are ranked based on Gestalt principles. We show that the proposed algorithm clearly outperforms three other recent methods for object discovery on the challenging Kitchen dataset.

1 Introduction

The human ability to detect arbitrary objects fast and reliably is a very important competence for everyday life. It enables us to interact with our environment and reason about it. Also computational systems would strongly profit from such capabilities, for example by being able to detect new objects without explicit instructions. This would increase the autonomy of such systems while decreasing the interaction time spent with them.

Recently, interest in this detection of arbitrary, previously unknown objects, called *object discovery*, has increased strongly. Several methods have been proposed that address this problem in the computer vision community [2,5,14] as well as in the field of robotics [8,11,13,16]. We follow here the approach of Manén et al. [14], which is a recent approach that has been very successful. The method starts from an over-segmentation of the image and iteratively grows object hypotheses by adding segments to a random seed segment. This is done by representing the segmented image as a graph and then randomly sampling partial spanning trees that correspond to object candidates.

We modify and extend Manén's approach [14] in several ways to improve the detection quality. First, we add the processing of depth data from an RGB-D device to the processing pipeline. Second, we modify the random selection strategy of Manén to an informed search based on saliency. Saliency detection, as the bottom-up part of visual attention, is an important ability of human perception that guides the processing to regions of potential interest [15]. The saliency

L. Nalpantidis et al. (Eds.): ICVS 2015, LNCS 9163, pp. 34–44, 2015.
DOI: 10.1007/978-3-319-20904-3_4

information affects the selection of the seed segment as well as the selection of iteratively added segments. Third, we adapt the computation of edge weights of the graph to integrate a new feature called *common border saliency*. Fourth, we adapt the termination criterion that determines when to stop the growing of a candidate by considering the internal similarity as well as the external difference of the current candidate to a new segment. This idea is borrowed from the segmentation method of [4] and fits very well here. And finally, we add an SVM-learned ranking of the resulting object candidates based on Gestalt principles. These principles are descriptive rules from psychology that aim to explain how humans segregate objects from background, especially, which visual properties of objects support our perception [17]. Gestalt principles have recently been successfully used in machine vision approaches to evaluate the shape of objects, e.g., in [8,11,13,16], and we show that ranking based on these principles clearly improves the detection quality.

We have tested our method on the recently introduced Kitchen dataset for object discovery [8] that contains several challenging real-world sequences and show that our approach clearly outperforms the approach from [14] as well as several other recent methods for object discovery in terms of precision and recall.

2   System Overview

This section describes the proposed approach in detail (overview in Fig. 1). Given an input RGB-D image, the data is first pre-processed, including the conversion to an opponent colorspace as well as an inpainting of missing depth values. We use the colorspace of [12], but shifted and scaled to the range $[0,1]$. Next, a saliency map and an over-segmentation are generated from the color data. From the oversegmented map, a graph is constructed which has segments as vertices and stores the similarity of neighboring segments in edge weights. Then, we introduce the saliency-guided Prim's algorithm that generates object candidates by iteratively adding segments to a set of salient seed segments. Finally, we rank the candidates by a combination of Gestalt principles which is learned with an SVM. The output of the system is a list of object candidates sorted by objectness.

2.1   Saliency Computation

For saliency computation, we use the recently introduced VOCUS2 saliency system [7][1], which is a re-implementation of the VOCUS system [6]. The main structure is similar to traditional attention systems such as the one from Itti [9]: the system computes intensity and color features by Difference-of-Gaussian filters (center-surround ratio: $2:4$) on different scales (here: 2) and octaves (here: 5) before fusing them to a single saliency map (example in Fig. 2). We chose this system since it has shown to outperform many state-of-the-art methods for salient object segmentation, is real-time capable, and works on cluttered real-world scenes [7].

---

[1] Code: http://www.iai.uni-bonn.de/~frintrop/vocus2.html.

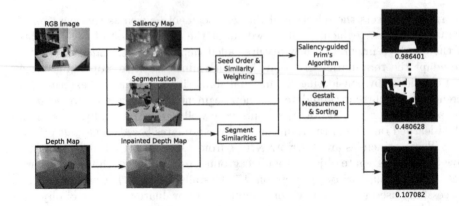

Fig. 1. Overview of the proposed approach: given an RGB-D input, the algorithm produces a list of object candidates, sorted by quality, here from 0.986401 (best) to 0.107082 (worst) (Color figure online).

In the following, the saliency map is used to determine the seeds of the candidate generation process and as a feature for determining object boundaries.

2.2 Graph Representation

Since our candidate generation method is based on finding minimum spanning trees in graphs, it is necessary to transform the input image into an appropriate graph representation. The graph representation is generated from an oversegmentation S of the image, obtained with the algorithm of [4].

We construct the graph $G = (V, E)$ so that each segment $s_i \in S$ becomes a vertex $v_i \in V$, and for each neighboring pair of segments s_i and s_j, an undirected edge $e_{i,j} \in E$ is introduced. To each edge $e_{i,j}$, a weight $w_{i,j}$ is assigned that represents the similarity of the corresponding segments (cf. Fig. 3).

The appearance similarity of two neighboring segments $svm(f_{i,j})$ is evaluated using an SVM that receives a feature vector $f_{i,j}$ extracted from the corresponding segments s_i and s_j. It computes the likelihood that both segments are part of the same object. The $4 + 4 + 1 = 9$ features that are used are:

- Intersection of the normalized 16 bin histograms of the four feature channels (3 color + 1 depth)
- Absolute differences of average value per feature channel
- Common-border ratio as defined in [14]

To overcome possible problems that come with inconsistent appearances of objects, an additional feature which relies on saliency is used to measure the similarity of segments. The measure is called *common border saliency* and is based on the observation that along boundaries of perceptually different regions (e.g., object/background boundaries) a center-surround based saliency operator produces a low response (cf. Fig. 2). It is defined as the average saliency along

Fig. 2. Common-border saliency: The Difference-of-Gaussian (DoG) operator that is used to computed center-surround contrasts has a low response when located at object boundaries (green = center, red = surround of the DoG filter) (Color figure online).

the common border of the two segments. This information can be utilized later to enforce the candidate generation process to respect such boundaries. The final edge weight/similarity value is defined as

$$w_{i,j} = svm(f_{i,j}) \cdot cbs(s_i, s_j), \tag{1}$$

which is the likelihood of belonging to the same object $svm(f_{i,j})$ weighted by their common border saliency $cbs(s_i, s_j)$.

2.3   Candidate Generation Process

Motivated by [14], the candidate generation process is formulated as the problem of finding partial maximal spanning trees using the Prim's algorithm. The differences to [14] are: (i) instead of random vertices the seeds are chosen according to their saliency, which enforces the inspection of the most promising regions first; (ii) segments are chosen in a greedy manner based on the similarity measure of Eq. 1; and finally, we introduce a deterministic stopping criterion compared to the randomized one from [14].

Given the graph G of an image, we extract several partial maximal spanning trees that serve as object candidates. The main idea is to select a starting segment (seed) s_{h_0} as the initial candidate $h_0 = \{s_{h_0}\}$ and to iteratively add the most similar neighboring vertices until a termination criterion is met. After t iterations, this results in candidate h_t consisting of segments $\{s_{h_0}, ..., s_{h_t}\}$. The termination predicate, inspired by the one in [4], takes into account the *internal dissimilarity* between the segments of the candidate, the *external dissimilarity* of the candidate to a given segment, and the size of the candidate.

Given a candidate h_t at iteration t and a vertex (segment) v_i, the external dissimilarity is recursively defined as

$$Ext(h_t, v_i) = 1 - \frac{1}{|E_{v_i \leftrightarrow h_t}|} \sum_{e_{j,k} \in E_{v_i \leftrightarrow h_t}} w_{j,k}, \tag{2}$$

where $E_{v_i \leftrightarrow h_t}$ is the subset of edges connecting vertex v_i with any vertex in h_t. In other words, the external dissimilarity is the average dissimilarity of the vertex v_i to the current candidate h_t. The final termination predicate is defined as

$$Ext(h_t, v_i) > \min\left(k, Int(h_t) + \frac{k}{t+1}\right), \tag{3}$$

which compares the external dissimilarity to the next vertex with current maximal external dissimilarity. As in [4], parameter k regulates how much extra internal variability is accepted within the candidates; the less segments the candidate has, the more influence k has. If the predicate holds, the vertex v_i is rejected and the growing process stops. Otherwise, the vertex is accepted and added to the current hypothesis. In such case, the internal dissimilarity $Int(h_{t+1})$ of the candidate at time $t+1$ is updated as

$$Int(h_{t+1}) = \max\left(Int(h_t), Ext(h_t, v_i)\right), \tag{4}$$

which is the maximal external dissimilarity obtained so far.

We generate object candidates for several values of k: we use $k = 0.6$ to $k = 0.9$ in steps of 0.05. A small example of the candidate generation process on an artificial graph is shown in Fig. 3. There it can be seen that 3 vertices are accepted due to their high similarity whereas the next candidate vertex is not similar enough and therefore rejected.

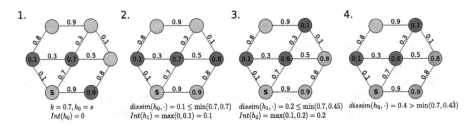

Fig. 3. Small example of the candidate generation process on an artificial graph: small example of the candidate generation process on an artificial graph: Green = current candidate, red = pool of next segments, blue = final candidate. The vertex weights are their external similarity to the current candidate and the edge weights reflect the similarity of the connected vertices (Color figure online).

2.4   Candidate Ranking Using Gestalt Measurements

After all object candidates are generated, a scoring mechanism is applied to each candidate h to evaluate its visual objectness. Several measures that correspond to different Gestalt principles are derived and evaluated on the candidates.

Color/Depth Contrast: Since objects usually have a strong contrast to their surround, a contrast measure is derived. For each feature channel, each segment within the candidate is compared with the neighbors outside the candidate, based on the intersection of normalized 16 bin histograms and the difference of color averages of the corresponding segments.

Good Continuation: Objects usually have smooth contours. Thus, the mean curvature of the contour of the candidate is a good indicator for its objectness. As in [13], we define good continuation as the average angular change of contour.

Symmetry: Symmetry is a non-accidental property and is known to have influence on human object perception [10]. Based on [11], we measure the overlap O_1 and O_2 of the candidate with itself after mirroring along both of its principle axes (eigenvectors of the scatter matrix). The two measures describing the symmetry are the *maximal symmetry* ($max(O_1, O_2)$) and the *weighted average symmetry* ($\frac{1}{\lambda_1 + \lambda_2}(\lambda_1 O_1 + \lambda_2 O_2)$) weighted by the corresponding eigenvalues.

Convexity: Convexity is also an important part in human object perception [10]. We propose three measures that capture the convexity of a candidate based on its convex hull. The first one, motivated by [11], is the *average convex distance*, which is the average distance of the candidate boundary to the closest point on the convex hull. Since it depends on the size of the candidate, it is normalized by the number of points that contributed and the largest observed distance. The second and third measure are the *perimeter ratio* and the *area ratio* of the convex hull and the candidate.

Compactness: The compactness measure consists of three values. The *average centroid distance* is computed as the average distance of the boundary points to the center of mass of the candidate. It is normalized by the number of boundary points and the maximal observed distance. The second measure is the *circularity*, that measures the similarity to a perfect circle of the same size. The measure is based on the ratio of perimeter P and area A of the candidate and is defined as $\frac{4\pi A(h)}{P(h)^2}$. The last measure is the *eccentricity* and is defined as the ratio of extensions λ_2, λ_1 along both principle axes by $\sqrt{1 - \frac{\lambda_2}{\lambda_1}}$.

Combination of Measures: After all measures are computed, their concatenation is fed to an SVM that evaluates the objectness of the corresponding candidate and assigns a real value to it. Based on the objectness, the list of object candidates is sorted so that those that are likely to correspond to a real object appear first. Finally, non-maxima suppression is applied to remove duplicate candidates with lower objectness. Whether a candidate is a duplicate, is determined using the *Intersection-over-Union (IoU)* measure and a threshold of 0.5 [3]. The output of our system is a list of object candidates, sorted by their decreasing objectness value.

3   Training, Evaluation and Results

In this section, we evaluate the performance of our algorithm and compare it to other state-of-the-art methods. We use the Kitchen dataset [8], which consists of five video sequences showing different cluttered, real-world indoor scenes. The sequences contain 600 frames and 80 objects on average. Ground truth labels are available for every 30*th* frame. Furthermore, the labels are consistent over the sequences, making it possible to evaluate the candidates on a sequence level.

3.1   Parameter Evaluation

We use the first of the sequences in [8] as training data and for parameter estimation. The rest are used as test sequences.

Saliency System: Following the method of [1], we evaluated saliency maps for several sets of parameters using the training sequence's ground truth. The optimal parameters are introduced in Sect. 2. A detailed description of the saliency evaluation and the results can be found in [18].

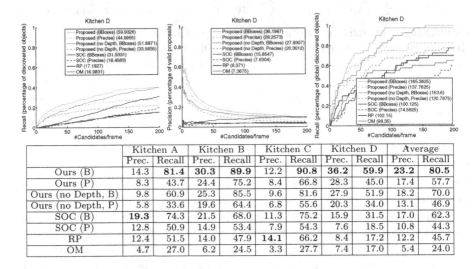

	Kitchen A		Kitchen B		Kitchen C		Kitchen D		Average	
	Prec.	Recall	Prec.	Recall	Prec.	Recall	Prec.	Recall	Prec.	Recall
Ours (B)	14.3	**81.4**	30.3	**89.9**	12.2	**90.8**	**36.2**	59.9	**23.2**	**80.5**
Ours (P)	8.3	43.7	24.4	75.2	8.4	66.8	28.3	45.0	17.4	57.7
Ours (no Depth, B)	9.8	60.9	25.3	85.5	9.6	81.6	27.9	51.9	18.2	70.0
Ours (no Depth, P)	5.8	33.6	19.6	64.4	6.8	55.6	20.3	34.0	13.1	46.9
SOC (B)	**19.3**	74.3	21.5	68.0	11.3	75.2	15.9	31.5	17.0	62.3
SOC (P)	12.8	50.9	14.9	53.4	7.9	54.3	7.6	18.5	10.8	44.3
RP	12.4	51.5	14.0	47.9	**14.1**	66.2	8.4	17.2	12.2	45.7
OM	4.7	27.0	6.2	24.5	3.3	27.7	7.4	17.0	5.4	24.0

Fig. 4. Evaluation on the Kitchen dataset sequences with three reference methods RP [14], OM [2] and SOC [8]. Top: Frame-based recall (left), precision (middle) and scene-based recall (right) on the Kitchen D sequence. Bottom: Overview of area under curve (AUC) values for precision and recall on all kitchen sequences. Highest values shown in bold. B: bounding boxes, P: pixel-precise.

SVMs: Within the proposed method two SVMs are used. The first one is trained to estimate the visual similarity of two segments (Sect. 2.2), a problem which is treated here as a classification problem. Training is performed as follows: (i) Given the training sequence, an over-segmentation as described in Sect. 2.2 is generated, (ii) positive and negative segment pairs are extracted, (iii) the corresponding feature vector from Sect. 2.2 is extracted and (iv) the feature vectors and positive/negative class labels are fed to the SVM. A positive segment pair consists of two neighboring segments belonging to the same object, and a negative pair is a set of two neighboring segments that either belong to different object or one belongs to an object and the other to the background. A segment is part of an object if its area is covered by the object by at least 50 %. To find the best parameters, the training of the SVM is done using a grid search in the parameter space and 10-fold cross-validation. The best parameter set is the one that has the lowest average error over all 10 rounds.

The second SVM is used to evaluate the objectness of object candidates (Sect. 2.4), which is treated as a regression problem. Training is performed as follows: (i) As before, an over-segmentation of the training data is produced, (ii) all ground truth objects are extracted by forming candidates of all covered segments, (iii) for each candidate the feature vector introduced in Sect. 2.4 is extracted and the IoU with the ground truth is measured, and (iv) for each candidate the feature vector is the input to the SVM, which regresses on the IoU. Like before, the best parameter set is obtained using a grid search and 10-fold cross validation. A detailed description of the training process and the results can be found in [18].

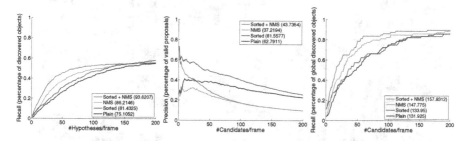

Fig. 5. Evaluation of the effect of different ranking methods. Plain: ranking by average saliency; sorted: ranking by Gestalt features; NMS: ranking after non-maxima-suppression (removes dublicates). Each individual step as well as their combination increases the quality of the candidates.

3.2 Comparison to Other Methods

We compare our approach to the methods *RP* [14], *OM* [2] and *SOC* [8]. We measure precision and recall in terms of the number of valid candidates (IoU ≥ 0.5). Additionally, we measure global, scene-based recall as the number of objects that were found throughout the whole sequence. We use the four sequences that were not used for training of the Kitchen dataset [8] as test data.

Although the dataset is annotated with pixel-precise ground truth, all evaluations are also performed using bounding boxes. This way a fair comparison of the methods is guaranteed, since *RP* and *OM* only produce bounding boxes. Our method is evaluated with and without depth information, since the reference methods are also developed to work only with color data.

Figure 4 shows the evaluation results exemplarily for the Kitchen D sequence. It contains recall, precision and global recall (from left to right) along with the corresponding area under curve values for each method. The proposed method outperforms all reference methods in terms of recall as well as precision. The recall plot shows that around 40 % of the objects in a frame are detected and that almost all objects in the sequence are detected at least once. The precision plot shows that when taking few candidates, e.g. 20, many of them match an

Fig. 6. Top 10 object hypotheses for some images. From top to bottom: input image, ground truth, OM [2], RP [14], SOC [8], Ours (sorted + NMS).

object. The results on the other sequences are consistently good and can be seen in the table in Fig. 4: our method has on average the highest precision and recall, and outperforms all the other methods in each sequence in terms of recall.

In Fig. 5 we compare different ranking strategies: the default ranking strategy according to the average saliency ('Plain' in the figure), sorting according to the Gestalt measures ('Sorted'), and the non-maxima suppression ('NMS'). The results can be explained as follows: sorting the candidates by their objectness will cause good candidates to appear first which explains the high precision for few candidates and the early increase of the recall. On the other hand, the non-maxima suppression removes duplicate candidates (also good ones) which explains the overall high recall as well as the drop in precision. For the recall the removal of duplicates has only positive effects, since duplicates will at most only re-discover objects or will not discover any object at all.

In Fig. 6 the ten best candidates per method are shown. It can be seen that two of the reference methods (RP and OM) generally produce very large candidates that capture either multiple objects or very large structures. The proposed method on the other hand adequately produces candidates for the individual objects.

4   Conclusion

We have presented a method for finding arbitrary, unknown objects in RGB-D data that utilizes principles of human object perception —visual attention and Gestalt psychology. This enables a fast and reliable generation of object candidates even for complex scenes containing many objects. We have shown that the presented method outperforms several state of the art methods and is able to detect more than 50 % of the objects in a frame and more than 90 % of the objects visible in the scene.

References

1. Achanta, R., Hemami, S., Estrada, F., Süsstrunk, S.: Frequency-tuned salient region detection. In: Proceedings of the CVPR (2009)
2. Alexe, B., Deselaers, T., Ferrari, V.: Measuring the objectness of image windows. Trans. on PAMI **34**(11), 2198–2202 (2012)
3. Everingham, M., Van Gool, L., Williams, C.K.I., Winn, J., Zisserman, A.: The pascal visual object classes (VOC) challenge. Int. J. of Comput. Vis. **88**(2), 303–338 (2010)
4. Felzenszwalb, P.F., Huttenlocher, D.P.: Efficient graph-based image segmentation. Int J. of Comput. Vis. **59**(2), 167–181 (2004)
5. Frintrop, S., Martín García, G., Cremers, A.B.: A cognitive approach for object discovery. In: Proceedings of ICPR (2014)
6. Frintrop, S.: 6 sensor fusion. In: Frintrop, S. (ed.) VOCUS: A Visual Attention System for Object Detection and Goal-Directed Search. LNCS (LNAI), vol. 3899, pp. 129–147. Springer, Heidelberg (2006)
7. Frintrop, S., Werner, T., Martín García, G.: Traditional saliency reloaded: a good old model in new shape. In: Proceedings of CVPR (2015)
8. Horbert, E., Martín García, G., Frintrop, S., Leibe, B.: Sequence level object candidates based on saliency for generic object recognition on mobile systems. In: Proceedings of ICRA (2015). Dataset: http://www.mmp.rwth-aachen.de/projects/kod/
9. Itti, L., Koch, C., Niebur, E.: A model of saliency-based visual attention for rapid scene analysis. Trans. on PAMI **20**(11), 1254–1259 (1998)
10. Kanizsa, G., Gerbino, W.: Convexity and Symmetry in Figure-Ground Organization. Vision and artifact, New York (1976)

11. Karpathy, A., Miller, S.: Object discovery in 3D scenes via shape analysis. In: Proceedings of ICRA (2013)
12. Klein, D.A., Frintrop, S.: Salient pattern detection using W_2 on multivariate normal distributions. In: Proceedings of DAGM-OAGM (2012)
13. Kootstra, G., Kragic, D.: Fast and bottom-up object detection, segmentation, and evaluation using Gestalt principles. In: Proceedings of ICRA (2011)
14. Manén, S., Guillaumin, M.: Prime object proposals with randomized prim's algorithm. In: Proceedings of ICCV (2013)
15. Pashler, H.: The Psychology of Attention. MIT Press, Cambridge (1997)
16. Richtsfeld, A., Zillich, M., Vincze, M.: Implementation of Gestalt principles for object segmentation. In: Proceedings of ICPR (2012)
17. Wagemans, J., Elder, J.H., Kubovy, M., Palmer, S.E., Peterson, M., Singh, M., von der Heydt, R.: A century of Gestalt psychology in visual perception: I. Perceptual grouping and figure-ground organization. Psychol. Bull. **138**(6), 1172–1217 (2012)
18. Werner, T.: Saliency-driven object dicovery based on gestalt principles. Master thesis, Rheinische Friedrich-Wilhelms-Universität Bonn (2015)

Person Re-identification Based
on Multi-directional Saliency Metric Learning

Zhonghua Huo[1], Ying Chen[1(✉)], and Chunjian Hua[2]

[1] Key Laboratory of Advanced Process Control for Light Industry (Ministry of Education), Jiangnan University, Wuxi, Jiangsu Province 214122, China
chenying@jiangnan.edu.cn
[2] Jiangsu Key Laboratory of Advanced Food Manufacturing Equipment and Technology Key, Jiangnan University, Wuxi, Jiangsu Province 214122, China

Abstract. Aiming for the problem of inconsistent saliency between matched patches in person re-identification, a multi-directional salience similarity evaluation for person re-identification based on metric learning is proposed. A distribution analysis for salience consistency between the patches is taken, and the similarity between matched patches is established by weighted fusion of multi-directional salience. The weight of saliency in each direction is obtained using metric learning in the base of Structural SVM Ranking. It improves the discriminative and accuracy performance of re-identification. Compared with the similar algorithms, the method achieves higher re-identification rate with more comprehensive similarity measure.

Keywords: Person re-identification · Metric learning · Salience feature · Ranking

1 Introduction

Matching persons observed from non-overlapping camera views, known as person re-identification(re-id) [1, 2], has become one of the most important tasks in video surveillance systems, such as human retrieval [3] and activity analysis [4]. An effective person re-identification method needs to solve the problem: when a query person disappears from one camera view, he/she can be identified in another view among a group of candidates. This task is difficult due to clutters in background and inter-camera variations in illumination and individual pose.

In order to tackle this problem, most existing work has concentrated either on designing a feature representation [5–7] that can be both distinctive and robust to large appearance variations, or on machine learning [3, 8, 9] that can optimize parameters of the model for person re-id. The common designed features include BiCov [5] which combines Biologically Inspired Features(BIF) and covariance descriptor, and Symmetry-Driven Accumulation of Local Features(SDALF) [6] which exploits the property of asymmetry and symmetry for each pedestrian image to divide the body into parts. The feature design can be well generalized to new camera views without additional human labeling efforts. However, severe changes of viewpoints, poses, illumination and occlusion in large surveillance area would cause significant appearance variations,

© Springer International Publishing Switzerland 2015
L. Nalpantidis et al. (Eds.): ICVS 2015, LNCS 9163, pp. 45–55, 2015.
DOI: 10.1007/978-3-319-20904-3_5

which make it extremely hard to design features that are both distinctive and reliable. On the other hand, typical machine learning methods include distance model training [9] and semantic attributes learning [3]. The former maximized the probability of a true match pair having a smallest distance, and the latter tried to learn a selection model of mid-level semantic attributes to describe a subject. Re-id by this approach can easily lead to over-fitting especially when less training set is used. Furthermore, the complexity of the training is larger due to lots of attribute classification. Based on the assumption that certain salient patches are those which possess uniqueness property among a specific set, Zhao et al. [8] proposed an unsupervised salience learning method which improved re-id rate by learning the salience of each patch and utilizing it to weight similarity of two matching patches of two images. However, only inter-salience with respect to images of different person, which was unstable across different training set, was considered in [8]. In addition, they assume the salience of matched patches is the same across images of the same identity taken by different camera, ignoring the salience variations among matched patches.

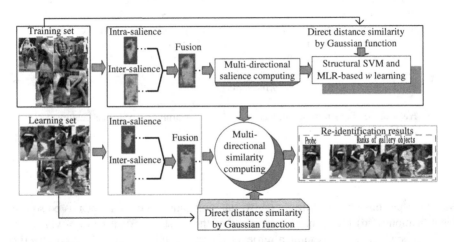

Fig. 1. Overview of approach of multi-directional saliency metric learning

Based on above considerations, a new person re-id approach based on multi-directional saliency metric learning(MSML) is proposed, which considers not only all possible saliency distribution of two matched patches but also the weight w of each saliency direction. As illustrated in Fig. 1, the true rank of query images in training set and the similarity vector based on multi-directional salience are used as the training input of Structural SVM Ranking [11, 12]. The trained weight w for each saliency direction is applied to saliency similarity computation between patches in test set, which helps to improve person re-id results. Fusion based saliency evaluation is also presented, combining inter-salience [8] and intra-salience based on Manifold Ranking (MR) [10]. The effectiveness of the proposed approach is validated on the VIPeR dataset [13] and the ETHZ dataset [14]. It outperforms the state-of-the-art methods on both datasets.

2 Person Re-identification Based on Multi-directional Saliency Metric Learning

Analysis on multi-directional salience is taken, based on which a salience weighting evaluation for similarity is designed. Then the multi-directional salience weight learning, based on the combination of Structural SVM [11] and Metric Learning to Rank(MLR) [12], is presented in detail.

2.1 Multi-directional Salience Analysis

We apply patch matching to tackle the misalignment problem as [8]. Let the patch features of an image be denoted as $x^{A,u}=\left\{x_{m,n}^{A,u}\right\}$, where $x_{m,n}^{A,u}$ denotes the patch centered at the m-th row and the n-th column of the u-th image in camera A. When conducting patch matching, each patch of the m-th row of image u from camera A has the same search set $\mathbb{Q}\left(x_{m,n}^{A,u},x^{B,v}\right)=\left\{x_{i,j}^{B,v}|j=1,\ldots,N, i=m\right\}$, where N is the number of column patches. After building patch matching between a test image and images in reference set, the most similar patch of each image in the reference set is obtained for each patch in the test image.

The purpose of person re-id is to find images of the given person in existing pedestrian image dataset. For this purpose, existing methods usually identify the associated images of the given person by estimate the similarity of two images. Given a pair of pedestrian images $x^{A,u}=\left\{x_{m,n}^{A,u}\right\}$ and $x^{B,v}=\left\{x_{i,j}^{B,v}\right\}$, a correspondence relation is established between two images after patch matching. Let q_i and q_{i*} denotes the correspondence, the direct distance similarity score of each pair of two patches is computed with the Gaussian function:

$$s\left(x_{q_i}^{A,u},x_{q_{i*}}^{B,v}\right)=\exp\left(-d\left(x_{q_i}^{A,u},x_{q_{i*}}^{B,v}\right)^2\bigg/2\sigma^2\right) \qquad (1)$$

where $d\left(x_{q_i}^{A,u},x_{q_{i*}}^{B,v}\right)=||x_{q_i}^{A,u}-x_{q_{i*}}^{B,v}||_2$ is the Euclidean distance between patch $x_{q_i}^{A,u}$ and $x_{q_{i*}}^{B,v}$, and σ is the bandwidth of the Gaussian function.

Zhao et al. [8] assumed images of the same person captured by different cameras have some consistent property on salience distributions, like situation ① and ② in Fig. 2. ① indicates bi-directional salience (Bi-Sal) in which both patches have large salience, and ② indicates bi-directional non-salience (Bi-nSal) in which both patches have small salience. So they compute the similarity between two images by a bi-directional salience weighting:

$$Sim\left(x^{A,u},x^{B,v}\right)=\sum_{m,n}sal\left(x_{m,n}^{A,u}\right)\times sal\left(x_{i,j}^{B,v}\right)\times s\left(x_{m,n}^{A,u},x_{i,j}^{B,v}\right) \qquad (2)$$

where sal is the salience score, which we viewed as inter-salience in this paper.

However, inconsistent salience appears between matched patches from images of the same person captured from different illumination, background and poses, like situation ③ and ④ in Fig. 2. ③ indicates unidirectional query-patch salience (Uni-qSal) in which query-patch has large salience while gallery-patch has small salience, and ④ indicates unidirectional gallery-patch salience (Uni-gSal) in which gallery-patch has large salience while query-patch has small salience. If Eq. (2) is taken for similarity evaluation, the salience inconsistency would reduce the similarity of the true matched patches with large gallery saliency and enhance the importance of patches with small gallery saliency. To solve the problem, an improved similarity evaluation based on weighted multi-directional saliency is proposed in the paper, where the weights are learned from training set.

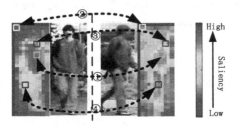

Fig. 2. Four saliency conditions of matched patches of real image pair

2.2 Similarity Based on Multi-directional Salience

For an image pair $x^{A,u} = \left\{ x_{q_i}^{A,u} \right\}$ and $x^{B,v} = \left\{ x_{q_{i*}}^{B,v} \right\}$, let $sal_{q_i}^A$ denotes the salience score of $x_{q_i}^{A,u}$, and $sal_{q_{i*}}^B$ denotes the salience score of $x_{q_{i*}}^{B,v}$. The multi-directional salience weighting evaluation can be represented as:

$$\mu_{\text{patch}}\left(x_{q_i}^{A,u}, x_{q_{i*}}^{B,v}; sal_{q_i}^A, sal_{q_{i*}}^B \right) = w_{q_i,1} \times sal_{q_i}^A \times sal_{q_{i*}}^B + w_{q_i,2} \times sal_{q_i}^A + w_{q_i,3} \times sal_{q_{i*}}^B \\ + w_{q_i,4}$$

$$(3)$$

where $w_{q_i,1} \sim w_{q_i,4}$ are weights of the four directional saliency. Therefore, the final similarity of each pair of patches based on multi-directional salience can be written as:

$$f_{\text{patch}}\left(x_{q_i}^{A,u}, x_{q_{i*}}^{B,v}; s, sal_{q_i}^A, sal_{q_{i*}}^B \right) = \mu_{\text{patch}}\left(x_{q_i}^{A,u}, x_{q_{i*}}^{B,v}; sal_{q_i}^A, sal_{q_{i*}}^B \right) \times s\left(x_{q_i}^{A,u}, x_{q_{i*}}^{B,v} \right) \quad (4)$$

where $s\left(x_{q_i}^{A,u}, x_{q_{i*}}^{B,v} \right)$ is the direct distance similarity between matched patches. Image pair's similarity can be estimated through final similarity of all patches:

$$f_{im}\left(x^{A,u}, x^{B,v}; s, sal^A, sal^B, q^{u,v}\right) = \sum_{i=1}^{M \times N} f_{patch}\left(x_{q_i}^{A,u}, x_{q_{i*}}^{B,v}; s, sal_{q_i}^A, sal_{q_{i*}}^B\right)$$

$$= w\phi\left(x^{A,u}, x^{B,v}; q^{u,v}\right) \tag{5}$$

where $q^{u,v}$ denotes the correspondence of image pair, and w is the weight of directional saliency of matched patches. $\phi(x^{A,u}, x^{B,v}; q^{u,v})$ denotes a feature map between feature space and similarity space of image pair:

$$\phi\left(x^{A,u}, x^{B,v}; q^{u,v}\right) = \left[\varphi\left(x_{q_1}^{A,u}, x_{q_1*}^{B,v}\right), \ldots, \varphi\left(x_{q_{MN}}^{A,u}, x_{q_{MN}^*}^{B,v}\right)\right]^T \tag{6}$$

$$w = \left[\left\{w_{q_1 j}\right\}_{j=1,2,3,4}, \ldots, \left\{w_{q_{MN} j}\right\}_{j=1,2,3,4}\right]$$

where $\varphi\left(x_{q_i}^{A,u}, x_{q_{i*}}^{B,v}\right)$ is a four dimensional weighted similarity vector:

$$\varphi\left(x_{q_i}^{A,u}, x_{q_{i*}}^{B,v}\right) = \left[sal_{q_i}^A \times sal_{q_{i*}}^B, sal_{q_i}^A, sal_{q_{i*}}^B, 1\right] \times s\left(x_{q_i}^{A,u}, x_{q_{i*}}^{B,v}\right).$$

For each query image $x^{A,u}$, the images in the gallery are ranked according to the similarities between query and each gallery image in Eq. (5). To obtain the similarity of image pair via Eq. (5), the similarity weighting should be known. The remaining problem is how to learn similarity weighting w.

2.3   Multi-directional Saliency Weight Learning

Taking person re-id as a ranking problem, we employ the Structural SVM which optimizes over ranking differences to learn the similarity weighting w. The objective function can be written as:

$$(w, \xi) \leftarrow \mathrm{argmin}_{w,\xi} \frac{1}{2} w^T w + C\xi$$

$$s.t. \frac{1}{V} w^T \sum_{v=1}^{V} \left[\Psi_{po}\left(x^{A,u}, \hat{y}_v^{A,u}; x^{B,v}, q^{u,v}\right) - \Psi_{po}\left(x^{A,u}, y_v^{A,u}; x^{B,v}, q^{u,v}\right)\right] \geq \frac{1}{V} \sum_{v=1}^{V} \Delta\left(\hat{y}_v^{A,u}, y_v^{A,u}\right) - \xi \tag{7}$$

$$\forall y_v^{A,u} \in \mathcal{Y}^{A,u}, \xi \geq 0, \quad for\, u = 1, \ldots, U$$

where $x^{A,u}$ is query image and $x^{B,v}$ is gallery image; $\mathcal{Y}^{A,u}$ denotes all possible partial orders of gallery image; $C > 0$ is a slack trade-off parameter; U is the total number of images in camera A and V is the total number of images in camera B. $\Delta\left(\hat{y}_v^{A,u}, y_v^{A,u}\right) \in (0, 1)$ denotes loss incurred for predicting a ranking $y_v^{A,u}$ rather than the ground truth ranking $\hat{y}_v^{A,u}$, and we employ Mean Average Precision(MAP) [12] to measure the loss function $\triangle$. ψ_{po} is a feature map between input-output pairs $(x^{A,u}, x^{B,v})$, and we employ partial order feature [12] to represent feature map according to considering person re-id as ranking problem, i.e., for query image which has its relevant images $\chi^+_{x^{A,u}} \subseteq \chi$(same identity) and irrelevant images $\chi^-_{x^{A,u}} \subseteq \chi$(different identities), ψ_{po} has the form as follows:

$$\psi_{po}\left(x^{A,u}, y_v^{A,u}; x^{B,v}, q^{u,v}\right) = \sum_{x^{B,v} \in \chi^+_{x^{A,u}}} \sum_{x^{B,v'} \in \chi^-_{x^{A,u}}} y_{v,v'}^{A,u} \left(\frac{\phi(x^{A,u}, x^{B,v}; q^{u,v}) - \phi\left(x^{A,u}, x^{B,v'}; q^{u,v'}\right)}{|\chi^+_{x^{A,u}}||\chi^-_{x^{A,u}}|}\right)$$

(8)

where

$$y_{v,v'}^{A,u} = \begin{cases} +1 & x^{B,v} \prec_{y_v^{A,u}} x^{B,v'} \\ -1 & otherwise \end{cases},$$

where $x^{B,v} \prec_{y_v^{A,u}} x^{B,v'}$ indicate that image $x^{B,v}$ is placed before $x^{B,v'}$ in order $y_v^{A,u}.q^{u,v}$ denotes the correspondence of image pair, and $\phi(x^{A,u}, x^{B,v}; q^{u,v})$ is a feature map between feature space and similarity space of image pair in Eq. (6). For each relevant-irrelevant pair $(x^{B,v}, x^{B,v'})$,the difference vector $\phi(x^{A,u}, x^{B,v}; q^{u,v}) - \phi\left(x^{A,u}, x^{B,v'}; q^{u,v'}\right)$ is added if $x^{B,v} \prec_{y_v^{A,u}} x^{B,v'}$, and subtracted otherwise.

Besides, note that the set $\mathcal{Y}^{A,u}$ of possible output structures is generally quite large, so margin constraints in Eq. (7) may not be feasible in practice. However, cutting planes can be applied to find a small working set of active constraints which are sufficient to optimize w [11]. The key component of the cutting plane method is the separation oracle, which has relationship with the sum of feature map and loss function. After the establishment of above function, the corresponding separation oracle of optimal partial order $y_v^{A,u}$ can be formed as maximizing following sum function:

$$y_v^{A,u} \leftarrow \underset{y_v^{A,u} \in \mathcal{Y}^{A,u}}{argmax} \triangle\left(\hat{y}_v^{A,u}, y_v^{A,u}\right) + w^T \psi_{po}\left(x^{A,u}, y^{A,u}; x^{B,v}, q^{u,v}\right)$$

(9)

where $\mathcal{Y}^{A,u}$ is all possible permutations of the training set. Intuitively, this computes the order $y_v^{A,u}$ with simultaneously large loss $\triangle\left(\hat{y}_v^{A,u}, y_v^{A,u}\right)$ and margin score $w^T \psi_{po}$.

The similarity weighting w can be optimized by using the learning algorithm based on ranking Structural SVM. For robust Structural SVM learning, the trade-off C is varied over $\{10^{-2}, 10^{-1}, 10^0, ..., 10^4\}$. Experimental results show that, when $C = 1$, the output weight of the model correspond to the highest re-id rate. In this paper, the experimental results are obtained in the case of $C = 1$.

3 Multi-Salience Fusion

To obtain a more accurate salience description for objects, a multi-salience fusion is proposed, combining inter-salience [8] with intra-salience based on MR [10].

In this work, we modify MR-based approach [10] to compute intra-salience of image patches. The intra-salience indicates the inherent salience of the patch in the original image and is independent to training set. Two modifications are introduced to adapt MR to intra-salience learning. First, we replace the superpixel segmentation with dense local patch segmentation. Second, we take patches at four corners as background queries to replace four boundary's superpixel. More details about MR can be found in [10]. Patch salience score is obtained by the fusion of intra-salience and inter-salience:

$$score_{patch}\left(x_{m,n}^{A,u}\right) = \beta_1 \times score_{intra}\left(x_{m,n}^{A,u}\right) + \beta_2 \times score_{inter}\left(x_{m,n}^{A,u}\right) \quad (10)$$

where $score_{intra}\left(x_{m,n}^{A,u}\right)$ denotes intra-salience of patch $x_{m,n}^{A,u}$, and $score_{inter}\left(x_{m,n}^{A,u}\right)$ denotes inter-salience of patch $x_{m,n}^{A,u}$, which is computed by K-Nearest Neighbor (KNN) method introduced in [8]. β_1 and β_2 are corresponding to the weight of inter- and intra-salience. In our experiment, β_1 and β_2 are set to 0.5.

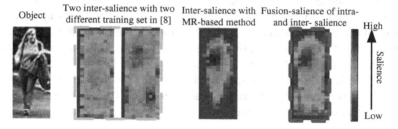

Fig. 3. Illustration of inter- salience, intra-salience and fusion-salience

As seen in Fig. 3, the inter-salience in [8] varies for different training set. Intra-salience is more robust and is independent to the training set. It is an inherent property of the image itself. Therefore, a more accurate salience description for objects is formed by the fusion of inter- and intra- salience.

4 Experimental Results

In this section we show extensive experiments to evaluate our approach, providing comparisons with other methods in the state of the art on two publicly datasets, the single-shot VIPeR dataset [13], and the multiple-shot ETHZ dataset [14]. The results are reported in standard Cumulated Matching Characteristics(CMC) curves. Rank-r recognition rate is the expectation of the matches at rank r, and the CMC curve is the cumulated values of recognition rate at all ranks. The recognition rate of $r = 1$

represents the correct matched pair. But when r is low, people can identify target assisted by human eyes, therefore it also has practical significance.

We apply the parameter settings as [8]: the size of patches are 10×10; 32-bin color histograms are computed in L, A, B channels respectively, and in each channel 3 levels of down sampling are used with scaling factors 0.5, 0.75 and 1; color histograms features are connected with SIFT features extracted in 3 color channels and thus produces a $32 \times 3 \times 3 + 128 \times 3$ feature vector for each patch.

VIPeR Dataset [13]. This dataset contains two views of 632 pedestrians. Each pair is made up of images of the same pedestrian taken from different camera views. Most of the examples contain a viewpoint change of 90 degrees. It is the most challenging dataset currently available for pedestrian re-id.

Following the evaluation protocol in [15], we randomly sample k image pairs of the dataset for training, and the remaining for test. Considering images from CAM B as the gallery set, and images from CAM A as the probe set, each image of the probe set is matched with the images of the gallery. This provides a ranking for every image in the gallery with respect to the probe. 10 trials of evaluation are repeated to achieve stable statistics, and the average result is reported.

Figure 4 reports the comparison results considering the number of training pairs $k = 316$. To indicate the advantage of the proposed method (MSML for the proposed re-id method with fused salience and MSML_interS for the one with inter-salience), we compare it with three existing unsupervised methods, $i.e.$, SDALF [6], ELF [15], and the algorithm proposed in [8]. As seen from Fig. 4(a), the proposed approach outperforms all these methods achieving 30 % at rank 1. And with Rank-r larger, the recognition rate of the proposed method improves obviously. The matching rate at rank 15 is around 72 % for MSML, and 70 % for MSML_interS, versus 68.5 % for paper [8], 58.7 % for SDALF, and 54 % for ELF. In Fig. 4(b), the recognition results before weight training is obtained by normalizing each weight into 0.25. It is observed that the proposed methods enhance re-id rate greatly.

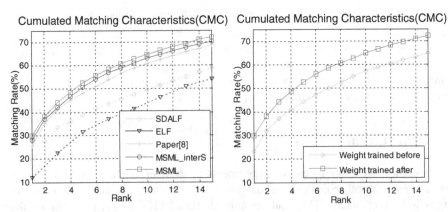

(a) Comparison with existing methods   (b) Comparison of weights trained before and after

Fig. 4. Performances on VIPeR dataset with 316 training set

Table 1. Comparison with existing re-id methods with 100 and 200 training pairs (%)

Method	k = 100				k = 200			
	r = 1	r = 5	r = 10	r = 20	r = 1	r = 5	r = 10	r = 20
Paper [8]	18.51	35.18	43.96	54.36	19.65	35.83	45.32	55.39
KISSME [16]	11.30	29.40	42.10	56.20	17.60	42.60	56.60	**71.50**
PRDC [17]	9.10	24.20	34.40	48.60	12.60	32.00	44.30	60.00
RPML [18]	11.00	28.00	38.00	52.00	20.00	42.00	56.00	71.00
MSML	**20.86**	**36.32**	**45.75**	**56.56**	**25.94**	**46.20**	**57.06**	68.85

Table 1 shows the comparison on re-id results of different learning methods with different scale of training set. The representative metric learning approaches, such as KISSME [16], PRDC [17], RPML [18], and the learning method used in [8] are taken for the comparison. The number of training pair k is chosen over 100 and 200 for testing. The lower of k, the harder of training and matching. When $k = 100$, the matching rate of the proposed method is higher than other learning based methods, even when the number of training pair of learning based methods is up to 200. It is clear that the proposed method outperforms the existing learning based methods, and can still get state-of-the-art performance even if the size of the training pair is small.

ETHZ Dataset [14]. This dataset is captured from moving cameras. Illumination changes and occlusions are obvious compared to VIPeR dataset. All images are normalized to 128 × 48 pixels. The dataset is structured as follows: SEQ.#1 contains 83 pedestrians, for a total of 4857 images; SEQ.#2 contains 35 pedestrians, for a total of 1936 images; SEQ.#3 contains 28 pedestrians, for a total of 1762 images.

For generalization verification, we take VIPeR dataset for weight learning, and ETHZ dataset for testing. The same settings of experiments in [6, 8] are reproduced, *i.e.*, using a single image as gallery, and several frames as query. For each person, we randomly sample one frame to establish gallery set, and the remaining form the probe set. Each image in probe is matched to every gallery image. The whole procedure is repeated for 10 times, and the average CMC curves are plotted in Fig. 5.

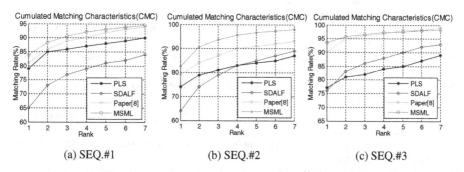

(a) SEQ.#1   (b) SEQ.#2   (c) SEQ.#3

Fig. 5. Performances comparison with one frame as gallery and several frames as query

As shown in Fig. 5, the proposed approach outperforms the existing feature design based method SDALF [6], and supervised learning based method PLS [19] on all three sequences. On SEQ.#1 and SEQ.#2, the proposed MSML outperforms paper [8]. On SEQ.#3, the MSML has similar re-id rate with paper [8], but rank 1 matching rate is higher than paper [8] reaching 93.5 %.

5 Conclusion

In this paper, a novel person re-id method based on multi-directional salience metric learning is proposed. Instead of bi-directional salience weighting for similarity evaluation, we design a similarity score as a weighted combination of four components, considering different patch salience directional distribution. Then, we adopt metric learning in the base of Structural SVM Ranking method to learn the weight of saliency in each direction. Experimental results clearly show that the proposed method outperforms the existing person re-id methods.

Acknowledgement. This work was supported by the National Natural Science Foundation of China (61104213), Natural Science Foundation of Jiangsu Province (BK2011146).

References

1. Doretto, G., Sebastian, T., Tu, P., et al.: Appearance-based person reidentification in camera networks: problem overview and current approaches. J. JAIHC **2**, 127–151 (2011)
2. Vezzani, R., Baltieri, D., Cucchiara, R.: People reidentification in surveillance and forensics: a survey. J. CSUR **46**, 29 (2013)
3. Layne, R., Hospedales, T.M., Gong, S., et al.: Person re-identification by attributes. In: BMVC, p. 8. (2012)
4. Gong, S., Cristani, M., Yan, S., et al.: Person re-identification. Springer, London (2014)
5. Ma, B., Su, Y., Jurie, F.: Bicov: a novel image representation for person re-identification and face verification. In: BMVC, p. 11 (2012)
6. Farenzena, M., Bazzani, L., Perina, A., et al.: Person re-identification by symmetry-driven accumulation of local features. In: CVPR, pp. 2360–2367 (2010)
7. Prosser, B., Zheng, W.S., Gong, S., et al.: Person re-identification by support vector ranking. In: BMVC, p. 6. (2010)
8. Zhao, R., Ouyang, W., Wang, X.: Unsupervised salience learning for person re-identification. In: CVPR, pp. 3586–3593 (2013)
9. Zheng, W.S., Gong, S., Xiang, T.: Reidentification by relative distance comparison. J. PAMI **35**, 653–668 (2013)
10. Yang, C., Zhang, L., Lu, H., et al.: Saliency detection via graph-based manifold ranking. In: CVPR, pp. 3166–3173 (2013)
11. Joachims, T., Finley, T., Yu, C.N.J.: Cutting-plane training of structural SVMs. J. Mach. Learn. **77**, 27–59 (2009)
12. McFee, B., Lanckriet, G.R.: Metric learning to rank. In: Proceedings of the 27th International Conference on Machine Learning, pp. 775–782 (2010)

13. Gray, D., Brennan, S., Tao, H.: Evaluating appearance models for recognition, reacquisition, and tracking. In: PETS, 3 (2007)
14. Ess, A., Leibe, B., Van Gool, L.: Depth and appearance for mobile scene analysis. In: ICCV, pp. 1–8 (2007)
15. Gray, D., Tao, H.: Viewpoint invariant pedestrian recognition with an ensemble of localized features. In: Forsyth, D., Torr, P., Zisserman, A. (eds.) ECCV 2008, Part I. LNCS, vol. 5302, pp. 262–275. Springer, Heidelberg (2008)
16. Kostinger, M., Hirzer, M., Wohlhart, P., et al.: Large scale metric learning from equivalence constraints. In: CVPR, pp. 2288–2295 (2012)
17. Zheng, W.S., Gong, S., Xiang, T.: Person re-identification by probabilistic relative distance comparison. In: CVPR, pp. 649–656 (2011)
18. Hirzer, M., Roth, P.M., Köstinger, M., Bischof, H.: Relaxed pairwise learned metric for person re-identification. In: Fitzgibbon, A., Lazebnik, S., Perona, P., Sato, Y., Schmid, C. (eds.) ECCV 2012, Part VI. LNCS, vol. 7577, pp. 780–793. Springer, Heidelberg (2012)
19. Schwartz, W.R., Davis, L.S.: Learning discriminative appearance-based models using partial least squares. In: XXII Brazilian Symposium on Computer Graphics and Image Processing (SIBGRAPI), pp. 322–329 (2009)

Sleep Pose Recognition in an ICU Using Multimodal Data and Environmental Feedback

Carlos Torres[1]([✉]), Scott D. Hammond[1], Jeffrey C. Fried[2],
and B.S. Manjunath[1]

[1] Department of Electrical and Computer Engineering,
University of California Santa Barbara, Santa Barbara, USA
{calostorres,manj}@ece.ucsb.edu, shammond@tmrl.ucsb.edu
http://vision.ece.ucsb.edu
[2] Santa Barbara Cottage Hospital, Santa Barbara, USA
jfried@sbch.org

Abstract. Clinical evidence suggests that sleep pose analysis can shed light onto patient recovery rates and responses to therapies. In this work, we introduce a formulation that combines features from multimodal data to classify human sleep poses in an Intensive Care Unit (ICU) environment. As opposed to the current methods that combine data from multiple sensors to generate a single feature, we extract features independently. We then use these features to estimate candidate labels and infer a pose. Our method uses modality trusts – each modality's classification ability – to handle variable scene conditions and to deal with sensor malfunctions. Specifically, we exploit shape and appearance features extracted from three sensor modalities: RGB, depth, and pressure. Classification results indicate that our method achieves 100 % accuracy (outperforming previous techniques by 6 %) in bright and clear (ideal) scenes, 70 % in poorly illuminated scenes, and 90 % in occluded ones.

1 Introduction

The tenets of evidence-based medicine implore clinicians and researchers to collect and process all available data in a specific healthcare setting. New methods for non-disruptive monitoring and analysis of patient sleep poses, patterns, and quality add objective metrics for predicting and evaluating health-related scenarios. There are clear clinical examples where patient poses are correlated to medical conditions. For example, sleep positions affect the symptoms of sleep apnea – where airway obstructions are greatest in supine positions [20]. The symptoms of gastroesophageal reflux disease (GERD) are reduced by laying on the side [11]. Body positioning is important in acute lung injury and prone positioning has been shown to improve outcomes in adult respiratory distress syndrome [5]. Prone and

This project is supported in part by the Institute for Collaborative Biotechnologies (ICB) through grant W911NF-09-0001 from the U.S. Army Research Office. The content of the information does not necessarily reflect the position or the policy of the Government, and no official endorsement should be inferred.

supine positions worsen back and spine problems, so lateral positioning is recommended by medical experts [4]. Physicians recommend that pregnant women lay on their sides to improve fetal blood flow [16]. The standard of care for immobile ICU patients is to rotate them every two hours to prevent decubitus ulcers, but this is rarely accomplished or effective [22].

The previous examples show that poses can be manipulated to improve patients' health. Therefore, accurate pose detection and classification is relevant to healthcare. The findings in [2,10,23] correlate body positions to various effects on health and quality of sleep of ICU patients. The authors state that identification of sleep poses in natural scenarios helps to evaluate sleep and to improve diagnosis and treatment of sleep disorders. Current physiological systems use machines that physically connect to the patients, making them disruptive and intrusive. Purely observational systems use images and pressure arrays to estimate poses but have been unable to handle natural scenes – indoor ICU scenes with variable illumination and occlusions such as blankets and pillows.

There are two major approaches for the study of sleep. One approach uses bio-status data to monitor a patient's metabolic state during sleep [12,14,18]. The polysomnogram is the standard equipment used in these studies. Its motion-restricting probes connect to the patient's head, face, and respiratory system, monitoring brain activity, rapid-eye-motion (REM) signals, and levels of oxygen and carbon-dioxide in the blood. The second approach is based on the identification of sleep patterns using non-intrusive equipment and human observers [7,15]. Computer vision methods are used in [13,15,18] but are limited to ideal scenes. In both approaches, the staging needed for observation affects the measurements. In order to overcome these issues, we propose to use three non-invasive, independent sensor modalities: RGB, depth, and pressure. Existing techniques are able to estimate human poses in ideal scenes using these modalities independently, but they fail in challenging ones. In [24] the authors present a generative approach that uses deformable parts model (DPM), commonly used in RGB images. Unfortunately, the DPM method requires images with relatively uniform illumination and with only minor self-occlusions. The discriminative approach from [21] uses depth images and is robust to illumination changes. However, this method requires clean depth segmentation and contrast, and it fails under occlusions. Neither of these methods works in unconstrained ICU scenarios.

Our work is most similar to [9], where standard RGB images and a low-resolution pressure array were used to classify sleep poses from static images. Their method used normalized geometric and load distribution features that depended on a clear view of the scene and the actor. They used interdependent data from RGB and pressure sensors – if one modality failed, no result was produced. Our method uses data from three modalities independently and then combines their estimation results using modality trusts to infer the final pose label. Moreover, our classification method is independent of body type and we use it to improve the unimodal decision of two common classifiers: Linear Discriminant Analysis (LDA) and Support Vector Classifier (SVC). The major contributions of this work are:

1. A new system configuration of complementary sensors to analyze sleep poses in healthcare scenarios. This modular system can be easily adapted to address a number of healthcare tasks and natural indoor scene constraints.
2. A new set of tuned features that capture the shape and appearance of human sleep poses.
3. The formulation of a novel multimodal concept for this application called modality trust, which leverages the ability of each individual modality for reliably representation of the human sleep poses.

2 System Description

The proposed system shown in Fig. 1 uses three sensor modalities: a single Carmine camera, with standard RGB and depth sensors by Primesense, and a high-resolution, pressure-sensing mattress by Tekscan. The Carmine and Tekscan devices are controlled by DuoCore computers, which communicate via TCP-IP and are synchronized using Network Time Protocol (NTP). The sensors monitor the bed and actors in a variety of poses and scenes as described in Sect. 2.1. The scene context (e.g., illumination and occlusions) is captured by the illumination, proximity, and radio-frequency identification (RFID) sensors.

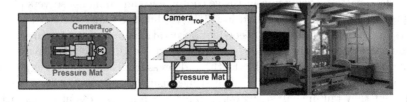

Fig. 1. Top and side profiles (left) of the multimodal system with top camera view (red) and pressure mat (green) and mock-up ICU (right) for data collection and testing (Color figure online).

2.1 Data Collection

Sleep poses are collected from five actors, who were asked to assume each of the ten poses from set Z = {Background, Soldier U, Soldier D, Faller R, Faller L, Log R, Log L, Yearner R, Yearner L, Fetal R, Fetal L}. The set Z has size L and is indexed by l. The letters in the labels U and D stand for facing-Up and facing-Down and L and R stand for laying-on-Left and laying-on-Right. The letter and subscript z_l is used to identify a specific pose label (e.g., z_0 = Background). The scene conditions are simulated using three illumination levels: bright (light sensor within 70–90 % saturation), medium (50–70 %), and dark (below 50 %) and four occlusion types: clear (no occlusion), blanket (covering 90 % of the actor's body), blanket and pillow, and pillow (between actor's upper body and the pressure mat). The illumination intensities are assigned using the percent saturation

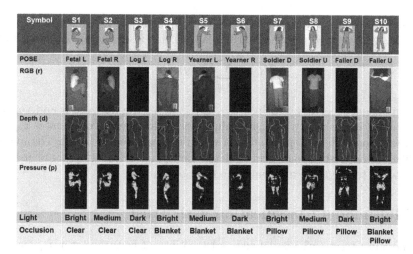

Fig. 2. Sample dictionary of sleep poses showing one actor in various poses and scenes. The top row shows the pose symbol, configuration, and orientation. The second row shows the pose names, where L and R indicates Left or the Right orientation, and U and D indicate facing Up or Down. The third, fourth, and fifth rows are the R, D, P pose representations. The D images on the fourth row are manually delineated to highlight the background and body differences. Finally, the bottom two rows describe the scene.

values and the occlusions are detected using inexpensive RFID and proximity sensors, all by .NET Gadgeteer. The combination of the illumination levels and occlusion types generates a 12-element scene-set $C = \{(\text{bright, medium, dark}) \times (\text{clear, blanket, pillow, blanket} + \text{pillow})\}$. Single illumination and occlusion combination (e.g., bright and clear) is represented using $c \in C$. The dataset is created assuming one scene to be the combination of one actor in one pose and under a single scene condition. From one scene four measurements are collected – three modalities from one camera view (RGB, depth, and a synthetic binary mask) and one pressure image. The data collection included background (bed without actor) images, and images of the actors in each of the 10 poses (11 classes including the background) under each of the 12 scene conditions. The process is repeated ten times for each of the five actors; this generates a dataset of 26,400 images (5 actors × 10 sessions × 4 images × 11 classes × 12 scenes). The modalities are calibrated using the methods from [6]. Sample data is shown in Fig. 2 and the complete set is available online at http://vision.ece.ucsb/research.

2.2 Feature Extraction

Features are extracted from R, D, P images after subtracting the background, converting them grayscale, and normalizing their pixel intensities.

Histogram of Oriented Gradients (HOG). The proposed formulation uses the HOG feature descriptor [3], extracted from R images, based on its ability to represent human limb structures, which is demonstrated in [24].

Image Geometric Moments (gMOM). Moments [8] extracted from the D and P images are used to describe the shape of the poses and are computed via:

$$\hat{M}_{i,j} = \sum_{x,y} I(x,y) x^j y^i, \tag{1}$$

where moment order is given by $i + j$, $i, j \geq 0$ are the horizontal and vertical orders, and I is the binary intensity value (0 or 1) for pixel at coordinates x, y. Its abilities for pose shape representation were demonstrated in [1, 19]. The images are tiled using a six-by-six grid and the raw pixel values ([0,1]) are used to compute up to the third moment from each block.

3   Multimodal Classification with Trust

The modality trust (w_m^c) is defined as the ability of feature vector f_m for pose classification. The vector f_m is extracted from modality m under scene conditions c. The trusts are estimated at training, using all the features in the subset X_{train}^c to compare estimated pose label $\hat{z}_k$ to the ground-truth label z_k^* and to record the matches. The learned trusts are used to infer a final multimodal label.

3.1   Trust Estimation

The set of modality trusts $\{w_1, w_2, \ldots w_M\}^c$ is estimated for modalities in N and condition c. The estimation of the modality trusts is divided into three stages: unimodal training, classifier validation, and trust normalization.

Unimodal Training. In this step unimodal SVC and LDA classifiers CLF_m^c are trained using the features f_m in X_{train}^c. Each of the unimodal classifier outputs a vector of length L of the form $[\hat{s}_{l,k}(f_m)] = [\hat{s}_{1,k}(f_m), \ldots, \hat{s}_{L,k}(f_m)]$. Given a datapoint X_k (with M unimodal feature vectors f_m), the $\hat{s}$ elements contain the scores for each of the L labels in Z.

Classifier Validation. At this stage the estimated unimodal labels $Z_{\hat{l},k}^{(m)}$ are compared to the ground truth label $Z_{l,k}^*$ from data point X_k. The label matches are stored in the array $\mathbf{b}$ of dimensions $[K, M]$ for all k datapoints ($1 \leq k \leq K$, and $K = |X_{train}|$) using Algorithm 1.

Trust Normalization. Finally, the trusts are estimated with following equation:

$$w_m = \frac{\sum\limits_{k=1}^{K} \mathbf{b}[k, m]}{K}, \tag{2}$$

and normalized so that the sum is one.

Algorithm 1. Unimodal Classifier Validation Vector (**b**)

1: **procedure** COMPARE($Z_{\hat{l},k}{}^{(m)}, Z_{*_{l,k}}$)   ▷ Estimated and ground truth labels
2:     **b** ← 0, $m, k = 0$,   ▷ Initialize array
3:     **for** k **do**
4:         **for** m **do**
5:             **if** $Z_{\hat{l},k}{}^{(m)} = Z_{*_{l,k}}$ **then**
6:                 b[k, m] ← 1
7:             **else**
8:                 b[k, m] ← 0
9:             **end if**
10:         **end for**
11:     **end for**
12:     **return b**   ▷ Vector of size K, M
13: **end procedure**

3.2 Multimodal Formulation

The overall description of the system is shown in Fig. 3. It uses the unimodal sensor training data (features) to estimate the trust values. Then the system uses the trusts to refine mulitmodal classification and produce a final pose label for a given test datapoint. First, the system applies a weighted scoring formulation to the unimodal label candidates obtained from the features $[f_1, f_2, f_3] = [\text{HOG}(R), \text{gMOM}(D), \text{gMOM}(P)]$ of datapoint X_k. Finally, the multimodal label $Z_{\hat{l},k}$ is the one with the maximum weighted score as follows:

$$S_{m,k}^c = S^c(X_k[f_m]) = w_m^c \text{CLF}_m^c(f_m), \tag{3}$$

where w_m^c represents the predictive power of feature f_m with scene conditions c, and CLF_m^c is the unimodal classifier score vector $[\hat{s}_{1,k}(f_m), \ldots, \hat{s}_{L,k}(f_m)]$

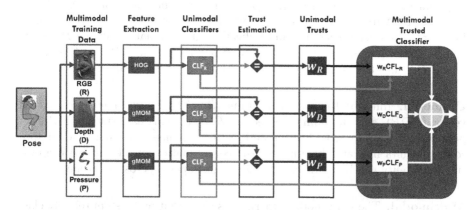

Fig. 3. Diagram of our proposed multimodal sleep pose classification method. The system uses modalities to exploit various scene and sensor properties. Second, features are extracted from the R, D, P pose representations and used to train unimodal classifiers and estimate modality trusts. Finally, trusts are used to refine the output.

(elements are label scores). Thus $S_{m,k}^c$ has L elements representing the unimodal label scores for an input X_k. The multimodal score is computed using:

$$S_k^c = \sum_{m=1}^M S_{m,k}^c = \sum_{m=1}^M \left(w_m^c [\hat{s}_{1,k}(f_m), \ldots, \hat{s}_{L,k}(f_m)]^c \right), \tag{4}$$

The vector S_k^c has L candidate scores values for each k and is computed via:

$$S_k^c = \sum_{m=1}^M \left(w_m^c \{\hat{s}_{l,k}(f_m)\}_L^c \right). \tag{5}$$

Therefore, given an input vector $X_k = \{f_m\}_M$ from scene c the estimated pose label is $Z_{\hat{l}}$, and the index $\hat{l}$ is computed using the following equations:

$$\hat{l} = \arg\max_{l \in L} \left(S_k^c \right), \tag{6}$$

where $\hat{l}$ is the index of the label with the highest trusted score from:

$$\hat{l} = \arg\max_{l \in L} \left(\sum_{m=1}^M w_m^c \{\hat{s}_{l,k}(f_m)\}_L^c \right). \tag{7}$$

Missing Modalities. Hardware malfunctions were simulated by omitting information from one modality (set its value to zero), proportionally adjusting the trusts of the remaining ones, and testing the system with the new trust values.

4 Experiments

Experiments are conducted using two classification methods: multi-class linear SVC and LDA from [17]. The experiments use five-fold cross-validation scheme for all reported accuracies. Results indicate that illumination affects R performance, while the performances of D and P remain constant. Recognition using R and D is affected by visual occlusions (blankets) and P is affected by pillows.

Unimodal. Initially, the system is trained/tested with a single concatenated vector (RDP), and the unimodal vectors R, D, P. This assessment provides a performance basis for classification and justifies the need for a multimodal approach. Results indicate that neither the concatenation of all nor the use of a single modality can be used directly to recognize poses across all scenes.

Multimodal. The multimodal experiments show that our system reliably classifies sleep poses in ICU scenarios using modality trust. To the best of our knowledge, there is no other method that considers our range of scenarios. Performance contrast of the system in various scenes is shown in Table 1. The table includes classification accuracies of the trusted multimodal system, a Majority-Vote-Learner (MaVL), and an in-house implementation of the method from [9].

Table 1. Mean multimodal sleep pose classification accuracy of two competing methods and our proposed multimodal trust using SVM (SVC) and LDA classifiers. Our method matches the performance of two competing methods in bright clear scenes and it outperforms them by a range of approximately 30 to 50 %.

Scene		Competing		Proposed	
Illumination	Occlusion	MaVL (*RDP*)	Huang (*RP*)	SVC (*RDP*)	LDA (*RDP*)
Bright	Clear	80	100	100	100
	Blanket	82	8	85.8	80.4
	Blanket + Pillow	65	6	85.8	83.6
	Pillow	54	58	90	90
Medium	Clear	80	88	100	100
	Blanket	65	7	85.3	80.6
	Blanket + Pillow	57	7	85.3	83.6
	Pillow	78	37	90	90
Dark	Clear	17	–	81.2	85
	Blanket	20	–	20.0	19.2
	Blanket + Pillow	32	–	17.7	18.6
	Pillow	60	–	24.5	22.3

Table 2. Mean classification accuracy with incomplete multimodal information. One modality is removed (\) and the modality trust values of the remaining ones is adjusted for SVC and LDA estimated labels.

Scene		SVC			LDA		
Illumination	Occlusion	$RD \setminus P$	$RP \setminus D$	$DP \setminus R$	$RD \setminus P$	$RP \setminus D$	$DP \setminus R$
Bright	Clear	100	100	100	100	100	100
	Blanket	85	90	95	80	85	92
	Blanket + Pillow	80	85	90	88.6	83.6	83.6
	Pillow	85	88	87	90	85	95
Medium	Clear	100	100	100	100	100	100
	Blanket	70	80	75	68.6	78.6	88.6
	Blanket + Pillow	65	70	71	73.5	81.6	83.6
	Pillow	81	85	87	77.3	82	85
Dark	Clear	54.1	47.7	72.7	29.5	74.1	76.4
	Blanket	7.5	30	35	23.2	68.6	76.8
	Blanket + Pillow	6	27	30	12.8	53	68.9
	Pillow	12	37	45	36.3	65.1	73.7

Missing Modalities. We test the limits of our system by omitting one modality and adjusting the contributions of the remaining modalities. We report SVC and LDA accuracies for all considered scenes in Table 2. Results show that our system performs poorly without pressure information, achieving a classification accuracy of 6 % using SVC and 12.8 % using LDA for dark and occluded scenes.

Confusion Matrices. The confusion matrices of our method and [9] are compared in Fig. 4. The main diagonal on the right shows that our method outperforms the competing method in challenging scenarios.

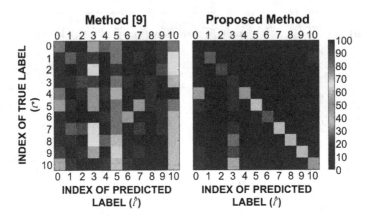

Fig. 4. Confusion matrices of implemented method from [9] with 16 % and our proposed method with 70 % accuracies for dark and occluded scenarios. The confusion matrices show how the indexes of the estimated labels $\hat{l}$ (x-axis) match the actual labels l^* (y-axis). The main diagonal indicates that our method (right) performs better.

5   Discussion

The parameters used for the computation of HOG features are: four orientations, 16×16 pixels per cell, and two-by-two cells per block. The geometric moment parameters were empirically tuned to achieve the highest pose classification accuracy possible. First, moments were extracted from the whole image (one-by-one grid) and their classification performance was tested. The one-by-one grid pose descriptors achieved a mean classification accuracy of 21 % over all scenes and 31 % for the bright, clear one. The grid dimensions were sequentially increased and revealed that a six-by-six grid yielded the highest accuracy without dramatically increasing computation time. Using the six-by-six grid, the system achieved a mean accuracy of 79 % over all scenes and 97 % for the bright and clear scene. Concatenation of features from the whole image and the six-by-six grid did not improve classification. The moment order was tuned alongside the grid dimensions. Shape descriptors were generated by computing up to the third geometric moment from each block; this yielded a ten-element vector per block or 360-element vector per image. Greater order moments increased estimation errors as reported in [8] and did not improve classification. The implementation of [9] to classify poses achieved an accuracy of 100 % in scenarios with bright and medium illumination. The performance increase (the authors reported a 94 % accuracy) is likely due to tunning parameters, higher resolution and complete bed coverage of the Tekscan mat. The $C = 0.5$ parameter for SVC was estimated during training with a validation dataset.

5.1 Conclusion

In this work, we presented a multimodal system to classify sleep poses in natural ICU scenarios. The system handles challenging conditions by relying on measurable variables from environmental sensors. We validated the sensor selection and features experimentally and showed that they provide accurate representations of sleep poses. Quantitative results indicate that the system has a performance increase of 6 % with respect to two existing methods in ideal scenarios and outperforms them significantly in dark and occluded ones. Reliability of the method was tested by sequentially omitting information from one modality and adjusting the remaining modalities via interpolation. With this scheme, the multimodal system achieved a pose classification accuracy of 47 % in challenging scenes.

6 Future Work

The multimodal system achieved high classification accuracies for most conditions; however, some scenarios caused a performance drop (e.g., 70 % in dark scenes) as shown in Table 1 and require further investigation. The system performs reliable classification of sleep poses in natural static ICU scenes. Nevertheless, we are exploring methods that integrate temporal information for the analysis of pose transitions and patterns. Extensions of this work will investigate new methods that are robust to an unconstrained set of body pose configurations, which better represent the poses of bed-ridden patients. Clinical deployment may impede the use of pressure mats due to sanitation requirements, so we are actively devising techniques that do not require this modality. Future work will explore new methods to estimate trust and combine multimodal classifiers (i.e., boosting), avoid the use of pressure mats, and integrate temporal information.

References

1. Ahad, M.A.R., Tan, J.K., Kim, H., Ishikawa, S.: Motion history image: its variants and applications. Mach. Vis. Appl. **23**(2), 255–281 (2012)
2. Bihari, S., McEvoy, R.D., Matheson, E., Kim, S., Woodman, R.J., Bersten, A.D.: Factors affecting sleep quality of patients in intensive care unit. J. Clin. Sleep Med. Official Publ. Am. Acad. Sleep Med. **8**(3), 301 (2012)
3. Dalal, N., Triggs, B.: Histograms of oriented gradients for human detection. In: Proceedings of the IEEE Conference Computer Vision and Pattern Recognition (2005)
4. Gordon, S.J., Grimmer, K.A., Trott, P.: Understanding sleep quality and waking cervico-thoracic symptoms. Int. J. Allied Health Sci. Pract. **5**, 1–12 (2007)
5. Guérin, C., Reignier, J., Richard, J.C., Beuret, P., Gacouin, A., Boulain, T., Mercier, E., Badet, M., Mercat, A., Baudin, O., et al.: Prone positioning in severe acute respiratory distress syndrome. New Engl. J. Med. **368**(23), 2159–2168 (2013)
6. Hartley, R.I., Zisserman, A.: Multiple View Geometry in Computer Vision, 2nd edn. Cambridge University Press (2004). ISBN: 0521540518
7. Hsia, C.C., Liou, K., Aung, A., Foo, V., Huang, W., Biswas, J.: Analysis and comparison of sleeping posture classification methods using pressure sensitive bed system. In: IEEE International Conference on Engineering in Medicine and Biology Society (2009)

8. Hu, M.K.: Visual pattern recognition by moment invariants. IEEE Trans. Inform. Theory **8**(2), 179–187 (1962)
9. Huang, W., Wai, A.A.P., Foo, S.F., Biswas, J., Hsia, C.C., Liou, K.: Multi-modal sleeping posture classification. In: IEEE International Conference on Pattern Recognition (2010)
10. Idzikowski, C.: Sleep position gives personality clue. BBC News, 16 September 2003
11. Khoury, R.M., Camacho-Lobato, L., Katz, P.O., Mohiuddin, M.A., Castell, D.O.: Influence of spontaneous sleep positions on nighttime recumbent reflux in patients with gastroesophageal reflux disease. Am. J. Gastroenterol. **94**(8), 2069–2073 (1999)
12. Koprinska, I., Pfurtscheller, G., Flotzinger, D.: Sleep classification in infants by decision tree-based neural networks. Artif. Intell. Med. **8**(4), 387–401 (1996)
13. Kuo, C.H., Yang, F.C., Tsai, M.Y., Ming-Yih, L.: Artificial neural networks based sleep motion recognition using night vision cameras. Biomed. Eng. Appl. Basis Commun. **16**(02), 79–86 (2004)
14. Lewicke, A., Sazonov, E., Corwin, M.J., Neuman, M., Schuckers, S.: Sleep versus wake classification from heart rate variability using computational intelligence: consideration of rejection in classification models. IEEE Trans. Biomed. Eng. **55**(1), 108–118 (2008)
15. Liao, W.H., Yang, C.M.: Video-based activity and movement pattern analysis in overnight sleep studies. In: IEEE International Conference on Pattern Recognition (2008)
16. Morong, S., Hermsen, B., de Vries, N.: Sleep position and pregnancy. In: de Vries, N., et al. (eds.) Positional Therapy in Obstructive Sleep Apnea, pp. 163–173. Springer, New York (2015)
17. Pedregosa, F., Varoquaux, G., Gramfort, A., Michel, V., Thirion, B., Grisel, O., Blondel, M., Prettenhofer, P., Weiss, R., Dubourg, V., Vanderplas, J., Passos, A., Cournapeau, D., Brucher, M., Perrot, M., Duchesnay, E.: Scikit-learn: machine learning in Python. J. Mach. Learn. Res. **12**, 2825–2830 (2011)
18. Penzel, T., Conradt, R.: Computer based sleep recording and analysis. Sleep Med. Rev. **4**(2), 131–148 (2000)
19. Ramagiri, S., Kavi, R., Kulathumani, V.: Real-time multi-view human action recognition using a wireless camera network. In: International IEEE Conference on Distributed Smart Cameras (2011)
20. Sahlin, C., Franklin, K.A., Stenlund, H., Lindberg, E.: Sleep in women: normal values for sleep stages and position and the effect of age, obesity, sleep apnea, smoking, alcohol and hypertension. Sleep Med. **10**(9), 1025–1030 (2009)
21. Shotton, J., Girshick, R., Fitzgibbon, A., Sharp, T., Cook, M., Finocchio, M., Moore, R., Kohli, P., Criminisi, A., Kipman, A., et al.: Efficient human pose estimation from single depth images. IEEE Trans. Pattern Anal. Mach. Intell. **35**(12), 2821–2840 (2013)
22. Soban, L., Hempel, S., Ewing, B., Miles, J.N., Rubenstein, L.V.: Preventing pressure ulcers in hospitals. Jt Comm. J. Qual. Patient Saf. **37**(6), 245–252 (2011)
23. Weinhouse, G.L., Schwab, R.J.: Sleep in the critically ill patient. Sleep-New York Then Westchester **29**(5), 707 (2006)
24. Yang, Y., Ramanan, D.: Articulated human detection with flexible mixtures of parts. IEEE Trans. Pattern Anal. Mach. Intell. **35**(12), 2878–2890 (2013)

Hardware-Implemented
and Real-Time Vision Systems

A Flexible High-Resolution Real-Time Low-Power Stereo Vision Engine

Stefan K. Gehrig[1]([⊠]), Reto Stalder[2], and Nicolai Schneider[3]

[1] Daimler AG Group Research, 71059 Sindelfingen, Germany
stefan.gehrig@daimler.com
[2] SCS AG, Technoparkstr. 11, 8005 Zuerich, Switzerland
[3] IT-Designers, Entennest 2, 73730 Esslingen, Germany

Abstract. Stereo Vision has been a focus of research for decades. In the meantime, many real-time stereo vision systems are available on low-power platforms. Several products using stereo vision exist on the market. So far, all of them are based on image sizes up to 1 MP. They either use a local correlation-like stereo engine or perform some variant of Semi-Global Matching (SGM).

However, many modern cameras deliver 2 MP images (full High Definition) at framerates beyond 20 Hz. In this contribution we propose a stereo vision engine tailored for automotive and mobile applications, that is able to process 2 MP images in real-time. Note that also the disparity range has to be increased when maintaining the same field of view with higher resolution. We implement the SGM algorithm with search space reduction techniques on a reconfigurable hardware platform, yielding a low power consumption of under 1 W. The algorithm runs at 22 Hz processing 2 MP image pairs and computing disparity maps with up to 255 disparities. The conducted evaluations on the KITTI Dataset and on a challenging bad weather dataset show that full depth resolution is obtained for small disparities and robustness of the method is maintained at a fraction of the resources of a regular SGM engine.

Keywords: Disparity estimation · Semi-global matching · FPGA

1 Introduction

Stereo vision has a long research history. The Middlebury benchmark to compare stereo algorithms with respect to accuracy was established in 2002 [16]. A more realistic benchmark for outdoor navigation and robotic scenarios is the KITTI Dataset [7]. There, we found Semi-Global Matching (SGM) [8] variants several times in the top 20. SGM offers a good compromise between performance and efficiency. So we focus on this algorithm for the rest of this paper.

Our main application focus is on outdoor scenarios for driver assistance. There, contradictory requirements push stereo algorithms to the limit: One one hand, a good disparity resolution for small disparities (large distances) is vital for far range obstacle detection, requiring high resolution images. On the other hand, all

© Springer International Publishing Switzerland 2015
L. Nalpantidis et al. (Eds.): ICVS 2015, LNCS 9163, pp. 69–79, 2015.
DOI: 10.1007/978-3-319-20904-3_7

objects in front of the car must be measured, demanding a large disparity range to be computed. We tackle this challenge by reducing the disparity search space and proper subsampling without loss of disparity resolution. Robotics scenarios benefit from this strategy as well. In this paper, we introduce a flexible real-time low-power stereo implementation that runs at 22 Hz using 2 MP imagery with less than 1 W power consumption. An example result is shown in Fig. 1.

In a nutshell, the base SGM algorithm performs an energy minimization in a dynamic-programming fashion on multiple 1 D paths crossing each pixel and thus approximating the 2 D image. The energy consists of three parts: a data term for similarity, a small penalty term for slanted surfaces that change the disparity slightly (parameter P_1), and a penalty term for depth discontinuities (parameter P_2).

Fig. 1. Left example image from the Zynq stereo system overlaid with the color-coded disparity result. Red pixels depict near, green far pixels. Right: corresponding confidence image, the brighter the pixel, the higher the confidence (Color figure online).

This paper is organized in the following way: Prior work of the field is presented in Sect. 2. Section 3 explains our system design. The next section describes FPGA implementation details to obtain real-time performance. Results of the hardware setup can be found in Sect. 5. An evaluation on the KITTI Dataset and on a challenging bad weather dataset is included. Conclusions and future work comprise the final section.

2 Related Work

2.1 Embedded Stereo Systems

Today, several real-time stereo vision systems are available on low-power platforms. One of the first stereo hardware engines is described in [12]. The Census-based stereo system by the company Tyzx is a popular choice [21].

Field-programmable gate-array (FPGA) stereo implementations have emerged frequently in the last decade. Dynamic programming stereo [15] has been implemented on an FPGA as an early example. SGM on an FPGA using two SGM passes with different resolutions is presented in [5]. An SGM implementation limited to 4 paths is described in [1] and [17]. A memory-efficient

SGM version is presented in [11]. A good overview of stereo vision algorithms with focus on resource-limited systems is presented in [19].

In the automotive field, stereo cameras are mounted behind the windshield. The system introduced in Mercedes models uses SGM at its heart [4]. Toyota offers a stereo object detection system for Lexus models [20]. Similar to this, all other available automotive stereo engines operate with local-correlation variants.

Furthermore, several global stereo algorithms have been implemented in real-time on the graphics card (GPU). For example, SGM is reported to run at 27 Hz on XGA size images [2]. However, the power consumption of such GPUs is above 100 W which does not qualify for a low-power embedded system.

2.2 Reduced Search Space Techniques

A traditional way to speed up stereo computation is to use image pyramids e.g. [3] or downsized images which also reduce the disparity range. There, only disparities around the optimum disparity from the smaller image are searched. However, small objects might be missed this way.

A similar technique to image pyramids is introduced in [5] and [6]. However, the different image sizes are all processed with SGM independently, resulting in several disparity maps. The merge is performed based on the chosen disparity range, being largest (scaled to full resolution) for the smallest image. This procedure is error-prone for match validation (do I keep the match when one SGM invalidates the match but one keeps it?).

Another search space reduction procedure closest to our proposed approach uses disparity space compression reducing the number of tested disparity hypotheses [18]. The full image resolution is maintained but for larger disparities (small distance errors) only every 2nd or 4th disparity is tested. Here, it is assumed that an optimal disparity at an untested position will deliver minimal matching costs at either the left or right neighboring position.

Despite the remarkable progress on real-time stereo vision systems, there is still a need for a stereo method working on high-resolution images at low-power and high frame rates. We close this gap with our contribution.

3 System Design

Disparity estimation, here exemplified for SGM, consists of the following main steps: Cost computation, cost aggregation, minimum cost finding, subpixel interpolation, and Right-Left consistency check.

We follow the design from [5] for the parts of cost aggregation, minimum cost finding, and subpixel interpolation. For the matching cost we pick the popular Census transform [22] that has been used very successfully in combination with SGM [10]. We choose a 9×7 window. For the Right-Left consistency check (RL-check) we pick the fast variant [13] without the need to compute SGM twice.

The main limitation of FPGA-based architectures are mostly internal memory storage (block RAMs, BRAMs) and external bandwidth. According to [5], the number of disparities multiplied by the number of image columns determine the BRAM consumption. This limitation can be pushed, when we apply the disparity compression trick from [18] and when we reduce the number of disparity measurements by subsampling.

Concretely, we design the system to operate with up to 2048 × 1024 px image pairs delivering 16 bits/px. For typical fields of view around 50° and 20 cm baseline, this results in maximum disparities of around 200 for objects at the own bumper. We reduce the disparity space to 64 steps, maintaining single steps for small disparities (large depth uncertainty), and increasing disparity step size up to 4 at large disparities (small uncertainty), trying to maintain similar depth uncertainties across the disparity range. In addition, a full resolution disparity image is not needed for mobile navigation or driver assistance. However, the full disparity resolution for large distance is vital for long range object detection. To account for this we average two lines to one line, ending with a 2048 × 512 resolution. This adds the nice property of being less prone to small calibration errors [9] without losing much information. In horizontal direction we evaluate the disparity at every other (even) pixel but we use the full horizontal resolution image for matching. Note that the resulting diagonal SGM paths still operate at 45° this way and the disparity image is 1024 × 512 px in size. We call these two steps of image size reduction in vertical direction and image subsampling in horizontal direction simply UV-subsampling (Vbinning and Hstep in Fig. 3).

4   FPGA Implementation

4.1   Hardware Platform

The experimental system (see Fig. 2) runs on a hardware accelerator box[1], based on the Xilinx Zynq 7045 SOC (System On Chip). The Zynq 7045 provides two ARM Cortex-A9 cores with neon engine and a Kintex-based FPGA fabric. Each core runs at 1 GHz and has its own 32 kByte first level cache. From the various on chip periphery 1 Gigabit Ethernet, 2 CAN and 1 USB Host interface are accessible to the user.

The FPGA fabric offers 218'000 6-input lookup tables (LUTs), 545 36 kBit embedded block rams (BRAMs) and 900 multiply-accumulate engines (DSP slices). It has access to two dedicated, independent DDR/3 memories. They offer capacities of 512 MBytes and 256 MBytes and are working 16-bit wide at 400 MHz. Additionally two Gigabit Ethernet ports are attached for the data transfer between FPGA fabric and external systems.

The ecosystem surrounding the SGM algorithm on the FPGA consists basically of a stereo image pipeline at the input and a data packer engine at the output which distributes the result over two Gigabit Ethernet channels. The neon engines are available for high-level algorithms using the disparity information.

The stereo image pipeline removes the Bayer pattern from the incoming images. SGM depends on rectified input images. Therefore lens distortions and

---

[1] http://www.scs.ch/ueber-scs/departments/felix-eberli.html.

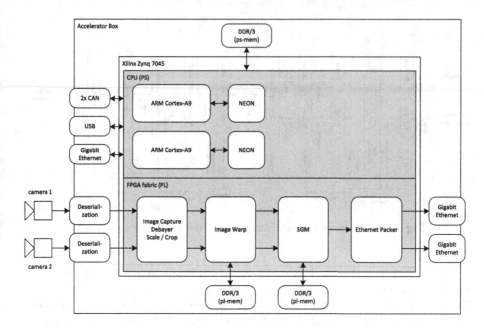

Fig. 2. Basic hardware and FPGA logic blocks of the experimental system.

mounting errors are removed by the rectification step which is effectively an image warper. This engine calculates the output images by bilinear interpolation of the required pixels from the input images. A lookup based algorithm finds the correspondence between pixels of the input and output images. Cache allocation and fitting of the interpolation are optimized offline by software. This facilitates a very resource-efficient FPGA implementation, consuming only 2000 Flip-Flops, 2000 6-input LUTs, 6 36 kBit BRAMs and 4 DSP slices.

4.2 SGM Implementation

General Considerations: We have designed the FPGA implementation of SGM for input images as large as 2048×1024 px. Disparity maps with 1024×512 px in size are generated at a frame rate of 22 Hz. When lowering the frame rate, the engine is also capable of delivering disparity maps at full input image size. The frame rate is limited by the available bandwidth to the external memory. Internally the SGM engine is running at 200 MHz clock speed. Considering that the calculations are divided into a scan-down and a scan-up phase (both calculating costs for 4 path directions, see [5]) we have a computation time of 8 clocks per pixel (or 25 MHz pixel clock). Or viewed differently: in scan-down and scan-up, for every pixel, and for each of the 4 paths, 64 path cost values are calculated. This computation is done in 8 clock cycles, resulting in 32 path cost values per clock and thus 32 parallel path cost calculation engines (see Fig. 3).

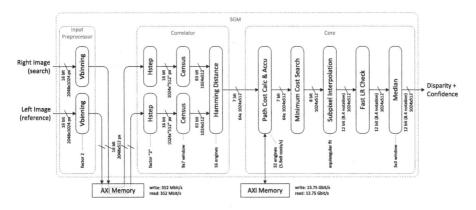

Fig. 3. Overview of the SGM implementation on the Zynq system.

Input Preprocessor: Fig. 3 shows that first each input image passes a vertical binning (Vbinning) engine, where the image heights are (optionally) halved. This is achieved by merging every two rows together in taking the arithmetic mean of the two pixels located one below the other. The preprocessed images are then written to the external memory.

Correlator: The preprocessed images are read twice by the correlator, first top-down in the scan-down phase and then bottom-up in the scan-up phase. Optionally, their widths are virtually halved (Hstep in Fig. 3). In fact the arithmetic mean of two subsequent pixels is taken for the reference image and the original value of every second pixel for the search image. Then for both images Census is computed. Finally the hamming distance is taken for every pixel in the reference image and their 64 disparity hypothesis counterparts in the search image.

Thanks to using Census as cost criterion (in contrast to ZSAD in [5]) the cost bandwidth is reduced to 10 bit. The Census operates on a 9×7 window. Compared to [9], the window size is extended to 18 px to add more stability when compressing the disparity space (see below). Every two subsequent pixel in horizontal direction are averaged, resulting in the 9×7 window. Thereon, the actual Census is applied. While the window moves, 8 of the 9 window columns remain the same. Therefore, we implement the Census in a sliding window manner, which saves internal memory bandwidth. However, as the center pixel changes every time, all 62 comparisons and the sum of their results must be repeated, resulting in parallel computation logic.

The hamming distance block in the correlator implements disparity space compression. In contrast to [5], where costs for 64 linearly distributed disparity hypotheses are computed over a range of 0–63, this implementation maintains the total number of 64 hypotheses per pixel, while increasing the range of native disparities to 0-255. The 64 hypotheses are distributed non-linearly with the aid of a so-called spacing configuration. Three spacing configurations are supported. They are illustrated in Fig. 4. As the Figure shows, spacing 4 averages

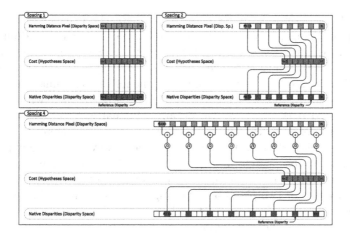

Fig. 4. Valid spacing configurations for the disparity space compression.

two hamming distances as a measure to avoid aliasing artifacts in contrast to
[18]. This has the impact that first the native (reference) disparity shifts by one
position compared to the hamming distances and second twice the computation
power is needed in comparison to spacings 1 and 2. That is why we have resigned
considering all intermediate hamming distances. A spacing configuration applies
to 8 subsequent hypotheses at a time. So for example the setting [1,1,2,2,4,4,4,4]
results in the following tested disparities which are also used for our evaluations
below: 0, 1, ... 14, 15, 16, 18, 20, ..., 44, 46, 49, 53, ..., 173.

Core: The core performs the actual SGM algorithm. Path cost calculation, path
cost accumulation, minimum cost search and median filter are conceptually similar to [5], except that the throughput grows by a factor of 4.7 due to changes in
image size and frame rate. Two confidence measures (local curve and peak ratio
native [14]) are added. Due to disparity compression, the subpixel interpolation
(equiangular fit) accounts for non-equidistant disparities.

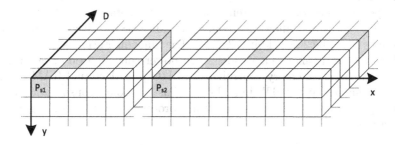

Fig. 5. Location of the virtual costs for a pixel in the original cost cube. Example for
spacing configurations 1 (P_{s1}) and 2 (P_{s2}).

RL-check: In contrast to a full RL-check the fast RL-check avoids a second SGM engine with exchanged reference and search images [13]. It is based on the following idea: assuming the left image is the reference, we compare the left image pixel $P_L(x, y)$ with the right image pixel $P_R(x - D, y)$ to calculate the cost for disparity D. The same calculation would be done for the right image as the reference: namely when $P_R(x, y)$ is compared to $P_L(x + D, y)$. Thus with reordering the accumulated path costs we can obtain a virtual cost cube similar to the one we would have when calculating SGM with exchanged reference and search images. Using this virtual cost cube, we calculate the virtual optimum disparities (by minimum cost search) and check them for similarity against the original optimum disparities. Figure 5 exemplifies the location of the virtual costs in the original cost cube for two pixels and spacing configurations. Unfortunately, the fast RL-check consumes large amounts of buffer space. The memory consumption is a linear function of the maximum native disparity.

5   Results

The results shown here are all conducted with a disparity range 0 to 173 as described above. UV-subsampling is performed. $P_1 = 20$ and $P_2 = 100$ is set for all evaluations.

5.1   Hardware Performance Results

The proposed system is synthesized on a Xilinx Zynq 7045 FPGA utilizing 32500 LUTs and 206 36 kbit BRAMs, leaving many resources for further processing. When running at 200 MHz clock speed, 2048 × 1024 images can be processed at 22 Hz, utilizing the full memory bandwidth of 13.75 Gbit/s. The resource increase for a classic SGM engine operating on 2 MP images would be at least twofold for all quantities at a lower frame rate. A comparison to other published SGM methods is shown in Table 1. Note that [1] and [17] use only 4 SGM paths yielding anisotropic results but mostly avoiding external memory communication hence getting higher frame rates. Resource comparisons are listed in Table 1 but note that the optimization goals are very different for the published methods.

   The performance of the current FPGA implementation would allow even higher frame rates and allows for computing all 2048 px without subsampling (consuming 60 of the 206 36 kbit BRAMs). The implementation is limited by the available external memory bandwidth. The power consumption of SGM is less than 1 W, including memory controllers and I/O pins. External RAM communication consumes up to 0.6 W in addition. This low power consumption results from the proper choice of hardware (28 nm process) and a careful algorithmic optimization.

5.2   KITTI Results

We perform our accuracy evaluations on the KITTI training set. The KITTI Dataset uses typical stereo traffic images under good weather conditions using

Table 1. SGM FPGA performance figures from published implementations.

method	resolution [px]	max. disp	fps [Hz]	LUTs	BRAM [kB]	power	clock [MHz]
[5]	680 × 400	127	27	60000	300	3W	133
[1]	640 × 480	127	30	22000	104	-	39
[11]	640 × 480	63	17	-	-	-	125
[17]	1242 × 375	159	199	109072	135	-	92
ZynqSGM	2048 × 1024	255	22	32500	824	1W	200

8 bits/px. We compare our proposed system, ZynqSGM, with a traditional SGM using the full image resolution (FullResSGM) and an SGM version at half image resolution (HalfResSGM) [14]. The results of FullResSGM and HalfResSGM are similar, even slightly better for half resolution. This is due to the more discriminative Census cost and better smoothing properties at half resolution. The proposed stereo method ZynqSGM performs actually slightly better than FullResSGM with the default KITTI error metric counting outliers beyond 3 disparities deviation. All runs have been conducted with a full RL-check and standard KITTI background interpolation. With parameter tuning ($P_1 = 28$, $P_2 = 140$), HalfResSGM yields 6.01 % error rate, on par with the best SGM methods in the KITTI benchmark.

The improvements in small disparity measurements become visible when evaluating the RMS for disparities under 16 px. The RMS of ZynqSGM is 0.24 px vs. 0.26 px for HalfResSGM, thus improving the small disparity sub-pixel quality using disparity compression.

If we use the fast RL-check for efficiency, the error rates for all three methods increase due to the less discriminative check, at slightly higher stereo densities. With this fast RL check, the ZynqSGM method obtains the best error rate (Table 2).

5.3 Ground Truth Stixel Dataset Results

As a second evaluation source, we use the challenging automotive dataset including rainy highway scenes, called the Ground Truth Stixel Dataset [14]. There, the stereo quality is evaluated using so-called stixels, an intermediate representation used in driver assistance. The robustness can be measured by considering the false positive stixel rate. The stixel detection rate indicates the density of the disparity data.

FullResSGM and HalfResSGM deliver similar results to our proposed algorithm, confirming no unwanted artifacts due to the disparity space compression and the adapted fast RL-check. Table 3 summarizes the results, the variants in parentheses utilize stereo confidence information with local curve fit as confidence measure [14].

Table 2. Pixel error rates on KITTI training set, evaluated for all pixels (disparity data interpolated). Results using fast RL-check in parentheses.

method	stereo density %	error rate %
FullResSGM	87.57 (89.71)	7.81 (10.13)
HalfResSGM [14]	**92.79 (94.25)**	**6.97** (9.11)
ZynqSGM	84.65 (89.31)	7.75 (**9.04**)

Table 3. False positive point rates, false positive stixels (fp), and detection rates for different SGM variants on a 3000-frames stixel database. Results using stereo confidence are shown in parentheses.

	false positive points/stixels			detections
	% fp point	#fp	#fp frames	all %
FullResSGM	**0.31**	**508 (202)**	**176** (101)	82.1 (81.8)
HalfResSGM	0.40	1552 (291)	242 (**98**)	**84.0 (84.0)**
ZynqSGM	0.41	829 (426)	230 (143)	83.0 (82.9)

6   Conclusions and Future Work

A flexible disparity estimation engine has been presented being able to process 2 MP images at 22 Hz with a maximum disparity of up to 255. Its performance is on par with a full resolution SGM engine at a fraction of the silicon resources. The evaluations on KITTI data and on the Stixel Ground Truth data show, that no relevant performance was sacrificed with the chosen resource optimizations.

The stereo engine can be configured flexibly with free choice where to put the highest disparity resolution. In a driver monitoring camera setting, this allows to measure the driver precisely, while the vehicle surroundings are measured in a coarser way. If resolutions beyond 2 MP become relevant in real-time systems, it is also possible to subsample the images with a larger factor than two, allowing the rest of the engine to keep operating the same way and still exploiting the full disparity resolution in the chosen area. In the future, we will reduce the resource consumption for the RL-check where more than 60 BRAMs are spent. We expect this engine to be a basis for future driver assistance and robotic systems.

References

1. Banz, C., et al.: Real-time stereo vision system using SGM disparity estimation: architecture and FPGA-implementation. In: SAMOS Conference (2010)
2. Banz, C., Blume, H.: Real-time semi-global matching disparity estimation on the GPU using SGM. In: Mobile Vision Workshop ICCV (2011)
3. Franke, U., Joos, A.: Real-time stereo vision for urban traffic scene understanding. In: Intelligent Vehicles (2000)

4. Franke, U. et al.: Making bertha see. In: Computer Vision for Autonomous Vehicles Workshop ICCV (2013)
5. Gehrig, S.K., Eberli, F., Meyer, T.: A real-time low-power stereo vision engine using semi-global matching. In: Fritz, M., Schiele, B., Piater, J.H. (eds.) ICVS 2009. LNCS, vol. 5815, pp. 134–143. Springer, Heidelberg (2009)
6. Gehrig, S., Rabe, C.: Real-time semi-global matching on the CPU. In: ECVW 2010 CVPR, June 2010
7. Geiger, A., Lenz, P., Urtasun, R.: Are we ready for autonomous driving? the KITTI vision benchmark suite. In: CVPR, June 2012
8. Hirschmueller, H.: Accurate and efficient stereo processing by semi-global matching and mutual information. CVPR **2**, 807–814 (2005). (San Francisco, CA)
9. Hirschmueller, H., Gehrig, S.: Stereo matching in the presence of sub-pixel calibration errors. In: CVPR, Miami, FL, June 2009
10. Hirschmueller, H., Scharstein, D.: Evaluation of stereo matching costs on images with radiometric distortions. IEEE PAMI **31**(9), 1582–1599 (2009)
11. Hirschueller, H., Buder, M., Ernst, I.: Memory-efficient semi-global matching. In: XXII ISPRS Congress (2012)
12. Konolige, K.: Small vision systems. In: Proceedings of the International Symposium on Robotics Research, Hayama, Japan (1997)
13. Muehlmann, K., et al.: Calculating dense disparity maps from color stereo images, an efficient implementation. IJCV **47**(1–3), 79–88 (2002)
14. Pfeiffer, D., Gehrig, S., Schneider, N.: Exploiting the power of stereo confidences. In: CVPR, June 2013
15. Sabihuddin, S., MacLean, W.J.: Maximum-likelihood stereo correspondence using field programmable gate arrays. In: ICVS, Bielefeld, Germany, March 2007
16. Scharstein, D., Szeliski, R.: Middlebury online stereo evaluation. http://vision. middlebury.edu/stereo. Accessed 12 March 2013
17. Schumacher, F., Greiner, T.: Matching cost computation algorithm and high speed fpga architecture for high quality real-time semi global matching stereo vision for road scenes. In: ITSC (2014)
18. Spangenberg, R., Langner, T., Adfeldt, S., Rojas, R.: Large scale semi-global matching on the CPU. In: Intelligent Vehicles (2014)
19. Tippets, B., et al.: Review of stereo vision algorithms and their suitability for resource-limited systems. Journal of Real-Time Image processing. Springer, Heidelberg, January 2013. http://rd.springer.com/article/10.1007%2Fs11554-012-0313-2
20. Usami, M., et al.: Stereo vision system for advances vehicle safety system. In: SAE World Congress, Technical paper. 2007-01-0405 (2007)
21. Woodfill, J.I., et al.: The TYZX deepsea G2 vision system, a taskable, embedded stereo camera. In: Embedded Computer Vision Workshop. pp. 126–132 (2006)
22. Zabih, R., Woodfill, J.: Non-parametric local transforms for computing visual correspondence. In: Eklundh, J.-O. (ed.) ECCV 1994. LNCS, vol. 801, pp. 151–158. Springer, Heidelberg (1994)

Real Time Vision System for Obstacle Detection and Localization on FPGA

Ali Alhamwi[1]([✉]), Bertrand Vandeportaele[1,2], and Jonathan Piat[1,2]

[1] LAAS-CNRS, 7 Avenue du Colonel Roche,
31077 Toulouse Cedex 4, France
{aalhamwi,bvandepo,jpiat}@laas.fr
[2] University of Toulouse,
31077 Toulouse Cedex 4, France

Abstract. Obstacle detection is a mandatory function for a robot navigating in an indoor environment especially when interaction with humans is done in a cluttered environment. Commonly used vision-based solutions like SLAM (Simultaneous Localization and Mapping) or optical flow tend to be computation intensive and require powerful computation resources to meet low speed real-time constraints. Solutions using LIDAR (Light Detection And Ranging) sensors are more robust but not cost effective. This paper presents a real-time hardware architecture for vision-based obstacle detection and localization based on IPM (Inverse Perspective Mapping) for obstacle detection, and Otsu's method plus Bresenham's algorithm for obstacle segmentation and localization under the hypothesis of a flat ground. The proposed architecture combines cost effectiveness, high frame-rate with low latency, low power consumption and without any prior knowledge of the scene compared to existing implementations.

1 Introduction

Obstacle detection is a fundamental ability of mobile robots to operate in an cluttered indoor environment and it is essential in order to perform basic functions of mobile robots like avoidance and navigation. This critical task is often addressed with high cost sensors (LIDAR, RADAR) or computation intensive algorithms (Optical Flow, SLAM ...) that prevent to limit the cost of a robotic system.

Sonar based methods prove to be unreliable because of the system noise. LIDAR sensors provide an accurate information and work independently of the ambient light. However, LIDAR sensors are expensive, and provide a performance with low level of vertical resolution.

The detection of obstacles based on images can determine the type of obstacle, and with the reduction of cameras cost it is possible to integrate a large number of cameras; Furthermore, they are compact, accurate and well modelled. However, a software implementation of SLAM and optical flow algorithms in real time requires a great computational load because of the complexity of these

© Springer International Publishing Switzerland 2015
L. Nalpantidis et al. (Eds.): ICVS 2015, LNCS 9163, pp. 80–90, 2015.
DOI: 10.1007/978-3-319-20904-3_8

algorithms [6]. Vision approaches based on classification need a prior knowledge about environment to separate ground pixels from obstacle pixels. Vision approaches based on IPM allow obstacle detection under the hypothesis of a flat ground, this method is based on the perspective effect perceived from a scene when observed from two different points of view [3]. This method was introduced in [9] and exploited for obstacle detection in [2]. While this method is based on homographic transformation, it requires an important amount of computations. Architectures based on GPU (Graphic Processing Unit) platform provide a good pipeline performance but they don't meet power requirements. An FPGA (Field Programmable Gate Array) solution can provide better trade-off for power consumption and pipeline requirements of an embedded platform.

This paper is organized as follows: Sect. 2 describes the theoretical background and related work. Section 3 describes the proposed hardware design. Discussion and conclusion are detailed in Sects. 4 and 5.

2   Theoretical Background

Inverse Perspective Mapping is a technique based on a geometric transformation applied on frames acquired with different point of view (either using multiple camera, or frames acquired at different time). This method belongs to the resampling effect family; an initial image is transformed to generate a view from a different position. Taking advantage of the perspective effect, this generated image is compared to a real image acquired from the new position. This comparison generates high differences for object sticking out of the ground plane. Detecting and localizing these differences in the ground plane allows to compute the object position relative to the camera.

2.1   Inverse Perspective Mapping

In Mono Inverse perspective mapping [3], a single camera is used, two frames are acquired at distinct instants t_n and t_{n+1}, as the robot moves. Odometry sensors are used as input to compute the homography matrix. This matrix encodes the effect on the images of the relative movement of the robot between the two positions for a given plane in the scene which is the ground plane in our case. The camera is considered already calibrated; i.e., it's intrinsic parameters (focal, principal point and distortion coefficients) have been determined off line. Thanks to this knowledge, optical distortions can be removed and it is possible to consider the simple Pinhole camera model to perform IPM. With this model, a 3D point of the scene (X_w, Y_w, Z_w) in the world frame is projected to pixel coordinates (u, v) in the pinhole image with the Eq. 1. As noted in Eq. 1, K is the camera intrinsic matrix and (R, t) encodes the rotation and translation from the world frame to the camera frame. These former parameters are named the camera extrinsic parameters. As IPM is intended to detect the ground pixels, the world frame which is the robot frame as depicted in Fig. (1)(a) is chosen such

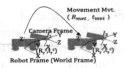 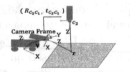

(a) Mono IPM system performing a movement M_vt.

(b) Bird's Eye transformation.

Fig. 1. Inverse perspective mapping

as the $X_w Y_w$ plane is the ground plane. Therefore, for 3D points in the world frame laying in the ground plane, $Z_w = 0$ is applied to (1) as shown in the Eq. 2:

$$\begin{bmatrix} su \\ sv \\ s \end{bmatrix} = K\,R \begin{bmatrix} X_w \\ Y_w \\ Z_w \end{bmatrix} + K\,t \tag{1}$$

$$\begin{bmatrix} su \\ sv \\ s \end{bmatrix} = K\left(R \begin{bmatrix} X_w \\ Y_w \\ 0 \end{bmatrix} + t\right) \tag{2}$$

Applying Algebraic properties to (2):

$$\begin{bmatrix} su \\ sv \\ s \end{bmatrix} = K \begin{bmatrix} r_1\ r_2\ t \end{bmatrix} \begin{bmatrix} X_w \\ Y_w \\ 1 \end{bmatrix} \tag{3}$$

In the first acquisition, the robot frame is considered as the world frame. Therefore, each pixel coordinates are represented with the Eq. (4):

$$\begin{bmatrix} s_1 u_1 \\ s_1 v_1 \\ s_1 \end{bmatrix} = K \begin{bmatrix} r_{r1}^c\ r_{r2}^c\ t_r^c \end{bmatrix} \begin{bmatrix} X_w \\ Y_w \\ 1 \end{bmatrix} = H_1 \begin{bmatrix} X_w \\ Y_w \\ 1 \end{bmatrix} \tag{4}$$

In the second acquisition, the position of the robot frame origin in the second acquisition is represented in the robot frame of the first acquisition.

$$\begin{bmatrix} s_2 u_2 \\ s_2 v_2 \\ s_2 \end{bmatrix} = K \begin{bmatrix} r_{w1}^c\ r_{w2}^c\ t_w^c \end{bmatrix} \begin{bmatrix} X_w \\ Y_w \\ 1 \end{bmatrix} = H_2 \begin{bmatrix} X_w \\ Y_w \\ 1 \end{bmatrix} \tag{5}$$

The transformation (R_w^c, t_w^c) is computed from the Eq. (6) as shown in the Fig. (1)(a):

$$\begin{bmatrix} R_w^c\ t_w^c \\ 0\ \ 1 \end{bmatrix} = \begin{bmatrix} R_r^c\ t_r^c \\ 0\ \ 1 \end{bmatrix} \begin{bmatrix} R_{mvt}\ t_{mvt} \\ 0\ \ \ 1 \end{bmatrix} \tag{6}$$

from the Eq. (4) and (5):

$$
\begin{bmatrix} s_2 u_2 \\ s_2 v_2 \\ s_2 \end{bmatrix} = K \begin{bmatrix} r^c_{w1} & r^c_{w2} & t^c_w \end{bmatrix} \begin{bmatrix} r^c_{r1} & r^c_{r2} & t^c_r \end{bmatrix}^{-1} K^{-1} \begin{bmatrix} s_1 u_1 \\ s_1 v_1 \\ s_1 \end{bmatrix} \tag{7}
$$

Therefore, each ground point is represented in the camera frame I_1 and represented with the coordinates (u_1, v_1) in the image frame will be presented in the camera frame I_2 with the coordinates (u_2, v_2) in the image frame from the Eq. (7):

$$
H = T_{ipm} = K \begin{bmatrix} r^c_{w1} & r^c_{w2} & t^c_w \end{bmatrix} \begin{bmatrix} r^c_{r1} & r^c_{r2} & t^c_r \end{bmatrix}^{-1} K^{-1} \tag{8}
$$

The transformation (8) is only correct for ground points. Therefore, the pixel to pixel value subtraction between $T_{ipm}[I_1]$ and I_2 generates low absolute values for the ground points.

2.2 Segmentation of Obstacles

In obstacle detection systems, one of the important steps to extract obstacle pixels is the segmentation of binary image and thresholding is a fundamental tool for segmentation. Otsu's thresholding [10] is known as a good method. The optimal threshold is computed by minimizing the mean square errors between original image and the resultant binary image. A threshold based on Otsu's algorithm is calculated from the Eqs. (9) and (10) [10]:

$$
\sigma_0^2(t) = \sum_{i=1}^{k} [i - \mu_0(t)]^2 \frac{p_i}{\omega_0} \tag{9}
$$

$$
\sigma_1^2(t) = \sum_{i=k+1}^{L} [i - \mu_1(t)]^2 \frac{p_i}{\omega_1} \tag{10}
$$

The threshold produced by the Eqs. (9) and (10) minimizes the weighted within class variance. The problem of searching the optimal threshold can be reduced to search a theshold that maximizes the between-class variance as shown in the Eq. (11):

$$
\sigma_B^2 = \omega_0 \omega_1 (\mu_1 - \mu_0)^2 \tag{11}
$$

For quicker calculation and optimal performance in hardware implementation the Eq. (11) is used to find the threshold from the histogram extracted of gray-level image.

2.3 Bird's-Eye Transformation

This transformation allows the distribution of obstacle information among image pixels [2] and leads to efficient implementation of polar histogram in order to localize obstacles. The binarized image is projected on the ground plane in the robot frame as depicted in Fig. (1)(b), up to a rotation around the vertical axis and a translation in XY. C_1 and C_2 represent camera frames as shown in Fig. (1)(b). Any point on the ground plane P has a 3D position represented with respect to the camera C_1 is r_{C1} [7]

$$\frac{n_{C_1}^T . r_{C_1}}{d_{C_1}} = 0 \tag{12}$$

$$r_{C_2} = R_{C_2 C_1}(r_{C_1} - t_{C_1}^{C_2 C_1}) \tag{13}$$

n_{C_1} is the ground plane normal represented in camera C_1 coordinates and d_{C_1} is the distance of the ground plane from the origin of camera C_1. The position vector r_{C_2} of the same point represented in camera C_2 is computed from Eq. (13). $R_{C_2 C_1}$ is the rotation matrix from C_1 to C_2 and $t_{C_1}^{C_2 C_1}$ is the translation from C_1 to C_2 presented in C_1 coordinates. The transformation required from the Original Camera C_1 to the virtual camera C_2 presenting bird's-eye view is:

$$r_{C_2} = H_{C_2 C_1} r_{C_1},$$

$$H_{C_2 C_1} = R_{C_2 C_1} - \frac{1}{d_{C_1}} t_{C_2}^{C_2 C_1} . n_{C_1}^T \tag{14}$$

By using the Eq. (14), the homography matrix of bird's-eye view for the cameras is calculated. To use this matrix in image coordinates (pixels), camera intrinsic matrix K is required as shown in the Eq. (15):

$$H_{bird} = K(R_{C_2 C_1} - \frac{1}{d_{C_1}} t_{C_2}^{C_2 C_1} . n_{C_1}^T) K^{-1} \tag{15}$$

The bird's eye image of the ground plane is generated by applying the homography to each pixel.

2.4   Obstacle Localization

Obstacle Bearing Measurement. Straight lines perpendicular to ground plane are parallel in the world frame. By intersecting image plane with a ray parallel to these lines in the camera frame through the camera center [7], vanishing point in the image frame is obtained to represent a point called *focus* [2]. Thus a beam of lines is originating from *focus* through the image to represent polar histogram. So binarized image is scanned using polar histogram to localize obstacle shapes in the image, and the tracking of pixels located in each line is done by using Bresenham's algorithm.

$$v = PX_\infty = K\,[I|0] \begin{bmatrix} d \\ 0 \end{bmatrix} = Kd \tag{16}$$

$X_\infty = (d^T, 0)^T$ is the vanishing point represented in the world frame, and v is its projection in the image frame. P being projection matrix, K is intrinsic matrix. Since two points coordinates are required to perform a line equation, the first point (u_0, v_0) is a pixel belonging to the first row of image whereas the second point is $focus\ (0, 0)$. As noted already, image frame is translated to $focus$. Bresenham's algorithm [4] is initially presented in Algorithm 1 for a line having a point coordinates (u_0, v_0) in the first row of image for the octant where $(u_0 < 0, v_0 > 0)$ and the vertical projection $|v_0|$ is longer than the horizontal projection $|u_0|$ as depicted in Fig. (3). $I(u, v)$ is pixel value at the coordinates (u, v). $Dens$ being the number of overthreshold pixels located in line. The implementation of the algorithm is generalized to produce and trace lines in different octants.

Data: u_0, v_0
Result: $Dens$
$dv = v_0,\ du = -u_0,\ D = 2du - dv,\ v = v_0$;
for $v = v_0 \rightarrow 0$ **do**
  if $D > 0$ **then**
    $u \leftarrow u + 1$;
    $D \leftarrow D + 2du - 2dv$;
  else
    $D \leftarrow D + 2du$;
  end
  if $I(u, v) > 0$ **then**
    $dens \leftarrow dens + 1$;
end
Algorithm 1. Bresenham's method implemented for a specific octant

Obstacles Localization in the Ground Plane. Obstacle shapes produced by IPM and binarization often have an isosceles triangular shape where the peak corresponds to the intersection point between ground plane and obstacle object. A method is proposed to find isosceles triangles crossed by Bresenham's lines and extract the peak of each isosceles triangle; meanwhile polar histogram is calculated. For each pixel $I(u, v)$ located in a defined line traced by Bresenham's algorithm, a factor a_r defined as a sum of neighbouring pixels located in the same image row r as shown in the Eq. (18):

$$a_r = \sum_{k=-l}^{l} I(u + k, v) \tag{17}$$

$$Sc = f(a_r, a_{r+1}) = \begin{cases} Sc + 1, & \text{if } a_{r+1} \leq a_r \\ 0, & \text{otherwise} \end{cases} \tag{18}$$

l being window width, and Sc is a score refering to the possibility whether an isosceles triangle is found or not. Since pixels of lines traced by Bresenham's algorithm don't include all image pixels, extracted points don't represent the ideal points.

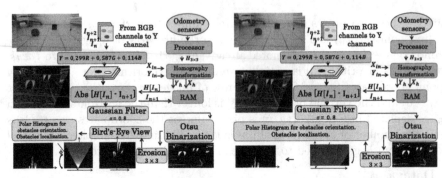

(a) First Hardware System design.   (b) Second Hardware System design.

Fig. 2. The two proposed architectures

3   Hardware Design

Two hardware architectures are proposed as depicted in Fig. (2). In the first architecture, bird's eye transformation is applied to the whole image produced by erosion module, while this transformation is only applied to the contact points in the second architecture. Figure (2) shows the general hardware system design with the differences between the two proposed architectures. Figures (3) and (4) show details of an implementation done for images of VGA resolution.

3.1   Homography and Bird's Eye Transformation

Homography transformation is a pixel-level operation that maps input pixel coordinates to computed output pixels coordinates (mapping operation). This operation requires to store image frames in memory. This transformation can be performed in hardware design by two methods detailed in [3]. As depicted in Fig. (4)(a), non-sequential reads of the input image and sequential writes of the output image are performed. Each output pixel is mapped to an input pixel. Thus the calculation of inverse matrix of homography matrix produced by the Eq. (8) is required, this process is performed in software as proposed in [3]. An approximation is done for the non integer output coordinates, and a null pixel value is assigned to the coordinates having no correspondence with the input image. The same process is performed for bird's eye transformation. The main difference between these two transformations is that the values of the transformation matrix can be computed off-line if we assume camera movement only over x, y, ϕ_z. The drawback of this transformation in hardware implementation is the high bit-depth required for fractional of the fixed point elements of the bird's eye matrix elements and the high cost of latency time. Since bird's eye matrix is a constant matrix, the maximum value of $|y_h - y_{in}|$ is calculated off-line and is used to perform the minimum size of Block Random Access Memories (BRAMs) required for the transformation. In our implementation done for VGA resolution, 191 rows of eroded image are stored in BRAMs in order to start bird's eye transformation.

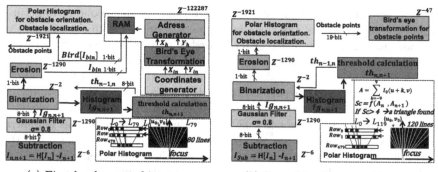

(a) First hardware architecture.   (b) Second hardware architecture.

Fig. 3. Differences between the two proposed architectures

3.2 IPM and Binarization

As shown in Fig. (3)(a)(b), the image transformed $H[I_n]$ is generated from the previous process. A subtraction is performed between pixels from $H[I_n]$ acquired at t_n and pixels from I_{n+1} at t_{n+1} as shown in the Fig. (3). A FIFO module is used in order to synchronize the stream of image transformed $H[I_n]$ acquired at t_n to the image I_{n+1} acquired at t_{n+1}. The image I_{n+1} will be written in the memory replacing the image I_n. The output image of subtraction passes through a gaussian filter to remove noise and insure an optimal performance in Otsu's binarization. This gaussian filter for a standard deviation $\sigma = 0.8$ is implemented as 3×3 as a kernel. The image filtered by the gaussian kernel called $Ig_{n,n+1}$ is binarized using Otsu's threshold; This threshold $th_{n-1,n}$ is already computed from the histogram of the image filtered $Ig_{n-1,n}$. As the computation of histogram used to perform Otsu's method to find optimal threshold requires a high latency time, the threshold which binarizes the image filtered $Ig_{n,n+1}$ is a threshold $th_{n-1,n}$ calculated from the image filtered $Ig_{n-1,n}$ as depicted in Fig. (3). Since there is not a high variation in intensities between two sequential frames, this binarization threshold remains valid and allows to save on processing latency. The resulting binary image is then eroded with a kernel element 3×3. As erosion process and gaussian filter use a 3×3 kernel, two image rows and two pixels are stored in BRAMs to perform these operations. Thus an additional cost to latency time is imposed as depicted in Fig. (3). In the first architecture, a definite number of eroded image rows is stored in BRAMs to perform bird's eye transformation and provide bird's eye image $Bird[I_{bin}]$. In the second architecture, eroded image pixels simply pass to the localization module.

3.3 Localization

In the first architecture as depicted in Fig. (3)(a), polar histogram makes use of bird's eye image for obstacles localization. However, the potential presence of two or more obstacles will complicate the process [2]. Therefore, eroded image is used to perform polar histogram, and this is done for the second architecture. For pipeline requirements, two rotating registers of image width size are used to store two image rows, the first register is used to determine which pixels belong to lines drawn by Bresenham's algorithm, count overthreshold pixels, detect isosceles triangles and their peaks, and to compute the next coordinates in the next register. The second register stores pixels read from memory while applying Bresenham's algorithm to the first register. Figure (3)(a) introduces an example how to scan bird's Eye image 640 × 480 by 80 lines. The output of this module is stored in BRAMs. Each address refers to a scanned sector of the image, and the content of memory represents the number of overthreshold pixels. Figure (3)(b) introduces an example showing how to scan an eroded image 640 × 480 by 120 lines in the second architecture, and an example is shown to implement the Eqs. (17) and (18) for extracting obstacles contact points with ground plane. A selection process is performed to choose the best points. Extracted points are divided into clusters, each cluster represents points assigned to same obstacle object. In the second architecture, the extracted pixels coordinates which are considered as contact points between ground plane and obstacles are transformed by bird's eye matrix to produce occupancy grid map for robot.

4   Discussion and Results

In the second architecture, Bird's eye transformation is not applied to eroded image, this is advantageous in hardware implementation because this transformation requires a high latency time, many BRAMs to store a specific number of eroded image rows, and a large amount of hardware resources.

The two proposed architecture are implemented using Xilinx Virtex 6 platform. A hardware accelerator for homography transformation and IPM algorithm has been developed in [3]. Table 2 shows the differences between our architecture and [3]. The software part of our architecture includes the calculation of homography matrix produced by the Eq. (8). A software solution is proposed in [3] to implement this equation by using a soft-processor, this solution is adopted and used in our architecture. In [1], a hardware system based on stereovision is proposed for obstacle detection, this architecture requires two cameras to perform the system while our architecture is a monocular vision system; furthermore, the maximum frequency of our system is better than the maximum achieved

Table 1. Comparison with other obstacle detection system

	Platform	OD method	Frame rate
[8]	CPU + GPU	optical flow	25 fps 640 × 480
[11]	PC 1.73 GHz	IPM coarse detection	30 fps 720 × 480
[5]	GPU	3D reconstruction	45.8 fps 640 × 480
[1]	FPGA	stereovision	Fmax = 51.7 Mhz, 180 fps 640 × 480
ours	FPGA	IPM	Fmax = 61.9 Mhz, 201 fps 640 × 480

Table 2. Comparison of our system with [3](640 × 480)

	FPGA [3]	Our FPGA
IPM	Yes	Yes
Binarization	No	Yes
Localization	No	Yes
Bird's Eye	No	Yes
Frame rate	30 fps (SDRAM)	201 fps (BRAMs)

Table 3. Resources required for the two architectures

Architecture	Slice Reg	Luts	RAMB36E1
First	35469	101479	87
second	34746	153623	78

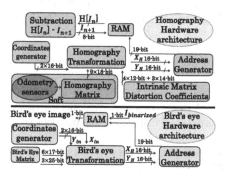

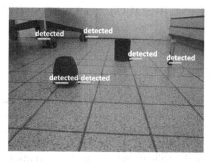

(a) Implementation of homography and bird's eye.

(b) Results of obstacles localization in the ground plane.

Fig. 4. Results and homography hardware architecture

frequency in [1]. Latency time in [1] (minimum detection time) is $5.5ms$ for VGA resolution while latency time (computed to produce contact points between obstacles and ground plane) of our architecture is $7.49\mu s$ for the second architecture and $2.05ms$ for the first architecture, the computational latency time is ~ 4610 clock cycles for the second architecture, while ~ 126897 clock cycles are required to perform the first architecture, Fig. (3) shows the required clock cycles for each part in the two proposed architectures. Table (1) shows the comparison of the proposed system to other obstacle detection systems. In [8], a system based on Optical flow, a computational intensive method, is used for obstacle detection. The estimation of power consumption in our architecture is around 3.9 *watt* which is clearly less than power consumption in GPU platform as [8]. In [11], a method based on IPM is used to perform a system with localization of obstacles using polar histogram. However, three sequential frames are needed to perform the system; furthermore, the proposed method is limited to vertical edges of obstacles. Figure (4)(b) shows the results of an implementation done for 640 × 480 images of the second architecture. Most of obstacles contact points with ground plane are detected. However, two contact points are detected as two obstacle objects, this is because of the selection process for contact points. An optimization is still required to overcome that problem (Table 3).

5   Conclusion

This paper presents a hardware architecture for obstacle detection and localization implemented on FPGA. An efficient solution combines Mono IPM for detection and Otsu's method, plus Bresenham's algorithm for localization. This architecture produces a pipelined design with a high frame rate. The results show the high frame rate of the system. In future, the proposed architecture will be optimized to consume less resources, and extended to a multi-camera system to generate occupancy grid map of the environment around robot.

This work has been performed by Ali Alhamwi, paid by the FUI-AAP14 project AIR-COBOT, co-funded by BPI France, FEDER and the Midi-Pyrénées region.

References

1. Bendaoudi, H., Khouas, A., Cherki, B.: FPGA design of a real-time obstacle detection system using stereovision. In: 24th International Conference on Microelectronics (ICM), 2012, pp. 1–4. IEEE (2012)
2. Bertozzi, M., Broggi, A., Fascioli, A.: Stereo inverse perspective mapping: theory and applications. Image Vis. Comput. **16**(8), 585–590 (1998)
3. Botero, D., Piat, J., Chalimbaud, P., Devy, M.: FPGA implementation of mono and stereo inverse perspective mapping for obstacle detection. In: Design and Architectures for Signal and Image Processing (DASIP), pp. 1–8. IEEE (2012)
4. Bresengham, J.: Algorithm for computer control of a digital plotter. IBM Syst. **4**(1), 25–30 (1965)
5. Cesar, C., Mendes, T., Osorio, F.S., Wolf, D.F.: An efficient obstacle detection approach for organized point clouds. In: Intelligent Vehicles Symposium, pp. 1203–1208. IEEE (2013)
6. Ha, J., Sattigeri, R.: Vision-based obstacle avoidance based on monocular slam and image segmentation for UAVs. In: Infotech@Aerospace 2012, pp. 1–9. AIAA (2012)
7. Hartley, R., Zisserman, A.: Multiple View Geometry in Computer Vision. Cambridge University Press, UK (2004)
8. He, C.Y., Hongand, C.T., Lo, R.C.: An improved obstacle detection using optical flow adjusting based on inverse perspective mapping for the vehicle safety. In: International Symposium on Intelligent Signal Processing and Communications Systems (ISPACS), 2012, pp. 85–89. IEEE (2012)
9. Mallot, H.A., Blthoff, H.H., Little, J.J., Bohrer, S.: Inverse perspective mapping simplifies optical flow computation and obstacle detection. Biol. Cybern. **64**(3), 177–185 (1991)
10. Otsu, N.: Threshold selection method from gray-level histogram. IEEE Trans.Syst. **SMC–9**(1), 62–66 (1979)
11. Yankun, Z., Chuyang, H., Norman, W.: A single camera based rear obstacle detection system. In: Intelligent Vehicles Symposium, pp. 485–490. IEEE (2011)

Bayesian Formulation of Gradient Orientation Matching

Håkan Ardö[(✉)] and Linus Svärm

Centre for Mathematical Sciences, Lund University, Lund, Sweden
ardo@maths.ith.se

Abstract. Gradient orientations are a common feature used in many computer vision algorithms. It is a good feature when the gradient magnitudes are high, but can be very noisy when the magnitudes are low. This means that some gradient orientations are matched with more confidence than others. By estimating this uncertainty, more weight can be put on the confident matches than those with higher uncertainty. To enable this, we derive the probability distribution of gradient orientations based on a signal to noise ratio defined as the gradient magnitude divided by the standard deviation of the Gaussian noise. The noise level is reasonably invariant over time, while the magnitude, has to be measured for every frame. Using this probability distribution we formulate the matching of gradient orientations as a Bayesian classification problem.

A common application where this is useful is feature point matching. Another application is background/foreground segmentation. This paper will use the latter application as an example, but is focused on the general formulation. It is shown how the theory can be used to implement a very fast background/foreground segmentation algorithm that is capable of handling complex lighting variations.

1 Introduction

A common feature used in computer vision applications is gradient orientations. It is the base of common descriptors such as SIFT [13] and HOG [5] as well as used in stereo matching [3] and motion estimation [12]. However, there has been little attention to probabilistic models of the gradient orientation.

While the theory presented in this paper is useful in many situations dealing with gradient directions, the application considered is background/foreground segmentation. This is a common initial step used by more advanced video analytics algorithms. In practical situations it is important that it is computational efficient, to free up resources for further processing.

Numerous foreground/background segmentation algorithms have been suggested. However, many of them are either quite computationally intensive or fail to model variations in the background caused by for example lighting variations. The trend of late have been to tackle complex dynamic backgrounds and a lot of impressive results have been achieved using a lot of processing power. However in many application those complex backgrounds are not present and it would

© Springer International Publishing Switzerland 2015
L. Nalpantidis et al. (Eds.): ICVS 2015, LNCS 9163, pp. 91–103, 2015.
DOI: 10.1007/978-3-319-20904-3_9

be more efficient to use this processing power elsewhere. Traffic surveillance is one example where you have static pavement as background and not swaying trees. You might however have the shadow of a swaying tree cast upon the pavement. The focus of the proposed algorithm is thus to handle static backgrounds observed under complex varying lighting conditions.

Friedman and Russel [7] have suggested to use a 3 component mixture of Gaussian where the three components represent pavement, pavement in shadow and foreground. This will work nicely on a sunny day when shadows consist of sharp shadows cast by road users. But on a cloudy day the diffuse clouds will generate a lighting of the scene that varies smoothly both spatially and temporary. There will no longer be two distinct components, but a continuous variation. In Sect. 4.3 we are looking at the even more complex lighting situation of underwater scenes. Here the rippling of the pool surface gives complex variations in the lighting of the scene below and it can change abruptly as someone swims past.

A different approach is to preprocess the input image to extract intensity independent features and base the background model on those instead. These methods typically assumes that the effect of the lighting variations are linear. While this might be the case with expensive industrial cameras, it is typically not the case with standard off-the-shelf surveillance cameras or webcams. Those kind of cameras often do a lot of non-linear preprocessing of the sensor data such as gamma compensation, noise reduction, wide dynamic range adjustments and back light compensations. The benefit of using gradient directions in this case is that they are very robust to these kind of transformations.

An issue with many intensity independent features, including gradient directions, is that they break down in dark or uniform areas. Take for example the normalised rgb, that transforms the colour pixel (r, g, b) into $\left(\frac{r}{r+g+b}, \frac{g}{r+g+b}, \frac{b}{r+g+b} \right)$. When r, g and b all are small, the denominator becomes close to zero and the noise is scaled up out of proportion. Gordon et $al.$ [8] has suggested to ignore normalised rgb features in dark areas and there rely on other features instead. A fix threshold was used to decide if the features were reliable or not. In the same fashion Hu et $al.$ [10] used 3 different models for background patches with different amount of structures. Also, Wayne and Schoonees [18] suggests to use two thresholds on the background likelihood to classify pixel into background, foreground or unknown depending on how close to the background model the current frame is.

This property of features being unreliable in some cases and reliable in other cases is not a discrete property. It is a property that varies continuously from for example a very dark pixel to a very light pixel. Features can be utilized much more efficiently by, instead of thresholding them into reliable or not reliable, using a continuous estimate of how reliable they are and weight the different features accordingly.

Theoretical distributions of the gradient orientation is derived in Sect. 2. It depends on a single parameter, the signal to noise ratio. The signal here refers to the magnitude of the gradient and noise level is represented as the standard deviation of the Gaussian noise. The noise level is fairly constant over time and can be estimated precisely by using several frames in the estimate. However the gradient magnitude can vary significantly from one frame to the next (as the lighting changes) This means that the distribution can change significantly from one frame to the next, and we only have a single sample from which to estimate it. That is not possible without additional information. The additional information available in this case is samples from related distributions (observations of the same pixel under different lighting conditions). This rules out non-parametric approaches or Gaussian approximations, which require multiple samples from the same distribution.

Combining this distribution with a uniform foreground model using Bayes rule, the probability of each gradient showing background or foreground can be calculated. This makes it possible to use the gradient direction feature for all gradients even if the magnitude is small. In that case, the foreground probability will be close to 0.5 and represent an uncertain state. The segmentation will there rely more on other features or on neighbours. This means that there will be no fix point where the measurements suddenly become uncertain. Instead the signal to noise ratio is measured and the parametrised model will move continuously from being very certain about gradients with large magnitude to being unsure about gradients with small magnitude.

Section 3 describes the background/foreground segmentation algorithm and experiments are presented in Sect. 4, with some conclusions in Sect. 5.

2   Gradient Distribution

Consider a video sequence consisting of frames, I_t, for $t = 1, 2, \cdots$, where each pixel, $I(x, y)$, is disturbed with Gaussian noise with some standard deviation I^σ. A common way to estimate gradients is to convolve the image with some kernel $D_x = (d_{i,j})$ and its transpose to form the x and y derivatives. Those components of the gradient will in that case also be disturbed by Gaussian noise, but with variance $\sigma^2 = \sum (|d_{i,j}| I^\sigma)^2$. The distribution of the magnitude and orientation of this gradient is given by Lemma 1 and Lemma 2 respectively.

Lemma 1. *Let* $\mathbf{x} = (a, b) = r(\cos\alpha, \sin\alpha)$ *be a two-dimensional stochastic variable with* a *and* b *Gaussian distributed with mean* $\bar{a} = \bar{r}\cos\bar{\alpha}$ *and* $\bar{b} = \bar{r}\sin\bar{\alpha}$ *respectively, and variance* σ^2. *The distribution of the squared magnitude,* r^2, *is*

$$f_{r^2}\left(r^2 \,\big|\, \bar{r}^2, \sigma^2\right) = \frac{1}{\sigma^2} f_{nc\chi^2}\left(\frac{r^2}{\sigma^2} \,\bigg|\, 2, \frac{\bar{r}^2}{\sigma^2}\right), \tag{1}$$

where $f_{nc\chi^2}(x \,|\, k, \lambda)$ *is the non-central* χ^2 *distribution with* k *degrees of fredom and non-centrality parameter* λ.

Proof. The expression $\frac{a^2}{\sigma^2} + \frac{b^2}{\sigma^2}$ *is non-central* χ^2 *distributed according to its the definition. Rescaling it with a constant factor* σ^2 *gives* $a^2 + b^2 = r^2$, *and the lemma follows.*

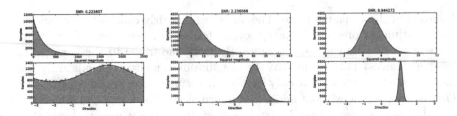

Fig. 1. Distribution of the gradient magnitude and orientation for different signal to noise ratios. Grey bar are histograms from simulations and the black curve is the theoretical distribution suggested.

Lemma 2. *Let* $\mathbf{x} = (a, b) = r\left(\cos\alpha, \sin\alpha\right)$ *be a two-dimensional stochastic variable with a and b Gaussian distributed with mean $\bar{a} = \bar{r}\cos\bar{\alpha}$ and $\bar{b} = \bar{r}\sin\bar{\alpha}$ respectively, and variance σ^2. The distribution of the orientation, α, is*

$$f_\alpha\left(\alpha - \bar{\alpha} \left| \frac{\bar{r}^2}{\sigma^2}\right.\right) = f_\alpha\left(\alpha_0 \left| s^2\right.\right) = \frac{e^{-\frac{s^2}{2}}}{2\pi}\left(1 + \sqrt{2\pi}s\cos\left(\alpha_0\right)\Phi\left(s\cos\left(\alpha_0\right)\right)e^{\frac{s^2\cos(\alpha_0)^2}{2}}\right), \tag{2}$$

where Φ is the cumulative Gaussian distribution function.

Proof. The two dimensional Gaussian distribution of the vector (a, b) can be written

$$\frac{1}{2\pi\sigma^2}e^{-\frac{(a-\bar{a})^2 + (b-\bar{b})^2}{2\sigma^2}}\,dadb. \tag{3}$$

Changing variables into polar coordinates yields

$$\frac{1}{2\pi\sigma^2}re^{-\frac{(r\cos\alpha - \bar{r}\cos\bar{\alpha})^2 + (r\sin\alpha - \bar{r}\sin\bar{\alpha})^2}{2\sigma^2}}\,drd\alpha. \tag{4}$$

The coordinate system can now be rotated (by changing variables again), to place $\bar{\alpha}$ at 0, which will place α at $\alpha_0 = \alpha - \bar{\alpha}$ and give the distribution

$$\frac{1}{2\pi\sigma^2}re^{-\frac{(r\cos\alpha - \bar{r})^2 + (r\sin\alpha)^2}{2\sigma^2}}\,drd\alpha = \underbrace{\frac{1}{2\pi\sigma^2}e^{-\frac{\bar{r}^2}{2\sigma^2}}}_{g}\underbrace{re^{-\frac{r^2 - 2r\bar{r}\cos\alpha}{2\sigma^2}}}_{h(r)}\,drd\alpha. \tag{5}$$

To get the distribution of α only, r needs to be integrated out. The first two factors, g, does not depend on r, and a primitive function for the last two factors, $h(r)$, is $H(r) =$

$$-e^{-\frac{r^2 - 2r\bar{r}\cos\alpha}{2\sigma^2}} - \frac{\bar{r}\cos\alpha\sqrt{\pi}}{\sqrt{2}\sigma}e^{-\frac{\bar{r}^2\cos^2\alpha}{2\sigma^2}}\mathrm{erf}\left(\frac{-r + \bar{r}\cos\alpha}{\sqrt{2}\sigma}\right), \tag{6}$$

which can be verified by differentiating it. Integrating r from 0 to ∞ and introducing $s = \frac{\bar{r}}{\sigma}$ gives $H(\infty) - H(0) =$

$$1 + \frac{s\cos\alpha\sqrt{\pi}}{\sqrt{2}}e^{\frac{s^2\cos^2\alpha}{2}}\left(\mathrm{erf}\left(\frac{s\cos\alpha}{\sqrt{2}}\right) + 1\right). \tag{7}$$

Replacing the erf *function with the* Φ *function using the relationship*

$$\Phi(u) = \frac{1}{2} + \frac{1}{2}\text{erf}\left(\frac{u}{\sqrt{2}}\right),\tag{8}$$

and multiplying with the first two constant factors, g, of 5 concludes the proof.

2.1 Simulations

The probability distributions were verified using simulations. 10^5 random samples of Gaussian noise with standard deviation, σ, of 10, 1 and 0.25 was added to a fix vector $(\bar{a}, \bar{b}) = (1, 2)$ and histograms were formed. They are presented in Fig. 1 together with the theoretical distributions. The correspondence is very good.

To utilize these distributions we need the magnitude of the gradient without any noise and the noise level. These are typically impossible to get exactly, as only the noisy data is available. The noise level is fairly constant over time, which means that standard deviation of the noise can be estimated precisely by measuring over several frames. However the gradient magnitude can change from frame to frame so it needs to be estimated from one single noisy sample. The relation between the noisy gradient magnitude, r, and the noise free $\bar{r}$ is given by Lemma 1. This relationship was investigated using simulations, similar to those above, for different signal-to-noise ratios. Results are plotted in Fig. 2.

For low signal to noise ratios, r significantly overestimates $\bar{r}$. This is not surprising as in those cases r would be more related to the noise than to $\bar{r}$. However the parameter of interest is the signal to noise ratio $s^2 = \frac{r^2}{\sigma^2}$, which is also plotted in Fig. 2. Here we see that the estimate is slightly biased, but not all that much. The bias seem to be constant and not depend on the signal to noise ratio. A numerical estimation of this bias gives 1.0, which can be removed from the estimates to compensate for this bias.

2.2 Measurements

The assumptions of the model were tested by recording video from a camera observing a completely static scene during several hours allowing the cloud cover

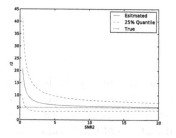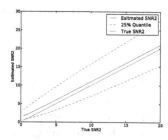

Fig. 2. Estimations of the gradient magnitude, r^2, (left) and signal to noise ratio, $\frac{r^2}{\sigma^2}$ (right) from noisy samples. The doted lines are the true values while the estimations are shown in blue with median solid while the 25 % and 75 % quantiles are dashed (Color figure online).

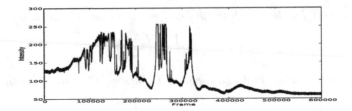

Fig. 3. Intensity of a single pixel from a static scene showing a lot of lighting variations due to the changing cloud cover and the setting of the sun.

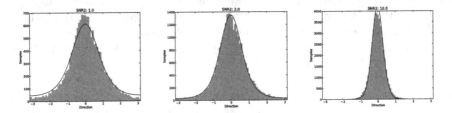

Fig. 4. Distribution of the gradient magnitude and orientation for different signal to noise ratios. Grey bar are histograms from recordings and the black curve is the theoretical distribution suggested.

and the setting of the sun to produce significant lighting variations. Figure 3 shows how the intensity of a single pixel varies due to the lighting over the entire recording.

Histograms over the observed gradient directions were produced. The observed signal to noise ratios were (after the bias compensation) used to partition the observations and one histogram was formed for each partition. The width of each partition is 20 % of the center signal to noise ratio. Some of the histograms are presented in Fig. 4 together with the theoretical distributions. Gaussian noise with standard deviation 0.5 was added to the observed intensities to remove discretization effects, which were otherwise quite prominent. The observed histograms correlates very well with the theoretical distributions. Especially for high signal to noise ratios.

3   Application

In the application of background/foreground segmentation, the idea is to extract moving objects in a video sequence, I_t, acquired by a static camera. The background in such an image is not perfectly static due to effect such as noise and lighting variations. However the gradient directions of the background is invariant to quite large lighting variations and Sect. 2 models how it varies due to Gaussian noise. If a background model consisting of gradient directions and a noise level is estimated from the video sequence, this model can be compared with the current frame. In every pixel it will then be possible to calculate the probability of whether this pixel originates from this background model or some uniform foreground model. This probability will typically become very uncertain (close to 0.5) in regions with little structure and quite certain (close to 0 or 1) in regions with a lot of structure.

3.1   Background Modelling

A background model consists, for each pixel, (x, y), of an estimate of the background gradient direction, $\bar{\alpha}_t$, and a noise level, I_t^σ. The noise level is represented as the standard deviation of the pixel intensities, I_t. Both are estimated continuously from the input video sequence I_t using recursive quantile estimation [14]. This means that they can vary slowly over time to adapt to more permanent changes in the background. The noise level is estimated from the temporal median, q_t, of $d_t = |I_t - I_{t-1}|$, which is related to the the standard deviation of I_t by

$$I_t^\sigma = \frac{\sqrt{2}}{\mathcal{N}^{-1}(0.75) - \mathcal{N}^{-1}(0.25)} q_t \approx 1.048358 q_t, \tag{9}$$

where $\mathcal{N}^{-1}$ is the inverse of the Gaussian cumulative distribution function with mean 0 an variance 1. The recursive quantile estimation updates the estimated median recursively using a control sequence $c_t = \max\left(\frac{c_0}{t}, c_{\min}\right)$,

$$q_t = \begin{cases} q_{t-1} + c_t \text{ if } q_{t-1} < d_t \\ q_{t-1} - c_t \text{ if } q_{t-1} > d_t \\ q_{t-1} \quad\quad \text{ if } q_{t-1} = d_t \end{cases} \tag{10}$$

The parameter $c_{\min}$ controls how fast the estimate adapts to more permanent changes in the background, and c_0 controls the initial behaviour and how fast the estimate converges.

The background gradient direction, $\bar{\alpha}_t$, is estimated as the median over the observed gradient directions, α_t. The quantile estimation update equation has to be modified slightly as the calculations here have to be performed modulus 2π. Using the range $0 \cdots 2\pi$ to represent angles, and $\Delta_t = \alpha_t - \bar{\alpha}_{t-1} \mod 2\pi$, the update equation becomes

$$\bar{\alpha}_t = \begin{cases} \bar{\alpha}_{t-1} + c_t \mod 2\pi \text{ if } 0 < \Delta_t < \pi \\ \bar{\alpha}_{t-1} - c_t \mod 2\pi \text{ if } \Delta_t \geq \pi \\ \bar{\alpha}_{t-1} \quad\quad\quad\quad \text{ if } \Delta_t = 0 \end{cases} \tag{11}$$

This gives a very robust measure of the dominant gradient direction observed for each pixels, and the assumption made is that this is the gradient direction of the background. Even for background gradients with fairly low magnitude, this gives a good estimate after the background have been observed for a long time. However in extreme cases, discretisation and truncation effects caused by the intensities being represented as integers in the range $0 \cdots 255$ can destroy the estimates. To mitigate those effects we have chosen to let $\bar{\alpha}_t = \bar{\alpha}_{t-1}$ if the observed intensities are within 2σ of 0 or 255.

Also, for very low noise levels the estimate of q_t becomes too low as the variation caused by the noise is lost in the discretisation. This effect can be modelled by assuming that in addition to the Gaussian noise we also have a discretisation noise of ± 1. This additional noise is incorporated simply by replacing q_t with $q_t + 1$ in Eq. 9. This will only have a noticeable effect for situations where q_t is close to 1.

3.2 Foreground Extraction

For each pixel (x, y) of each input frame, I_t, a gradient direction, α_t, and a gradient magnitude, r_t, is calculated. Lemma 2 gives the likelihood that this observation originates from the estimated background model,

$$l_{\text{bg}} = f_\alpha \left(\alpha_t - \bar{\alpha}_t \left| \frac{\bar{r}^2}{\sigma^2} \right. \right) \approx f_\alpha \left(\alpha_t - \bar{\alpha}_t \left| \frac{r_t^2}{\sigma_t^2} \right. \right). \tag{12}$$

The distribution of gradient directions in the foreground is assumed to be uniform. That gives the likelihood that the observation originates from the foreground model, $l_{\text{fg}} = \frac{1}{2\pi}$. Using a Bayesian approach gives the probability of foreground

$$p_{fg} = \frac{l_{\text{fg}} p_{\text{prior}}}{l_{\text{fg}} p_{\text{prior}} + l_{\text{bg}} \left(1 - p_{\text{prior}} \right)}, \tag{13}$$

where p_{prior} is the prior probability that a random pixel is foreground. It is set to 0.4 for the experiments below.

4   Experiments

The background foreground/segmentation have been tested on several video sequences with varying complexity. The output is a probabilistic background/foreground segmentation. It can be used as an input to tracking algorithms that uses probabilistic background/foreground segmentation directly [2], or it can be used as the unary-weights in a Markov random field (MRF) [4,11]. In the experiments below a MRF is used with $-\log\left(p_{\text{fg}}\right)$ as unary terms for foreground pixels, and $-\log\left(1 - p_{\text{fg}}\right)$ as unary term for background pixels. For binary terms, 4-connectivity with the value $-\log\left(0.9\right)$ for pixels belonging to the same class is used, and $-\log\left(0.1\right)$ for pixels belonging to different classes.

4.1   Wallflower

The proposed algorithm was tested on the WallFlower [16] dataset available online[1], which is also used by [15]. This dataset consists of 7 sequences with

---

[1] http://research.microsoft.com/users/jckrumm/WallFlower/TestImages.htm.

Input

GT

Fg.prob.

MRF seg.

Fig. 5. Results from applying the proposed algorithm on the wallflower [16] dataset. One input frame and its ground truth is shown for each sequence together with the probabilistic background/foreground segmentation produced by the proposed algorithm and a MRF segmentation of that probability (Color figure online).

resolution 160×120. For each sequence one frame has been manually segmented into foreground and background. The result from the proposed algorithm followed by a binary MRF segmentation was compared to those ground truth frames and results are presented in Table 1 and Fig. 5. The same parameters were used for all the videos, $(c_0, c_{min}) = (\pi, \pi/100)$ for the median estimate and $(c_0, c_{min}) = (10, 0.1)$ for the noise estimate.

Results are very accurate. Worst case is the LightSwitch sequence (4th column of Fig. 5) which consists of a person that enters a dark room, turns on the light and pulls out a chair to sit down. In addition the false positives detected at the previous position of the chair there are also some false positives on the background. Those originate mostly from areas of the image that was underexposed while the room was dark and thus the estimation of the background gradient direction fails here. In the WavingTrees sequence (last column of Fig. 5) the swaying tree in the background causes extra false positives.

On average 6.06% of the pixels are misclassified, which is better than many previous results presented of 7.82% [16], 7.33% [15] and 12.19% [1]. It does not beat the result of 4.5% presented by Wang and Suter [17], but with the exception of the cases discussed above the result is very close and for two of the sequences it is actually better (see Table 1). The proposed algorithm is also significantly faster. The probabilistic segmentation of those 160×120 sequences are generated at 1830 fps and the binary at 188 fps on a single core of a Intel Core i7-3770 CPU at 3.40 GHz. Wang and Suter [17] reports a speed of 6-10 fps (depending on parameter settings) on a 1.6 GHz Pentium M processor. This speed together with its robustness for varying lighting are the main benefits of the proposed algorithm.

The wallflower paper [16] also present results from applying frame-to-frame difference, as well as several other classic methods with very low computational demands, to the wallflower sequences. Frame-to-frame difference gives on aver-

Table 1. Results from applying the proposed algorithm to the dataset from [16]. For each of the 7 sequences the percentages of misclassified pixels are presented separately for false positives and false negatives. The last column contains the results of Wang and Suter [17] for comparison.

Sequence	FP (%)	FN (%)	Tot (%)	[17]
TimeOfDay	1.23	5.95	1.55	**1.99**
ForegroundAp	5.80	2.43	**4.93**	10.56
Bootstrap	5.38	5.17	**5.35**	6.64
Camouflage	3.99	1.93	2.89	**2.6**
LightSwitch	18.64	1.68	16.02	**8.43**
MovedObject	0.10	0.00	0.10	**0.00**
WavingTrees	15.90	1.78	11.58	**1.41**

age 17.08 % miss-classified pixels, a thresholded difference with a mean value background estimate gives 20.22 %, the pfinder aproach gives 22.60 % and the mixture of gaussians 17.91 %.

4.2   Change Detection Video Database

Additional exepriemts were performed on the Change Detection Video Database [9], also available online[2]. The same parameters as for the Wallflower sequences were used. Results, presented in Table 2, are competitive except for DynamicBackground and CameraJitter. They contain effects outside the scope of this paper, which are thus not modelled.

In the most relevant category, Shadow, we achieve 1.55 % wrong classified pixels, which is close the current state of art [6] of 1.25 %. They report a runtime of 34 fps for 320×240 sequences on a single core of a AMD Phenom II X4 CPU at 3.00 GHz. The proposed method is significantly faster. It can produce a probabilistic 320×240 segmentation at 509 fps on a single core of a Intel Core i7-3770 CPU at 3.40 GHz. In the experiments, the MRF segmentation is solved exactly which results in a binary segmentation at 51 fps.

4.3   Detecting Swimmers

Analyzing athletic swimming techniques using video analytics is a demanding task for several reasons. One of the issues is that the rippling of the pool surface gives complex variations in the lighting of the scene below. Also, the nature of the lighting variations can change abruptly as someone swims past which causes swirls. The proposed algorithm was tested on video sequences from this kind of application and the result is presented in Fig. 6.

---

[2] http://www.changedetection.net/.

Table 2. Results from applying the proposed algorithm to the Change Detection Video Database [9]. For each of the sequences the average pwc (Percentage of Wrong Classifications) is presented as well as the result of Evangelio and Sikora [6]

Sequence	PWC (%)	[6]
Baseline:	1.9594	0.5494
CameraJitter:	13.3695	2.3608
IntermittentObjectMotion:	6.1012	2.5238
Shadow:	1.5555	1.2534
Thermal:	3.4605	1.6846
DynamicBackground:	40.4967	0.6041

The algorithm performs very well for pixels strictly below the surface, despite the complex lighting situation there. On the surface itself it fails to find one single dominant gradient direction due to the rippling, and thus a lot of false positives show up there. However the result is good enough to detect swimmers, as it can be assumed that a significant part of them are below the surface. To show this we implemented a simple detector that sums up the foreground probability within a window of known dimensions. The image was scanned in a sliding window fashion detecting objects by thresholding this sum. The results are shown as red boxes in Fig. 6.

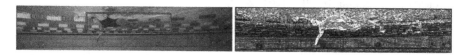

Fig. 6. One example frame from the swimming sequence (left) with the detected swimmer marked with a box and the probability of foreground (right) (Color figure online).

The sequence consists of 1297 frames with a single swimmer who enters the scene during frame 163-207 and exits it during frame 391-437 and is thus fully visible during frame 207-391 (limbs are ignored here). The swimmer is detected in frame 225 - 467, which means that the detection misses in about 18 of the initial frames the swimmer is fully present and produces false detections in about 30 frames after she has left the scene. The false detections are probably due to bubbles of air kicked down into the water by the swimmer that is slowly raising again.

This gives a fast way of detecting the swimmers, which allows more advanced and computational expensive algorithms to be focused on those areas of the image. Execution time for the background/foreground segmentation of those images on a single core of a 2.93 GHz Core 2 Duo E7500 are 37.95 for 2044 × 400 images, 152 fps for 1024 × 200 images and 466.80 for 512 × 100 images.

5 Conclusions

We have presented the probability distribution of the gradient orientation which can be used to asses the quality of matched gradient directions based on the signal to noise level. It is defined as the gradient magnitude divided by the standard deviation of the Gaussian noise. We have shown how this can be utilized to produce a background/foreground segmentation algorithm that is both computational light and capable of handling complex variations in the scene lighting. The suggested algorithm gives only 6.06 % miss-classified pixels on the Wall-Flower dataset [16]. Our current implementation uses a uni-modal background model, but it is straight forward to extend that to a multi-modal model to better handle rippling water surfaces or swaying trees.

The suggested algorithm can produce probabilistic 320×240 segmentations at 509 fps and we demonstrate how such an segmentation can be used for object detection without producing a binary segmentation first.

References

1. Ardö, H., Åström, K.: Bayesian formulation of image patch matching using cross-correlation. J. Math. Imaging Vis. **43**(1), 72–87 (2012)
2. Ardö, H., Berthilsson, R., Åström, K.: Real time viterbi optimization of hidden markov models for multi target tracking. In: IEEE Workshop on Motion and Video Computing (2007)
3. Baha, N., Larabi, S.: Accurate real-time neural disparity map estimation with fpga. Pattern Recogn. **45**(3), 1195–1204 (2012)
4. Boykov, Y., Kolmogorov, V.: An experimental comparison of min-cut/max-flow algorithms for energy minimization in vision. IEEE Trans. Pattern Anal. Mach. Intell. **26**(9), 1124–1137 (2004)
5. Dalal, N., Triggs, B.: Histograms of oriented gradients for human detection. In: IEEE Computer Society Conference on Computer Vision and Pattern Recognition, CVPR 2005, vol. 1, pp. 886–893, June 2005
6. Evangelio, R., Sikora, T.: Complementary background models for the detection of static and moving objects in crowded environments. In: 2011 8th IEEE International Conference on Advanced Video and Signal-Based Surveillance (AVSS), pp. 71–76 (2011)
7. Friedman, N., Russell, S.: Image segmentation in video sequences: a probabilistic approach. In: Thirteenth Conference on Uncertainty in Artificial Intelligence, pp. 175–181 (1997)
8. Gordon, G., Darrell, T., Harville, M., Woodfill, J.: Background estimation and removal based on range and color. In: IEEE Computer Society Conference on Computer Vision and Pattern Recognition, vol. 2, p. 464 (1999)
9. Goyette, N., Jodoin, P., Porikli, F., Konrad, J., Ishwar, P.: Changedetection.net: A new change detection benchmark dataset. In: 2012 IEEE Computer Society Conference on Computer Vision and Pattern Recognition Workshops (CVPRW), pp. 1–8 (2012)
10. Hu, W., Gong, H., Zhu, S.-C., Wang, Y.: An integrated background model for video surveillance based on primal sketch and 3d scene geometry. In: IEEE Conference on Computer Vision and Pattern Recognition, CVPR 2008, pp. 1–8, June 2008

11. Kohli, P., Torr, P.H.S.: Dynamic graph cuts for efficient inference in markov random fields. IEEE Trans. Pattern Anal. Mach. Intell. **29**(12), 2079–2088 (2007)
12. Kondo, T.: Motion estimation using gradient orientation structure tensors. In: Proceedings of the Second International Conference on Innovative Computing, Informatio and Control, ICICIC 2007, p. 450. IEEE Computer Society, Washington (2007)
13. Lowe, D.G.: Distinctive image features from scale-invariant keypoints. Int. J. Comput. Vision **60**(2), 91–110 (2004)
14. Möller, E., Grieszbach, G., Schack, B., Witte, H., Maurizio, P.: Statistical properties and control algorithms of recursive quantile estimators. Biometrical J. **42**(6), 729–746 (2000)
15. Noriega, P., Bernier, O.: Real time illumination invariant background subtraction using local kernel histograms. In: Proceedings of the British Machine Vision Conference, BMVA Press, pp. 100.1–100.10 (2006). doi:10.5244/C.20.100
16. Toyama, K., Krumm, J., Brumitt, B., Meyers, B.: Wallflower: principles and practice of background maintenance. In: The Proceedings of the Seventh IEEE International Conference on Computer Vision, vol.1, pp. 255–261 (1999)
17. Wang, H., Suter, D.: Background subtraction based on a robust consensus method. In: 18th International Conference on Pattern Recognition, ICPR 2006, vol. 1, pp. 223–226 (2006)
18. Wayne, P., Johann, P., Schoonees, A.: Understanding background mixture models for foreground segmentation. In: Proceedings Image and Vision Computing (2002)

Can Speedup Assist Accuracy? An On-Board GPU-Accelerated Image Georeference Method for UAVs

Loukas Bampis[✉], Evangelos G. Karakasis, Angelos Amanatiadis, and Antonios Gasteratos

Department of Production and Management Engineering, Democritus University of Thrace, Xanthi, Greece
lbampis@pme.duth.gr

Abstract. This paper presents a georeferenced map extraction method, for Medium-Altitude Long-Endurance UAVs. The adopted technique of projecting world points to an image plane is a perfect candidate for a GPU implementation. The achieved high frame rate leads to a plethora of measurements even in the case of a low-power mobile processing unit. These measurements can later be combined in order to refine the output and create a more accurate result.

1   Introduction

Remote sensing Unmanned Aerial Vehicles (UAVs) are increasingly used in various civilian domains such as agriculture, environmental monitoring, wildfire detection and urban geodata tasks. High-accuracy georeferenced mosaics are required in many remote sensing applications such as coastal erosion monitoring, post-disaster assessment, micro-topography and urban geoinformation [10]. The precision and correctness of the models however, are affected by many parameters such as the accuracy of the on-board inertial measurement units, the Global Positioning Systems (GPS) and the optical image sensors.

Image georeferencing has extensively been investigated in the last decades. A variety of approaches have been introduced in the literature which address this issue using the flat world assumption [8,13]. Such kind of methods are limited to high flight altitudes or planar terrains. In order to create a georeferenced map for terrains with rough geomorphology one could distinguish two main trends: (1) algorithms that derive information about the world morphology from Digital Terrain Models (DTMs) or Digital Surface Models (DSMs) [1,3,11] and (2) techniques that are based on the correlation between the optical information from consecutively acquired images [6,10,12]. In addition to the aforementioned trends, there is also an increased interest in accelerating the production of georeferenced maps using GPGPU computing [11].

Taking advantage of the continuous progress in the precision of the aforementioned sensors, recent sophisticated computer vision algorithms can provide in real-time, significantly improved accuracies in high resolution spatial data. This improvement however, comes with a critical trade off, which is the necessity for more computational power on the on-board processing units, especially

© Springer International Publishing Switzerland 2015
L. Nalpantidis et al. (Eds.): ICVS 2015, LNCS 9163, pp. 104–114, 2015.
DOI: 10.1007/978-3-319-20904-3_10

when on-board real-time processing is required. Since power consumption and weight limitations are two of the most fundamental constraints in a UAV design, an approach of utilizing low-weight and low-power processing boards is highly essential.

In this paper, a method for real-time on-board georeferenced map extraction for Medium-Altitude Long-Endurance (MALE) UAVs is proposed, based on the projection of the world points to the grabbed camera frames. The algorithm extends well on a GPU, providing the possibility of high processing frequencies. The achieved frame rates offer multiple measurements which can be used to increase the accuracy of the final extracted map.

2   Proposed Method

In this section the proposed method, which is based on GPS and Inertial Measurement Unit (IMU) sensors as well as on terrain information, using available Digital Elevation Models (DEMs), is presented. Through a process of a forward and backward projection between UAV camera sensor images and the used DEMs, the method produces a colored and georeferenced 3D point cloud. An orthographic projection of this point cloud to the image plane produces an orthorectified, georeferenced image. At this point it should be noted that the z-axis of the camera is always pointing to nadir, so as its image plane is parallel to the ground.

According to Karakasis et al.[5], a DEM produced by a fusion process between different DEMs, like SRTM and ASTER, is characterized by more accurate elevations. Since the proposed method depends on the sensors and DEMs accuracy, a fused version of ASTER and SRTM is selected to be used.

Although basic in principle and sensitive to GPS, IMU and DEMs accuracy, the proposed algorithm is a perfect candidate for a GPU implementation, since its mathematical foundation is consistent with that of graphics and thus, a great acceleration can be achieved. The advantage of speeding up the proposed algorithm is that it increases the measurements density for the 3D point cloud by allowing a corresponding increase of the camera's frame rate. This fact lead us to conclude that we can reduce the overall error of georeference by averaging measurements which correspond to the same world point. Furthermore, it is worth noticing, that the suitability of the proposed methodology for a GPU implementation, allows the use of cheaper and less power consuming equipment.

2.1   DEMs Fusion

A four-step fusion process based on the Chebyshev spectral expansion [5], is used in order to produce a fused version of the freely available ASTER and SRTM DEMs. The fusion steps are the following: (1) the preprocessing process, which addresses resolution issues of the used DEMs, (2) the forward transform of the DEMs using the Chebyshev spectral expansion, which produces a set of spectral expansion coefficients, (3) the weighted average of the expansion coefficients, which produces a set of fused coefficients and finally, (4) the inverse spectral transform of the fused coefficients in order to produce the fused DEM.

2.2 Mathematical Foundation and Error Reduction

The provided measurements from the GPS and IMU can be represented using two vectors, namely a 3-dimensional for the position and a 4-dimensional quaternion for the orientation:

$$
{}^{uav\_m}_{w}\boldsymbol{p}^{(i)} = \begin{bmatrix} x \\ y \\ z \end{bmatrix} = {}^{uav\_m}_{uav\_t}\boldsymbol{p}^{(i)} + {}^{uav\_t}_{w}\boldsymbol{p}^{(i)} \qquad and \qquad (1)
$$

$$
{}^{uav\_m}_{w}\boldsymbol{q}^{(i)} = \begin{bmatrix} k_x\sin(\theta/2) \\ k_y\sin(\theta/2) \\ k_z\sin(\theta/2) \\ \cos(\theta/2) \end{bmatrix} = {}^{uav\_m}_{uav\_t}\boldsymbol{q}^{(i)} \otimes {}^{uav\_t}_{w}\boldsymbol{q}^{(i)} \qquad (2)
$$

where $\hat{\boldsymbol{k}} = [k_x\ k_y\ k_z]^T$ is a unit vector on the rotation axis, while θ is the rotation angle. The vector ${}^{uav\_m}_{w}\boldsymbol{p}^{(i)}$ represents the measured and ${}^{uav\_t}_{w}\boldsymbol{p}^{(i)}$ the true position of the UAV with respect to the global frame of reference, while ${}^{uav\_m}_{uav\_t}\boldsymbol{p}^{(i)}$ is an error factor introduced by the GPS. Similarly, ${}^{uav\_m}_{w}\boldsymbol{q}^{(i)}$ represents the measured and ${}^{uav\_t}_{w}\boldsymbol{q}^{(i)}$ the true orientation of the UAV with respect to the global frame of reference, while ${}^{uav\_m}_{uav\_t}\boldsymbol{q}^{(i)}$ is a quaternion representing the error introduced by the IMU. It is safe to assume that both error parameters follow a zero mean Gaussian distribution [9]: ${}^{uav\_m}_{uav\_t}\boldsymbol{p}^{(i)} \sim N(0, Q_T)$ is the error of translation with covariance matrix Q_T and $\theta_e^{(i)} \sim N(0, \sigma_R^2)$ the error angle corresponding to ${}^{uav\_m}_{uav\_t}\boldsymbol{q}^{(i)}$ with σ_R^2 variance. Additionally, we introduce the expression $\boldsymbol{R}\left({}^{uav\_m}_{w}\boldsymbol{q}^{(i)}\right)$ as the rotation matrix corresponding to the quaternion ${}^{uav\_m}_{w}\boldsymbol{q}^{(i)}$. Note that the superscript (i) is a notation indicating the measurements in different points in time.

On the other hand, every point in the world can be represented with respect to the global frame of reference as:

$$
{}^{w}\boldsymbol{p} = \begin{bmatrix} x \\ y \\ z \end{bmatrix} \qquad (3)
$$

and given the position and the orientation of the UAV, one can express a world point with respect to the UAV frame of reference as:

$$
{}^{uav}\boldsymbol{p}^{(i)} = \boldsymbol{R}\left({}^{uav\_m}_{w}\boldsymbol{q}^{(i)}\right){}^{w}\boldsymbol{p} + {}^{uav\_m}_{w}\boldsymbol{p}^{(i)} \qquad (4)
$$

Finally, given the transformation between the GPS, IMU and camera $\left({}^{cam}_{uav}\boldsymbol{T}\right)$, as well as the camera intrinsics matrix $\left({}^{img}_{cam}\boldsymbol{C}\right)$, the point ${}^{uav}\boldsymbol{p}^{(i)}$ can be expressed as coordinates on the camera frame using homogenous coordinates:

$$
\boldsymbol{px}_L^{(i)} = \begin{bmatrix} u_L \\ v_L \\ w_L \end{bmatrix} = {}^{img}_{cam}\boldsymbol{C}\,{}^{cam}_{uav}\boldsymbol{T}\begin{bmatrix} {}^{uav}\boldsymbol{p}^{(i)} \\ 1 \end{bmatrix} = {}^{img}_{uav}\boldsymbol{C}\begin{bmatrix} {}^{uav}\boldsymbol{p}^{(i)} \\ 1 \end{bmatrix} \qquad (5)
$$

Using Eqs. (4) and (5), a color measurement for the world points inside (i)th's camera frustum can be obtained and assigned to a global image representing the georeferenced map as $I_G\left(\boldsymbol{px}_G^{(i)}\right) = I_L^{(i)}\left(\boldsymbol{px}_L^{(i)}\right)$. Furthermore, it is easy to extract the correlation between $\boldsymbol{px}_L^{(i)}$ and $\boldsymbol{px}_G^{(i)}$ on the common plane from an equation like:

$$\boldsymbol{px}_G^{(i)} = \begin{bmatrix} u_G \\ v_G \\ w_G \end{bmatrix} = \boldsymbol{Q}^{(i)}\,\boldsymbol{px}_L^{(i)} + \boldsymbol{J}^{(i)} \tag{6}$$

where the matrix $\boldsymbol{Q}^{(i)}$ and vector $\boldsymbol{J}^{(i)}$ are derived from the Eqs. (4) and (5) for a plane and contain information from ${}_{w}^{uav\_m}\boldsymbol{p}^{(i)}$ and ${}_{w}^{uav\_m}\boldsymbol{q}^{(i)}$ [13].

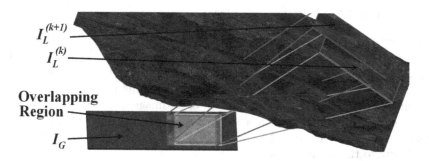

Fig. 1. Grabbed frames projected to a global georeferenced map through Eq. (6).

Figure 1 illustrates the aforementioned procedure for an example of two grabbed frames. Images $I_L^{(k)}$ and $I_L^{(k+1)}$ are added to the global map I_G through the projection process encompassing though an error introduced by the IMU and GPS measurements.

Considering the noise reduction, instead of assigning one absolute color measurement on a world point, the plethora of available measurements is exploited. Thus, a better estimation for the georeferenced color of each world point can be obtained by taking the average of all the associated measurements.

The intuition behind that logic was the fact that noises introduced to the system by the measurement units have zero mean. With that in mind and from Eq. (1) we can easily prove that:

$$_{w}^{uav\_m}\bar{\boldsymbol{p}} = {}_{uav\_t}^{uav\_m}\bar{\boldsymbol{p}} + {}_{w}^{uav\_t}\bar{\boldsymbol{p}} = {}_{w}^{uav\_t}\bar{\boldsymbol{p}} \tag{7}$$

where the notation ($^-$) above the factors is used to describe their average value for all the acquired measurements over time.

For the rotation on the other hand, the small angle approximation needs to be considered. In general, if the rotation angle that a quaternion represents is small enough (like the case of noise); the quaternion can take the form:

$$\delta q = \begin{bmatrix} \hat{k} \sin(\delta\theta/2) \\ \cos(\delta\theta/2) \end{bmatrix} \approx \begin{bmatrix} \frac{1}{2}\delta\theta \\ 1 \end{bmatrix} \tag{8}$$

In that case the rotation matrix that corresponds to the quaternion is:

$$R(\delta q) \approx I_{3x3} - \lfloor \delta\theta \rfloor \tag{9}$$

where $\lfloor \delta\theta \rfloor$ is the skew-symmetric matrix of the $\delta\theta$ vector.

Taking into account Eq. (9), the rotation matrix $R\left(^{uav\_m}_{w} q^{(i)}\right)$ given by

$$R\left(^{uav\_m}_{w} q^{(i)}\right) = R\left(^{uav\_m}_{uav\_t} q^{(i)}\right) R\left(^{uav\_t}_{w} q^{(i)}\right) \tag{10}$$

and the fact that $\theta_e^{(i)}$ noise have zero mean, one can get:

$$\bar{R}\left(^{uav\_m}_{w} q\right) = \overline{R\left(^{uav\_m}_{uav\_t} q\right) R\left(^{uav\_t}_{w} q\right)} = \bar{R}\left(^{uav\_m}_{uav\_t} q\right) \bar{R}\left(^{uav\_t}_{w} q\right) = \bar{R}\left(^{uav\_t}_{w} q\right) \tag{11}$$

Starting from $\bar{I}_G(px_G) = \bar{I}_L(px_L)$, we need to associate the color information of the global map to its pixel coordinates. At this point, an assumption regarding the local luminosity distribution of an image needs to be introduced. We are going to assume that in a small global frame region, where the measurements for the same world point will fall, the image function will behave accordingly to the bilinear model:

$$I_G\left(px_G^{(i)}\right) = diag\left(\begin{bmatrix} a \\ b \\ c \end{bmatrix}\right) px_G^{(i)} \quad or \quad \bar{I}_G(px_G) = diag\left(\begin{bmatrix} a \\ b \\ c \end{bmatrix}\right) \bar{px}_G \tag{12}$$

or in other words that the color remains stable or relates bilinearly, with coefficients a, b and c, to the pixel coordinates, for a small patch of the image. The combination of the above with Eq. (6), relates the average of the global pixel coordinates with the local ones, while the $\bar{Q}$ and $\bar{J}$ factors exclude their noise as it was proven with Eqs. (7) and (11).

To test the aforementioned assumption's strength, an experiment was conducted where the image presented in Fig. 2(a) was trimmed into many subimages. A 20×20 neighborhood was extracted for every pixel of the image, as well as the neighborhood's best fitted plane accordingly to the luminosities. The extracted plane together with the corresponding luminosity values is shown in Fig. 2(b). Figure 2(c) presents a histogram of the absolute differences between those planes and the corresponding luminosities, while Fig. 2(d) indicates the mean absolute difference for the individual coordinates of all tested patches. Since the error between the true pixel intensities and the assumed plane is sufficiently small, it is justified to carry on having in mind that Eq. (12) locally holds but it is expected to create a blurring effect to the produced map. Another approach which doesn't require this assumption, would be to keep track of the average of the local pixel coordinates and later combine it with the local pixel

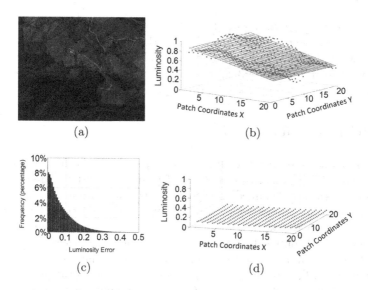

Fig. 2. (a) Tested image. (b) Extracted plane with corresponding luminosity values for a 20×20 size patch. (c) Histogram of the absolute differences between the plane and the luminosities for all the pixel of the tested image. (d) Average absolute difference for the 20×20 patch coordinates. Note that the range of the pixel intensities is [0 1].

luminosities. That methodology, though better in principle, is computationally more expensive for a GPU implementation and that is why it was not initially adopted. However, an extension of the methodology including the aforementioned approach is in authors' future plans.

Continuing the derivations, from Eq. (5):

$$\overline{p}\overline{x}_L = \overline{\substack{img \\ uav}C \begin{bmatrix} uav\,p \\ 1 \end{bmatrix}} \quad or \quad \overline{p}\overline{x}_L = \substack{img \\ uav}C \begin{bmatrix} uav\,\overline{p} \\ 1 \end{bmatrix} \tag{13}$$

since the $\substack{img \\ uav}C$ matrix is constant. Additionally, from Eq. (4) we obtain:

$$uav\,\overline{p} = \overline{R\left(\substack{uav\_m \\ w}q\right) {}^w p} + \substack{uav\_m \\ w}\,\overline{p} \tag{14}$$

Once again, given that the position of the world points is not changing over time, the term $^w\overline{p}$ can be substituted with $^w p$. Furthermore, from the above equation, together with (7) and (11):

$$uav\,\overline{p} = \overline{R\left(\substack{uav\_m \\ w}q\right) {}^w p} + \substack{uav\_m \\ w}\,\overline{p} = \overline{R}\left(\substack{uav\_t \\ w}q\right) {}^w p + \substack{uav\_t \\ w}\overline{p} \tag{15}$$

Finally, the combination of Eqs. (12), (13) and (15) provides a more accurate measurement for the georeferenced color of a world point, since the noise factors are eliminated.

At this point, the importance of a measurement plethora becomes clear. As the number of available measurements for a world point grows bigger, the average GPS and IMU input is better approximated and the noise is closer to zero. This result is verified in Subsect. 4.3, where the accuracy improvement with respect to the growth of measurements for a world point is presented.

3   GPU Implementation

Inspired by modern graphics rendering techniques, we introduce an early step in the aforementioned algorithm. Instead of projecting all the individual world points of the area to be scanned on every grabbed frame from the UAV, we narrow down the world candidates by using an opposite projection. The technique of narrowing down the world candidates is well known in computer graphics, where the lighting is only calculated for the world points that can be seen by the camera. Therefore, in our case the pixels of each individual image are projected on a flat world [13], providing an estimation about the world points possibly inside the field of view of the camera. Only those points are projected again on the image plane and the ones that fall out of the image dimensions are rejected.

As it is stated before, the whole process of projection is a perfect candidate and can be efficiently implemented on a GPU. The process of assigning one new color measurement to every world point inside the camera's field of view, is passed on to GPU threads and executed in parallel. The transformation matrices are stored in the GPU constant memory, allowing all threads to access their values simultaneously. Furthermore, the DEM data are stored in the texture memory of the GPU, enabling fast hardware bilinear interpolation in order to achieve the desired analysis.

The GPU algorithm was implemented using nVidia's CUDA API [4] following its Single Instruction on Multiple Threads (SIMT) possibilities and constraints, while the reader is able to examine the specifics of the implementation online[1].

4   Experimental Results

This section aims to evaluate the proposed methodology in terms of both, computation time and accuracy of the resulted orthorectified and georeferenced map. As has already been mentioned, the GPU implementation of the proposed algorithm significantly accelerates the computation time leading to the conclusion that a faster camera could be used. High frame rates increase the density of the produced point cloud allowing a corresponding improvement of the overall resulting accuracy. Since, the construction of the UAV has not been finished yet, a simulation environment has been built in order to evaluate the algorithm's performance.

---

[1] http://tinyurl.com/CUDA-AerialImgGeoref.

4.1   Simulation

The simulated environment is based on the usage of DEMs and satellite images in order to construct a realistic scene. A dense lidar DEM dataset [7], which represents the area (*Longitude range: 2°24′00.0"W to 2°25′48.0"W and Latitude range: 43°18′00.0"N to 43°19′48.0"N*), with resolution 1 m is used as ground truth in order to evaluate the resulted orthorectified map of the proposed algorithm. Furthermore, Gaussian noise is added to the position and orientation of the simulated UAV in order to further simulate the errors, which are owed to sensors (GPS & IMU) accuracy. This procedure creates a position error about ±5 meters from the exact position, while such orientation error, so as to have at most 2° degrees error from the vertical axis (nadir).

4.2   CPU Vs GPU - Time Performance Comparison

In order to present timing evaluations and comparisons, a CPU version of the aforementioned methodology was also implemented. Both algorithms (CPU & GPU) where executed and timed on a nVidia Jetson TK1 board. This board is equipped with a Tegra K1 GPU and a quad-core ARM Cortex-A15 CPU. The low power consumption ($\sim 14\,W$ at most) and the lightness ($\sim 120\,gr$) of this board (crucial requirements for modern systems [2]) enables the processing to be done online on the UAV without the need of extra communications, hardware and flight load.

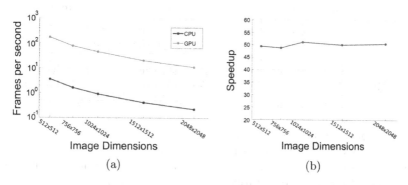

Fig. 3. (a) Fps comparison for the CPU and the GPU implementations (note the logarithmic scale). (b) GPU over CPU achieved speedup.

Figure 3(a) presents the frames per second achieved for both CPU and GPU implementations over 5 different image resolutions, viz 512 × 512, 756 × 756, 1024×1024, 1512×1512 and 2048×2048. Real time performance was achieved for image up to 1512 × 1512 size. In general, modern cameras provide the possibility of choosing between several combinations of image resolution and frame rate. The most efficient choice for a real setup scenario would be the one that lies closer to a point of the presented graph. Figure 3(b) on the other hand, depicts the speedup of the GPU over the CPU implementation. Note that the speedup remains constant as the resolution grows, proving a consistent scalability of the implemented algorithm.

4.3   GPU Implementation - Accuracy Evaluation

The number of measurements acquired for a world point depends on the factors of flight height and speed, the frame rate of the camera and the algorithm, as well as the image dimensions. We choose to carry out the presented experiments with a setup where the UAV would fly at $1\,km$ height with $150\,km/h$ using a camera with 756×756 resolution, although our method is scalable for any other combination.

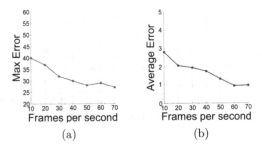

Fig. 4. (a) Maximum measured error. (b) Average measured error. Note that the error scale is [0 255] for visualization purposes.

In order to relate the georeferenced map accuracy with the achieved speed of the algorithm, a variety of different frame rates were tested. The absolute difference between the ground truth georeferenced map and the map produced from the proposed algorithm (with introduced noise), is selected as a measure of error. As one can see in Fig. 4, the error is inversely proportional to the frame rate and consistently to the number of measurements for the individual points.

Finally, the ground truth and the generated georeferenced-orthorectified map of the scanned area, can qualitatively be compared to each other in Fig. 5(a) and (b) respectively. Since the number of measurements for the points of the world is not uniformly distributed, i.e. the density is smaller at the beginning and the end of the UAV trajectory, only the region in the middle exhibits the optimum noise reduction. The measurement density is illustrated in Fig. 5(c), where the red coloring represents the territory with less measured world points, while moving towards blue the number of measurements grows bigger. At this point it should be noticed that although the output has blur appearance, the georeference quality in the middle region is increased, since there are no ghost effects (as in the bottom and upper area) and the color information is better positioned in the world.

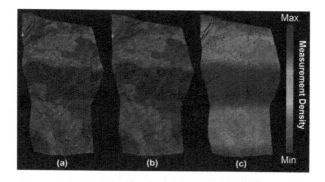

Fig. 5. (a) Georeferenced ground truth map. (b) Georeferenced produced map. (c) Measurements density of the scanned area.

5   Conclusions

In this work, a GPU accelerated method able to generate a georeferenced map for a scanned area from a UAV, is proposed. Although the method is influenced by GPS and IMU noise, a high frame rate can be achieved by the algorithm (even for a mobile GPU), enabling the acquisition of a measurement plethora which subsequently was proven to create more precise results.

References

1. Amanatiadis, A., Karakasis, E., Bampis, L., Giitsidis, T., Panagiotou, P., Sirakoulis, G.C., Gasteratos, A., Tsalides, P., Goulas, A., Yakinthos, K.: The hcuav project: electronics and software development for medium altitude remote sensing. In: IEEE International Symposium on Safety, Security, and Rescue Robotics, pp. 1–5 (2014)
2. Amanatiadis, A., Bampis, L., Gasteratos, A.: Accelerating single-image super-resolution polynomial regression in mobile devices. IEEE Trans. Consum. Electron. **61**(1), 63–71 (2015)
3. Choi, K., Lee, I.: A UAV-based close-range rapid aerial monitoring system for emergency responses. Int. Arch. Photogramm. Remote Sens. Spat. Inf. Sci. **38**, 247–252 (2011)
4. Cuda™: Nvidia corp. http://www.nvidia.com/object/cuda_home_new.html
5. Karakasis, E.G., Bampis, L., Amanatiadis, A., Gasteratos, A., Tsalides, P.: Digital elevation model fusion using spectral methods. In: IEEE International Conference on Imaging Systems and Techniques, pp. 340–345 (2014)
6. Küng, O., Strecha, C., Beyeler, A., Zufferey, J.C., Floreano, D., Fua, P., Gervaix, F.: The accuracy of automatic photogrammetric techniques on ultra-light uav imagery. In: UAV-g 2011-Unmanned Aerial Vehicle in Geomatics (2011)
7. The lidar DEM data website. http://b5m.gipuzkoa.net/
8. Paull, L., Thibault, C., Nagaty, A., Seto, M., Li, H.: Sensor-driven area coverage for an autonomous fixed-wing unmanned aerial vehicle. IEEE Trans. Cybern. **44**(9), 1605–1618 (2014)

9. Qi, H., Moore, J.B.: Direct kalman filtering approach for gps/ins integration. IEEE Trans. Aerosp. Electron. Syst. **38**(2), 687–693 (2002)

10. Remondino, F., Barazzetti, L., Nex, F., Scaioni, M., Sarazzi, D.: Uav photogrammetry for mapping and 3d modeling-current status and future perspectives. Int. Arch. Photogramm. Remote Sens. Spat. Inf. Sci. **38**(1), C22 (2011)

11. Thomas, U., Kurz, F., Rosenbaum, D., Mueller, R., Reinartz, P.: Gpu-based orthorectification of digital airborne camera images in real time. In: Proceedings of the XXI ISPRS Congress (2008)

12. Wang, Y., Fevig, R., Schultz, R.R.: Super-resolution mosaicking of UAV surveillance video. In: IEEE International Conference on Image Processing, pp. 345–348 (2008)

13. Xiang, H., Tian, L.: Method for automatic georeferencing aerial remote sensing (rs) images from an unmanned aerial vehicle (UAV) platform. Biosyst. Eng. **108**(2), 104–113 (2011)

High-Level Vision

Surface Reconstruction from Intensity Image Using Illumination Model Based Morphable Modeling

Zhi Yang$^{(\boxtimes)}$ and Varun Chandola

C.S.E Department of SUNY-Buffalo, Buffalo, NY, USA
{zhiyang,chandola}@buffalo.edu
http://www.cse.buffalo.edu/~zhiyang
http://www.cse.buffalo.edu/~chandola

Abstract. We present a new method for reconstructing depth of a known object from a single still image using deformed underneath sign matrix of a similar object. Existing Shape from Shading(SFS) methods try to establish a relationship between intensity values of a still image and surface normal of corresponding depth, but most of them resort to error minimization based approaches. Given the fact that these reconstruction approaches are fundamentally ill-posed, they have limited successes for surfaces like a human face. Photometric Stereo (PS) or Structure from Motion (SfM) based methods extend SFS by adding additional information/constraints about the target. Our goal is identical to SFS, however, we tackle the problem by building a relationship between gradient of depth and intensity value at the corresponding location of image of the same object. This formula is simplified and approximated for handing different materials, lighting conditions and, the underneath sign matrix is also obtained by resizing/deforming Region of Interest(ROI) with respect to its counterpart of a similar object. The target object is then reconstructed from its still image. In addition to the process, delicate details of the surface is also rebuilt using a Gabor Wavelet Network(GWN) on different ROIs. Finally, for merging the patches together, a Self-Organizing Maps(SOM) based method is used to retrieve and smooth boundary parts of ROIs. Compared with state of art SFS based methods, the proposed method yields promising results on both widely used benchmark datasets and images in the wild.

Keywords: 3d surfaces · Depth reconstruction · SFS · Morphable modeling · Surface deforming · Human perception

1 Introduction

Humans have a remarkable capability to perceive the 3D shape by looking at a 2D monocular image. Enabling computer vision systems to do the same still remains a challenging task. The exact problem, as formulated as early as in 1970 [7], to obtain the shape of a smooth opaque object from a single view, is

© Springer International Publishing Switzerland 2015
L. Nalpantidis et al. (Eds.): ICVS 2015, LNCS 9163, pp. 117–127, 2015.
DOI: 10.1007/978-3-319-20904-3_11

Fig. 1. The input data and generated data. From left to right: input raw sensor range data; input target image; output reconstructed 3D surface.

called *shape-from-shading* problem. Significant research has been done in this area over the past four decades with varying levels of success [12]. The classical SFS problem is typically solved under assumptions such as single point light source, constant albedo, and Lambertian reflectance. The key challenge faced by these methods is that ambiguity needs to be solved is fundamentally ill-posed, i.e., for the given intensity there could be multiple valid surfaces [12].

There have been recent advances to resolve the ambiguity. However, most methods either seek additional images corresponding to the target (e.g., *photometric-stereo* [16] and *structure-from-motion* [18]), or require knowledge of the context, such as the illumination model [11,15,17]. Recently, the work by Barron and Malik [8,10] has made advances in the field of *intrinsic image model* and SFS by simultaneously extracting multiple aspects of an image, including *shape, albedo*, and *illumination* from a single intensity image.

In this paper, we are trying to solve the same problem without using any additional context based constraints and knowing depth information of target object, instead, we propose a new method based on illumination model and an object similar to the target. The illumination model establish a relationship between gradient at each point and its corresponding intensity value. The input raw data, still image and generated data of our method are shown in Fig. 1.

As the workflow shown in Fig. 2, our approach has 5 steps. In step 1, we identify ROIs from both reference depth and target image in the following manner: first, we identify keypoints in reference depth by finding local maximum/minimum where $\frac{\partial z}{\partial x} = 0$ and $\frac{\partial z}{\partial y} = 0$ (usually we select the region around local maximum where local minimum determine boundaries). next, we determine corresponding ROIs in target image manually(in the Sect. 2.2, we will be introducing a semi-automated way doing this). In step 2, the ROIs of reference depth is resized to match the size of its counter parts of target image. In step 3, we could build a sign matrix for the target(along x or y axis, 1,0,-1 indicate the slope of depth is growing up, non-changed, down, respectively, e.g. we can decide the sign of the first row and then the sign of columns below that row),and then the depth of target image is reconstructed. In step 4, for recovering details of target image, a GWN based method is used. In the final step, a SOM based method is used to retrieve and smooth boundaries of ROIs.

2   3D Reconstruction Method

2.1   Basic Illumination Model

To make our work easier to be comprehended, we want to address the idea before giving any formula. Mathematically, in two dimensional euclidean space, say z

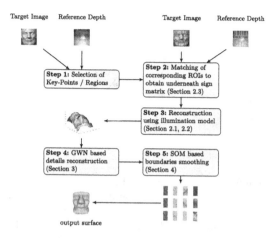

Target Image   Reference Depth   Target Image   Reference Depth

Step 1: Selection of
Key-Points / Regions

Step 2: Matching of
corresponding ROIs to
obtain underneath sign
matrix (Section 2.3)

Step 3: Reconstruction
using illumination model
(Section 2.1, 2.2)

Step 4: GWN based
details reconstruction
(Section 3)

Step 5: SOM based
boundaries smoothing
(Section 4)

output surface

Fig. 2. Overview of proposed tasks. The inputs to the reconstruction algorithm are the target image, a reference depth. The algorithm expects general correspondence between the target and reference images. Mathematically, the correspondence should be such that the *depth-intensity relationship* for the reference object is the same as that of the target object(we shall explain the relationship using a formula and a sign matrix in Sec. 2). For practical purposes, given the target object, we choose a much similar reference object.

and x are axis orthogonal to each other, as long as the gradient $\frac{\Delta z}{\Delta x}$ is known, the depth z at any point could be integrated from a known point x_{start}. In other words, if we regard the space is discrete, and step-wise Δz (with respect to *equal-length* step Δx) could be inferred or calculated at every point, then the summation of Δz from starting point x_{start} to ending point x_{end} along the path of summation, i.e., $\Sigma \Delta z_i$, is the relative height $z_{end} - z_{start}$.

Therefore, the problem, in our case, is to find the relationship between partial gradient $\frac{\partial z}{\partial x}$(or $\frac{\partial z}{\partial y}$), of given point (x, y), with respect to the intensity value I_{xy} at the point:

$$\frac{\partial z}{\partial x} = f_x(I_{xy}) \qquad or \qquad \frac{\partial z}{\partial y} = f_y(I_{xy}) \qquad (1)$$

This is much the same formula as stated in the traditional SFS problem: $I(x) = s(n(x))$, where the $n(x)$ is the normal vector of the location vector x.

As shown in Fig. 3, $\hat{n}_{max}$, which gives us $\theta = 2\beta$, or $\beta = \frac{1}{2}\theta = \mp\frac{1}{2}$ arccos $\left(\frac{I_x}{I_{max}}\right)$. We notice here the gradient of surface point x has exact the same angle as $\tan(\alpha - \beta)$, or in other words, $\frac{\partial z}{\partial x} = \tan(\alpha - \beta)$. Put above formulas together, we have:

$$\frac{\partial z}{\partial x} = \tan(\alpha - \beta) = \tan\left(\alpha \pm \frac{1}{2}\arccos\left(\frac{I_x}{I_{max}}\right)\right) \qquad (2)$$

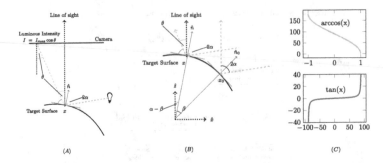

Fig. 3. In (A), the luminance, or often called brightness, from the observer's perspective, or *line of sight*, can be represented as the luminous intensity per projected area normal to the line of observation [6] (notice in (B), we assume that a single light source is located at infinity such that light falls on each point of the surface from the same direction). To be more accurate, the angle between line of sight and incoming light ray, i.e., θ, at point x, can be inferred by the angle between normal of x, i.e. $\hat{n}$ and normal of maximum intensity value received by observer, i.e., $\hat{n}_{max}$, which gives us $\theta = 2\beta$.

2.2 Handling Issues Caused by Lighting Condition and Material

Of course, it would be straight forward to think of implementing the formula (2) directly, and that will lead to 2-dimensional integration. However, the formula only works well in ideal conditions, and for the image in the wild, shading, especially material of surface will play important roles in the surface reconstruction. Therefore, we introduce an approximation of above formula, and an offset factor, to counterbalance the non-ideal situations.

We consider firstly of the linear attribute of arccos and tan functions. See Fig. 3(C), most values for both Inverse Cosine function and Tangent function, in their domain of definition, can be approximated using linear relation. Thus, we make following approximation: $\tan(x) = k_1 x + b_1$ and $\arccos(x) = k_2 x + b_2$ (from Fig. 3(C), we can see the values k_1, k_2, b_1 and b_2 are constant values). Using discrete manner of partial derivative for the purpose of digital computation, the formula (2) can be rewritten as: $\frac{\Delta z}{\Delta x} = k_1 \left(\alpha \pm \frac{1}{2} \left(k_2 \frac{I}{I_{max}} + b_2 \right) \right) + b_1$. As discussed, issues caused by lighting condition, different materials, impose an offset value for intensity values received by observer/camera. The offset, we empirically assume it has constant value b_{offset}.[1] Simplified from above formula, we have:

$$\frac{\Delta z}{\Delta x} = \pm(k \cdot I + b) + b' + b_{offset} = \pm(k \cdot I + b) + \tilde{b} \qquad (3)$$

Because we do not know the sign before the quantity $\frac{1}{2} \arccos \left(\frac{I_x}{I_{max}} \right)$ in (2), we cannot find the exact expression for the gradient. Let $\rho(x) \in \{-1, +1\}$ be a

---

[1] Usually we prefer to use the principles of photometry to match the luminance of the grayscale image to the luminance of the original color image(in reality, RGB model has different weight combination as compared with YUV model) [13].

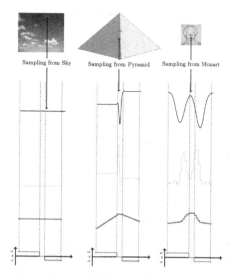

Fig. 4. An experiment to prove the approximated illumination model. The 1_{st} row: input images; 2_{nd} row: a slice of intensity values sampled from images above; 3_{rd} row: recovered absolute value of Δz using formula (4); 4_{th} row: reconstructed depth; 5_{th} row: underneath sign vector. Notice all these 3 experiments use the same sign vector. We assume the color of sky(dark blue), pyramid(light yellow), and face(misty rose), and empirically select b_{offset} for them(in our case, these values are -112, -201, -212 respectively and,the numbers are represented in signed 16-bit integer fashion). Given the same the sign function at the bottom row, the step-wise Δz is calculated(3_{rd} row) and the summation(4_{th}row) proves the reconstructed depth is correct(4_{th} row) (Color figure online).

binary indicator function which indicates the direction of the gradient. If $\rho(x)$ is known, we get:

$$\frac{\Delta z}{\Delta x} = \rho(x)(k \cdot I + b) + \tilde{b} \qquad (4)$$

Using the formula (4), we can determine candidate local maximum/minimum points from target image by letting $\frac{\Delta z}{\Delta x} = 0$ and $\frac{\Delta z}{\Delta y} = 0$, then manually prune unnecessary points. Given the gradient in (4), we can reconstruct the relative depth for the x_{start} and x_{end} as:

$$z = \sum_{x_{start}}^{x_{end}} \left[\rho(x)(k \cdot I_x + b) + \tilde{b} \right] \Delta x \qquad (5)$$

To prove formula (5) is correct, we did a very interesting experiment as shown in Fig. 4. In this experiment, the calculated Δz for sky is always 0, and so, no matter what sign function is, the depth will be summed up to 0. But we can see that the Δz for pyramid and mozart's face take on different values, and without alignment of sign function below, the depth could not be reconstructed correctly. Therefore in our method, the purpose of resizing similar object's ROIs, is to obtain correct alignment of the sign matrix/function.

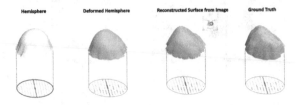

Fig. 5. Reconstructed surface using sign matrix from a deformed hemisphere. From left to right: original hemisphere, deformed hemisphere, reconstructed depth from a still image on its up-right corner(within pink color circle); ground truth of the depth in the pink color circle. Notice here, the summation sequence start from centerline, and then to both sides (Color figure online).

2.3 Reconstruction Using Sign Matrix

Finally we consider double summation over more general regions. Suppose that the region R is defined by $G_1(x) \leqslant y \leqslant G_2(x)$ with $x_{start} \leqslant x \leqslant x_{end}$. This is called a vertically simple region. The double summation is given by

$$
z = \sum_{x_{start}}^{x_{end}} \sum_{G_1(x)}^{G_2(x)} \left[\rho_{xy}(k_x \cdot I_{xy} + b_x) + \tilde{b}_x \right] \left[\rho_{xy}(k_y \cdot I_{xy} + b_y) + \tilde{b}_y \right] \Delta x \Delta y
$$

$$
= \sum_{x_{start}}^{x_{end}} \left[\rho_{xy}(k_x \cdot I_{xy} + b_x) + \tilde{b}_x \right] \Delta x \sum_{G_1(x)}^{G_2(x)} \left[\rho_{xy}(k_y \cdot I_{xy} + b_y) + \tilde{b}_y \right] \Delta y \quad (6)
$$

As shown in formula (6), recovering the shape of object is still determined by the two important factors: one is the underneath sign matrix, the other is intensity values. Of course, the offset plays an import role here too. This introduce an interesting topic: The sign matrix ρ_{xy} could be easily obtained by deforming a similar object's surface, i.e., by deforming an existing object, not only the depth of the morphable object at each location is changed, but also the underneath sign matrix is changed.

To prove our idea using formula (6), we did another interesting experiment as shown in Fig. 5. Here we have a hemisphere, and our target is to reconstruct target object using its still image. The first step is to estimate underneath sign matrix. It can be seen in the Fig. 5, by deforming surface of a hemisphere, the sign matrix is obtained exactly the same as that of the ground truth.[2] Next, using formula (6), we are able to recover the surface from the intensity values within the pink circle. The result is pretty similar to the shape of ground truth, which confirm proposed idea and the approximation are correct.

---

[2] This can be obtained by output of Heaviside function on difference of depth's gradient.

3   Reconstruction of Surface Details

Since deformed shape keep original features of reference object, the details of target object needs to be reconstructed too. In terms of imposing details, traditional SFS can perform well. Here we adopt a strategy using a GWN, which will keep the details of target image and not disturb the rough surface.

Proposed method take all ROIs as a whole, and minimize errors in batch manner:

$$[s, \theta, w] = \arg \min_{s, \theta, w} \sum_{i=1}^{N} \left(||I_i - \sum_{j=1}^{K_i} w_{ij}\psi_i||_2^2 + \beta \sum_{j=1}^{K_i} |w_{ij}| \right) \tag{7}$$

θ and s orientation factor and scale factor of Gabor wavelets, w_{ij} and ψ_{ij} the jth coefficient and its corresponding wavelet on ith ROI respectively. In order to prevent over-fitting, we add a regularization term $\beta \sum_{j=1}^{K_i} |w_{ij}|$. Here β is penalty factor for the L_1 norm of vector $[w_{i1}, ..., w_{iK_i}]$.

4   Self-Organizing Maps

Before merging different ROIs, their boundaries are usually rough and a smoothing process is required. Instead of finding out a smoothing strategy, here we propose a depth retrieval method using existing surface boundary parts. This issue has been addressed by an interesting recent paper [20], where input depth is divided into five facial parts via the alignment, and each facial part is matched independently to the dataset resulting in five high-resolution meshes. They use azimuth angle and elevation angle for measuring the similarity between two patches. Our method make stored depth "learn" target boundaries and therefore the best match are gradually smoothed by learning two boundaries. The depth patches comes from public dataset [2, 4].

Traditionally, there are two operational modes for a SOM, training and mapping. During training, the learning example is compared to the weight vectors associated with each neuron and the closest winning neuron is selected. The weights of all the neurons are then updated using the following update equation:

$$\omega_k(t + 1) = \omega_k(t) + \alpha(t)\eta(\nu, k, t)||\omega_k(t) - x||_2 \tag{8}$$

Here $\omega_k(t)$ is the weight for the kth neuron at t^{th} iteration, x is the input vector, and ν is the index of the winning neuron. $\alpha()$ gives the learning rate which monotonically decreases with is t. A neighborhood function which measures the distance between a given neuron and the winning neuron. Typically, η takes a Gaussian form, $\eta(\nu, k, t) = \frac{\Delta_{\nu,k}}{2\sigma(t)^2}$, where $\Delta(,)$ is the distance between two neurons on the grid, and σ is the monotonically decreasing neighborhood width. The SOM algorithm assumes that the input vectors are semantically homogeneous.

In our case, we attach the stored depth map of boundary parts at each neuron. During the training, in each round, the errors between two adjacent ROIs w.r.t. the boundary part are calculated, and the winning neuron should have the least errors. We summarize the idea in Algorithm 1.

Input : Adjacent Patch R, Adjacent Patch $\bar{R}$, Number of rounds n.
Output: Patch $N_{\hat{i},\hat{j}}$.

Initialize 2-dimensional matrix N of size $a \times b$ with stored depth of the same type of patches;
Initialize set of training set $S = \{R, \bar{R}\}$;
for $c \leftarrow 1$ *to* n **do**
  for $k \leftarrow 1$ *to* 2 **do**
    Find winning neuron $\nu = N_{\hat{i},\hat{j}}$ *for* S_k *using formula* (8);
    for $i \leftarrow 1$ *to* a **do**
      for $j \leftarrow 1$ *to* b **do**
        | *Update* N_{ij} *w.r.t.* ν *and* S_k;
      end
    end
  end
  Finding final winning neuron $N_{\hat{i},\hat{j}}$;
end

Algorithm 1. Parallel SOM Algorithm

5 Experiments

In order to demonstrate robustness of our method, we test our method on both benchmark data and images in the wild.

5.1 Benchmark Datasets

The first set of evaluation was conducted on a public RGB-D dataset [1,3,5]. In Fig. 6, we show comparison of our method with enhanced SFS in terms of depth errors. For all three benchmark objects, our method can achieve better reconstruction result compared with enhanced SFS on average. This phenomenon comes majorly from the fact that our result is calculated using an integration/summation process, which leads to a fair accurate output as a whole. Instead, traditional SFS-based method focus on local ambiguity, even in natural lighting environment, reconstructed surface converges to the value of gray-scale or intensity values. Some SFS based methods will inevitably converge to global minimum/maximum if their models are fundamentally convex or concave. Take MPI vase for example(the first row in Fig. 6), the boundary part are successfully reconstructed and perform better than our method, however, for the bulge part of this vase, the enhanced SFS simply did not recover the depth, compared with ground truth and, the error amounts to around $14cm$ to $15cm$.

The next set of experiments are performed on benchmark [5] for comparing normal errors among traditional SFS, enhanced SFS and our method. We maintain the similar lighting condition as [11](see leftmost figure of Mozart in the first row of Fig. 7). It can be seen that traditional SFS-based method converges to local intensity values, which give effect of "deep trench", while enhanced SFS overcome the the problem by adding natural illumination constraints. In our

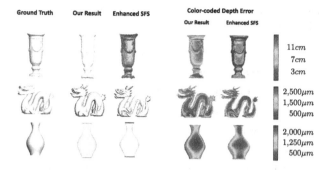

Fig. 6. A comparison in terms of depth errors between our method and enhanced SFS(*best viewed in color*) (Color figure online).

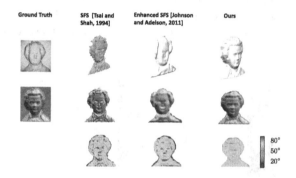

Fig. 7. A comparison in terms of normal errors among our method, traditional SFS and enhanced SFS(*best viewed in color*). The first row: target image(leftmost column) and reconstructed surface; the second row: normal map of target surface and reconstructed surface; the third row: normal error of reconstructed surface (Color figure online).

case, however, the depth information comes from accumulation of a portion of intensity, and therefore, the rough normal error is minimized. Moreover, using Gabor wavelet makes sure mean value and covariance are allocated along the direction to minimize error of reconstruction. This gives our method advantages over both traditional and enhanced SFS methods.

Then we numerically compare our method to three state of art methods: traditional SFS [14], PS, and the recent SAIFS method [10][3] on Stanford benchmark [3]. Result is shown in Table 1. The proposed method outperforms both SFS and SAIFS on all three benchmark images by a factor of 2 or 3.

5.2 Images in the Wild

We especially wish to see how our method can handle the issue of shading and natural lighting condition, as well as the problems caused by different materials.

---

[3] http://www.cs.berkeley.edu/~barron/SIRFS_release1.5.zip.

Table 1. Comparison of average reconstruction error of proposed method and existing methods. Error is measured in μm.

Model	Dragon	Armadillo	Buddha
SFS	962.4	1067.4	1251.7
SAIFS	1915.6	2217.1	2405.2
PS	492.7	515.3	603.1
Ours	417.1	497.5	542.9

We select images of famous people from internet. Take Fig. 8 for example, eye brow, mustache hair take different "color" compared with regular skin. What is more, the lighting condition is natural such that our assumption of a single source of light does not hold too. The results are shown in Fig. 8. This result is especially interesting in the sense, as long as the corresponding underneath sign matrix is similar enough to the counterpart of target, reconstructing a satisfactory surface is possible.

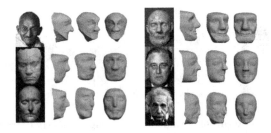

Fig. 8. Result of reconstruction for images in the wild (Color figure online)

6   Conclusions and Future Work

We have shown a depth recovery method for certain object from a still image by deforming the underneath sign matrix of a similar object. The contribution of this paper is four folds:

- introduces an illumination model;
- handles reflectance problem from different material or lighting condition;
- the details of the surface is recovered using GWN for each ROI on target;
- to merge the different ROIs, a SOM based method is used to retrieve and smooth boundary parts of ROIs.

In terms of recovery, unlike PS based methods, given the fact that very little depth knowledge is known of target, our method can effectively reconstruct complex surface like face. The current ROIs are manually selected according to the number of local maximum points, so in the future, we would like to explore an automatic way for finding regions.

References

1. MPI-Inf 3d data. http://gvv.mpi-inf.mpg.de/files/
2. VAP dataset. http://www.vap.aau.dk/rgb-d-face-database/
3. Stanford 3d repository. http://graphics.stanford.edu/data/3Dscanrep/
4. Thingiverse. http://www.thingiverse.com/
5. UCF shape database. http://www.cs.ucf.edu/~vision/
6. RCA: RCA Electro-Optics Handbook, pp. 18–19, RCA (1974)
7. Horn, B.K.: Shape from shading. Doctoral Thesis MIT. MA, USA (1970)
8. Barron, J.T., Malik, J. : High-frequency shape and albedo from shading using natural image statistics. In: CVPR, pp. 2521–2528 (2011)
9. Horn, B.K., Brooks, M.J.: The variational approach to shape from shading. Comput. Vis. Gr. Image Process **33**, 174–208 (1986)
10. Barron, J.T., Malik, J.: Shape, albedo, and illumination from a single image of an unknown object. In: CVPR, pp. 334–341 (2012)
11. Johnson, M.K., Adelson, E.H.: Shape estimation in natural illumination. In: CVPR, pp. 2553–2560 (2011)
12. Zhang, R., Tsai, P.-S., Cryer, J.E., Shah, M.: Shape from shading: a survey. IEEE Trans. PAMI **21**, 690–706 (1999)
13. Volz, H.G.: Industrial Color Testing: Fundamentals and Techniques. Wiley-VCH, New York (2001)
14. Tsai, P.-S., Shah, M.: Shape from shading using linear approximation. Image Vis. Comput. **12**, 487–498 (1994)
15. Han, Y., Lee, J-Y., Kweon, I.S.: High quality shape from a single RGB-D image under uncalibrated natural illumination. In: ICCV, pp. 1617–1624 (2013)
16. Woodham, R.J.: Photometric method for determining surface orientation from multiple images. Opt. Eng. **19**, 139–144 (1980)
17. Yu, L.-F., Yeung, S.-K., Tai, Y.-W., Lin, S.: Shading-based shape refinement of RGB-D images. In: CVPR, pp. 1415–1422 (2013)
18. Bregler, C., Hertzmann, A., Biermann, H.: Recovering non-rigid 3d shape from image streams. In: CVPR, vol. 2, pp. 690–696 (2000)
19. Rusinkiewicz, S., Hall-Holt, O., Levoy, M.: Real-time 3d model acquisition. ACM Trans. Graph. **21**, 438–446 (2002)
20. Liang, S., Kemelmacher-Shlizerman, I., Shapiro, L.G.: 3D face hallucination from a single depth frame. In: International Conference on 3D Vision (3DV) (2014)

Learning Appearance Features for Pain Detection Using the UNBC-McMaster Shoulder Pain Expression Archive Database

Henrik Pedersen[✉]

Department of Engineering, Aarhus University,
Finlandsgade 22, Aarhus, Denmark
hpe@eng.au.dk

Abstract. We propose a supervised approach to solve the task of automatic pain detection from facial expressions. A pain detection algorithm should be both robust to face pose and the identity of the face (identity bias). In order to achieve invariance to face pose, we use an Active Appearance Model (AAM) to warp all face images into frontal pose. The main contribution of our paper is a discriminative feature extractor that addresses identity bias by learning appearance features that separate pain-related factors from other factors, such as those related to the identity of the face. The system achieves state-of-the-art performance on the UNBC-McMaster Shoulder Pain Expression Archive Database.

Keywords: Pain detection · Facial expression recognition · Feature learning

1 Introduction

Automatic detection of spontaneous facial expression has been studied extensively over the past decade [19,23]. Likewise, automatic pain monitoring from facial expression has received increased attention due to its applications in health care, ranging from back pain to severe neurological disorders [3,7,9–13,20]. Automatic pain assessment is crucial in patients who are unable to verbally communicate, including newborns and patients in intensive care units. The main challenges in automatic pain assessment from facial expressions are head-pose variations and identity bias. While the former can be addressed by warping the face to frontal pose, the latter requires a feature representation that can tell identity-related appearance and shape cues apart from pain-related cues.

To date, relatively few works have addressed the problem of automatic pain detection from facial expressions [3,7,9–13,20]. Most schemes focus on activation and deactivation of facial action units (AUs) known to be linked with pain [22]. Facial AUs, which originate from the Facial Action Coding System (FACS) [6], describe basic facial configurations such as nose wrinkling and cheek-raising. The

© Springer International Publishing Switzerland 2015
L. Nalpantidis et al. (Eds.): ICVS 2015, LNCS 9163, pp. 128–136, 2015.
DOI: 10.1007/978-3-319-20904-3_12

presence and intensity of a selected subset of these AUs can be used to calculate a quantitative measure of pain using the so-called Prkachin and Solomon Pain Intensity (PSPI) score [15,16].

The UNBC-McMaster Shoulder Pain Expression Archive Database [13] consists of 200 video sequences of 25 patient's faces (suffering from shoulder pain) while they were moving the affected and the non-affected shoulder. The database provides pain-related AUs for each frame, coded by certified FACS coders, and the PSPI score is provided for each frame as well. For a detailed description and analysis of the database, the reader is referred to [12]. In order to detect pain automatically, Lucey et al. [13] use an Active Appearance Model (AAM) [5,14] to extract the position of 66 facial landmark points in each video frame. They subsequently use Support Vector Machines (SVMs) to predict the presence of pain-related AUs in a given frame, as well as presence of PSPI scores above zero, using the spatial configuration of the facial landmarks as input. SVM cross-validation is performed using a leave-one-subject-out strategy, i.e., training is performed on data from all subjects except one, who's data are used for testing the accuracy of the pain detection. In addition to the spatial configuration, Lucey et al. also propose a *canonical normalized appearance* as input to the pain prediction. This input is generated for each frame by warping the face into the mean shape (of all faces in the database) based on the positions of the facial landmark points. This step eliminates all identity bias related to shape. The canonical normalized appearance performs slightly better than the spatial configuration for detecting pain (defined as a PSPI score above zero), which may be explained by the higher dimensionality - and consequently the higher expressiveness - of the appearance features (number of dimensions = $87 \times 93 = 8091$) compared with the spatial landmark features (number of dimensions = $2 \times 66 = 132$).

A potential problem that arises when using appearance-based features, such as those proposed in [13], is the so-called identity bias [19]. Appearance features are derived directly from the raw pixel intensities and without any further processing they naturally cluster into regions corresponding to the identities of the subjects present in the database. When training an SVM to predict pain in the presence of identity bias, the decision boundaries essentially end up being estimated separately for each cluster (or subject), which ultimately results in poor generalization of the trained SVM to unseen subjects. One way to overcome the problem associated with identity bias is to reduce the dimensionality of the input data in such a way that the reduced data representation does not cluster into subjects. By far the most popular dimensionality reduction technique is Principal Component Analysis (PCA), which is essentially a data compression technique. Other common techniques include sparse coding and non-negative matrix factorization. Another closely related category of dimensionality reduction techniques that has achieved much attention over the last decade is auto-encoders. Auto-encoders provide a flexible framework for unsupervised feature learning and have been widely used for pre-training of deep neural networks (e.g., [2,8]). The flexibility lies in the choice of cost function, including the type of reconstruction error and regularization terms, and also the choice of activation function (e.g., sigmoid or rectified linear units). The latter is particularly important, as it provides a means to derive a non-linear encoding of the input, which again allows stacking auto-encoders to learn very high-level abstractions of the input [1,21].

In this paper, we propose a discriminative feature extractor for automatic pain detection which learns appearance-based features that separate out the factors related to pain. Inspired by [17], we construct a feature extractor that divides the set of features into two blocks. The two blocks are trained to cooperate to reconstruct the input image, but one block is also trained to predict pain. The overall structure of the discriminative feature extractor closely resembles that of traditional auto-encoders, with the addition of a logistic regression module that encourages the features of one of the two blocks to encode pain-related features. The trained feature encoders can be stacked similar to stacked auto-encoders to obtain high-level representations of the input. Subsequently, the learned features are used as input to train an SVM to predict pain.

2   Approach

The proposed method for pain detection builds on the framework of [13]. The annotated facial landmark points of all video frames are used to derive a mean shape, and subsequently non-linear warping is used to register all faces to the mean shape (see Fig. 1). Following conversion to gray-scale and intensity normalization, the warped facial images are used to train the proposed discriminative feature extractor. Finally, following the standard procedure, the learned features are used to train a linear SVM to predict pain, defined here as a PSPI score above zero.

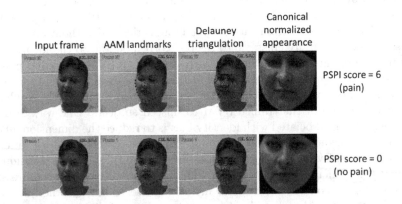

Fig. 1. Image registration pipeline. Each input frame in the database has been annotated with 66 facial landmark points using an AAM. Using Delauney triangulation, each face is non-rigidly warped to frontal pose (the mean of all shapes). This frontalized view is dubbed the *canonical normalized appearance*. The figure shows the image registration pipeline for a painful face (top row) and a neutral face (bottom row).

2.1   Image Registration

The initial step of many facial expression recognition techniques consists of an image registration step, where the face is located and warped into frontal pose. Some authors refer to this step as *frontalization*. The motivation of this step is that head pose variation renders subsequent facial expression analysis difficult, if not dealt with. By far the most popular method for registration of facial images is AAMs. In our case, since the face database has already been annotated using an AAM, the image registration step is straight forward to implement. Given a (randomly chosen) reference video frame, the facial landmark points of all other frames are registered to the reference using Procrustes alignment, comprising global scaling, rotation, and translation. In order to reduce bias towards the initial reference, a new reference is generated by averaging over all aligned shapes, and the Procrustes alignment is repeated to obtain the final mean shape.

Once the mean shape has been obtained, a given video frame is registered to the mean shape using a piece-wise affine warping that acts separately on each triangle spanned by the facial landmark points (triangles are obtained by Delauney triangulation). For facial expression recognition, the resulting frontalized face image is typically converted to gray-scale before further processing. In line with [13], we refer to the frontalized face image as the *canonical normalized appearance*. In our study, the canonical normalized appearance has size 48×48. The image registration pipeline is illustrated in Fig. 1.

2.2   Preprocessing

When using the sigmoid as activation function in auto-encoders, the input data must be scaled to lie within the range from 0 to 1 (or better yet, between 0.1 and 0.9, as explained below). In addition, it is desirable to whiten the data to make the feature dimensions uncorrelated, or one should at least standardize the data to have zero mean and unit variance along each feature dimension. This paper uses the latter approach. In order to avoid saturation of the sigmoid activation functions at the beginning of training, it is a common trick to scale each input dimension such that the values lie within the range from 0.1 to 0.9. This squeezes the data into the roughly linear range of the sigmoid function, thus preventing vanishing gradients during the initial training phase and ultimately leading to faster convergence of the auto-encoder.

2.3   Discriminative Feature Extractor

The traditional auto-encoder learns an encoder function, $h(x) = f(Wx + b)$, where $x \in R^{n \times 1}$ is the input, $W \in R^{m \times n}$ is a linear transformation, $b \in R$ is a bias term, and f is the element-wise sigmoid function. With tied weights the decoding of $h(x)$ is the reconstructed input, $\hat{x} = f(W^T h(x) + c)$, where W^T is the matrix transpose of W, and $c \in R^{n \times 1}$ is the bias of the decoder. The learnable parameters $\{W, b, c\}$ are trained to minimize the reconstruction error $\|x - \hat{x}\|^2$.

The semi-supervised version of auto-encoders proposed in [17] learns two encoder functions: one that encodes discriminative factors of the input, $h^d(x) = f(Wx+b)$, and one that encodes all other factors, $h^o(x) = f(Vx+a)$. The reconstructed input is $\hat{x} = f(W^T h^d(x) + V^T h^o(x) + c)$, and as before the parameters are trained to minimize $L_{recon} = \|x - \hat{x}\|^2$. In addition, the discriminative features, $h^d(x)$, are also trained to predict the facial expression label $y(x)$ similarly to logistic regression. Specifically, if there are only two possible labels ($y = 1$ for pain and $y = 0$ for no pain), the predicted probability of pain given the input is $\hat{y} = P(y = 1|x) = f(U h^d(x) + d)$, where the feature vector U maps the discriminative features, $h^d(x)$, to the prediction for pain, and d is the bias. The corresponding loss function is $L_{disc} = -y \log(\hat{y}) + (1 - y) \log(1 - \hat{y})$. The learnable parameters $\{W, V, U, a, b, c, d\}$ are trained to minimize $L_{recon} + \gamma L_{disc}$, where γ can be used to adjust the tradeoff between reconstruction error and classification error.

While [17] uses a regularization penalty inspired by contractive auto-encoders [18], we use a simple $L1$ penalty that promotes sparsity in V and W. In our experience, using conventional $L1$ regularization results in features that are very similar to those obtained using contractive regularization, but at higher computational speed.

Finally, in order to further encourage the two feature blocks to learn distinct features, an orthogonality promoting penalty is added to the loss function. This term sums the squared inner product of all feature vectors in V with all feature vectors in W, i.e., $L_{orth} = \sum (W^T V)^2$.

The total loss function to minimize is

$$L_{recon} + \gamma L_{disc} + \lambda(|V| + |W|) + \eta L_{orth} \tag{1}$$

where $|\cdot|$ denotes the $L1$ norm, λ controls the level of $L1$ regularization, and η determines the weight of the orthogonality promoting penalty.

The learned feature representation consisting of the concatenation of $h^d(x)$ and $h^o(x)$ (for all training x) can be used as input to train a second discriminative feature extractor in the same way as described above. The resulting stacked feature extractor thus has two hidden layers.

2.4   Classification

Once the discriminative feature extractor has been trained, the resulting features can be used to predict pain. As in the original work inspiring our paper [13], we use a linear SVM for classification [4]. The SVM is trained to predict the label, y, corresponding to the sign of the pain-related PSPI score annotated in the database. A value of $y = 0$ corresponds to a PSPI score of zero (no pain), whereas $y = 1$ corresponds to a PSPI score above zero (pain). In the most general case, the features that are used as input to the SVM are both the discriminative features, $h^d(x)$, and the other features, $h^o(x)$. Alternatively, one could also choose to use only the discriminative features as input. This was not considered in the present paper, because in our experience using both $h^d(x)$ and $h^o(x)$ gives the best performance.

3 Experiments and Results

Our experiments were conducted on the UNBC-McMaster Shoulder Pain Expression Archive Database [13]. The total number of frames in the database is 48398, of which 8369 frames (17.3 %) are associated with pain (PSPI>0). Due to the over-representation of frames with no behavior of interest, the results of the classification can be somewhat skewed. To address this issue, Lucey et al. [13] use the area under the curve (AUC) of the receiver-operator characteristic (ROC) curve as a performance measure. Alternatively, if samples are drawn from the 'pain' and 'no pain' frames with equal probability, and classification performance is evaluated over multiple runs, the average percentage of correctly classified images also provides a reliable performance measure. Here, we report the performance using both measures.

In all experiments conducted, a leave-one-subject-out strategy was used and both the discriminative feature extractor and the SVM-based pain detector were trained on data from all other subjects. In each run, 2000 training frames were sampled randomly with 50 % probability from the 'pain' frames and 50 % probability from the 'no pain' frames. After training of the feature extractor and the SVM, classification performance was tested on frames picked from the left-out subject. Again, test frames were sampled randomly with 50 % probability from the 'pain' frames and 50 % probability from the 'no pain' frames. The number of test frames was chosen such that all 'pain' frames of the selected subject were included in the test set. We performed 10 such runs for each of the 25 subjects and averaged classification performance over all runs. For comparison, we also trained and evaluated the SVM classifier using the canonical normalized appearance as input (as originally proposed in [13]).

The first layer of the feature extractor was trained to extract 400 discriminative features and 400 non-discriminative features. The weights of the terms in the loss function were $\gamma = 10, \lambda = 0.001, \eta = 0.1$. Figure 2 shows typical examples of the features extracted. In general, the features are sparse and difficult to semantically interpret. It is hard to see the difference between the discriminative and non-discriminative features, except maybe that the discriminative feature set shows some redundancy (i.e., some of the learned features are nearly identical).

All classification results are summarized in Table 1. Using first layer features as input to the SVM classifier, the average AUC was 0.857, and the average accuracy was 71.6 %. To demonstrate that the discriminative feature block is indeed important to obtain good classification results, we also tested the performance without the discriminative loss term (L_{disc}), i.e., using $\gamma = 0$. The orthogonality promoting penalty term (L_{orth}) ensures that the two feature blocks will be different, but learning is completely unsupervised, meaning that no attempt is made to learn discriminative features. In this case, the AUC was reduced to 0.806 and the accuracy to 67.8 %. This shows that the discriminative loss term is necessary in order to obtain good classification performance.

The second layer of the feature extractor was trained using the feature representation of the first layer as input. The second layer was trained to extract

64 discriminative features and 64 non-discriminative features, and the weighting of the terms in the loss function was the same as for the first layer. Using the second layer features as input to the SVM classifier, the average AUC increased to 0.96 and the average accuracy to 86.1 %. Without the discriminative loss term ($\gamma = 0$) and using the discriminatively trained first layer features to encode the input, the AUC dropped to 0.633 and the accuracy to 55.4 %. This is significantly worse than for the first layer with γ set to zero, which may be attributed to the fact that the dimensionality of layer two is much lower (2×64 for the second layer vs. 2×400 for the first layer).

The above results should be compared with those obtained using the canonical normalized appearance [13] as input. With our training and testing scheme, where 'pain' and 'no pain' frames are sampled with equal probability, the canonical normalized appearance yielded in an average AUC of 0.781 and an average accuracy of 66.7 %.

While the first layer features moderately improve performance compared with the traditional canonical normalized appearance, the second layer features significantly surpass the first layer features, achieving a generalization accuracy that is nearly 15 % higher. This dramatic improvement suggests that high-level features are needed in order to achieve good performance in pain detection. We did not experiment with deeper architectures, nor did we consider other deep learning techniques in the present study.

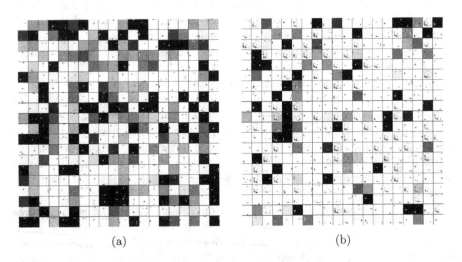

(a)   (b)

Fig. 2. Examples of first layer features. (a) and (b) respectively show the 400 non-discriminative features and the 400 discriminative features.

4   Discussion

In this paper, we have presented and investigated an approach to learn appearance features for pain detection from facial expressions. Invariance to head pose

Table 1. Performance of pain classification

	AUC	Accuracy (%)
Canonical normalized appearance [13]	0.781 ± 0.125	66.7 ± 12.3
First layer features ($\gamma = 10$)	0.857 ± 0.097	71.6 ± 12.8
First layer features ($\gamma = 0$)	0.806 ± 0.102	67.8 ± 12.0
Second layer features ($\gamma = 10$)	$\mathbf{0.965 \pm 0.027}$	$\mathbf{86.1 \pm 10.2}$
Second layer features ($\gamma = 0$)	0.633 ± 0.189	55.4 ± 9.55

variation and shape-related identity bias is achieved by warping all faces to a common shape. However, the resulting canonical normalized appearance is sensitive to identity bias and, with an accuracy of 66.7 %, acts as a relatively poor predictor of pain. To address this issue, we introduce a discriminative feature extractor that learns appearance features that separate pain-related factors from other factors, such as those related to the identity of the face. When stacking two such feature extractors, we achieve state-of-the-art performance on the UNBC-McMaster Shoulder Pain Expression Archive Database [13] with an average generalization accuracy of 86.1 %. We also show that disabling the discriminative part of the feature extractor (by setting γ to zero) results in poor classification results, showing that the learned discriminative features are indeed sensitive to pain.

References

1. Bengio, Y.: Learning deep architectures for AI. Found. Trends® Mach. Learn. **2**(1), 1–127 (2009)
2. Bengio, Y., Lamblin, P., Popovici, D., Larochelle, H., et al.: Greedy layer-wise training of deep networks. Adv. Neural Inf. Process. Syst. **19**, 153 (2007)
3. Brahnam, S., Chuang, C.F., Shih, F.Y., Slack, M.R.: Machine recognition and representation of neonatal facial displays of acute pain. Artif. Intell. Med. **36**(3), 211–222 (2006)
4. Chang, C.C., Lin, C.J.: Libsvm: a library for support vector machines. ACM Trans. Intell. Syst. Technol. **2**(3), 27:1–27:27 (2011)
5. Cootes, T.F., Edwards, G.J., Taylor, C.J.: Active appearance models. IEEE Trans. Pattern Anal. Mach. Intell. **23**(6), 681–685 (2001)
6. Essa, I.A., Pentland, A.P.: Coding, analysis, interpretation, and recognition of facial expressions. IEEE Trans. Pattern Anal. Mach. Intell. **19**(7), 757–763 (1997)
7. Gholami, B., Haddad, M., Tannenbaum, A.R.: Agitation and pain assessment using digital imaging. In: Annual International Conference of the IEEE Engineering in Medicine and Biology Society, EMBC 2009, pp. 2176–2179. IEEE (2009)
8. Hinton, G., Osindero, S., Teh, Y.W.: A fast learning algorithm for deep belief nets. Neural Comput. **18**(7), 1527–1554 (2006)
9. Kaltwang, S., Rudovic, O., Pantic, M.: Continuous pain intensity estimation from facial expressions. In: Bebis, G., Boyle, R., Parvin, B., Koracin, D., Fowlkes, C., Wang, S., Choi, M.-H., Mantler, S., Schulze, J., Acevedo, D., Mueller, K., Papka, M. (eds.) ISVC 2012, Part II. LNCS, vol. 7432, pp. 368–377. Springer, Heidelberg (2012)

10. Littlewort, G.C., Bartlett, M.S., Lee, K.: Automatic coding of facial expressions displayed during posed and genuine pain. Image Vis. Comput. **27**(12), 1797–1803 (2009)
11. Lucey, P., Cohn, J.F., Matthews, I., Lucey, S., Sridharan, S., Howlett, J., Prkachin, K.M.: Automatically detecting pain in video through facial action units. IEEE Trans. Syst. Man Cybern. B Cybern. **41**(3), 664–674 (2011)
12. Lucey, P., Cohn, J.F., Prkachin, K.M., Solomon, P.E., Chew, S., Matthews, I.: Painful monitoring: automatic pain monitoring using the unbc-mcmaster shoulder pain expression archive database. Image Vis. Comput. **30**(3), 197–205 (2012)
13. Lucey, P., Cohn, J.F., Prkachin, K.M., Solomon, P.E., Matthews, I.: Painful data: the unbc-mcmaster shoulder pain expression archive database. In: IEEE International Conference on Automatic Face and Gesture Recognition and Workshops (FG 2011), pp. 57–64. IEEE (2011)
14. Matthews, I., Baker, S.: Active appearance models revisited. Int. J. Comput. Vision **60**(2), 135–164 (2004)
15. Prkachin, K.M.: The consistency of facial expressions of pain: a comparison across modalities. Pain **51**(3), 297–306 (1992)
16. Prkachin, K.M., Solomon, P.E.: The structure, reliability and validity of pain expression: evidence from patients with shoulder pain. Pain **139**(2), 267–274 (2008)
17. Rifai, S., Bengio, Y., Courville, A., Vincent, P., Mirza, M.: Disentangling factors of variation for facial expression recognition. In: Fitzgibbon, A., Lazebnik, S., Perona, P., Sato, Y., Schmid, C. (eds.) ECCV 2012, Part VI. LNCS, vol. 7577, pp. 808–822. Springer, Heidelberg (2012)
18. Rifai, S., Vincent, P., Muller, X., Glorot, X., Bengio, Y.: Contractive auto-encoders: explicit invariance during feature extraction. In: Proceedings of the 28th International Conference on Machine Learning (ICML 2011), pp. 833–840 (2011)
19. Sariyanidi, E., Gunes, H., Cavallaro, A.: Automatic analysis of facial affect: a survey of registration, representation and recognition. IEEE Trans. Pattern Anal. Mach. Intell. **37**(6), 1113–1133 (2014)
20. Sikka, K., Dhall, A., Bartlett, M.S.: Classification and weakly supervised pain localization using multiple segment representation. Image Vis. Comput. **32**(10), 659–670 (2014)
21. Vincent, P., Larochelle, H., Lajoie, I., Bengio, Y., Manzagol, P.A.: Stacked denoising autoencoders: learning useful representations in a deep network with a local denoising criterion. J. Mach. Learn. Res. **11**, 3371–3408 (2010)
22. Williamdes, A.C.: Facial expression of pain: an evolutionary account. Behav. Brain Sci. **25**(4), 439–455 (2002)
23. Zeng, Z., Pantic, M., Roisman, G.I., Huang, T.S.: A survey of affect recognition methods: audio, visual, and spontaneous expressions. IEEE Trans. Pattern Anal. Mach. Intell. **31**(1), 39–58 (2009)

How Good Is Kernel Descriptor on Depth Motion Map for Action Recognition

Thanh-Hai Tran[1][(✉)] and Van-Toi Nguyen[1,2,3]

[1] International Research Institute MICA, HUST-CNRS/UMI-2954-INP Grenoble,
Hanoi, Vietnam
{thanh-hai.tran,van-toi.nguyen}@mica.edu.vn
[2] L3i Laboratory, University of La Rochelle, La Rochelle, France
[3] University of Information and Communication Technology Under
Thai Nguyen University, Thai Nguyen, Vietnam

Abstract. This paper presents a new method for action recognition using depth data. Each depth sequence is represented by depth motion maps from three projection views (front, side and top) to exploit different aspects of the motion. However, different from state of the art works extracting local binary pattern or histogram of oriented gradients, we describe an action based on gradient kernel descriptor. The proposed method is evaluated on two benchmark datasets (MSRAction3D and MSRGestures3D) and obtains very competitive performances with the best state of the arts methods. Our best recognition rate is 91.57 % on MSRAction3D and 100 % on MSRGestures3D dataset whereas [1] achieved 93.77 % and 94.60 % respectively.

Keywords: Action recognition · Depth motion map · Kernel descriptor

1 Introduction

Action recognition is an active topic in computer vision because of its wide range of practical applications, more specifically, home abnormal activity, sport activity, human gestures, human interaction, pedestrian traffic, healthcare, gaming. Research on human action recognition initially employed video sequences provided by conventional RGB camera. With the development of new and low-cost depth sensors such as Microsoft Kinect, new opportunities for action recognition have emerged.

Kinect sensor provides multi-modal data for processing such as RGB, Depth, Skeleton. RGB data is strongly affected by illumination changing. Skeleton is usually computed from a long training on a very large data [2]. Sometimes, the skeleton is not available or not precise due to the (self-)occusion of the human. As a result, conventional approaches based on color information could not perform well. Currently, numerous approaches for action recognition usually exploit the depth data [3] with different aspects: point cloud, surface normals, etc.

In this paper, we propose a novel method based upon depth motion map and kernel descriptor. Depth motion map (DMM) is a technique to compress depth

© Springer International Publishing Switzerland 2015
L. Nalpantidis et al. (Eds.): ICVS 2015, LNCS 9163, pp. 137–146, 2015.
DOI: 10.1007/978-3-319-20904-3_13

sequence into one map representing the motion history of the action. It has been applied successfully in [4] and [1]. However, instead of extracting histogram of oriented gradients (HOG) in [4] or local binary pattern (LBP) in [1], we use a new gradient descriptor based on kernel.

Kernel descriptor has been initially introduced by [5] for general visual recognition problem. Kernel descriptor provides an unified framework to define different descriptors such as SIFT, HOG, LBP. Kernel descriptor computed on RGB images has been shown to be one of the best descriptors for object recognition on several public datasets. However, original kernel descriptor has some limitations that is it is not invariant to rotation and scale changes. In addition, it has never been proved on motion depth data.

In this paper, we improve the original kernel descriptor in [5] to make it more robust to scaling and rotation. We then study on how the proposed kernel descriptor is good on depth motion maps for action recognition. The proposed method is extensively evaluated with different configurations of machine learning techniques such as Support Vector Machine (SVM) and Kernel based Extreme Machine Learning (KEML) on each projection view of the motion map. The experiments show that our method outperforms state of the art works on MSRGesture3D dataset until now and obtains comparable results on MSRAction3D dataset in term of accuracy (Table 3).

2   Related Works

Human action recognition has been mentioned since more than twenty years ago. There are many methods that have been proposed to aim this goal [6]. In the section, we are not ambitious to update the survey but we focus on methods that employ depth data for action representation and recognition.

In [4], the authors proposed to represent the depth sequence by depth motion map. To make use of the additional body shape and motion information from depth maps, each depth frame is projected onto three orthogonal Cartesian planes. Then region of interest (ROI) corresponding to the bounding box of the human is extracted and normalized to a fixed size to avoid the intra-class variation. Then HOG feature is computed on the ROI which is the input to a linear SVM classifier for human action recognition. Experiments have been done with MSRAction3D dataset. The accuracy is computed with different sub-sets of data. The method achieves the best result (96.2 %) on the third subset with cross validation.

Inspired from the idea of Spatio temporal Interest Point (STIP) computed on RGB sequence, L. Xia and J.K.Aggarwal extended to depth data by extracting STIPs on each depth map of the sequence (so called DSTIP) [7]. Then they built a depth cuboid similarity feature (DCSF) to describe the local 3D depth cuboid around the DSTIPs with an adaptable supporting size. To model an action, Bag of Word (BoW) model was employed. Each action sequence is represented by a distribution of code-words computed on all depth maps of the sequence. Finally, SVM with histogram intersection kernel is applied for classification. This method has been tested on two public datasets (MSRAction3D and MSRActivity3D) and obtained 89.3 % and 88.2 % respectively in term of accuracy with a half data for training and the rest for testing.

In [8], the authors claimed that the existing features for action representation are usually based on shape or motion independently. These features fail to capture the complex joint shape-motion cues at pixel-level. Therefore, in the paper, the authors consider the depth sequence as a function from R^3 (spatial coordinates, time) to R^1 (depth) that constitutes a surface in 4D space (time, depth and spatial coordinates). They then proposed to describe depth sequence by a histogram capturing the distribution of surface normal orientations in 4D space (HON4D). Following the author, HON4Ds capture richer information than 3D gradient orientation (HOG3D) [4] therefore the representation is more discriminant. The proposed method has been evaluated on three public datasets (MSRAction3D, MSRGesture3D, MSRDailyActivity3D). The best recognition rate on MSRAction3D is 88.89 % while the best on MSRGesture3D is 92.45 %.

In [9], the authors in [4] proposed a new method for human action recognition which based on the polynormal which is a group of hypersurface normals in depth sequences. For representing a depth video, firstly, the depth video is subdivided into a set of spate-time grids. An adaptive spatio-temporal pyramid is proposed to capture the spatial layout and temporal order in a global way. Then they concatenate the vector extracted from all the space-time grids as the final representation of super normal vector (SNV). The method has been tested on four datasets (MSRAction3D, MSRGesture3D, MSRActionPairs, MSRDaily-Activity3D) and shown to ourperform all published works at that time (93.09 %, 94.72 %, 98.89 %, 86.25 % respectively).

Currently, L. Bo *et al.* have introduced kernel descriptor for visual recognition problem [5] that shown to be the best descriptor for visual recognition on some challenging datasets. In this paper, we improved kernel descriptor to be more robust to scaling and rotation. We would like to investigate how the improved kernel descriptor is good for action recognition based on depth motion map.

3   Proposed Approach

3.1   General Framework

We propose a framework for action recognition which composes of three main steps (Fig. 1):

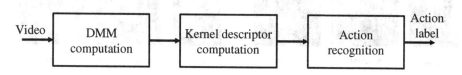

Fig. 1. Main steps of action recognition

- Motion representation: Given a video, we compute depth motion map from three projection views (front, side, top).
- Action modeling: For each depth motion map, we compute gradient based kernel descriptor to output the final feature vector.
- Action recognition: The feature vector inputs to a multiclass classifier (SVM, KEML) to decide the class that the action belongs to. At this step, two fusion solutions (feature level fusion and classifier level fusions) will be studied.

In the next sections, we will describe in detail each step of the framework.

3.2   Depth Motion Map

Depth Motion Map was firstly introduced in [4]. Given a sequence of N depth maps $D_1, D_2, ..., D_N$, the depth motion map is defined as follows:

$$DMM = \sum_{i=1}^{N-1} (|D^{i+1} - D^i| > \epsilon) \tag{1}$$

where ϵ is a threshold to make binary the difference between two consecutive maps D^{i+1} and D^i. The binary map of motion energy indicates motion regions or where movement happens in each temporal interval. So the DMM represents sum of motions through entire video sequences.

Different from [4], in [1], the authors modified the procedure to obtain DMM. Specifically, instead of computing the sum on binary maps, [1] take the absolute difference:

$$DMM = \sum_{i=1}^{N-1} |D^{i+1} - D^i| \tag{2}$$

In [4], the authors proposed to project depth frames onto three orthogonal Cartesian planes to characterize the motion of an action. Specifically, each 3D depth frame is used to generate three 2D projected maps corresponding to front, side and top views, denoted by D_f, D_s, D_t respectively. By this way, we obtain three DMMs corresponding to three views.

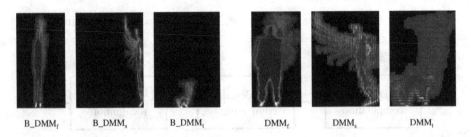

B_DMM$_f$ B_DMM$_s$ B_DMM$_t$ DMM$_f$ DMM$_s$ DMM$_t$

Fig. 2. Three DMMs computed from front, side, top projection views of depth sequence

We apply also a bounding box to extract the non-zero region as the foreground in each DMM. Figure 2 shows three DMMs computed following (1) (we call B_DMM with B means Binary) and (2) respectively from an action sequence in MSRAction3D dataset. Obviously, we see that (2) gets richer motion information than (1). We have tested both procedures of computing DMM and found that the binary DMM gives worse performance. Therefore, in the following, we will use DDM computed according to (2).

3.3 Gradient Based Kernel Descriptor

Kernel descriptor was initially introduced by [5]. This method for object representation has been shown to outperform all state of the art descriptors on several published datasets.

When working with the original kernel descriptor presented in [5], we observe some problems. Firstly, the gradient based kernel considers the current gradient vector of a pixel on the patch, it is therefore not invariant to rotation. In addition, the size of patch is fixed for all images. As consequent, the description is not invariant to scale change.

We have studied deeply on kernel descriptor and propose two improvements to make the original kernel descriptor more robust to rotation and scale changes. The computation of kernel descriptor is presented in Fig. 3. It comprises three main steps:

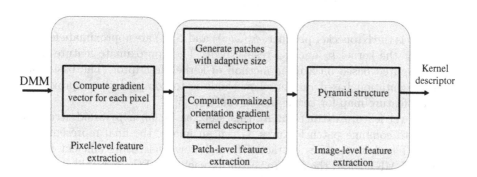

Fig. 3. Computation of kernel descriptor

– Pixel-level feature extraction: At this level, a normalized gradient vector is computed for each pixel of the image. The normalized gradient vector at a pixel z is defined by its magnitude $m(z)$ and normalized orientation $\omega(z) = \theta(z) - \bar{\theta}(P)$, where $\theta(z)$ is orientation of gradient vector at the pixel z, and $\bar{\theta}(P)$ is the dominant orientation of the patch P that is the vector sum of all the gradient vectors in the patch. This normalization will make patch-level features invariant to rotation. In practice, the normalized orientation of a gradient vector will be $\tilde{\omega}(z) = [sin(\omega(z))\ cos(\omega(z))]$. Note that in the original kernel descriptor proposed in [5], the gradient orientation was not normalized.

- Patch-level feature extraction: A set of patches is generated with adaptive size. The size of the patch is directly proportional to the size of the image. This adaptive size ensures the number of patches to be considered unchanged. This adaptive patch makes the patch descriptor more robust to scale change. Note that in [5], the patch size was fixed for all images. Therefore the number of generated patches from two images was very different that leads to two different representations of the same scene observed at different two scales. Roughly speaking, such representation was not invariant to scale change.

  For each patch, we compute a patch feature based on a given definition of match kernel. The gradient match kernel is constructed from three kernels that are gradient magnitude kernel $k_{\widetilde{m}}$, orientation kernel k_o and position kernel k_p.

$$K_{gradient}(P, Q) = \sum_{z \in P} \sum_{z' \in Q} k_{\widetilde{m}}(z, z') k_o(\widetilde{\omega}(z), \widetilde{\omega}(z')) k_p(z, z') \qquad (3)$$

where P and Q are patches of two different images that we need to measure the similarity. z and z' denote the 2D position of a pixel in the image patch P and Q respectively. Let $\varphi_o(.)$ and $\varphi_p(.)$ the feature maps for the gradient orientation kernel k_o and position kernel k_p respectively. Then, the approximate feature over image patch P is constructed as:

$$\overline{F}_{gradient}(P) = \sum_{z \in P} \widetilde{m}(z) \phi_o(\widetilde{\omega}(z)) \otimes \phi_p(z) \qquad (4)$$

where $\otimes$ is the Kronecker product, $\phi_o(\widetilde{\omega}(z))$ and $\phi_p(z)$ are approximate feature maps for the kernel k_o and k_p, respectively. The approximate feature maps are computed based on a basic method of kernel descriptor. The basic idea of representation based on kernel methods is to compute the approximate explicit feature map for kernel match function [5].

- Image-level feature extraction: At this step, as in [5], a pyramid structure is used to combine patch features. Given an image, the final representation is built based on features extracted from lower levels using efficient match kernels (EMK). First, the feature vector for each cell of the pyramid structure is computed. The final descriptor is the concatenation of feature vectors of all cells.

  Let C be a cell that has a set of patch-level features $X = \{x_1, ..., x_p\}$ then the feature map on this set of vectors is defined as:

$$\overline{\phi}_S(X) = \frac{1}{|X|} \sum_{x \in X} \phi(x) \qquad (5)$$

Where $\phi(x)$ is approximate feature maps for the kernel $k(x, y)$. The feature vector on the set of patches, $\overline{\phi}_S(X)$, is extracted explicitly.

Given an image, let L be the number of spatial layers to be considered. In our experiment $L = 3$. The number of cells in layer l-th is (n_l). $X(l, t)$ is set of patch-level features falling within the spatial cell (l, t) (cell t-th in the l-th level). A patch is fallen in a cell when its centroid belongs to the cell. The feature map on the pyramid structure is:

$$\overline{\phi}_P(X) = [w^{(1)}\overline{\phi}_S(X^{(1,1)}); ...; w^{(l)}\overline{\phi}_S(X^{(l,t)}); ...; w^{(L)}\overline{\phi}_S(X^{(L,n_L)})] \quad (6)$$

In (6), $w^{(l)} = \frac{\frac{1}{n_l}}{\sum_{l=1}^{L}\frac{1}{n_l}}$ is the weight associated with level l.

3.4   Action Classification

Once kernel descriptor is computed, the classification could be simplified by a linear classifier. In this paper, we use multi-class SVM classifier. However, to compare the efficiency of the descriptors, we employ also KELM method as in [1]. The input of these classifier is the action descriptor vector that is computed in the previous steps.

Feature Level Fusion. As we consider three project views of the depth map, we obtain three depth motion maps corresponding to front, side and top view. A straightforward solution to combine these information is to concatenate kernel descriptors computed from three views to make the final representation of the action sequence.

Decision Level Fusion. The second solution is to build three independent classifiers for each descriptor and then fuse the result from three classifiers. We follow the same approach for decision fusion as presented in [1]. More specifically, the SVM/KEML classifier outputs a value $f_L(x)$ which is the distance between a given feature x and the model. This value is normalized to $[0, 1]$ and the posterior probability is approximated using sigmoid function according to Platt's empirical analysis.

$$p(y_k|x) = \frac{1}{1 + exp(Af_L(x)_k + B)} \quad (7)$$

In our experiment, A = -1, B = 0. This probability is used to estimate a global membership function:

$$logP(y_k|x) = \sum_{q=1}^{Q} \alpha_i p_q(y_k|x) \quad (8)$$

where Q is the number of classifiers and $\{\alpha_q\}_{q=1}^{Q}$ are uniformly distributed classifier weights. The final class label $y*$ is selected as follows:

$$y* = argmaxP(y_k|x) \quad (9)$$

4   Experimental Results

We evaluate the proposed method on two published datasets: MSRAction3D [10] and MSRGesture3D [11]. Both datasets are built by depth camera.

4.1 MRSAction3D Dataset

The MSRAction3D dataset includes 20 action types realized by 10 subjects, each subject performs each action 2 or 3 times. The resolution is 320×240. There are 567 depth map sequences in total. However, as reported in [12], 10 sequences are not used in experiment because the skeletons are either missing or too erroneous and to be comparible with the current work, we will use only 557 sequences. The actions are: *high wave, horizontal wave, hammer, hand catch, forward punch, high throw, draw x, draw tick, draw circle, hand clap, two hand wave, side boxing, bend, forward kick, side pick, jogging, tennis swing, tennis serve, golf swing, and pickup throw.*

We follow the experiment setting in [13] in which one half of the subjects (1, 3, 5, 7, 9) are used for training and the remaining are used for testing. This dataset is challenging because of the number of action classes is large while the samples for training is not numerous. To normalize the size of DMM, we follow the setting in [1]. Specifically, the size of DMM_f, DMM_s, DMM_t are 102×54, 102×75, 75×54 respectively.

4.2 MSRGesture3D Dataset

The MSRGesture3D dataset is a dynamic hand gesture dataset that contains a subset of gestures defined by American Sign Language (ASL). It includes 12 gestures: *bathroom, blue, finish, green, hungry, milk, past, pig, store, where, j, z.* The dataset comprises 333 depth sequences. We follows the same experimental setting as in [12] that uses leave-one-subject-out cross-validation. The size of DMM_f, DMM_s, DMM_t are 118×133, 118×29, 29×133.

4.3 Analysis

Different features, classifiers have been combined to make the comparison. We label feature level fusion approach as FF, decision level fusion as DF. Tables 1 and 2 show the comparative performance of the original kernel descriptor (OKD), local binary pattern (LBP) and the proposed kernel descriptor (PKD) computed on three depth motion maps. Globally, we make some conclusions:

Table 1. Comparison of recognition accuracy (%) on MSRAction3D dataset

DepthMap	OKD-SVM [5]	PKD-SVM	PKD-KELM	LPB-KELM [1]
DMM_f	79.85	83.15	**83.88**	78.75
DMM_s	71.06	73.62	**73.99**	68.13
DMM_t	67.39	72.16	**71.79**	64.10
DMM_{FF}	81.68	88.64	89.01	**91.94**
DMM_{DF}	81.97	88.65	91.57	**93.77**

Table 2. Comparison of recognition accuracy (%) on MSRGesture3D dataset

DepthMap	OKD-SVM [5]	PKD-SVM	PKD-KELM	LPB-KELM [1]
DMM_f	96.67	100	**100**	84.58
DMM_s	81.11	85.56	**93.33**	68.47
DMM_t	68.37	70.55	**76.66**	64.30
DMM_{FF}	96.66	93.34	**96.67**	93.40
DMM_{DF}	93.33	94.44	90.00	**94.60**

- The proposed kernel descriptor outperforms the original one in all tests with each projection view independently. It shows the robustness of out descriptor w.r.t scaling and rotation.
- The proposed kernel descriptor outperforms LPB features for each projection view. The use of KELM classification instead of SVM helps to improve lightly the performance. Once again, we show the efficiency of kernel descriptor on depth motion map.
- The combination of projection views according to the decision fusion solution does not improve the performance as in case of LPB descriptor. The reason for this is this the kernel descriptor gives stable performances for all classes on each project view. For MSRGesture3D dataset, the feature level fusion obtain better accuracy than the case of LPB.

Table 3. Recognition accuracy (%) on two datasets

Dataset	Best in [8]	Best in [9]	Best in [1]	Our best
MSRAction3D	88.89	93.09	93.77	91.57
MSRGesture3D	92.45	94.72	94.60	100

5   Conclusion

In this paper, we have presented a novel method for action recognition. The method compresses the video sequence into one image using Depth Motion Map technique then describes the DMM using kernel descriptor. In comparison with the original kernel descriptor [5], the proposed kernel descriptor is more robust to scaling and rotation because we have performed a normalization in gradient orientation as well as selection of adaptive patch size. Using the new descriptor help to improve significantly the classification rate on each projection view of the depth map. In the future, we will analyse in more detail how the kernel descriptor acts on each projection view and propose a new solution to efficiently fuse these information.

Acknowlegment. This research is funded by Vietnam National Foundation for Science and Technology Development (NAFOSTED) under grant number FWO.102.2013.08.

References

1. Chen, C., Jafari, R., Kehtarnavaz, N.: Action recognition from depth sequences using depth motion maps-based local binary patterns. In: WACV, pp. 1092–1099 (2015)
2. Shotton, J., Fitzgibbon., A., Cook, M., Sharp, T., Finocchio, M., Moore, R., Kipman, A., Blake, A.: Real-time human pose recognition in parts from a single depth image. In: PAMI (2012)
3. Ye, M., Zhang, Q., Wang, L., Zhu, J., Yang, R., Gall, J.: A survey on human motion analysis from depth data. In: Grzegorzek, M., Theobalt, C., Koch, R., Kolb, A. (eds.) Time-of-Flight and Depth Imaging. LNCS, vol. 8200, pp. 149–187. Springer, Heidelberg (2013)
4. Yang, X., Zhang, C., Tian, Y.: Recognizing actions using depth motion maps-based histograms of oriented gradients. In: ACM Multimedia (MM), pp. 1057–1060 (2012)
5. Bo, L., Ren, X., Fox, D.: Kernel descriptors for visual recognition. In: Advances in Neural Information Processing Systems, pp. 244–252 (2010)
6. Turaga, P., Chellappa, R., Subrahmanian, V.S., Udrea, O.: Machine recognition of human activities: a survey. IEEE Trans. Circ. Syst. Video Technol. 18(11), 1473–1488 (2008)
7. Xia, L., Aggarwal, J.K.: Spatio-temporal depth cuboid similarity feature for activity recognition using depth camera. In: CVPR, pp. 2834–2841 (2013)
8. Omar, O., Liu, Z.: HON4D: histogram of oriented 4D normals for: activity recognition from depth sequences. In: CVPR, pp. 716–723 (2013)
9. Yang, X., Tian, Y.: Super normal vector for activity recognition using depth sequences. In: CVPR, pp. 804–811 (2014)
10. Li, W., Zhang, Z., Liu, Y.: Action recognition based on a bag of 3D points. In: CVPR Workshop, pp. 9–14 (2010)
11. Kurakin, A., Zhang, Z., Liu, Z.: A real time system for dynamic hand gesture recognition with a depth sensor. In: EUSIPCO, pp. 1975–1979 (2012)
12. Wang, J., Liu, Z., Wu, Y., Yuan, J.: Mining actionlet ensemble for action recognition with depth cameras. In: CVPR (2012)
13. Wang, J., Liu, Z., Chorowski, J., Chen, Z., Wu, Y.: Robust 3D action recognition with random occupancy patterns. In: Fitzgibbon, A., Lazebnik, S., Perona, P., Sato, Y., Schmid, C. (eds.) ECCV 2012, Part II. LNCS, vol. 7573, pp. 872–885. Springer, Heidelberg (2012)

An Informative Logistic Regression for Cross-Domain Image Classification

Guangtang Zhu[1], Hanfang Yang[1], Lan Lin[2], Guichun Zhou[1],
and Xiangdong Zhou[1(✉)]

[1] School of Computer Science, Shanghai Key Laboratory of Data Science,
Fudan University, Shanghai, China
xdzhou@fudan.edu.cn
[2] School of Electronics and Information Engineering, Tongji University,
Shanghai, China

Abstract. Cross-domain image classification is a challenge problem in numerous practical applications and has attracted a lot of interests from research and industry communities. It differs from traditional closed set image classification due to the variance between the training and testing datasets. Although the semantics of the image categories are the same, the image variance between testing and training often results in significant loss of performance. To solve the problem, most previous works resort to data pre-processing approaches, such as minimizing the difference between the distributions of the training and testing datasets. In this paper, we propose a novel informative feature preserving classifier for cross-domain image classification. We introduce the idea of maximizing the variance of unlabeled training data into a L1 based logistic regression model, so that the informative features can be preserved in the model training which consequently leads to performance improvement in the testing. Experiments conducted on commonly used benchmarks for cross-domain image classification show that our method significantly outperforms the state-of-the-art.

1 Introduction

Traditional image classification assumes that the training and testing data are collected from similar sources, such that the training and testing data obey the same or similar distributions. However, considering the limitations in real world applications, such as the insufficiency of training data or the high cost of human labeling, we face a great challenge of cross-domain image classification: Images are usually taken in different illumination, different background environment and different time. As a result, the characteristics of training and testing datasets often differ in practice. In this case, the previous trained model can not handle the successive practical classification (testing) very well. Figure 1 shows some sample images from cross-domain datasets for illustration.

Cross-domain image classification has attracted a lot of research interests recently [1,13,17]. Data preprocessing [3,4] is the mainstream for dealing with

© Springer International Publishing Switzerland 2015
L. Nalpantidis et al. (Eds.): ICVS 2015, LNCS 9163, pp. 147–156, 2015.
DOI: 10.1007/978-3-319-20904-3_14

Sample Images from Caltech Dataset   **Sample Images from Amazon Dataset**

Fig. 1. Sample images from Caltech and Amazon datasets [13]. We can see that although the semantics of the categories (each row) are the same, the images are various. Specifically, the images of Caltech dataset have complex background, on the country the images of Amazon dataset are clean. So we can imagine that the classification model trained on Caltech dataset can not fit the Amazon dataset very well and vice versa, since the different background of the images is a noisy for the classification.

this problem, that is through data transformation, the difference between the distributions of the training data and the testing data are diminished. Expectation and variance are two standard metrics for distribution evaluation and widely used in data transformation and analysis. Most of the previous works make use of expectation based data pre-processing for cross-domain image classification. For instance, Gretton et al. [5] propose computing and minimizing the difference between the means of the testing and training datasets to improve classification performance. However, there is very few previous works which explore the distribution variance in dealing with this problem.

In this paper, we propose a novel classifier for cross-domain image classification. The main challenge of cross-domain classification is the significant deviation between the training and testing datasets. Consequently, the optimal parameters estimated on the training data may not fit the testing data very well, which in essence is similar to the over-fitting problem in machine learning. Since regularization plays an important role in dealing with the over-fitting problem, it motivates us to investigate the regularization approach from the aspect of data distribution for cross-domain image classification. Our method is built on L1 regularization based logistic regression. In this framework, the sparse L1 regularization extends the logistical regression with the ability of feature selection. Our method enhances the adaptability of the feature selection to improve the performance of cross-domain image classification. Specifically, we propose to maximize the variance of the unlabeled testing images into the logistic regression framework.

Although there are very few works of investigating the classifier model to solve the problem, in this work we demonstrate it is a promising pathway of improving the performance of cross-domain image classification. Besides, our model can easily integrate with the data pre-processing approach. To evaluate our work, experiments are conducted on commonly used benchmarks for cross-domain image classification. The experimental results show that our method significantly outperforms the strong baselines and the state-of-the-arts.

In Sect. 2, we review the related work. Our informative logistic regression classifier is described in detail in Sect. 3. In Sect. 4, we present experimental results on several cross-domain images classification dataset and compare our method with the strong baselines and the state-of-the-arts.

2   Related Work

To solve the cross-domain image classification problem, most of the previous works make use of data pre-processing techniques. For instance, the feature vectors of training and testing images are transferred into a new data space in order to reduce the discrepancy between the two data distributions. In [15], Sinno et al. propose the Transfer Component Analysis (TCA) method. It tries to learn some transfer components across the datasets of training and testing, and in the subspace spanned by these transfer components, data distributions of training and testing datasets are close to each other. Long et al. [4] propose a novel transfer learning method called Joint Distribution Adaptation (JDA). In JDA, the difference of marginal and conditional distributions between training and testing dataset is considered in the data transfer. In [17], Long et al. present the Transfer Sparse Coding (TSC) approach which combines the transfer method and sparse coding method to construct robust sparse representations for cross-domain image classification. All the above methods investigate the data distributions by employing the method of Maximum Mean Discrepancy(MMD) [5]. In this paper, we propose a novel cross-domain image classification model, which keeps the informative features in the model learning by exploiting the variance of the data distribution.

3   A Novel Logistic Regression for Cross-Domain Image Classification

Without loss of generality, we assume all the images concerned in this work can be regarded as high dimensional vectors in the same feature (data) space, since we can employ the same procedures to extract visual features.

3.1   Logistic Regression

Our basic model is the logistic regression. Given a set of training images $X^i = [x_1^i, \ldots, x_n^i] \in R^{n \times p}$ and their label set $Y^i = [y_1^i, \ldots, y_n^i]^T$, and a set of test images $X^j = [x_1^j, \ldots, x_m^j] \in R^{m \times p}$, the probability of class label $y_k^j = 1$ on condition of observing image x_k^j can be described by a logistic function as follows:

$$P(y_j = 1|x_k^j) = \frac{1}{1 + e^{-w^T x_k^j}}, \tag{1}$$

where w is the weight vector and x_j is represented by a p-dimensional vector.

3.2 Maximum Variance

The expectation and variance are two commonly used metrics for data distribution evaluation. The variance is mainly used to measure the degree of data dispersion. A large variance indicates that the data points tend to be far from the expected value, which also indicates these data points are more informative. As a metric of data distribution, variance is maturely applied in many fields, such as Principle Component Analysis (PCA) for dimension reduction. In this paper, instead of exploiting expectation metric to dealing with cross-domain image classification, we explore the variance metric for informative feature preserving. The idea is inspired by the target function of PCA, which maximizes the variance of the first principal component as follows:

$$w = \arg\max_{\|w\|=1} w^T X^T X w$$

There are many extensions of the traditional PCA. For instance, the sparse PCA approach is proposed in [8], which is then applied for feature extraction [9]. In this paper, we propose to maximize the variance of unlabeled testing samples in our classification model to enhance the adaptability of feature selection to solve the cross-domain classification problem.

3.3 Model for Cross-Domain Image Classification

The objective of our cross-domain image classification model is to minimize the negative logarithm of the Maximum Likelihood Estimation(MLE) as following:

$$\min_{\alpha} \sum_{i=1}^{n} log(1 + exp(-y_i^s \alpha^T x_i^s)) + \lambda_1 \|\alpha\|_1 + \\ \lambda_2 \sum_{j=1}^{m} \frac{1}{1 + \|\beta^T x_j^t\|^2} + \lambda_3 \|\beta\|_1 + \lambda_4 f(\alpha - \beta), \tag{2}$$

where n is the number of training images and m is the number of unlabeled testing images. α is weight vector of the decision hyperplane, and the β is the weight vector of the first principal component. f is a distance function which measures the distance between two vectors:

$$f(\alpha - \beta) = \|\alpha - \beta\|_2^2$$

The terms in Eq. 2 can be divided into three parts: the first and the second terms are the L1 regularized logistic regression, which aims to select the proper features for better classification [21]; The goal of the third and the fourth terms is to maximize the variance of the unlabelled testing images and selecting the high informative features by L1 regularization; The last term is to minimize the differences between the two parametrized spaces of training and testing and keep them consistent to coordinate the overall optimal objective. However,

Eq. 2 is rather complicated and difficult to solve, therefore we propose a simpler and condensed form in which the coefficient α and β in Eq. 2 are merged and denoted by w. That is, we propose using one parameterized space to achieve our overall optimization goal. The new objective function is given as follows:

$$\min_w \sum_{i=1}^n log(1 + exp(-y_i^s w^T x_i^s)) + \lambda_1 \sum_{j=1}^m \frac{1}{1 + \|w^T x_j^t\|_2^2} + \lambda_2 \|w\|_1, \qquad (3)$$

where the parameter λ_1 and λ_2 are used for balancing the effects of different terms. λ_1 is used for balancing the testing dataset variance, while λ_2 controls the sparsity of w. In Eq. 3, the procedures of maximizing the likelihood and the variance of the first principal component are integrated with a sparse regularization term for feature selection.

3.4   Parameter Estimation

In this paper, we use gradient descent to estimate the parameters in our model. L1- regularized logistic regression solution is a well studied problem. Gradient descent and coordinate descent are commonly used to solve the optimization problem, and many other variations such as stochastic gradient descent [10] and stochastic coordinate decent [11] are also proposed. In our method, we use the idea of gradient descent to optimize our problem. Let

$$G(w) = \sum_{i=1}^n log(1 + exp(-y_i^s w^T x_i^s)) + \lambda_1 \sum_{j=1}^m \frac{1}{1 + \|w^T x_j^t\|_2^2} \qquad (4)$$

be the function of loss and the constraint of variance. Then in our solution, we update w_i according the following rule.

$$w_i^{k+1} = w_i^k + \eta^k \frac{\partial}{\partial w}(G(w) + \lambda_2 \sum_i \|w_i\|), \qquad (5)$$

where k indicates the kth iteration, η is the learning rate. Let $g(w)$ represent the variance constraint term in Eq. 4:

$$g(w) = \sum_{j=1}^m \frac{1}{1 + \|w^T x_j^t\|_2^2}.$$

Its gradient is:

$$\frac{\partial g}{\partial w} = -\sum_{j=1}^m \frac{2x_j^T x_j w}{(1 + \|w^T x_j^t\|_2^2)^2}$$

Following the typical gradient decent approach, we have the gradient of the Eq. 4 as follows:

$$\frac{\partial G(w)}{\partial w} = \sum_{i=1}^n \frac{-y_i^s x_i^s}{1 + exp(-y_i^s w^T x_i^s)} + \sum_{i=1}^m \frac{-2x_j^T x_j w}{(1 + \|w^T x_j^t\|_2^2)^2}.$$

Since the L1 regularization is not differentiable, we adopt the subgradient approach to deal with this problem:

$$w_i^{k+1} = w_i^k + \eta^k \frac{\partial}{\partial w} G(w) + \lambda_2 \eta^k sign(w_i) \qquad (6)$$

$sign(x)$ is a sign function: $sign(x) = 1$ if $x > 0$, $sign(x) = -1$ if $x < 0$, $sign(x) = 0$ if $x = 0$. To deal with the value of w at zero point, we use the method [19].

4   Experiments

In this section, we evaluate our cross-domain image classification approach using both the classical SURF feature and Convolutional Neural Network (CNN) feature [18] and compare its performance to other methods for cross-domain classification.

4.1   Experimental Setup

The datasets used in our experiments are Office/Caltech [13] and VOC/MSRC [17]. The Office dataset consists of three subsets of Amazon images, Webcam images and SLR camera images. It contains 4652 images of 31 different categories. Caltech-256 is a commonly used dataset for object recognition. It has 256 categories and contains 30,607 images. According to [13], the Caltech-256 includes 10 classes with 8 to 151 images per category, and 2533 images in total. For VOC/MSRC, we follow the configuration of [17] and selected 1530 images in VOC07 and 1269 images in MSRC.

In the experiments, we compare our method to several baselines, such as logistic regression (LR), L1 regularized logistic regression (L1-LR) and Support Vector Machine (SVM) and the state-of-arts, such as the transfer feature learning with joint distribution adaptation (JDA+KNN)[4] and SVM with transfer component analysis (TCA) [15] Table 1.

4.2   Experimental Results

Deep Learning based feature for image classification achieves significant improvement [20], hence we also use CNN features [18] to evaluate our approach in cross-domain classification. The result is given in Tables 2 and 3. We can see from the two Tables that there are significant improvements by using CNN feature on Office/Caltech and VOC/MSRC datasets respectively compared with SURF feature. In this situation, for the comparison with LR model, our method still achieves higher accuracy, about 2%-4% improvements.

Table 1. Accuracy (%) on cross-domain dataset Office and Caltech using SURF feature

Training	Testing	LR	L1-LR	JDA+LR	JDA+KNN[4]	SVM	TCA[15]	Our
Caltech	Amazon	46.97	49.43	46.66	44.78	55.64	54.70	55.11
Caltech	Dslr	38.85	43.31	39.49	45.22	43.73	46.44	46.50
Caltech	Webcam	38.31	40.32	39.66	41.69	45.22	40.76	48.81
Amazon	Caltech	37.31	39.80	41.41	39.36	45.77	45.33	42.39
Amazon	Dslr	35.03	35.85	35.67	39.49	39.66	39.32	42.04
Amazon	Webcam	33.90	34.58	33.56	37.97	42.04	36.31	37.29
Dslr	Caltech	34.86	33.72	34.66	33.09	26.62	37.79	37.27
Dslr	Amazon	32.41	30.56	30.99	31.52	29.39	33.84	33.57
Dslr	Webcam	80.68	79.46	78.31	89.49	63.39	82.37	81.36
Webcam	Caltech	37.16	35.85	37.68	32.78	34.76	38.00	37.79
Webcam	Amazon	32.86	32.24	33.57	31.17	31.43	33.66	35.80
Webcam	Dslr	79.62	77.16	78.34	89.17	82.80	87.90	84.08
Avg		**44.00**	**44.36**	**44.17**	**46.31**	**45.04**	**48.03**	**48.50**

Table 2. Accuracy (%) on cross-domain dataset Office and Caltech using CNN feature

Training set	Test set	LR	Our method
Caltech	Amazon	90.71	92.59
Caltech	Dslr	84.07	86.62
Caltech	Webcam	82.37	82.95
Amazon	Caltech	83.44	86.29
Amazon	Dslr	91.08	91.72
Amazon	Webcam	84.07	85.63
Dslr	Caltech	87.31	90.92
Dslr	Amazon	79.32	82.81
Dslr	Webcam	96.95	97.63
Webcam	Caltech	82.05	84.51
Webcam	Amazon	73.37	76.40
Webcam	Dslr	98.09	98.73
Avg		**86.07**	**88.07**

Table 3. Accuracy (%) on MSRC and VOC using CNN feature

Training set	Test set	LR	L1-LR	Our method
MSRC	VOC	73.32	75.63	77.49
VOC	MSRC	93,54	93.71	95.51

4.3   Discussion

In this subsection, we give some analysis and discussion to further understand and evaluate our proposed method. The left side of Fig. 2 shows the performance increments of our method com pared with LR on the four datasets: Caltech, Amazon, Dslr and Webcam. Form the Figure we have the following observations and discussions: First of all, the experimental results show that our method can improve the cross-domain image classification performance in all of our experiments. Particulary, most of the significant performance improvements are occurred when the Caltech dataset is used as training data, please see the bright yellow bars in the Fig. 2. This means that our method is very effective to handle the problem of cross-domain classification, since the Caltech data is more various and the difference of the distributions between Caltech and the other datasets are larger, which leads a more serious problem of cross-domain classification. The right side of Fig. 2 shows some sample images of the four datasets for reference.

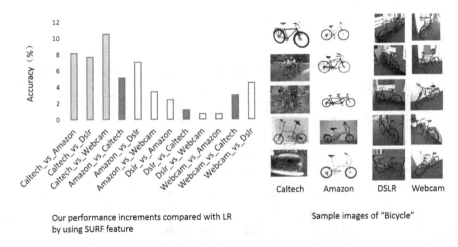

Fig. 2. Discussion. The left side shows our performance increment compared with LR method, and the right side shows some samples images of the four image datasets for discussions

However, we also note that when Caltech is used as testing data, the performance increments are not as good as in the previous case. See those blue bars in Fig. 2. For this phenomenon, our analysis is: It is related to our proposed method of how to preserve the most informative features, recall that we introduce maximizing the variance of the first principal component of training dataset in our objective function. Therefore, when the data distribution is simple (for instance, when the Amazon, Dslr and Webcam are used as testing datasets), the variance constraint on the first principal component is good enough to catch the most informative feature. The experimental results have shown that the performance can be increased significantly in this situation. However, when the Caltech data is used for testing, its data distribution is very complex, the variance constraint on the first principal component can not handle the problem very well. As a consequence, the performance improvement is not very significant compared with the previous case. These observations and discussions also give out a direction for our future work to improve our study on the cross-domain image classification.

5   Conclusion

This paper proposes a novel classification model for cross-domain image classification. We introduce the data distribution constraints into the classification model. Specifically, maximizing variance for informative feature preserving is exploited and integrated into the sparse regularization based logistic regression. The experiments conducted on commonly used benchmarks of cross-domain image classification show that our method achieves the best performance compared with baselines and several the state-of-the-art methods. For future work, we will study to improve the ability of preserving the informative features with complex distribution for cross-domain image classification

Acknowledgements. This work was partially supported by the NSFC No.61370157, NSFC No.61373106 and Shanghai Science and Technology Development Funds No.13dz2260200, 13511504300 and 14511107403.

References

1. Scheirer, W.J., Rocha, A.R., Sapkota, A., Boult, T.E.: Toward open set recognition. Pattern Anal. Mach. Intell. **35**(7), 1757–1772 (2013)
2. Baktashmotlagh, M., Harandi, M.T., Lovell, B.C., Salzmann, M.: Domain adaptation on the statistical manifold. In: Proceedings of IEEE Conference on Computer Vision and Pattern Recognition (CVPR), pp. 2481–2488 (2014)
3. Pan, S.J., Yang, Q.: A survey on transfer learning. Trans. Knowl. Data Eng. **22**(10), 1345–1359 (2010)
4. Long, M., Wang, J., Ding, G., Sun, J., Yu, P.S.: Transfer feature learning with joint distribution adaptation. In: ICCV, pp. 2200–2207 (2013)
5. Gretton, A., Borgwardt, K.M., Rasch, M.J., Schölkopf, B., Smola, A.J.: A kernel method for the two-sample-problem. In: NIPS, pp. 513–520 (2006)
6. Dong, Y., Guo, H., Zhi, W., Fan, M.: Class imbalance oriented logistic regression. In: International Conference on Cyber-Enabled Distributed Computing and Knowledge Discovery, pp. 187–192 (2014)
7. Tan, M., Tsang, I.W., Wang, L.: Minimax sparse logistic regression for very high-dimensional feature selection. Trans. Neural Netw. Learn. Syst. **24**(10), 1609–1622 (2013)
8. Zou, H., Hastie, T., Tibshirani, R.: Sparse principal component analysis. Comput. Graph. Stat. **15**(2), 265–286 (2006)
9. Naikal, N., Yang, A.Y., Sastry, S.: Informative feature selection for object recognition via sparse PCA. In: ICCV, pp. 818–825 (2011)

10. Shwartz, S.S., Tewari, A.: Stochastic methods for L1-regularized loss minimization. In: Machine Learning Research, pp. 1865–1892 (2011)
11. Yuan, G., Chang, K., Hsieh, C., Lin, C.: A comparison of optimization methods and software for large-scale L1-regularized linear classification. Mach. Learn. Res. **11**, 3183–3234 (2010)
12. Bradley, J.K., Kyrola, A., Bickson, D., Guestrin, C.: Parallel coordinate descent for l1-regularized loss minimization. In: Proceedings of ICML, pp. 321–328 (2011)
13. Shi, B.G.Y., Sha, F., Grauman, K.: Geodesic flow kernel for unsupervised domain adaptation. In: Proceedings of IEEE Conference on Computer Vision and Pattern Recognition (CVPR), pp. 2066–2073 (2012)
14. Hastie, T., Tibshirani, R.: The Elements of Statistical Learning. Springer, Heidelberg (2009)
15. Pan, S.J., Tsang, I.W., Kwok, J.T., Yang, Q.: Domain adaptation via transfer component analysis. Trans. neural Netw. **22**(2), 199–210 (2011)
16. Long, M., Wang, J., Sun, J., Yu, P.S.: Domain invariant transfer kernel learning. Trans. Knowl. Data Eng. **11**, 1–14 (2014)
17. Long, M., Ding, G., Wang, J., Sun, J., Guo, Y., Yu, P.S.: Transfer sparse coding for robust image representation. In: Proceedings of IEEE Conference on Computer Vision and Pattern Recognition(CVPR), pp. 407–414 (2013)
18. Jia, Y., Shelhamer, E., Donahue, J., Karayev, S., Long, J., Girshick, R.B., Guadarrama, S., Darrell, T.: Caffe: convolutional architecture for fast feature embedding. In: Proceedings of ACM International Conference on Multimedia, pp. 675–678 (2014)
19. Tsuruoka, Y., Tsujii, J., Ananiadou, S.: Stochastic gradient descent training for L1-regularized log-linear models with cumulative penalty. In: ACL and AFNL, pp. 477–485 (2009)
20. Krizhevsky, A., Sutskever, I., Hinton, G.: ImageNet classification with deep convolutional neural networks. In: NIPS (2012)
21. Ji, C., Zhou, X., Lin, L., Yang, W.: Labeling images by integrating sparse multiple distance learning and semantic context modeling. In: Fitzgibbon, A., Lazebnik, S., Perona, P., Sato, Y., Schmid, C. (eds.) ECCV 2012, Part IV. LNCS, vol. 7575, pp. 688–701. Springer, Heidelberg (2012)

Robust Facial Feature Localization using Data-Driven Semi-supervised Learning Approach

Yoon Young Kim[1], Sung Jin Hong[1], Ji Hye Rhee[2],
Mi Young Nam[3], and Phill Kyu Rhee[1(✉)]

[1] Department of Computer Science and Engineering, Inha University,
Incheon, South Korea
Yoonyoung.kim@inha.edu, sjhong0117@gmail.com,
pkrhee@inha.ac.kr
[2] Department of Computer Science, Yonsei University, Seoul, South Korea
jhrhee@yonsei.com
[3] YM-Naeultech, Incheon, Korea
nammiyoung@gmail.com

Abstract. In this paper, we present a novel localization method of facial feature points with generalization ability based on a data-driven semi-supervised learning approach. Even though a powerful facial feature detector can be built using a number of human-annotated training data, the collection process is time-consuming and very often impractical due to the high cost and error-prone process of manual annotations. The proposed method takes advantage of a data-driven semi-supervised learning that optimizes a hybrid detector by interacting with a hierarchical data model to suppress and regularize noisy outliers. The competitive performance comparing to other state-of-the-art technology is also shown using benchmark datasets, Bosprous, BioID.

Keywords: Facial feature localization · Hybrid detector · Hierarchical data model · Hirerarchical soft K-means algorithm · Data-driven semi-supervised learning

1 Introduction

Facial feature localization has much impact on face-image based applications such as animation, expression recognition, and face registration [1]. Facial feature detectors can be categorized based on their focusing information that is observed from face images. Local detectors usually employ texture descriptors relying on sliding-window based search. Commonly used texture descriptors are the SIFT [2] and histogram of gradients (HOG) [3]. Global detectors focus more on global models such as geometrical distributions and structural relationships between facial feature points. Facial features are characterized by shape distribution models [4] or probability distribution of a feature point from other locations [5].

Local feature detectors can obtain precise localization, but they are sensitive to even small noises and are prone to generate frequent false alarms. Global detectors can

© Springer International Publishing Switzerland 2015
L. Nalpantidis et al. (Eds.): ICVS 2015, LNCS 9163, pp. 157–166, 2015.
DOI: 10.1007/978-3-319-20904-3_15

prevent such local noise sensitivity, however localization accuracy cannot approach to real world requirements in general. To avoid such a contradictory dilemma, many facial feature detectors combine the local detector and global detector. Zhu and Ramanan [3] represent patches using HOG features, and employ a quadratic spring scheme as a global shape model. RANSAC-like approach was addressed by Belhumeur et al. [6], where a Bayesian formulation allows to integrate local detectors into a global structure. A robust detector with generalized performance can be acquired using a number of data labeled correctly. However, in many real-world applications the collection of large volume of well-labeled dataset is not easy due to the high cost and error-prone processes of manual annotations. We propose an outlier-aware hybrid detector based on a data-driven semi-supervised learning approach. Generalization ability can be achieved using both labeled and unlabeled data [7] based on semi-supervised learning approaches. Recently, Tong et al. [8] presented an automatic method to avoid labor-intensive and error-prone manual processes in feature annotation. In their experiment, only a small portion of faces was manually labeled, and the remaining images are automatically annotated. However, Tong et al.'s approach is only a pioneer study on automatic facial feature annotation to obtain training data easily, not aims at robust facial feature localization with generalization ability applied for noisy and uncertain real-world environments.

The interactive data-driven semi-supervised learning framework consists of the hybrid detector (abbreviated by H-DTR) and the hierarchical data model (abbreviated by HDM). We explores the adaptive outlier suppression in the H-DTR, the outlier regularization of noisy or contaminated troublesome data in the HDM, and the interactive updates of the H-DTR and the HDM for better generalization ability. The HDM is constructed based on the hierarchical outlier-aware soft K-means clustering algorithm [9]. In Sect. 2, the overview of our approach is given. We discuss the HDM and the formulation of proposed H-DTR in Sect. 3 and Sect. 4, respectively. In Sect. 5, the data-driven semi-supervised learning algorithm using the HDM is discussed. Section 6 shows the superiority of the proposed method to other state-of-the-art localization technologies by experiments. Finally, conclusion is given in Sect. 7.

2 Overview of the Approach

In general, better generalization performance can be obtained with more training data labeled correctly, however the accumulation of a number of labeled data usually requires heavy labor-intensive processes and is very often error-prone. In this section, we outline a data-driven semi-supervised approach combining a hybrid detector and a hierarchical data model which can take advantage of both labeled data and unlabeled data. The proposed method provides a robust and generalization performance in real-life noisy environments, and is a fully automatic without human supervision except initial annotation of labeled dataset which is much smaller than unlabeled dataset.

The novelty of this paper is the effective combination of the HDM and H-DTR in an interactive manner (Fig. 1). The H-DTR consists of the global detector and the local detectors. Given an image, the global detector locates the face region and facial component regions using the Haar-like feature–based boosting method [10], and the detected face region is normalized over the scale to reduce the effects of scale

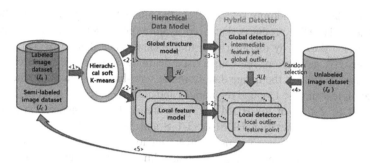

Fig. 1. The data-driven semi-supervised learning framework, where the optimization for a robust localization performance with generalization ability is obtained based on the iterative constructions of the HDM and H-DTR using both labeled data set and unlabeled image dataset.

uncertainty. Facial feature distributions are initialized based on pre-complied positions. The global detector produces the confidence search areas of individual feature points which are constrained by the Procrustes analysis [11]. The local detectors localize the feature points using k-NN regression algorithms in terms of SIFT descriptors [2]. Both the global and local detectors have outlier detection mechanisms using the HDM to obtain a robust performance. The HDM is defined by a two-level cluster tree consisting of the heterogeneous data models: the regularized global structure and local appearance models in the 1st and 2nd levels of the HDM, respectively (Fig. 2). The HDM is built using a semi-labeled image dataset. The semi-labeled dataset includes both labeled image data annotated by hand and annotated by the H-DTR during the interactive/incremental learning.

We construct a HDM (1st generation) from a given labeled dataset ($< 1>$, $< 2\text{-}1 >$, and $< 2\text{-}2 >$ in Fig. 1) in the initial data-driven learning step. The 1st level of the HDM represents different clusters of the global model which represent the global structures of feature point distributions in terms of Hausdroff vectors, and the 2nd level denotes different clusters of the local SIFT features for each facial feature point. We establish the 1st generation H-DTR based on the 1st generation HDM ($< 3\text{-}1 >$ and $< 3\text{-}2 >$), and

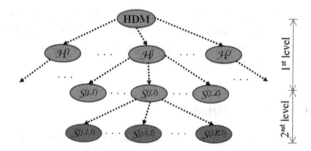

Fig. 2. An illustration of the HDM: H^j denotes the jth global structure model of the 1st level ($j \in \{1, \ldots, J\}$); $S^{(j,k,l)}$ indicates the kth local appearance model of the lth feature point label $S^{(j,l)}$ of the jth global structure model H^j in the 2nd level ($l \in \{1, \ldots, L\}$).

partial image data are randomly selected from the unlabeled image dataset (< 4>). The 1st generation H-DTR produces localized feature point sets, and constitutes the semi-supervised dataset by merging with the labeled image dataset (< 5>). Next, we perform the 2nd generation semi-supervised learning, where the hierarchical soft K-means algorithm takes the image data from the semi-labeled dataset produced in the 1st generation learning (< 1>), and regularizes and constructs the 1st level (< 2-1 >) and the 2nd level (< 2-1 >) of the HDM (2nd generation). The 2nd generation H-DTR is ready using the 2nd generation HDM (< 3-1 > and 3-2 >), selects randomly partial unlabeled data from, and so on until converging to a target performance. One can notice that well-managements of semi-labeled image dataset and regularized data models are essential to obtain incremental robust performance with generalization ability.

3 Hierarchical Data Model

The proposed framework employs the HDM (Hierarchical Data Model) which is established using the labeled training dataset initially, and updated by the H-DTR using randomly selected samples from the unlabeled dataset interactively until it converges or a predefined iteration limit. The HDM is two-level clusters generated by the soft K-means algorithm. In this paper, the global information represents the geometrical distribution of feature points and structural relationships between them, and the local information represents the appearances of individual feature points using the SIFT descriptors (Fig. 2). We first build the 1st level of the HDM (called "global structure models") using the global information and the 2nd level (called "local appearance models") for each 1st level cluster using the local information.

The global structure models are represented by the clusters centroids of the global Hausdroff vectors which consist of the positions of all feature points and Hausdroff distances between them. The local appearance models are represented by the cluster centroids of the SIFT vectors of individual feature points.

4 Hybrid Detector

H-DTR is a relatively simple, but has a flexible algorithm architecture so that it can be efficiently applied in real-life environments. H-DTR consists of the global detector for localizing an global structure of feature points and local detectors for more precise localization of individual feature points.

4.1 Outlier-Aware Hybrid Detector

Let $\mathbf{X} = \{ X^1, \ldots, X^L \}$ be a set of random variable spaces, where X^l is the space of a facial feature point that can be labeled by $l \in \{1, \ldots, \mathbf{L}\}$. The localization of facial feature points is formalized as multiclass ($\mathbf{L}$ classes) classification problem as follows. Let x (= $[x, y]^T$) denote a facial feature point. If x belongs to $\mathbf{X}^l$, (i.e.,), x is denoted by (x,*l*) or x^l meaning that a facial feature label *l* can be assigned to the feature point x. The feature localization is to assign a label *l* to a best feature point x that is estimated by a classifier. Given a face image *I*, the H-DTR finds a best facial feature vector $\mathbf{X} = \{ x^1, \ldots, x^L \}$ with $x^i \in \mathbf{X}^i$ using both global and local detectors. The global detector is based on Procustes analysis, constrained by the global structure models of the HDM, and decides the search areas of the facial feature points. The search area of a feature label *l* denoted by $\mathbf{A}(l), l \in \{1, \ldots, \mathbf{L}\}$ indicates the area within which the best point of feature label *l* can be found with high probability. It is decided empirically and the details can be found in [12]. The local detector for a feature point carries out more a precise localization using the SIFT descriptors [2] constrained by the local appearance models of the HDM and local Hausdroff distances. The global detector allows the local detectors are conditionally independent each other. Given a face image *I* and a training dataset D, assuming that a prior distribution over $\mathbf{X}$ exists, $\mathbf{X}$ can be treated as random variable in Bayesian statistics. The posterior distribution of $\mathbf{X}$ is represented by:

$$p(\mathbf{X}|I, \mathrm{D}) = \frac{p(I|\mathbf{X},\mathrm{D})p(\mathbf{X}|\mathrm{D})}{\int} \tag{1}$$

In this paper, the priors of a local detector for a feature point labeled *l* are the search area A(*l*). Since the H-DTR is divided into global detector and local detectors, Eq. 1 is rewritten by

$$p(\mathbf{X}_G, \mathbf{X}|I, \mathrm{D}) = p(\mathbf{X}_G|I, \mathrm{D})p(\mathbf{X}|\mathbf{X}_G, I, \mathrm{D}) =$$
$$\frac{p(I|\mathbf{X}_G,\mathrm{D})p(\mathbf{X}_G,\mathrm{D})}{\int} \frac{p(I|\mathbf{X}, \mathbf{X}_G,\mathrm{D})p(\mathbf{X}|\mathbf{X}_G,\mathrm{D})}{\int}, \tag{2}$$

where $\mathbf{X}_G$ and $\mathbf{X}$ are localized feature points in the global and local steps, respectively. The H-DTR is looking for optimal facial feature vectors $\mathbf{X}_G$ and $\mathbf{X}$, satisfying

$$(\hat{\mathbf{X}}_G, \hat{\mathbf{X}})_{\mathrm{MAP}}(I, \mathrm{D}) = \arg \max_{\mathbf{X}_G, \mathbf{X}} [p(I|\mathbf{X}_G, \mathrm{D})p(\mathbf{X}_G|\mathrm{D}) \prod_{l=1}^{L} \{p(I|x^l, x^l \in \mathbf{A}(l))p(x^l, x^l \in \mathbf{A}(l))\}$$

$$\tag{3}$$

where $p(I|\mathbf{X}, \mathbf{X}_G,\mathrm{D}) = \prod_{l=1}^{L} p(I|x^l)$ and $p(\mathbf{X}|\mathbf{X}_G,\mathrm{D}) = \prod_{l=1}^{L} p(x^l)$, since the global structure $\mathbf{X}_G$ constrains feature points by the search areas, a feature point x^l can treated as conditionally independent of each other. Note that $p(I|\mathbf{X}^G, \mathrm{D})$ and $p(I|x^l, x^l \in \mathbf{A}(l))$ are the likelihood functions of $\mathbf{X}_G$ and $x^l \in \mathbf{X}(l = 1, \ldots, \mathrm{L})$, and are estimated by the global detector and local detectors. Finally, we minimize the negative of the logarithm the posterior rather than maximizing (Eq. 3).

$$(\hat{\mathbf{X}}_G, \hat{x}^l, \ldots, \hat{x}^L | I, D) = \underset{\mathbf{X}_G \in \mathbf{X}}{\arg \min} f(\mathbf{X}_G; x^1, \ldots, x^L, I, D) +$$

$$\sum_{l=1}^{L} \underset{x^l \in X^l}{\arg \min} f(x^l; \mathbf{X}_G, \tilde{x}^l, I, D) + R(\mathbf{X}_G, x^1, \ldots, x^L | I, D) \qquad (4)$$

where $\{\tilde{x}^l\} = \{x^i\}_{i=1}^{L} - \{x^l\}$ and $R(\mathbf{X}_G, x^1, \ldots, x^L) = R(\mathbf{X}_G) + \sum_{i=1}^{L} R(x^i)$. The first term is a global detector error that encourages a good intermediated feature point localization based on Procustes analysis, and the second term is a local detector error for more precise localizations based on the local appearance model and local Hausdroff constraints with neighboring feature points. The third term is the regularization for control global sparsity and local sparsity using the priors of the HDM, where $R(\mathbf{X}_G)$ and $R(x^i)$ are global and regularizations, respectively.

4.2   Hierarchical Outlier Suppression

We carried out two types of outlier suppressions: global and local outlier suppressions. The global detector determines the global structure, $\mathbf{X}_G$, based on the Procustes analysis and investigates whether or not the $\mathbf{X}_G$, is a global outlier. If $\mathbf{X}_G$ is not an outlier, the global detector decides the search area of each feature point, otherwise a global localization error is declared. The local detector explores the search area to find a feature point with highest probability. The localized feature point is checked whether or not it is a local outlier. If the localized feature point is not an outlier, the localization is reported as success, otherwise a local localization error is declared. The outlier constraints are measured based on the global structure and local appearance data models in the HDM, and used to prevent global and local outliers, respectively.

4.3   Optimization

The solution of (Eq. 4) is nonconvex, but it is convex w.r.t. each of optimization variables, $x^1, \ldots, x^L$, and $\mathbf{X}_G$. We develop a local optimal algorithm based on the block-coordinate decent method [13], which minimizes (Eq. 4) iteratively w.r.t. each variable while the other variables are fixed. Algorithm 1 represents our optimization procedure. Localized points with the maximum likelihood may not always be correct facial feature points, and not consistent with other feature points. There are many reasons making the detectors unstable such as noises, pose variances, cluttered background, and illuminant changes. In this context, we introduce a data-driven semi-supervised framework which can learn incrementally using both labeled and unlabeled datasets to minimize the effects of troublesome patterns and to prevent outliers in cooperative with the HDM in Sect. 5.

Algorithm 1. Block Coordinate Descent based Optimization for H-DTR

Input: Image (I), the HDM

Output: $\hat{\mathbf{X}} = \{\hat{x}^1, \ldots, \hat{x}^L\}$

Method:

Initialize $\mathbf{X}_G, \mathbf{x}^1, \ldots, \mathbf{x}^L$

$k \leftarrow 0$

repeat

$$\mathbf{X}_G^{k+1} \leftarrow \underset{\mathbf{B}}{\arg\min} J_0(\mathbf{X}_G; \mathbf{x}^{(L,k)}, \ldots, \mathbf{x}^{(L,k)})$$

$$\mathbf{x}^{(1,k+1)} \leftarrow \underset{\mathbf{C}}{\arg\min} J_1(\mathbf{x}^{(1,k)}; \mathbf{X}_G; \mathbf{x}^{(2,k)}, \ldots, \mathbf{x}^{(L,k)})$$

$$\vdots$$

$$\mathbf{x}^{(i,k+1)} \leftarrow \underset{\mathbf{C}}{\arg\min} J_i(\mathbf{x}^i; \mathbf{X}_G; \mathbf{x}^{(1,k)}, \ldots, \mathbf{x}^{(i-1,k)}, \mathbf{x}^{(i+1,k)} \ldots, \mathbf{x}^{(L,k)})$$

$$\vdots$$

$$\mathbf{x}^{(L,k+1)} \leftarrow \underset{\mathbf{C}}{\arg\min} J_L(\mathbf{x}^L; \mathbf{X}_G; \mathbf{x}^{(1,k)}, \ldots, \mathbf{x}^{(L-1,k)})$$

until convergence.

5   Data-Driven Semi-supervised Learning

In the proposed method, the semi-supervised learning steps iteratively construct the HDM's and H-DTR's using randomly selected image data from the unlabeled dataset. We initialize the 1st generation HDM and H-DTR using a labeled image dataset. Remind that the semi-labeled image dataset indicates both human-annotated data given initially and machine-annotated data that may be wrong during semi-supervised learning steps. The data-driven semi-supervised learning is controlled by the hierarchical soft K-means clustering algorithm. The machine-annotated data is produced by the current H-DTR, and it is used to construct a next generation HDM.

5.1   Semi-Labeled Dataset Update

The newly labeled dataset is merged to the semi-supervised dataset, and constitutes the next semi-supervised dataset. The H-DTR finds a best matched global structure model for $\mathbf{X}_G$ based on the similarity measure of global Hausdroff vectors. If there is no matched global structure satisfying the global outlier constraint, it is rejected. Once the global structure, $\mathbf{X}_G$ is determined, the local detector finds a best matched local appearance model for a feature point $x^l \in A(l)$. In the local detection phase, the current H-DTR performs a local matching using k-NN regression. Algorithm 2 summarizes the update process of the semi-labeled dataset in the proposed learning framework.

Algorithm 2. Update process of semi-labeled dataset

Input: randomly selected unlabeled dataset $I = \{I_i\}_{i=1}^{N}$, and the current semi-supervised labeled dataset L .

Output: updated semi-labeled dataset (i.e., $L = L_{current} \cup \{\mathbf{X}_i\}_{i=1}^{N}$ where $\mathbf{X}_i = \{\mathbf{x}_i^l\}_{l=1}^{\mathcal{L}}$).

Method:

$L = L_{current}$

for $i = 1$ to N

   Step 1. global detector

      1.1 Produce a global feature $\mathbf{X}_G$

      1.2 Find a best matched global structure cluster $\mathcal{H}^* \subset \mathcal{H}$ ($* = 1, \ldots, J$) by scanning the global structure modes (the 1st level) of the HDM.

         if $\mathcal{R}(\mathbf{X}_G) \neq 0$, $\mathcal{H}^* = \mathcal{H}^{\mathcal{R}(\mathbf{X}_G)}$, otherwise $\mathcal{H}^* = \varnothing$ (global outlier).

   Step 2. **If** $\mathcal{H}^* \neq \varnothing$ (local detector)

      2.1 Perform the local detection using $\mathcal{H}^*$ based on NN regression algorithm.

      2.2 Set *localOutlierFlag* = False.

      2.3 **for** $l = 1$ **to** $\mathcal{L}$

      Determine the optimal feature point l.

      if $\mathcal{R}(\mathbf{x}^l) \neq 0$, set *localOutlierFlag* = True .

      endfor

      2.4 **if** *localOutlierFlag* = False , $\mathbf{X}_i = \{\mathbf{x}^1, \ldots, \mathbf{x}^{\mathcal{L}}\}$, otherwise, $\mathbf{X}_i = \varnothing$ (local outlier).

     Step3. $L = L \cup \mathbf{X}_i$

endfor

6   Experimental Results

The localization performance was evaluated from several points of views using popular face datasets such as Bosphorus [14], BioID [15]. Our method is compared to the state-of-the-art of technologies reported in [16]. The experiments were performed on an Intel Core(TM)2 Quad CPU Q8400 2.66 GHz with C ++.

6.1   Performance Evaluation

Our localization method is compared to that of STASM V.4 [17] and that of 3-Level IMoFA [16]. We used 200 and 500 labeled and unlabeled samples for the

Table 1. The localization accuracies of our method compared to those of STASM V.4 and 3-Level IMoFA using Bosphrus. Facial feature points: OEC (Outer eye corners), IEC (Inner eye corners), NT (Nose tip), MC (Mouth corners), OE (Outer eyebrows), IE (Inner eyebrows), PC (Pupil centers), NS (Nose saddles), and LOM (Lip center of mouth).

Landmark	CSSL(200,500)		3-Level IMoFA		STASM	
	Success	Mean error	Success	Mean error	Success	Mean error
OEC	96.89	2.63	97.98	3.16	94.17	3.32
IEC	99.75	2.48	98.46	2.54	99.67	2.70
NT	97.89	2.22	94.68	3.65	97.75	2.19
MC	90.56	3.13	90.74	4.94	89.56	3.13
OE	81.17	3.64	91.42	4.80	81.83	3.49
IE	96.23	2.44	94.79	4.35	97.22	2.38
PC	99.60	2.37	98.84	2.37	99.56	2.44
NS	94.98	2.77	86.51	4.93	94.72	2.77
LOM	93.22	2.58	88.76	5.85	92.50	2.53
Average	94.48	2.70	93.58	4.07	94.11	2.77

semi-supervised learning of local detectors of our method, respectively. 500 samples from Bosphorus are used for testing. The comparison results are given in Table 1. Our method shows better performance in average localization accuracies and mean errors than 3-Level IMoFA and STASM V.4.

In Fig. 3, the cumulative correct localization rates of the proposed method is compared to other state-of-the art methods reported by Dibeklioglu et al. [16]. The performance of our method is comparable to other approaches [16] such as 3-Level IMoFA, Generative, Sliwiga, AAM, CLM, and BorMaN.

Semi-supervised learning is carried out simultaneously with testing using the unlabeled test data samples to make fair comparisons.

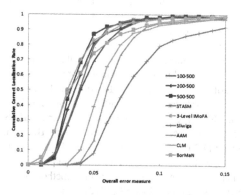

Fig. 3. Cumulative correct localization rate with respect to entire feature localization error m_e of our method and other state-of-the-art technologies [16] using BioID dataset

7 Conclusion

Most state-of-the-art face feature detectors rely on only labeled training data, and thus have much difficulty in obtaining robust performances when the variability of images hardly be predicted in prior. Instead of using a number of labeled training data, unlabeled data that can be easily gathered is employed for improving the generalization ability of feature localization. We presented an iterative algorithm for robust facial feature localization, where the H-DTR improves the localization performance of facial feature points with incremental generalization ability.

References

1. Celiktutan, O., et al.: A Comparative Study of Face Landmarking Techniques, EURASIP Journal on Image and Video Processing (2013)
2. Lowe, D.G.: Distinctive image features from scale-invariant keypoints. Int. J. Comput. Vision 60(2), 91–110 (2004)
3. Zhu, X., Ramanan, D.: Face detection, pose estimation and landmark estimation in the wild. In: IEEE Conference on Computer Vision and Pattern Recognition (2012)
4. Cristinacce, D., Cootes, T.: Feature detection and tracking with constrained local models. In: Proceedings BMVC, pp. 929–938 (2006)
5. Cristinacce, D., Cootes, T., Scott, I.: A multi-stage approach to facial feature detection. Proc. British Mach. Vis. Conf. 1, 231–240 (2004)
6. Belhumeur, P.N., Jacobs, D.W., Kriegman, D.J., Kumar, N.: Localizing parts of faces using a consensus of exemplars. In: CVPR (2011)
7. Blum, A., Mitchell, T.: Combining labeled and unlabeled data with co-training. In: Proceedings of the 11th Annual Conference on Computational Learning Theory, pp. 92–100 (1998)
8. Tong, Y., Liu, X., Wheeler, F.W., Tu, P.: Semi-supervised facial landmark annotation. Comput. Vis. Image Underst. (CVIU) 116(8), 922–935 (2012)
9. Forero, P.A.: Robust clustering using outlier-sparsity regularization. IEEE Trans. Sig. Process. 60(8), 4163–4177 (2012)
10. Viola, P., Jones, M.J.: Robust real-time face detection. Int. J. Comput. Vis. 57(2), 137–154 (2004)
11. Goodall, C.: Procrustes methods in the statistical analysis of shape. J. Roy. Statist. Soc. Ser. B 53(2), 285–339 (1991)
12. Hong, S., Khim, S., Lee, P.K.: Efficient face landmark localization using spatial-context adaboost algorithm. In: Proceedings Journal of Visaul Communication and Image Presentation (2013)
13. Mareček1, J., Richtárik2, P., Takáč, M.: Distributed Block Coordinate Descent for Minimizing Partially Separable Functions, Math.OC 2 June 2014
14. Savran, A., Alyüz, N., Dibeklioğlu, H., Çeliktutan, O., Gökberk, B., Sankur, B., Akarun, L.: Bosphorus database for 3D face analysis. In: Schouten, B., Juul, N.C., Drygajlo, A., Tistarelli, M. (eds.) BIOID 2008. LNCS, vol. 5372, pp. 47–56. Springer, Heidelberg (2008)
15. http://www.bioid.com/downloads/software/bioid-face-database
16. Dibeklioglu, H., Salah, A.A., Gevers, T.: A statistical method for 2-D facial landmarking. IEEE Trans. Image Process. 21(2), 844–858 (2012)
17. Milborrow, S., Nicolls, F.: Active Shape Models with SIFT Descriptors and MARS. VISAPP (2014)

Quantitative Analysis of Surface Reconstruction Accuracy Achievable with the TSDF Representation

Diana Werner[✉], Philipp Werner, and Ayoub Al-Hamadi

University of Magdeburg, Magdeburg, Germany
{Diana.Werner,Philipp.Werner,Ayoub.Al-Hamadi}@ovgu.de

Abstract. During the last years KinectFusion and related algorithms have facilitated significant advances in real-time simultaneous localization and mapping (SLAM) with depth-sensing cameras. Nearly all of these algorithms represent the observed area with the truncated signed distance function (TSDF). The reconstruction accuracy achievable with the representation is crucial for camera pose estimation and object reconstruction. Therefore, we evaluate this reconstruction accuracy in an optimal context, i.e. assuming error-free camera pose estimation and depth measurement. For this purpose we use a synthetic dataset of depth image sequences and corresponding camera pose ground truth and compare the reconstructed point clouds with the ground truth meshes. We investigate several influencing factors, especially the TSDF resolution and show that the TSDF is a very powerful representation even for low resolutions.

Keywords: TSDF · Reconstruction accuracy · KinectFusion

1   Introduction

In the last years several works approached the simultaneous localization and mapping (SLAM) problem using the truncated signed distance function (TSDF) for representing the observed area. The first was KinectFusion [7,12], followed by Kintinuous [17–19]. An open source implementation of KinectFusion without limitation in the volume of reconstruction is KinfuLargeScale [13,14]. All these methods use a depth camera to capture the environment and the TSDF to represent the observed area. They convert the TSDF to a point cloud after each frame to localize the camera with help of an iterative closest point algorithm (ICP) and the current point cloud obtained from the measured depth image. Divergently, in [1] the camera pose estimation is computed directly from TSDF.

These methods were evaluated mostly qualitatively, due to a lack of ground truth in most datasets. Some quantitative results are presented in [5,6,8,10], but with a clear focus on the camera pose estimation error. Few works [6,10] include quantitative results on reconstruction accuracy. However, they only analyze one to three sequences.

© Springer International Publishing Switzerland 2015
L. Nalpantidis et al. (Eds.): ICVS 2015, LNCS 9163, pp. 167–176, 2015.
DOI: 10.1007/978-3-319-20904-3_16

None of these works analyzed the TSDF itself, decoupled from effects that originate from pose estimation errors. To our knowledge, only [16] analyzes reconstruction accuracy with TSDF as map representation, but the work is limited to the 2D case with a single observation. However in fact, in all SLAM methods, the precision of the computed point cloud for ICP and therefore the localization accuracy, depends directly on the accuracy we can achieve with the TSDF as world representation. It is the same for the reconstruction of the observed area.

Therefore in this paper we will investigate the question: How accurate can a reconstruction of an given object or area be given the TSDF as world representation? We do especially look at the voxel sizes used for representing the world grid. To evaluate only the influence of TSDF representation for reconstructing with different voxel sizes, we decided to conduct our experiments with synthetic depth map sequences generated from publicly available 3D models. We also use ground truth camera movement during reconstruction, to analyze the reconstruction accuracy, while avoiding that uncertainties of localization done with ICP does have influence on reconstruction.

We examine different scenarios with different levels of detail. The used depth sequences include several camera movements and frequencies of observations per surface point. In this way, we will not only look at variable voxel sizes, but also on the different kinds of depth sequences you could be faced to when performing SLAM or object reconstruction.

In the following, we will at first give a brief theoretical overview for TSDF. In Sect. 3 we will shortly introduce the used dataset. In Sect. 4 we present the conducted experiments and discuss the results. We will finish with conclusion and future work.

2   Theory

To represent the environment we use the truncated signed distance function (TSDF), which had been introduced in [2].

For this you firstly choose the dimension of an cube in front of your camera; in our case the edge length is 3 m. The surfaces observed in the real world inside this cube will now be transformed into TSDF. The cube is subdivided in a regular grid of voxels (world grid). For each voxel you save the distance from voxel center to the nearest object surface. The distance is truncated to a chosen length. You also save a second value, representing the confidence of the distance saved. So every time you see a surface for a voxel, this value is incremented. To merge several points of view for the same world grid, you add the already saved distance value for each voxel with the current given distance weighted with the certainty value. Therefore the equations for distance value $tsdf_i$ and certainty value w_i for each current seen voxel[1] i with currently given distance d_i are as follows:

$$tsdf_i := \frac{w_i \cdot tsdf_i + d_i}{w_i + 1} \tag{1}$$

---

[1] Voxels are currently seen if they are in the field of view of camera, no matter if they are occluded by a surface.

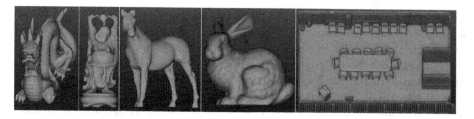

Fig. 1. Meshes used for the dataset.

After this, the $tsdf_i$ value needs to be truncated.

$$w_i := w_i + 1; \tag{2}$$

To be able to update TSDF you need depth data and the correct position of your camera. After integrating several points of view, we can reconstruct the observed scene from the TSDF. We used the StandaloneMarchingCubes algorithm from PCL [14] for that.

3 Dataset

To evaluate the reconstruction error of a scene or object we need a large dataset with scene ground truth and depth image sequences with corresponding ground truth camera poses. Since the available datasets are limited regarding size, availability of ground truth and its quality, we generated a synthetic dataset. It is based on publically available mesh models. For each sequence we defined a series of camera poses. These are saved as camera movement ground truth and used to render the corresponding depth image of the selected mesh. The images were rendered with a virtual Kinect camera [9]. We decided to simulate the camera without noise or the holes typically seen when using a Kinect camera, because we want to test the TSDF reconstruction under optimal circumstances.

With this kind of dataset it is possible to evaluate both, the accuracy of reconstruction and of camera pose estimation. In this work we focus on reconstruction.

For the dataset we choose several types of objects with varying level of detail: a planar wall, a horse [3], the stanford bunny, dragon and buddha [15]. For scene reconstruction we used a model of a conference room [11] with moderate level of detail. You can get an impression from Fig. 1. Each sequence contains one of the objects and each object is always used at the same scale. The dataset is publically available on www.iikt.ovgu.de/Diana_Werner.html.

4 Experiments and Discussion

In this section we describe our error analysis for object or scene reconstruction when using TSDF as the world representation. We conducted our experiments with the open source C++ implementation KinfuLargeScale [13], but several adaptations were necessary: (1) Our aim is to test the reconstruction capabilities of TSDF under optimal circumstances. Therefore we do not estimate the camera pose for each depth image as done in KinectFusion, but use the given ground truth camera movement instead. (2) We want to evaluate the influence of the TSDF resolution on the accuracy of reconstruction. In the original implementation the world grid size is fixed to 512 voxels along each dimension. We adapted the software to make this parameter arbitrarily changeable, which required several bug fixes. (3) To simplify the analysis of results, we directly calculate and save the complete surface point cloud fused from multiple TSDF world cubes. Further, it gets aligned correctly for direct comparison with the ground truth mesh.

We evaluate the reconstruction accuracy with several tests to analyze influencing factors. We will now describe the tests and evaluations in detail. In every evaluation figure you will see the mean value for absolute distance error from surface point to ground truth mesh. We also show the standard deviation. Both are given as *mean value ± standard deviation*. All results are presented in mm. The resolution is the world grid resolution and is chosen the same for all world grid dimensions. For the resolution 64 the voxels have width, height and depth of 46.8 mm. For resolution 128, 256 and 512 the voxel edges have a length of 23.4 mm, 11.7 mm and 5.9 mm respectively. The errors had been computed using CloudCompare [4].

We do the tests with these resolutions because of the fact that you need much less memory space for lower resolutions to represent the same scene size. In this context it is interesting to evaluate the achievable reconstruction accuracy for low resolutions.

4.1 Influence of Distance to Surface

In this test we look at a wall from several distances. At the start we look vertically at the wall and rotate the camera in the next frames around the y-axis in camera coordinates from 30 degree to 0 degree. We want to evaluate the accuracy of reconstruction in dependence of resolution and distance in a sequence with varying viewing angles on a very low detail object. You can the the evaluation in Fig. 2.

Like you can see in this figure the mean absolute errors are always small compared to size of voxels, especially for small resolutions. So for low detail objects you can choose a very low resolution nearly without loosing reconstruction accuracy for computed surface points. For every resolution, we found that distances from 1.5 m to 2 m obtain the worst reconstruction accuracy.

4.2 Influence of Viewing Angle

In this test we look at a wall in several angles. So for this test we evaluate the dependence of resolution and viewing angle for a low detail object. The sequences are generated in a way, that we start for every angle at a 2 m distances and move

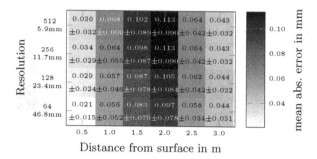

Fig. 2. Evaluation for distance from surface.

1 m ahead and reverse. We choose several angles to test the influence of rotation of surface normal in the world grid. For this we rotated the camera around its y-axis (upper vector). The results are shown in Fig. 3.

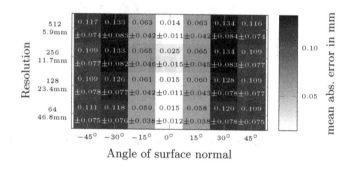

Fig. 3. Evaluation for angle of surface normal.

From this experiment it is obvious that the angle between surface normal and world grid coordinate system is important for accuracy of reconstruction. The best results for angle 0°, which means looking frontally at the wall. The differences between the different resolutions are not significant. The error is really small compared to voxel size for all resolutions, especially for lower resolutions. Therefore, for low detailed objects you can use low resolutions without loosing reconstruction accuracy for computed surface points.

4.3 Influence of Distance and Resolutions for More Detailed Objects

For this test we look at several objects with different levels of detail. We move around these objects in several distances. For the far distance, where we choose the distance around 2.3 m from surface, we only translate the camera in the first

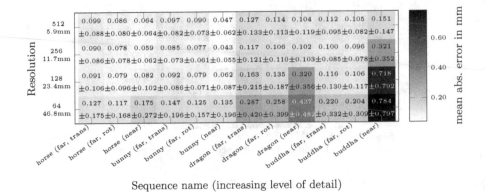

Fig. 4. Evaluation for each sequence for different levels of detail and distance.

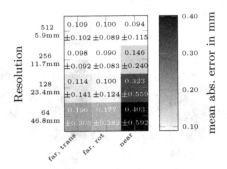

Fig. 5. Evaluation for sequences with same distance and movement.

test and in the second one we only rotate it around its y-axis and x-axis. In the near distance, which we choose to be around 0.6 m from surface, we rotate and translate the camera. So for this test we evaluate the influence of resolution and distance for objects with different level of detail. The *horse* object has the lowest level of detail, followed by *bunny*, *dragon* and *buddha* with higher levels of detail.

In Fig. 4 you can see the results for all sequences. In all cases the mean absolute errors are small compared to voxel size especially for small resolutions. You can see that the level of detail influences the reconstruction accuracy. The mean absolute error and the standard deviation are up to two times higher for objects with higher levels of detail particularly with regard to the near distance. However, in relation to voxel size these differences are low.

In Fig. 5 we show the mean absolute errors over all sequences with same distance and camera movement. You can see, that for the really low resolution 64 it is slightly better to have a higher distance to the object, whereas for resolution 512 it is better to be near. Like in the tests before the changes of mean absolute error and standard deviation for the chosen distances and camera movements are low compared to voxel size for all resolutions.

4.4 Influence of Resolutions for Sequences with Arbitrary Distances and Movement

In this test we are looking at a conference scene. We are moving arbitrarily to cover a wide range of observation differences and movements. The scene has many objects with moderate level of detail (chairs, tables, walls, doors etc.) and some detailed objects (exit sign, fire-extinguisher). We also try to have different times of measurements within the scene. So the camera movement and the scene itself should be quite general for SLAM problems. In this test we want to evaluate the accuracy of scene reconstruction in a general SLAM problem, but with given and therefore optimal camera pose estimation. You can see the results for each of the 5 sequences and the mean over all sequences in Fig. 6.

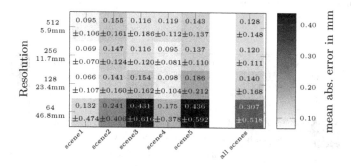

Fig. 6. Evaluation with arbitrary camera movement and distances.

Over all sequences, resolution 256 is slightly better compared to the others. But compared to voxel size the differences are low. For scene3 and scene5 resolution 64 and 128 show a drop of reconstruction accuracy compared to the other scenes. This is because of a curtain in this scene forming a regular depth pattern which can not be reconstructed very well with this resolution. For resolution 512 and 256 scene2 is worst among all scenes, because it contains very detailed objects (exit sign, fire-extinguisher). No other objects in the conference room show this level of detail. Like in all other experiments all mean absolute errors and standard deviations are very small for all resolutions compared to voxel size.

You can get a qualitative impression for the reconstruction results from Fig. 7. There you can see the computed surface points and absolute errors compared with the given ground truth mesh for all resolutions. The highest errors are at the edges of the objects.

4.5 Influence of Times of View

In this test we are looking at a wall with quite chaotic, really small movements. We translated in 1 cm steps in such a way, that we moved back to start position nearly immediately and same for rotation in 1 degree steps. The sequences used

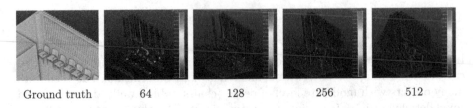

| Ground truth | 64 | 128 | 256 | 512 |

Fig. 7. Ground truth and computed surface points with absolute errors for scene3.

have different numbers of frames and therefore we want to evaluate the influence of times of views for each voxel. Because of the way we are moving the camera we assume that we always see the same clipping of the wall. In this way, the times of view for each seen voxel is either zero or the number of frames. We present our results in Fig. 8.

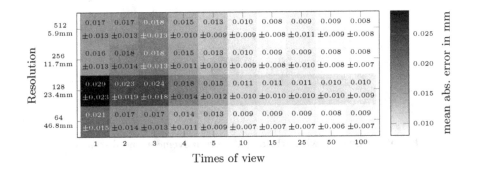

Fig. 8. Evaluation for different times of view.

This experiment shows, that you should have at least ten observations for each voxel to obtain optimal resolution accuracy for very low detailed objects. Therefore the integration of depth data is an important benefit for reconstruction accuracy. This is even more important when considering real depth maps, which are noisy to some degree. Like in all experiments the mean absolute error is very small compared to voxel size especially for low resolutions.

4.6 Qualitative Analysis

In all experiments the errors for the reconstructed surfaces points in every resolution where very small in comparison to voxel size, especially for low resolutions. So the quantitative errors are nearly the same for all resolutions. We will now show the computed surface meshes for the *buddha* object in Fig. 9 to give an qualitative impression for the different resolutions. This objects has been seen frontal in the used sequence. It is obvious, that computing the same number of surface points like in resolution 512 for all the other resolutions, for example

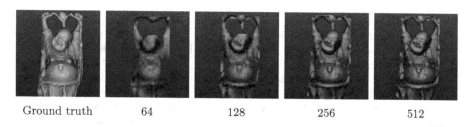

Ground truth   64   128   256   512

Fig. 9. Ground truth and meshes from computed surface points for used resolutions.

with interpolation, would induce a much higher quantitative error. We believe that the most important shape, with level of detail reconstructible by the chosen resolution, is reconstructed very well. With this knowledge it is possible to choose a low resolution and therefore considerably save memory space if you are not interested in reconstructions with high level of detail, assuming optimal camera pose estimation and depth measurement.

5 Conclusion

In this paper we presented an evaluation for surface reconstruction accuracy achievable for TSDF as world grid representation. We used KinfuLargeScale [13] with given and therefore correct camera poses. For evaluation we utilized ground truth object meshes and synthetic depth sequences from a simulated Kinect camera [9] without noise.

We assert that in this optimal context the rotation of surface normal, distance to surface, level of detail for observed objects, times of viewing each voxel in world grid and world grid resolution only have a slight influence on reconstruction accuracy. All mean absolute errors from generated surface points to given ground truth mesh are far beyond the voxel sizes, especially for low resolution.

In future work we will investigate the influence of world grid resolution for camera pose estimation.

Acknowledgments. This work was supported by Transregional Collaborative Research Centre SFB/TRR 62 (Companion-Technology for Cognitive Technical Systems) funded by the German Research Foundation (DFG).

References

1. Bylow, E., Sturm, J., Kerl, C., Kahl, F., Cremers, D.: Real-time camera tracking and 3d reconstruction using signed distance functions. In: Robotics: Science and Systems (RSS) Conference 2013, vol. 9 (2013)
2. Curless, B., Levoy, M.: A volumetric method for building complex models from range images. In: Proceedings of the 23rd Annual Conference on Computer Graphics and Interactive Techniques, pp. 303–312. ACM (1996)

3. Georgia Institute of Technology: Large geometric models archive. http://www.cc.gatech.edu/projects/large_models/
4. Girardeau-Montaut, D.: CloudCompare (2015). http://www.danielgm.net/cc/
5. Hemmat, H.J., Bondarev, E., Dubbelman, G., With, P.: Improved ICP-based pose estimation by distance-aware 3d mapping. In: International Conference on Computer Vision Theory and Applications (VISAPP), pp. 360–367. SciTePress (2014)
6. Hemmat, H.J., Bondarev, E., de With, P.H.N.: Exploring Distance-Aware weighting strategies for accurate reconstruction of Voxel-Based 3D synthetic models. In: Gurrin, C., Hopfgartner, F., Hurst, W., Johansen, H., Lee, H., O'Connor, N. (eds.) MMM 2014, Part I. LNCS, vol. 8325, pp. 412–423. Springer, Heidelberg (2014)
7. Izadi, S., Kim, D., Hilliges, O., Molyneaux, D., Newcombe, R., Kohli, P., Shotton, J., Hodges, S., Freeman, D., Davison, A.: KinectFusion: real-time 3d reconstruction and interaction using a moving depth camera. In: Proceedings of the 24th Annual ACM Symposium on User Interface Software and Technology, pp. 559–568. ACM (2011)
8. Jiang, S.Y., Chang, N.C., Wu, C.C., Wu, C.H., Song, K.T.: Error analysis and experiments of 3d reconstruction using a rgb-d sensor. In: IEEE International Conference on Automation Science and Engineering (CASE), pp. 1020–1025 (2014)
9. Kinect: Kinect (2014). http://www.xbox.com/en-us/kinect/
10. Meister, S., Izadi, S., Kohli, P., Hammerle, M., Rother, C., Kondermann, D.: When can we use kinectfusion for ground truth acquisition? In: Workshop on Color-Depth Camera Fusion in Robotics, IROS (2012)
11. Morgan McGuire: Computer graphics archive. http://graphics.cs.williams.edu/data/meshes.xml
12. Newcombe, R.A., Davison, A.J., et al.: KinectFusion: real-time dense surface mapping and tracking. In: IEEE International Symposium on Mixed and Augmented Reality (ISMAR), pp. 127–136. IEEE (2011)
13. PCL: Kinectfusion in PCL 1.7.1 (2014). http://www.pointclouds.org/
14. Rusu, R., Cousins, S.: 3d is here: Point Cloud Library (PCL). In: IEEE International Conference on Robotics and Automation (ICRA), pp. 1–4 (2011)
15. Stanford University: The stanford 3d scanning repository. http://graphics.stanford.edu/data/3Dscanrep/
16. Werner, D., Al-Hamadi, A., Werner, P.: Truncated signed distance function: experiments on voxel size. In: Campilho, A., Kamel, M. (eds.) ICIAR 2014, Part II. LNCS, vol. 8815, pp. 357–364. Springer, Heidelberg (2014)
17. Whelan, T., Johannsson, H., Kaess, M., Leonard, J., McDonald, J.: Robust tracking for real-time dense RGB-D mapping with Kintinuous. Tech. Rep. MIT-CSAIL-TR-2012-031, Computer Science and Artificial Intelligence Laboratory, MIT, September 2012
18. Whelan, T., Johannsson, H., Kaess, M., Leonard, J.J., McDonald, J.: Robust real-time visual odometry for dense RGB-D mapping. In: IEEE International Conference on Robotics and Automation (ICRA), pp. 5724–5731. IEEE (2013)
19. Whelan, T., Kaess, M., Fallon, M., Johannsson, H., Leonard, J., McDonald, J.: Kintinuous: spatially extended kinectfusion. In: RSS Workshop on RGB-D: Advanced Reasoning with Depth Cameras (2012)

Learning and Adaptation

An Online Adaptive Fuzzy Clustering and Its Application for Background Suppression

Thanh Minh Nguyen[1]([✉]), Q.M. Jonathan Wu[1], and Dibyendu Mukherjee[1,2]

[1] University of Windsor, Windsor, ON N9B3P4, Canada
nguyen1j@uwindsor.ca
[2] Duke University, Durham, NC 27708, USA

Abstract. Background suppression in video sequences has attracted growing attention and is one of the heated issues in almost every task of video processing. An online fuzzy clustering for automatic background suppression is presented in this paper. First, in the classical fuzzy clustering methods, we have to wait until all data have been generated before the learning process begins. It is impractical because in real application for background suppression, the video length is unknown and the video frames are generated dynamically in a streaming environment and arrive one at a time. Our method has an ability to adapt and change through complex scenes in a true online fashion. Secondly, different from previous works for background suppression, where the information of the detected background is ignored, we propose a new way to incorporate this information. Finally, to estimate the model parameters, the scoring method is adopted to minimize the fuzzy objective function with the Kullback-Leibler divergence information. Experiments on real datasets are presented. The performance of the proposed model is compared to that of other background modeling techniques, demonstrating the robustness and accuracy of our method.

Keywords: Fuzzy clustering · Background suppression · Online unsupervised learning

1 Introduction

The study of background suppression in video sequences is an attractive research topic in computer vision [1–4]. In most of the applications, the motion is considered to be part of the foreground while the background is assumed to be relatively static. Many previous works have been carried out on background suppression, in particular, statistical model based approaches [5–7] has received great attention for separating the foreground objects, as it aims to reduce the sensitivity of the segmentation result with respect to noise.

Many algorithms are based on the statistical model based approaches to achieve highly accurate segmentation results. Among these algorithms, the Gaussian mixture model (GMM) [1] is a well-known method. It is a flexible and powerful statistical modeling tool for background suppression. In this method,

© Springer International Publishing Switzerland 2015
L. Nalpantidis et al. (Eds.): ICVS 2015, LNCS 9163, pp. 179–187, 2015.
DOI: 10.1007/978-3-319-20904-3_17

the static background is modeled by a mixture of Gaussian distributions. Following this work, several researchers have improved the statistical models [8–11]. Among them, one of the simplest and fastest converging approaches in this domain is the effective Gaussian mixture model (EGMM) [9]. Conditional random field based GMM (CRF) [11] is a notable approach. The main advantage of this method is that the spatial information between the neighboring pixels is incorporated and influenced in the learning process. In order to improve the robustness of the algorithm, a self adaptive GMM (SAGMM) with shadow removal has been proposed in [12]. The main advantage of this model is that it can deal with rapid illumination changes.

Another way to assign a set of data into different labels so that the objects in the same label are more similar to each other is to adopt the fuzzy clustering algorithm [13–17]. Although, methods in [16,17] has been successfully applied for segmentation, they are mostly based on algorithms for segmenting static images. In [18], a dynamic fuzzy clustering with the Kullback-Leibler (KL) divergence information has been presented to view video sequences as dynamic textures, where a sample from stochastic processes is defined over space and time. This model provides a natural way to cluster video sequences based on the fuzzy membership function. However, in this method, we have to wait until all data have been generated before learning begins. It is impractical because in real application for background suppression, the video length is unknown and the video frames are generated dynamically in a streaming environment and arrive one at a time.

Motivated by the aforementioned observations, we present an online fuzzy clustering for background suppression. The work presented in this paper is an extension and improvement on the idea of fuzzy clustering. Hence, it is simple and easy to implement. Our method has an ability to adapt and change through complex scenes in a true online fashion. We do not have to wait until all data have been generated before learning begins. Different from previous works for background suppression, where the information of the detected background is ignored, we propose a new way to incorporate this information. In order to estimate the model parameters, the scoring method is adopted to minimize the fuzzy objective function with the KL divergence information. Experiments are presented where the proposed model is tested on real datasets.

The remainder of this paper is organized as follows: Sect. 2 presents the related works; Sect. 3 describes the proposed method in detail; Sect. 4 sets out the experimental results; and Sect. 5 presents our conclusions.

2   Related Works

Notations used throughout this paper are as follows. A video is represented as a sequence of still images. The values of a pixel at position (u,v) over time is described using the set $\mathbf{x} = \{\mathbf{x}_1, \mathbf{x}_2, ..., \mathbf{x}_\tau\}$, where $\mathbf{x}_t = \{x_{t,1}, x_{t,2}, ..., x_{t,D}\}$, $t = (1,2,...,N)$. N is the length of the video. D denotes the number of available features (dimension of each image). And K denotes the number of clusters (components).

Let us consider the problem of clustering N observations into K labels, fuzzy clustering algorithms rely on the dissimilarity function $d_{t,j}$ to assign a unique label to each observation. In the standard fuzzy clustering [13], the objective function is given by

$$J(\Psi) = \sum_{t=1}^{N} \sum_{j=1}^{K} z_{t,j}^{\gamma} d_{t,j} \tag{1}$$

where Ψ is the model parameter, and the fuzzy membership $z_{t,j}$ satisfies the constraints $z_{t,j} \geq 0$ and $\sum_{j=1}^{K} z_{t,j} = 1$. In (1), $\gamma \geq 1$ is the weighted exponent for each fuzzy membership, which determines the degree of fuzziness of the clustering algorithm. If γ equal to one, then the algorithm reduces to the hard c-means algorithm [14]. However, for several researchers [15–18], the degree of fuzziness γ in the context of the hard c-means algorithm yielding the standard fuzzy clustering in (1) has been considered as an unnatural element. In order to overcome this problem, a fuzzy clustering with the KL divergence information is introduced

$$J(\Psi) = \sum_{t=1}^{N} \sum_{j=1}^{K} z_{t,j} d_{t,j} + \gamma \sum_{t=1}^{N} \sum_{j=1}^{K} z_{t,j} \log \frac{z_{t,j}}{\pi_{t,j}} \tag{2}$$

where $\pi_{t,j}$ is the prior probability. In (2), the KL divergence information works as the fuzzifier. As discussed in [15–18], if the negative log-likelihood of the Gaussian distribution is used to define the dissimilarity function $d_{t,j}$, the method in (2) yields a fuzzy clustering alternative to the EM algorithm for Gaussian mixture model. As shown in (2), the fuzzy objective function used to estimate the parameters Ψ is simple and easy to implement.

3   Proposed Method

As shown in Sect. 2, existing fuzzy clustering has been applied for offline learning, where all of the observations are available before they need to act. It is impractical because in real application for background suppression, the number of the observations (N) is unknown. Also, in the previous works for background suppression [1,10–12], the information from the detected background (previous frame: $\hat{y}_{t-1}$) is ignored. In order to update the model parameters, the method in [1] relies on two learning rates (α and β), which are sensitive to sudden changes in illumination. Based on these considerations, we proposed an online adaptive fuzzy clustering for automatic background suppression in this section. The objective function in our method is given at the t-th frame is given by

$$J(\Psi_t) = \sum_{k=1}^{M} \sum_{j=1}^{K} z_{t,k,j} d_{t,k,j} + \gamma \sum_{k=1}^{M} \sum_{j=1}^{K} z_{t,k,j} \frac{\log z_{t,k,j}}{\log \pi_{t,k,j}} \tag{3}$$

In (3), M is the background level, which is defined by the user ($M = 2$ in this paper). The prior probabilities $\pi_{t,k,j}$ satisfies the constraints $\pi_{t,k,j} \geq 0$ and

$\sum_{j=1}^{K} \pi_{t,k,j} = 1$. Adopting the idea from [19], in our method, the distribution of the fuzzy membership $z_{t,k}$ given the prior probabilities $\pi_{t,k}$ is given

$$p(z_{t,k}|\pi_{t,k}) = \prod_{j=1}^{K} \pi_{t,k,j}^{z_{t,k,j}} \qquad (4)$$

where $z_{t,k,j}$ satisfies the constraints $\sum_{j=1}^{K} z_{t,k,j} = 1$ and $z_{t,k,j} \geq 0$. In (3), the dissimilarity function $d_{t,k,j}$ is derived as

$$d_{t,k,j} = -\sum_{l=1}^{D} \log \Phi(y_{t,k,l}|\mu_{t,k,j,l}, \sigma_{t,k,j,l}^{2}) \qquad (5)$$

where $\Phi(y_{t,k,l}|\mu_{t,k,j,l}, \sigma_{t,k,j,l}^{2})$ is the Gaussian distribution with two parameters: mean $\mu_{t,k,j,l}$ and variance $\sigma_{t,k,j,l}^{2}$. Different from previous works for background suppression [1, 10–12], where the information of the detected background (previous frame: $\hat{y}_{t-1}$) is ignored, we propose a new way to incorporate this information into the observation $y_{t,k,l}$. The observation $y_{t,k,l}$ in our method is derived as

$$\begin{aligned} y_{t,1,l} &= x_{t,l} \\ y_{t,2,l} &= |y_{t-1,1,l} - \hat{y}_{t-1,1,l}| \\ &\cdots \\ y_{t,M,l} &= |y_{t-1,M-1,l} - \hat{y}_{t-1,M-1,l}| \end{aligned} \qquad (6)$$

In (6), $x_{t,l}$ is the original observation. And $\hat{y}_{t-1,k,l}$, $k = (1,2,...,M-1)$ is the detected background of the l-th feature at the previous frame $(t-1)$. The idea to define observation $y_{t,k,l}$ is based on a fact that the detected backgrounds at the neighborhood frame are similar in some sense. Also, the detected background may be corrupted by noise and contain some background information.

Note that, the objective function $J(\Psi_t)$ in (3) can be regarded as an error function. Therefore, minimizing $J(\Psi_t)$ is then equivalent to maximizing the negative error function $Q(\Psi_t) = -J(\Psi_t)$

$$\begin{aligned} Q(\Psi_t) = \sum_{k=1}^{M}\sum_{j=1}^{K} z_{t,k,j} \sum_{l=1}^{D} \log \Phi(y_{t,k,l}|\mu_{t,k,j,l}, \sigma_{t,k,j,l}^{2}) \\ - \gamma \sum_{k=1}^{M}\sum_{j=1}^{K} z_{t,k,j} \frac{\log z_{t,k,j}}{\log \pi_{t,k,j}} \end{aligned} \qquad (7)$$

To maximize this function, the scoring method [20–23] is adopted. Each iteration of the algorithm consists of two steps. In the first step, we calculate the fuzzy membership $z_{t,k,j}$ with the current parameters. Then, in the second step, the new parameter is computed based on the fuzzy membership $z_{t,k,j}$

$$\begin{cases} z_{t,k,j} = \arg\max_{z} Q(\Psi_t) \\ \Psi_{t+1} = \Psi_t + \frac{1}{t+1}[I_c(\Psi_t)]^{-1}\nabla_{\Psi}[Q(\Psi_t)] \end{cases} \qquad (8)$$

In (8), $I_c(\Psi_t)$ is the Fisher information matrix

$$I_c(\Psi_t) = -\mathbb{E}\left[\frac{\partial^2 Q(\Psi_t)}{\partial \Psi_t \partial \Psi_t^T}\right] \tag{9}$$

where $\mathbb{E}[\cdot]$ stands for the expectation. In order to estimate the parameter $\Psi_t = \{\pi_{t,k,j}, \mu_{t,k,j,l}, \sigma^2_{t,j,l,k}\}$ and to present conveniently, we subdivide this section into two subsections.

3.1   The Fuzzy Membership $z_{t,k,j}$

In order to maximizing the function $Q(\Psi_t)$ in (7), we now consider the derivative of the function $Q(\Psi_t)$ with the fuzzy membership $z_{t,k,j}$. We use the Lagrange's multiplier η for each observation

$$\frac{\partial}{\partial z_{t,k,j}}\left[Q(\Psi_t) - \eta\left(\sum_{j=1}^{K} z_{t,k,j} - 1\right)\right] = 0 \tag{10}$$

The constraint $\sum_{j=1}^{K} z_{t,k,j} = 1$ enables the determination of the parameter set $z_{t,k,j}$

$$z_{t,k,j} = \frac{\pi_{t,k,j}\exp(-\gamma^{-1}d_{t,k,j})}{\sum_{m=1}^{K} \pi_{t,k,m}\exp(-\gamma^{-1}d_{t,k,m})} \tag{11}$$

where $d_{t,k,j}$ is the dissimilarity function, which is given in (5).

3.2   The Parameter $\Psi_t = \{\pi_{t,k,j}, \mu_{t,k,j,l}, \sigma^2_{t,j,l,k}\}$

In order to update the parameter Ψ_t, we need to calculate the Fisher information matrix $I_c(\Psi_t)$ in (9). Invoking a property of the Bernoulli distribution in (4) and a property of the Gaussian distribution $\Phi(y_{t,k,l}|\mu_{t,k,j,l}, \sigma^2_{k,j,l})$, we can write the following specification

$$\mathbb{E}[(y_{t,k,l} - \mu_{t,k,j,l})^2] = \sigma^2_{t,k,j,l} \quad \text{and} \quad \mathbb{E}[z_{t,k,j}] = \pi_{t,k,j} \tag{12}$$

Now we can apply (12) to the Fisher information matrix $I_c(\Psi_t)$ in (9), after some manipulation, we have

$$\begin{aligned}
I_c(\pi_{t,k,j}) &= \lambda\frac{1}{\pi_{t,k,j}} \\
I_c(\mu_{t,k,j,l}) &= \sigma^{-2}_{t,k,j,l}\pi_{t,k,j} \\
I_c(\sigma^2_{t,k,j,l}) &= \frac{1}{2}\pi_{t,k,j}\sigma^{-4}_{t,k,j,l}
\end{aligned} \tag{13}$$

Note that $\pi_{t,k,j}$ should satisfy the constraints $\pi_{t,k,j} \geq 0$ and $\sum_{j=1}^{K}\pi_{t,k,j} = 1$. Apply (13) to (8), the parameters $\Psi_t = \{\pi_{t,k,j}, \mu_{t,k,j,l}, \sigma^2_{t,j,l,k}\}$ are updated as follows

$$
\begin{aligned}
\pi_{t,k,j} &= \pi_{t-1,k,j} + (1+t)^{-1}(z_{t,k,j} - \pi_{t-1,k,j}) \\
\mu_{t,k,j,l} &= \mu_{t-1,k,j,l} + (1+t)^{-1} \times \\
&\quad \pi_{t,k,j}^{-1} z_{t,k,j}(y_{t,k,l} - \mu_{t-1,k,j,l}) \\
\sigma_{t,k,j,l}^2 &= \sigma_{t-1,k,j,l}^2 + (1+t)^{-1} \times \\
&\quad \pi_{t,k,j}^{-1} z_{t,k,j}[(y_{t,k,l} - \mu_{t,k,j,l})^2 - \sigma_{t-1,k,j,l}^2]
\end{aligned}
\tag{14}
$$

So far, the discussion has focused on estimating the parameter $\Psi_t = \{\pi_{t,k,j}, \mu_{t,k,j,l}, \sigma_{t,j,l,k}^2\}$ of the proposed model. Our online algorithm is applied for background suppression. The various steps of our algorithm can be summarized as follows

Step 1: Initialize the parameters Ψ_t: the initialization of the parameters $\Psi_t = \{\pi_{t,k,j}, \mu_{t,k,j,l}, \sigma_{t,j,l,k}^2\}$ in our method is the same as that of GMM [1].

Step 2: Evaluate the variables $z_{t,k,j}$ in (11).

Step 3: Update parameters $\Psi_t = \{\pi_{t,k,j}, \mu_{t,k,j,l}, \sigma_{t,j,l,k}^2\}$ by using (14). It is worth mentioning that, for the learning rate $\beta = (1+t)^{-1}$ in these equations, we have selected $\beta = 0.01$ for the for the first 400 frames. After that, we set $\beta = (1+t)^{-1}$.

Step 4: If there is a new observation, then go to step 2.

In this paper, in order to extract the foreground $\hat{y}_{t,k,l}$, $k = (1,2,...,M)$, $l = (1,2,...,D)$, we adopt the concept of background suppression in [1]. The final detected background in our method is given by $\hat{y}_{t,l} = \hat{y}_{t,1,l} + \frac{1}{M-1}\sum_{k=2}^{M}\hat{y}_{t,k,l}$. In the next section, we demonstrate the accuracy and effectiveness of the proposed model compared to others.

4   Experiments

In this section, the performance of the proposed method is compared to the GMM [1], EGMM [9], CRF [11], and SAGMM [12]. All compared methods are initialized similar to the initialization of the proposed algorithm. It is worth mentioning that all experiments in this paper do not consist of any pre/post-processing step. For our method, the thresholds Th is assigned a value of 0.1 ($Th = 0.1$). The value of the degree of fuzziness of the fuzzy membership is set to one ($\gamma = 1$). The selected value of the background level is set to two ($M = 2$). Except for CRF which uses 3 ($K = 3$) components, the number of components in all compared methods is assigned a value of 5 ($K = 5$). For all methods, the R, G, and B channels of the RGB color space are used in this paper ($D = 3$).

In the first experiment, a real-world video from DynTex is used to compare the performance of the proposed algorithm with others. The original video was downloaded from http://projects.cwi.nl/dyntex. This video contains 723 frames. One difficulty in this experiment is that the sequence is very congested. Thus, the background road is difficult to be constructed due to the high amount of vehicles present. From 2nd column to 6th column of Fig. 1, we present the foreground results in the frame 600 and 680 obtained by employing GMM, EGMM,

CRF, SAGMM, and the proposed method, respectively. It can be seen that the accuracy of the CRF method is poor compared to the GMM and EGMM. The SAGMM reduces the error significantly and can segment the foreground well. However, It can be seen in the marked box that there is a region that has been misclassified. The vehicle is well constructed by the proposed method in 6th column of Fig. 1.

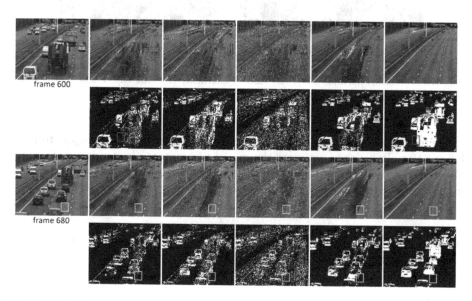

Fig. 1. The first experiment: foreground and background, (1st column): original image (Dyntex, ID = 645c610), (2nd column): GMM, (3rd column): EGMM, (4th column): CRF, (5th column): SAGMM, (6th column): our method.

In the second experiment, one real-world video clip with 717 frames, as shown in Fig. 2(a), from the DynTex dataset is used. From Figs. 2(b) to 2(f), we present the background results obtained by employing GMM, EGMM, CRF, SAGMM, and our method, respectively. In Fig. 2(e), the SAGMM method demonstrates better performance compared to the GMM, EGMM, and CRF methods. Looking closely at the marked boxes of Fig. 2(f), our method reduces the error significantly and can obtain the background well. The foreground results are shown in Figs. 2(g) to 2(k).

5   Relation to Prior Works and Conclusions

We have a fuzzy clustering for automatic background suppression in this paper. In the classical fuzzy clustering methods, we have to wait until all data have been generated before the learning process begins. Our method has an ability to adapt and change through complex scenes in a true online fashion. Different from previous works for background suppression, where the information of

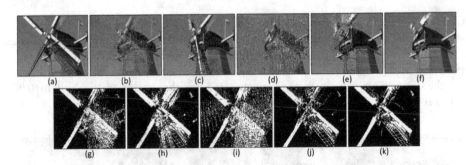

Fig. 2. The second experiment: foreground and background, (a): original image (Dyn-tex, ID = 648ab10, frame 450), (b) and (g): GMM, (c) and (h): EGMM, (d) and (i): CRF, (e) and (j): SAGMM, (f) and (k): our method.

the detected background is ignored, we propose a new way to incorporate this information. In order to estimate the model parameters, the scoring method is adopted to minimize the fuzzy objective function with the KL divergence information. Real datasets have demonstrated the accuracy and effectiveness of our method.

Acknowledgements. This research has been supported in part by the Canada Research Chair Program and the NSERC Discovery grant.

References

1. Stauffer, C., Grimson, W.: Adaptive background mixture models for real-time tracking. In: IEEE Computer Vision and Pattern Recognition, vol. 2, pp. 246–252 (1999)
2. Vargas, M., Milla, J., Toral, S., Barrero, F.: An enhanced background estimation algorithm for vehicle detection in urban traffic scenes. IEEE Trans. Veh. Technol. **59**(8), 3694–3709 (2010)
3. Kasturi, R., Goldgof, D., Soundararajan, P., Manohar, V., Garofolo, J., Bowers, R., Boonstra, M., Korzhova, V., Zhang, J.: Framework for performance evaluation of face, text, and vehicle detection and tracking in video: data, metrics, and protocol. IEEE Trans. Pattern Anal. Mach. Intell. **31**(2), 319–336 (2009)
4. Mukherjee, D., Wu, Q.M.J., Thanh, M.N.: Gaussian mixture model with advanced distance measure based on support weights and histogram of gradients for background suppression. IEEE Trans. Industr. Inf. **10**(2), 1086–1096 (2014)
5. Han, B., Comaniciu, D., Davis, L.: Sequential kernel density approximation and its application to real-time visual tracking. IEEE Trans. Pattern Anal. Mach. Intell. **30**(7), 1186–1197 (2008)
6. Vargas, M., Milla, J., Toral, S., Barrero, F.: An enhanced background estimation algorithm for vehicle detection in urban traffic scenes. IEEE Trans. Veh. Technol. **59**(8), 3694–3709 (2010)
7. Thanh, M.N., Wu, Q.M.J.: A nonsymmetric mixture model for unsupervised image segmentation. IEEE Trans. Cybern. **43**(2), 751–765 (2013)

8. Greenspan, H., Goldberger, J., Mayer, A.: Probabilistic space-time video modeling via piecewise GMM. IEEE Trans. Pattern Anal. Mach. Intell. **26**(3), 384–396 (2004)
9. Lee, D.S.: Effective Gaussian mixture learning for video background subtraction. IEEE Trans. Pattern Anal. Mach. Intell. **27**(5), 827–832 (2005)
10. Zivkovic, Z.: Improved adaptive Gaussian mixture model for background subtraction. In: IEEE International Conference on Pattern Recognition, vol. 2, pp. 28–31 (2004)
11. Wang, Y., Loe, K.F., Wu, J.K.: A dynamic conditional random field model for foreground and shadow segmentation. IEEE Trans. Pattern Anal. Mach. Intell. **28**(2), 279–289 (2006)
12. Chen, Z., Ellis, T.: Self-adaptive Gaussian mixture model for urban traffic monitoring system. In: IEEE International Conference on Computer Vision Workshops, pp. 1769–1776 (2011)
13. Bezdek, J.C.: Pattern Recognition with Fuzzy Objective Function Algorithms. Springer, New York (1981)
14. Jain, A.K., Dubes, R.C.: Algorithms for Clustering Data. Prentice-Hall, Upper Saddle River (1988)
15. Miyamoto, S., Mukaidono, M.: Fuzzy c-means as a regularization and maximum entropy approach. In: International Fuzzy Systems Association World Congress, pp. 86–92 (1997)
16. Ichihashi, H., Miyagishi, K., Honda, K.: Fuzzy c-means clustering with regularization by K-L information. In: IEEE International Conference on Fuzzy Systems, pp. 924–927 (2001)
17. Chatzis, S.P., Varvarigou, T.A.: A fuzzy clustering approach toward hidden Markov random field models for enhanced spatially constrained image segmentation. IEEE Trans. Fuzzy Syst. **16**(5), 1351–1361 (2008)
18. Thanh, M.N., Wu, Q.M.J.: Dynamic fuzzy clustering and its application in motion segmentation. IEEE Trans. Fuzzy Syst. **21**(6), 1019–1031 (2013)
19. Bishop, C.M.: Pattern Recognition and Machine Learning. Springer, New York (2006)
20. Titterington, D.M.: Recursive parameter estimation using incomplete data. J. Roy. Stat. Soc. B **46**(2), 257–267 (1984)
21. Titterington, D.M., Smith, A.F.M., Makov, U.E.: tatistical Analysis of Finite Mixture Distributions. Wiley, New York (1985)
22. Allou, S., Christophe, A., Gerard, G.: An online classification EM algorithm based on the mixture model. Stat. Comput. **17**(3), 209–218 (2007)
23. Yao, J.F.: On recursive estimation in incomplete data models. Statistics **34**(1), 27–51 (2000)

Object Detection and Terrain Classification in Agricultural Fields Using 3D Lidar Data

Mikkel Kragh$^{(\boxtimes)}$, Rasmus N. Jørgensen, and Henrik Pedersen

Department of Engineering, Aarhus University, Finlandsgade 22, Aarhus, Denmark
{mkha,rnj,hpe}@eng.au.dk

Abstract. Autonomous navigation and operation of agricultural vehicles is a challenging task due to the rather unstructured environment. An uneven terrain consisting of ground and vegetation combined with the risk of non-traversable obstacles necessitates a strong focus on safety and reliability. This paper presents an object detection and terrain classification approach for classifying individual points from 3D point clouds acquired using single multi-beam lidar scans. Using a support vector machine (SVM) classifier, individual 3D points are categorized as either ground, vegetation, or object based on features extracted from local neighborhoods. Experiments performed at a local working farm show that the proposed method has a combined classification accuracy of 91.6 %, detecting points belonging to objects such as humans, animals, cars, and buildings with 81.1 % accuracy, while classifying vegetation with an accuracy of 97.5 %.

Keywords: Object detection · Terrain classification · Agriculture · Lidar

1 Introduction

Autonomous farming is the concept of automatic agricultural machines operating safely and efficiently without human intervention. In order to ensure safe autonomous operation, robust real-time risk detection is crucial. Humans, animals, trees, other machines, etc. must be detected in due time to perform risk avoidance.

A lidar sensor measures range data to a set of surrounding points and generates a point cloud where each point is represented by a 3D position. It provides very accurate depth information in 360° horizontally and is robust towards changing lighting conditions. The lidar sensor has been used extensively in the automotive industry for detecting and localizing objects in urban environments by distinguishing between ground and obstacles [11]. In agriculture, however, a subdivision between objects and vegetation is necessary, since some apparent obstacles actually represent traversable crops. Therefore, a classification of points into ground, vegetation, and objects is needed. The ground class identifies accessible terrain, whereas the object class identifies obstacles/risks. The vegetation class serves as an intermediate category identifying both crops, bushes,

© Springer International Publishing Switzerland 2015
L. Nalpantidis et al. (Eds.): ICVS 2015, LNCS 9163, pp. 188–197, 2015.
DOI: 10.1007/978-3-319-20904-3_18

and trees. Depending on the agricultural context, vegetation can thus be either obstacles or a natural part of the field area.

In the literature, different approaches have been used to detect objects and characterize terrain in agricultural environments. [1,12–14] use single-beam lidar sensors and a mathematical density function for homogeneous grass to discriminate obstacles from grass and foliage. [6,15] use multi-beam lidars to perform ground plane identification in rough terrain. However, vegetation is not discriminated from objects. [8,9,18] use a feature-based approach for classifying individual points into the classes: scatter, linear, and surface. The objective is to identify vegetation (scatter); wires and tree branches (linear); and ground surfaces, rocks, and tree trunks (surface). [19] adds to this the objective of differentiating between vegetation and objects for increasing safety. This is done with a feature-based approach using online adaptation allowing the system to automatically collect and interpret training data. However, the results of this approach are only visually verified, and only a few specific cases are handled.

In this paper, we present an object detection approach for classifying individual points from 3D point clouds acquired with a vehicle-mounted Velodyne HDL-32E lidar. Our method calculates for each point 13 different features based on a local neighborhood. In order to account for the varying point density experienced with a vehicle-mounted lidar, we propose an adaptive neighborhood radius depending on the distance ensuring high resolution at short distance and preventing noisy features at far distance. Using a support vector machine (SVM), each point is categorized into one of three classes: ground, vegetation, or object.

The paper is divided into 5 sections. Section 2 presents the proposed approach including preprocessing, feature extraction, and classification. Section 3 presents the experimental setup and results followed by a discussion in Sect. 4. Ultimately, Sect. 5 presents a conclusion and future work.

2   Approach

The proposed method for object detection and terrain classification builds on individual point classification of single multi-beam lidar scans. A single lidar scan provides a 3D point cloud consisting of N points. For each point, 13 features are calculated using statistics from a local neighborhood. These features describe the distribution of points into surfaces, linear structures, clutter volumes, etc. and serve to distinguish between points representing the three classes: ground, vegetation, and object. Using hand labeled data, an SVM classifier is trained to classify individual points based on their calculated features.

2.1   Preprocessing

An initial step before extracting features performs a rotation and translation of the point cloud according to a globally estimated plane. This ensures that ground points in general lie close to the xy-plane. Due to variations in point density, the point cloud is first resampled using a minimum filter with a fixed sized radius of 15 cm. A global plane is then estimated using a RANSAC-based plane fitting algorithm [5]. The point cloud is finally translated and rotated according to the normal vector of this plane. The resulting point cloud has an approximately vertically oriented z-axis.

2.2   Feature Extraction

When analyzing 3D data points from a point cloud, the notion of scale is extremely important in order to obtain both robust and accurate information. Point features are calculated using a local neighborhood such that the points located close to an evaluated point contribute with information of the point's context. For instance, one feature might describe how well a point fits with a local planar surface estimated on its neighborhood. The radius of the neighborhood should depend on the desired accuracy but also on the noise levels and the density of the point cloud. Depending on the sensor used for acquiring 3D data, a point cloud can be categorized as either dense or sparse [4]. A dense point cloud has an approximately constant point density, whereas the density of a sparse point cloud (e.g. from a single lidar scan) varies with the distance. Therefore, the process of feature extraction should incorporate information of the local point density and possibly also adjust the radius of the neighborhood accordingly.

Traditionally, the neighborhood radius is kept constant by dividing all points into a global voxel representation [7,8,19]. This approach allows for easy feature calculation and comparison since all voxels are the same size. However, it has the unfortunate property that it does not exploit the high point resolution close to the sensor, and at far distances only few measurements are available resulting in too noisy features. Different approaches have been made to handle this issue of varying point density. An automatic scale selection method estimates the optimal neighborhood radius that minimizes the error of local normal estimation [9]. Another approach is to perform feature extraction on multiple scales and choose the local scale that has the highest saliency [10,17]. However, these approaches both rely on a specific measure that cannot be generalized across all possible features and structures. Also, computing features at multiple scales significantly increases the computational complexity.

Therefore, in this paper we propose a simple heuristic approach that scales the neighborhood radius r linearly with the sensor distance d. This has the benefit of computational simplicity while allowing fine estimation close to the sensor and a more coarse estimate far from the sensor. The specific relationship is given as

$$r = 0.0276d + 0.25 \tag{1}$$

such that a radius of 0.3 m is used at a distance of 2 m, whereas a radius of 3.0 m is used at a distance of 100m.

It is important that all features are made scale-invariant such that the neighborhood radius does not directly influence the features. A common normalization technique is not applicable since the features express different characteristics. Hence, we need to consider normalization for each feature separately.

A total of 13 features related to the height, shape, orientation, distance, and reflectance are calculated. In the following, these are explained in detail, and individual normalization techniques are discussed.

f_1, f_2, f_3, f_4: **Height.** Four height related features are calculated inspired by the work in [15]. Height features capture structures that protrude from the ground either positively (upwards) or negatively (downwards). f_1 is simply the z-coordinate of the evaluated point i. f_2 is the minimum z-coordinate of the neighborhood. f_3 is the average z-coordinate of all points in the neighborhood. f_4 is the standard deviation of all z-coordinates. Since the standard deviation depends directly on the size of the neighborhood, it is normalized by dividing by the neighborhood radius r. In the following equations, z_i denotes the z-coordinate of the i'th point, and k denotes the number of points within a neighborhood of radius r. k thus varies with r and the specific point density locally around point i.

$$f_1 = z_i \tag{2}$$

$$f_2 = min\,(z_1 \ldots z_k) \tag{3}$$

$$f_3 = \overline{z} = \frac{1}{k}\sum_{j=1}^{k} z_j \tag{4}$$

$$f_4 = \frac{\sigma_z}{r} = \frac{1}{r}\sqrt{\frac{1}{k}\sum_{j=1}^{k}(z_j - \overline{z})^2} \tag{5}$$

f_5, f_6, f_7, f_8: **Shape.** Principal component analysis (PCA) of the point neighborhood can be used to describe the shape/saliency of the point cloud [8,18,19]. Let $\lambda_1 < \lambda_2 < \lambda_3$ be the eigenvalues of the 3×3 covariance matrix. In case of scattered points (random point distribution), $\lambda_1 \approx \lambda_2 \approx \lambda_3$. For points on planes, $\lambda_2, \lambda_3 \gg \lambda_1$, whereas for linear structures $\lambda_3 \gg \lambda_1, \lambda_2$. Using this intuition, λ_1 captures vegetation, $\lambda_2 - \lambda_1$ captures linear structures, whereas $\lambda_3 - \lambda_2$ captures planar-like data.

Constructing scale-invariant PCA features can be done in different ways. [10] scales λ_2 and λ_3 by the neighborhood radius but leaves λ_1 intact. This results in scale-invariant eigenvalues for planar-like data, whereas scatteredness is left unscaled. [16], on the other hand, uses the ratio of PCA values.

In this paper, we utilize the eigenvalue differences as described above and scale them by the largest eigenvalue. This guarantees scale-invariant features (always adds up to 1) while allowing for the differentiation between scatter, linear, and planar structures.

$$f_5 = \frac{\lambda_1}{\lambda_3} \tag{6}$$

$$f_6 = \frac{\lambda_2 - \lambda_1}{\lambda_3} \tag{7}$$

$$f_7 = \frac{\lambda_3 - \lambda_2}{\lambda_3} \tag{8}$$

In addition to the three PCA shape features, we use a normalized orthogonal residual sum of squares (RSS) proposed by [15].

$$f_8 = \frac{1}{k} \sum_{j=1}^{k} \left((\boldsymbol{p}_j - \overline{\boldsymbol{p}}) \cdot \boldsymbol{v}_1 \right)^2 \tag{9}$$

where $\boldsymbol{v}_1$ is the eigenvector corresponding to the smallest eigenvalue λ_1, $\boldsymbol{p}_i$ is the 3D vector of the i'th point, and $\overline{\boldsymbol{p}}$ is the neighborhood mean (centroid).

f_9, f_10, f_11: **Orientation.** From the principal component analysis, the eigenvector $\boldsymbol{v}_1$ is equal to the normal vector of a locally estimated plane. $\boldsymbol{v}_1$ thus describes the orientation of the plane. The z-component of the vector has been used to capture ground points assuming that the terrain is fairly flat and not sloped [10,15]. In this paper we include all the components.

$$f_9 = \boldsymbol{v}_1 \cdot (1, 0, 0) \tag{10}$$

$$f_{10} = \boldsymbol{v}_1 \cdot (0, 1, 0) \tag{11}$$

$$f_{11} = \boldsymbol{v}_1 \cdot (0, 0, 1) \tag{12}$$

f_12: **Distance.** Although the distance-dependent point density to some degree is handled by the varying neighborhood radius, the distance from a point $\boldsymbol{p}_j$ to the sensor $\boldsymbol{s}$ can also be used as a predictor [19].

$$f_{12} = \sqrt{(\boldsymbol{p}_i - \boldsymbol{s}) \cdot (\boldsymbol{p}_i - \boldsymbol{s})} \tag{13}$$

f_13: **Reflectance.** The lidar sensor utilized in the experiments provides for each point a reflectance intensity. This can help differentiate between different materials, although it depends also on the distance and incident angle [10,19].

$$f_{13} = \text{intensity}_i \tag{14}$$

2.3   Classification

A support vector machine (SVM) classifier is trained on hand-labeled data and used to differentiate between ground, vegetation, and object. In order to balance the training data, a number of ground and vegetation points, corresponding to the number of object points, are drawn by random. We use the LIBSVM implementation [2] with a radial basis function (RBF) kernel and default SVM parameters $C = 1$ and $\gamma = \frac{1}{\#features} = \frac{1}{13}$. Prior to feeding the classifier, features are normalized by subtracting the mean and dividing by the standard deviation for each dimension across the training data. The normalization parameters are then stored for subsequent use in the test procedure.

3 Experiments and Results

An experimental dataset was acquired on a local working farm in Denmark in November 2014. Figure 1 shows the custom-built vehicle-mounted sensor platform including a Velodyne HDL-32E lidar [3]. In addition to the lidar sensor, a number of visual and pose sensors were mounted for subsequent analysis. The recordings include high and low grass, a large number of trees, 2 buildings, 2 cars, 5 men, 7 children, and 2 dogs, all from different angles and distances. 15 lidar frames from 7 different trials (recordings) were subsequently hand labeled into the three classes: ground, vegetation, and object. Results have been obtained using leave-one-out cross-validation (with 7 folds corresponding to the different trials), thereby training on 6 and testing on a single fold at a time. Separating trials in the cross-correlation should prevent overfitting, which would otherwise occur due to high correlation between frames within the same trial.

Table 1 presents a confusion matrix showing the accumulated counts of points across the 7 folds classified correctly or incorrectly compared to the ground truth. As mentioned above, the uneven distribution of ground, vegetation, and object points is evened out by drawing by random a number of these, corresponding to the number of object points, from individual frames. The results show a combined classification accuracy of 91.6 %. Points belonging to the ground are correctly predicted as ground with 96.4 % accuracy, and points belonging to vegetation are correctly predicted as vegetation with 97.5 % accuracy. Object points, however, are more often mistaken for vegetation, resulting in an object detection accuracy of 81.1 %.

Fig. 1. Sensor platform mounted on tractor.

Table 1. Confusion matrix relating predictions (columns) to ground truth (rows).

	Ground	Vegetation	Object
Ground	44806 (96.4%)	1234 (2.7%)	437 (0.9%)
Vegetation	724 (1.6%)	43372 (97.5%)	381 (0.9%)
Object	728 (1.6%)	8041 (17.3%)	37708 (81.1%)

Figure 2 illustrates examples of two frames with ground truth labels and classifier predictions. The problem of object/vegetation confusion is particularly visible in Fig. 2b on the side of the building. Here, around half of the building is incorrectly predicted as vegetation.

Two feature selection techniques were used to investigate the individual importance of the 13 features. Both techniques use only a subset of all combinations of features, since exhaustive search is impractical with $\sum_{f=1}^{13} \binom{13}{f} = 8191$ combinations. In order to evaluate a feature combination, a common metric is needed. Since the features are ultimately used for classification, a wrapper method detecting possible interactions between features was used. The SVM classifier was thus trained on each feature combination, and the accuracy was used as a score.

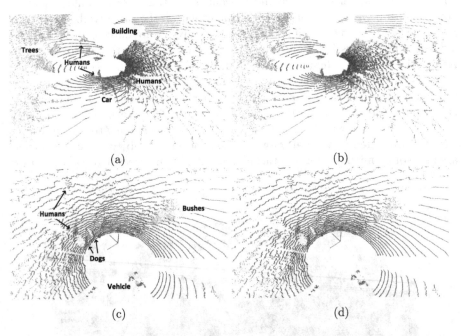

(a)   (b)

(c)   (d)

Fig. 2. Examples of classification results. a) and b) respectively show ground truth and classification results of a scene with ground, trees, humans, a car, and a building. c) and d) respectively show ground truth and classification results of a scene with ground, bushes, humans, and dogs. Blue denotes ground, green denotes vegetation, and red denotes objects (Colour figure online).

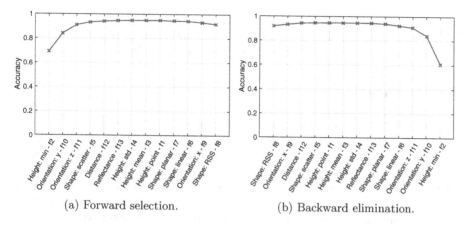

(a) Forward selection.   (b) Backward elimination.

Fig. 3. Feature selection using greedy forward selection and backward elimination.

Greedy forward selection starts by evaluating all features individually and assigns for each a classification score. The feature with the highest score is added to a set of used features, and this set is gradually increased by iteratively adding the highest scoring feature of the remaining unused features. Figure 3a shows the relevance sorting of this approach. The most relevant feature is considered to be f_2 (minimum height), whereas the least relevant is f_8 (RSS).

Greedy backward elimination, on the other hand, starts by evaluating all features in combination leaving out a single feature. The feature that gives the smallest decrease in score is then eliminated, and the process is continued iteratively until a single feature is left. Figure 3b shows the relevance sorting of this approach. As for the forward selection, the most relevant feature is considered to be f_2 (minimum height), and the least relevant is f_8 (RSS).

All computations were performed using C++ on a laptop with an Intel i7 Quad-core CPU at 2.7GHz and 16GB of RAM. The average execution time is 705ms per frame. Preprocessing takes 2.4ms, feature extraction takes 324.9ms, and classification takes 377.9ms.

4   Discussion

Due to the interaction of features, the two feature selection techniques do not fully agree about the sorting of all relevances. However, some observations can be made from the graphs. Using more than 5 features seems to be unnecessary, as it does not significantly increase the accuracy. This is an important observation, since utilizing fewer features results in decreased computational complexity. Another common trend of the two graphs is seen by looking at the three feature categories: height, shape, and orientation. Only one or two features within each category are considered relevant. This implies (but does not prove) that features within each of the categories are correlated and thus redundant. Although the two techniques do not agree about the specific features, they both include a height, shape, and orientation feature among the most relevant four features. A reasonable choice of feature reduction would therefore be to select the intersection of the 5 most significant features from the two selection techniques.

5   Conclusion

In this paper, we have presented an object detection approach for classifying individual points from 3D point clouds acquired with a vehicle-mounted lidar. Our method calculates for each point 13 different features based on a local neighborhood. In order to account for the varying point density experienced with a vehicle-mounted lidar, the neighborhood radius depends on the distance ensuring high resolution at short distance and preventing noisy features at far distance. Using a support vector machine, each point is categorized into one of three classes: ground, vegetation, or object.

The proposed method shows promising results on an experimental dataset recorded on a working farm including grass, trees, buildings, cars, humans, and animals. It has a combined classification accuracy of 91.6 %. Ground points are correctly classified with an accuracy of 96.4 %, and points belonging to vegetation are correctly predicted as vegetation with 97.5 % accuracy. Object points, however, are more often mistaken for vegetation, resulting in an object detection accuracy of 81.1 %.

In order to increase differentiation performance, further work will focus on temporal accumulation of lidar frames using odometry information from GPS and IMU sensors. Also, further differentiation and characterization of objects will require additional information possibly by fusing lidar and vision sensors.

Acknowledgements. This research is sponsored by the Innovation Fund Denmark as part of the project "SAFE - Safer Autonomous Farming Equipment" (project no. 16-2014-0).

References

1. Castano, A., Matthies, L.: Foliage discrimination using a rotating ladar. In: 2003 IEEE International Conference on Robotics and Automation, vol. 1, pp. 1–6 (2003)
2. Chang, C.C., Lin, C.J.: Libsvm: a library for support vector machines. ACM Trans. Intell. Syst. Technol. **2**(3), 1–27 (2011). Article No. 27
3. Christiansen, P., Kragh, M., Steen, K.A., Karstoft, H., Jørgensen, R.N.: Advanced sensor platform for human detection and protection in autonomous farming. In: 10th European Conference on Precision Agriculture (ECPA 2015) (2015)
4. Douillard, B., Underwood, J., Kuntz, N., Vlaskine, V., Quadros, A., Morton, P., Frenkel, A.: On the segmentation of 3D lidar point clouds. In: Proceedings - IEEE International Conference on Robotics and Automation, pp. 2798–2805. IEEE (2011)
5. Fischler, M.A., Bolles, R.C.: Random sample consensus: a paradigm for model fitting with applications to image analysis and automated cartography. Commun. ACM **24**(6), 381–395 (1981)

6. Hadsell, R., Bagnell, J.A., Huber, D., Hebert, M.: Space-carving kernels for accurate rough terrain estimation. Int. J. Robot. Res. **29**(8), 981–996 (2010)
7. Hebert, M., Vandapel, N.: Terrain classification techniques from ladar data for autonomous navigation. In: Collaborative Technology Alliances Conference (2003)
8. Lalonde, J.F., Vandapel, N., Huber, D.F., Hebert, M.: Natural terrain classification using three-dimensional ladar data for ground robot mobility. J. Field Robot. **23**(10), 839–861 (2006)
9. Lalonde, J.F., Unnikrishnan, R., Vandapel, N., Hebert, M.: Scale selection for classification of point-sampled 3D surfaces. In: Proceedings of International Conference on 3-D Digital Imaging and Modeling, 3DIM, pp. 285–292 (2005)
10. Lim, E.H., Suter, D.: 3D terrestrial LIDAR classifications with super-voxels and multi-scale conditional random fields. CAD Comput. Aided Des. **41**(10), 701–710 (2009)
11. Luettel, T., Himmelsbach, M., Wuensche, H.J.: Autonomous ground vehiclesconcepts and a path to the future. In: Proceedings of the IEEE, vol. 100, (Special Centennial Issue), pp. 1831–1839, May 2012
12. Macedo, J., Manduchi, R., Matthies, L.: Ladar-based discrimination of grass from obstacles for autonomous navigation. In: Proceedings of the International Symposium on Experimental Robotics VII (ISER 2001), pp. 111–120 (2001)
13. Manduchi, R., Castano, A., Talukder, A., Matthies, L.: Obstacle detection and terrain classification for autonomous off-road navigation. Auton. Robots **18**(1), 81–102 (2005)
14. Matthies, L., Bergh, C., Castano, A., Macedo, J., Manduchi, R.: Obstacle detection in foliage with ladar and radar. In: Proceedings of ISRR, pp. 291–300 (2003)
15. McDaniel, M.W., Nishihata, T., Brooks, C.A., Lagnemma, K.: Ground plane identification using LIDAR in forested environments. In: Proceedings - IEEE International Conference on Robotics and Automation, pp. 3831–3836 (2010)
16. Spinello, L., Arras, K.O., Triebel, R., Siegwart, R.: A layered approach to people detection in 3d range data. In: Proceedings of the AAAI Conference on Artificial Intelligence: Physically Grounded AI Track (AAAI) (2010)
17. Unnikrishnan, R., Hebert, M.: Multi-scale interest regions from unorganized point clouds. In: 2008 IEEE Computer Society Conference on Computer Vision and Pattern Recognition Workshops, CVPR Workshops (2008)
18. Vandapel, N., Huber, D., Kapuria, A., Hebert, M.: Natural terrain classification using 3-D ladar data. In: Proceedings of IEEE International Conference on Robotics and Automation, ICRA 2004, vol. 5, pp. 5117–5122 (2004)
19. Wellington, C., Stentz, A.: Online adaptive rough-terrain navigation in vegetation. In: Proceedings of IEEE International Conference on Robotics and Automation, ICRA 2004, vol. 1, pp. 96–101 (2004)

Enhanced Residual Orientation for Improving Fingerprint Quality

Jing-Wein Wang[1(✉)], Ngoc Tuyen Le[1], and Tzu-Hsiung Chen[2]

[1] Institute of Photonics and Communications, National Kaohsiung University
of Applied Sciences, Kaohsing 807, Taiwan
jwwang@cc.kuas.edu.tw, tuyennl75@gmail.com
[2] Computer Science and Information Engineering, Taipei Chengshih University
of Science and Technology, Taipei 112, Taiwan
thchen@tpcu.edu.tw

Abstract. Fingerprint possesses unique, hard to lose, and reliable characteristics. In the recent years, it has been widely applied in biometrics. However, in fingerprint identification, blurred images often occur owing to uneven pressing force; and result in recognition errors. This study proposes an innovative fingerprint quality improvement algorithm to enhance the contrast of fingerprint image and to reduce blurs. By employing D4 discrete wavelet transformation, images are transformed from spatial domain to four frequency domain subbands. Then interactive compensation is performed on each band through the multi-resolution characteristic of wavelet transformation and singular value decomposition. Finally, compensated images are reconstructed through inverse-wavelet transformation. After going through our developed fuzzy fingerprint detection system, the fuzzy extent of compensated images can be effectively improved for later backend identification. This study employed NIST-4 and FVC fingerprint databases. The experimental results showed that our method actually could effectively improve blurs in fingerprint.

1 Introduction

Fingerprint sampling is currently divided into contact and non-contact types. Non-contact type mainly uses CCD to capture fingerprint images for processing; the relevant research literatures are fewer. The current mainstream research is still the contact type fingerprint handling. When capture contact type fingerprint images, owing to uneven pressing force of fingers, blurred images of poor-quality often occur and lead to failure in fingerprint feature extraction and recognition errors. Past relevant researches on improving the quality of fingerprint are reviewed as follows. Jirachaweng et al. [1] divided fingerprint into three layers. Then speculated the orientation field pertaining to poor quality and unidentified blocks; and reconstructed, estimated the new orientation field. Ryu et al. [2] tried to find the fingerprint characteristics prior to image processing. If failure occurred due to poor quality, then adjusted the noise level according to input image and added in Gaussian noise. Fingerprint characteristics were enhanced through the noise resonance effect. The research of Zhang et al. [3] adopted the strategy of

© Springer International Publishing Switzerland 2015
L. Nalpantidis et al. (Eds.): ICVS 2015, LNCS 9163, pp. 198–206, 2015.
DOI: 10.1007/978-3-319-20904-3_19

hardware improvement. Through changing the distances between prisms and lens and between lens and charge-coupled devices in fingerprint machine, the captured image resolution of fingerprint machine was enhanced. From the high-resolution fingerprint images, fingerprint minutiae and pores were picked out as identification features to improve the recognition rate. Xie et al. [4] designed orientation field reliable levels by use of fingerprint image characteristic values; and, according to reliable levels, divided the input images into four categories. Then found out the corresponding feature number of each level according to different levels. Finally, the above-mentioned features were classified through radial basis functions and supportive vector machines to achieve the best classification results. In pre-handling, Saquib et al. [5] first determined the fingerprint quality and removed the low-quality images via detection. They suggested a hierarchical analysis method, including eight qualities, three fingerprint overall shapes and five partial blocks. Each hierarchical analysis was given a corresponding score. Then the scores were combined into a single quality score to determine the fingerprint quality. Liu et al. [6] captured fingerprint images using non-contact type fingerprint capture devices; and obtained three fingerprint images through simultaneous shooting from three different angles. Then SIFT (scale-invariant feature transform) and TPS (thin plate spline) were used to capture features and combine the three images into one image. Liu and Yap [7] proposed PCMs (polar complex moments); and captured the rotation invariant features by means of PCMs to reconstruct the fingerprint orientation field. Zhao et al. [8] used a high-resolution contact type fingerprint machine. From the high-resolution images, PVD (pore-valley descriptors) were used to capture the pore characteristics for identification. Lee et al. [9] first calculated the two-dimensional gradient values of the fingerprint image. Then converted the two-dimensional gradient values into two sets of one-dimensional gradient values RR (ridge to ridge direction) and RV (ridge to valley direction). According to different gradient values, the corresponding pdf (probability density function) were applied to calculate the DQD (degree of quality degradation) of the fingerprint image. By observing the aforementioned literatures, it is found that most studies in resolving fuzzy fingerprints intend to reconstruct the orientation field. Galar et al. [10] paid attention on the different learning models considered to build the classifiers used to label new fingerprints. The combination based on taxonomy and classification for the feature extraction, singular point detection, orientation extraction, and learning method was presented. However, these techniques can only be used in block reconstruction which is originally blurred or its orientation field cannot be determined. It is not only inaccurate but also can damage the original information of image. This study proposes a method to improve the fuzzy fingerprint, as shown in Fig. 1. We first employed D4 discrete wavelet conversion [11] to transform the images from space domain to frequency domain, using its multi-resolution characteristic to conduct SVD compensation against different sub-bands. Then the inverse wavelet conversion was conducted to reconstruct the images. Finally, to ensure the extent in improvement, we used the fuzzy fingerprint detection method proposed in this study to determine the effect in improvement of blurred images.

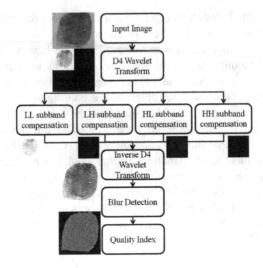

Fig. 1. System flow chart.

2 Proposed System

To improve a fuzzy fingerprint, after obtaining the fingerprint image, making use of the multi-resolution characteristic of D4 discrete wavelet conversion to conduct light compensation in four different frequency sub-bands. Different resolutions contained different types of features, as shown in Fig. 2.

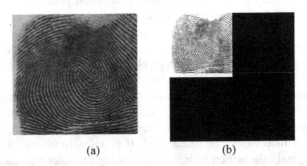

Fig. 2. Wavelet conversion (a) original image, (b) the result after wavelet conversion.

Based on the multi-resolution characteristic, and combining with SVD, the image is undergone D4 discrete wavelet conversion to improve its blurred issue. After D4 wavelets are filtered through low-pass and high-pass filters, the image is decomposed into sub-bands a_{ll}, d_{lh}, d_{hl}, and d_{hh}, representing the images of sub-band frequency domains LL, LH, HL, and HH respectively after image decomposition. Next, we conduct singular value decomposition on the four individual wavelet frequency sub-bands. Equation (1) is the singular value decomposition.

$$s_i = U_i \sum_i V_i^T, \tag{1}$$

s_i is the original image composed of wavelet coefficients. U_i and V_i are all orthogonal matrices, i.e., $U_i^T = U_i^{-1}$, $V_i^T = V_i^{-1}$. Σ_i is the diagonal matrix composed of eigenvalues, corresponding to the energy magnitudes of image. In order to improve the blurred fingerprint images caused by fingerprint pressing, we have designed a compensation coefficient ξ, so that the singular value decomposition has compensation effect as in Eq. (2):

$$s_{ai} = U_i(\xi\Sigma_i)V_i^T, \tag{2}$$

s_{ai} is the image after compensation. After image going through singular value decomposition, the first root is the maximum value, corresponding to the energy of image background. The first root versus second root ratio of singular values corresponds to the contrast of the image; they are negatively related. We achieve the separated effect between fingerprint and background by adjusting the compensation value ξ_{LL} of the LL frequency band. By applying the relationship between the aforementioned ratio of first root and second root of singular values and the contrast of the image to determine the ξ_{LL} value, Eq. (3) is derived.

$$\begin{cases} \frac{\lambda_1}{\lambda_2} > \mu_r + \sigma_r, \xi_{LL} = 1.4 \\ \mu_r + \sigma_r \geq \frac{\lambda_1}{\lambda_2} > \mu_r - \sigma_r, \xi_{LL} = 1.5, \\ \frac{\lambda_1}{\lambda_2} \leq \mu_r - \sigma_r, \xi_{LL} = 1.6 \end{cases} \tag{3}$$

λ_1 and λ_2 are the two roots of singular values prior to inputting images. μ_r is the average value of the ratio of the first two roots of all the image singular values in database. σ_r is the standard deviation of the ratio of the first two roots of all the image singular values in database. Based on the experimental results of NIST-4 fingerprint database [12], we obtain 8.2 and 3.2 respectively for μ_r and σ_r. If the ratio exceeds $\mu_r + \sigma_r$, ξ_{LL} is 1.4; if the ratio exceeds $\mu_r - \sigma_r$ and is less than or equal to $\mu_r + \sigma_r$, ξ_{LL} is 1.5; if it is less than $\mu_r - \sigma_r$, ξ_{LL} is 1.6. The fingerprint image after compensation can effectively remove the background without destroying the fingerprint lines; hence accurate foreground and background separation is achieved. Complete division of fingerprint blocks is useful for rear end handling. It can remove the background noise interference and completely maintain the image information. Input image goes through D4 discrete wavelet conversion prior to compensation. It is necessary to define individual compensation values and weight coefficients in the three frequency domains LH, HL and HH, as shown in the following equation:

$$\text{Max}(\mu_{I_{LL}}, \mu_{I_{LH}}, \mu_{I_{HL}}, \mu_{I_{HH}}) = \mu_{I_M}, \tag{4}$$

$$\xi_{LH} = \sqrt[3]{\left(\frac{\mu_{I_M}}{\mu_{I_{LH}}}\right) * \left(\frac{\text{Max}(\Sigma_{G_{LH}(\mu,\sigma)})}{\text{Max}(\Sigma_{I_{LH}})}\right)}, \tag{5}$$

202   J.-W. Wang et al.

$$\xi_{HL} = \sqrt[3]{\left(\frac{\mu_{I_M}}{\mu_{I_{HL}}}\right) * \left(\frac{\text{Max}\left(\Sigma_{G_{HL}(\mu,\sigma)}\right)}{\text{Max}(\Sigma_{I_{HL}})}\right)},$$ (6)

$$\xi_{HH} = \sqrt[3]{\left(\frac{\mu_{I_M}}{\mu_{I_{HH}}}\right) * \left(\frac{\text{Max}\left(\Sigma_{G_{HH}(\mu,\sigma)}\right)}{\text{Max}(\Sigma_{I_{HH}})}\right)}.$$ (7)

Where, $\mu_{I_{LL}}$, $\mu_{I_{LH}}$, $\mu_{I_{HL}}$, and $\mu_{I_{HH}}$ are the average values of wavelet coefficients in frequency bands LL, LH, HL, and HH respectively; ξ_{LH}, ξ_{HL}, and ξ_{HH} are the individual compensation coefficients of frequency bands LH, HL, and HH respectively. The singular value first root ratio of Gaussian reference image and input image is the basic framework for compensation coefficient. Since the adjustment weights calculated by the maximum singular value corresponding to the wavelet coefficients of input image and the maximum singular value corresponding to the wavelet coefficients of Gaussian reference image may not be suitable for frequency bands LL, LH, HL, and HH, the automatic adjustment of compensation weight method is used here to solve the defects caused by individual adjustment in each frequency band. The method should first calculate the corresponding average value of wavelet coefficients in the four frequency bands LL, LH, HL, and HH; then the maximum average value in the four frequency bands is taken as a reference. The average values of the remained three frequency bands are used to compare with the reference value for dynamic adjustment. Further, the corresponding weights for compensation in each band are determined. Eventually, wavelet inverse conversion is performed on the compensated sub-bands to reconstruct the image. The process is shown in Fig. 3.

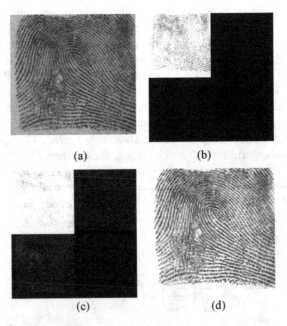

(a)   (b)

(c)   (d)

Fig. 3. Fingerprint image reconstruction (a) original image, (b) the image of original image after D4 discrete wavelet conversion, (c) the image of wavelet coefficients after compensation, (d) the final reconstructed composite image.

3   Fingerprint Fuzzy Detection

So far, there is no unified definition for fuzzy fingerprint. We propose an innovative fuzzy fingerprint detection system as a reference before and after fuzzy fingerprint repair. In this study, through the use of multi-resolution characteristics in two-dimensional non-discrete wavelet conversion, different type of features can be obtained under different frequency resolution. Based on this characteristic, we can conduct two-dimensional non-discrete wavelet conversion on the image. Through the low-pass and high-pass filters, the image is decomposed into two sub-bands d_h and d_l, representing the sub-images of high frequency and low frequency in frequency domain after image decomposition, where d_h band image information representing feature details of image edges. Fingerprint fuzzy blocks in d_h band do not have edge detailed information. Through this characteristic, image information amount in d_h band can be calculated

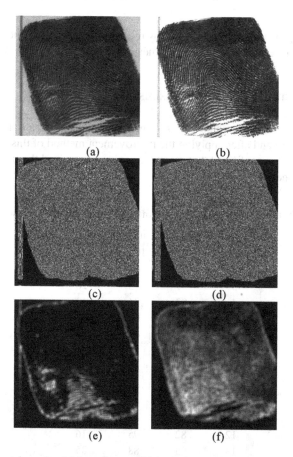

Fig. 4. Experimental results: (a) input image, (b) input image after compensation of this study, (c) entropy mean of input image, (d) entropy mean of input image after compensation of this study, (e) normalized entropy mean of input image (normalized average: 57), (f) normalized entropy mean of input image after compensation of this study (normalized average: 72).

through the average entropy, so as to determine the fuzzy block size. Equation (8) is the judgment method applicable to fuzzy fingerprint detection via average entropy. The results are normalized to facilitate visual observation.

$$e_{dwt} = \frac{-1}{n^2} \sum_{x,y=0}^{n-1} |d_h(x,y)| \log_2 |d_h(x,y)|, \qquad (8)$$

In Eq. (8), d_h is the high-frequency information after two-dimensional non-discrete wavelet conversion; e_{dwt} is the coefficient distribution after doing average entropy against d_h; n is the filter magnitude of average entropy ($n = 13$). To quantify the extent in fuzzy improvement, we have designed a fuzzy progressive value κ. It is defined in Eq. (9),

$$\kappa = \frac{|\mu_{neo} - \mu_{nei}|}{\mu_{nei}} \times 100\%. \qquad (9)$$

In Eq. (9), μ_{nei} is the normalized entropy mean of input image of the original image; μ_{neo} is output image normalized entropy mean of output image (Fig. 4).

4   Experimental Result and Discussion

Table 1 shows the average value variation in entropy mean of partial NIST-4 fingerprint images before and after applying the improvement method of this study. Since the mean of κ is 2.2, it is confirmed that most images have improved the fingerprint quality after using this method.

Table 1. Experimental result of NIST-4 fingerprint database.

Image	μ_{nei}	μ_{neo}	$\kappa(\%)$
1	82	104	27
2	91	106	16
3	57	72	26
4	82	84	2
5	49	60	22
6	44	60	36
7	13	37	185
8	21	29	38
9	12	44	267
10	30	48	60
11	28	44	57
12	82	95	16
13	65	88	35
14	77	86	12
15	57	70	23
Avg.	52.6	68.47	54.8

Through experiments and observations, it was discovered that the κ value of a few images dropped. In the experimental process, we summarized that LL frequency band compensation value would affect background brightness. Too small a compensation value could not separate the foreground from background; too large would fade the fingerprint lines and damage the image. The compensation values in frequency bands LH, HL, and HH mainly affect the edges of fingerprint lines. Too small in compensation value would have no enhancing effect; too large would enhance image noise and cause image distortion. Currently, most images in NIST-4 database can be effectively improved. There are still a few images, owing to too low in contrast, after the compensation of this study, have declined in κ value due to too large in compensation values and hence the destruction of original images.

5   Conclusion

Unlike the general fingerprint researches which look for accurate identification methods but skip and do not discuss fuzzy fingerprints or rebuild the fingerprint orientation field to guess the orientation field characteristics, this study conducts research and discussion without destroying the original image information. Making use of the multi-resolution characteristic in D4 discrete wavelet conversion, we divide into four frequency bands to identify the relevance and conduct singular value interactive compensation in different sub-bands. Then perform inverse wavelet conversion to obtain the output image. Later, through fuzzy fingerprint detection, it is confirmed that this method can significantly improve fuzzy fingerprints. The method proposed not only changes relevant researchers' perceptions in fuzzy fingerprint, but also substantially improves backend fingerprint classification and identification.

Acknowledgment. The authors would like to acknowledge the support received from MOST through project number 103-2221-E-151-037.

References

1. Jirachaweng, S., Hou, Z., Yau, W.Y., Areekul, V.: Residual orientation modeling for fingerprint enhancement and singular point detection. Patt. Recog. **44**, 431–444 (2011)
2. Ryu, C., Kong, S.G., Kim, H.: Enhancement of feature extraction for low-quality fingerprint images using stochastic resonance. Patt. Recog. **32**, 107–113 (2011)
3. Zhang, D., Liu, F., Zhao, Q., Lu, G., Luo, N.: Selecting a reference high resolution for fingerprint recognition using minutiae and pores. IEEE Trans. Instrum. Measure **60**, 863–871 (2011)
4. Xie, S.J., Yang, J.C., Yoon, S., Park, D.S.: An optimal orientation certainty level approach for fingerprint quality estimation. In: Second International Symposium on Intelligent Information Technology Application (IITA), vol. 3, pp. 722–726 (2008)
5. Saquib, Z., Soni, S.K., Vig, R.: Hierarchical fingerprint quality estimation scheme. In: International Conference on Computer Design and Applications, vol. 1, pp. 493–500 (2010)

6. Liu, F., Zhang, D., Song, C., Lu, G.: Touchless multiview fingerprint acquisition and mosaicking. IEEE Trans. Instrum. Measure **62**, 2250–2492 (2013)
7. Liu, M., Yap, P.T.: Invariant representation of orientation fields for fingerprint indexing. Patt. Recog. **45**, 2532–2542 (2012)
8. Zhao, Q., Zhang, D., Zhang, L., Luo, N.: High resolution partial fingerprint alignment using pore-valley descriptors. Patt. Recog. **43**, 1050–1061 (2010)
9. Lee, S., Choi, H., Choi, K., Kim, J.: Fingerprint-quality index using gradient components. IEEE Trans. Inform. Fore. Secu. **3**, 792–800 (2008)
10. Galar, M., Derrac, J., Peleralta, D., Triguero, I., Paternain, D., Lopez-Molina, C., García, S., Benítez, J.M., Pagola, M., Barrenechea, E., Bustince, H., Herrera, F.: A Survey of Fingerprint Classification Part I: Taxonomies on Feature Extraction Methods and Learning Models. Knowledge-based systems (2015)
11. Gonzalez, R.C., Woods, R.E. (eds.): Digital Image Processing, 3rd edn. Prentice Halll, New Jersey (2008)

Learning Human Priors for Task-Constrained Grasping

Martin Hjelm[1], Carl Henrik Ek[1]([✉]), Renaud Detry[2], and Danica Kragic[1]

[1] Autonomous Systems and the Computer Vision and Active Perception Lab,
CSC, KTH Royal Institute of Technology, Stockholm, Sweden
{martinhjelm,chek,danik}@csc.kth.se
[2] University of Liège, Liège, Belgium
renaud.detry@ulg.ac.be

Abstract. An autonomous agent using manmade objects must understand how task conditions the grasp placement. In this paper we formulate task based robotic grasping as a feature learning problem. Using a human demonstrator to provide examples of grasps associated with a specific task, we learn a representation, such that similarity in task is reflected by similarity in feature. The learned representation discards parts of the sensory input that is redundant for the task, allowing the agent to ground and reason about the relevant features for the task. Synthesized grasps for an observed task on previously unseen objects can then be filtered and ordered by matching to learned instances without the need of an analytically formulated metric. We show on a real robot how our approach is able to utilize the learned representation to synthesize and perform valid task specific grasps on novel objects.

1 Introduction

This paper focuses on the problem of how an autonomous agent can discover how different tasks, conditions grasping. The challenge in task based grasping is twofold, first the agent needs to understand the task requirements, secondly it needs to translate these to the object. Formulating the requirements explicitly is not likely to scale beyond simple tasks and objects. Therefore a promising approach is to try to infer the requirements from data using a learning by demonstration approach.

As an example, given a set of demonstrations of pouring, the agent should realize and generalize that the actual constraints lies in, not covering the opening, and in the additional constraints that makes a placed grasp on a specific object successful. This is the fundamental challenge facing data-driven task based grasping.

An important body of work on task based grasping, using a generative model, is Song et al. [1,2]. The authors build a Bayesian Network around gripper, object,

---

This work was supported by the Swedish Foundation for Strategic Research, the Belgian National Fund for Scientific Research (FNRS), the Swedish Research Council, and the EU project EU ERC FLEXBOT.

L. Nalpantidis et al. (Eds.): ICVS 2015, LNCS 9163, pp. 207–217, 2015.
DOI: 10.1007/978-3-319-20904-3_20

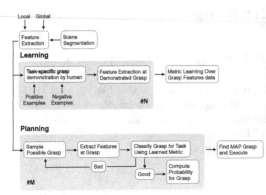

(a) Flow diagram over learning and grasp planning.

(b) Grasps executed using learned task constraints. Handle, cork, pouring, and lift up.

Fig. 1. (a) Flow diagram over learning and grasp planning. (b) Grasps executed using learned task constraints. Handle, cork, pouring, and lift up.

and task parameters; making it possible to condition on task and synthesize task based grasps. Even though the approach shows impressive results on synthetic data, building statistical models of all observations, will place significant constraints on the dimensionality of the observations. It is thus questionable how the approach will perform when the number of tasks and objects increase.

A number of papers instead applies a discriminative approach and learns distributions over local features of the object, Saxena et al. [3], Boularis et al. [4], etc. This avoids the complexity of the generative model but still requires a substantial amount of, often manually, labeled data, which is expensive to obtain.

Rather than using features a successful approach is to represent objects as a set of local templates. Grasping can then be learned on a template basis allowing for transfer of grasps between different objects. The template systems of Detry et al. [5], Herzog et al. [6], Kroemer et al. [7], and Ying et al. [8] have been shown to give good results. The main drawback of these template based systems is their analytical approaches to similarity and the complexity in constructing the template structure. Our method avoids both these drawbacks by learning similarity from the data by learning a representation and utilizing it for matching when synthesizing grasps.

Selecting the features that are relevant for a task to model task constraints is linked with affordances. Stark et al. [9] detects affordance cues, functional parts of the object that the human demonstrator uses for grasping. The agent then uses the cues to plan grasps on objects. Aleotti et al. [10] presents a similar idea which represents objects as a topology. Each demonstrated grasp is associated with one part of the topology. The agent then formulates task constraints around the associated parts.

Instead of trying to decompose or detect functional parts of objects our method revolves around relating previous grasping experience and grounding task constraints in sensory data, similarly to our work in [11]. The features captured from the human demonstrator can therefore be considered as object specific affordance cues that our method learns to generalize.

2   Methodology

Our aim is to be able generate a set of grasps on a previously unseen object that are compatible with a given task, and order them according to relevance.

In the learning process we observe a set of objects and grasps, placed by a human demonstrator, that are suitable to achieve the task. For each grasp on an object we extract a set of features, which capture global and local aspects, which we combine into a vector x. The features, x, captured from a demonstration are labeled with a task variable, t.

Global features describe the object as a whole, for example, how well it approximates a shape primitive, etc. Local features, are features at the grasp of the human demonstrator, for example, local curvature or color. We do not collect any pose information of the demonstrator, since robot-human pose transforms are not the aim of this paper. The demonstration procedure is illustrated in Fig. 3 and the features we capture are described in the feature section.

Given a novel object, and a desired task we wish to infer from a set of synthesized grasps, $G = \{g_i\}_{i=1}^M$, which of them are compatible with the task. For each synthesized grasp we extract a feature vector in the same manner as in the demonstration process, $X_G = \{x_i\}_{i=1}^M$; this is explained further in the Grasp Synthesis section. To select valid grasps from the synthesized set we apply k-Nearest Neighbor (k-NN) classification using the learned instances.

After extracting the set of valid grasps we want to produce a ranking, which reflects how similar a synthesized grasp is to learned instances. We use a Kernel Density Estimate (KDE) over the set of observed instances to produce a likelihood for each of the grasps. The KDE is formed using a Gaussian Kernel and the assumption that a suggested grasp, x^*, is conditionally independent of all other grasps except for the k nearest neighbors, that is,

$$p(x^*|\mathbf{X}_t) = \frac{1}{k} \sum_{x \in \mathbf{X}_k} \mathcal{N}(x^*; x, \mathbf{\Sigma}), \qquad (1)$$

where $\mathbf{X}_k$ is the set of k closest neighbors to x^* found in $\mathbf{X}_t$, the observed instances of the specific task, and $\mathbf{\Sigma}$ is a diagonal matrix. To execute the grasp on the object we choose the most likely synthesized grasp.

2.1   Metric Learning for Feature And Transfer-Selection

Both k-NN and the Gaussian Kernel uses a Euclidian metric to measure feature proximity. It has several shortcomings, as the dimension of the features increases it becomes susceptible to noise, and the inclusion of irrelevant features. Further on, different features have different natural distance measures, and it is unclear how one can weight these.

We instead consider the problem of measuring similarity as a representation learning problem, where we want to learn a task dependent embedding from the data such that similarity is translated into proximity in the embedding. In addition, we want the embedding to reflect which features are relevant to the task.

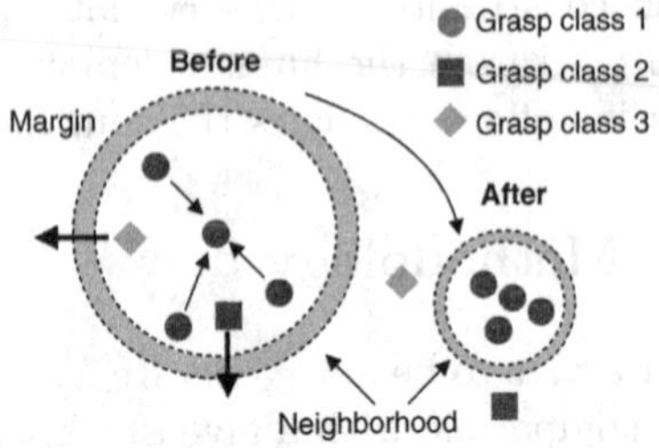

One set of metric learning algorithms, that approaches the problems specified above, are those that try to learn a Mahalanobis metric; that is, a positive semidefinite matrix (PSD), $\mathbf{M}$, that reflects information given about instance distances in the training data.

Since $\mathbf{M}$ is PSD the Mahalanobis

Fig. 2. Figuratively LMNN optimization decides on a set of neighbors for each instance and then tries to push those neighbors towards the instance, while pushing non-class members out of the perimeter of the neighborhood.

metric is equivalent to applying a transform, $\mathbf{L}$ to the data points, where $\mathbf{M} = \mathbf{L}^T\mathbf{L}$, and then computing the Euclidian distance; that is,

$$D(x,y) = (x-y)^T\mathbf{M}(x-y) = \parallel \mathbf{L}(x-y) \parallel_2^2 . \qquad (2)$$

The method we employ in this paper is the Large Margin Nearest Neighbor Classification (LMNN) algorithm [12]. [12] formulates the learning of $\mathbf{M}$ as a semidefinite program (SDP) which tries to compress distances between subsets of instances of the same class, called target neighborhoods, while pushing out non-class members, called impostors, outside a specified margin. See Fig. 2 for an illustration.

minimize

$$(1-\mu)\Sigma_{i,i\rightsquigarrow j}(x_i - x_j)^T\mathbf{M}(x_i - x_j) + \mu\Sigma_{i,i\rightsquigarrow j,l}(1-y_{il})\xi_{ijl}$$

subject to

$$(x_i - x_l)^T\mathbf{M}(x_i - x_l) - (x_i - x_j)^T\mathbf{M}(x_i - x_j) \geq 1 - \xi_{ijl}$$

$$\xi_{ijl} \geq 0$$

$$\mathbf{M} \succeq 0$$

(3)

The first term in the objective function is the Mahalanobis distance which penalizes large distances between target neighbors. The second term is the slack variables that mimics the convex hinge loss. The indices i,j specify target neighbors, and l impostors. The slack variables, ξ_{ijl}, are over all triplets of target neighborhoods and measure the amount of violation of the margin in the transformed space.

The target neighbors subsets are determined by either a priori specified information about similarity or in the absence as the instances with minimum

Euclidian distance in the original space. The cardinality of the target neighborhoods is set manually.

M is learned by exploiting the fact that most target neighborhoods are homogenous allowing the optimization to work on subsets of the constraints involving the neighborhoods. **M** can thus be found using sub-gradients of the loss function with standard hill-climbing algorithms, together with a step where **M** is projected onto the cone of all positive semidefinite matrices [12].

Learning **M**, for D-dimensional data, requires learning D^2 entries of the matrix, the parameters of the model. With few data points that are high-dimensional overfitting can occur. Since data points are expensive to obtain we want to reduce the number of parameters. By letting **M** be diagonal, we only need to learn D parameters. Instead of penalizing any non-zero off-diagonal elements in **M** in the objective function we set all off-diagonal elements to zero, in the update step. The optimization process will thus find the diagonal matrix that minimizes the cost function.

LMNN translates neatly into our feature representation for grasps. The diagonalization of **M** allows us to treat the diagonal elements as feature weights, where low values indicates non-discriminative features and therefore irrelevant features for a task. The matrix found by LMNN thus implicitly facilitates feature selection. By analyzing the magnitudes for a specific task we can compare with our expectations of which features are important.

2.2 Features

We are interested in exploiting the fact that objects with similar function follow similar form. There is also evidence that humans make inference about the world by considering both global and local observations, [13], [14], and that both aspects enhance inference [15].

Given the above observations we are interested formulating features that capture both global and local aspects of the object. Since we a priori cannot know which of them will be important for a task it is reasonable to select many simple and broad features over those that are more discriminatory. In addition, having multiple features will help when sensors fails, or give incorrect information.

We capture information from a grasp by extracting features from a bounding box around the grasp and merging them with global descriptors of the object into a 104 dimensional vector. The process is illustrated in Fig. 3. We go over the features briefly below and provide motivation when needed.

[**Shape Primitives**] - Scoring function for how well the object resembles a spherical, cylindrical, and cuboid.

[**Elongatedness**] - The ratio of the minor axes to the major axis.

[**Relative Free volume**] - The volume of the part of the object enclosed by the grasp cuboid divided by the volume of the object.

[**Relative Grasping Position**] - The relative position of the grasp on the axes of the object, that is, the ratio of the position of the grasp on the main axes divided by the axes

[**Openings**] - The opening feature detects openings on objects, parametrized as a 3D circle, and produces: - A binary value for the existence of an opening. - The angle the grasp cuboid center makes with respect to the openings normal - The signed relative orthogonal distance to the openings plane.

[**Bag of Words Histogram over Fast Point Feature**] - To encode local curvature we create a Bag of Words model over the Fast Point Feature Histogram (FPFH) [16] using a small set of 30 keywords. For each of the points in a recorded grasp we extract count-normalized histogram (CNH) over the keywords.

[**Intensity and Gradient Filters**] - We apply gradient filters of first, second, and third order over the 2D window containing the object. We also extract the intensity values. For each of the points in a recorded grasp we compute CNHs for each of the filter values and the intensity values.

[**Color Quantization**] - We are interested in comparing color against color at the grasp point, as there are reoccurring color patterns in human design. We segment the image using the segmentation algorithm of [17] and encode each patch with its closest color from a chart of 15 different colors, in CIELab space. Each point in the point cloud of the object thus gets a quantized color assigned to it. For a grasp we compute the CNH of the quantized colors of the points captured by the grasp.

[**Color Uniformity**] - We are also interested in the uniformity of the colors since objects, usually have areas that have a single colors to indicate some form of function, for a grasp we compute the entropy, mean and variance of the CNH color quantization.

2.3   Grasp Synthesis

Generating constructive grasps on a partial point cloud of an object is difficult. Models that rely on collision detection are not applicable due to the partial representation of the object. Our method for generating grasps mimics the method found in [18] but instead uses the information found in the point cloud and point cloud normals. In short, we slice the object with a plane constructed by points in the point cloud, and select an approach vector that is orthogonal to the plane. The width of gripper is computed by taking the minimum point spread of the two orthogonal directions to the plane. The height of the gripper is set to a random value. The bounding box generated by the gripper is used to extract the feature representation for the synthesized grasp.

3   Experiments

In evaluating our approach, we want to verify a number of things: - That our method can order its nearest neighbors better than k-NN - That the ordering is reasonable - That the approach can separate different groupings of grasps reasonably well - That the features that LMMN picks out resonates with what could be expected for the specific task - That the grasps we generate are in fact useful, placed at the proper positions and executable

The object is placed in front of the robot, who examines it and records a set of global and local features from image and point cloud data.	A human demonstrates a set of grasps on the object to the robot. For each grasp the robot records a bounding box around the grasp and extracts the local features contained in the box. Each grasp is annotated for belonging to classes of tasks that the grasps is valid for. In the figure the first and second grasp are positive grasps for pouring, while the third is a negative example.

Fig. 3. Procedure for learning from demonstration.

3.1 Data Collection

We perform the collection of object-grasp data using a Kinect camera with objects placed on a flat surface in front of the robot. The robot observes and segments out the object and records features over the object. A human demonstrator performs both positive and negative grasp examples for four different tasks: *lift up, pouring, handle, and corks*. The robot observes the grasp placement and the local features as captured by a box around the hand placement. The procedure is illustrated in Fig. 3.

3.2 Learning

We preprocess the non-histogram features by scaling to unit variance. To evaluate the learning we run the LMNN and k-NN a 100 times, using random splits of the collected data with a ratio of 70 % training and 30 % test data. We also make sure that each split contains at least 25 % positive and negative examples. The reason for this lies in the formulation of LMNN that allows instances some slack in fulfilling the optimization constraints. The gradient descent optimization is thus prone to allowing the smaller class to violate the constraints while optimizing for the bigger class. If the positive example's relevant features have been erased by the feature learning process then comparison to previously learned instances in the grasp synthesis phase becomes reliant on comparison to irrelevant features.

We use 5 nearest neighbors to evaluate the classification rate. As can be seen in Fig. 4 LMNN is superior to k-NN performing better, roughly by 3–7 % for all grasps classes. The curves for the class agreement as a function of the nearest neighbor in Fig. 6, are also consistent for the LMNN while k-NN declines quite rapidly as the order increases. Further on, k-NN has much more variance. A possible explanation for the decline in the lift up task is that the features that explain a correct grasping position might be less distinct compared to handles or corks.

	Pouring	Lift Up	Handle	Cork
k-NN	[92.3%, 9.8]	[77.6%, 9.3]	[77.0%, 8.4]	[88.5%, 7.0]
LMNN	[95.2%, 5.5]	[80.5%, 10.2]	[84.5%, 7.6]	[95.5%, 3.9]

Fig. 4. k-NN and LMNN mean accuracy and standard deviation in classification of demonstrated grasp instances.

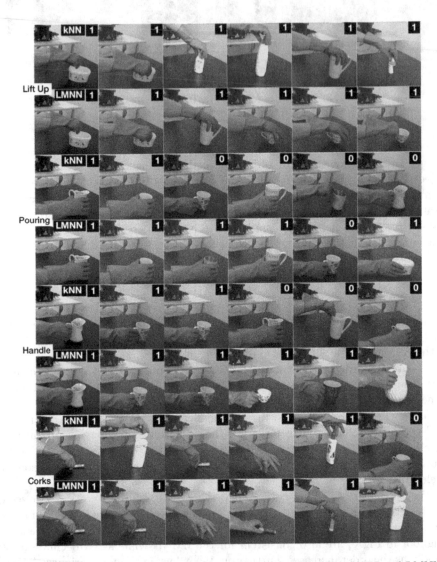

Fig. 5. 5 Nearest Neighbors to test instances for the four tasks for k-NN and LMNN. The number 0 and red overlay indicates an instance of another class than the test instance. The LMNN ordering is much more sensical than the k-NN. For example in the corks task, k-NN chooses the cork of a cleaning fluid bottle as the nearest neighbor while LMNN picks the cork of similar looking pen as the nearest neighbor. In the pouring task, where we have defined the handle grasps as not good for pouring for the robot's limited gripper, LMMN manages produce a much more sensical ordering than the k-NN which includes several handle grasps instances.

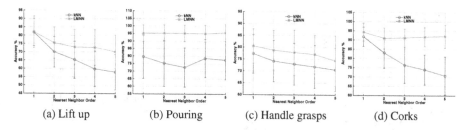

| (a) Lift up | (b) Pouring | (c) Handle grasps | (d) Corks |

Fig. 6. k-NN versus LMNN accuracy if using only the k-th neighbor for classification. The low negative incline of the LMNN versus the k-NN indicates that learned transform improves consistency.

Quantitatively LMNN outperforms k-NN as could be expected. Less clear is if the embedding actually re-orders objects in an order that is sensical to a human observer. In Fig. 5 we have included a set of grasp instances and their 5 closest neighbors. As can be seen the ordering in the LMNN embedding makes more sense. For example, in the case of the pen cork k-NN has it that the nearest neighbor is the cork of a cleaning fluid bottle while LMNN puts a similar pen as the nearest neighbor. Similar orderings can be observed in the other examples and indicates that LMNN through the embedding finds a more sensical ordering.

3.3   Feature Selection

Feature selection in our context means that the LMNN diagonal have low to zero values for irrelevant features and high for relevant. One way of analyzing the selection is to look at the mean value and standard deviation across the 100 runs. A detailed analysis is provided in Fig. 7.

3.4   Grasping

To evaluate how the model is able to transfer the demonstrated instances to grasp novel objects we select a set of unseen objects for each task and generate a 10000 positive samples using 1-NN for classification. We pick the most likely grasp as the one to perform on the object. The final grasps are illustrated in Fig. 1.

4   Conclusion

We have presented an approach for task based grasping based on metric learning. Our approach use demonstrations to learn a task-specific representation with the characteristic that distances reflect grasp similarity according to the demonstrated semantic. This allows us to use simple distance based heuristics to transfer grasps from objects in the training data-base to novel objects. We show experiments on a real robot where execution is performed on previously unseen objects according to the semantic learned during demonstration. In future work

216   M. Hjelm et al.

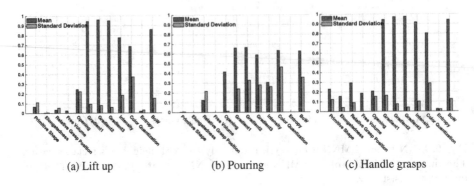

(a) Lift up   (b) Pouring   (c) Handle grasps

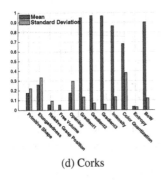

(d) Corks

Fig. 7. Mean values and standard deviation of the LMNN transformation matrix diagonal as per feature. A value close to zero means that the feature is considered irrelevant for separation by the LMNN. A value close to 1 and low standard deviation indicates that the feature is always present and of low relevance for separation by the LMNN. In (**a**), the lift up task, we expect that no feature is predominant since lift-up is more pose dependent than feature dependent. And as can be seen intensity, color quantization, and the BoW are the most relevant features. In (**b**), the pouring task, we would expect the opening to be the most relevant feature, and it has a value of around 0.4 with low standard deviation as could be expected. The BoW, gradient and intensity are all significant factors which can be explained by the similarity of objects that affords pouring. In (**c**), the handle grasp task, we would expect the shape to play a predominant role. However, as the diagram indicates the relative grasping position, color quantization and the opening features are also factors. In (**d**), the grasping of corks, the color quantization is an important factor as could be expected. Primitive shape and elongatnedness are also factors which can be explained by the fact that most items with corks are elongated and have a more cylindrical shape.

we plan to extend the model to include information about how the human demonstrator grasped the object, such as approach vector, type of grasp, etc. Including this information will give the agent the ability to understand how the human demonstrator's grasp relates to its own embodiment.

References

1. Song, D., Huebner, K., Kyrki, V., Kragic, D.: Learning task constraints for robot grasping using graphical models. In: IROS (2010)
2. Song, D., Ek, C.H., Huebner, K., Kragic, D.: Embodiment-specific representation of robot grasping using graphical models and latent-space discretization. In: IROS, pp. 980–986 (2011)
3. Saxena, A., Driemeyer, J., Ng, A.Y.: Robotic grasping of novel objects using vision. Int. J. Robot. Res. **27**(2), 157–173 (2008)
4. Boularias, A., Kroemer, O., Peters, J.: Learning robot grasping from 3-D images with Markov Random Fields. In: IROS, pp. 1548–1553 (2011)
5. Detry, R., Ek, C.H., Madry, M., Kragic, D.: Learning a dictionary of prototypical grasp-predicting parts from grasping experience. In: ICRA (2011)
6. Herzog, A., Pastor, P., Kalakrishnan, M., Righetti, L., Asfour, T., Schaal, S.: Template-based learning of grasp selection. In: ICRA (2012)
7. Kroemer, O., Ugur, E., Oztop, E., Peters, J.: A kernel-based approach to direct action perception. In: ICRA, pp. 2605–2610 (2012)
8. Ying, L., Fu, J.L., Pollard, N.S.: Data-driven grasp synthesis using shape matching and task-based pruning. IEEE Trans. Visual Comput. Graphics **13**(4), 732–747 (2007)
9. Stark, M., Lies, P., Zillich, M., Wyatt, J.C., Schiele, B.: Functional object class detection based on learned affordance cues. In: Gasteratos, A., Vincze, M., Tsotsos, J.K. (eds.) ICVS 2008. LNCS, vol. 5008, pp. 435–444. Springer, Heidelberg (2008)
10. Aleotti, J., Caselli, S.: Part-based robot grasp planning from human demonstration. In: ICRA, pp. 4554–4560 (2011)
11. Hjelm, M., Detry, R., Ek, C.H., Kragic, D.: Cross-object grasp transfer. In: ICRA, Representations for Cross-task (2014)
12. Weinberger, K.Q., Saul, L.K.: Distance metric learning for large margin nearest neighbor classification. J. Mach. Learn. Res. **10**, 207–244 (2009)
13. Bertenthal, B.I.: Origins and early development of perception, action, and representation. Annu. Rev. Psychol. **47**(1), 431–459 (1996)
14. Berthier, N.E., Clifton, R.K., Gullapalli, V., McCall, D.D., Robin, D.J.: Visual information and object size in the control of reaching. J. Mot. Behav. **28**(3), 187–197 (1996)
15. Csurka, G., Dance, C., Fan, L., Willamowski, J., Bray, C.: Visual categorization with bags of keypoints. In: Workshop on Statistical Learning in Computer Vision, ECCV, vol. 1, pp. 1–2. Prague (2004)
16. Rusu, R.B., Blodow, N., Beetz, M.: Fast Point Feature Histograms (FPFH) for 3D registration. In: ICRA, pp. 3212–3217 (2009)
17. Felzenszwalb, P.F., Huttenlocher, D.P.: Efficient graph-based image segmentation. Int. J. Comput. Vis. **59**(2), 167–181 (2004)
18. Bergström, N., Bohg, J., Kragic, D.: Integration of visual cues for robotic grasping. In: Fritz, M., Schiele, B., Piater, J.H. (eds.) ICVS 2009. LNCS, vol. 5815, pp. 245–254. Springer, Heidelberg (2009)

Region-of-Interest Retrieval in Large Image Datasets with Voronoi VLAD

Aaron Chadha and Yiannis Andreopoulos[(✉)]

Department of Electrical and Electronic Engineering,
University College London (UCL), London, UK
i.andreopoulos@ucl.ac.uk

Abstract. We investigate the problem of visual-query based retrieval from large image datasets when the visual queries comprise arbitrary regions of interest (ROI) rather than entire images. Our proposal is a compact image descriptor that combines the vector of locally aggregated descriptors (VLAD) of Jegou *et. al.* with a multi-level, Voronoi-based, spatial partitioning of each dataset image, and it is termed as the Voronoi VLAD (VVLAD). The proposed multi-level Voronoi partitioning uses a spatial hierarchical K-means over interest-point locations, and computes a VLAD over each cell. In order to reduce the matching complexity when handling very large datasets, we propose the following modifications. First, we utilize the tree structure of the spatial hierarchical K-means to perform a top-to-bottom pruning for local similarity maxima, rather than exhaustively matching against all cells (Fast-VVLAD). Second, we propose to aggregate VLADs of adjacent Voronoi cells in order to reduce the overall VVLAD storage requirement per image. Finally, we propose a new image similarity score for Fast-VVLAD that combines relevant information from all partition levels into a single measure for similarity. For a range of ROI queries in two standard datasets, Fast-VVLAD achieves comparable or higher mean Average Precision against the state-of-the-art Multi-VLAD framework while offering more than two-fold acceleration.

1 Introduction

Image retrieval based on visual queries is now a topic of intensive research interest since it finds many applications in visual search, detection of copyright violation, recommendation services, object or person identification, etc. [1]. The state-of-the-art for image retrieval is to first describe salient points in images using a locally-invariant feature descriptor, such as SIFT [2]. A visual vocabulary is then learned using K-means or a mixture of Gaussians (MoG), which quantize the feature space into cells (visual words). The SIFT cell assignments are then aggregated over the image to obtain a compact image representation [3]. Notable contributions in this domain have relied on the bag-of-words (BoW) image representation, or its derivatives [1,4,5], where the number of SIFTs assigned to each visual word is aggregated into a histogram used for retrieval purposes.

This work was funded in part by Innovate UK, project REVQUAL (101855), and EPSRC (Industrial PhD CASE award, co-sponsored by BAFTA).

© Springer International Publishing Switzerland 2015
L. Nalpantidis et al. (Eds.): ICVS 2015, LNCS 9163, pp. 218–227, 2015.
DOI: 10.1007/978-3-319-20904-3_21

Despite the success of BoW approaches, their large storage and memory access requirements make them unsuitable for image retrieval within very large image datasets (e.g., tens of millions of images). For such problems, the current state-of-the-art is the vector of locally aggregated descriptors (VLAD) [6], which is a non-probabilistic variant of the Fisher vector image descriptor [7] that encodes the distribution of SIFT assignments according to cluster centers. VLAD has been shown to achieve very competitive retrieval performance to BoW methods with substantially smaller complexity and memory footprint, i.e., requiring 16–256 bytes per image instead of tens of kilobytes, as in BoW methods [6].

We are interested in the problem of designing a visual-query based retrieval system that is capable of handling both small and large-size "object", or, more broadly, region-of-interest (ROI) queries over very large image datasets. Given a ROI representing a visual query, the proposed system should return all images from the database containing this query, with matching complexity and storage requirements that remain of the order of VLAD. This is considerably more challenging than whole-image retrieval systems, as the query object may be occluded or distorted, or be seen from different viewpoints and distances in relevant images [8]. This is also the reason why the original VLAD proposal does not perform well for this problem [9]. We therefore propose a new compact image descriptor based on VLAD, termed as Voronoi VLAD (VVLAD), in which we spatially partition the image, using a hierarchical K-means, into Voronoi cells and thus compute multiple VLADs over cells. We couple this with an adaptive search algorithm via which we minimize the overall computation for similarity identification by first finding the cells most representative to the query and then computing a single score for the image over these cells. Our system design for object retrieval adheres to the following principles:

1. The system should improve on the VLAD mean Average Precision (mAP) when ROI queries are small relative to the image size.
2. The system should maintain competitive mAP to VLAD under ROI queries occupying a sizeable proportion (or the entirety) of images.
3. The system should be amenable to big-data processing, i.e., its image descriptors' size and matching complexity should be closer to that of VLAD rather than BoW descriptors.

In the following section we discuss the background and related work. In Sect. 3 we present the offline and online components of our proposed system, including the VVLAD descriptor upon which our system is derived. Section 4 presents experimental results on the Holidays [10] and Caltech Cars (Rear) datasets [11], and Sect. 5 draws concluding remarks.

2   Background and Related Work

2.1   VLAD

VLAD is a fixed-size compact image representation that stores first order information associated with clusters of image salient points. In essence, VLAD is intrinsically related to the Fisher vector image descriptor [12].

In the offline part of the VLAD encoding, a visual word vocabulary is first learned using K-means and comprises K clusters with cluster centers $\mathbf{M} = \{\boldsymbol{\mu}_1, \boldsymbol{\mu}_2, \ldots, \boldsymbol{\mu}_K\}$. For each image I, N interest points are detected using an affine invariant detector and described using d-dimensional SIFT descriptors, thus forming a descriptor ensemble $\mathbf{X} = \{\boldsymbol{x}_1, \boldsymbol{x}_2, \ldots, \boldsymbol{x}_N\}$. The descriptors $\boldsymbol{x}_n$, $1 \leq n \leq N$, are assigned to the nearest cluster in the vocabulary via a cluster assignment function $f(\boldsymbol{x}_i)$. VLAD then stores the residuals of the SIFT assignments from their associated cluster centers. The VLAD d-dimensional encoding $\boldsymbol{v}_k$ for the k-th cluster is given by $(1 \leq k \leq K)$ $\boldsymbol{v}_k = \sum_{\forall \boldsymbol{x}_i : f(\boldsymbol{x}_i) = k} (\boldsymbol{x}_i - \boldsymbol{\mu}_k)$. The VLAD encodings for each cluster are concatenated into a single descriptor $\boldsymbol{\phi}(I) = [\boldsymbol{v}_1, \ldots, \boldsymbol{v}_K]^{\mathrm{T}}$ with fixed dimension Kd, which is independent of the number of the SIFT descriptors found in the image. The VLAD vectors are then sign square rooted and L_2-normalized [13] and the vectors across all W images of a dataset are thus aggregated into a single $Kd \times W$ matrix $\boldsymbol{\Phi} = [\boldsymbol{\phi}_1, \ldots, \boldsymbol{\phi}_W]$.

In a practical system, the SIFT descriptor length d is typically 128; if the feature space is coarsely quantized with K set to 64, then the VLAD image descriptor has 8192 dimensions. Further dimensionality reduction is achieved with principal component analysis (PCA) and whitening, thus further minimizing the memory footprint per image descriptor [14,15]. The $D \times Kd$ projection matrix used by VLAD comprises only the D largest eigenvectors of the covariance matrix [14,15]. The projected VLAD $\tilde{\boldsymbol{\phi}}_{\text{test}}$ of each test image is then L_2-normalized, thereby completing the offline part of the VLAD generation.

During online ROI-query based retrieval, after the VLAD encoding of the ROI query has been generated, the similarity between that and the VLAD of a test image, $\tilde{\boldsymbol{\phi}}_{\text{ROI}}$ and $\tilde{\boldsymbol{\phi}}_{\text{test}}$, is simply measured by:

$$S_{\text{ROI,test}} = \left\langle \tilde{\boldsymbol{\phi}}_{\text{ROI}}, \tilde{\boldsymbol{\phi}}_{\text{test}} \right\rangle. \tag{1}$$

With L_2 normalized vectors, $S_{\text{ROI,test}}$ ranges between -1 (completely dissimilar) to 1 (perfect match).

2.2   Multi-VLAD

For ROI-based retrieval, VLAD and the similarity measure of (1) will produce suboptimal results because information encoded from the remaining parts of the dataset image will distort the similarity scoring [9]. The recently-proposed Multi-VLAD descriptor [9] attempts to resolve this issue by spatially partitioning the dataset images into rectangular blocks over three scales and computing a VLAD descriptor per block. At the finest scale (level 2), nine VLADs are encoded over a 3×3 rectangular grid. At medium scale (level 1), four VLADs are encoded over a 2×2 grid, where each block is composed of 2×2 blocks from the finest scale. Finally, a single VLAD is encoded over the whole dataset image (level 0). At each scale, Multi-VLAD excludes featureless regions near image borders by adjusting the grid boundary. Moreover, each VLAD is PCA projected and truncated to a 128-dimensional vector. The similarity is thus computed between the VLAD encoded over the query ROI and each of the 14 VLAD descriptors via

(1) and the dataset image is assigned a similarity score to the ROI equal to the maximum similarity over its constituent VLADs.

For ROI queries occupying about 11 % of image real estate, the Multi-VLAD descriptor has been shown to outperform the single (128×14)-D VLAD (computed over the whole image) in terms of mAP. However, Multi-VLAD achieves 20 % lower mAP than the (128×14)-D VLAD when queries occupy a sizeable proportion of the image [9]. In addition, it incurs a 14-fold penalty in storage and matching complexity in comparison to the baseline 128-D VLAD.

3   Proposed Voronoi-Based VLAD and its Fast Variant

The proposed VVLAD encoding, described in Subsect. 3.1, constitutes the offline component of our system. The remaining two subsections describe of the proposed acceleration for online VVLAD-based ROI query search and the memory compaction to reduce storage requirements for very large image datasets.

3.1   VVLAD Encoding

Instead of spatially partitioning the images into rectangular blocks, we propose to partition the image into Voronoi cells over L levels (scales), using hierarchical spatial K-means clustering. The key intuition is that objects that may constitute ROI queries tend to appear as clusters of salient points, potentially interspersed with featureless regions in the image. Therefore, a ROI-oriented partitioning must attempt to adaptively isolate these spatial clusters at multiple levels.

Initially, the entire image is VLAD-encoded; this comprises level 0 of VVLAD. For level 1, a spatial K-means is computed over the interest point locations in the whole image, which effectively partitions the image into V_1 Voronoi cells. Next, for level 2, a spatial K-means is computed over the interest point locations within each level-1 Voronoi cell, thus partitioning each cell into V_2 constituent cells. In general, for level l, $1 \leq l < L$, each of the V_{l-1} cells of the previous level is partitioned into V_l cells, with $V_0 \triangleq 1$. A VLAD descriptor is encoded over each cell following the description of Sect. 2.1, giving a total of $V_{tot} = 1 + \sum_{l=1}^{L-1} \prod_{m=1}^{l} V_m$ VLADs per image. As such, we construct a single PCA projection matrix for the utilized image training set. When PCA projecting the VLAD of each cell, we aggregate each level l into a single matrix Φ_l.

A three-level Voronoi partitioning for an image from the Caltech Cars image dataset with $V_1 = V_2 = 3$ is illustrated in Fig. 1. The detected points are shown in color in the left image of Fig. 1, and the level-1 and level-2 Voronoi cells are superimposed with dashed lines on the middle and right image (resp.), with their corresponding descriptors appearing with different colors. Evidently, there is an intrinsic dependency on the characteristics of the feature point detector. For ROI-based retrieval, we require a detector robust to scale and viewpoint changes, which detects enough points in salient regions to allow for reliable partitioning. Therefore, we use the Hessian Affine detector [16,17], which is based on the multi-scale determinant of the Hessian matrix (computed locally), and detects affine

Fig. 1. Three-level Voronoi partitioning for an image from Caltech Cars dataset. For illustration purposes, SIFT descriptors are color-differentiated for each cell (Color figure online).

covariant regions. SIFT descriptors are then produced based on the detected points. Importantly, unlike Multi-VLAD, there is no need to preprocess the image and exclude featureless regions: as shown in Fig. 1, smaller Voronoi cells are adaptively formed around regions of tight clusters of detected points.

3.2   Adaptive Search for Fast-VVLAD and Image Score

For the standard VVLAD encoding we assign an image score as the global maximum similarity over cells, using (1) for each cell. However, the proposed Voronoi partitioning essentially gives us a tree of spatial Voronoi cells where, for L levels, $\prod_{l=1}^{L-1} V_l$ "leaf" Voronoi cells exist at the bottom of the tree. Given that there is inherent mutual information between a cell and its constituent cells, rather than accessing data for all levels and measuring VLAD similarity over all V_{tot} cells of the tree indiscriminately, we can design an adaptive search with top-to-bottom tree pruning to find the most relevant Voronoi cells to the query. This reduces the overall execution time and memory accesses when a query is processed, which makes our proposal applicable to very large image databases that would contain millions of images. The top-to-bottom search is carried out in two phases.

Phase-1: Considering the cell of level $l-1$ with maximum similarity to the query [measured via (1)], in Phase-1 of the search, we assume that either this cell or a constituent cell within it (at level l) will attain high similarity to the query. If the cell of level $l-1$ is found to attain the highest similarity to the query, we terminate the search for that image at level $l-1$ and proceed to Phase-2. On the other hand, if we find that a constituent cell of level l attains the maximum similarity, we repeat Phase-1 for that cell and its constituent cells at the next level $(l+1)$, until we reach the bottom of the tree, in which case we move to Phase-2.

Phase-2: Let us denote the maximum similarity found by Phase-1 for each level l as S_l^* and assume that Phase-1 exited at level l_{ph1}, $0 \leq l_{\text{ph1}} \leq L-1$. Rather than assigning $S_{l_{\text{ph1}}}^*$ as the similarity score between the ROI query and the test image I in the dataset, we perform a weighted sum over all $S_0^*, \ldots, S_{l_{\text{ph1}}}^*$. To this end, we first compute the difference d_l, $0 \leq l \leq l_{\text{ph1}}$, between the number of interest points in the query and the number of interest points in the image dataset cell corresponding to S_l^*. This difference is subsequently used within a scaled

Gaussian function, which serves as a smoothing function and also handles cases where $d_l = 0$. The weight for S_l^* ($0 \leq l \leq l_{\text{ph1}}$) is thus defined as $w_l = \exp\left(\frac{-d_l^2}{\sigma^2}\right)$ and the level of smoothing is controlled by σ. The weight vector over all levels is L_1-normalized so that the image score can be ranked independently of the level l_{ph1} at which Phase-1 terminated. Denoting the L_1-normalized weight as $\hat{w}_l$, the proposed similarity score between a ROI query and dataset image I after Phase-2 is:

$$S_{\text{ROI},I} = \sum_{l=0}^{l_{\text{ph1}}} \hat{w}_l S_l^*. \tag{2}$$

For example, for a three-level partition, if a query object is small relative to the image size, we expect that the total number of interest points over the query would be more comparable to that of a level-2 cell. Hence, the level-2 maximum dot product S_2^* should receive the largest weighting $\hat{w}_2$ when computing the similarity score. This is expected to be a more robust similarity scoring than just taking a global maximum over all $S_0^*, \ldots, S_{l_{\text{ph1}}}^*$ (as in Multi-VLAD) as the similarity score, since we account for relevant information from all levels.

Summary: We term this two-phase search for VVLAD as the Fast-VVLAD, because it reduces the expected number of cell VLADs that are accessed at runtime. The upper bound for the Fast-VVLAD's matching complexity is $1 + \sum_{l=1}^{\min\{l_{\text{ph1}}+1, L-1\}} V_l$ inner products per image instead of the V_{tot} inner products required by VVLAD. Finally, due to the weights of (2), per image I, along with the VVLAD vector we also store the number of interest points per cell, comprising V_{tot} additional values. These values can be quantized to four bits each in order to reduce their storage requirement.

3.3 Level Projection for VVLAD Storage Compaction

Beyond the online matching complexity reduction offered by Fast-VVLAD, we can adhere to memory constraints of a practical deployment for very-large image datasets by only storing offline the PCA projected VLADs for the last level, $L-1$ and computing the VLADs for levels $0, \ldots, L-2$ at runtime by aggregating smaller-cell VLADs. Specifically, in the storage-efficient VVLAD, the VLAD descriptor over two constituent cells x and y (i.e., spatially-neighboring cells belonging to the same cell of the upper level), is simply found as the sum of their VLADs:

$$\tilde{\phi}_{x \cup y} = \tilde{\phi}_x + \tilde{\phi}_y. \tag{3}$$

This holds because both PCA and whitening are linear mappings, therefore, if we do not consider the L_2 normalization of the individual VLAD vectors, the additivity property holds in the projected domain as well. Given that directionality is preserved under normalization, (3) provides a close approximation to the normalized VLAD computed directly over the two cells. Therefore, we can trade-off computation for memory by solely storing the last-level PCA-projected VLADs (level $L-1$) and computing all other VLADs for all lower levels at runtime via repetitive application of (3) amongst constituent cells and renormalizing before carrying out the similarity measurement of (1). We remark that vectorized addition and scaling for normalization is extremely inexpensive in modern SIMD-based architectures. As such, this approach requires offline storage for only $\prod_{l=1}^{L-1} V_l$, instead of V_{tot} VLAD vectors.

4 Experimental Evaluation

4.1 Datasets and Evaluation Procedure

We measure performance on the Holidays and Caltech Cars (Rear) image datasets. For both datasets, a set of predefined queries and hand-annotated ground truth is used. The Hessian Affine rotation-and-affine-invariant detector [17] is used for feature detection and SIFT is used for feature description.

Caltech Cars (Rear) [11]: This dataset consists of 1155 (360 × 240) photographs of cars taken from the rear. For the purposes of this paper, we take a subset 800 images and use 400 images for learning the PCA projection matrix and visual word centers and 400 as test images. We select 10 image queries and perform three tests: (i) we mimic a surveillance test by selecting only the license plates as ROI-queries; (ii) we select as mid-scale ROI-queries a section of the car trunk, and (iii) use the whole images as queries. An example of the query subset is given in the left part of Fig. 2. For the license plate test, we manually create "good" and "junk" ground-truth files over matching images [8]; "junk" ground truth comprises any image in which the query (i.e., the license plate) is not visible or not distinguishable by the interest point detector.

Holidays + Flickr10k [10]: The Holidays dataset consists of 1491 high resolution images, mainly consisting of personal holiday photos. There are 500 queries of a distinct scene or object. To simulate large-scale retrieval and further diversify the test, we merge the Holidays dataset with a 10,000 (10k) subset from the Flickr1M dataset [10], which we denote Flickr10k. The visual word centers are learnt on an independent image dataset, Flickr60k, and the PCA projection

Fig. 2. (Left) Example queries for the Caltech Cars dataset. (Right) Example ROI query (top left) and matching image set for the Holidays dataset (remaining images).

matrix is learnt on a different 10k subset of the Flickr1M image dataset [10]. We use the publicly available SIFT descriptors [10] for both training and testing and select salient regions from a subset of 40 query images as ROI queries into our system. An example ROI query with its corresponding matching image set is shown in the right part of Fig. 2.

Evaluation Process: The retrieval performance is measured by creating a ranked list and computing the mAP over all queries. For VVLAD, we set: $K = 64$, $L = 3$, $V_1 = V_2 = 3$, 128-D VLAD per cell, and the maximum similarity score considered for the ranked list. Additionally, for Fast-VVLAD we set σ^2 to 0.5×10^7 for the weighting function in (2). For VLAD, for the Holidays+Flickr10k, we use: 128-D, (128×4)-D and (128×16)-D sizes, in order to align our VLAD results with the ones reported by Jegou et al. [13]. For the Caltech Cars dataset, given that no previous VLAD results are reported, we use 128-D and (128×13)-D sizes in order to align VLAD with the VVLAD storage requirement. The Multi-VLAD descriptor produces (128×14)-D size per image for both datasets [9]. Finally, per descriptor, we report the matching complexity averaged over all tests and normalized to the baseline 128-D VLAD complexity.

4.2 Performance and Results

Table 1 summarises the retrieval performance of all methods on the Caltech Cars dataset. The first observation is that the larger (128×13)-D VLAD actually performs considerably worse than the 128-D VLAD. Previous work [6] has also reported performance drop when increasing the VLAD dimension, and this can be explained by the fact that, in the case of VLAD, the additional dimensions are adding noise to the descriptor. On the other hand, Fast-VVLAD performs significantly better than the 128-D VLAD on small license plate queries, yielding substantial mAP gain of 26 %. Importantly, both Fast-VVLAD and VVLAD maintain consistently-good mAP even with the larger ROIs of car trunks and whole-image queries. Between them, Fast-VVLAD remains competitive to VVLAD, while requiring half of the average matching complexity. Interestingly, the Fast-VLAD outperforms VVLAD for whole image queries. While this may appear to be counterintuitive, this is due to the Fast-VVLAD similarity score of (2) considering all partition levels, which provides robustness against false

Table 1. Complexity and mAP results for the Caltech Cars (Rear) image dataset [11].

	D	Matching Complexity	License Plates	Trunk	Whole Image
VLAD [13]	128	1	0.504	0.738	0.726
	128×13	13	0.232	0.320	0.383
Proposed VVLAD	128×13	13	0.646	0.801	0.657
Proposed Fast-VVLAD	128×13	6.74	0.636	0.797	0.700
Multi-VLAD [9]	128×14	14	0.610	0.818	0.655

positives. Finally, both Fast-VVLAD and VVLAD outperform Multi-VLAD for small queries (license plates), whilst being lower dimensional.

The Holidays+Flickr10k dataset provides a less controlled test for our system. Crucially, in this dataset, the scale of the selected ROI and the whole images tends to vary more. Table 2 summarises the retrieval performance for the 500 whole-image queries and 40 smaller ROI queries. The Fast-VVLAD is again found to outperform VVLAD for whole image queries due to its superior similarity score of (2). The (128×4)-D VLAD performs best for whole image queries, but only by a small margin. Fast-VVLAD outperforms all tested VLADs for ROI queries (gains of 13 % to 48 % in mAP over VLAD). Finally, while Fast-VVLAD achieves only around 6 % higher mAP than Multi-VLAD in this dataset, it provides for more than two-fold reduction in matching complexity.

Table 2. Complexity and mAP results for the Holidays + Flickr10k dataset [10].

	D	Matching Complexity	Query ROI	Whole Image
VLAD [13]	128	1	0.185	0.473
	128×4	4	0.242	0.514
	128×16	16	0.227	0.449
Proposed VVLAD	128×13	13	0.282	0.459
Proposed Fast-VVLAD	128×13	6.74	0.274	0.485
Multi-VLAD [9]	128×14	14	0.259	0.459

5   Conclusion

We proposed a novel descriptor design, termed Voronoi-based vector of locally-aggregated descriptors (VVLAD), for region-of-interest (ROI) retrieval in very large datasets that is less dependent on the size of ROI. We have shown how VVLAD could fit into a practical large-scale ROI-based retrieval system via the proposed fast search, memory-efficient design and robust similarity scoring mechanisms. Our results show that the proposed VVLAD and its fast version maintain competitive retrieval performance over diverse ROI queries on two datasets and significantly improve on the retrieval performance (or implementation efficiency) of VLAD and Multi-VLAD when dealing with smaller ROI queries.

References

1. Arandjelovic, R., Zisserman, A.: Three things everyone should know to improve object retrieval. In: IEEE International Conference on Computer Vision and Pattern Recognition (CVPR), pp. 2911–2918 (2012)
2. Lowe, D.G.: Distinctive image features from scale-invariant keypoints. Int. J. of Comput. Vis. **60**(2), 91–110 (2004)

3. Lazebnik, S. et al.: Beyond bags of features: spatial pyramid matching for recognizing natural scene categories, In: IEEE International Conference on Computer Vision and Pattern Recogonition, vol. 2, pp. 2169–2178 (2006)
4. Philbin, J. et al.: Lost in quantization: improving particular object retrieval in large scale image databases. In: IEEE International Conference on Computer Vision and Pattern Recogonition, pp. 1–8 (2008)
5. Chum, O. et al.: Total recall: automatic query expansion with a generative feature model for object retrieval, In: IEEE International Conference on Computer Vision, pp. 1–8 (2007)
6. Jégou, H., Douze, M., Schmid, C., Pérez, P.: Aggregating local descriptors into a compact image representation, In: IEEE International Conference on Computer Vision and Pattern Recogonition, pp. 3304–3311 (2010)
7. Perronnin, F., Dance, C.: Fisher kernels on visual vocabularies for image categorization. In: IEEE International Conference on Computer Vision and Pattern Recogonition, pp. 1–8 (2007)
8. Philbin, J., Chum, O., Isard, M., Sivic, J., Zisserman, A.: Object retrieval with large vocabularies and fast spatial matching. In: IEEE International Conference on Computer Vision and Pattern Recogonition, pp. 1–8 (2007)
9. Arandjelovic, R., Zisserman, A.: All about VLAD. In: IEEE International Conference on Computer Vision and Pattern Recogonition, pp. 1578–1585 (2013)
10. Jegou, H., Douze, M., Schmid, C.: Hamming embedding and weak geometric consistency for large scale image search. In: Forsyth, D., Torr, P., Zisserman, A. (eds.) ECCV 2008, Part I. LNCS, vol. 5302, pp. 304–317. Springer, Heidelberg (2008)
11. Fergus, R., Perona, P., Zisserman, A.: Object class recognition by unsupervised scale-invariant learning. In: IEEE International Conference on Computer Vision and Pattern Recogonition, vol. 2, pp. II-264–II-271 (2003)
12. Perronnin, F., Liu, Y., Sánchez, J., Poirier, H.: Large-scale image retrieval with compressed fisher vectors. In: IEEE International Conference on Computer Vision and Pattern Recogonition, pp. 3384–3391 (2010)
13. Jégou, H., Perronnin, F., Douze, M., Sánchez, J., Pérez, P., Schmid, C.: Aggregating local image descriptors into compact codes. In: IEEE Transaction on Pattern Analysis and Machine Intelligence, vol. 34, no. 9, pp. 1704–1716 (2012)
14. Jégou, H., Chum, O.: Negative evidences and co-occurences in image retrieval: the benefit of pca and whitening. In: Fitzgibbon, A., Lazebnik, S., Perona, P., Sato, Y., Schmid, C. (eds.) ECCV 2012, Part II. LNCS, vol. 7573, pp. 774–787. Springer, Heidelberg (2012)
15. Chum, O., Matas, J.: Unsupervised discovery of co-occurrence in sparse high dimensional data. In: IEEE International Conference on Computer Vision and Pattern Recogonition, pp. 3416–3423 (2010)
16. Mikolajczyk, K., et al.: A comparison of affine region detectors. Int. J. of Comput. Vis. **65**(1–2), 43–72 (2005)
17. Mikolajczyk, K., Schmid, C.: An affine invariant interest point detector. In: Heyden, A., Sparr, G., Nielsen, M., Johansen, P. (eds.) ECCV 2002, Part I. LNCS, vol. 2350, pp. 128–142. Springer, Heidelberg (2002)

Geostatistics for Context-Aware Image Classification

Felipe Codevilla[1]([✉]), Silvia S.C. Botelho[1], Nelson Duarte[1], Samuel Purkis[2], A.S.M. Shihavuddin[3], Rafael Garcia[3], and Nuno Gracias[3]

[1] Center of Computational Sciences (C3), Federal University of Rio Grande (FURG), Rio Grande, Brazil
[2] National Coral Reef Institute, Nova Southeastern University, Dania Beach, FL 33004, USA
[3] Computer Vision and Robotics Institute, Centre d'Investigació En Robòtica Submarina, Universitat de Girona, 17003 Girona, Spain
`felipe.codevilla@furg.br`

Abstract. Context information is fundamental for image understanding. Many algorithms add context information by including semantic relations among objects such as neighboring tendencies, relative sizes and positions. To achieve context inclusion, popular context-aware classification methods rely on probabilistic graphical models such as Markov Random Fields (MRF) or Conditional Random Fields (CRF). However, recent studies showed that MRF/CRF approaches do not perform better than a simple smoothing on the labeling results.

The need for more context awareness has motivated the use of different methods where the semantic relations between objects are further enforced. With this, we found that on particular application scenarios where some specific assumptions can be made, the use of context relationships is greatly more effective.

We propose a new method, called *GeoSim*, to compute the labels of mosaic images with context label agreement. Our method trains a transition probability model to enforce properties such as class size and proportions. The method draws inspiration from Geostatistics, usually used to model spatial uncertainties. We tested the proposed method in two different ocean seabed classification context, obtaining state-of-art results.

Keywords: Context adding · Underwater vision · Geostatistics · Conditional random fields

1 Introduction

The idea of context information is fundamental for image classification and object recognition [4,9]. The contextual information is usually associated with some object relations that are fundamental for object identification. These, called *Semantic Relations* [9], are associated with object distance probability (objects

© Springer International Publishing Switzerland 2015
L. Nalpantidis et al. (Eds.): ICVS 2015, LNCS 9163, pp. 228–239, 2015.
DOI: 10.1007/978-3-319-20904-3_22

tend to appear close to each other), size (objects usually have a predefined size) and position (objects have usually a predefined position).

A large number of recently proposed methods aim to increase the classification accuracy by using context [5,6,16] and enforcing *Semantic Relations*. In this area, the use of probabilistic graphical models such as Conditional Random Fields (CRF) or Markov Random Fields (MRF) are common approaches to include the spatial context.

However, *Lucchi et al.* [13] illustrated that simpler global features can produce results comparable to those achieved with complex CRF or MRF models. The need to obtain better results than with a simple global feature, motivates new methods to enforce the *Semantic Relations* more directly.

In this paper, we argue that for some important application scenarios, it is easier to enforce *Semantic Relations* by exploring the particularities of those scenarios. To demonstrate this, we present examples that utilize underwater seabed mapping. These scenarios have useful properties, since they typically tend to be acquired by a down-looking camera at constant distance to the scene, thus having similar spatial statistics over the extent on the input images.

Considering these circumstances, we propose to use and adapt tools from the Geostatistics field, to model spatial uncertainty. Geostatistics modeling tools are commonly used in applications such as reservoir simulation in the hydrocarbon industry [3], and for geologic mapping [14]. We combine the Geostatistics mechanisms with the modeling used by the CRF methods in order to successively maximize context agreement on label assignment.

Our model considers spatial properties such as size, proportions and juxtaposition tendencies by training a Markov chain transition probability model between classes. These relations are iteratively added by randomly sampling patches in different image neighborhoods until a convergence is obtained. Finally, we test our method in two different ocean seabed classification images and are able to obtain state-of-art results.

2   Problem Formulation

We assume an image to be represented as a vector $X = (x_1, ..., x_n)$, where each x_i is a *patch* from the image. For a given image X, the objective is to obtain a vector of labelled patches $Y = (y_1, ..., y_n)$ where, each y_i can assume a $k \in 1...K$ value.

One can consider the problem of assigning a label as a probability distribution $P(Y|X)$ where each label y_i has a probability to be of each possible class from the set of classes. With this, we are interested on finding the maximum a-posteriori distribution (MAP), that is the optimal solution given a model, *i.e.* the set of labels that has the maximum probability. This is showed by:

$$Y* = arg\ max\ P(Y|X). \tag{1}$$

The main difficulty for the MAP is the high complexity of modelling, *i.e.* to learn the probability distribution, also leading to a high computational cost to compute $Y*$ [17].

An common solution to approximate $P(X|Y)$ is by the CRF model that uses a graph representation of the image X. Let $G(v, \varepsilon)$ be the representation of the image, being v the set of vertex and ε the set of edges. According to the Hammersley-Clifford theorem [10] the probability $P(X|Y)$ can be written as a normalized exponential of a energy function $E(X)$. The energy function of a the graph G is a function of an unitary factor (φ_i^u) and a local factor (φ_{ij}^L). Hence, we define the energy of a certain set of labels $Y = (y_1, ..., y_n)$ given a model graph G and a set of parameters θ_u and θ_l as:

$$E(X|G, \theta_u, \theta_l) = w_u \sum_{y_i \in X}^{u} \varphi_i^u(y_i, \theta_u) + w_l \sum_{(y_i, y_j) \in \varepsilon}^{\varepsilon} \varphi_{ij}^L(y_i, y_j, \theta_l), \tag{2}$$

where the θ parameters are associated with the spatial likelihood training. The optimal labelling assignment (MAP) of Eq. 2 is related to minimizing the energy function $Y* = arg\ min\ E(X|G, \theta_u, \theta_l)$. However, direct minimization is unfeasible due to the extremely large domain of $E(X)$ [5].

Algorithmic approximations have been proposed to tackle this problem, such as *belief propagation* (BP) [18], which computes an approximation of the MAP for a given model graph. Each node patch label probability $p_i(y_i)$ will be updated by a message passing algorithm that takes into consideration both unary and local probability distributions:

$$p_i(y_i) = \frac{1}{Z} \varphi_i^u(y_i) \prod_{j \in N(i)} m_{ji}(y_i), \tag{3}$$

where $m_{ji}(y_i)$ are the messages from j to i, $N(i)$ is the set of all the nodes neighbouring i, and $m_{ji}(y_i)$ is computed as:

$$m_{ij}(y_j) \leftarrow \sum_{y_i} \varphi_i^u(y_i)\ \varphi_{ij}^L(y_i, y_j) \prod_{k \in N(i) \setminus j} m_{ki}(y_i). \tag{4}$$

The belief propagation passes messages until a convergence condition is obtained.

3   Proposed Approach

We show that the same maximum a-posteriori problem of Eq. 1 (MAP) can be solved by the application of a Sequential Indicator Simulation (SIS) adapted from Geostatistical reservoir simulation methods [7]. We call it the *GeoSim* technique.

To simulate the probability of a certain label y_0 in a patch x_0, for a given class k from the set K, a certain number N of random sample positions x_α are computed around the position x_0 in a radius r. An iterative function is applied on the image lattice X until convergence is obtained:

$$P(y_0 = k|X)^{(n)} = (P(y_0 = k|X)^{(n-1)})^{g_p} (\frac{1}{Z} \sum_{\alpha=1}^{N} \sum_{j=1}^{K} P(y_\alpha = j|X)^{(n-1)} w_{jk,\alpha})^{g_l} \tag{5}$$

where $P(y_0 = k|X)^{(n)}$ is the probability of a given patch x_0 to be labelled as class k at a certain iteration n. The equation is divided into two parts: (1) the left fraction, $(P(y_0 = k|X)^{(n-1)})^{g_p}$ is related to the previous probability distribution and is weighted by the constant g_p. (2) the right fraction (weighted by g_l), is related to the sampled positions used to add the spatial context information, being $P(y_\alpha = j|X)^{(n-1)}$ the probability of a sampled position x_α. Z is the normalization factor.

The probability for the basis $(n = 0)$ is the prior unary probability, obtained by using a trained classifier:

$$P(y_0 = k|X)^{(0)} = P_u(y_0 = k|X). \tag{6}$$

The function $w_{jk,\alpha}$ is a weighted transition function that is related to the probability of patch x_α of class j being at a distance $h = d(x_0, x_\alpha)$ from a patch x_0 of class k, so:

$$w_{jk} = t_{jk}(h)\, u(x_0, x_\alpha),\ j \in K,\ k \in K, \tag{7}$$

where $t_{jk}(h)$ is the transition probability function for a pair of classes over a distance h. An heuristic function $u(x_0, x_\alpha)$ is used to weight the transition. We computed $u(x_0, x_\alpha)$ as a weighting function that assigns larger weights to smaller distances $d(x_0, x_\alpha)$. For some Geostatistics applications the weight is related to the a estimated variogram [7].

As showed by [7], the transition matrix T can be modelled as a exponential function of distance h_ϕ under a direction ϕ.

$$T(h_\phi) = e^{R_\phi h_\phi} \tag{8}$$

We assume that the transition function is the same regardless of the direction ϕ, which is valid for the cases where the objects to be classified are approximately isomorphic. Figure 1 shows an example of the matrix T containing the transition function $t_{jk}(h)$, for each pair of classes, on a three classes example.

T can be estimated by measuring the matrix R from a set of annotated training data [7]. The rate of transition between a pair of classes j and k are a measure proportional to the average size of the classes and to the frequency of transition between the pairs. Where each element of R, r_{jk}, is computed as:

$$r_{jk} = \frac{f_{jk}}{L_j \sum_{k \neq j} f_{jk}}. \tag{9}$$

The L_j, in Geostatistics, is computed as the mean length of a certain class. By considering the objects as isomorphic shapes, we consider the mean length as a 2D mean radius L_j. We approximate the shapes as circles and we define the shapes by a single radius parameter. With this approximation, we compute the radius of all circles and subsequently compute the mean radius L and variance V.

The transition frequency f_{jk} in Eq. 9 is computed as the number of times of the class j occurs *and* class k occur with a tolerance radius determined by the mean radius L_j and L_k, and the variances V_j and V_k.

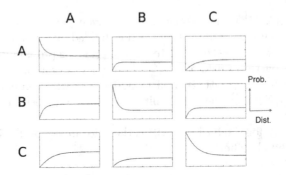

Fig. 1. Example of transition probabilities for a 3 classes case. Each plot shows the transition probabilities (y axis) as function of the distance (x axis, in pixels) from each class (A,B,C) to all classes.

The transition matrix T is computed from R using eigenvalue analysis [1], as:

$$T(h) = e^{Rh} = \sum_{i=1}^{K} e^{\lambda_k h} Z_k, \qquad (10)$$

where λ_k and Z_k denote the eigenvalues and the spectral component matrices of R. The spectral components matrix can be directly computed from the eigenvalues, as

$$Z_k = \frac{\prod_{m \neq k}(\lambda_k I - R)}{\prod_{m \neq k}(\lambda_m - \lambda_k)} \quad k = 1, ..., K. \qquad (11)$$

3.1   *GeoSim* Algorithm

Given a trained transition probability matrix T and a image with the prior unary probabilities already computed, the following algorithm computes Eq. 5.

While $error(\epsilon) \ \forall \ x \ \epsilon \ X > thresh$ increase n:

- Select a position x_0 pseudo-randomly, with preference on selecting positions where $max(P(y_0|X)^{(n-1)})$ is smaller;
- Sample N positions x_α around x_0 in radius r;
- Obtain the w_{jk} for each pair of positions x_0 , x_α, following Eq. 7;
- Compute the $P(y_0 = k|X)^{(n)}$ for each possible class k using Eq. 5;

Finally, the algorithm selects the class k with maximum probability for the function $P(y = k|X)$ for each position x_i. The error ϵ is monotonically reduced through each additional iteration. However, the convergence rate is greatly dependant on the weights g_p and g_l. The larger the magnitude of g_p, less the spatial information considered by each iteration and therefore the faster the convergence of the solution.

Figure 2 illustrates the algorithm sequence. The uncertainty, represented by color intensity is reduced over the iterations reaching into a final classification (Fig. 2c).

3.2   Quenching Step

The entire results are based on the initial configuration of probability $P_u(Y|X)$ (Eq. 6). If there are considerable tendencies on a patch being assigned to a wrong class, this tendency can propagate on the map culminating into a decrease of accuracy.

A *Quenching* step is employed to minimize the image disagreement with the measured L and proportions *i.e.* the prior probability of a class appearing on the training set [8].

In a conceptually similar way to simulated annealing algorithms, we induce perturbations after some iterations, by changing some classes probabilities distributions. These perturbations are done mainly on classes for which the distributions do not correlate to the previously trained mean radius and proportions.

Figure 2b shows a quenching iteration. For this case, the yellow class had, on the basis of the training set, an average radius of 56 pixels and a proportion of 0.05 % of the scene. For the Fig. 2b, the proportions and average size was about of about 15 times higher. The changes were mainly done on this class, allowing the *GeoSim* algorithm to propagate less information of this class.

3.3   Relation to Previous Works

The proposed method is closely related to the belief propagation method used with CRF. The similarity in the methods stands from the fact that both propagate context information based on prior assumptions and trained local relationships. The two main differences between *GeoSim* and *Belief Propagation* are: (1) the *GeoSim* method uses direct longer range interactions between nodes, but with loosen connection properties, *i.e.* just N sampled nodes are connected. (2) The *GeoSim* approach also incorporates the idea that context comes not only from between-objects but also from object size and scene proportions.

4   Experiments

4.1   Datasets

We tested the algorithms on two different seabed datasets. The datasets consist of mosaics obtained by merging several hundred digital still images.

The *Redsea* dataset contains images captured in very shallow waters close to the city of Eilat, as part of a survey of coral reef ecology [19]. For the classification, we considered five classes: *Urchin, Branching Coral, Brain Coral, Favid Coral* and the *Background*. We used one mosaic of 3256×2939 pixels for validation and the spatial likelihood training for both CRF and *GeoSim*. Another mosaic of dimensions 3256×2939 pixels was used for testing. The mosaic was created with a resolution of 1.1 pixel/mm.

The *Marker* dataset was captured in the Bahamas. We divided this set into General Corals, Gorgonians (sea fans), Sand and the Background. We use one mosaic of 2592×3963 for validation and the spatial likelihood training for both CRF and *GeoSim*. Another mosaic of 2592×3963 pixels was used for testing. The mosaic was captured in a 2.2 pixels/mm resolution.

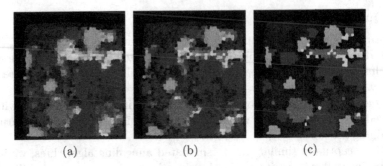

(a)   (b)   (c)

Fig. 2. Different iterations on the classification step for a five classes example (yellow, green, blue, magenta and black). Each color represent a different class. The less mixed is the color, the higher is the probability of a patch assuming a certain class, *i.e.* there is a class k for where $P(y_i = k|X)^{(n)}$ is close to 1 for k and close to zero for all the other classes. (a) Shows the initial configuration of the map where all positions x_i are equal to the unary probability distribution $P_u(y_i = k|X)$. (b) Shows the map after quenching step application, the yellow class was reduced since it did not attend to the proportions and class size. (c) Shows the final result after convergence (Color figure online).

4.2 Testing Configuration

The used test configuration to generate the unary probabilities is based on the framework by *Shihav et al.* [15]. The underwater environment tends to produce color non-uniformity and subdues the overall contrast. For the cases where the images are not severely degraded, like in our test data, the application of simple methods for contrast correction and color correction are sufficient to facilitate the use of the texture and color features. The main selected features are based on a mix of texture based features. We used a mix of Gabor filters, CLBP and GLCM [15] feature kernels.

By using the set of textures descriptors , we compute the $P_u(y_i|X)$ based on the confidence function training as explained by [2]. This is computed for each patch, where each is a superpixel computed with the *TurboPixels* algorithm [12]. The confidence curve is computed in order to produce a more meaningful unary probability distribution.

After having $P_u(y_i|X)$, the algorithm of Sect. 3.1 can be applied to compute the the results. For the weights g_p and g_l we used respectively 1.5 and 1.

We compared our implementation with a CRF incremented with the Potts potential [16].

4.3 Results

Figures 4 and 3, shows the results for both the *Redsea* and the *Marker* datasets. Each color represent a different class of seabed object being classified, black begin the background.

We can see the advantages of the more specific assumptions and richer statistics considerations of the *GeoSim* method as compared to the CRF approach.

This is seen specially for the *Marker* dataset (Figs. 3a,b,d,e) where the results for *GeoSim* were about seven percentage points larger than CRF. As discussed in *Lucchi et. al.* [13], the common probabilistic graphical models normally assure no more than local smoothness. However, we can perceive for the *GeoSim* method that the context measures such as sizes and proportions helped to improve the

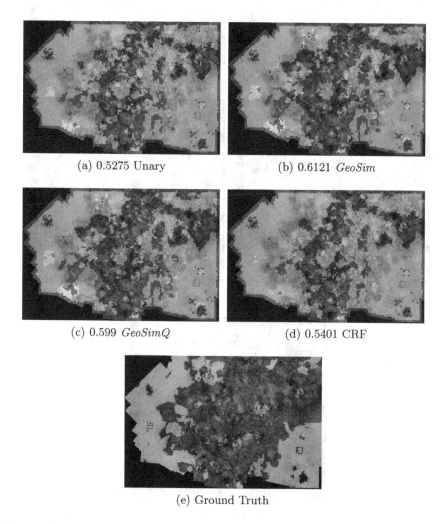

(a) 0.5275 Unary   (b) 0.6121 *GeoSim*

(c) 0.599 *GeoSimQ*   (d) 0.5401 CRF

(e) Ground Truth

Fig. 3. The final results for the *Marker* seabed dataset. The figures show the data classified by a color label. The dataset contains four different classes: Background (black), Gorgonians (yellow), Sand (green) and General Corals (blue). In this case, we can perceive a significant improvement of the *GeoSim* (in (b)) when compared to the CRF model (in (d)) (Color figure online).

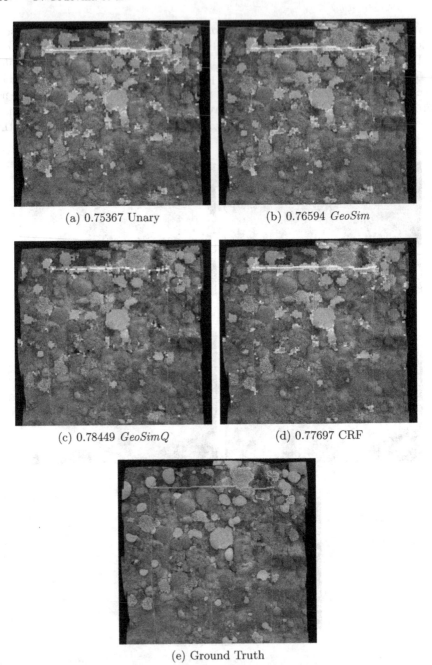

(a) 0.75367 Unary

(b) 0.76594 *GeoSim*

(c) 0.78449 *GeoSimQ*

(d) 0.77697 CRF

(e) Ground Truth

Fig. 4. The final results for *Redsea* seabed dataset. The figures show the data classified by a color label. The dataset contains five different classes: Background (black), Urchin(yellow), Branching Corals (magenta), Brain Corals (green) and Faviid Corals (blue). We can see a better performance of the *GeoSim* method in (b) (Color figure online).

Table 1. Results of the average accuracy for multiple random samples of 1200×1200 pixels.

Algorithm	Unary	GeoSim	GeoSimQ	CRF
Accuracy *RedSea*	80.49 %	**81.2%**	**81.64%**	**82.21%**
Accuracy *Marker*	45.17 %	**54.53%**	**54.49%**	46.11 %

results. The green area on Fig. 3a was greatly reduced on the *GeoSim* results (Fig. 3b). This happened since the green area did not respected the proportions and sizes, allowing an increment on the classification accuracy. CRF, on the other hand, in fact only enhanced the local smoothness, having marginal improvements on accuracy (Fig. 3b). However, the *Quenching* step (*GeoSimQ* on Fig. 3c), was not beneficial, since there was no large amount of patches with labels out of the measured statistics with high probability for a single class.

For the *Redsea* dataset (Figs. 4a,c,d,e) there was less room for improvement with context information, since the unary accuracy is higher. However, the quenching step was able to improve the results. This happened since, the perturbations reduced the yellow class size (Fig. 4c). This reduction is expected because the *Urchin* class is usually small (This can be perceived at the Ground Truth 4e).

In order to simulate more visual variability, we tested our algorithm with multiple patches from the mosaics dataset. We cropped 15 randomly sampled square patches of size 1200×1200 pixels and averaged their computed accuracy for a different set of methods. The Table 1 shows the results. We can still perceive the best results for the *GeoSim* method over the CRF on the *Marker* dataset. For the *Redsea* dataset, the differences were marginal. Again we perceived the benefits of the quenching mainly for the *Redsea* dataset.

5   Conclusions

In this work we presented a novel method for context aware image classification called *GeoSim*. The method is inspired by the techniques of spatial uncertainty modelling. Our method is designed to work in a specific scenario that has low scale variance. Examples of applications that have this properties are oceanic, aerial and satellite mapping of natural scenes.

For these conditions, *GeoSim* was able to obtain significantly better results than CRF, which was only able to enforce local smoothness. It contributes to the field by being the first to combine techniques from two distinct topics, Geostatistics and Probabilistic Graphical Models, and to illustrate its benefit with respect to the state-of-the-art.

As a future work, this method will be compared with more complex forms of context addition such as the fully connected CRF [11] and auto-context [17].

Acknowledgements. The authors would like to thank to the Brazilian National Agency of Petroleum, Natural Gas and Biofuels(ANP), to the Funding Authority for Studies and Projects(FINEP) and to Ministry of Science and Technology (MCT) for their financial support through the Human Resources Program of ANP to the Petroleum and Gas Sector - PRH-ANP/MCT.

This paper is also a contribution of the Brazilian National Institute of Science and Technology - INCT-Mar COI funded by CNPq Grant Number 610012/2011-8.

Additional support was granted by the Spanish National Project OMNIUS (CTM2013-46718-R), and the Generalitat de Catalunya through the TECNIOspring program (TECSPR14-1-0050) to N. Gracias.

References

1. Agterberg, F.: Mathematical geology. In: General Geology. Encyclopedia of Earth Science, pp. 573–582. Springer, US (1988). http://dx.doi.org/10.1007/0-387-30844-X_76
2. Aßfalg, J., Kriegel, H.-P., Pryakhin, A., Schubert, M.: Multi-represented classification based on confidence estimation. In: Zhou, Z.-H., Li, H., Yang, Q. (eds.) PAKDD 2007. LNCS (LNAI), vol. 4426, pp. 23–34. Springer, Heidelberg (2007)
3. Beattie, C., Mills, B., Mayo, V.: Development drilling of the tawila field, yemen, based on three-dimensional reservoir modeling and simulation. In: SPE Annual Technical Conference, pp. 715–725 (1998)
4. Biederman, I., Mezzanotte, R.J., Rabinowitz, J.C.: Scene perception: detecting and judging objects undergoing relational violations. Cogn. Psychol. **14**(2), 143–177 (1982)
5. Boix, X., Gonfaus, J.M., van de Weijer, J., Bagdanov, A.D., Serrat, J., Gonzàlez, J.: Harmony potentials. Int. J. Comput. Vision **96**(1), 83–102 (2012)
6. Carbonetto, P., de Freitas, N., Barnard, K.: A statistical model for general contextual object recognition. In: Pajdla, T., Matas, J.G. (eds.) ECCV 2004. LNCS, vol. 3021, pp. 350–362. Springer, Heidelberg (2004)
7. Carle, S.F., Fogg, G.E.: Transition probability-based indicator geostatistics. Math. Geol. **28**(4), 453–476 (1996)
8. Deutsch, C.V., Journel, A.G., et al.: The application of simulated annealing to stochastic reservoir modeling. SPE Adv. Technol. Ser. **2**(02), 222–227 (1994)
9. Galleguillos, C., Belongie, S.: Context based object categorization: a critical survey. Comput. Vis. Image Underst. **114**(6), 712–722 (2010)
10. Grimmett, G.R.: A theorem about random fields. Bull. Lond. Math. Soc. **5**(1), 81–84 (1973)
11. Krähenbühl, P., Koltun, V.: Efficient inference in fully connected CRFS with Gaussian edge potentials. In: Shawe-Taylor, J., Zemel, R.S., Bartlett, P.L., Pereira, F., Weinberger, K.Q. (eds.) Advances in Neural Information Processing Systems, vol. 24, pp. 109–117. Curran Associates, Inc (2011)
12. Levinshtein, A., Stere, A., Kutulakos, K.N., Fleet, D.J., Dickinson, S.J., Siddiqi, K.: Turbopixels: fast superpixels using geometric flows. IEEE Trans. Pattern Anal. Mach. Intell. **31**(12), 2290–2297 (2009)
13. Lucchi, A., Li, Y., Boix, X., Smith, K., Fua, P.: Are spatial and global constraints really necessary for segmentation? In: IEEE International Conference on Computer Vision (ICCV), pp. 9–16. IEEE (2011)

14. Purkis, S., Vlaswinkel, B., Gracias, N.: Vertical-to-lateral transitions among creta-ceous carbonate facies: a means to 3-d framework construction via markov analysis. J. Sediment. Res. **82**(4), 232–243 (2012)
15. Shihavuddin, A., Gracias, N., Garcia, R., Gleason, A.C.R., Gintert, B.: Image-based coral reef classification and thematic mapping. Remote Sens. **5**(4), 1809–1841 (2013). http://www.mdpi.com/2072-4292/5/4/1809
16. Shotton, J., Winn, J., Rother, C., Criminisi, A.: Textonboost for image understand-ing: multi-class object recognition and segmentation by jointly modeling texture, layout, and context. Int. J. Comput. Vision **81**(1), 2–23 (2009)
17. Tu, Z.: Auto-context and its application to high-level vision tasks. In: IEEE Con-ference on Computer Vision and Pattern Recognition. CVPR 2008, pp. 1–8. IEEE (2008)
18. Yedidia, J.S., Freeman, W.T., Weiss, Y., et al.: Generalized belief propagation. In: Leen, T.K., Dietterich, T.G., Tresp, V. (eds.) Advances in Neural Information Processing Systems, vol. 13, pp. 689–695. MIT Press (2001)
19. Zvuloni, A., Artzy-Randrup, Y., Stone, L., Kramarsky-Winter, E., Barkan, R., Loya, Y.: Spatio-temporal transmission patterns of black-band disease in a coral community. PLoS One **4**(4), e4993 (2009)

Robot Vision

Querying 3D Data by Adjacency Graphs

Nils Bore[(✉)], Patric Jensfelt, and John Folkesson

Centre for Autonomous Systems at KTH Royal Institute of Technology,
Stockholm, Sweden
nbore@kth.se

Abstract. The need for robots to search the 3D data they have saved is becoming more apparent. We present an approach for finding structures in 3D models such as those built by robots of their environment. The method extracts geometric primitives from point cloud data. An attributed graph over these primitives forms our representation of the surface structures. Recurring substructures are found with frequent graph mining techniques. We investigate if a model invariant to changes in size and reflection using only the geometric information of and between primitives can be discriminative enough for practical use. Experiments confirm that it can be used to support queries of 3D models.

1 Introduction

Rapid advances in computing and 3D sensing have led to larger and larger 3D data sets being collected by robots and stored for future reference. With the advent of digital cameras and the Internet, a similar situation arose for 2D images, spurring the development of ways to analyze and mine the large amounts of data; these needs now arise for 3D data.

The ability to represent a robot's working environment with simple structures of composite geometric primitives enables both compact representations and the possibility for the robot to reason about its surroundings at a more abstract level. For example, at a high level a bookshelf consists of two vertical sides and horizontal shelves. Most indoor environments consist of combinations of simple substructures repeated throughout the space. Take an office space as an example. It is typically made up of tables, chairs, bookshelves, doorways, pillars, etc. which could be further broken down to simpler parts, e.g. corners or edges.

We would like our robot to be able to look back over its stored data to find specific structures. This would be helpful in a semantic mapping context; perhaps instructed to put a label 'doorway' on all structures that 'look like' some example. It can also be used in an unsupervised transfer learning context, e.g. the robot learns to associate a certain human behavior near a sink in a kitchen. It then finds a similar structure in another room and infers a similar human behavior as a prior. The capability needed is one of being able to query 3D data with representative examples of a structure.

Our approach is based on the idea of having a qualitative representation that can be queried for parts that might be similar. We focus on finding general structures by looking at the surface topology of an indoor environment.

© Springer International Publishing Switzerland 2015
L. Nalpantidis et al. (Eds.): ICVS 2015, LNCS 9163, pp. 243–252, 2015.
DOI: 10.1007/978-3-319-20904-3_23

We believe that identification of frequent substructures could be an important part of a robot's understanding of space. The structures could potentially be used as building blocks for a robotic map representation, enabling efficient representation of 3D data gathered by modern robots.

We build on the work in [1] and adapt a popular adjacency graph model to represent configurations of geometric primitives. To find the frequent substructures we look for frequent subgraphs using the *gSpan* algorithm [2].

We contribute a new way of defining discrete pairwise relations in the adjacency graph and propose to have full connectivity locally. This enables us to achieve greater consistency between matched structures. In addition, we extend the approach by learning a graph to search for from a set of example pointclouds.

2   Related Work

The use of frequent patterns for image detection and classification has been studied within the computer vision community. In [3], Nowozin *et al.* demonstrate good classification results with a method based on a combination of graph mining and boosting. The authors suggest that a representation of spatial relations between features is powerful compared to bag-of-words representations, and note that it has the important advantage of easier human interpretation. Jiang & Coenan [4], like [5], propose to use frequent patterns across a set of images as features for classification. As in this paper, both approaches utilize some variant of the popular *gSpan* graph mining algorithm [2]. Within a robotics context, Aydemir *et al.* [6] use *gSpan* to predict what may lie beyond the explored part of the environment.

Many recent papers both in 2D and 3D contexts use over-segmentation to partition a scene into areas that are to be labeled. Those often employ graphical models over adjacent areas to infer semantic labels, primarily by using some kind of probabilistic inference over the graph. An early example of this kind of inference on a stitched point cloud map was presented by Anand *et al.* [7]. As is natural in a 3D context, they use e.g. local shape features for the patches and geometric relations such as co-planarity as pairwise features. Silberman *et al.* [8] focus primarily on inferring geometrical structure in the form of support relations. They demonstrate that segmenting the scene simultaneously with inferring scene topology improves segmentation quality.

Another approach within the scene analysis context that is more similar to ours is the work by Nüchter *et al.* [9]. Their method segments a scene into planes and form discrete pairwise angle features over the segments. Using pre-compiled knowledge of typical angle and co-planarity constraints between plane classes, the system labels each plane according to e.g. floor, ceiling or doorway. Their algorithm achieves this by finding a global labeling that satisfies the local interplanar constraints.

Farid & Sammut [10] use a similar model for supervised classification of compounds of planes. To achieve this they use a classification scheme based on *inductive linear programming*. Given a set of object groups that are to be classified, a set of *Prolog* clauses are learned for each object such that at least one returns true upon being shown an object example but none returns true when shown a negative.

In robotics, several papers have dealt with the problem of finding furniture-sized objects from 3D data without supervision. Common to all such methods is that they look for recurring objects. Shin *et al.* [11] use the relation of gradually discovered shape parts in addition to features to gain more information about potential objects. The authors propose a variant of the branch-and-bound joint compatibility test to find multiple object instances. In [12] the authors find repetitive objects in precise indoor LIDAR data. Using a segmentation of point clouds into locally planar patches, the authors group combinations of patches into spatially consistent objects. They use shape descriptors of the patches together with geometric consistency within the objects. To limit the possible number of necessary combinations, several pruning steps based on patch size and individual patch is similarity is required.

The idea to model perception of 3D objects through their decomposition into primitive parts was introduced by Biederman [13]. Adjacency graphs over planes have been used for 3D roof detection from aerial LIDAR data, see e.g. [14]. In [15], Schnabel *et al.* present a representation of adjacency graphs over primitives that is similar to ours. The authors demonstrate a system that allows a user to look for a structure by specifying a query graph that can then be found within large scale environments. Our model differs in how we define discrete pairwise relations and have full connectivity locally. This enables us to search the graph for repeated structure and achieve greater consistency between matched structures. In addition, we extend their approach by learning a graph to search for from a set of example point clouds.

Our work differs from unsupervised object detection approaches like [12] in that, instead of looking for repeating structures, we look for functional parts by finding the *most frequently* repeating structures globally. We also consider more of the environment, including building structure. This is enabled by frequent subgraph mining techniques, which, to the best of our knowledge, is applied here for the first time to extract patterns in 3D point cloud data. A trade-off when using these techniques is that we have to derive precise discrete attributes.

3   Method

A popular approach to model semantic properties of a space has been to study graphs constructed over-segmented scenes [7,8]. Our approach is to similarly construct an adjacency graph over the scene but to instead identify topological structures within that graph. However, to do so, we need a graph that for one type of 3D structure consistently returns the same segmentation and graph structure. This means that over-segmentation is not an option. Instead we need to make the assumption that the surfaces that we study are unambiguous. Therefore, similar to [9,10,15], we make the assumption that interesting parts can be represented by geometric primitives such as planes or cylinders. This makes

sense at a larger scale where much of the environment is made up of constellations of such shapes. It further enables us to define clear pairwise relations
through the relative angles and the primitive types provide us with node labels.
The algorithm works with discrete properties, an inherent trait of this kind of
graph mining.

We assume that we have an algorithm for segmenting a point cloud into
planes, cylinders and spheres. First, some general graph concepts are introduced.

3.1 Preliminaries

A *labeled graph* is defined as a tuple $G = (V, E, \alpha)$ of nodes V and edges $E \subseteq$
$V \times V$ together with a function $\alpha : V \cup E \to \mathbb{L}$ that maps nodes and edges to
discrete labels. The *order* of a graph is $|V|$, the number of nodes. Two graphs
$G_1 = (V_1, E_1, \alpha_1)$ and $G_2 = (V_2, E_2, \alpha_2)$ are said to be *isomorphic* if there exists
a bijective function $f : V_1 \to V_2$ such that

- $\alpha_1(v_1) = \alpha_2(f(v_1)), \forall v_1 \in V_1$
- $\forall e_1 = (v_1, v_1') \in E_1 \ \exists e_2 = (f(v_1), f(v_1')) \in E_2$
  s.t. $\alpha_1(e_1) = \alpha_2(e_2)$ and conversely,
- $\forall e_2 = (v_2, v_2') \in E_2 \ \exists e_1 = (f^{-1}(v_2), f^{-1}(v_2')) \in E_1$
  s.t. $\alpha_2(e_2) = \alpha_1(e_1)$.

This simply means that there is a mapping f that associates every node in G_1
with a node in G_2 in such a way that all the labels and edges are maintained.
A graph G is called a *subgraph* of $\hat{G} = (\hat{V}, \hat{E}, \alpha)$ if there exists some subset
$(V \subseteq \hat{V}, E \subseteq \hat{E}, \alpha)$ isomorphic to G.

A collection of graphs $D = \{G_1, \dots, G_n\}$ is said to form a *graph dataset*.
Further we define $D_G = \{G_i \in D; G \text{ subgraph of} G_i\}$. The *support* of G in D is
then the number of times G appears as a subgraph in D, namely $|D_G|$.

3.2 Graph Construction

In our graph, the nodes $v \in V$ correspond to primitives. Each pair of primitives
in a scene are connected through an edge, with one exception discussed later.
Edges $e = (v_1, v_2) \in E$ describe the spatial relation between two primitives, as
described by the *distance* and *angle* labels, $\alpha(e) = (l_d, l_a)$. The distance label l_d
can assume two values, *close* and *distant*. A *close* edge connects two primitives
(v_1, v_2) if any two points of the surfaces are closer than 0.01m (0.25m when
looking at large structure data), otherwise the edge is labeled *distant*.

To assign each edge an angle label l_a, we first define the meaning of an
angle γ between two primitives. Generally, the idea is to define it as the angle
between the rotational symmetry axes n_1 and n_2 of the two primitives, i.e.
$\gamma = \arccos(|n_1 \cdot n_2|)$. Of course, in the case of the sphere, that is ambiguous
and any pair involving one is defined to have angle zero. Planes, however, have
a notion of direction since they are rotationally symmetric around the surface
normal. If the normals n_1 and n_2 are taken to be unit length and on the visible

sides of the planes, the angle between two *distant* planes is $\gamma = \arccos(n_1 \cdot n_2)$. Another exception is *close* planes, where we define the angle based on the angle of intersection. An inwards edge (e.g. wall facing the floor) will have angle 90° whereas an outwards edge (e.g. corner of a building) will have angle 270°.

The angles in our data are mostly parallel or orthogonal, with few exceptions. This justifies a discretization of the angles. To find the angle label l_a of an edge, we discretize the angle of its connecting primitives around multiples of 90°. In order not to include shapes not conforming to this model, all primitive pairs with relative angle further away than $\sim 11°$ from this are discarded in the following analysis. Additionally, we introduce an extra label for distant co-planar planes, enabling us to represent e.g. walls interrupted by cabinets or doors.

3.3 Subgraph Extraction

Given a collection of point clouds from different scenes, a graph of primitives is extracted for each scene. The graphs together form a graph dataset D. We want to study which substructures are the most frequent for different substructure complexities. Within our framework, this translates to finding the subgraphs of order n with the highest support in the graph dataset. We use the *gSpan* algorithm for this purpose. The algorithm expands each graph to a unique *Depth First Code* (DFC). It then does a depth-first search of the graphs to effectively find the most frequent subgraphs in a graph dataset. The algorithm has found extensive use in e.g. molecule mining for finding common molecule substructures [16]. We use a *gSpan* implementation by Kudo *et al.* [17]. To make sure that the internal relations between the primitives in all scenes corresponding to a certain subgraph are consistent, we require that the frequent graphs be complete. We therefore limit the *gSpan* algorithm to look only for subgraphs $G = (V, E)$ with $|E| = \frac{n(n-1)}{2}$. Further, for the subgraphs to represent something connected in the scene, most of the primitives need to belong to the same surface structure. A number of *close* edges greater than or equal to a constant n_{adj} is therefore also required. If nothing else is stated, at least half of the edges have to be *close*. One could require that the subgraph be connected by *close* edges but as we will see this was not necessary on our data. It can easily be added if needed.

3.4 Study of Isomorphic Graphs

We are investigating to what extent we can use pure surface topology to characterize the typical structures. Within one group of isomorphic subgraphs we can therefore have nodes corresponding to primitives of different sizes. However, in the following analysis, it will prove useful to be able to remove instances with large size deviations. To do this, we construct from each instance of a subgraph in a scene, a vector u_i where each element represents a measure of the size of one primitive. For example, in Sect. 5.2 we use the areas of the extracted planes. Thus, a subgraph found in m scene instances will have vectors $U = \{u_1, \ldots, u_m\}$ describing the different sizes. To separate the subgraphs based on size also, one could imagine doing clustering over this vector space. For this paper, we are only interested in removing matched graph instances with sizes dissimilar from the provided examples. Based on the nearest neighbor distance between an instance and the example set size vectors, we remove far-away matches.

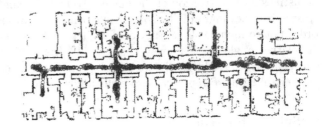

Fig. 1. The Scitos G5 robot, during the capturing of the data set with the snapshot positions overlaid on the floor map. The camera is looking down at 43°.

4   Experimental Setup

4.1   Primitive Extraction

One major challenge with using geometric primitives is that they can be costly to extract, especially in noisy sensor data. We use a RANSAC algorithm [18] since it is known to be robust to noise in the form of outliers. The basic algorithm in the context of shape recognition works by sampling a number of points, called a *minimal set*, from which a shape hypothesis can be formed. Several hypotheses are formed by sampling minimal sets of points repeatedly. The algorithm returns the shape hypothesis that is supported by the most inlier points. An *inlier* to a shape is defined as a point whose minimal distance to the shape surface is less than some threshold λ.

However, using this algorithm to extract several shapes from one point cloud can be unnecessarily costly since the minimal sets are sampled across the entire cloud, with no prior on size or locality. We therefore use a RANSAC modification which was introduced by Schnabel *et al.* [1]. Their algorithm makes use of the observation that points in a smaller neighborhood are more likely to belong to the same surface. The result of the method is a segmentation of a point cloud into primitives, with some points remaining.

4.2   Environment & Setup

We conduct our experiments using a Scitos G5 platform with an Asus Xtion depth-sensing camera mounted in front. We did two experiments, one in which the robot drives around autonomously and captures individual RGB-D images and another in which many point clouds were combined into a single 3D map.

In the first experiment we want to avoid having many images from nearly the same camera pose so we only save images from distinct view points. A new image is captured only when the robot has turned more than the field of view or traveled more than a certain distance. Granted, this does not mean that the same structure is not observed several times during a run but the intention is to make the distribution of the scans roughly uniform across the floor. The robot performed two runs over approximately three hours each, together making up a dataset of 1846 frames, see Fig. 1. Along the way, it went in to three offices and a kitchen. In this first experiment we extract planes, cylinders and spheres.

To construct the 3D map for the second experiment, we drove the robot around the office and collected local 3D sweeps using a camera pan-tilt unit (PTU) mounted on the head. These were then assembled into a big map using the transform from the PTU and stock laser localization [19]. To form a graph and search this very large point cloud was computationally infeasible. We therefore build graphs and search inside a window of a fixed size. The window is then slid to a partially overlapping position and the search repeated until the entire map is covered. Since planes are dominating at this more coarse level of resolution, we limit ourselves to plane primitives. Also, as the robot always knows the position of the floor, so it is given its own label with edge definitions equivalent to other planes.

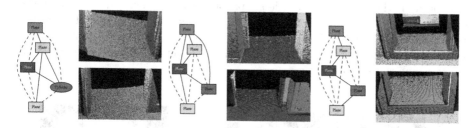

Fig. 2. Graphs representing the doors and the classified scenes. The color of primitives in the scenes and the corresponding nodes of the graph match. The *far* edges are dotted, while the *close* edges are solid. From left to right: Open from outside, open from inside and closed from outside. The bottom middle frame has similar geometry to an open door from the inside and is falsely classified as such.

5   Results

5.1   Experiment 1

In the first experiment we search a set of individual RGB-D snapshots. We show the robot doors in three different configurations: open from outside, open from inside, and closed from outside. Our robot was positioned to take twelve snapshots of different doors in each configuration. The framework then extracts the most frequent subgraph from each door configuration, defining a "template" graph for each type. The doors are re-identified by finding instances of these graphs within the set of 1846 scene graphs. To make the subgraphs more discriminative, we choose a graph order of $n = 5$ with $n_{adj} = 4$.

The results can be seen in Fig. 2. Apart from the floor, all graphs have the door frames and parts of the door in common. Among all frames, the robot successfully found five instances of open doors from the outside, seven open doors from the inside and 33 closed doors from the outside. For each of the open door categories, one false positive was found, containing some primitives not part of the doors. Among the 33 extracted closed doors, all were found to be correctly classified. The most common subgraph for each configuration together with some instances of the graph are presented in Fig. 2. This is an encouraging result and confirms that the representation can be descriptive enough to find instances of one particular structure.

As might be expected, the sphere primitives found little use in this data set as they were detected in only a few places. The cylinders were detected more often, most consistently in specific structures like the trash cans. While simple primitives other than planes were not as common in this particular environment, we note that they allow the method to represent some more of these special cases.

Many doors were not detected, probably partly because the entire structure was not in the field of view of one of our snapshots. This is a limitation of our method when applied to single snapshots as we did here. If we look at the example of the closed doors, the method is sensitive to the degree of occlusion between the door and the floor since that can determine if the corresponding edge will be labeled as *close* or *distant*. The following section explores one approach to overcome these problems.

Fig. 3. Top row: Result of a bookshelves query. The blue rectangles are graph template matches removed by size constraints. Bottom row: Here we show the most frequent structures found using a $3\,m \times 3\,m$ window size; mostly doorways.

5.2   Experiment 2

In the second experiment we search a very large point cloud map. A user selects windows by clicking points in a display of the point cloud map. In this experiment we select four areas with bookcases. The average width of these windows determine the scale at which we look for similar structures. From the examples, the most frequent subgraph of order 5 is extracted, giving us a template graph representing the bookcase. The top row of Fig. 3 summarizes the result. On the left are all the locations of returns from the query. On the right is one instance. In this case the query returns many false candidates. We can then use other information, size in this case, to further remove candidates. From the example graph instances, we create a vector set U over plane areas, constructed as in Sect. 3.4. By removing found instances with size vector further than a certain nearest-neighbor distance from U we can remove all instances not representing a bookcase. These are shown as blue rectangles while the red ones are all true bookcases. We also looked at the most frequent structures over the sliding windows. The result for a $3\,m \times 3\,m$ sliding is presented in the bottom row of Fig. 3. The most frequent graph represents most of the doors found in the environment. As should be expected, when the user queries for doors by marking four doorways, the result is mostly the same. A four times larger window finds structures matching walls and ceiling of a room.

The results show that the problems observed in the door identification are fixed by considering a full view of the scenes instead of partial views; this time 14 out of 18 doors in the office floor are detected without any false positives.

6   Conclusion and Future Work

We proposed a method to construct adjacency graphs over geometric primitives from point cloud data. We demonstrated the ability to re-identify structures. The approach was also verified to be able to search for structure in a large scale 3D map. Our results indicated that we can combine topology with other cues, here size but one could extrapolate to for example color, for reliable classification. An advantage of the graph mining in 3D versus the case with traditional images is that we can define clear, descriptive relations between local features.

We see this as a first step towards building a general 3D point cloud query framework. This would extend the search criteria to include such things as the separation of the point cloud by planes which could lead to concepts such as "enclosed by". One could for example then look for structures "inside" the rooms that we found here.

Acknowledgments. The work presented in this papers has been funded by the European Union Seventh Framework Programme (FP7/2007–2013) under grant agreement No 600623 ("STRANDS"), VR project "XPLOIT", and the Swedish Foundation for Strategic Research (SSF) through its Centre for Autonomous Systems.

References

1. Schnabel, R., Wahl, R., Klein, R.: Efficient ransac for point-cloud shape detection. Comput. Graph. Forum **26**, 214–226 (2007)

2. Yan, X., Han, J.: gspan: Graph-based substructure pattern mining. In: Proceedings of the 2002 IEEE International Conference on Data Mining, ICDM 2002, pp. 721–729. IEEE Computer Society, Washington, DC, USA (2002)

3. Nowozin, S., et al.: Weighted substructure mining for image analysis. In: Conference on Computer Vision and Pattern Recognition, pp. 1–8. IEEE (2007)

4. Jiang, M.C., Coenen, F.: Graph-based image classification by weighting scheme. In: Allen, T., Ellis, R., Petridis, M. (eds.) Applications and Innovations in Intelligent Systems XVI, pp. 63–76. Springer, London (2009)

5. Cheng, H., Yan, X., Han, J., Hsu, C.-W.: Discriminative frequent pattern analysis for effective classification. In: IEEE 23rd International Conference on Data Engineering, ICDE 2007, pp. 716–725. IEEE (2007)

6. Aydemir, A., Jensfelt, P., Folkesson, J.: What can we learn from 38,000 rooms? reasoning about unexplored space in indoor environments. In: IEEE/RSJ International Conference on Intelligent Robots and Systems, pp. 4675–4682 (2012)

7. Anand, A., et al.: Contextually guided semantic labeling and search for three-dimensional point clouds. Int. J. Robot. Res. **32**(1), 19–34 (2013)

8. Silberman, N., Hoiem, D., Kohli, P., Fergus, R.: Indoor segmentation and support inference from RGBD images. In: Fitzgibbon, A., Lazebnik, S., Perona, P., Sato, Y., Schmid, C. (eds.) ECCV 2012, Part V. LNCS, vol. 7576, pp. 746–760. Springer, Heidelberg (2012)

9. Nüchter, A., Hertzberg, J.: Towards semantic maps for mobile robots. Robot. Auton. Syst. **56**(11), 915–926 (2008)

10. Farid, R., Sammut, C.: A relational approach to plane-based object categorization. In Robotics Science and Systems Workshop on RGB-D Cameras (2012)

11. Shin, J., Triebel, R., Siegwart, R.: Unsupervised discovery of repetitive objects. In: IEEE International Conference on Robotics and Automation, ICRA 2010, Anchorage, Alaska, USA, pp. 5041–5046. IEEE, 3–7 May 2010

12. Mattausch, O., Panozzo, D., Mura, C., Sorkine-Hornung, O., Pajarola, R.: Object detection and classification from large-scale cluttered indoor scans. Comput. Graph. Forum **33**, 11–21 (2014)

13. Biederman, I.: Recognition-by-components: a theory of human image understanding. Psychol. Rev. **94**(2), 115 (1987)

14. Verma, V., Kumar, R., Hsu, S.: 3d building detection and modeling from aerial lidar data. In: IEEE Computer Society Conference on Computer Vision and Pattern Recognition, vol. 2, pp. 2213–2220. IEEE (2006)

15. Schnabel, R., Wessel, R., Wahl, R., Klein, R.: Shape recognition in 3d point-clouds. In: Proceedings of Conference in Central Europe on Computer Graphics, Visualization and Computer Vision, vol. 2. Citeseer (2008)

16. Jahn, K., Kramer, S.: Optimizing gspan for molecular datasets. In: Proceedings of the Third International Workshop on Mining Graphs, Trees and Sequences (MGTS-2005), pp. 77–89 (2005)

17. Kudo, T., et al.: An application of boosting to graph classification. Adv. Neural Inf. Process. Syst. **17**, 729–736 (2004)

18. Fischler, M.A., Bolles, R.C.: Random sample consensus: a paradigm for model fitting with applications to image analysis and automated cartography. Commun. ACM **24**(6), 381–395 (1981)

19. Fox, D., Burgard, W., Dellaert, F., Thrun, S.: Monte carlo localization: efficient position estimation for mobile robots. AAAI/IAAI **1999**, 343–349 (1999)

Towards a Robust System Helping Underwater Archaeologists Through the Acquisition of Geo-referenced Optical and Acoustic Data

Benedetto Allotta[1], Riccardo Costanzi[1], Massimo Magrini[2], Niccoló Monni[1],
Davide Moroni[2], Maria Antonietta Pascali[2(✉)], Marco Reggiannini[2],
Alessandro Ridolfi[1], Ovidio Salvetti[2], and Marco Tampucci[2]

[1] Department of Industrial Engineering, University of Florence,
Via di Santa Marta 3, 50139 Florence, Italy
[2] SILab, Institute of Information Science and Technololgies - CNR,
Via G. Moruzzi 1, 56124 Pisa, Italy
maria.antonietta.pascali@isti.cnr.it

Abstract. In the framework of the ARROWS project (September 2012 -
August 2015), a venture funded by the European Commission, several
modular Autonomous Underwater Vehicles (AUV) have been developed
to the main purposes of mapping, diagnosing, cleaning, and securing
underwater and coastal archaeological sites. These AUVs consist of modular mobile robots, designed and manufactured according to specific suggestions formulated by a pool of archaeologists featuring long-standing
experience in the field of Underwater Cultural Heritage preservation. The
vehicles are typically equipped with acoustic modems to communicate
during the dive and with different payload devices to sense the environment. The selected sensors represent appealing choices to the oceano-
graphic engineer since they provide complementary information about
the surrounding environment. The main topics discussed in this paper
concern (i) performing a systematic mapping of the marine seafloors,
(ii) processing the output maps to detect and classify potential archaeological targets and finally (iii) developing dissemination systems with
the purpose of creating virtual scenes as a photorealistic and informative
representation of the surveyed underwater sites.

1 Introduction

Marine water covers approximately the 72 % of the planet's surface and, being
largely unexplored nowadays, it represents an unlimited source of discovery
and knowledge in several fields, from ecology to archeology. Since the marine
environment represents an extreme setting to the man, exploring these locations typically requires large amounts of funding, knowledge and expertise, and
finally, it can be seriously dangerous for the explorer. During the ARROWS
project (end August 2015), funded by the European Commission, a modular
Autonomous Underwater Vehicle (AUV) called MARTA, acronym for MARine
Tool for Archeology, has been developed. The ARROWS project is devoted to

© Springer International Publishing Switzerland 2015
L. Nalpantidis et al. (Eds.): ICVS 2015, LNCS 9163, pp. 253–262, 2015.
DOI: 10.1007/978-3-319-20904-3_24

advanced technologies and tools for mapping, diagnosing, cleaning, and securing underwater and coastal archaeological sites. MARTA AUV is a modular mobile robot designed and constructed according to the requirements formulated by a team of expert archaeologists operators, belonging to outstanding Cultural Heritage institutions (the Department of Cultural Heritage and Sicilian Identity, and the Estonian Maritime Museum). MARTA is equipped with acoustic modems to communicate when submerged and it hosts two different payload sensor to capture data: a pair of synchronised digital cameras coupled with visible light as well as structured light (blue laser) illuminators and a forward looking multibeam echo-sounder or a side looking sonar.

The data collected during the mission campaigns will be processed in order to detect targets of interest located on the seabed. These data are affected by multiple typologies of distortions, relating to both systematic as well as environmental sources of corruption (Blondel 2009). Consider the example of the geometrical distortions affecting the sonar signal, such as the central black stripe in the side scan sonar maps (Fig. 2), generated by the acoustic propagation through the water column, or the random distortions in the sonogram formation, generated by unpredictable fluctuations in the AUV attitude.

Under the hypothesis that the noise can be properly filtered out and that the geometry distortions can be corrected by exploiting the geo-referencing of the data described in Sect. 2, the relevant goal is to analyze the output data to provide a highly informative description of the environment. The main approach adopted for the detection procedures is to emphasize the amount of regularity in the captured data. This can be pursued by exploiting machine learning algorithms that perform (i) the recognition of geometrical curves (ii) the classification of seafloor areas by means of textural pattern analysis and (iii) a reliable object recognition process performing the integration of the available multimodal data. Moreover the collected raw data, together with the analysis output results, will be stored to allow for an offline accurate analysis of the archaeological findings. This will represent a powerful tool for expert users as well as for disseminating to the general public the increased knowledge about the underwater sites.

2   MARTA AUV

The specific features required during a typical underwater archaeological mission concern two main situations: in a preliminary stage the AUV surveys a large scale area with the purpose of detecting interesting areas while, in case of a detected anomaly, a further survey stage is dedicated to obtain finer details about the detected site. Each configuration requires a proper choice in terms of the sensor suite to be installed on-board the AUV. To this purpose acoustic sensors are better exploited in large scale mapping of the environment while optical sensors work at their best in small range regimes. The two cited configurations are:

– Search AUV: AUV equipped with acoustic sensors, such as Side-Scan Sonar (SSS) or MultiBeam Echo Sounder (MBES), used for fast and large surveys, searching for targets of interest;

– Inspection AUV: the AUV aim is to reach the targets, identified as potentially interesting thanks to the data acquired by the Search AUV, and to acquire optical and/or acoustic images to obtain more details.

In order to fulfill the various requirements arising in an underwater archaeological mission, one of the main design criterion for MARTA has been the **modularity**. Depending on the mission to perform, MARTA is configurable with several payloads and different propulsion systems: this way, the vehicle can play both the role of search and inspection AUV. MARTA's payload can be:

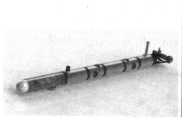 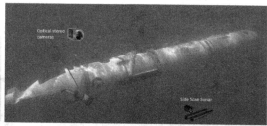

Fig. 1. MARTA final CAD (left); housing of the side scan sonar and of the cameras (right).

– Acoustic payload: a Multibeam Echo Sounder (MBES - Teledyne BlueView M900) is housed in the bow;
– Optical payload: MARTA houses a couple of Basler Ace cameras, a C-laser Fan from Ocean Tools, four illuminators.

MARTA has 5 degrees of freedom which can be fully controlled by means of 6 actuators (electrical motors plus propellers). More in detail they consist of 2 rear propellers, 2 lateral thrusters and 2 vertical thrusters. The described actuation system enables the vehicle to perform hovering. The technical features of MARTA are summarized in Table 1; Fig. 1 (left) shows the final 3D CAD outline of MARTA AUV.

The first sea trials of MARTA AUV are scheduled fro the end of March 2015, but the vehicle payload, both acoustic and optical, has been already tested at sea. This was possible by exploiting the **Typhoon** (see Fig. 1 right), an AUV that has been designed, developed and built by the UNIFI MDM Lab in the framework of the previous THESAURUS project (Allotta et al. 2014a; Allotta et al. 2014b). Typhoon AUV proved to be an useful tool for archaeologists and already performed several missions at sea with suitable payload on board. Figure 2 shows an example of side scan sonar (SSS) data captured during a Typhoon mission at the Baratti Gulf, Italy, July 2014 (the Caligola wreck is visible in the right channel). The acquisition system is based on two different PC housed on board the vehicle:

Table 1. MARTA AUV technical features.

AUV parameter	Value
Reachable depth (m)	120
Maximum longitudinal speed (kn)	4
Battery autonomy (hr)	$4 \div 6$
Length (m)	$3 \div 4$
External diameter (in)	7
Weight (kg)	~ 90
Power supply voltage (V)	24 (LiPo batteries)
Main components material	Anticorodal (corrosion-resistant **Al** alloy)
Redundant propulsion system	6 thrusters plus 2 buoyancy modules
Hovering capability	5 DOFs (except roll) fully controllable

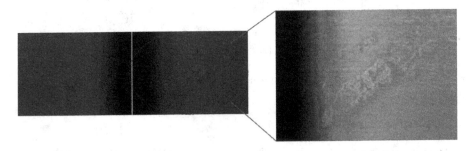

Fig. 2. Acoustic image from SSS of the Caligola wreck (right channel), Gulf of Baratti, Italy

– Vital PC: it is a very reliable industrial PC dedicated to the vital aspects that include the motion control and navigation tasks in addition to the unsafe conditions detection and response. Its capabilities are not very high as this kind of task is not very demanding from a computational point of view;
– Payload PC: it is a high performance SBC (Single Board Computer) with an i7 processor dedicated to the acquisition and the process of high amount of payload data as optical and acoustic images are.

From the software point of view, all the various modules are interfaced by means of ROS (Robots Operating System, http://www.ros.org/), a popular middleware that allows a simplified management of the data flow within the system. ROS is used also to ensure an accurate synchronization of all the available data; each piece of data is logged through the so call rosbag method along with a timestamp corresponding to the instant when it has been generated. By means of the comparison between the timestamp associated to payload data and the one associated to the navigation state, calculated through the navigation filter for the AUV pose estimation running in real-time, an accurate geo-referencing of the payload data is available since the end of the mission. Also raw navigation data (not processed output data from navigation sensors) are logged with timestamp so that, in case the real time pose estimation filter fails, payload data georeferencing can be achieved in post processing. The navigation strategy used to guarantee a valid georeferencing of the payload data is based on two independent algorithms, respectively an orientation estimation one and a position estimation one. The former exploits the use of the 3D accelerometer, the 3D gyroscope and the 3D magnetometer mounted on board; data from these sensors are fused within a Nonlinear Complementary Filter based on Mahony et al. (2008). The latter, exploiting all the navigation sensors available, follows a Kalman filtering approach within an Unscented Kalman Filter developed in the framework of the ARROWS project itself (Allotta et al. 2015).

3 Payload Data Processing

The main goal of the AUV mission is to perform a systematic mapping of the marine seafloors (e.g. in Elibol et al. (2014), for the optical mapping) and to detect and classify potential archaeological targets. To that aim the underwater vehicles will be equipped with two acquisition payloads (as described in the previous section), providing complementary information about the surrounding environment: acoustic sensors are exploited to create large scale maps of the environment while cameras provide more detailed images of the targets. Since the two sensor typologies operate on different principles the captured data are affected by different distortions, relating to both systematic as well as environmental sources of corruption. The cameras introduce geometrical distortions in the images because of the propagation of electromagnetic waves through the optical unit. Moreover the optical signal is affected by strong degradation due to energy absorption in the water medium. On the other hand acoustic sonars are affected as well by geometrical distortions. That is due to the peculiar perception of the environment: e.g. side scan sonar maps contain a central black stripe which is generated by the propagation of acoustic waves through the water column. That represents useless piece of information that has to be erased in order to restore the correct geometrical properties of the data. Also the fluctuation in the pose of the vehicle hosting the sensors may represent a relevant source of geometry distortion of the data. In case of strong oscillations of the vehicle induced by intense waves or currents this can represent a dominant issue.

This issue highlights the strong need for the synchronization of the optical and acoustic data with the navigation data records, in order to get a proper correction. Under the hypothesis that the whole set of noise sources can be reduced by proper restoration and geometry correction techniques the successive goal is to analyse the output data to provide an informative description of the environment.

3.1 Geometry Assessment

The ARROWS project is conceived to supply with technological tools the archaeological operators, hence a scene understanding procedure has to be mainly focused on man-made object recognition tasks. To that purpose the adopted criterion is to highlight the regularity content in the data. In this framework we consider regular those areas containing parts of primitive curves, like lines, circles and ellipses. Moreover regularity can be found in repeating patterns in the image spatial intensity.

Based on those features, we can perform attentive analysis of the environment by giving to an area a label of interest proportional to the regularity content: more regular areas are marked with higher ranks while chaotic and unstructured area will be marked with low ranks.

Fig. 3. Application of the curve detection algorithm to a side scan sonar image detail (image taken from http://www.jwfishers.com/).

The assessment of primitive curves segments in an image is a typical computer vision issue that has been tackled in many ways. In order to fulfill the curve detection purpose, a dedicated procedure has been developed. The implemented algorithm is based on a statistical approach in order to provide the system with enough reliability and computational performances. The application of the algorithm, based on the Gestalt theory (Desolneux et al. 2004; Patraucean et al. 2012), is more thoroughly described in Moroni et al. (2013a). Some results are shown in Fig. 3.

3.2   Texture Analysis

Texture is a descriptor of the surface appearance of objects. This parameter can be exploited to discern between different kinds of objects and to assign each of them to a specific class. In the special case of underwater mapping, textural analysis is employed to classify the surveyed environment into seafloor categories (sand, rock, vegetation). This enables the detection of anomalies that can be related to potentially interesting objects.

Within the many descriptors available in the literature we chose a method based on the Gabor filters (Jain et al. 1991). Mathematically speaking a Gabor filter is a 2D sinusoid, with specific orientation and frequency values, modulated by a Gaussian function. The convolution of this filter with an image results in a map where the regions exhibiting frequency and orientation values similar to the filter ones are emphasized. By varying frequency and orientation and repeating the convolution operation a set of filter responses is obtained. Those responses can be clustered according to the dominant component. This way every pixel in the image will be assigned to a specific class. The application of Gabor filters for textural analysis purposes is illustrated in Fig. 4.

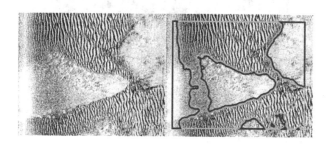

Fig. 4. SSS map segmentation by exploiting of a Gabor filtering technique (image taken from http://www.ise.bc.ca/)

3.3 Data Integration

As stated in the previous sections, each sensor employed in the survey missions will provide an individual description of the environment. As far as a robust object recognition process is pursued, it is interesting to conceive a synthesis structure summarizing all the informative content related to an area of the seabed. This can be formally expressed by introducing a multi-dimensional map, made up of multiple layers. A point in this map gives details about the whole information available for the corresponding point in the world (Moroni et al. 2013b). This refers to information concerning (i) the raw captured data, (ii) the results of data analysis algorithms and (iii) the bathymetry collected by proper sensors or estimated by computer vision procedures. It is expected that considering the whole set of available information can be an efficient way to perform a robust object recognition, reliable with respect to false alarms rejection. An example of data integration result, obtained by stitching the camera images mosaic on the multi-beam bathymetry is illustrated in Fig. 5.

4   3D Rendering and the Virtual Environment

The whole set of data acquired in each acquisition campaign is the base for (i) the 3D modelling of the archaeological inspected, and (ii) the virtual reconstruction of the archaeological site where the finds are located. These two outputs are of great importance for both the community of archaeologists and the general public. The availability of detailed data about an object of interest allows

Fig. 5. Bathymetric map, obtained by means of a multi-beam echo-sounder, integrated with an optical mosaic. The data have been captured during an experiment performed in the small pool facility of the Ocean Systems Lab, Heriot Watt University, Edinburgh (Scotland)

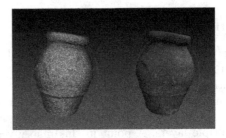

Fig. 6. Detailed reconstruction of an amphora: only mesh (left) and textured (right)

building a detailed 3D model to be studied by experts. The visualization and comparison with existing findings will lead to a deeper knowledge of the inspected site without any risk for the people involved in the acquisition campaign. The method used for the 3D modelling is based mainly on multi-view stereo algorithms applied to the optical data. The detailed reconstruction of the mesh (geometric structure) and the texture (appearance) of a single object of interest will be semi-automated in order to fulfill the archaeological validation (see Fig. 6). The virtual reconstruction will be interactive (enabling the user to explore the environment) and possibly multimodal (linking videos, pictures, text, 3D models to specific points of interest in the scene). This way the fruition will ensure an immersive and informative setting for promoting access and exploiting the rich underwater cultural heritage. The reconstructed mesh is refined through advanced 3D computer graphics tools (e.g. Blender, MeshLab). Then the meshes (objects and terrain) are integrated together in a virtual environment exploiting advanced game engine functionalities (e.g. Unity) in order to obtain a more immersive and better detailed scene (see Fig. 7). The scene fruition can be performed also through the most recent 3D interaction devices, like Oculus Rift (see Fig. 8), and gestural interfaces, like Kinect and Hot Hand.

Fig. 7. Scene reconstruction exploiting Unity game engine.

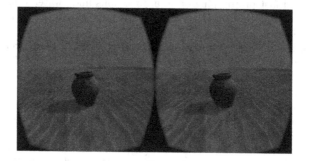

Fig. 8. View of the 3D Virtual Environment through Oculus Rift

5   Conclusions

The robotic and automation technology presented in this paper will make easier the underwater archaeologist work, carried out in a hostile and complex environment. The archaeologist will be provided with techniques to perform indirect measurements and to formulate historical interpretations on the findings. Moreover, in order to disseminate knowledge regarding the underwater cultural heritage and to increase the sensitivity for its preservation, the developed tools allow to address different audiences, including the general public. In particular, one of the purposes of the project is to devise new dissemination channels making use of 3D immersive environments to make more attractive the collected information. In the next months, the developed methodology will be tested by organizing specific campaigns in two European sites, one in Italy, in the Egadi Archipelagos, and one in the Baltic sea. All the collected data will be processed using the methods reported in this paper and will be used for assessing the validity of our approach. As a result, a set of 3D scenes will be produced, with the aim of replicating the experience of wreck exploration and survey.

The activity described in this paper has been supported by the ARROWS project, funded by the European Union 7th Framework Programme for research, technological development and demonstration under grant agreement no. 308724. The authors would like to thank Dr. Pamela Gambogi, Executive Archaeologist and Coordinator of the Underwater Operational Team of the Tuscany Archaeological Superintendence. The authors would also like to thank Prof. Yvan Petillot and Prof. David Lane from Heriot Watt University of Edinburgh, for kindly providing access to the facilities of the Ocean Systems Laboratory.

References

Allotta, B., Costanzi, R., Meli, E., Pugi, L., Ridolfi, A., Vettori, G.: Cooperative localization of a team of AUVs by a tetrahedral configuration. In: Robotics and Autonomous Systems, vol. 62, pp. 1228–1237. Elsevier (2014)

Allotta, B., Pugi, L., Bartolini, F., Ridolfi, A., Costanzi, R., Monni, N., Gelli, J.: Preliminary design and fast prototyping of an autonomous underwater vehicle propulsion system. Proc. Inst. Mech. Eng., Part M, J. Eng. Marit. Environ. (2014). doi:10.1177/1475090213514040

Allotta, B., Caiti, A., Chisci, L., Costanzi, R., Di Corato, F., Fantacci, C., Fenucci, D., Meli, E., Ridolfi, A.: Development of a navigation algorithm for autonomous underwater vehicles. In: IFAC Workshop on Navigation Guidance and Control of Underwater Vehicles (NGCUV 2015), Girona, Spain (2015)

Blondel, P.: The Handbook of Sidescan Sonar. Springer Praxis Books, New York (2009)

Desolneux, A., Moisan, L., Morel, J.M.: Gestalt theory and computer vision. In: Seeing, Thinking and Knowing. vol. 38, pp. 71–101. Kluwer (2004)

Elibol, A., Kim, J., Gracias, N., Garcia, R.: Efficient image mosaicing for multi-robot visual underwater mapping. Pattern Recognit. Lett. **46**, 2026 (2014)

Jain, K.A., Farrokhnia, F.: Unsupervised texture segmentation using gabor filters. Pattern Recognit. **24**(12), 1167–1186 (1991)

Mahony, R.E., Hamel, T., Pflimlin, J.M.: Nonlinear complementary filters on the special orthogonal group. IEEE Trans. Autom. Control **53**(5), 1203–1218 (2008)

Moroni, D., Pascali, M.A., Reggiannini, M., Salvetti, O.: Curve recognition for underwater wrecks and handmade artefacts. In: IMTA13, 3rd International Workshop on Image Mining. Theory and Applications (2013)

Moroni, D., Pascali, M.A., Reggiannini, M., Salvetti, O.: Underwater scene understanding by optical and acoustic data integration. In: Proceedings of Meeting on Acoustics, vol. 17 (2013)

Pătrăucean, V., Gurdjos, P., von Gioi, R.G.: A parameterless line segment and elliptical arc detector with enhanced ellipse fitting. In: Fitzgibbon, A., Lazebnik, S., Perona, P., Sato, Y., Schmid, C. (eds.) ECCV 2012, Part II. LNCS, vol. 7573, pp. 572–585. Springer, Heidelberg (2012)

3D Object Pose Refinement in Range Images

Xenophon Zabulis[✉], Manolis Lourakis, and Panagiotis Koutlemanis

Institute of Computer Science, Foundation for Research and Technology - Hellas,
Nikolaou Plastira 100, 70013 Heraklion, Greece
{zabulis,lourakis,koutle}@ics.forth.gr

Abstract. Estimating the pose of objects from range data is a problem of considerable practical importance for many vision applications. This paper presents an approach for accurate and efficient 3D pose estimation from 2.5D range images. Initialized with an approximate pose estimate, the proposed approach refines it so that it accurately accounts for an acquired range image. This is achieved by using a hypothesize-and-test scheme that combines Particle Swarm Optimization (PSO) and graphics-based rendering to minimize a cost function of object pose that quantifies the misalignment between the acquired and a hypothesized, rendered range image. Extensive experimental results demonstrate the superior performance of the approach compared to the Iterative Closest Point (ICP) algorithm that is commonly used for pose refinement.

1 Introduction

Human-made environments abound with textureless objects and several applications demand knowledge of their position and orientation (i.e., pose) in 3D space. Examples include household object manipulation in service robotics or bin picking and intelligent assembly in industrial settings. In such scenarios, the pose of textureless objects cannot be estimated with state of the art techniques like [5,14] that capture object appearance via photometric local patch detectors and descriptors.

When visual texture is not available, depth measurements provided by range sensors become a natural choice of input for determining object pose. The recent proliferation of low-cost RGB-D sensors such as the Kinect has renewed interest in depth-based object recognition and localization. Pose estimation in range images is often addressed as a final step in model-based object detection and recognition pipelines [15]. Such approaches typically estimate pose in a geometric verification step that is aimed to confirm the agreement of a certain model with the depth data and thus eliminate false positives. Since an approximate pose is often provided as a byproduct of object recognition, the ICP algorithm whose initialization is requires such a pose is a highly popular choice for pose refinement with 3D data.

This work deals with accurately estimating the pose of arbitrary rigid objects for which a 3D model and an initial pose are available. Its contributions include (a) an algorithm for model-based pose refinement, that is based on the simultaneous evaluation of many pose hypotheses and is shown to perform better than

© Springer International Publishing Switzerland 2015
L. Nalpantidis et al. (Eds.): ICVS 2015, LNCS 9163, pp. 263–274, 2015.
DOI: 10.1007/978-3-319-20904-3_25

Fig. 1. Method overview; left to right: *(a)* input depth image and detected edges superimposed. Thumbnails show in magnification the depth values and edges (bottom) and color-coded surface normals (top, see text). *(b)* visualization of the initial poses for an electrical fuse and fusebox. *(c)* rendering of the fusebox, generated during hypothesis formulation, and detected edges superimposed; the illustrated pose is also the refined, output pose; thumbnails as in (a). *(d)* visualization of the refined poses (Color figure online).

ICP, (b) a novel objective function for comparing the alignment of two range images and (c) an efficient parallel implementation of the algorithm on the GPU. The proposed approach employs a range image and an initial, possibly crude, pose estimate which is assumed to originate from an object recognition algorithm. The accuracy of this pose is improved using exclusively depth information and making no assumptions regarding the presence of texture. Apart from the provision of an initial pose, the approach is oblivious to the object recognition algorithm, details of which shall not concern us in this paper.

An overview of the proposed approach is illustrated in Fig. 1. It employs a hypothesize-and-test scheme that forms pose hypotheses and evaluates them by generating synthetic depth images and measuring their affinity to the acquired image. This measurement involves the depth values, the associated surface normals, and the edges of the two depth images. The evaluated pose that best accounts for the observed data is kept. Candidate and final resulting poses are visualized in Fig. 1 by overlaying upon intensity images renderings of the object models at these poses, along with the depth edges detected at the corresponding depth images. Intensity images are used solely for illustration.

Accurate pose estimation for small objects with consumer RGB-D sensors is challenging due to the wide FOV and medium imaging detail of the latter, resulting in noisy depth measurements of low precision and resolution [13]. The proposed approach strives to maximize the number of pixels involved in a comparison. No correspondences need to be established between the depth image and the 3D model. Furthermore, no assumptions are made regarding the richness of surface normal variations or surface texture, hence the approach has no issues with large planar faces or densely textured objects. Missing data and moderate occlusions are tolerated and the implementation greatly benefits from the availability of modern GPU hardware. The approach employs a fully projective imaging formulation and can readily accommodate new objects of arbitrary resolution without any parameter tuning.

2   Previous Work

Pose estimation from 3D data is often addressed in the broader context of object detection and recognition. Existing approaches use either object-centered or view-centered representations. In the first case, distinctive features of an object's shape are extracted and their properties are encoded in an object-centered coordinate system to form a model that is independent of an observation viewpoint. Given a depth image with an unknown object, the latter is recognized by matching its features with those of a model. The pose of the object can be estimated from the underlying geometries of corresponding features using standard absolute orientation techniques [11]. Most approaches in the literature fall in this category and a far from exhaustive list includes spin images [12], 3D shape contexts [9], point histograms [19] and oriented point pairs [6]. It should be noted that these approaches perform better on clean, high-resolution and complete 3D scans rather than on noisy, low-resolution 2.5D range images. In recent years, local point feature descriptors that combine texture and shape cues on a per pixel basis have appeared, e.g. [8,23]. Nevertheless, such works focus primarily on the aspect of description and do not address the issue of feature detection.

View-centered representations capture the appearance of an object using multiple descriptions, each dependent on the vantage point from which the object is observed. Such approaches are trained with several images of an object at different poses and distances from the viewer. Descriptions extracted from these images are stored in an associative index along with the pose of the object. Recognizing an object in an image then amounts to finding its best match among the descriptions stored in the index. A rough estimate of object pose is readily provided by the pose associated with the best matching description. For example, Hinterstoisser et al. devised an efficient template matching technique capable of detecting textureless 3D objects [10]. They rely on depth edges and surface normals to represent an object with a set of binary training templates. The pose retrieved from the best matching template is used as a starting point for subsequent refinement with ICP. Tejani et al. [22] converted an early version of [10] to a scale-invariant patch descriptor and combined it with a regression forest. Park et al. [16] use rendering to construct a database of reference range images from multiple viewpoints, identify in parallel the reference image among them that best aligns with the input one and finally refine its pose with ICP. Wang et al. [24] develop a descriptor which combines color and shape features. They employ surface patches and describe them using color histograms and shape features that depend upon the geometric relationship of patch points with the patch centroid and the sensor viewpoint. Descriptors extracted from images of unknown objects are used in a nearest neighbor search to determine the identity of objects and their approximate 3D pose. Choi and Christensen [4] augment oriented point pairs with color information and use them in a voting scheme to generate clusters of pose hypotheses the most voted of which are refined with ICP. Sun et al. [21] represent objects as collections of patch parts and propose a generalized Hough voting scheme for object detection, succeeded by pose estimation with ICP.

In view-centered approaches, the pose retrieved via the best matching template is approximate. This is due to the limited resolution of the pose sampling process in training and potentially slightly wrong matches during recognition. Therefore, the retrieved pose should be refined with an optimization step that typically employs ICP [1,18]. It is well-known that ICP is sensitive to initialization, converging correctly only when sufficient overlap exists between two point sets and no gross outliers are present. Otherwise, it can easily get stuck in local minima. This has motivated the recent trend to regularize the ICP error metric by using sparsity-inducing $\mathcal{L}_p$ norms for $p \leq 1$. In this work, we propose to substitute ICP with the optimization scheme described in Sect. 3. This scheme is compared in Sect. 4 with a modern ICP variant based on $\mathcal{L}_p$ norms [2].

3   Proposed Method

The proposed method estimates the pose of an object whose position and orientation in space are assumed to be approximately known. Its input is a mesh model of the object, an initial object pose $\{\mathbf{R}_0, \mathbf{t}_0\}$, the acquired depth image and the depth sensor's intrinsic parameters. The result is a refined pose $\{\mathbf{R}, \mathbf{t}\}$. Both the initial and the refined poses refer to the sensor coordinate frame. Objects are represented with arbitrary 3D triangle meshes, which can originate from CAD drawings or digital scans. A mesh $\mathcal{M}$ is comprised of an ordered set of 3D vertex points V and an ordered set G of triplet indices upon V that define the mesh triangles. The 3D oriented bounding box B of each model is precomputed using the eigenvectors of V's covariance matrix.

The method generates candidate poses $\{\mathbf{R}_i, \mathbf{t}_i\}$ and evaluates them with the aid of depth images S_i synthesized by rendering $\mathcal{M}$ at each $\{\mathbf{R}_i, \mathbf{t}_i\}$. An objective function yields score $o(i)$, which quantifies the similarity between the acquired depth image and each S_i. The proposed objective function effectively compares two depth images using depth, edge and orientation cues and is amenable to a parallel implementation. Derivative-free particle swarm optimization is used to efficiently explore the pose space and optimize the objective function. Finally, the pose whose rendering is found to be the most similar to the acquired depth image is selected. Details on the method follow next.

Initialization. The initial pose is used to bootstrap pose estimation and can be quite crude. The projection of the model at the initial pose determines a 2D, axis-aligned bounding box b. To mitigate possible initial pose inaccuracies, b is inflated proportionally to the initial camera-object distance. To suppress sensor noise, the acquired depth image is median filtered (with a 5×5 kernel) and the result is retained as image D. Depth shadows and other shortcomings of consumer depth sensors manifest as invalid pixels in D. Surface normals for valid depth pixels are estimated by local plane fitting and stored in N. A binary image E is computed by Sobel edge detection on D. The distance transform T of E [7] is also computed for later use. These operations are parallelized on the GPU at pixel level, while T uses the parallel formulation of [3]. Only D is uploaded to the GPU, which uses it to compute N and T.

Pose Hypotheses Rendering. A rendering process simulates depth images of the target object at a hypothesized pose against a blank background. The simulated depth sensor shares the same intrinsic and extrinsic parameters with the real sensor. A rendered image simulates the image that the latter would acquire if it imaged the target object in isolation, at the hypothesized pose. Pose rendering is formulated as follows. Transform $\{\mathbf{R}_0, \mathbf{t}_0\}$ brings the model to an approximate location and orientation, in the sensor's reference frame. Candidate poses are parametrized relative to this initial pose, using a relative translation $\mathbf{t}_i$ and an "in place" rotation $\mathbf{R}_i$. This rotation is with respect to the centroid $\mathbf{c}$ of points in V. Specifically, the model is first translated by $-\mathbf{c}$ to center it on the coordinate axes origin, then rotated by $\mathbf{R}_i$, and finally translated back in place by $\mathbf{c}$. Rotation $\mathbf{R}_i$ is thus the product of primitive rotations about the 3 axes: $\mathbf{R}_i = \mathbf{R}_x(\theta_i) \cdot \mathbf{R}_y(\phi_i) \cdot \mathbf{R}_z(\omega_i)$. The transformation model point $\mathbf{x}$ undergoes is, thus, $\mathbf{R}_i \cdot (\mathbf{x} - \mathbf{c}) + \mathbf{c} + \mathbf{t}_i$. To avoid repeated calculations, the initial and candidate poses are combined into the following overall transformation:

$$\mathbf{R}_i \cdot \mathbf{R}_0 \cdot \mathbf{x} + \mathbf{R}_i \cdot (\mathbf{t}_0 - \mathbf{c}) + \mathbf{c} + \mathbf{t}_i. \tag{1}$$

The model transformed according to Eq. (1) is rendered in depth image S_i. Depth edges and surface normals of S_i are computed and stored in binary image E_i and data structure N_i, respectively, for subsequent use.

Computation and storage of S_i, E_i, and N_i is delegated to the GPU. The process employs Z-buffering to respect visibility and realistically deal with self-occlusions. Parallelization is performed at two levels of granularity. At a fine level, rendering is parallelized upon the triangles of the rendered mesh. At a coarser level, multiple hypotheses are rendered together, with a composite image gathering all renderings (see Fig. 2). In this manner, multiple hypotheses are evaluated in a single batch, resulting in better utilization of GPU resources and reduced CPU communication. Edge detection is applied once, directly upon the composite image.

Fig. 2. A composite depth image for 50 pose hypotheses, all rendered in one batch. Each hypothesis is bounded by a rectangle and cropped when lying outside it, to avoid interference with its neighbors. Brighter pixels are further away from the sensor.

Pose Hypotheses Evaluation. A candidate pose is evaluated with respect to the extent to which it explains the acquired depth image. Ideally, rendering the object model at its true pose would produce an image identical to the acquired one. Function $o(\cdot)$ avails a score $o(i)$ by examining the similarity of depth values, surface normals, as well as edges between D and S_i. Two range images are corresponded in terms of their coordinates and are compared as follows. Depth values from D and S_i are compared pixelwise. For n pixel pairs, depth differences δ_k are computed and the cumulative depth cost term is given by Eq. (2), in which $|\delta_k|$ is set to ∞ if greater than a threshold d_T (20 mm in our implementation) to avoid comparing with background surfaces. For the same n pairs of pixels, the cost due to surface normal differences is as in Eq. (3), where γ_k equals the dot product of the two corresponding surface normals. Edge differences are aggregated in an edge cost using E and E_i. Let m be the number of edgels of E_i within bounding box b. For each such edgel j, let ϵ_j be the distance from its closest edgel in D which is looked up from T. The corresponding edge cost term is given by Eq. (4).

$$d_i = \sum_{k=1}^{n} \frac{1}{|\delta_k| + 1} \quad (2) \qquad u_i = \sum_{k=1}^{n} \frac{1}{|\gamma_k| + 1} \quad (3) \qquad e_i = \sum_{j=1}^{m} \frac{1}{\epsilon_j + 1} \quad (4)$$

Each of the cost terms in Eqs. (2)–(4) involves two ordered pixel sets, one from each image D and S_i, that contain the pixel locations to be compared. As d_i, u_i, and e_i have different numeric ranges, the combined cost is defined by their cubed geometric mean, i.e. $o(i) = -d_i \cdot e_i \cdot u_i$. The minus sign is used to ensure that optimal values correspond to minima, since d_i, e_i and u_i are non-negative. Summing the reciprocals of partial differences $|\delta_k|$, $|\gamma_k|$ and ϵ_j rewards poses that maximize the support (i.e., spatial overlap) between the compared regions of D and S_i: these partial sums are positive, thus the more pixels, the lower (better) the overall score becomes. The larger a difference, the smaller its induced decrease in the score. Hence, the objective function improves when more pixels in the rendered depth map overlap with the surfaces captured in the acquired image, whereas pose hypotheses based on little support do not yield good scores. Computation of $o(i)$ is parallelized per pixel on the GPU with minimal CPU communication. The scores of multiple pose hypotheses, evaluated together, are grouped and sent to the host CPU in a single message.

As no segmentation procedure is employed, during the evaluation of inaccurate pose hypotheses, the rendered object may be compared against pixels that correspond to background or occluding surfaces. To counter this effect, only pixels located within b are considered. Hypotheses that correspond to renderings partially outside b obtain a poor similarity score and thus the solution does not drift towards an irrelevant surface. Moreover, during the evaluation of each hypothesis, the oriented bounding box B_i that corresponds to hypothesis i is computed by transforming B according to Eq. (1). By so doing, depth pixels within b but corresponding to 3D points outside B_i are not considered, as they are irrelevant to the evaluated hypothesis.

Pose Optimization. The search space for pose estimation is constrained in a 6D neighborhood of the initial pose estimate $\{\mathbf{R}_0, \mathbf{t}_0\}$. As the cost of an exhaustive grid-based search is prohibitive, a numerical optimization approach is adopted to optimize objective function $o(\cdot)$ and find the pose that yields the highest similarity between the rendered and acquired image. Minimization of $o(\cdot)$ is based on PSO [17], which has proven to be an effective and efficient computational method for solving other vision optimization problems [25]. PSO stochastically evolves a population of candidate solutions dubbed particles that explore the parameter space in runs called generations. PSO does not require knowledge of the derivatives of the objective function, depends on very few parameters and requires a relatively small number of objective function evaluations until convergence. Compared to gradient-based optimization methods, PSO has a wider basin of convergence, exhibiting better robustness to local minima. Furthermore, as particles evolve independently at each generation, it is amenable to an efficient parallel implementation.

The rotational component of candidate poses is parameterized using Euler angles while translation is parameterized with Euclidean coordinates. Each dimension of the pose search space is bounded, defining a search hyperrectangle centered on the initial pose estimate. Particles are initialized with the aid of a 6D Sobol sequence [20], which ensures a good spatial distribution. PSO updates the state of each particle after the completion of each generation, whereas particles evolve independently within a generation. This observation suggests that the rendering and evaluation of particles representing pose hypotheses can be parallelized at every generation. As confirmed experimentally (see Sect. 4), such an optimization results into considerable computational savings.

4 Experiments

The proposed method was implemented in C++ and CUDA on a PC with an NVIDIA $GTX580$ programmable GPU. The Kinect 1 RGB-D sensor was employed for data acquisition in the experiments, thus D's resolution was 480×640 pixels and its field of view $57° \times 43°$. All experiments employed a PSO with parallelized hypotheses rendering. This PSO with 50 particles and 50 generations requires ≈ 0.1 s per frame to estimate the pose of a model with ≈ 7K triangles. Compared to the 1.2 s required when hypotheses are evaluated sequentially, this time constitutes a 12-fold speedup.

Experiments employed data from the public dataset[1] of [10]. This dataset consists of 15 RGB-D sequences of textureless objects captured with a Kinect sensor that scanned a mostly static scene from various viewpoints. Occlusions, background clutter and sensor noise contribute to the emergence of significant amounts of outliers in the depth data. A subset of 11 sequences were used in the experiments reported here, which were selected depending on whether a triangle mesh model for the corresponding object was included in the dataset. Thus, the selected sequences are the 'duck', 'cat', 'ape', 'benchviseblue', 'can', 'driller', 'glue', 'holepuncher', 'iron', 'lamp' and 'phone', comprised of approximately 1200 RGB-D frames each. The corresponding models have between 11.6 K

---

[1] http://campar.in.tum.de/Main/StefanHinterstoisser.

Fig. 3. Sample results from the experiments, for the 'duck', 'cat', and 'ape' sequences (left to right). For each result, shown is the RGB image on the left and a zoomed-in visualization of the estimated pose to its right (Color figure online).

and 467.5 K triangle faces. Objects measure from 5 to 15 cm in each dimension and are between 0.8 to 1.2 m away from the sensor. Figure 3 shows indicative pose estimation results with the proposed method.

Ground truth sensor poses obtained via marker-based extrinsic calibration from the RGB images are included in the dataset. To make the experiments independent of a particular object recognition method, the initial pose estimates required by our method were obtained by Monte Carlo-type simulations as random perturbations of the ground truth poses. More specifically, the ground truth pose for each frame was additively perturbed by a random vector following a multivariate uniform distribution. The marginal distributions of this vector were uniform in the interval $[-\tau\,\mathrm{mm},\,\tau\,\mathrm{mm}]$ for the translational components and $[-\alpha°,\,\alpha°]$ for the rotational ones; this perturbation is henceforth denoted as $U\{\tau\,\mathrm{mm},\alpha°\}$. Perturbations were applied independently to each pose parameter. This was repeated 10 times for each frame, estimating the pose for each perturbation and averaging the obtained pose estimation errors. Pose error was quantified by the misalignment between the true and estimated pose, as in [10]: for a ground truth pose $\{\mathbf{R}_g,\mathbf{t}_g\}$ and an estimated one $\{\mathbf{R}_e,\mathbf{t}_e\}$, the error is $e = (\sum_i |\mathbf{g}_i - \mathbf{e}_i|)/\nu$, where $\mathbf{g}_i = \mathbf{R}_g x_i + \mathbf{t}_g$, $\mathbf{e}_i = \mathbf{R}_e x_i + \mathbf{t}_e$, and i enumerates the ν vertices of V.

Impact of PSO Parameters. These experiments investigate the impact of key PSO parameters on the accuracy and speed performance of the proposed method. Its computational cost is determined by the number of objective function evaluations, which relates directly to the number of model renderings. PSO involves p particles that evolve for g generations, amounting to a total of $p \cdot g$ renderings. This product represents a tradeoff between accuracy and speed of execution and we refer to it as the "budget" of an optimization. A small budget will lead to premature termination and poor pose estimate, while a large budget will prolong execution without noticeable improvements in accuracy. An application of PSO with p particles and g generations is referred to as *configuration p/g*.

A set of exponentially decreasing budgets, namely configurations 200/200, 100/100, 50/50 and 25/25, examine the performance of the method with different settings. For each frame and configuration, the true pose was perturbed 10 times with $U\{20\,\mathrm{mm},20°\}$, then used to bootstrap the proposed method and finally the obtained pose estimation errors were averaged. Figure 4(left) summarizes the average execution time, whereas Fig. 4(right) illustrates the corresponding mean errors for the estimated poses. Sequences are enumerated in the order referenced in Sect. 4. As rendering time depends on the number of model trian-gles, pose estimation time was different for each object. From those figures, it is observed that configuration 50/50, amounting in 2500 renderings, constitutes a good tradeoff between accuracy and execution time.

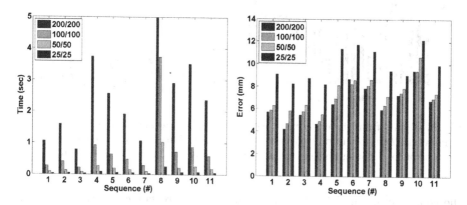

Fig. 4. Results from the decreasing budgets experiment from 533880 pose estimations. *Left:* execution times for the 4 configurations and all 11 sequences used. The vertical axis is limited to 5 s. The execution time for configuration #1 for sequence 8 is 15 s (its model has 467.5 K faces) and is off the chart. *Right:* accuracy obtained with the different configurations, shown by the mean error for each sequence.

Given a suitable budget, its allocation between particles and generations is investigated next. Towards this end, 7 configurations of particles and generations were considered, all with approximately the same budget of 2500 renderings: 125/20, 20/125, 100/25, 25/100, 63/40, 40/63, and 50/50. The same random perturbation $U\{20\,\text{mm}, 20°\}$ of the true pose was employed for the initial poses. Figure 5 shows the mean pose errors for the 7 configurations and all models. It is observed that for a given budget, a large number of particles is more beneficial than a large number of generations. This is because more particles avail a better coverage of pose space, reducing the possibility that the global minimum is missed for a local one. Besides, more particles entail increased parallelism among rendering calculations. For the configurations tested, it was also observed that PSO typically converged to a minimum in fewer than 50 generations, yielding more generations redundant. The most accurate configuration was 100/25 and, since it is also one of the most efficient, it is adopted when execution time is of primary concern.

Comparison with ICP. The accuracy of the proposed method was compared against a state-of-the-art ICP variant, chosen for its increased robustness to outliers. Specifically, the sparse ICP of [2] with the point-to-plane metric, referred to as "SICP" in the following, was employed for the comparison. The input to SICP was oriented 3D points produced by rendering models at the initial poses. Compared with the alternative of directly matching the range sensor data against

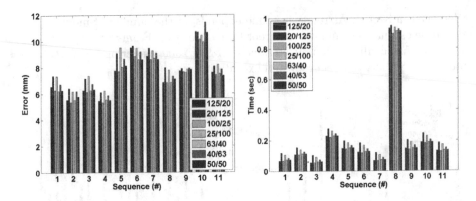

Fig. 5. Results from the experiment with the fixed budget, summarizing 934290 pose estimations. *Left:* execution times for the 7 configurations and all 11 sequences. *Right:* mean error for 7 configurations, grouped per each of the 11 employed sequences.

the complete 3D models, this choice enables a more fair comparison with the proposed method. The reason is that it prevents SICP from matching the input with self-occluded parts of the model and, at the same time, ensures that the point clouds being matched are of similar densities. PSO was applied with the configuration 100/100 as this was found in the previous experiment to yield accurate results within a moderate amount of time.

For each frame, ground truth poses were perturbed 10 times using $U\{20\,\text{mm}, 20°\}$, $U\{30\,\text{mm}, 30°\}$ and $U\{40\,\text{mm}, 40°\}$. For the larger of these perturbations, the corresponding initial poses differ considerably from the true ones. The pose for each perturbation was estimated with both the proposed method and SICP and the means of the pose estimate errors were computed. The results in Fig. 6, illustrate that the proposed method is more accurate than SICP. It is also more robust as indicated by the standard deviations of the errors (not included due to lack of space), which are much smaller for the proposed method.

We further report a wider basin of convergence for the proposed method. As the inaccuracy of the initial poses increases, SICP yields large errors, but this has only a marginal effect on the magnitude of the estimation errors for the proposed method which exhibits a graceful degradation: perturbations rising up to $U\{40\,\text{mm}, 40°\}$ still yield small errors for the proposed method, while SICP yields considerably larger errors that are comparable to the size of the objects and, therefore, can be regarded as pose estimation failures. In a view-centered pipeline (cf. Sect. 2), this facilitates a coarser sampling of training poses for the recognition step, while preserving pose estimation accuracy.

A direct comparison with [10] is not possible as its authors did not publish similarly detailed pose errors for these data. This is because they were only interested in comparing the pose errors against a threshold defined relative to the diameter of a model in order to determine whether a detected object corresponded to a true positive. It is noted that the performance of SICP constitutes

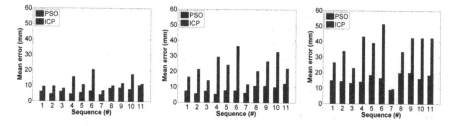

Fig. 6. Mean errors in mm for the PSO and SICP methods for perturbations $U\{20\,\text{mm}, 20°\}$ (left), $U\{30\,\text{mm}, 30°\}$ (middle), and $U\{40\,\text{mm}, 40°\}$ (right). Each pair of vertical bars summarizes errors from 800160 pose estimations.

an upper bound on the performance of standard ICP variants, which would perform considerably worse due to their sensitivity to outliers, clutter and occlusions. As a result, the performance of SICP is a good indication of what can at best be achieved with ICP-based approaches.

5   Conclusions

This paper has presented an approach for accurately localizing 3D objects in range images. Bootstrapped with an initial pose estimate, the proposed approach refines it using a scheme that combines population-based randomized optimization with rendering-based synthesis. Extensive experiments on publicly available data have demonstrated that it can successfully cope with the limitations of current consumer RGB-D sensors, while delivering superior accuracy, robustness and speed compared to the commonly used ICP algorithm.

Acknowledgements. This work has received funding from the EC FP7 programme under grant no. 270138 DARWIN and by FORTH-ICS internal RTD Programme "Ambient Intelligence and Smart Environments".

References

1. Besl, P., McKay, N.: A method for registration of 3-D shapes. PAMI **14**(2), 239–256 (1992)
2. Bouaziz, S., Tagliasacchi, A., Pauly, M.: Sparse iterative closest point. Comput. Graph. Forum **32**(5), 113–123 (2013)
3. Cao, T.-T., Tang, K., Mohamed, A., Tan, T.-S.: Parallel banding algorithm to compute exact distance transform with the GPU. In: I3D, pp. 83–90 (2010)
4. Choi, C., Christensen, H.: 3D pose estimation of daily objects using an RGB-D camera. In: IROS, pp. 3342–3349 (2012)
5. Collet, A., Martinez, M., Srinivasa, S.: The MOPED framework: object recognition and pose estimation for manipulation. Int. J. Robot. Res. **30**(10), 1284–1306 (2011)
6. Drost, B., Ulrich, M., Navab, N., Ilic, S.: Model globally, match locally: efficient and robust 3D object recognition. In: CVPR, pp. 998–1005, June 2010

7. Felzenszwalb, P., Huttenlocher, D.: Distance transforms of sampled functions. Theory Comput. **8**(19), 415–428 (2012)
8. Fischer, J., Bormann, R., Arbeiter, G., Verl, A.: A feature descriptor for textureless object representation using 2D and 3D cues from RGB-D data. In: ICRA, pp. 2112–2117 (2013)
9. Frome, A., Huber, D., Kolluri, R., Bülow, T., Malik, J.: Recognizing objects in range data using regional point descriptors. In: Pajdla, T., Matas, J.G. (eds.) ECCV 2004. LNCS, vol. 3023, pp. 224–237. Springer, Heidelberg (2004)
10. Hinterstoisser, S., Lepetit, V., Ilic, S., Holzer, S., Bradski, G., Konolige, K., Navab, N.: Model based training, detection and pose estimation of texture-less 3D objects in heavily cluttered scenes. In: Lee, K.M., Matsushita, Y., Rehg, J.M., Hu, Z. (eds.) ACCV 2012, Part I. LNCS, vol. 7724, pp. 548–562. Springer, Heidelberg (2013)
11. Horn, B.: Closed-form solution of absolute orientation using unit quaternions. J. Optical Soc. Am. A **4**(4), 629–642 (1987)
12. Johnson, A., Hebert, M.: Using spin images for efficient object recognition in cluttered 3D scenes. PAMI **21**(5), 433–449 (1999)
13. Khoshelham, K., Elberink, S.: Accuracy and resolution of kinect depth data for indoor mapping applications. Sensors **12**(2), 1437–1454 (2012)
14. Lourakis, M., Zabulis, X.: Model-based pose estimation for rigid objects. In: Chen, M., Leibe, B., Neumann, B. (eds.) ICVS 2013. LNCS, vol. 7963, pp. 83–92. Springer, Heidelberg (2013)
15. Mian, A., Bennamoun, M., Owens, R.: Automatic correspondence for 3D modeling: an extensive review. Int. J. Shape Model. **11**(02), 253–291 (2005)
16. Park, I., Germann, M., Breitenstein, M., Pfister, H.: Fast and automatic object pose estimation for range images on the GPU. Mach. Vis. Appl. **21**(5), 749–766 (2010)
17. Poli, R., Kennedy, J., Blackwell, T.: Particle swarm optimization. Swarm Intell. **1**(1), 33–57 (2007)
18. Rusinkiewicz, S., Levoy, M.: Efficient variants of the ICP algorithm. In: 3DIM, pp. 145–152 (2001)
19. Rusu, R., Blodow, N., Beetz, M.: Fast point feature histograms (FPFH) for 3D registration. In: ICRA, pp. 3212–3217 (2009)
20. Sobol, I.: Distribution of points in a cube and approximate evaluation of integrals. U.S.S.R. Comput. Maths. Math. Phys. **7**, 86–112 (1967)
21. Sun, M., Bradski, G., Xu, B.-X., Savarese, S.: Depth-encoded hough voting for joint object detection and shape recovery. In: Daniilidis, K., Maragos, P., Paragios, N. (eds.) ECCV 2010, Part V. LNCS, vol. 6315, pp. 658–671. Springer, Heidelberg (2010)
22. Tejani, A., Tang, D., Kouskouridas, R., Kim, T.-K.: Latent-class hough forests for 3D object detection and pose estimation. In: Fleet, D., Pajdla, T., Schiele, B., Tuytelaars, T. (eds.) ECCV 2014, Part VI. LNCS, vol. 8694, pp. 462–477. Springer, Heidelberg (2014)
23. Tombari, F., Salti, S., di Stefano, L.: A combined texture-shape descriptor for enhanced 3D feature matching. In: ICIP, pp. 809–812 (2011)
24. Wang, W., Chen, L., Liu, Z., Khnlenz, K., Burschka, D.: Textured/textureless object recognition and pose estimation using RGB-D image. J. Real-Time Image Process. 1–16 (2013)
25. Zhang, X., Hu, W., Maybank, S., Li, X., Zhu, M.: Sequential particle swarm optimization for visual tracking. In: CVPR, pp. 1–8 (2008)

Revisiting Robust Visual Tracking Using Pixel-Wise Posteriors

Falk Schubert[1]([✉]), Daniele Casaburo[2], Dirk Dickmanns[1],
and Vasileios Belagiannis[3]

[1] Airbus Group Innovations, Unterschleißheim, Germany
{falk.schubert,dirk.dickmanns}@airbus.com
[2] Technische Universität München, Munich, Germany
casaburo@in.tum.de
[3] Chair of Computer Aided Medical Procedures,
Technische Universität München, Munich, Germany
belagian@in.tum.de

Abstract. In this paper we present an in-depth evaluation of a recently published tracking algorithm [6] which intelligently couples rigid-registration and color-based segmentation using level-sets. The original method did not arouse the deserved interest in the community, most likely due to challenges in reimplementation and the lack of a quantitative evaluation. Therefore, we reimplemented this baseline approach, evaluated it on state-of-the-art datasets (VOT and OOT) and compared it to alternative segmentation-based tracking algorithms. We believe this is a valuable contribution as such a comparison is missing in the literature. The impressive results help promoting segmentation-based tracking algorithms, which are currently under-represented in the visual tracking benchmarks. Furthermore, we present various extensions to the color model, which improve the performance in challenging situations such as confusions between fore- and background. Last, but not least, we discuss implementation details to speed up the computation by using only a sparse set of pixels for the propagation of the contour, which results in tracking speed of up to 200 Hz for typical object sizes using a single core of a standard 2.3 GHz CPU.

Keywords: Segmentation · Visual tracking · Registration · Benchmark · Real-time tracking

1 Introduction

Visual tracking is a very active research field in which many different, competing methods have been proposed [20]. As many of them focus on similar applications, i.e. generic tracking of manually selected patches, it is important to understand the properties of the type of tracking category each method falls into. Only then it is possible to select the right algorithm from the obscure and overloaded pool of different approaches for a specific task. For instance if one needs to follow the

© Springer International Publishing Switzerland 2015
L. Nalpantidis et al. (Eds.): ICVS 2015, LNCS 9163, pp. 275–288, 2015.
DOI: 10.1007/978-3-319-20904-3_26

face of a presenter in a lecture hall using a camera, a fast face detector running as a tracking-by-detection approach might be a better choice than tailoring a generic patch tracking algorithm to that task. In that sense, tracking benchmarks have become increasingly popular to shed some quantitative light into the large pool of many methods. However, often the best performing methods rank almost equally well or their ranking differs depending on the benchmark. The best performing methods on the well-known "Online Object Tracking Benchmark" [28] were learning-based tracking-by-detection methods such as STRUCK [14] and TLD [18]. However, in the same year the "The Visual Object Tracking Challenge" [19] ranked their performance in middle of all methods compared, which was confirmed by the experiments run in the follow-up challenge 2014 [20]. As the selection of algorithms, which were compared and the pool of video sequences used for evaluation had a significant overlap, the conclusions that can be drawn from these results on the general tracking performance are not so obvious for an end-user. After all, these benchmarks only demonstrate that a computer vision algorithm solves a dataset, but not necessarily a target application.

One class of methods which has been under-represented in these state-of-the-art benchmarks are segmentation-based tracking approaches. In our view this is due to four reasons. First, many top-performing methods run usually not in real-time [8,12]. Second, the overlap computation using bounding boxes penalizes segmentation-based methods as these extract tight object contours, which are usually smaller than the coarse, surrounding groundtruth rectangle. Third, the appearance model is often based on color, which is considered a limitation as apposed to gradient-based descriptors, because color models tend to perform poorly on grayscale and low-contrast sequences. Fourth, segmentation automatically locks onto object boundaries, which prohibits tracking of patches that are not bound by a clear contour, e.g. upper part of a human face. In this paper we want to promote segmentation-based tracking algorithms for generic visual tracking. We demonstrate that the four reasons mentioned above do not always hold true.

On the contrary to the prejudices to segmentation-based tracking, there are quite a few advantages. Highly deformable objects are often impossible to describe with a bounding box. Hence, background information is also included in the foreground area, which misleads learning-based approaches during the online adaption step and can be a major source of drift. A segmentation step, which extracts the contour, could be very valuable to guide the sampling of positive and negative examples for a co-running tracking-by-detection method. Additionally, the contour itself is also a valuable descriptor, which can be used for downstream applications such as pose estimation. For very small objects or those with homogeneous appearance color might be the only valuable descriptor as opposed to the very popular gradient-based ones.

Recently a segmentation-based tracking algorithm was presented [6] which achieves impressive performance in terms of accuracy and run-time. The core power of this approach is the intelligent coupling of rigid registration and fast segmentation via level-sets. This combination allows very fast computation and yet accurate contour estimation. Both together allow the color-based modeling to achieve best performance even in very low-contrast scenarios, which are considered intractable for segmentation-based tracking. Due to the challenges in reimplementation and lack of a quantitative evaluation on state-of-the-art datasets, the method did not receive the attention it deserves. Therefore, we present in this paper such a quantitative evaluation using the latest datasets in the tracking community and compare it to the best methods. Furthermore, we extend the method in terms of color and shape model in order to overcome major limitations such as the confusion between fore- and background. Last, but not least, we provide details about an implementation trick using only a subset of the pixels around the contour, which results in tracking speeds of up to 200 Hz for typical object sizes using a single core of a standard 2.3 GHz CPU.

The paper is structured as follows. First, we provide an overview of relevant tracking methods and discuss our choice of the baseline segmentation-based tracking. In Sect. 3, we discuss the details of the baseline method. In Sect. 4, we present our extensions to the baseline method. In Sect. 5, we compare all methods against other state-of-the-art approaches using three common benchmark datasets. Last, but not least, we conclude our paper and give an outlook to future research.

2   Related Work

There is vast amount of literature on visual object tracking. For a detailed review we refer to [21,29]. In this section, we present related work to our method and we mainly focus on approaches that rely on segmentation and non-bounding object representations.

Learning-based object trackers have dominated the field of non-rigid object tracking. The first works on this direction have been published by Avidan [2] and Javed et al. [16], where tracking is defined as a classification problem. In [13] a semi-supervised algorithm was proposed, which learns from unlabeled data during the execution. Another popular learning-based tracker (TLD) was published in [18], which combines online updated random forest and a KLT tracker [4]. Finally, the margin-based trackers [7,14] have relied on a structured SVM and online updates for tracking, often at the cost of speed. However, all the above approaches are being trained with samples that come from a bounding-box. Consequently, background information can be included into the training process with the threat to drift the tracker. Also the online training inherently limits the run-time speed.

The idea of tracking-by-segmentation has been investigated extensively in the past [24]. In [5], a particle filter has been combined with a graph-based segmentation for sampling observations only from the foreground area. Segmentation-based approaches have also been combined with a Bayesian framework [1], Random walkers [23] and variational approaches [26]. In [8], the object is defined by fragments based on level-sets. Recently, Tsai et al. [25] have proposed an energy minimization scheme within a multi-label Markov Random Field model, but the method does not work online. A new approach based on level-sets was published in [6]. As opposed to the methods discussed before, the key insight of the authors is, that the contours of deformable objects have a significant rigid part, which can be propagated more efficiently via a registration rather than re-segmentation. The impressive results demonstrated accurate and very fast tracking. However, due to missing quantitative evaluation, the method never raised enough attention in the community to promote segmentation-based tracking. In this paper we adopted this approach and provide such as an evaluation as well as several extensions to it.

To leverage the power of both worlds, learning-based and segmentation-based tracking, approaches have been developed which combine them. In [12] a method called HoughTrack was proposed, merging random forests, hough voting and graph-cut segmentation. The classification output initializes the segmentation serving as a better refinement of the target object. The tracker is relatively slow, but it has produced promising results. PixelTrack [10] also relies on hough voting to detect the object, followed by segmentation between foreground and background. Both are few exceptions of approaches using segmentation that were considered in the two VOT-challenges [19,20]. In our evaluation we compare both methods against [6] and our extended version.

3   Segmentation-Based Tracking

In order to make the paper self-contained and to provide background information for our proposed extensions, we revisit the baseline method [6] which consists of three major steps as illustrated in Fig. 1. First, the appearance-model is constructed using a probabilistic formulation with a pixel-wise posterior. Second, using this model the level-set segmentation is carried out. Third, the rigid registration and contour propagation (i.e. tracking) is performed. In the following we will discuss each of the steps individually. Last, but not least, we present details on how to significantly speed up the computation by considering only a subset of the pixels as motivated in [6].

Appearance-Model. The segmentation and tracking procedures are derived from a probabilistic framework in which the representation of the object is

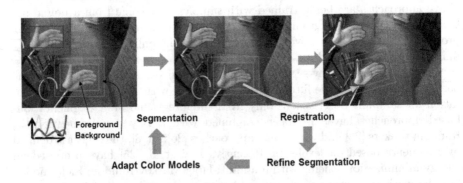

Fig. 1. Overview of the method presented in [6].

obtained by modeling the information coming from its location (defined by a warp $W(x,\mathbf{p})$ within the image and the shape of its contour C (the zero-level set $C = \{x|\Phi(x) = 0\}$, extracted from the embedding function $\Phi(x)$). The latter enable to define the foreground and background areas $\Omega_i, i = \{f, b\}$ from which the colors $\mathbf{y}$ at the pixels locations $\mathbf{x}$ are used to build the color histograms $M_i, i = \{f, b\}$ which serve as the appearance models $P(\mathbf{y}|M_i), i = \{f, b\}$. Within this framework, it is possible to infer the embedding function $\Phi(x)$ and the position $\mathbf{p}$ of the object by expressing the pixel-wise joint probability distribution:

$$P(\mathbf{x}, \mathbf{y}, \Phi, \mathbf{p}, M) = P(\mathbf{x}|\Phi, \mathbf{p}, M)P(\mathbf{y}|M)P(M)P(\Phi)P(\mathbf{p}) \qquad (1)$$

Conditioning on $\mathbf{x}$ and $\mathbf{y}$ and marginalizing over M yields the pixel-wise posterior [6]:

$$P(\Phi, \mathbf{p}|\mathbf{x}, \mathbf{y}) = \frac{1}{P(\mathbf{x})} \sum_{i=\{f,b\}} \left\{ P(\mathbf{x}|\Phi, \mathbf{p}, M_i)P(M_i|\mathbf{y}) \right\} P(\Phi)P(\mathbf{p}). \qquad (2)$$

For each pixel $\mathbf{x}$, the posteriors are merged with a logarithmic opinion pool assuming pixel-wise independence:

$$P(\Phi, \mathbf{p}|\Omega) = \prod_{i=1}^{N} \sum_{j=\{f,b\}} \left\{ P(\mathbf{x}_i|\Phi, \mathbf{p}, M_j)P(M_j|\mathbf{y}_i) \right\} P(\Phi)P(\mathbf{p}) \qquad (3)$$

In order to remove the need to re-initialize the level set during its evolution, Φ is forced to be as close as possible to a signed distance function by introducing a geometric prior:

$$P(\Phi) = \prod_{i=1}^{N} \frac{1}{\sigma\sqrt{2\pi}} \exp -\frac{(|\nabla\Phi(\mathbf{x}_i)| - 1)^2}{2\sigma^2}. \qquad (4)$$

By taking the log of Eq. 3, we obtain the objective function for the pixel-wise log posterior:

$$\log\left(P(\Phi, \mathbf{p}|\Omega)\right) \propto \sum_{i=1}^{N} \left\{ \log\left(P\left(\mathbf{x}_i|\Phi, \mathbf{p}, \mathbf{y}_i\right)\right) - \frac{(|\nabla\Phi(\mathbf{x}_i)| - 1)^2}{2\sigma^2} \right\} + N\log\left(\frac{1}{\sigma\sqrt{2\pi}}\right) + \log\left(P(\mathbf{p})\right) \quad (5)$$

Segmentation. The segmentation of the object foreground from its background is achieved by iteratively optimizing Eq. 5 w.r.t. Φ under the assumption of constant $\mathbf{p}$ using the following derivative of Eq. 5:

$$\frac{\partial P(\Phi, \mathbf{p}|\Omega)}{\partial \Phi} = \frac{\delta_\epsilon(\Phi)(P_f - P_b)}{P(\mathbf{x}|\Phi, \mathbf{p}, \mathbf{y})} - \frac{1}{\sigma^2}\left[\nabla^2\Phi - \text{div}\left(\frac{\nabla\Phi}{|\nabla\Phi|}\right)\right], \qquad (6)$$

in which $\delta_\epsilon(\Phi)$ is the derivative of the blurred Heaviside step function H_ϵ and ∇^2 is the Laplacian. The probabilities $P_i, i = \{f, b\}$ indicate how strong a color value $\mathbf{y}$ belongs to foreground/background and is defined as follows:

$$P_i = \frac{P(\mathbf{y}|M_i)}{\eta_f P(\mathbf{y}|M_f) + \eta_b P(\mathbf{y}|M_b)}, i = \{f, b\} \qquad (7)$$

Note, that the use of normalized histogram look-ups $(P(\mathbf{y}|M_i), i = \{f,b\})$ is crucial. We normalized via dividing the histograms by the number of fore-/background pixels and using discrete voting for the construction of them.

Tracking. Following the inverse compositional approach [4], the position of the object in a sequence is described by the warp transformation $\mathbf{W}(\mathbf{x}, \Delta \mathbf{p})$, where $\Delta \mathbf{p}$ represents the incremental warp and is calculated by optimizing Eq. 5 w.r.t. the parameter vector $\mathbf{p}$ while keeping the embedding function Φ constant. The resulting $\Delta \mathbf{p}$ is expressed as:

$$\Delta \mathbf{p} = \left[\sum_{i=1}^{N} \frac{1}{2P(\mathbf{W}(\mathbf{x}_i, \Delta \mathbf{p})|\Phi, \mathbf{p}, \mathbf{y}_i)} \left(\frac{P_f}{\sqrt{H_\epsilon(\Phi(\mathbf{x}_i))}} + \frac{P_b}{\sqrt{(H_\epsilon(\Phi(\mathbf{x}_i)))}} \right) \mathbf{J}^T \mathbf{J} \right]^{-1}$$

$$\times \sum_{i=1}^{N} \frac{(P_f - P_b)\mathbf{J}^T}{P(\mathbf{W}(\mathbf{x}_i, \Delta \mathbf{p})|\Phi, \mathbf{p}, \mathbf{y}_i)}, \tag{8}$$

in which $\mathbf{J} = \frac{\partial H_\epsilon}{\partial \Phi} \frac{\partial \Phi}{\partial \mathbf{x}} \frac{\partial \mathbf{W}}{\partial \Delta \mathbf{p}} = \delta_\epsilon(\Phi(\mathbf{x}_i)) \nabla \Phi(\mathbf{x}_i) \frac{\partial \mathbf{W}}{\partial \Delta \mathbf{p}}$ and $\frac{\partial \mathbf{W}}{\partial \Delta \mathbf{p}}$ is the warp Jacobian.

Speed-Up via Pixel-Subsets. In a straight-forward implementation the probability maps are computed dense on the area selected by the user which defines the foreground and some border padding which defined the background area. A drawback of this implementation is that the run-time significantly depends on the size of the user selection. Since the global color-model is not very sensitive to the resolution, the selection can be internally down-scaled to a maximum size (e.g. 80×80 px) which guarantees an upper bound on the run-time.

If we investigate the actually values that are considered for the computation, we see that the derivative of the Heaviside step function δ_ϵ defines a tight area along the contour in which values are greater than zero. Outside this area the values are very small and hence the influence of the other variables in Eq. 6 is suppressed. Therefore, we compute this area as a list of pixel indices and also store a precomputed index list for each neighbor. Then we iterate only over these index lists for all computations instead over the whole image matrix. To reduce the influence of the contour size on the run-time, we keep the width of the area constant at $\beta = 10$ px. The cut-off threshold of $\delta_\epsilon(x)$ is controlled by the decay function $c = \frac{2\exp(\beta)}{(1+\exp(2\beta))^2}$. Only indices relating to pixel positions x for which $\delta_\epsilon(x) > c$ are stored in the final index lists. On the "hand sequence" of [6] this increases the overall framerate from 60 Hz (using all pixels) to 200 Hz on average using a single core of a standard 2.3G Hz Intel i7 CPU.

4   Extensions

One of the major failure cases of the baseline method is confusion between fore- and background color which destroys the appearance models during run-time and often ends in tracking failure. In order to overcome this, we discuss three extensions. First, an additional prior which guides the smoothness of the contour can be added to the geometric one (see Eq. 4) as discussed in [22]. This prior penalizes long contours and therefore ones with high curvature. This slows down the expansion of the contour to wrong foreground pixels without generally shrinking it. Hence, in situations where fore- and background are hard to distinguish, the stiffness of the contour will temporarily aid as a guide.

As a second and third extension we propose modifications to the sampling for building and updating the color model. Both extensions aim to avoid sampling confusing colors either by assuming geometric locality of the foreground or by explicitly avoiding colors which also appear in the background. In the following we will discuss each one separately.

Color Locality. The fore- and background probability maps P_f and P_b in Eq. 6 are computed using two separate color-histograms. In the baseline method each pixel votes into them by equal weight. Hence, any information about spatial content is lost. Whereas this results in a rotation invariant description, it is quite sensitive to wrong pixel assignment to fore- and background in cases of bad contour estimation. Therefore we build the appearance histograms in a similar manner to the locality sensitive histogram algorithm [15]. Each pixel vote is weighted according to its distance from the window center, leading to a histogram expressed as:

$$H^L(b) = \sum_{p=1}^{W} \alpha^{|p-c|} \mathbb{I}(\mathbf{I}_p, b), \quad b = 1, \cdots, B \qquad (9)$$

where W is the number of pixels composing the window. The value B is the total number of bins and $\mathbb{I}(\mathbf{I}_p, b)$ is an indicator function resulting in zero except when the pixel information $\mathbf{I}_p$ belongs to bin b. The weight $\alpha \in [0,1]$ controls the decay of importance for pixels far away from the window center. The histograms are then normalized using the factor $n_f^L = \sum_{p=1}^{W} \alpha^{|p-c|}$. For the histogram relating to the foreground, the centroid of the bounding box is used for the distance calculation. Conversely, the background weighting scheme is computed considering the bounding box borders as the origins from which to calculate the distances.

Color Frequency. As discussed for the previous extension, two separate histograms for modeling the fore- and background are computed. This leads to controversy in scenarios where a color appears in both, background and foreground. A color bin is much more informative and distinctive if it appears only in either one of the histograms. Similarly problems have been discussed in the information retrieval community. Documents are commonly represented by a vector of frequencies of the composing words employing the 'term frequency-inverse document frequency'(tf-idf) weighting technique [3]. We propose to adopt a similar weighting scheme to emphasize the uniqueness of colors by computing:

$$P(\mathbf{y}|M_f) = \frac{|\mathbf{y}_f|}{n_f} \cdot \frac{1}{\max(|\mathbf{y}_b|, 1)} \qquad (10)$$

in which the first term accounts for the frequency of occurrence of the color **y** in the foreground while the second term considers how much the same color appears in the background. The same is applied to the background probability $P(\mathbf{y}|M_b)$.

5 Evaluations

In this section we will demonstrate that the baseline method and our proposed extensions rank among the top performers for two well known benchmark datasets. As a qualitative validation of our implementation, we reproduced the results on four sequences of [6][1]. All frames of the sequences were successfully tracked. Visual results for the "hand sequence" are depicted in Fig. 2.

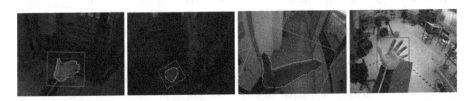

Fig. 2. Four frames with our results from the "hand sequence" presented in [6]. The contour is shown in yellow, the full 6DOF bounding box (including rotation) in green and rectified, tight predicted bounding box used for overlap computations in red (Color figure online).

OOT - Online Object Tracking. This benchmark[2] was presented in [28] and compared 29 state-of-art trackers on 50 sequences. For brevity we will compare the *Baseline* (i.e. our implementation of [6]) and our *Proposed Extensions* (using all extensions together) against the 5 top-ranked trackes from the *one-pass evaluation* (OPE) experiment, which were: ASLA [17], CXT [9], SCM [30], STRUCK [14] and TLD [18]. The evaluation scheme measured two values: success and precision rate. The first one measures the rate of overlap between the groundtruth bounding box and the predicted one considering various overlap thresholds. To summarize these values the area under the resulting curve (AUC) is measured. The second rate measures how often the centers of the groundtruth and predicted box are close enough, again considering various distance thresholds. To summarize these values, the precision rate at a distance threshold of 20 pixels is used. Since both the *Baseline* method and the *Proposed Extensions* of this paper intrinsically depend on color information, the evaluation is performed in two versions: one using all sequences and one using only color sequences (35 out of 50).

In Table 1 the results for the *Baseline* and the *Proposed Extensions* as well as the 5 best trackers are summarized (left using all 50 sequences, right considering only color sequences). The segmentation-based method successfully ranks

---

[1] Sequences were kindly provided by Esther Horbert from the Computer Vision Group, RWTH Aachen University.

[2] http://visual-tracking.net.

in the top for both success rate and precision rate, especially when considering only color sequences. Our *Proposed Extensions* always show an increased performance w.r.t. the *Baseline*. This demonstrates the power of color-based segmentation in respect to well-known learning-based techniques and motivates the combination of both worlds. Visual results for the sequences "FaceOcc1", "Woman" and "Lemming" are depicted in Fig. 3.

Table 1. OOT Benchmarks: left, top-5 as reported in [28] and our proposed methods using all 50 sequences; right, the results when considering only color-sequences. Highest result is marked in red, the second highest is marked in blue and the third highest is marked in green.

(a) OOT using all sequences.

OOT Benchmark (all sequences)			
Success AUC		Precision rate Location error at 20 px	
Tracker	Score	Tracker	Score
SCM [30]	0.5052	STRUCK[14]	0.7088
STRUCK[14]	0.4777	SCM [30]	0.7069
TLD[18]	0.4405	TLD[18]	0.6774
ASLA[17]	0.4387	Proposed Extensions	0.6389
CXT[9]	0.4288	CXT[9]	0.6121
Proposed Extensions	0.4217	ASLA[17]	0.6030
Baseline	0.4103	Baseline	0.5988

(b) OOT using only color sequences.

OOT Benchmark (only color sequences)			
Success AUC		Precision rate Location error at 20 px	
Tracker	Score	Tracker	Score
SCM [30]	0.4517	Proposed Extensions	0.6485
Proposed Extensions	0.45	STRUCK[14]	0.6364
Baseline	0.4411	Baseline	0.6288
STRUCK[14]	0.4304	SCM [30]	0.6242
TLD[18]	0.3859	TLD[18]	0.5957
ASLA[17]	0.3698	ASLA[17]	0.5172
CXT[9]	0.3499	CXT[9]	0.5107

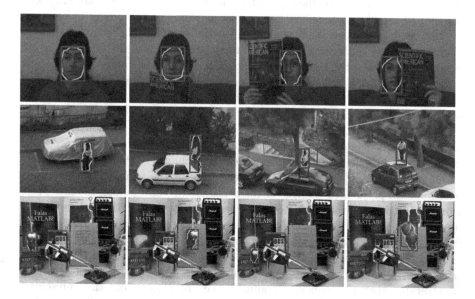

Fig. 3. Three videos from the OOT [28] dataset showing the groundtruth in blue and our method in yellow (for the contour) and red (for the final predicted bounding box) (Color figure online).

VOT - Visual Object Tracking. The idea of the OOT benchmark was to provide a reference dataset for better comparison of tracking methods. It compared publicly available trackers (using default parameter settings) on a manually defined collection of videos. The VOT2013 carried this idea further and created an open competition. All participants could individually tune their algorithm to the benchmark dataset for best performance guaranteeing a fair comparison. The 16 benchmark videos were automatically extracted from a pool of about 60 sequences. A whole committee supervised the challenge (i.e. selection of algorithms and dataset) and the results were published in [19]. Due the big success, the challenge will be continued (e.g. VOT2014 [20]). The evaluation scheme is similar to the OOT. The performances are captured by two measures: accuracy and robustness. The accuracy value measures how well the bounding box predicted by the tracker overlaps with the groundtruth bounding box. The robustness of a tracker is evaluated by the failure rate which expresses how many times the tracker completely loses the target within a sequence. The results are averaged over 15 runs. Three experiments were carried out: `Baseline`, in which a tracker is tested on all sequences by initializing it on the groundtruth bounding boxes; `Region noise`, like the `Baseline` but initialized with noisy bounding box; `Grayscale`, like the `Baseline` one but on grayscale converted sequences. Similarly to OOT benchmark, we exclude the last experiment as our segmentation-based methods heavily rely on color as a descriptor.

The official results are summarized in the left part of Table 2. The top performing trackers on all the experiments are PLT[3], FoT [27] and EDFT [11] respectively. Interestingly, the top-performing learning-based methods STRUCK [14] and TLD [18] from the OOT benchmark rank only in the middle. The reasons are not clear, other than that the dataset is different, yet the visual challenges in the videos are quite similar. We also report the scores of the state-of-the-art segmentation-based tracker HT [12] which also ranks in the lower part.

In the right part of Table 2, the results for our segmentation-based method (*Baseline* and the *Proposed Extensions*) are reported. The average overlap as well as the mean number of restarts are comparable to the two top-performing methods. As the ranking procedure was only accessible to the authors of the VOT2013 challenge, it was not possible to compute the exact rank our proposed methods would have reached. Nevertheless, in comparing the obtained performances in both parts of Table 2 w.r.t. the rank of the winning trackers, it is reasonable to place both versions of the considered tracker among the first ones. Our proposed extensions enhanced the performance of the baseline version in terms of *robustness*. The drop in accuracy is due to the intrinsic tendency to focus on unique colors, especially that ones close to the object center, leading to a smaller bounding-box. It is exactly that feature that allowed it to be less sensible w.r.t. noisy initializations keeping the track more steady on the target.

Overall, the experiments confirm the reliability of the presented segmentation-based tracking approach, especially in presence of challenging conditions such as changes in lighting condition (e.g. see top row of Fig. 4),

---

[3] No official publication available. Only a brief abstract in [19].

Table 2. VOT2013 challenge: results comparison. Highest result is marked in red, the second highest is marked in blue and the third highest is marked in green.

		VOT2013 CHALLENGE: Official Results						Evaluated Methods	
Experiment	Metric	#1: PLT	#2: FoT[27]	#3: EDFT[11]	#12: STRUCK[14]	#17: TLD[18]	#20: HT[12]	Baseline	Proposed Extensions
baseline	Accuracy	0.6185	0.6492	0.6	0.584	0.5962	0.4727	0.6316	0.6053
	Robustness	0	0.6545	0.4455	1.365	2.9383	1.6558	0.1875	0.125
region-noise	Accuracy	0.5892	0.6	0.5693	0.5275	0.5735	0.4723	0.6256	0.6054
	Robustness	0.0236	0.6921	0.6593	1.4710	2.9839	1.8432	0.2667	0.1375

Fig. 4. Three videos from the VOT2013 [19] dataset showing the groundtruth in blue and our method in yellow (for the contour) and red (for the final predicted bounding box) (Color figure online).

deformations, etc. The results strengthen the intuition to exploit more information related to the color appearance. Visual results for the three sequences "David", "Bolt" and "Bicycle" are depicted in Fig. 4.

Segmentation-Based Trackers. Since segmentation-based trackers are under-represented in the two benchmarks discussed above, we represent a comparison of three state-of-the-art methods using segmentation: PaFiSS [5], PixelTrack [10] and HT [12]. Following [10], we measure the percentage of frames in which the object is correctly tracked. The tracking is considered correct if the overlap measure between the output bounding box and the groundtruth is above 10 %. The evaluation is performed using the dataset presented in [10], which contains objects that undergo rigid and non-rigid deformations, large lighting variations as well as partial occlusions. In Table 3 the results are summarized by two average values. The first average value in the last row is the

Table 3. PixelTrack [10] comparison: percentage of correctly tracked frames. Highest result is marked in red, the second highest is marked in blue and the third highest is marked in green. The first average value in the last row is the performance considering all sequences. The second value only considers values for which PAFISS results were available.

Sequence	HT[12]	PixelTrack[10]	PaFiSS[5]	Baseline	Proposed Extensions
David	89.25	45.16	–	99.78	99.57
Sylvester	55.02	36.80	–	99.92	99.82
Girl	92.22	93.21	80.64	99.80	99.80
Face Occlusion 1	99.44	100	98.78	99.77	99.66
Face Occlusion 2	100	88.34	71.41	99.88	99.88
Coke	72.88	91.53	–	99.65	99.65
Tiger 1	26.76	46.48	–	99.72	99.72
Tiger 2	41.10	98.63	–	99.72	99.72
Cliff-dive 1	100	100	100	100	100
Motocross 1	100	57.59	23.78	99.39	99.39
Skiing	100	100	61.63	98.76	97.53
Mountain-bike	100	94.55	98.68	99.56	99.56
Cliff-dive 2	100	32.79	23.19	100	100
Volleyball	45.12	100	34.6	58.60	58.40
Motocross 2	100	100	100	69.56	69.56
Transformer	38.71	94.35	100	100	100
Diving	21.21	88.74	26.84	100	87.01
High Jump	77.87	94.26	9.02	65.57	66.39
Gymnastics	98.87	99.09	19.95	100	90.87
Average	77.13 / 84.32	82.18 / 88.78	- / 60.61	94.19 / 92.21	92.97 / 90.57

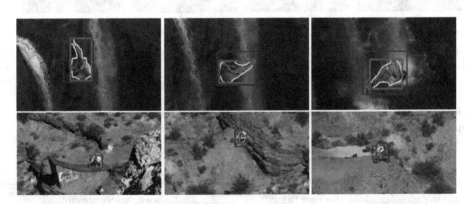

Fig. 5. Two videos from the PixelTrack dataset [10] showing the groundtruth in blue and our method in yellow (for the contour) and red (for the final predicted bounding box) (Color figure online).

performance considering all sequences. The second value only considers values for which PAFISS results were available. Our proposed approach outperforms all other methods. The extensions perform slightly worse due to the same reasons as reported for the VOT2013 dataset. Visual results for the sequences "Cliff-dive 1" and "Mountain-Bike" are depicted in Fig. 5.

6   Conclusions

In this paper we motivated the use of segmentation-based tracking. We adopted a baseline method [6] which intelligently couples rigid registration and fast level-set segmentation and reported impressive results. Our implementation verifies the conclusions of the authors as we could qualitatively reproduce the published results. However, the method did not receive the attention it deserves in the latest tracking benchmarks. We believe this is mainly due to the challenges in reimplementation and a missing quantitative evaluation on common datasets. In this paper we provide such an evaluation using the latest benchmark datasets and following the state-of-the-art evaluation protocols. The results show that this method ranks among the best performing trackers, which demonstrates the often underestimated power of segmentation-based tracking. In many applications contours and color-models are much more useful than the typically used gradient-based descriptors, making such a segmentation-based tracking algorithm an interesting alternative. Furthermore, we presented various extensions which aim to mitigate a major drawback of the global color-based appearance model. In future work, we would like to couple this segmentation-based tracker with a tracking-by-detection algorithm to increase the overall tracking performance even further.

Acknowledgments. We thank Esther Horbert (Computer Vision Group RWTH Aachen University) for providing four evaluation sequences and valuable feedback for resolving open questions on the hidden details of [6].

References

1. Aeschliman, C., Park, J., Kak, A.: A probabilistic framework for joint segmentation and tracking. In: CVPR (2010)
2. Avidan, S.: Ensemble tracking. PAMI **29**, 261–271 (2007)
3. Baeza-Yates, R., Ribeiro-Neto, B., et al.: Modern Information Retrieval. ACM Press, New York (1999)
4. Baker, S., Matthews, I.: Lucas-kanade 20 years on: a unifying framework. IJCV **56**, 221–255 (2004)
5. Belagiannis, V., Schubert, F., Navab, N., Ilic, S.: Segmentation based particle filtering for real-time 2D object tracking. In: Fitzgibbon, A., Lazebnik, S., Perona, P., Sato, Y., Schmid, C. (eds.) ECCV 2012, Part IV. LNCS, vol. 7575, pp. 842–855. Springer, Heidelberg (2012)
6. Bibby, C., Reid, I.: Robust real-time visual tracking using pixel-wise posteriors. In: Forsyth, D., Torr, P., Zisserman, A. (eds.) ECCV 2008, Part II. LNCS, vol. 5303, pp. 831–844. Springer, Heidelberg (2008)
7. Chen, D., Yuan, Z., Hua, G., Wu, Y., Zheng, N.: Description-discrimination collaborative tracking. In: Fleet, D., Pajdla, T., Schiele, B., Tuytelaars, T. (eds.) ECCV 2014, Part I. LNCS, vol. 8689, pp. 345–360. Springer, Heidelberg (2014)

8. Chockalingam, P., Pradeep, N., Birchfield, S.: Adaptive fragments-based tracking of non-rigid objects using level sets. In: ICCV (2009)

9. Dinh, T., Vo, N., Medioni, G.: Context tracker: exploring supporters and distracters in unconstrained environments. In: CVPR (2011)

10. Duffner, S., Garcia, C.: Pixeltrack: a fast adaptive algorithm for tracking non-rigid objects. In: ICCV (2013)

11. Felsberg, M.: Enhanced distribution field tracking using channel representations. In: ICCVW (2013)

12. Godec, M., Roth, P., Bischof, H.: Hough-based tracking of non-rigid objects. In: ICCV (2011)

13. Grabner, H., Leistner, C., Bischof, H.: Semi-supervised on-line boosting for robust tracking. In: Forsyth, D., Torr, P., Zisserman, A. (eds.) ECCV 2008, Part I. LNCS, vol. 5302, pp. 234–247. Springer, Heidelberg (2008)

14. Hare, S., Saffari, A., Torr, P.: Struck: structured output tracking with kernels. In: ICCV (2011)

15. He, S., Yang, Q., Lau, R., Wang, J., Yang, M.H.: Visual tracking via locality sensitive histograms. In: CVPR (2013)

16. Javed, O., Ali, S., Shah, M.: Online detection and classification of moving objects using progressively improving detectors. In: CVPR (2005)

17. Jia, X., Lu, H., Yang, M.H.: Visual tracking via adaptive structural local sparse appearance model. In: CVPR (2012)

18. Kalal, Z., Matas, J., Mikolajczyk, K.: P-N learning: bootstrapping binary classifiers by structural constraints. In: CVPR (2010)

19. Kristan, M., et al.: The visual object tracking VOT2013 challenge results. In: ICCVW (2013)

20. Kristan, M., et al.: The visual object tracking VOT2014 challenge results. In: Agapito, L., Bronstein, M.M., Rother, C. (eds.) ECCV 2014 Workshops. LNCS, vol. 8926, pp. 191–217. Springer, Heidelberg (2015)

21. Li, X., Hu, W., Shen, C., Zhang, Z., Dick, A., Hengel, A.V.D.: A survey of appearance models in visual object tracking. TIST **4**, 1–58 (2013)

22. Mitzel, D., Horbert, E., Ess, A., Leibe, B.: Multi-person tracking with sparse detection and continuous segmentation. In: Daniilidis, K., Maragos, P., Paragios, N. (eds.) ECCV 2010, Part I. LNCS, vol. 6311, pp. 397–410. Springer, Heidelberg (2010)

23. Papoutsakis, K., Argyros, A.: Integrating tracking with fine object segmentation. Image Vis. Comput. **31**, 771–785 (2013)

24. Paragios, N., Deriche, R.: Geodesic active contours and level sets for the detection and tracking of moving objects. PAMI **22**, 266–280 (2000)

25. Tsai, D., Flagg, M., Rehg, J.M.: Motion coherent tracking with multi-label MRF optimization. In: BMVC (2010)

26. Unger, M., Mauthner, T., Pock, T., Bischof, H.: Tracking as segmentation of spatial-temporal volumes by anisotropic weighted tv. In: Energy Minimization Methods Workshop in CVPR (2009)

27. Vojíř, T., Matas, J.: Robustifying the flock of trackers. In: CVWW (2011)

28. Wu, Y., Lim, J., Yang, M.H.: Online object tracking: a benchmark. In: CVPR (2013)

29. Yilmaz, A., Javed, O., Shah, M.: Object tracking: a survey. ACM Comput. Surv. (CSUR) **38**, 1–45 (2006)

30. Zhong, W., Lu, H., Yang, M.H.: Robust object tracking via sparsity-based collaborative model. In: CVPR (2012)

Teach it Yourself - Fast Modeling of Industrial Objects for 6D Pose Estimation

Thomas Sølund[1,3](✉), Thiusius Rajeeth Savarimuthu[2], Anders Glent Buch[2], Anders Billesø Beck[1], Norbert Krüger[2], and Henrik Aanæs[3]

[1] Center for Robot Technology, Danish Technological Institute, Odense, Denmark
{thso,anbb}@dti.dk
[2] Mærsk Mc-Kinney Møller Institute, University of Southern Denmark,
Odense, Denmark
{trs,anbu,norbert}@mmmi.sdu.dk
[3] Department of Applied Mathematics and Computer Science,
Technical University of Denmark, Kongens Lyngby, Denmark
aanes@dtu.dk

Abstract. In this paper, we present a vision system that allows a human to create new 3D models of novel industrial parts by placing the part in two different positions in the scene. The two shot modeling framework generates models with a precision that allows the model to be used for 6D pose estimation without loss in pose accuracy. We quantitatively show that our modeling framework reconstructs noisy but adequate object models with a mean RMS error at 2.7 mm, a mean standard deviation at 0.025 mm and a completeness of 70.3 % over all 14 reconstructed models, compared to the ground truth CAD models. In addition, the models are applied in a pose estimation application, evaluated with 37 different scenes with 61 unique object poses. The pose estimation results show a mean translation error on 4.97 mm and a mean rotation error on 3.38 degrees.

Keywords: 3D modeling · Pose estimation · Robot manipulation · Flexible automation

1 Introduction

European manufacturing industries are challenged due to high wages, a growing number of product variants as well as a need for product customization. These facts imply an increasing demand for agile and flexible manufacturing systems. Especially, small batch sizes is changing the production paradigm from mass production to high/mix low/volume production [1]. This shift has changed the requirements to automation and industrial robotic systems, where e.g. high flexibility, reconfigurability and fast programming time are demanded.

The research leading to these results has been funded by the Danish Ministry of Science, Innovation and Higher Education under grant agreement #11-117524. and CARMEN under grant agreement #12-131860.

© Springer International Publishing Switzerland 2015
L. Nalpantidis et al. (Eds.): ICVS 2015, LNCS 9163, pp. 289–302, 2015.
DOI: 10.1007/978-3-319-20904-3_27

This paper presents a vision system that enables fast learning of geometrical object models in a multi view camera set-up intended for perception tasks, such as pose estimation and object recognition. With three pre-calibrated stereo camera pairs covering the scene a point cloud model of the object is extracted. The object is then turned manually to cover previously occluded parts of the surface followed by surface registration and post processing, to complete the model.

Geometrical modeling of industrial objects combined with 6D pose estimation based on visual information facilitates the reconfiguration of a robotic systems by reducing the effort for precise positioning. Vision guided robot systems in industry have until now been dominated by 2D or 2.5D vision solutions, which are hard to handle by users without expert vision knowledge. This has three reasons in particular: First, the viewpoint of the cameras need to be adapted to the stored views of the object. Second, often a rather awkward process is required to make sure that the space of required viewpoints is sufficiently densely sampled with object views often requiring large amounts of training data. Third, methods based on 2D pattern matching require a cumbersome extrinsic camera calibration process to be able to compute a 3D object pose.

In this context, 3D object models serve as a suitable abstractions of the general perception problem by lowering the training efforts needed compared to 2D or 2.5D vision applications and increasing the flexibility of the vision system. One common way is to use 3D CAD models [2]. Certain steps are needed in order to prepare a mechanical model, before it can be applied in a typical pose estimation pipeline. Typical, CAD models of the objects are (1) converted to a proper CAD file format (2) loaded into the vision system and (3) (down)sampled to get a point cloud representation with a correct point resolution by rendering and ray casting different views. Each step requires vision knowledge to parametrize correctly. The point resolution of the model has to roughly match with the point cloud resolution from the scene, that is directly dictated by the scene cameras. Furthermore, pose estimation algorithms need parametrization to fit the scene resolution. Creating the object representation directly by utilizing the scene cameras removes all before mentioned steps, thus reducing the (re)configuration time. Occasionally, there is no 3D CAD model of the object, if (1) the batch size is small, (2) the manufacturing company is small, (3) the particular object is customized, or (4) only 2D technical drawings of the object exist. Typically, it is time consuming to design the part in a CAD program, thus online 3D modeling is an appealing technology. Furthermore, existing CAD models are sometimes inaccurate, contain errors and/or lack important features which make them unsuitable for 6D pose estimation.

Hence fast and intuitive methods to train a robot system to recognize objects and estimate their poses are wanted [3,4]. In this paper, we present a two shot learning method for 3D models and apply it to pose estimation. Figure 1 shows our reconstruction pipeline that extracts the object from the scene with super-voxel segmentation and clustering followed by a registration pipeline that registers two partial models into one full model.

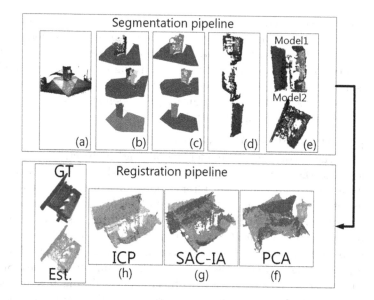

Fig. 1. Modeling steps: (a): *Step 1* - Transformation to camera frame and region-of-interest filtering of each view. **(b):** *Step 2* - Over segmentation of the scene. **(c):** *Step 3* - Clustering. **(d):** *Step 4* - Smoothing, up-sampling and filtering of each cluster. **(e):** - Output of the segmentation pipeline - two partial object models taken after the user has turned the object, **(f)**, **(g):** *Step 6* -Initial alignment with Principal component analysis or SAmple Consensus - Initial Alignment. The initial registration method applied, is selected by the user. **(h):** *Step 7* - ICP registration. The estimated model (**Est.**) is shown together with the ground truth model (**GT**)

The main contribution of our work can be summarized as follows. **(a)** we present a novel multi-view two shot modeling framework suited for fast on-site modeling of industrial objects. **(b)** we present a comparison of our object models with the ground truth CAD model with respect to completeness and accuracy. **(c)** we evaluate and compare pose estimation results by applying our object models and ground truth models.

This paper is structured as follows: Sect. 2 contains related work; Sect. 3 describes our approach to realize two shot 3D model acquisition together with a description of our multi-view robot platform. Our evaluation protocol is outlined in Sect. 4, followed by a presentation of the results in Sect. 5. We conclude the paper in Sect. 6.

2   Related Work

Accurate 3D model reconstruction from a visual representation originates from reverse engineering science where object models are needed for computer animation, methodology, quality inspection etc. Initially rotatory tables are used for moving the object in front of a sensor to get range images form each view [5], later robots are introduced to move the sensor or the object. A review of early work is presented in [6]. This review only considers geometric 3D model learning strategies of rigid objects with a robot. Learning object representation can basically be divided into four sub categories; (1) modeling by physical manipulation [7–9], (2) single view modeling using shape prior [3, 10–12] (3) surface registration of multiple views [13–16] and (4) multi-view modeling with 360 degree scene coverage [17]. Our work belong the latter.

Modeling by Physical Manipulation: *Ilonen et al.* [7] fuse visual and tactile data to reconstruct a complete 3D model by grasping an object. Visual data from a single view RGB-D camera and a gripper padded with tactile sensors are fused using an iterative extended Kalman filter. The reconstruction method assumes that the objects are symmetrical. *Björkman et al.* [8] use Gaussian process (GP) regression to model an implicit surface of an object from a single Kinect view followed by tactile touch. The GP uncertainty is used to guide the robot to touch the model at areas with highest uncertainty. In [9] textured objects are modelled by detecting and tracking piecewise planar surfaces patches. Surfaces are merged and split into separate 3D object models during pushing actions with a robot manipulator. The method requires detecting interest points on the object surface.

Single View Modeling Using Shape Prior: In many applications, planar or rotational symmetry of an object can be assumed, but estimating symmetry axis is computationally hard because of the large search space and limited data available from a single view. *Bohg et al.* [10] bootstrap the search by limiting the set of hypothesis by only considering a vertical axis perpendicular to a plan. *Marton et al.* [3] fit geometric primitives (Boxes and cylinders) to the data taken from a single view. Additionally, a RANSAC based method for detecting the symmetry axis and completing surfaces of revolution is presented. For some objects detecting symmetry is error prone and a method such as point cloud extrusion [11] is a complementary method. Instead of detecting the symmetry axis and mirror the point cloud, fitting superquadrics [12] or implicit surfaces [8] have shown promising results.

Surface Registration of Multiple Views: Estimating the complete geometric representation of objects without making inference on shape geometry e.g. symmetry axis, requires that a sensor is either moved around the object [13, 15] or the object is lifted by a robot and rotated in front of a camera [14, 16] to cover unseen areas. *Bone et al.* [13] combine 2D silhouette based modeling and laser stripe scanning to estimate the shape of an object. In [15] a robot with a range sensor in the hand explores a table with objects. After first scan the object of interest is lifted, rotated and placed on the table and scanned using the same robot motion. *Kraft et al.* [14] present a sparse model representation based on 3D primitives composed of edge, line, orientation, phase and color transition for interest points. Their object learning framework grasps objects in the scene with a simple grasping reflex based on 3D primitives. When a grasp succeed the object is rotated in front of a stereo camera to accumulate 3D primitives. This results in a sparse 3D representation of the model. *Krainin et al.* [16] show the same approach, but model the object as a dense surfel representation with a RGD-B camera. They introduce the articulated ICP which combines tracking of both the object and the robot manipulator while creating the model. The method combines a Kalman filter and ICP in an unified estimation process. With this approach they model symmetric objects, which in the case of general ICP is error prone due to ambiguities in object matching.

Our proposed method avoids some of the disadvantages of above mentioned methods e.g. no prior assumptions regarding object shape like symmetry [10] is required nor does our method fit geometrical primitives [3], superquadrics [12] or implicit surfaces [8]. Instead, the proposed method utilizes a multi-view calibration to align point clouds to capture the shape. With this, registration of different scans are avoided as in [14–16]. This enables us to model symmetric objects like cylinders and spheres with no texture which is difficult with classical registration of views, e.g., with the ICP algorithm. As the modeling framework takes two shots of the object, previous unseen surface patches, e.g., the bottom, are represented which is difficult with, e.g., single view modeling and fitting techniques without prior assumptions.

3   Two Shot 3D Object Modeling

The object modeling and all experiments are conducted on our experimental platform, consisting of two Universal robots[1] manipulators. The platform has three sensor clusters, each with a Microsoft Kinect v1 sensor, a BumbleeBee 2 stereo camera[2] and a XWGA projector for applying artificial texture to the scene in order to reconstruct industrial metallic objects. The three camera clusters give a 360-degree coverage of the scene and enables us to get a complete scene representations in one shot. Note, that only the BumbleBee stereo cameras and the XWGA projectors are used in this work. The platform is shown in Fig. 2 together with all 14 objects.

The extrinsic calibration of the platform is conducted in a single step multi camera and robot calibration procedure. As input for the calibration procedure, a rough model of the setup is needed including start guess on the robot and camera placements and the intrinsic calibration of the cameras. This allows the robot to automatically plan motions and move to valid positions where the cameras are able to detect a marker mounted in the tool of the robot. The extrinsic parameters of the camera and robot and the intrinsic parameters of the robot are computed using a set of detected marker poses and robot poses. In order to gain the required precision we calibrate two camera clusters at a time and let the robot move closer to these cameras. Based on a sample size of 402 corresponding images and robot poses we use 75 % of the samples to calibrate and the 25 % of the samples to verify the results. The residual of the calibration process shows an average error 2.8 mm in translation and 1.0 deg in rotation.

---

[1] Universal Robots - http://www.universal-robots.com/en/.

[2] http://www.ptgrey.com/bumblebee2-firewire-stereo-vision-camera-systems.

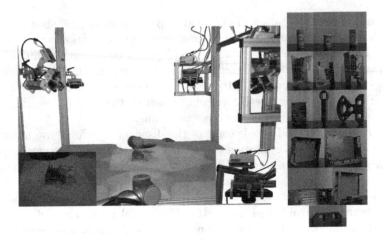

Fig. 2. Left image: The experimental platform. **Right image:** The 14 test objects.

Initially, the scene is reconstructed using Stereo Block Matching from OpenCV[3]. The reconstructed point clouds are aligned with the world frame located in the base of robot 1 by applying the extrinsic platform calibration, This allows the robot to grasp detected objects.

Extracting models from a 3D scene is basically a segmentation problem where points associated with the model have to be filtered. In robotics, traditionally it has been assumed that the object of interest is located on a dominant plane e.g. a table. The typical segmentation pipeline that has been used to remove the plane from the point cloud includes e.g. a RANSAC plane fitting algorithm followed by an Euclidean clustering algorithm. However, this pipeline is not optimal when it comes to model extraction because the plane removal algorithms, removes points in the transition between the object and the plane that belongs to the object. This fact is critical in our system, because a surface to surface registration is needed to finalize the two partial models into one full model. If the partial models lack correlated features, the registration of the surfaces is likely fail. Therefore we propose a different pipeline based on supervoxel segmentation proposed in [18] followed by a learning free segmentation algorithm that evaluates each supervoxel based on a local convexity criterion [19]. We extend this with a geometrical clustering algorithm based on a segment-to-plane and Euclidean distance criterion. In the following, we will outline the segmentation pipeline followed by the post-processing and surface to surface registration pipeline. An overview of the processing pipeline is given in Fig. 1.

3.1 Segmentation Pipeline

Our segmentation algorithm starts with segmenting each point cloud from the three views into supervoxels by applying the algorithm from [18] with a voxel

---

[3] OpenCV Stereo Block Matching: http://docs.opencv.org.

resolution equal 0.0035 and a seed resolution equal 0.020. The importance of color λ, spatial distance μ and normal direction ϵ in the computation of the seed expansion distance measure, is set to 2.0, 5.0, 8.0, respectively. A prerequisite for the algorithm in [19] is that the object is represented as a continuous point set and not containing discontinuities and large holes with missing points. The fact that we are reconstructing industrial objects with discontinues surfaces e.g. heatsinks with specular surface properties, will result in the algorithm not segmenting the object as one object. As a consequence we deliberately over-segment the scene into partial object segments and cluster these segments into one object representation. The algorithm segments the scene by considering the inclination angle of the super voxel normals direction to determine if the edge between two super voxels in the adjacency graph is concave or convex. The threshold that determines if an edge between two supervoxels is convex is set to 15.0 degrees and we remove supervoxels segments smaller that 10 to avoid noise.

The convexity based supervoxel segmentation algorithm described above results in an over-segmentation of the objects as shown in Fig. 1(b). We cluster the partial object segments into one object by examining the normal direction of the plane fitted each object segment. If the spherical inclination angle between the normal of the segment and the dominant plane in the scene e.g. a table, is larger than α and the plane-to-plane euclidean distance of the segment, is larger than β we accept the segment as a part of the object. We set α to 0.5 degrees and β to 5 mm. The clustering step is depicted in Fig. 1(c).

A post-processing step is conducted to refine the object model by smoothing and noise filtering. The surface is filtered by removing outliers based on two metrics; a statistical and a radius. The statistical outlier removal filter removes noisy measurement from the point cloud by considering the mean point distance in a local neighbourhood and remove points with a distance larger than a threshold. For removing spurious point clusters from the scene we filter the point cloud by looking in a radius around a point. If a point has less than 40 neighbouring points in a radius of 10 mm, the point is removed. The surface filtering is followed by an euclidean clustering step that select the largest cluster. A final step up-samples and smooth the surface by applying a moving least square filter with voxel grid dilation. The entire segmentation pipeline is implemented with use of the Point cloud Library[4].

3.2   Surface to Surface Registration

The segmentation pipeline extracts a partial object model that misses e.g. the bottom of the object. For covering previously occluded parts of the surface, the object is turned manually by the user and the segmentation pipeline is processed again which results in two partial object models, Fig. 1(e). The fact that the robot platform provides a full scene coverage gives us enough correlating object points between the two partial object models to register the two surfaces to one coherent object model. Initially, we roughly align the two object frames by computing the

---

[4] Point Cloud Library: http://pointclouds.org.

centroid and principal component of each model with PCA analysis, Fig. 1(f). The quality of this alignment is highly dependant on the object surface. The PCA analysis of pseudo-symmetrical objects with ambiguity tends to rotate the two object models differently. In order to cover this, the user has the possibility to initiate an additional alignment step before ICP registration. This step computes a new initial alignment based on shape features, in case the PCA misaligns the two partial object models. We adapt the SAC-IA method from [20] that compute an initial transformation for aligning the two surfaces by means of Fast Point Feature Histogram (FPFH) and SAmple Consensus, Fig. 1(g). The SAC-IA alignment is followed by a final ICP registration step, Fig. 1(h).

4   Evaluation Protocol

Two different experimental evaluations of the approach are presented. In Sect. 4.1 we outline the comparison of the object model obtained from our two shot modeling framework with the ground truth models, in terms of accuracy and completeness. This gives us a measure of how similar the object models are compared to the ground truth. In Sect. 4.2 we outline the protocol for testing and evaluating our models in pose estimation of industrial objects on our multi-view robot platform, presented in Sect. 3.

For evaluating the proposed method, the 14 different objects in Fig. 2 are reconstructed and categorized into three categories according to their surface properties. A sample of 4 of the 14 objects is illustrated in Fig. 3. The 14 objects include industrial parts with different surface properties as textured, non-textured, specular, non-specular, light and dark objects. Furthermore, some geometrical simple objects with few discriminative shape features, e.g., a cylinder and objects with many discriminative shape features are included. The objects are categories as following: (1) textured objects e.g. food containers with labels (Fig. 3 first row), (2) non-textured objects e.g. plastic parts for final assembly (fourth row) and (3) complex objects which posses some specular surface properties and high dynamic range (second row).

For evaluating the reconstructed model M_{est} with ground truth CAD model M_{gt} it is required that the two models are aligned to a common object frame. The alignment of the two models follows three steps, (1) manual selecting correspondences in M_{est} and M_{gt} (2) computing alignment transform that aligns M_{est} and M_{gt} using RANSAC and (3) run 500 ICP iterations with decreasing correspondence distance, to compute the final (rigid) alignment transform T.

4.1   Model Comparison

Comparing 3D models has formerly been conducted as a mesh to mesh comparison of watertight surfaces. Metrics like Hausdorff distance or Mean Square Error (MSE) are applied in order to compute an error map. This surface-to-surface methodology can be error prone when an accurate point-to-point error is required due to the natural vertex modification step in many reconstruction algorithms e.g. Possion or Marching Cube algorithms. Instead a point-to-point measure is applied to avoid introducing a reconstruction error term arising from vertex modification and choice of reconstruction parameter. We compare the point cloud model with the ground truth CAD model by computing the number of correct points and the point accuracy of the estimated object models. For each 14 models the accuracy and completeness is computed as an evaluation measure for the model quality, where:

- **Accuracy:** is measured as the root mean square distance from each Point P_{est} in the estimated model M_{est} to the nearest neighbouring point P_{gt} in the ground truth model M_{gt}. This measure expresses the quality of the reconstructed point P_{est} in M_{est}.
- **Completeness:** is measured as a percentage of correct reconstructed points in M_{est}. We compute the root mean square distance from each Point P_{gt} in the ground truth model M_{gt} to the nearest neighbouring point P_{est} in the estimated model M_{est}. We threshold this distance and count the number of correct points. The threshold is empirical chosen to be 3 times the average point resolution of the scene.

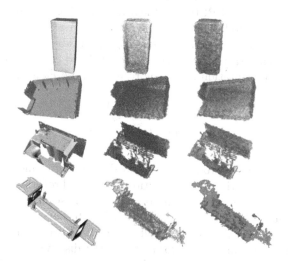

Fig. 3. Samples of the objects used in the evaluation. **First column:** Ground truth CAD model of the objects. **Second column:** Estimated models. **Third column:** Error model showing the noise distribution compared to ground truth.

The accuracy is reported in Sect. 5 as the average median error $\tilde{x}$, the standard deviation σ and RMS error M_{rms} of probability distribution functions (PDFs). We report the median error $\tilde{x}$ of the PDF to have a measure that is not biased by large outliers.

4.2   Pose Estimation

In order to quantify that our method is a valid visual learning method for computing 3D object representations, we evaluate the performance of a pose estimation algorithm with our estimated models and the ground truth models. This is to verify that learned object models result in an adequate pose accuracy and recognition rate compared to ground truth.

The objective of pose estimation is to estimate the (rigid) Transformation $T \in SE(3)$ that minimizes the mean square distances between each point P_{model} in an object model and the corresponding point P_{scene} in the scene. For the evaluation we have recorded 37 different multi-view scenes. For the evaluation we use 6 objects, paired three by three in two different sets of scenes. Each set consists of scenes with one, two and three objects such that all objects are represented by themselves and together with one or two other objects. Each set consists both of scenes where objects are touching each other and scenes where they are not. All scenes are recorded with the world frame in robot 1 base as global coordinate system. Ground truth data is obtained for all 37 scenes by manual annotation of 4 point in each point cloud, computing initial transformation followed by a large number of ICP iterations as described in Sect. 4.

We use a classic RANSAC 'hypothesis and test' algorithm together with Fast Point Feature Histogram (FPFH) local features [20]. For each scene and object, normals are estimated followed by feature estimation and RANSAC pose estimation. For all 6 models we measure the recognition rate for both the generated model and the ground truth. Each model is considered correct recognized if the translation t_r and the rotation R_r of the resulting pose P_r follows

$$t_r = ||t_{gt} - t_p|| \quad < 10\,mm \tag{1}$$

$$R_r = \arccos \frac{trace(R_p^T R_{gt} - 1)}{2} \quad < 10° \tag{2}$$

where t_{gt} and R_{gt} are the ground truth translation vector and rotation matrix and t_p and R_p are the estimated translation vector and rotation matrix. We use 10 mm as threshold value because all objects in all 37 scenes have a distance of more than one meter from the sensor. With a Bumblebee stereo camera with a focal length equals 1320 pixels and baseline equal 0.12 m, a one pixel disparity error will result in a 6 mm depth error at one meter distance, thus a 10 mm pose error threshold is a good compromise. In addition to the recognition rate the pose accuracy of the models are determined by computing the translation error from Eq. 1 and the rotation error from Eq. 2. The results are presented in Sect. 5.

5   Results

In Table 1 the results of the model comparison are presented. Our method reconstructs the 14 models with a completeness ranging from approximately 52 % to 87 %. The low level of completeness for some objects e.g. the *Pendulum* and

Angular_bracket has different reasons. In case of the *Pendulum*, the object suffers from an incomplete registration due to object ambiguities and the fact that the surface of the *Angular_bracket* has a highly reflecting surface which results in missing points in the reconstruction. In these cases, the system reconstructs objects with a lower level of completeness. On the other hand, objects with good surface properties and less ambiguities are reconstructed with 70–85 % correct surface points by our system, with a satisfying accuracy when compared to the scene point resolution and noise level.

Table 1. Results from comparing model M_{est} with the ground truth M_{gt}

Results models vs. ground truth				
Model ID	RMS error	Stddev σ	Median $\hat{x}$	Completeness %
*Marmalade**	3.43e-3	7.02e-6	2.31e-6	79.57
*Salt Box**	2.04e-3	3.81e-6	0.84e-6	85.87
*Salt Cylinder**	2.55e-3	9.77e-6	2.79e-6	86.82
*Potato box**	1.57e-3	5.89e-6	5.28e-6	78.59
Rear Part A1#	2.73e-3	57.1e-6	0.48e-6	75.69
Rear Part A2#	3.98e-3	86.2e-6	0.83e-6	82.16
Rear Part A3#	1.05e-3	2.57e-6	0.54e-6	80.63
Heatsink A1#	1.52e-3	6.35e-6	0.62e-6	68.41
Heatsink A2#	4.82e-3	9.64e-6	0.46e-6	58.19
Heatsink A3#	1.47e-3	8.38e-6	0.88e-6	60.77
Faceplate+	4.89e-3	74.7e-6	2.27e-6	54.54
Pendulum+	2.68e-3	11.6e-6	1.71e-6	55.91
Seperator+	2.96e-3	29.2e-6	2.23e-6	52.19
Bracket#	2.63e-3	35.7e-6	1.19e-6	64.46
Average	2.67e-3	24.8e-6	1.60e-6	70.27

objects from real industrial production sites, + Cranfield benchmark objects
*from KIT object database http://i61p109.ira.uka.de/ObjectModels WebUI/

The evaluation of the useability of the reconstructed models for pose estimation is conducted with a RANSAC pose estimation algorithm. The RANSAC algorithm runs for 5000 iterations with an inlier fraction at 0.2. The scene and the model are down-sampled to 5 mm and the pose estimation algorithm runs with an Euclidean inlier threshold at two times the scene point resolution. Each pose estimate is followed by a pose refinement step with 200 ICP iterations.

Our dataset consists of 37 different scenes with 61 unique object poses. We correctly estimate the pose of 38 object with our model and 33 with the ground truth model which result in a recognition rate at 62 % and 54 %, respectively. The quit low recognition rate is related to the difficulty of the scenes with many similar objects placed closely together or on top of each other. In Fig. 4 the pose error obtained from the reconstructed and the ground truth CAD model are presented as histograms. The results show that our models and ground truth are performing equal but our models have a slight lower average rotation error at 3.38 degrees, measured on all estimated poses of recognized objects. The ground truth has a slightly larger rotation error on 3.94 degrees. On the other hand, the ground truth has a lower average translation error on 3.0 mm compared to the estimated models having an average error on 4.97 mm. The overall conclusion is that the method has reconstructed the models with a completeness between 52 % to 87 % and a mean point accuracy between 2.04 to 4.89 mm. The result of the pose estimation evaluation shows that using the estimated models one get approximately the same pose accuracy than using ground truth CAD models. This result is satisfying for robot manipulation. The estimated models have a

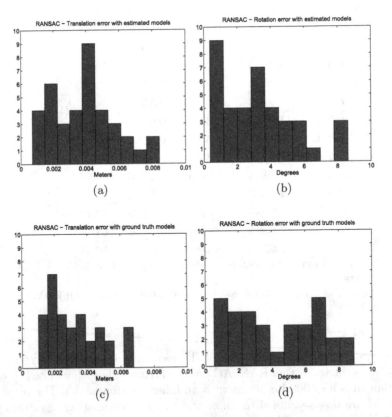

Fig. 4. Histogram of the pose error of all accepted pose estimates based on the criterion in Eqs. 1 and 2. **(a)** translation error of the pose estimation results with the reconstructed model. **(b)** rotation error with the reconstructed model. **(c)** translation error with the ground truth model. **(d)** rotation error with the ground truth model.

slightly better recognition rate than compared to ground truth. This could imply that having models which posses some of the scene characteristics in terms of noise levels and distortions of object borders, actually could improve the recognition rate abit. A more realistic representation of the object results in better surface normals and computed features that in the end favours pose estimation algorithms. However, to determine this correlation a larger dataset is required. This will be investigated in future work, together with a study concerning dexterous grasp simulation in combination with the reconstructed models.

6   Conclusion

We presented a multi view vision system able to reconstruct full 3D object models in only two shots. Our experiments show that object models larger than $(7.5 \times 7.5 \times 7.5)$ cm are reconstructed with an adequate accuracy and completeness. Furthermore, the models are useful in 6D pose estimation applications, without loss in recognition rate and precision compared to the ground truth CAD model. The combination of a 360-degree scene coverage from three calibrated stereo pairs and the two shot modeling methodology make the method useful for flexible reconfiguration of vision systems in industry. This flexibility makes the approach suited for few-of-a-kind production in industry where many new novel objects have to be handled by a robot thus reconfigurable vision systems reducing the set-up times.

References

1. Bannat, A., Bautze, T., Beetz, M., Blume, J., Diepold, K., Ertelt, C., Geiger, F., Gmeiner, T., Gyger, T., Knoll, A., Lau, C., Lenz, C., Ostgathe, M., Reinhart, G., Roesel, W., Ruehr, T., Schuboe, A., Shea, K., Wersborg, I., Stork genannt Wersborg, S., Tekouo, W., Wallhoff, F., Wiesbeck, M., Zaeh, M.F.: Artificial cognition in production systems. IEEE Trans. Autom. Sci. Eng. **8**(1), 148–174 (2011)
2. Buch, A., Kraft, D., Kamarainen, J.-K., Petersen, H., Kruger, N.: Pose estimation using local structure-specific shape and appearance context. In: IEEE International Conference on Robotics and Automation (ICRA), pp. 2080–2087, May 2013
3. Marton, Z., Pangercic, D., Blodow, N., Kleinehellefort, J., Beetz, M.: General 3D modelling of novel objects from a single view. In: 2010 IEEE/RSJ International Conference on Intelligent Robots and Systems, Taipei, Taiwan, pp. 3700–3705, October 2010
4. Mustafa, W., Pugeault, N., Kruger, N.: Multi-view object recognition using view-point invariant shape relations and appearance information. In: IEEE/RSJ International Conference on Robotics and Automation, Karlsruhe, Germany, pp. 4230–4237, May 2013
5. Chen, Y., Medioni, G.: Object modeling by registration of multiple range images. In: Proceedings of the 1991 IEEE International Conference on Robotics and Automation, Sacramento, California, pp. 2724–2729, April 1991
6. Bernardini, F., Rushmeier, H.: The 3D model acquisition pipeline. Comput. Graph. Forum **21**(2), 149–172 (2002)

7. Ilonen, J., Bohg, J., Kyrki, V.: Three-dimensional object reconstruction of symmetric objects by fusing visual and tactile sensing. Int. J. Robot. Res. **33**(2), 321–341 (2013)
8. Björkman, M., Bekiroglu, Y., Hogman, V., Kragic, D.: Enhancing visual perception of shape through tactile glances. In: IEEE/RSJ International Conference on Intelligent Robots and Systems, Tokyo, Japan, November 2013
9. Prankl, J., Zillich, M., Vincze, M.: Interactive object modelling based on piecewise planar surface patches. Comput. Vis. Image Underst. **117**(6), 718–731 (2013)
10. Bohg, J., Johnson-Roberson, M., Leon, B., Felip, J., Gratal, X., Bergstrom, N., Kragic, D., Morales, A.: Mind the gap - robotic grasping under incomplete observation. In: IEEE International Conference on Robotics and Automation (ICRA), Shanghai, China, May 2011
11. Kroemer, O., Ben Amor, H., Ewerton, M., Peters, J.: Point cloud completion using extrusions. In: IEEE-RAS International Conference on Humanoid Robots (Humanoids), Osaka, Japan, pp. 680–685, November 2012
12. Duncan, K., Sarkar, S., Alqasemi, R., Dubey, R.: Multi-scale superquadric fitting for efficient shape and pose recovery of unknown objects. In: IEEE/RSJ International Conference on Robotics and Automation, Karlsruhe, Germany, pp. 4238–4243, May 2013
13. Bone, G.M., Lambert, A., Edwards, M.: Automated modeling and robotic grasping of unknown three-dimensional objects. In: 2008 IEEE International Conference on Robotics and Automation, Pasadena, California, pp. 292–298, May 2008
14. Kraft, D., Detry, R., Pugeault, N.: Development of object and grasping knowledge by robot exploration. IEEE Trans. Auton. Mental Dev. **2**(4), 368–382 (2010)
15. Aleotti, J., Rizzini, D.L., Caselli, S.: Perception and grasping of object parts from active robot exploration. J. Intell. Robot. Syst. **76**, 401–425 (2014)
16. Krainin, M., Henry, P., Ren, X., Fox, D.: Manipulator and object tracking for in-hand 3D object modeling. Int. J. Robot. Res. **30**, 1311–1327 (2011)
17. Olesen, S.M., Lyder, S., Kraft, D., Krüger, N., Jessen, J.B.: Real-time extraction of surface patches with associated uncertainties by means of kinect cameras. J. Real-Time Image Process. **10**(1), 105–118 (2012). doi:10.1007/s11554-012-0261-x
18. Papon, J., Abramov, A., Schoeler, M., Wörgötter, F.: Voxel cloud connectivity segmentation - supervoxels for point clouds. In: 2013 IEEE Conference on Computer Vision and Pattern Recognition (CVPR), Portland, Oregon, 22–27 June 2013
19. Stein, S., Schoeler, M., Papon, J., Worgotter, F.: Object partitioning using local convexity. In: IEEE Conference on Computer Vision and Pattern Recognition (CVPR), pp. 304–311, June 2014
20. Rusu, R., Blodow, N., Beetz, M.: Fast point feature histograms (FPFH) for 3D registration. In: IEEE International Conference on Robotics and Automation, ICRA 2009, pp. 3212–3217, May 2009

Shape Dependency of ICP Pose Uncertainties in the Context of Pose Estimation Systems

Thorbjørn Mosekjær Iversen$^{(\boxtimes)}$, Anders Glent Buch, Norbert Krüger, and Dirk Kraft

The Mærsk Mc-Kinney Møller Institute, University of Southern Denmark, Odense, Denmark
{thmi,anbu,norbert,kraft}@mmmi.sdu.dk

Abstract. The iterative closest point (ICP) algorithm is used to fine tune the alignment of two point clouds in many pose estimation algorithms. The uncertainty in these pose estimation algorithms is thus mainly dependent on the pose uncertainty in ICP.

This paper investigates the uncertainties in the ICP algorithm by the use of Monte Carlo simulation. A new descriptor based on object shape and a pose error descriptor are introduced. Results show that it is reasonable to approximate the pose errors by multivariate Gaussian distributions, and that there is a linear relationship between the parameters of the Gaussian distributions and the shape descriptor. As a consequence the shape descriptor potentially provides a computationally cheap way to approximate pose uncertainties.

Keywords: Uncertainty modeling · Pose estimation · Robot vision · ICP

1 Introduction

To the present day the production industry has mainly focused on automating tasks involving mass production. Recently, however, several initiatives have been taken to develop flexible systems which can handle a large variety of workpieces [6]. One of the challenges in designing flexible systems is controlling the pose of the workpieces. Traditionally, the pose of objects in a production line is controlled by dedicated hardware which physically aligns the objects. However, this becomes infeasible in productions that experience rapid changes in product demands. To meet the needs for flexibility, the responsibility of determining object pose can be transferred to a vision system (see [10] for an overview of 3D object recognition and pose estimation systems).

Uncertainties are unavoidable when operating in a complex environment with vision sensors. To increase the robustness of the automation system, it is therefore important to incorporate knowledge of pose uncertainties into the system, such that subsequent actions that are dependent on the pose are designed appropriately. It has for instance been shown that peg-in-hole operations done using

© Springer International Publishing Switzerland 2015
L. Nalpantidis et al. (Eds.): ICVS 2015, LNCS 9163, pp. 303–315, 2015.
DOI: 10.1007/978-3-319-20904-3_28

trajectories which take the pose uncertainty into account are less prone to errors than if simpler trajectories are used [4]. It is therefore crucial to model the uncertainties of pose estimates provided by commonly used pose estimation algorithms.

Many pose estimation algorithms first compute an initial estimate of the pose—often using a robust feature matching algorithm—and then fine tune the pose using the *Iterative Closest Point* (ICP) algorithm [2]. Results of an analysis of the pose uncertainty in ICP are therefore applicable to a wide range of pose estimation systems.

There are two important aspects of uncertainty in ICP. One is the determination of a *basin of convergence* [7]: ICP is sensitive to the initial alignment, given by the initial pose estimation algorithm. If an inaccurate initial pose is supplied, ICP will likely converge to a pose far away from the true pose. The set of initial poses from which ICP converges to a proper solution is denoted the *basin of convergence*.

Given an initial pose estimate within the basin of convergence, the ICP algorithm converges to a pose close to the ground truth. However, due to noise, the errors between the estimated poses and the ground truth are distributed according to some unknown distribution. In this paper, this distribution is approximated by a multivariate Gaussian distribution. Based on this approximation, results indicate that there is a linear correlation between the parameters of the multivariate Gaussian error distribution and the shape of the object. For the remainder of this paper, all pose estimates are assumed to originate from initial alignments within the basin of convergence.

The ICP algorithm is based on the minimization of the sum of squared distances between nearest neighbors of an object and a scene point cloud. Due to this, the shape of an object plays an important role in the accuracy of the estimated pose. The ICP algorithm, when applied to a planar object in the xy-plane, will for instance have a higher accuracy in the z-direction than in the x- or y-direction, since a translation in x or y maintains an overlap between the object and the scene, which leads to incorrect point matches that maintain a small sum of squared distances. In contrast, a translation in the z-direction will increase the distance for all point matches, leading to a higher sum of squared distances. The overlap introduced by various translation directions is evident from Fig. 1a.

In the literature pose uncertainties in ICP have mainly been treated analytically by assuming that the points of the two point clouds that are being aligned have been matched correctly such that there is perfect one-to-one matching between the points in the two clouds. We argue that this is a bad assumption since a slightly wrong initial pose followed by nearest neighbor matching will result in many-to-one matches. The alternative is to use Monte Carlo simulation to estimate pose uncertainties, however this is computationally expensive. The aim of this article is to develop a descriptor of an object's shape which correlates with the uncertainty in the estimated pose. The shape descriptor can then be used to approximate pose uncertainties in ICP much faster than using Monte Carlo simulations.

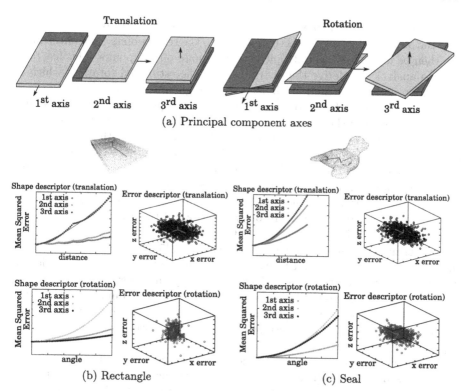

Fig. 1. (a) The three principal component axes of the rectangular box and the translation along and rotation around the axes, which are used to compute the shape descriptor. Notice how the amount of self-overlap introduced by a transformation is very
dependent on the axis. (b) Visualization of the shape descriptors and error descriptors
for the rectangular box. (c) The shape descriptors and the error descriptors for a point
cloud of a seal.

The structure of this article is as follows: First an overview of previous work
is presented (Sect. 2). Descriptors for both the shape of an object and the corresponding pose uncertainty are then formulated (Sect. 3). A model is then proposed, which, based on the descriptors, correlates an object's shape with the
uncertainty in pose as estimated by the ICP algorithm (Sect. 4). Finally Sect. 5
concludes the work.

2   State of the Art

While the ICP algorithm has received a lot of attention in the literature, the
problem of determining the uncertainty of the pose estimates has received less
attention. A topic related to pose uncertainty is the determination of degenerate
degrees of freedom: As ICP is based on object shape, there are objects where
there exist more than one pose which can be considered correct. An example of
this is the cylinder which has a single degenerate rotational degree of freedom
due to its rotational symmetry.

A popular approach to estimating the pose uncertainty in ICP is to assume that the object points are correctly matched to the scene points. The uncertainty can then be formulated as isotropic Gaussian noise on the points. This has been used to analytically derive the distribution of the estimated rotation, which in quaternion notation is the four dimensional Bingham distribution [9].

The assumption of a priori known object-scene point correspondences has also been applied in the derivation of pose uncertainty in the context of surface registration using normal-projection ICP [13]. To account for the fact that ICP is unable to distinguish between poses with degenerate degrees of freedom, a registration index is introduced as an indicator of near degeneracy. The near degeneracy can then be expressed as high uncertainty.

In [1] the covariance of the result of a minimization over a quadratic error function is shown to be dependent on the Hessian of the error function. This is applicable for an individual step of the ICP algorithm where point matches have been determined from a nearest-neighbor search. In [5] it is however argued that the uncertainty in ICP cannot be explained by the shape of the error function as determined from a particular set of observational points. Instead the covariance of the estimated pose describes how the position of the minimum of the error function changes with regard to different observations. An analytic expression for the covariance of an ICP pose estimate, based on the covariance of observations, is presented as an alternative.

Principal component analysis of the covariance matrix of the pose estimate has been used as a tool for improving ICP by selecting suitable sampling points. This was introduced to avoid failure in near degenerate cases. It was found that the eigenvalues of the covariance matrix can be used as a measure for the stability of the ICP algorithm [8].

Due to the complexity of analyzing the uncertainty while taking into account the lack of a priori knowledge of object-scene correspondences, Monte Carlo simulation has been used to analyze the performance of ICP. This has been carried out in the context of point registration to non-uniform rational B-spline surfaces [3]. It was concluded that one of the most important factors affecting registration performance was the shape of the object and the degree of symmetry.

The concept of a basin of convergence has been formulated both in relation to general optimization and in relation to ICP [7]. An investigation into 3D correspondence estimation has shown that the basin of convergence of ICP is very dependent on the shape of the object [14].

The contribution of this article is the formulation of a shape descriptor, which can be used to estimate the pose uncertainty in ICP without performing time consuming Monte Carlo simulations or relying on the questionable assumption of correct object-scene point matching.

3   Descriptors of Shape and Pose Error and Their Computation

As previously mentioned, successful pose estimates will often deviate from the ground truth. When doing pose estimation on simple objects, such as the planar object discussed in the introduction, it is clear that there is some correlation between the shape of the object and the accuracy of the estimated pose. To find and quantify this correlation, both the shape of the object and the pose error must be described using some descriptors, which can then be investigated for correlation. We introduce two descriptors in this paper named the *shape descriptor* and the *error descriptor*.

The shape descriptor is a measure of self-overlaps introduced by applying controlled transformations to the point cloud. It is thus independent of ICP. The error descriptor, on the other hand, is strongly connected to ICP, as it is a measure of the uncertainty of the estimated poses.

A correlation between the two descriptors is of interest because it enables the estimation of pose uncertainty based on the shape descriptor. This is computationally much cheaper than performing Monte Carlo simulations.

3.1   Shape Descriptor

Due to noise in the scene point cloud, there might not exist a pose which causes all points to be correctly matched to their corresponding points in the object cloud. This causes the estimated pose to be different from the ground truth pose. The amount of incorrect matches affecting the uncertainty is dependent on the shape of the object. Again using the example of a planar object in the xy-plane, a translation in the z-direction will increase the squared distance between all point pairs, whereas translation in x or y will lead to an increased squared distance for only a few points pairs. As a result, the pose error in the z-direction is mainly due to noise, while the incorrectly matched points due to overlap are the major factor in the x- and y-direction.

The shape descriptor is a quantitative measure of how fast the mean squared distance between nearest neighbors increases with translation along, or rotation around, the principal axes of an object in the absence of noise. The translational and rotational parts of the shape descriptor for a rectangular box are shown in Fig. 1. It shows that the relationship between a translation along, or rotation around, a principal axis and the corresponding mean squared distance between matched points can be approximated by a second-order polynomial.

A large mean squared distance for a given translation or rotation is due to there being only few incorrect matches originating from point cloud overlap. When there are only few incorrect matches, the error on the pose estimate will be small. The curvature of the second order polynomial can thus be hypothesized to be inversely proportional to the magnitude of the pose errors. Due to this the shape descriptor has been chosen to be the inverse of the curvature. The principal components have been chosen to be ordered from largest to smallest, so in the shape descriptor the inverse curvatures are ordered according to magnitude of their corresponding principal components.

The principal axes have been chosen for two reasons. Firstly, they are unique and thus provide an object-fixed coordinate frame, leading to a rotation and position invariant descriptor.[1] Secondly, the principal axes indicate the directions of largest point variance, which are directions where an object-scene overlap is most likely to occur.

The shape descriptor is split up into a translational component and a rotational component. Algorithm 1 describes the computation of the translational component. Figure 1a illustrates this as well.

Algorithm 1. Computation of the translational component of the shape descriptor

---

1 Compute the principal components of the object point cloud;
2 **for** *each of the principal axes* a_p **do**
3   **for** *increasing distances* $\Delta_{translation}$ **do**
4   Translate a copy of the cloud by $\Delta_{translation}$ along a_p;
5   Find the nearest neighbors between the original cloud and the translated copy;
6   Calculate the mean squared distance d between the matched points;
7   **end**
8   Fit the data points of d vs. $\Delta_{translation}$ with a second order polynomial;
9 **end**
10 Compute the inverse curvature of the fitted polynomials and order them according to the size of their corresponding principal component.

To compute the rotational component of the descriptor, Algorithm 1 is repeated using a rotation of $\Delta_{rotation}$ around the principal axes.

The final shape descriptor is thus the value of six inverse curvatures ordered according to their corresponding principal components.

3.2   Error Descriptor

Monte Carlo simulation was used to investigate the distribution of the pose errors. First isotropic Gaussian noise is added to a copy of the object point cloud. This new point cloud is denoted the scene cloud.

To test the ICP algorithm, a random transformation is applied to the scene cloud. The rotation is defined by a magnitude drawn from a normal distribution, and an axis is chosen by picking a random point on the unit sphere. The translation is a vector from a three-dimensional isotropic Gaussian distribution.

The difference between the pose of the object cloud and the scene cloud simulates an initial alignment of the object to the scene, which would normally

---

[1] It is possible to construct point clouds where some of the principal axes are degenerate, such as for a sphere or cylinder. If the degeneracy is due to rotational symmetry in the object, arbitrary axes can be chosen, since the corresponding pose error will display the same symmetry. Other causes for the degeneracy are not investigated in this paper.

be performed by a preprocessing pose estimation algorithm. The computation of the ICP pose errors is then done by performing ICP and calculating the estimated pose deviation from the ground truth pose by

$$t_{error} = t_{icp} - t_{gt} \qquad R_{error} = R_{icp}R_{gt}^{-1} \tag{1}$$

where t is the translation, R is the rotation matrix, and the subscripts $error$, icp and gt refer to the error, ICP and ground truth. The rotational part is then converted to the axis angle representation allowing the pose errors to be represented by two 3-dimensional vectors: One representing the translation error and one the rotation error.

The repeated application of this process leads to a set of translational and rotational error points. These are then each fitted with a multivariate Gaussian distribution. The distribution is described by the direction of its axes and its variance along these axes. It is these variances which constitute the error descriptor.

To find a correlation between the shape descriptor and the error descriptor, the principal axes of the object and the axes of the error descriptor have to be matched. However, there is no guarantee that the two sets of axes have the exact same directions. Each axis of the error descriptor is therefore matched to the principal axis to which it has the shortest angle.[2] With the axes matched, the values of the shape descriptor can be compared to the variances in the error descriptor.

There are some objects for which the error cloud is clearly non-Gaussian. However, with the exception of objects with rotational symmetry around an axis different from a principal axis, the Gaussian approximation has proven to be adequate. The situations where it is not adequate are discussed in Sect. 4.3.

4 Evaluation

To investigate the correlation between the shape descriptor and the error descriptor, ten different point clouds were used. Four of these are simple geometric shapes, five are clouds sampled from objects from the "KIT ObjectModels Web Database - Grasp bundle" [11], and one is from the "UWA database - Recognition bundle" [12]. The clouds used in the simulations have been picked so various classes of objects are represented. The set thus includes shapes with different properties such as irregularly shaped clouds and clouds with various degrees of symmetry. Figure 2 shows the point clouds used in addition to the two shown in Fig. 1.

4.1 Experiment Setup

Figure 3 shows the pipeline used for the simulated experiment. The computation of shape descriptors and the Monte Carlo simulation of the pose errors are shown

---

[2] As the choice of positive direction of both principal axes and error axes are arbitrary, they are always chosen so the angle between them is $0 \leq angle \leq \pi/2$.

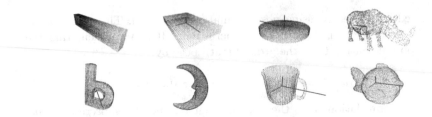

Fig. 2. Images of the point clouds used in addition to the two shown in Fig. 1

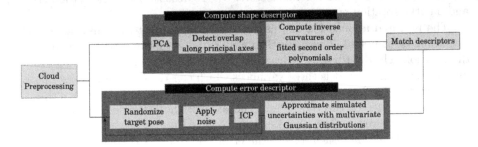

Fig. 3. The pipeline for the computation of the descriptors and the comparison of the results.

as being done in parallel. In reality they were done sequentially, but since they are independent from each other, they could have been carried out in parallel without changing the outcome.

First all point clouds were approximately normalized by translating them to the center of gravity, and then scaling them so they were comparable in size (the maximum distance between two points in a cloud after normalization is in the range of 2–10 m). The shape descriptor was then computed using the algorithm presented in Sect. 3.1, with $\Delta_{translation} = 0$ m to 0.5 m in steps of 0.01 m, and $\Delta_{rotation} = 0$ rad to 0.5 rad (28.6°) in steps of 0.01 rad (0.57°).

In the Monte Carlo simulation of the pose uncertainties, a number of parameters for the noise, target pose and ICP have been defined. The Point Cloud Library 1.7 base implementation of ICP was used.[3] All the parameters were defined once and held constant throughout the experiment. The chosen values for the normal distributions were: Standard deviation of the rotation magnitude of the ground truth pose $= \frac{2\pi}{9}$ rad (20°), standard deviation of the translational part of the ground truth pose $= 2$ m, standard deviation of the isotropic noise on the points of the scene point cloud $= 0.1$ m, ICP max correspondence distance $= 10$ m, ICP max number of iterations $= 200$, ICP transformation epsilon $= 10^{-8}$ m, ICP Euclidean fitness epsilon $= 10^{-5}$ m.

---

[3] The base implementation in Point Cloud Library 1.7 is a modified version of the original ICP algorithm. See the Point Cloud Library documentation for details: http://docs.pointclouds.org/1.7.0/classpcl_1_1_iterative_closest_point.html.

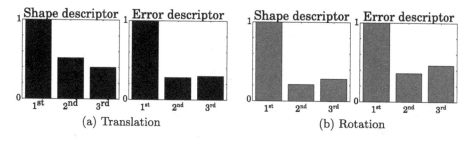

Fig. 4. Comparison of the shape and error descriptor for the seal point cloud.

The correspondence between shape descriptor and error descriptor is initially done qualitatively by comparing the two descriptors normalized so the largest value in each descriptor equals one. To investigate if there is a quantitative correspondence between the descriptors, the non-normalized error variances are finally plotted against the non-normalized inverse curvatures.

4.2   Results

This section presents the results of the evaluation. It should be noted that although each point cloud has some distinctive features, all but the disc and the moon show a good correspondence between shape and error descriptor. The data for the disc and the moon is not included in the analysis of this section. Furthermore this section only discusses the qualitative descriptor comparisons for the rectangular box and the seal point cloud in detail as they are representative of the rest of the point clouds.

Figure 1 shows a visualization of both the shape descriptor and the error descriptor for the rectangular box and the seal point cloud. By comparing the axes of Fig. 1a with the shape descriptors in Fig. 1b it is clear that a large overlap results in a small curvature. It can also be seen that the corresponding error distribution correlates with the shape descriptor.

As mentioned in Sect. 4.1, the comparison between the shape descriptor and the error descriptor can be done qualitatively by normalizing the two descriptors so the largest value is one. Figure 4 shows the normalized descriptors for the seal.

The angles between the matched descriptor axes are also computed. Given in degrees these are $\{3; 23; 23\}$ for the translational descriptors and $\{17; 41; 44\}$ for the rotational descriptors. The smaller the angle between the axes the better the match. A large angle might indicate some degree of symmetry in the object, causing the direction of the axes to be weakly defined, which means some uncertainty in the correspondence between the shape and error descriptors can be expected. The computed results for the seal show a relatively good correspondence between the shape and error descriptor.

In order to use the shape descriptor to predict the ICP pose uncertainty, and thus avoid carrying out time consuming Monte Carlo simulation for every new object, a quantitative correlation valid for all point clouds must be determined. Figure 5 shows a plot of the variances in the error descriptor vs. the inverse

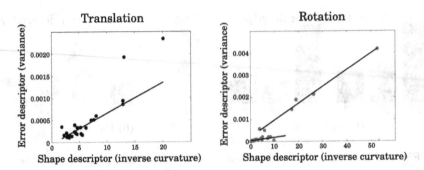

Fig. 5. A plot summarizing the relationship between the error descriptor and shape descriptor for all the point clouds which are within the domain of the model (see Sect. 4.3 for limitations). It shows the variance of the error descriptor vs. the corresponding inverse curvature in the shape descriptor.

curvatures in the shape descriptors before they are normalized. The figure indicates that there is a linear relationship between the descriptors. For the translational part the data seems to follow a simple linear relationship, while the rotational part is better described by two regressions—one for the low variance and one for the high variance data points. It should be noted that the analysis is based on a relatively small data set. Further studies are thus needed in order to confirm the hypothesis and provide reliable regressions.

The computation time of the shape and error descriptor is heavily dependent on the chosen ICP parameters and on the number of points in the point cloud. However to clarify the computational benefit of using the shape descriptor instead of Monte Carlo simulation to estimate pose uncertainties, the computation time for the seal's descriptors was recorded. The computation of the shape descriptor was a factor 460 faster than the Monte Carlo simulation, as the Monte Carlo simulation took 23 min while the shape descriptor was computed in three seconds.

4.3   Limitations

As the ICP algorithm uses the shape of an object to estimate its pose, the algorithm is not able to handle perfect rotational symmetry. In case of rotational symmetry, a rotation around the symmetry axis will introduce very small or even zero errors. This will lead to a very small curvature, or even a negative one due to noise in the process. As the shape descriptor is the inverse of the curvature, its value can go towards positive or negative infinity. As a consequence, objects with near perfect rotational symmetry are outside the domain of the model presented in this article. It should however be noted that the translational part of the descriptor still might provide reasonable results. The results for the disc, which is rotational symmetric, illustrates this (see Fig. 6).

Another limitation of the model is in regard to objects where the errors due to rotation and translation are strongly coupled. This is the case where there

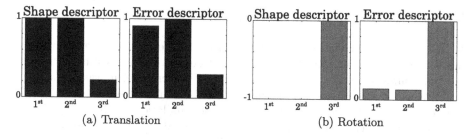

Fig. 6. Comparison of the shape and error descriptor for the disc point cloud.

is some degree of rotational symmetry, but around a different axis than the center of gravity. The shape descriptor only describes the overlap due to rotation around an axis through the center of gravity. It does not describe overlap due to combined translation and rotation, which is present in off-axis symmetric objects, such as the moon object. To confirm this theory a half donut was created, and the descriptors were computed using both an axis through the center of gravity and the symmetry axis as rotation axis. The result of using the axes through the center of gravity is shown in Fig. 7a and b. Using the symmetry axis results in the descriptors shown in Fig. 7c and d.

Although the descriptors correspond better to each other when using the symmetry axis, it introduces a bias in the translational error, which is not contained in the shape descriptor. For this reason objects with strongly coupled rotation and translation, such as off-axis rotation symmetry, are considered outside the model's domain.

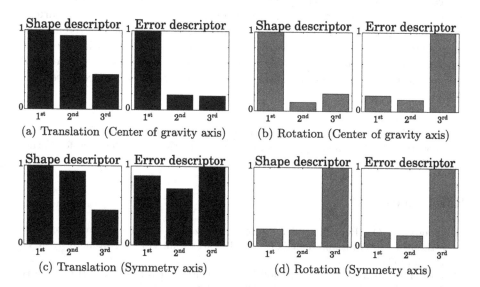

Fig. 7. Comparison of the shape and error descriptor for a half donut shaped point cloud.

5   Conclusions and Future Work

In this article the correlation between an object's shape and the pose uncertainty due to ICP has been investigated and modeled. Addressing pose estimates resulting from initial alignments within the basin of convergence, it was found that it is reasonable to approximate the uncertainty of estimated poses by multivariate Gaussian distributions. Using Monte Carlo simulations, it has been shown that there is a linear relationship between an error descriptor consisting of the variances of the multivariate Gaussian distributions and a novel shape descriptor presented in this paper. We have shown that there is a potential in our method to predict pose uncertainties in a principled and computationally efficient manner.

Beside validating the results using a larger dataset, future work should investigate whether a better correspondence between the shape and the error descriptor can be achieved if axes different from the principal component axes are chosen. Furthermore the model's dependency on ICP parameters and anisotropic noise parameters should be investigated.

It would also be interesting to investigate how the shape descriptor correlates with near degenerate degrees of freedom. The results in this paper indicate that the closer a degree of freedom is to being degenerate the larger the corresponding shape descriptor value is. Thus the descriptor provides a quantification of the gradual shift from high uncertainty to degeneracy. Unfortunately this will not detect periodic degrees of freedom which is present in for instance a cube which can be rotated $pi/2$ to produce the same appearance. It can however be speculated that if the mean squared distance vs. Δ plot used to compute the shape descriptor was extended beyond the basin of convergence, the periodic degrees of freedom would become visible as zero points in the plot. This could be used to detect if a pose outside the basin of convergence is degenerate in regard to the defined ground truth pose. In the context of pose estimation systems, the knowledge of near degenerate degrees of freedom outside the basin of convergence might provide insight into which poses are likely to be returned when ICP fails to find the correct pose. However, further investigation is needed to confirm this hypothesis.

Acknowledgements. The research leading to these results has been funded in part by Innovation Fund Denmark as a part of the project "MADE - Platform for Future Production".

References

1. Bengtsson, O., Baerveldt, A.J.: Robot localization based on scan-matching - estimating the covariance matrix for the IDC algorithm. Robot. Auton. Syst. **44**(1), 29–40 (2003)
2. Besl, P., McKay, N.D.: A method for registration of 3-D shapes. IEEE Trans. Pattern Anal. Mach. Intell. **14**(2), 239–256 (1992)
3. Brujic, D., Ristic, M.: Monte carlo simulation and analysis of free-form surface registration. Proc. Inst. Mech. Eng. Part B: J. Eng. Manuf. **211**(8), 605–617 (1997)

4. Buch, J.P., Laursen, J.S., Sørensen, L.C., Ellekilde, L.-P., Kraft, D., Schultz, U.P., Petersen, H.G.: Applying simulation and a domain-specific language for an adaptive action library. In: Brugali, D., Broenink, J.F., Kroeger, T., MacDonald, B.A. (eds.) SIMPAR 2014. LNCS, vol. 8810, pp. 86–97. Springer, Heidelberg (2014)
5. Censi, A.: An accurate closed-form estimate of ICP's covariance. In: 2007 IEEE International Conference on Robotics and Automation, pp. 3167–3172, April 2007
6. Christensen, H.I., et al.: A roadmap for u.s. robotics: from internet to robotics. Computing Community Consortium and Computing Research Association, Washington, DC (US) (2013)
7. Fitzgibbon, A.W.: Robust registration of 2D and 3D point sets. Image Vis. Comput. 21(13), 1145–1153 (2003)
8. Gelfand, N., Ikemoto, L., Rusinkiewicz, S., Levoy, M.: Geometrically stable sampling for the ICP algorithm. In: Proceedings of the Fourth International Conference on 3-D Digital Imaging and Modeling, 3DIM 2003, pp. 260–267 (2003)
9. Glover, J., Popovic, S.: Bingham procrustean alignment for object detection in clutter. In: 2013 IEEE/RSJ International Conference on Intelligent Robots and Systems (IROS), pp. 2158–2165 (2013)
10. Guo, Y., Bennamoun, M., Sohel, F., Lu, M., Wan, J.: 3D object recognition in cluttered scenes with local surface features: a survey. IEEE Trans. Pattern Anal. Mach. Intell. 36(11), 2270–2287 (2014)
11. Kasper, A., Xue, Z., Dillmann, R.: The kit object models database: an object model database for object recognition, localization and manipulation in service robotics. Int. J. Robot. Res. (IJRR) 31(8), 927–934 (2012)
12. Mian, A.S., Bennamoun, M., Owens, R.: Three-dimensional model-based object recognition and segmentation in cluttered scenes. IEEE Trans. Pattern Anal. Mach. Intell. 28(10), 1584–1601 (2006)
13. Stoddart, A.J., Lemke, S., Hilton, A., Renn, T.: Estimating pose uncertainty for surface registration. Image Vis. Comput. 16(2), 111–120 (1998)
14. Zinßer, T., Schmidt, J., Niemann, H.: A refined ICP algorithm for robust 3-D correspondence estimation. In: Proceedings of the 2003 International Conference on Image Processing, ICIP 2003, vol. 2, p. II-695 (2003)

D²CO: Fast and Robust Registration of 3D Textureless Objects Using the Directional Chamfer Distance

Marco Imperoli and Alberto Pretto[✉]

Department of Computer, Control,
and Management Engineering "Antonio Ruberti",
Sapienza University of Rome, Rome, Italy
marcoimperoli@gmail.com, pretto@dis.uniroma1.it

Abstract. This paper introduces a robust and efficient vision based method for object detection and 3D pose estimation that exploits a novel edge-based registration algorithm we called Direct Directional Chamfer Optimization (D²CO). Our approach is able to handle textureless and partially occluded objects and does not require any off-line object learning step. Depth edges and visible patterns extracted from the 3D CAD model of the object are matched against edges detected in the current grey level image by means of a 3D distance transform represented by an image tensor, that encodes the minimum distance to an edge point in a joint direction/location space. D²CO refines the object position employing a non-linear optimization procedure, where the cost being minimized is extracted directly from the 3D image tensor. Differently from other popular registration algorithms as ICP, that require to constantly update the correspondences between points, our approach does not require any iterative re-association step: the data association is implicitly optimized while inferring the object position. This enables D²CO to obtain a considerable gain in speed over other registration algorithms while presenting a wider basin of convergence. We tested our system with a set of challenging untextured objects in presence of occlusions and cluttered background, showing accurate results and often outperforming other state-of-the-art methods.

1 Introduction

A reliable object instance detection and localization system is an essential requirement for most robotics applications, from robot-aided manufacturing to service robotics applications, where a robot needs to grasp and manipulate objects in an accurate and reliable way. Many very promising image-based object detection systems usually assumes that the searched objects are characterized by salient visual patterns or textures, to be extracted using robust invariant detectors (e.g., [15]) and matched against precomputed image-based models [18,23]. Unfortunately, these methods can't handle untextured, non-Lambertian objects: this often prevents the use of these methods for industrial applications,

© Springer International Publishing Switzerland 2015
L. Nalpantidis et al. (Eds.): ICVS 2015, LNCS 9163, pp. 316–328, 2015.
DOI: 10.1007/978-3-319-20904-3_29

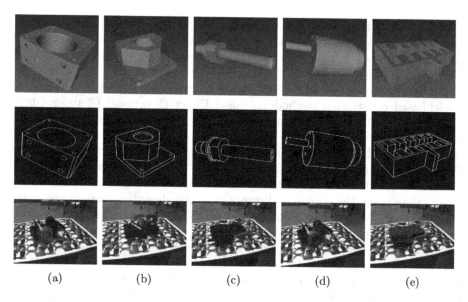

(a)   (b)   (c)   (d)   (e)

Fig. 1. [Top row]: The 3D CAD models of the untextured objects used in the experiments. (a),(b) and (c) are metal objects with high-reflectance surfaces, while (d) and (e) are black, plastic objects, and present a strong visible-light absorption. [Center row]: The edge templates extracted from the CAD models. [Bottom row]: Some registration results obtained using the D²CO algorithm, the initial guess is reported in blue, while the final position estimate in red (Color online figure).

where objects are usually untextured and made with non-Lambertian materials as metal or glass. Thanks to the availability of many commercial depth sensor as RGB-D cameras, laser triangulation systems and 3D laser range finders, many vision systems are currently moving toward these 3D sensors (e.g., [20,21]). Although these systems benefit of a full 3D representation of the workspace, they still have some important limitations: (i) The cost of a 3D industrial sensor is still from 3 to 10 times higher than a conventional high resolution industrial camera; (ii) Current consumer RGB-D cameras can't handle small objects due to the limited resolution and the minimum viewing distance. Actually, we tested the Microsoft Kinect RGB-D camera with the objects used in our experiments (Fig. 1), and we found that the object (c) is often not even perceived from the depth sensor, even at small distances.

In many cases, edge-based vision algorithms for object detection and localization still provide superior performances. In this context, state-of-the-art methods (e.g., [11,14]) usually perform an efficient and exhaustive template matching over the whole image. Templates usually represents shapes extracted from the 3D CAD of the object, seen from a number of viewpoints. Unfortunately, in our experience we found that, given as input a single grey level image and no accurate scale priors, none of the tested state-of-the-art matching algorithms provide as first output the best, true-positive, match. Actually, without accurate scale priors, the searching space is huge, imposing a coarse-grained viewpoint discretization. It is usually required to perform many time-consuming object registration steps over a large set of object candidates, extracted from the matching algorithm, in order to accurately detect the true best matches.

To address this problem, in this work we introduce an efficient and robust model-based registration method we called Direct Directional Chamfer Optimization (D^2CO). D^2CO works on grey level images: the backbone of our method is represented by the 3D distance transform proposed in [14] we call here Directional Chamfer Distance (DCD). This distance improves the accuracy of the Chamfer matching by including edge orientation. The DCD is computed using a 3D image tensor that, for each image pixel coordinates and for each (discretized) direction, provides the minimum distance in a joint direction/location space. In our experience, DCD-based matching provides the best matching results compared with other state-of-the-art matching algorithms in case of clutter and undetected image edges. [14] also introduced a refinement algorithm based on ICP that exploits the DCD to re-compute the point-to-point correspondences. In the following, we will refer to this algorithm with the acronym DC-ICP. DC-ICP provides state-of-the-art registration results, but it is very slow since it requires many iterations to converge. D^2CO aims to overcome these limitations, taking advantage of the DCD while boosting the convergence rate. The idea is to refine the parameters using a cost function that exploits the DCD tensor in a *direct way*, i.e., by retrieving the costs and the derivatives directly from the tensor. Being a piecewise smooth function of both the image translation and the (edge) orientation, the DCD ensures a wide basin of convergence. Differently from DC-ICP, D^2CO does not require to re-compute the point-to-point correspondences, since the data association is implicitly encoded in the DCD tensor. Experiments and quantitative evaluations performed on challenging scenes show the effectiveness of our registration method.

1.1   Related Work

Vision systems for learning, detecting and localizing objects have been widely studied in the computer vision and robotics communities for many years.

Image-based systems (e.g., [18,23]) usually represents objects through collections of distinctive local features (e.g., [15]) extracted form a number of viewpoints. An overview of general image-based object recognition and localization techniques can be found in [22], along with a performance evaluation of many types of visual local descriptors used for 6 DoF pose estimation. Even if this class of methods achieved impressive object recognition and categorization results, they can't be easily applied to textureless objects. Moreover, image-based systems usually fails to obtain accurate object localization results, due to the discrete nature of the collected viewpoints.

Model-based systems use instead 3D CAD models of the searched objects, or the shapes extracted from the model, seen from a number of viewpoints. This class of methods are well suited for robot-aided manufacturing or service robotics applications: actually, besides ensuring greater accuracy in the localization task, they can deal with untextured objects. In this context, many object detection and registration techniques have been presented.

Recently, we presented a model-based vision system for 3D localization of planar textureless objects [17]. This system exploits a modified Generalized Hough Transform to select object candidates, and an iterative optimize-and-score registration procedure that employs a constrained optimization to be robust against local minima. Although the registration is very accurate, this system can deal only with planar objects rotated up to ±40 *degrees* around x and y axes. The iterative closest point (ICP) [2] is probably the best known point registration method: at each iteration, given the current parameters (i.e., a rigid-body transformation), ICP re-computes the correspondences between points and then updates the parameters as a solution of a least square problem. Fitzgibbon [8] proposed to use the Levenberg-Marquardt algorithm to solve the ICP inner loop, while employing a fast distance lookup based on the Chamfer Distance Transform. Jian *et al.* [12] proposed a generalization of the ICP algorithm that represents the input point sets using Gaussian mixture models. Unfortunately, an initial data association far from the correct one, dramatically increase the chances of ICP to get stuck in a wrong local minima. To mitigate this problem, Gold *et al.* [9] proposed to relax the ICP assumption of fixed correspondences between point sets: they proposed to assign "soft" correspondences between points by means of scalar values in the range [0..1]. This method, called robust point matching (RPM), has been recently extended by Lian and Zhang [13]: they proposed a concave optimization approach for the RPM energy function, that is globally optimal and it can handle the presence of outliers. Unfortunately, these methods include in the parameters set the whole point correspondences matrix, making them often unsuitable to real-world problems.

The Chamfer Distance Transform ([1,3]), used also for registration in [8], has played an important role in many model-based detection and matching algorithms. Even if the original formulation suffers from not being robust to outliers, Chamfer matching and especially its variations still remain powerful tools used for edge-based object detection and matching. Choi and Christensen [5] employed Chamfer matching inside a particle filtering framework for textureless object detection and tracking. In [19] Shotton *et al.* presented a matching scheme called Oriented Chamfer Matching (OCM): they proposed to augment the Chamfer distance with an additional channel that encodes the edge points orientations. Cai *et al.* [4] used sparse edge-based image descriptor to efficiently prune object-pose hypotheses, and OCM for hypotheses verification. Danielsson *et al.* [7] proposed an object category detection algorithm based on a voting scheme that employs a set of distance transform maps, each one computed for a discretized orientation. Recently, Liu *et al.* [14] extended this idea proposing the Fast Directional Chamfer Matching (FDCM) scheme, that exploits a 3D distance transform reporting the minimum distance to an edge point in a joint direction/location space: reported results show that FDCM outperform OCM. [14] also presented an ICP-based registration algorithm that exploits the proposed distance transform. The method presented in this paper was inspired from [14] and [8].

Other recent model-based object matching algorithms use spread image gradient orientations saved in a cache memory-friendly way [11] and multi-path edgelet constellations [6].

2   Object Detection

In this section, we describe our object detection approach, that exploits the DCD tensor in order to extract a set of objects candidates (i.e., their 'rough' 3D locations) from the input image, based on the given model template.

2.1   Object Model

Edges represent the most informative image features that characterize untextured objects: edges are usually generated by occlusions (depth edges) and high curvature. Given a 3D CAD model of an object (e.g., first row of Fig. 1), we need to extract a 3D template that includes only these edges. We start from the 3D model wireframe, preserving only edges that belong to high curvature parts or to the external object shape, while using the OpenGL z-buffer to deal with occlusions. Some results of this procedure are shown in the second row of Fig. 1. It is important to note that, in the general case, this procedure should be repeated for each viewpoint, i.e., for each object position.

We finally produce a *rasterization* of this template, i.e. we extract from the template a set of m sample points $\mathcal{M} = \{\mathbf{o}_1, \ldots, \mathbf{o}_m\} \in \mathbb{R}^3$, in the object reference frame. Typically we employ a rasterization step of $1 - 2$ mm. We also collect another set of m points, $\bar{\mathcal{M}} = \{\bar{\mathbf{o}}_1, \ldots, \bar{\mathbf{o}}_m\} \in \mathbb{R}^3$, where:

$$\bar{\mathbf{o}}_i = \mathbf{o}_i + \hat{\tau}(\mathbf{o}_i) \cdot dr \tag{1}$$

$\hat{\tau}(\mathbf{o}_i)$ is a function that provides the unit tangent vector, i.e. the unit direction vector of the 3D edge the raster point belongs to, while dr is a small scalar increment, $dr \ll 1$. Given a transformation $\mathbf{g}_{cam,obj} \in \mathbb{SE}(3)$ from the object frame to the camera frame, we can project the raster points on the image plane as:

$$\mathbf{x}_i = \pi(\mathbf{o}_i, \mathbf{g}_{cam,obj}) \in \mathbb{R}^2, i = \{1, \ldots, m\} \tag{2}$$

The idea behind these two set of 3D points is simple: by projecting on the image plane the raster points $\mathcal{M}$ along with the points $\bar{\mathcal{M}}$, it is possible to easily recover also the 2D local directions (orientations) of the projected edge points in the image plane.

2.2   Edge Points Extraction

In order to match the edge template extracted from the CAD model, we need to detect edges in the input image. We adopt here the concept of *edgelet*, a straight segment that can be part of a longer, possibly curved, line, extracted using a state-of-the-art detection algorithm for line segment detector called LSD [10].

This algorithm searches the input image for edgelets starting from pixels with higher gradient magnitude, looking in the neighbourhood for pixels with similar gradient directions. A line-support region is therefore selected and validated in order to discard the outliers. We employ the LSD algorithm on a Gaussian pyramid of the input image, enabling to include in the final set also edgelets that appear in higher scales. This technique increases the sensitivity of the edge detector, at the cost of a reduced accuracy in the localization of the edgelets. For each detected edgelet, we also compute its orientation in the image reference frame. We define as $\mathcal{E} = \{\mathbf{e}_1, \dots, \mathbf{e}_n\} \in \mathbb{R}^2$ the set of pixels (*edgels*) that belong to edgelets.

2.3 Directional Chamfer Distance

As introduced above, our approach leverages the Directional Chamfer Distance tensor in both the detection and registration steps. The DCD tensor $(DT3_V)$ is represented by an ordered sequence of distance transform maps[1], each one representing a *discretized edge direction*. The basic idea behind the Directional Chamfer Distance is simple:

- Divide the set of edgelets computed in Sec. 2.2 into several subsets by quantizing their directions;
- draw each edgelets set in a different binary image;
- compute one distance transform map for each subset using the binary images computed above.

In this way, each map reports the minimum distance from a set of edges with almost the same direction. Liu *et al.* [14] extended this idea enabling the DCD tensor $DT3_V$ to encode the minimum distance to an edge point in a joint location and orientation space. Be $\mathbf{x}_i$ the 2D projection on the image plane of a 3D raster edge point $\mathbf{o}_i$ with $\Xi(\mathbf{x}_i)$ a function that provides its (scalar) direction in the image reference frame, computed projecting also $\bar{\mathbf{o}}_i$ (see Sec. 3). The minimum distance to an edge point (edgel) $\mathbf{e}_j$ can be recovered as:

$$DT3_V(\mathbf{x}_i, \Xi(\mathbf{x}_i)) = \min_{\mathbf{e}_j \in \mathcal{E}} (\|\mathbf{x}_i - \mathbf{e}_j\| + \lambda \|\phi(\Xi(\mathbf{x}_i)) - \phi(o(\mathbf{e}_j))\|) \qquad (3)$$

where $o(\mathbf{e}_j)$ is the edgel orientation and $\phi(.)$ is an operator that provides the nearest quantized orientation. The tensor $DT3_V$ can be easily computed by applying a forward and backward recursions to the sequence of distance transform maps described above, see [14] for the details. Since our optimization framework employs the tensor $DT3_V$ in a direct way (see Sec. 3), we need to ensure that the function $DT3_V : \mathbb{R}^3 \to \mathbb{R}$ that it represents is piecewise smooth. To this end, we smooth the tensor along the direction (orientation) dimension using a simple Gaussian filter. In all our experiments, we use 60 discretized orientations and we set λ to 100 and σ^2 (the variance the Gaussian filter) to 1.

---

[1] In our case, a distance transform is an image where each pixel reports the distance to the closest edge pixel (edgel).

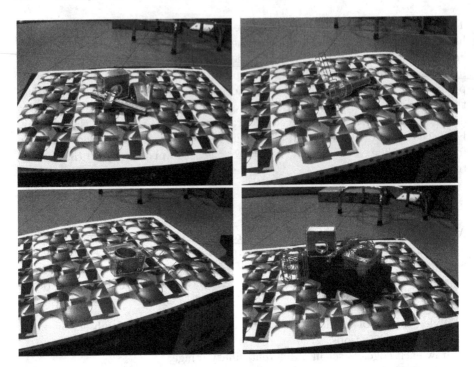

Fig. 2. Some examples of objects candidates extraction. The red template represents the ground truth position of the object, green and blue templates represent the true and false positives, respectively (Color online figure).

2.4   Candidate Extraction

Since we perform the object detection task without knowing any accurate scale prior, the huge 6D searching space imposes a coarse-grained viewpoint discretization. In order to speedup the process, for each object in the dataset we pre-compute the (projected) raster templates along with their image orientations for a large number of possible 3D locations. Each template includes in such a way a set of image points along with their orientation: by performing a set of lookups on the tensor $DT3_V$, we can compute the average distance in an efficient way. Finally, we sort the templates for increasing distance: the top rated templates (e.g., see Fig. 2) represent our objects hypothesis (or "object candidates"), to be registered and validated.

3   Object Registration

Once we have obtained a set of objects candidates, we need to precisely locate each true positive object, while discarding the outliers. D^2CO refines the object position employing a non-linear optimization procedure that minimizes a tensor-based cost function.

Given a set of m raster points extracted from the 3D CAD model, from Eq. 2 we can obtain the corresponding image projections $\mathbf{x}_i$. We can also express the transformation $\mathbf{g}_{cam,obj}$ in terms of a translation vector $\mathbf{T} = [t_x\ t_y\ t_z]^T$ and a orientation vector $\boldsymbol{\Omega} = [r_x\ r_y\ r_z]^T$, both in $\mathbb{R}^3$. We make explicit this fact using the notation $\mathbf{g}(\mathbf{T}, \boldsymbol{\Omega}) = \mathbf{g}_{cam,obj}$. $\mathbf{R}(\boldsymbol{\Omega}) \doteq \exp(\widehat{\boldsymbol{\Omega}})$ is the rotation matrix corresponding to the rotation vector $\boldsymbol{\Omega}$, where $\widehat{\boldsymbol{\Omega}}$ is the skew-symmetric matrix corresponding to $\boldsymbol{\Omega}$, and $Log_{\mathrm{SO}(3)}(\mathbf{R}(\boldsymbol{\Omega})) \doteq \boldsymbol{\Omega}$ is the rotation vector $\boldsymbol{\Omega}$ corresponding to the rotation matrix $\mathbf{R}(\boldsymbol{\Omega})$ [16]. Our optimization procedure aims to find the parameters $(\tilde{\mathbf{T}}, \tilde{\boldsymbol{\Omega}}) \in \mathbb{R}^6$ that minimize:

$$E(\mathbf{T}, \boldsymbol{\Omega}) = \frac{1}{2} \sum_{i=1}^{m} DT3_V\left[\pi(\mathbf{o}_i, \mathbf{g}(\mathbf{T}, \boldsymbol{\Omega})), \Xi(\pi(\mathbf{o}_i, \mathbf{g}(\mathbf{T}, \boldsymbol{\Omega})))\right]^2 \qquad (4)$$

While we can assume that, for small viewpoint transformations, the 3D raster points do not change (i.e., we can neglect changes in the occlusions), this fact does not apply for their image projections. Moreover, Eq. 4 also requires to constantly update the projected (edge) point orientations. We first project also the point set $\bar{\mathcal{M}}$: $\bar{\mathbf{x}}_i = \pi(\bar{\mathbf{o}}_i, \mathbf{g}_{cam,obj})$, $i = \{1, \dots, m\}$. If we define $\mathbf{d}_i \triangleq \bar{\mathbf{x}}_i - \mathbf{x}_i$, for each iteration of the optimization we can compute the updated orientations as:

$$\Xi(\pi(\mathbf{o}_i, \mathbf{g}(\mathbf{T}, \boldsymbol{\Omega}))) = \Xi(\mathbf{x}_i) = atan\left(\frac{\mathbf{d}_i(1)}{\mathbf{d}_i(0)}\right) \qquad (5)$$

In order to apply a non-linear minimization on $E(\mathbf{T}, \boldsymbol{\Omega})$, we have to compute its derivatives ∇E. Application of the chain rule yields:

$$\nabla E = \sum_{i=1}^{m} \{\nabla DT3_V\ \nabla\left[\pi(\mathbf{o}_i, \mathbf{g}(\mathbf{T}, \boldsymbol{\Omega})), \Xi(\pi(\mathbf{o}_i, \mathbf{g}(\mathbf{T}, \boldsymbol{\Omega})))\right]\} \qquad (6)$$

Since $DT3_V$ is only defined at discrete points, its derivatives $\nabla DT3_V$ should be computed in a numerical, approximate way. To this end, we compute the x and y derivatives as the image derivatives of the currently selected distance map and, in a similar way, the derivative along the orientation direction ξ as:

$$\frac{\delta DT3_V}{\delta \xi}(\mathbf{x}, \xi) = \frac{DT3_V(\mathbf{x}, \xi + 1) - DT3_V(\mathbf{x}, \xi - 1)}{2} \qquad (7)$$

We lookup the $DT3_V$ tensor employing a bilinear interpolation operator, adapted to the 3D nature of $DT3_V$: this enables to improve the level of smoothness of the cost function.

We perform the optimization using the Levenberg-Marquardt algorithm and, as suggested in [8], a Huber loss function in order to reduces the influence of outliers.

3.1 The Scoring Function

Some of the selected hypothesis used as initial guess for the registration may represent false positive objects: after the position refinement presented above, we need to employ a metrics that allows us to discard the outliers and to select the best match. We use a simple but effective scoring function based on local image gradient directions. Given $\mathbf{x}_i$ a raster point projected on the image plane, we can compute its image normal direction $n_{dir}(\mathbf{x}_i)$: in the ideal case of a perfect match, this direction should correspond to the local gradient direction $\mathbf{I}_\theta(\mathbf{x}_i)$ (up to a rotation of π *radians*), where $\mathbf{I}_\theta$ is the gradient direction image computed directly from the input image. We define the scoring function as:

$$\Psi(\mathbf{g}_{cam,obj}) = \frac{1}{m} \sum_1^m |\cos(\mathbf{I}_\theta(\mathbf{x}_i) - n_{dir}(\mathbf{x}_i))| \tag{8}$$

Clearly $\Psi(\mathbf{g}_{cam,obj})$ can get values from 0 to 1, where 1 represents the score for a perfect, ideal match. In our experiments, all good matches (inliers) obtain a score greater than 0.8. We discard all the matches with a score less than this threshold: they can be outliers (false positive objects) or real objects heavily occluded.

4   Experiments

We present two different experimental validations. The first experiment aims to show that FDCM [14], that is the backbone of D^2CO, outperforms in our dataset another recent state-of-the-art object detection algorithm. In a second experiments, we compare D^2CO to other registration techniques, showing state-of-the-art performances with a gain in speed up to a factor 10.

Our dataset[2] is composed by 60 1024x768 grey level images of scenes that contain up to 5 untextured objects[3] (see Fig. 1) disposed in arbitrary 3D positions, often mutually occluded. In some images we added a background board with multiple patterns in order to simulate a (visual) crowded background (e.g., see Fig. 4). Each image is provided with the ground truth positions of the objects, obtained with an externally guided procedure. All the experiments were performed running the algorithms on a standard laptop with an Intel Core i7-3820QM CPU with 2.70GHz, using a single core. All the compared algorithms has been implemented in C++ without any strong optimization. When possible, they share the same codebase and the same parameters, enabling an objective performance and timing comparison.

4.1   Object Detection

In the first experiment, we compare our object matching approach, that is strongly related with FDCM presented in [14], with a state-of-the-art object detection approach (called in the plots GRM, from Gradient Response Maps) described in [11] (since we are using only images, we use the LINE-2D version).

---

[2] The dataset is available at http://www.dis.uniroma1.it/~labrococo/D2CO.

[3] The objects used in the experiments are currently employed in the RoCKIn@Work competitions, http://rockinrobotchallenge.eu.

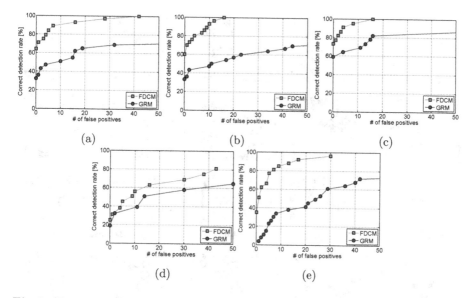

Fig. 3. True positives rate plotted against the number of false positives (the letters (a),..(e) refer to the objects of Fig. 1).

In our experiments we don't perform any memory linearization as in [11], since we don't assume that the object projection remain the same every $x - y$ translation. Anyhow, this modification does not affect the performance of GRM: it just runs slower.

We perform object matching starting from a set of 1260 pose candidates for each one of the 60 scenes of our dataset. Each of these candidates are acquired by sampling a large cubic scene region containing the target objects. Figure 3 shows how FDCM outperforms GRM in terms of correct detection rate against the number of false positives for each image.

4.2 Object Registration

We compared our approach (D²CO) to DC-ICP [14], LM-ICP [8], C-ICP (ICP that exploits the Chamfer distance) and Direct (a simple coarse-to-fine object registration strategy that uses a Gaussian pyramid of gradient magnitudes images). All the tested algorithms share the same inner loop's stopping criteria parameters. We set the number of external ICP iterations to 50: we verified that this is a good trade-off in order to reach reliable results in our dataset. For each image and for each object in the image, we sampled 100 random positions around the ground truth position (e.g., the blue templates reported in Fig. 4). We used these positions as initial guesses for the registration algorithms we are testing. The final estimated position (e.g., the red templates reported in Fig. 4) is checked against the ground truth: if the total angular error was less than 0.1 radians, and the total error of translation was less than 5 mm, the registration

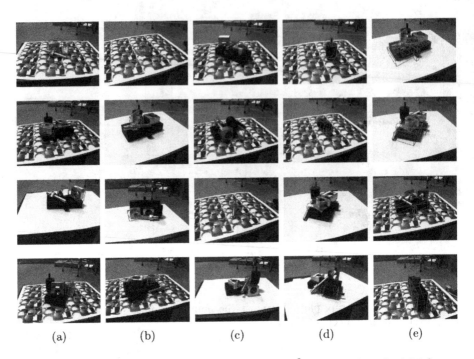

(a)   (b)   (c)   (d)   (e)

Fig. 4. Other registration results obtained using the D²CO algorithm, the initial guess is reported in blue, final position estimate in red (the letters (a),..(e) refer to the objects of Fig. 1) (Color figure online).

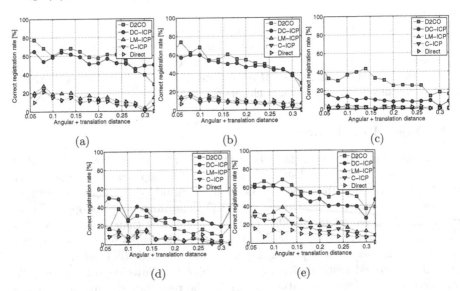

Fig. 5. Correct registrations rate plotted against the distance (angle + translation) of the initial guess from the ground truth position (the letters (a),..(e) refer to the objects of Fig. 1).

was considered correct. The proposed D²CO algorithm outperforms the other methods in almost all tests (Fig. 5), while getting a gain in speed of a factor 10 compared to the second most competitive approach (see Table 1).

Table 1. Average object registration time (milliseconds).

Algorithm	D²CO	DC-ICP	LM-ICP	C-ICP	Direct
Time (msec)	56.49	659.09	68.43	601.10	65.83

5 Conclusions and Future Works

In this paper, we have proposed an object detection and localization system that combines a state-of-the-art untextured object detection algorithm with a novel registration strategy that leverages the Directional Chamfer Distance tensor in a direct and efficient way. We tested our system with a set of challenging untextured objects in presence of occlusions and cluttered background, getting state-of-the-art results while saving computation time.

We are currently improving our system by enabling the optimization to work directly on the directional integral images representation of the DCD tensor, in order to further speedup the registration process.

Acknowledgement. This research has been supported by the European Commission under: 644227-Flourish and FP7-ICT-601012 (RoCKIn Project).

References

1. Barrow, H.G., Tenenbaum, J.M., Bolles, R.C., Wolf, H.C.: Parametric correspondence and chamfer matching: two new techniques for image matching. In: Proceedings of 5th International Joint Conference on Artificial Intelligence, pp. 659–663 (1977)
2. Besl, P.J., McKay, N.D.: A method for registration of 3-d shapes. IEEE Trans. Pattern Anal. Mach. Intell. **14**(2), 239–256 (1992)
3. Borgefors, G.: Hierarchical chamfer matching: a parametric edge matching algorithm. IEEE Trans. Pattern Anal. Mach. Intell. **10**(6), 849–865 (1988)
4. Cai, H., Werner, T., Matas, J.: Fast detection of multiple textureless 3-D objects. In: Chen, M., Leibe, B., Neumann, B. (eds.) ICVS 2013. LNCS, vol. 7963, pp. 103–112. Springer, Heidelberg (2013)
5. Choi, C., Christensen, H.I.: 3d textureless object detection and tracking: an edge-based approach. In: Proceedings of: IEEE/RSJ International Conference on Intelligent Robots and Systems (IROS), pp. 3877–3884 (2012)
6. Damen, D., Bunnun, P., Calway, A., Mayol-Cuevas, W.W.: Real-time learning and detection of 3d texture-less objects: a scalable approach. In: Proceedings of British Machine Vision Conference, pp. 1–12 (2012)

7. Danielsson, O.M., Carlsson, S., Sullivan, J.: Automatic learning and extraction of multi-local features. In: Proceedings of IEEE 12th International Conference on Computer Vision, pp. 917–924 (2009)
8. Fitzgibbon, A.W.: Robust registration of 2D and 3D point sets. In: British Machine Vision Conference, pp. 662–670 (2001)
9. Gold, S., Rangarajan, A., Lu, C.P., Mjolsness, E.: New algorithms for 2d and 3d point matching: pose estimation and correspondence. Pattern Recogn. 31, 957–964 (1997)
10. Jakubowicz, J., Morel, J.-M., Randall, G.: Lsd: a fast line segment detector with a false detection control. IEEE Trans. Pattern Anal. Mach. Intell. 32(4), 722–732 (2010)
11. Hinterstoisser, S., Cagniart, C., Ilic, S., Sturm, P.F., Navab, N., Fua, P., Lepetit, V.: Gradient response maps for real-time detection of textureless objects. IEEE Trans. Pattern Anal. Mach. Intell. 34(5), 876–888 (2012)
12. Jian, B., Vemuri, B.C.: Robust point set registration using gaussian mixture models. IEEE Trans. Pattern Anal. Mach. Intell. 33(8), 1633–1645 (2011)
13. Lian, W., Zhang, L.: Point matching in the presence of outliers in both point sets: a concave optimization approach. In: Proceedings of the IEEE Conference on Computer Vision and Pattern Recognition, pp. 352–359 (2014)
14. Liu, M.-Y., Tuzel, O., Veeraraghavan, A., Taguchi, Y., Marks, T.K., Chellappa, R.: Fast object localization and pose estimation in heavy clutter for robotic bin picking. I. J. Robotic Res. 31(8), 951–973 (2012)
15. Lowe, D.G.: Distinctive image features from scale-invariant keypoints. Int. J. Comput. Vis. 60(2), 91–110 (2004)
16. Ma, Y., Soatto, S., Kosecka, J., Sastry, S.: An invitation to 3D vision: from images to models. Springer, New York (2003)
17. Pretto, A., Tonello, S., Menegatti, E.: Flexible 3d localization of planar objects for industrial bin-picking with monocamera vision system. In: Proceedings of IEEE International Conference on Automation Science and Engineering (CASE), pp. 168–175 (2013)
18. Savarese, S., Li, F.-F.: 3d generic object categorization, localization and pose estimation. In: Proceedings of IEEE 11th International Conference on Computer Vision, pp. 1–8 (2007)
19. Shotton, J., Blake, A., Cipolla, R.: Multiscale categorical object recognition using contour fragments. IEEE Trans. Pattern Anal. Mach. Intell. 30(7), 1270–1281 (2008)
20. Sun, M., Kumar, S.S., Bradski, G.R., Savarese, S.: Object detection, shape recovery, and 3d modelling by depth-encoded hough voting. Comput. Vision Image Underst. 117(9), 1190–1202 (2013)
21. Tang, J., Miller, S., Singh, A., Abbeel, P.: A textured object recognition pipeline for color and depth image data. In: Proceedings of the IEEE International Conference on Robotics and Automation (2012)
22. Viksten, F., Forssén, P.-E., Johansson, B., Moe, A.: Comparison of local image descriptors for full 6 degree-of-freedom pose estimation. In: Proceedings of the IEEE International Conference on Robotics and Automation (2009)
23. Yeh, T., Lee, J.J., Darrell, T.: Fast concurrent object localization and recognition. In: Proceedings of IEEE Computer Society Conference on Computer Vision and Pattern Recognition (CVPR), pp. 280–287 (2009)

Comparative Evaluation of 3D Pose Estimation of Industrial Objects in RGB Pointclouds

Bjarne Großmann[✉], Mennatullah Siam, and Volker Krüger

Robotics, Vision and Machine Intelligence Lab,
Department of Mechanical and Manufacturing Engineering,
Aalborg University Copenhagen,
Copenhagen, Denmark
{bjarne,menna,vok}@m-tech.aau.dk

Abstract. 3D pose estimation is a crucial element for enabling robots to work in industrial environment to perform tasks like bin-picking or depalletizing. Even though there exist various pose estimation algorithms, they usually deal with common daily objects applied in lab environments. However, coping with real-world industrial objects is a much harder challenge for most pose estimation techniques due to the difficult material and structural properties of those objects. A comparative evaluation of pose estimation algorithms in regard to these object characteristics has yet to be done. This paper aims to provide a description and evaluation of selected state-of-the-art pose estimation techniques to investigate their object-related performance in terms of time and accuracy. The evaluation shows that there is indeed not a general algorithm which solves the task for all different objects, but it outlines the issues that real-world application have to deal with and what the strengths and weaknesses of the different pose estimation approaches are.

Keywords: Robot vision · Pose estimation · Feature descriptor · Pointcloud registration · Performance evaluation

1 Introduction

3D pose estimation of objects has been heavily investigated during the past years. The pose estimation is an important module of robotic perception [5, 11, 18], especially in industrial environments [21]. Bin-picking or depalletizing, for example, need high-accurate pose estimations of industrial objects for machine feeding tasks as in [4]. Plethora of work was conducted on pose estimation in 2D images, but with the rise of depth sensors, the focus has been shifting towards 3D data. As 3D data contains more geometrical information and encodes the exact surface dimensions, it naturally supersedes 2D image data. The features extracted from it are mostly not affected by scale or rotation changes and thus provide more accurate pose estimates.

B. Großmann and M. Siam—Contributed equally to this work.

© Springer International Publishing Switzerland 2015
L. Nalpantidis et al. (Eds.): ICVS 2015, LNCS 9163, pp. 329–342, 2015.
DOI: 10.1007/978-3-319-20904-3_30

A variety of sensors can be used, like RGBD cameras, time of flight cameras or laser scanners. However, most of the previous work in the industrial domain was focused on laser scan data as it is less noisy. But since RGBD cameras are recently spreading due to their cheap price, there is an increasing need of performance evaluation on RGBD data. At the same time, most of the previous benchmarks were aimed at ordinary non-industrial objects, but the 3D pose estimation of industrial parts is in particular a challenge due to the nature of their surface and material properties - they can be reflective, very small or have a complex structure. Previous surveys or comparative studies like in [2,9] provide an overview of 3D descriptors and object recognition techniques, however, they are not focused on the industrial domain and RGBD data. In contrast, this paper addresses this gap and focuses on the performance evaluation of 3D pose estimation of industrial objects using RGBD cameras.

The available approaches can be differentiated by their Feature Descriptors reviewed in Sect. 2, the Model Representation as discussed in Sect. 3 and Registration methods as presented in Sect. 4. Section 5 demonstrates a detailed experimental analysis followed by a conclusion and potential directions in Sect. 6.

2   Feature Descriptor

2.1   Global Features

Global features characterize the global shape of 3D data. In [15] the Viewpoint Feature Histogram (VFH) is introduced which is closely related to the local FPFH feature [13] that will be discussed later. It is computed by constructing point pairs between each point and its local neighbourhood. For each point pair (p_i, p_j), a reference frame (u, v, w) centered on p_i is computed where u denotes the normal n_i on point p_i, $v = u \times \frac{p_i - p_j}{\|p_i - p_j\|_2}$ and $w = u \times v$. Furthermore, three angles $\alpha = v^T \cdot n_i$, $\phi = u^T \cdot \frac{p_i - p_j}{\|p_i - p_j\|_2}$ and $\theta = arctan(w^T \cdot n_i, u^T \cdot n_i)$ are computed. The angles and the distances between the points and the center are binned into a 45-bin histogram respectively. Finally, due to the dependency on the viewpoint direction, the angle between the normals and the central viewpoint direction is binned as well into a 128-bin histogram.

Another variant presented in [1] is the Clustered Viewpoint Feature Histogram (CVFH). It initially selects stable regions of the object and removes points with high curvature. The point cloud is then split into disjoint smooth regions and for each a VFH descriptor is computed.

In [20], the Ensemble Shape Function (ESF) is used as a global descriptor based on shape functions for distance, angle and area distribution. It computes ten 64-bin histograms, three for distance, three for angle, three for area distribution and finally one distance ratio histogram.

However, a disadvantage of the global features in general is the high computational needs which make them much slower to compute compared to local features. Additionally, they are not discriminative about object details resulting in a less precise object description and they suffer from failure with incomplete data due to occlusions which renders them often useless in scenarios where objects are e.g. located inside a robot gripper. Even though they are applicable for certain problems like 3D shape retrieval, they are not suitable for pose estimation in industrial domains which demand high accuracy.

2.2 Local Features

In contrast to the global features, local features only describe a local neighbourhood of points. Thereby, they are not only faster to compute, but also describe object details more accurately while being robust to partial occlusions.

Due to possible large sizes of pointclouds, it is often more feasible to reduce the points used for computing feature descriptors to avoid computational overhead. This can for example be done by using a voxelized grid of the pointcloud and compute the descriptor for the averaged points. A more sophisticated way to improve the performance is to use a 3D keypoint extraction method which robustly detects descriptive points in the pointcloud. In [16], a recent performance evaluation of the different 3D keypoint detectors is presented.

Regarding the local feature descriptors, [10] presents spin images as a surface representation. For each surface point, the author computes an image that contains a 2D histogram of the surface locations around this point with respect to a local basis and associates it with the surface point.

Point Feature Histograms (PFH) [14] describe the local neighborhood by encoding the relationships between the neighborhood points and their normals in a histogram. It is similar to VFH [15] but only describes the object locally and doesn't depend on the viewpoint direction. First, point pairs between each point and its local neighborhood are constructed. Second, for each point pair (p_i, p_j) a reference frame and the three angles (α, ϕ, θ) as in VFH are computed which are then binned into a histogram. The speeded up version of it Fast Point Feature Histogram (FPFH) [13] is done by caching previously computed values and using the simplified point features. The latter encodes the relationships between a point and its neighbours in two passes instead of iterating through all point-pairs as PFH does.

The algorithm in [6] uses point pair features (PPF) for two points (p_i, p_j) with normals (n_i, n_j) respectively. The descriptor is defined as $(\|p_j - p_i\|_2, \angle(n_i, p_j - p_i), \angle(n_j, p_j - p_i), \angle(n_i, n_j))$. But this type of features is then used in a certain model representation that is discussed in the next section.

Finally, Unique Signatures of Histograms for Surface and Texture Description (SHOT) [19] describes the local neighborhood by computing local weighted histograms over a 3D grid which is aligned with a previously computed reference frame. Additionally, an extended version of the SHOT descriptor is presented which also uses texture information. The colored SHOT (CSHOT) encodes both geometric and texture description of the local surface. It is based on the CIELab color space which is perceptually more uniform than RGB color space.

3   Model Representation

Another perspective that differentiates the approaches is the way of the model representation. Most approaches for global and local features will use the feature descriptors directly for representing models. However, some approaches will work in a rather hybrid fashion between global and local descriptors. A variety of algorithms using this approach but only two methods are discussed here as they are state of the art algorithms and within the focus of the paper.

The work of [6] presents a method to model the object globally while applying matching on local PPF features as described previously. The representation of the model is built offline using all point pair features to capture the global geometric information of the model. The distances and angles are discretized into certain number of steps and features with similar discrete representations are grouped in a hashtable. In the online phase, point pair features are computed for the scene but instead for all point pairs, only pairs with respect to selected reference points are used. Finally, for each pair in the scene, a constant-time lookup in the hashtable is performed to find the corresponding entry for similar pairs in the model. This work was utilized as part of the commercial product HALCON in their 3D surface-based matching.

Another work demonstrated in [18] has the model represented as a multi-resolution surfel map (MRSMap). An octree is built with each node (surfel) containing statistical information along with the feature descriptor. The statistical information include the mean and covariance of the joint spatial and color distribution. The feature descriptor incorporates both shape and texture information similar to the FPFH [13]. A histogram is built for the three angular surfel pair relations between each surfel and its 26 neighbours.

4   Registration

After establishing the model representation, the next step in the pose estimation is the registration of the model to the scene. One of the most established and popular methods for registering two point sets due to its simple and intuitive nature is the Iterative Closest Point Method (ICP) [3, 22].

This iterative method is purely based on geometric information and alternates between point-wise correspondence matching and transformation estimation. The correspondences are simply matched by choosing the closest point respectively, thereby minimizing the overall Euclidean distance of the residuals.

However, due to the local nature of the approach, it is also known for being prone to get trapped in local minima and therefore requiring a good initial alignment of the point sets. Especially with noisy data, where a lot of outliers can be present, the algorithm might estimate a transformation far away from the optimal solution. Several variation of the ICP algorithm have been proposed to overcome these issues by smoothing out the error function or "jumping" out of local minima [12, 17].

Another strategy for point set registration are heuristic approaches. One of the most prominent approach is the Random Sampling Consensus (RANSAC) which is a general technique for fitting a mathematical model to data points [7]. It only uses three randomly chosen point correspondences to compute a hypothesis of a pose transformation between the model and the data set. This transformation is then applied and tested by evaluating the error function. Points over a certain threshold are rejected and are not used anymore, whereas points supporting this transformation stay inliers. For robustness, the process is usually repeated multiple times. The advantage of this approach is the robustness against outliers and that it does not need a dense data set. However, correspondences between the model and the data points have to be established beforehand. Typically, these initial correspondences are obtained by a feature-based matching process.

The authors of [13] extend the RANSAC approach by integrating feature descriptors within the alignment process known as Sample Consensus Initial Alignment (SAC-IA). Instead of choosing the points for the hypothesis generation randomly, they restrict the selected points to those which have a similar feature histogram. This selection strategy increases the registration speed significantly while still providing a good alignment. However, this alignment has to be refined to generate a more accurate pose estimation. In their approach, this is achieved by applying the non-linear Levenberg-Marquardt (LM) algorithm [8] afterwards. This refinement step is nevertheless not only bound to LM, but could also be replaced by a classical ICP approach or another registration method.

One rather new registration method is presented by [18] where the authors exploit an octree structure to match surfels on multiple resolution and thereby implementing a fast pose estimation method which can be used for RGBD-SLAM. Similar to the SAC-IA, this approach consists of two alternating steps: First, the correspondences between surfels on the finest resolution are established using a viewpoint-dependent shape-texture descriptor. Only similar surfels get associated and if an octree node has no associated child surfels, the association process is repeated for the next coarser resolution. Second, the pose estimate is evaluated by computing the observation likelihood for a transformation hypothesis which then can be optimized by applying the Levenberg-Marquardt method.

Even though these approaches have been proven to give good results in different scenarios, a detailed comparison and evaluation of their behaviour for differently sized and shaped objects has not been made yet.

5 Expermiments

5.1 Dataset

The focus in this paper is on industrial parts, therefore a dataset of ten industrial objects belonging to different (especially automotive) industries are used like Peugeot Citroen, Daimler, Ford and BMW. Figure 1 shows the different industrial parts, their pointclouds and their names that are used throughout the experiments. The parts were picked to have a variety between large and small parts, and complex- and simple-structured objects as shown in Fig. 4. Each part has different properties: the Alternator is a highly structured, large object that contains lots of holes and differently oriented curvatures. The Starter is of relatively complex shape but not as fine-grained as the Alternator. The Engine Support and Thermal Shield are large objects with a relatively simple structure. The Daimler is a medium-sized simple object while the Salzgitter is a medium-sized complex part. The Tube, BMW Part, Prism and Small Ford are small parts with varying dimensions.

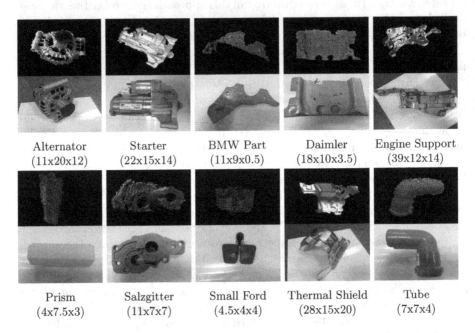

Alternator	Starter	BMW Part	Daimler	Engine Support
(11x20x12)	(22x15x14)	(11x9x0.5)	(18x10x3.5)	(39x12x14)

Prism	Salzgitter	Small Ford	Thermal Shield	Tube
(4x7.5x3)	(11x7x7)	(4.5x4x4)	(28x15x20)	(7x7x4)

Fig. 1. Evaluated industrial objects, their pointcloud representation and their dimension (WxHxD) in cm.

5.2 Setup

For the experimental analysis, the short-ranged PrimeSense Carmaine 1.09 is used. Mainly two sets of experiments were carried out. The first experiment evaluates and compares multi-resolution surfel maps (MRSMaps) [5] and iterative closest point (ICP) [3,22] to show how they are performing as a refinement registration. A special focus was put on the refinement registration since an accurate pose estimation is crucial in the industrial domain. Afterwards, a detailed analysis of pose estimation pipelines are presented and compared over objects with different properties. The implementations of the tested pose estimation pipelines are all open source, commercial software like HALCON[1] is not included in the analysis. The used techniques include Fast Point Feature Histogram (FPFH) [13] followed by SAC-IA and two variants

---

[1] http://www.halcon.com.

of this, one refined by ICP (FPFH+ICP) [3,22] and the other one refined by MRSMap (FPFH+MRSMap) [5]. Finally, Point Pair Feature (PPF) described in [6] and another one followed by ICP (PPF+ICP) are evaluated.

The experimental setup for the refinement registration analysis compares two scenes from the same viewing direction to each other. One scene is considered as the model whereas the second scene becomes the target scene after applying a random transformation on it. The randomly generated transformations are within the range of 10 to 30 degrees and 1 to 5 cm translation resulting in 5000 different scenes. Both, the object and the scene, are previously extracted using a simple tabletop segmentation.

For the analysis of the pose estimation pipelines, for each object 800 scenes were generated resulting in 8000 point clouds in total. To evaluate the behavior of the algorithms in regard to translational and rotational offsets, these parameters are tested independently for each object. Therefore, a first evaluation is done by running the pose estimation for an increasing translational offset in a range between 0 and 5 cm while keeping the rotational offset between 0 and 10 degrees. Due to sensor noise, the observed translational error is averaged over 20 pose estimations for each of the 10 bins used in the tested range. A second test evaluates the pose estimation for an increasing rotational offset in a range of 0 and 50 degrees, while the translational offset is kept between 0 and 1 cm. As the previous experiment, the observed rotational error is averaged over 20 pose estimations using 10 bins in the tested range. The metrics used for evaluating the experiments are the translation error measured as the euclidean distance and the rotational error as the angle between two orientations.

5.3   Refinement Registration Experiments

In these experiments, the behavior of MRSMap and ICP is compared with respect to the increasing number of iterations. As the MRSMap requires size and distance dependent parameters, additional preliminary tests were carried out to find the most suitable parameters for each object.

In Fig. 2, the performance of both algorithms is exemplarily compared based on the evaluation of the Thermal Shield. It shows that MRSMap converges much faster than ICP and has almost constant performance behavior with increasing number of iterations. ICP, in contrast, shows a linear increasing behavior proportional to the iterations. Especially for large objects (or pointclouds), MRSMap exhibits a much better run-time behavior.

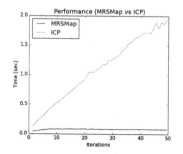

Fig. 2. Run-time behavior of the registration algorithms

As for the pose error, Fig. 3 shows both the translational and rotational error with respect to the introduced transformation. The color values denote the error, i.e. more saturated colors reflect higher errors while lighter colors represent lower errors.

The evaluation of the Engine Support, Thermal Shield and the Daimler show that MRSMap converges with only few iterations to the global minimum independent of the introduced error. ICP, however, even though resulting in a very good pose estimate, needs more iterations to converge. This can be explained by the nature of the objects, as they are relatively simple but rather large. The behavior of these objects is summarized in Fig. 3a.

Even though the Starter and the Alternator are also rather large objects, they do have a more complex surface structure. Hence, they exhibit a similar behavior to the large objects, however, MRSMap becomes unstable in the estimated orientation with respect to the ICP as shown in Fig. 3b, also with higher iterations. We can infer that the complex structure for the objects have a negative effect on the accuracy of the pose estimate derived from the MRSMap resulting in a noisier behavior.

Medium-sized objects like the Salzgitter and small objects like the Prism, the BMW and the Tube are performing much worse with the MRSMap (see Figs. 3c, d). ICP, however, shows a much more stable behavior in all the cases, although it needs more iterations to converge, especially for very small objects.

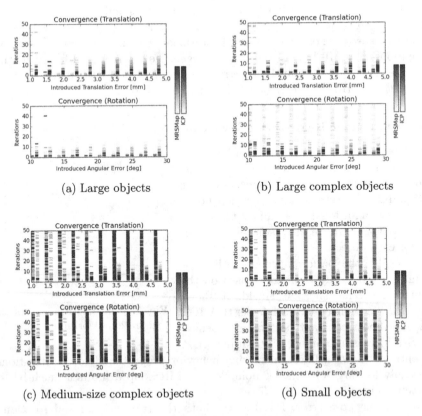

(a) Large objects

(b) Large complex objects

(c) Medium-size complex objects

(d) Small objects

Fig. 3. Convergence behavior of the algorithms in regard to the introduced error

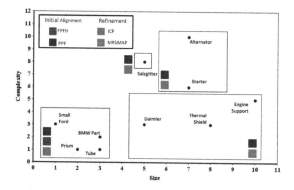

Fig. 4. Best-suited algorithms for object classes depending on their size and complexity.

The low performance of MRSMap is caused by the small sizes of the objects as MRSMap seems to need a good initial alignment that ensures a large enough overlap between model and scene pointclouds. With increasing enforced translations, the error increases and MRSMap will eventually fail to register at all if the objects are not overlapping.

The Salzgitter, even though not a very small object, performs worse with MRSMap as it combines the instability introduced by the complex surface structure and the smaller object size.

5.4 Pose Estimation Experiments

In these experiments, the overall performance of seven different pose estimation pipelines are evaluated. For the iterative algorithms ICP and MRSMap, we run these experiments with 50 iterations each to make sure that the algorithm has converged. The applied FPFH for initial alignment uses a constant feature radius of 2 cm and the scene is voxelized to a 5 mm grid. The applied PPF uses 1 cm, 7 mm, 5 mm voxel grid size and 3 cm, 1 cm, 1 cm normal radius for large, medium and small objects respectively. Additionally, it uses 1 cm for discretized distance steps and 12 degree for discretized rotation steps. Finally, for the rest of PPF parameters 10 reference points are used in the scene point cloud, and 30 degree, 10 cm for the clustering thresholds. Figures 5 and 6 show the observed errors in regard to the enforced transformation errors for each object.

The PPF with different objects shows different behaviour but its refined variant with ICP is notably improved compared to the original one for all objects. For the large simple-structured objects like the Thermal Shield and the Engine Support, ICP and MRSMap perform better than FPFH and PPF. The refined FPFH variants do not differ that much with respect to the original performance of ICP and MRSMap. MRSMap is performing relatively good and gives results in the range of 1 to 3 mm for the translational and 1 to 3 degrees for the rotational error. This confirms the previous experiments which suggest that MRSMap works

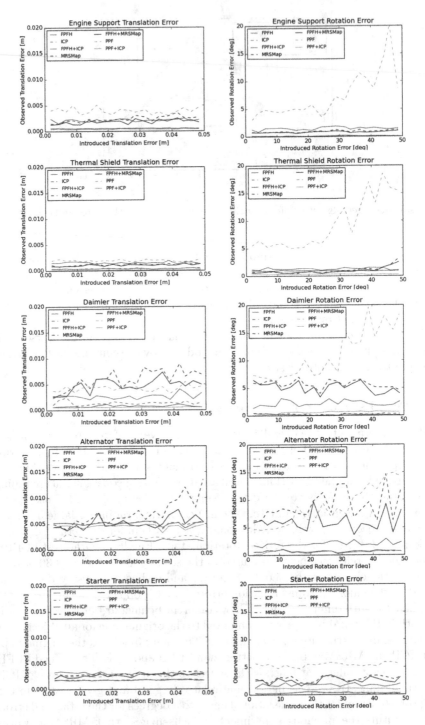

Fig. 5. Results of the pose estimation experiments (1)

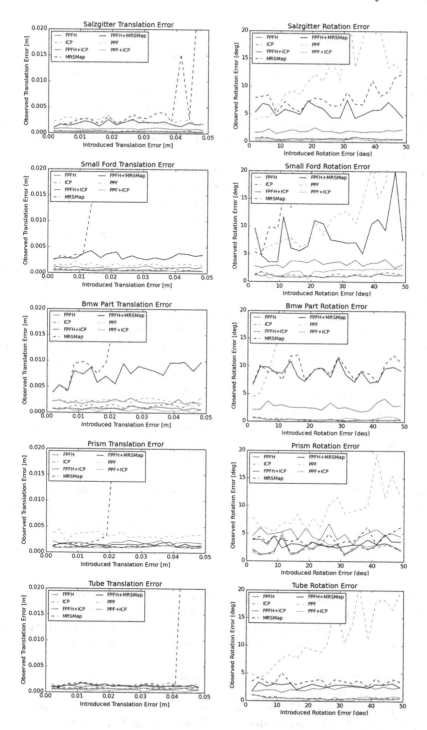

Fig. 6. Results of the pose estimation experiments (2)

stable with large objects despite its low running time which gives it an edge over other techniques.

For large complex-structured objects like the Alternator and Starter, the results show that MRSMap is not suitable for them. When initialized with FPFH though, it enhances the accuracy for the MRSMap, but is still worse than using FPFH by itself. This is due to the unstable behavior of MRSMap for complex objects predicted from the previous experiment. While both ICP and FPFH perform better, in the case of the Starter, ICP is performing much better than the FPFH.

Finally, for the Ford, Prism, BMW Part and Tube, which are all small objects, MRSMap has a bad performance consistent with the previous experiments. However, it is notably enhanced by using FPFH as an initial alignment. FPFH, in general, is improved using an additional refinement registration, especially the ICP, since it performs bad on small objects due to the size of the descriptor radius. Small radii for the descriptor lowers the descriptiveness while large radii will result in ambiguities. Both, the Salzgitter and Daimler as medium-sized objects, perform almost the same as the previous category of small objects.

In Fig. 4 all objects that are varying in size and complexity are plotted, while being graded according to the size and complexity on a scale from 1 to 10 subjectively. Suggested algorithms to be used with different clusters of objects are shown in colours. For large simple structured objects (Thermal Shield, Engine Support, Daimler), it is recommended to use PPF for initial alignment since the refined results are very accurate while, at the same time, being less computational intensive than FPFH as the model representation is computed in an offline training phase. Furthermore, it is recommended to use MRSMap for refinement since it shows stable behaviour while having much smaller running time than ICP.

As for small objects (Small Ford, BMW Part, Prism, Tube) it is advised to use either PPF or FPFH for initialization and to use ICP for refinement. Due to unstable behaviour with these objects, the usage of MRSMap is not recommended. Finally, for both medium complex object (Salzgitter) and large complex objects (Alternator, Starter), PPF with ICP refinement should be preferred.

6   Conclusions

In this paper, we focused on the pose estimation of objects from a real-world industrial environment with difficult structural and material properties. We discussed different classes of registration techniques, explaining the underlying algorithms and evaluating their behavior in a whole pose estimation pipeline.

The evaluation of the experiments show that there is no "best" algorithm for all the different object types - some algorithms are more suited for certain object classes or use-cases.

The FPFH with SAC-IA can handle most objects with good accuracy but becomes unstable with small objects and finely-grained structures due to the size of the used feature radius.

PPF on its own does not perform as good as FPFH, but in combination with the refinement strategies, it results in an accurate and stable pose estimation. Due to its precomputed model description, it has the advantage of being computationally less expensive during the actual pose estimation.

MRSMap depends strongly on the object sizes and the initial alignment. For large overlaps, MRSMap performs good and converges much faster then ICP while also using less computational time, however for small-sized objects, the MRSMap approach is less accurate and unstable. A good initial alignment, e.g. given by the FPFH, improves the stability of the algorithm significantly.

ICP performs stable on most objects, but suffers from slow convergence and intensive computation time with respect to MRSMap.

As the experiments were solely carried out for single-view pose estimations, further experiments should be conducted in the future. This includes in particular the evaluation of the algorithms for multi-view pose estimation and eventually CAD model pose estimation, as this is often needed in real-world industrial scenarios.

Acknowledgment. Special thanks to Jörg Stückler and Bertram Drost for providing us with the necessary information to evaluate their developed algorithms. This work has partly been funded by the European Commission through grant agreement number 610917 (STAMINA).

References

1. Aldoma, A., Vincze, M., Blodow, N., Gossow, D., Gedikli, S., Rusu, R., Bradski, G.: CAD-model recognition and 6DOF pose estimation using 3D cues. In: 2011 IEEE International Conference on Computer Vision Workshops (ICCV Workshops), pp. 585–592, November 2011
2. Alexandre, L.A.: 3D descriptors for object and category recognition: a comparative evaluation. In: Workshop on Color-Depth Camera Fusion in Robotics at the IEEE/RSJ International Conference on Intelligent Robots and Systems (IROS), Vilamoura, Portugal, October 2012
3. Besl, P.J., McKay, N.D.: A method for registration of 3-d shapes. IEEE Trans. Pattern Anal. Mach. Intell. **14**(2), 239–256 (1992)
4. Choi, C., Taguchi, Y., Tuzel, O., Liu, M.Y., Ramalingam, S.: Voting-based pose estimation for robotic assembly using a 3D sensor. In: 2012 IEEE International Conference on Robotics and Automation (ICRA), pp. 1724–1731, May 2012
5. Droeschel, D., Stückler, J., Behnke, S.: Local multi-resolution surfel grids for MAV motion estimation and 3D mapping. In: Proceedings of the 13th International Conference on Intelligent Autonomous Systems (IAS), July 2014
6. Drost, B., Ulrich, M., Navab, N., Ilic, S.: Model globally, match locally: efficient and robust 3D object recognition. In: 2010 IEEE Conference on Computer Vision and Pattern Recognition (CVPR), pp. 998–1005, June 2010
7. Fischler, M.A., Bolles, R.C.: Random sample consensus: a paradigm for model fitting with applications to image analysis and automated cartography. Commun. ACM **24**(6), 381–395 (1981)

8. Fitzgibbon, A.W.: Robust registration of 2D and 3D point sets. In: Proceedings of the British Machine Vision Conference, pp. 43.1–43.10. BMVA Press (2001)
9. Guo, Y., Bennamoun, M., Sohel, F., Lu, M., Wan, J.: 3D object recognition in cluttered scenes with local surface features: a survey. IEEE Trans. Pattern Anal. Mach. Intell. **36**(11), 2270–2287 (2014)
10. Johnson, A., Hebert, M.: Using spin images for efficient object recognition in cluttered 3D scenes. IEEE Trans. Pattern Anal. Mach. Intell. **21**(5), 433–449 (1999)
11. Kriegel, S., Brucker, M., Marton, Z.C., Bodenmuller, T., Suppa, M.: Combining object modeling and recognition for active scene exploration. In: IEEE/RSJ International Conference on Intelligent Robots and Systems (IROS), pp. 2384–2391, November 2013
12. Rusinkiewicz, S., Levoy, M.: Efficient variants of the ICP algorithm. In: Third International Conference on 3D Digital Imaging and Modeling (3DIM), June 2001
13. Rusu, R., Blodow, N., Beetz, M.: Fast point feature histograms (FPFH) for 3D registration. In: IEEE International Conference on Robotics and Automation, ICRA 2009, pp. 3212–3217, May 2009
14. Rusu, R., Blodow, N., Marton, Z., Beetz, M.: Aligning point cloud views using persistent feature histograms. In: IEEE/RSJ International Conference on Intelligent Robots and Systems, IROS 2008, pp. 3384–3391, September 2008
15. Rusu, R., Bradski, G., Thibaux, R., Hsu, J.: Fast 3D recognition and pose using the viewpoint feature histogram. In: 2010 IEEE/RSJ International Conference on Intelligent Robots and Systems (IROS), pp. 2155–2162, October 2010
16. Salti, S., Tombari, F., Di Stefano, L.: A performance evaluation of 3D keypoint detectors. In: 2011 International Conference on 3D Imaging, Modeling, Processing, Visualization and Transmission (3DIMPVT), pp. 236–243, May 2011
17. Segal, A., Hähnel, D., Thrun, S.: Generalized-ICP. In: Robotics: Science and Systems V, University of Washington, Seattle, USA, 28 June–1 July, 2009
18. Stückler, J., Behnke, S.: Model learning and real-time tracking using multi-resolution surfel maps. In: Proceedings of the AAAI Conference on Artificial Intelligence (AAAI 2012) (2012)
19. Tombari, F., Salti, S., Di Stefano, L.: Unique signatures of histograms for local surface description. In: Daniilidis, K., Maragos, P., Paragios, N. (eds.) ECCV 2010, Part III. LNCS, vol. 6313, pp. 356–369. Springer, Heidelberg (2010)
20. Wohlkinger, W., Vincze, M.: Ensemble of shape functions for 3D object classification. In: 2011 IEEE International Conference on Robotics and Biomimetics (ROBIO), pp. 2987–2992, December 2011
21. Yoon, Y., Desouza, G., Kak, A.: Real-time tracking and pose estimation for industrial objects using geometric features. In: IEEE International Conference on Robotics and Automation (ICRA), vol. 3, pp. 3473–3478, September 2003
22. Zhang, Z.: Iterative point matching for registration of free-form curves and surfaces. Int. J. Comput. Vision **13**(2), 119–152 (1994)

Object Detection Using a Combination of Multiple 3D Feature Descriptors

Lilita Kiforenko[✉], Anders Glent Buch, and Norbert Krüger

The Mærsk Mc-Kinney Møller Institute,
University of Southern Denmark,
Odense, Denmark
{lilita,anbu,norbert}@mmmi.sdu.dk

Abstract. This paper presents an approach for object pose estimation using a combination of multiple feature descriptors. We propose to use a combination of three feature descriptors, capturing both surface and edge information. Those descriptors individually perform well for different object classes. We use scenes from an established RGB-D dataset and our own recorded scenes to justify the claim that by combining multiple features, we in general achieve better performance. We present quantitative results for descriptor matching and object detection for both datasets.

Keywords: Object detection · Pose estimation · Feature combination

1 Introduction

Object detection and pose estimation is a challenging and still unsolved topic. Many researchers design a feature descriptor that will help to detect instances within a certain set of object classes. The results so far are promising, but we still do not have a more general feature descriptor. There exists a vast variety of feature descriptors, and many of them are improvements of existing ones, with some modifications. Typically, when creating a new descriptor, researchers are focusing on specific objects or scenes, for example texture-less objects [17]. While particular feature descriptors perform extremely well for some objects/datasets, for others they may have serious problems.

The underlying hypothesis of this paper is that by combining multiple features that perform good for different objects, it is possible to detect a larger variety of objects in different scenarios. In this paper we present a method that does not require any learning and is easily expandable with other feature descriptors.

To support our hyphothesis, we selected 3 different 3D features: SHOT [14], Cat3DEdge [9] and ECSAD [8]. The selection was based on availability and that they perform well for rather different objects. The SHOT descriptor is very good at recognising objects with large local shape variation, while Cat3DEdge is more suitable for planar objects, because it also covers edge information. ECSAD is a 3D shape feature designed for 3D shape edges, which performs good for objects

© Springer International Publishing Switzerland 2015
L. Nalpantidis et al. (Eds.): ICVS 2015, LNCS 9163, pp. 343–353, 2015.
DOI: 10.1007/978-3-319-20904-3_31

such as books and mobile phones, where there is a certain structure, but also clear edges. For testing our method, we have selected scenes from a well known RGB-D dataset [10], which contains objects on which a shape descriptor such as SHOT is expected to show high performance. We recorded another set of scenes containing objects with less shape variation, in which Cat3DEdge and ECSAD are expected to show good performance.

Feature descriptor combinations is not a new topic, and different methods exist in the area of visual 3D object detection and retrieval. The experiments in [11] include usage of various feature descriptors, for both shape based and image based inputs. This research also shows that selectively combining descriptors is better than using all feature descriptors naively. It is also proposed to use different descriptor selection and weighting methods. In [12], instead of putting weights on descriptors, it is proposed to use different distance measures between them. Multiple feature descriptor combinations are also used for pedestrian detection in [15]. The research in [7] shows that it is necessary to use various descriptors to get better object detection. They used SIFT, line and colour feature descriptors. But their primary focus was on environmental parameter changes, e.g. illumination and distance. The proposed solution was to use a probabilistic modeling for automatic descriptor selection. Compared to these works, this paper is focusing on object detection using 3D feature descriptors.

This paper has the following structure. Section 2 describes the applied feature descriptors, Sect. 3 explains the designed system flow, i.e. how the different feature descriptors were used and combined. Section 4 explains how the datasets for testing were created, and which data they represent. Section 5 presents the results achieved for each feature descriptor individually, and their combination. The last section, Sect. 6, summarises the achieved results and presents ideas for future improvements.

2   Feature Descriptors

In this section we give a short summary of the feature descriptors used in our system. We aim at a certain level completeness in our representation by choosing a purely shape based descriptor (SHOT), a purely edge based descriptor (Cat3DEdge) and a feature descriptor that places itself in between (ECSAD). These are all described below, and we refer to the original papers for further details. The implementation of SHOT is available in the Point Cloud Library (PCL [13]) on http://pointclouds.org, and Cat3DEdge and ECSAD are available in our own library on https://gitlab.com/caro-sdu/covis.

2.1   SHOT or Signature of Histograms of Orientation

SHOT is a surface feature descriptor, which for each input point computes a unique, repeatable local reference frame using an Eigen value decomposition. Using the reference frame it builds a spherical grid around the input point that divides supporting points into grid cells. At each cell it computes a weighted cosine of the relative normal angle and bins the result into a local histogram for that cell. SHOT combines all local histograms into one descriptor of length 352. In the last stage, the descriptor is normalized to an Euclidean norm of 1. The colour version of the descriptor (CSHOT [16]) is also available, the descriptor length of which is 1344. In this work we are using the original SHOT descriptor.

2.2 ECSAD or Equivalent Circumference Surface Angle Descriptor

ECSAD [8] is a surface-edge feature descriptor, which in the original work is also applied for the task of detecting edges in point clouds. The main focus of ECSAD is to represent the relative angles between opposite surface cells around an edge point. It uses a special azimuth binning to achieve this; the supporting sphere is split into 6 cells (60° each), then it splits each of the 6 cells depending on its radial increment (one split per each increment). A local reference frame is also computed using the Eigen value decomposition of the supporting points. Then, all support points are mapped to the corresponding spatial bins using radial and azimuth coordinates. For each of the bins, an average angle is computed, and interpolation is used to fill empty bins. These angles are used directly as the descriptor values. The recommended length of the descriptor is 30, which corresponds to 4 radial and 3 azimuth levels.

2.3 Cat3DEdge Descriptor

The Cat3DEdge feature descriptor is a local histogram descriptor that uses different types, or categories, of edges. We introduced it first in [9]. The edges and their types are extracted using the edge detection algorithm [5] that is available in PCL. This edge detection algorithm computes edges from organised RGB-D, Kinect-like point clouds. It introduces 5 different edge categories: *occluding* and *occluded* are edges computed from depth discontinuities, *high-curvature* edges appear at points with rapidly changing surface normals, *canny* edges are computed using the Canny edge detection algorithm [4] and *boundary* edges represent point cloud boundaries. 4 of the extracted edge types are used by the Cat3DEdge descriptor: *occluding, occluded, high-curvature* and *canny*. To make the descriptor more robust, one more category is added—*non-edge* or *surface*—representing all points in the support that are not an edge point. All categories, coded with different colours, are shown in Fig. 1.

The edge extraction is extended by also computing a 3D edge orientation from the local 2D RGB image gradient and the surface normal computed from the point cloud. This is done using the following formula:

$$edge\text{-}orientation = normal \times (gradient \times normal) \tag{1}$$

In order to remove noise in 3D edge orientation computation and to increase descriptor robustness, the 2D RGB image is smoothed by an 11×11 Gaussian kernel. Then for each channel of the RGB image, gradients are computed separately, and in the end the gradient from the channel that has the maximum response at each pixel is selected. The same strategy was used in [6].

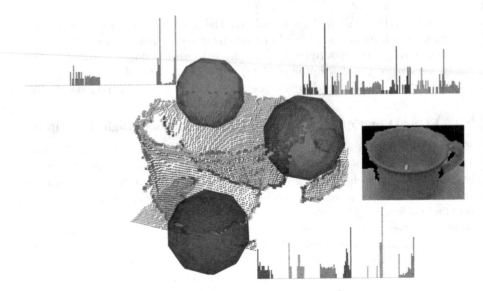

Fig. 1. Cat3DEdge descriptor example for three random edge input points on an object. The object *coffee_mug_6_2_43* is taken from the RGB-D dataset [10]. The image on the right is the RGB image of the object. The object template contains a small amount of table points. Different colours represent edge categories: *green - occluding, red - occluded, yellow - high-curvature, cyan - canny* and *grey - non-edge*. The sphere represents the support radius (3 cm). Next to each sphere we show the computed Cat3DEdge histogram, where different colours represent the different edge categories encoded in the descriptor (Color figure online).

For each input, point neighbours are found within an experimentally selected support radius of 3 cm. Each neighbour point belongs to one or more of the above mentioned categories.[1] Between the input point and its neighbours the two relative measures are computed—*distance* and *angle* using the point and orientation information. Depending on the neighbour type, the result is binned into a specific part of the histogram, i.e. a *sub histogram*. The category order is predefined; the first half is reserved for all the *distance* relations, and the last half for the *angle* relations. The *distance* and *angle* parts have the same order of categories: *occluding, occluded, high-curvature, canny* and *non-edge*. For distance computation we use the Euclidean distance. For angles we use the absolute dot product of the 3D edge orientations.

The Cat3DEdge descriptor length is 150, where 15 bins are reserved for every sub histogram. Empirical results have indicated that a good choice of bins for each sub histogram is between 10 and 20. An example is shown in Fig. 1. The figure shows three examples of histograms for three different points (centres of

---

[1] Indeed, any edge point is allowed to belong to multiple categories at once, e.g. *canny* and *occluding*, meaning an edge point detected by appearance, but also found to occlude parts of the scene from the depth image.

spheres). The spheres radius is 3 cm, the same radius we use for our experiments. The *magenta* sphere contains only *canny* edges and *surface (non-edge)* points. Therefore the histogram contains only 4 non-zero sub histograms. The centre point of the grey sphere contains all edge types in its neighbourhood, resulting in a more populated histogram.

3   System Description

This section presents the developed method for combining multiple feature descriptors as well as our evaluation system. Our end goal is to detect a known object (represented by a template) in a scene.

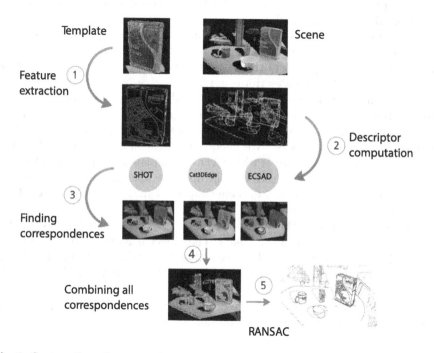

Fig. 2. System flow diagram. The *template* and *scene* is taken from RGB-D dataset [10]. Even though we display the method pipeline only for the *cereal* object, the last image shows all found objects (Color figure online).

The typical pose estimation steps for detecting an object [1,2] are: (i) feature point (keypoint) extraction (sometimes this is just done by point cloud down-sampling) (ii) feature descriptor estimation for each keypoint (iii) finding correspondences between template feature descriptors and scene descriptors (iv) template alignment (using e.g. RANSAC or other robust methods).

In our system, we are using a similar pose estimation pipeline. As it can be seen from Fig. 2, we have an object template and a scene point cloud. Then we extract 3D edges, using the method presented in [5]. In the next step, instead of computing only one descriptor, we compute the three chosen descriptors: SHOT, ECSAD and Cat3DEdge . Each set of template features is matched with the features in the scene by a nearest neighbour search, leading to three sets of correspondences. We define a correspondence as a pair of two points, where the first point represents the feature point in the template and the second point is the matched feature point in the scene. We concatenate all three correspondence vectors into one, and it serves as the input to the RANSAC algorithm.

Please note that we compute descriptors only for edge points, but still represent the underlying surface using all points in the support. The edge extraction can therefore be seen as a keypoint extractor, which determines which points on the surface to describe. Note also that while all features use all surface points in the support for description, the Cat3DEdge descriptor additionally encodes spatial relations to neighbouring edge points.

For each of the feature descriptors we found the optimal parameter settings using a small training set. For SHOT and ECSAD we are using a radius of 5 cm and the recommended length of the descriptor. For Cat3DEdge we use radius of 3 cm, and the length of the descriptor is 150.

We evaluate the proposed method in two different ways. Firstly, after we have computed correspondences for each descriptor, we calculate how many of those correspondences are correct using the ground truth pose, which we have obtained by a manual process. We denote a correspondence as correct, if the aligned template feature point is within 1 cm of its matched feature point in the scene. We have selected a relatively high distance tolerance here, because the point clouds used in our datasets, being captured from RGB-D devices, have quite high depth uncertainties.

The next evaluation is the detection rate, or the relative number of correctly found poses of the objects in the scenes. The object is correctly detected if the estimated pose is within a small distance and angle threshold of the ground truth pose. Small misalignments are acceptable, since these can always be corrected using the ICP algorithm [3].

The results of both evaluations are presented in Sect. 5, but before presenting these, we introduce the dataset used for our tests in the following section.

4   Dataset Description

For testing different feature descriptor performances, we created a dataset, which contains a variety of objects. First we selected 7 scenes (Fig. 3, bottom left) from the RGB-D dataset [10]. The RGB-D dataset provides a large amount of objects and scenes from 5 different indoor categories: *background, desk, kitchen_small, meeting_small, table_small*. Some of the categories have sub categories, for example, *desk* contains *desk_1, desk_2* and *desk_3*. Each indoor scene contains a limited number of object instances from the dataset. The RGB-D dataset does not provide the ground truth pose for objects in those scenes, therefore we selected one test scene from each sub category, except the background category, leading to 7 test scenes. For each of the objects appearing in the test scenes, we found a suitable object template from the object set. The RGB-D dataset provides many views around each object. We tried to select the closest view of an object to the instances in the scenes. We processed the selected view by removing the background as much as possible, while keeping the organised structure of the point cloud, which is required for the edge extraction method [5] to work. After

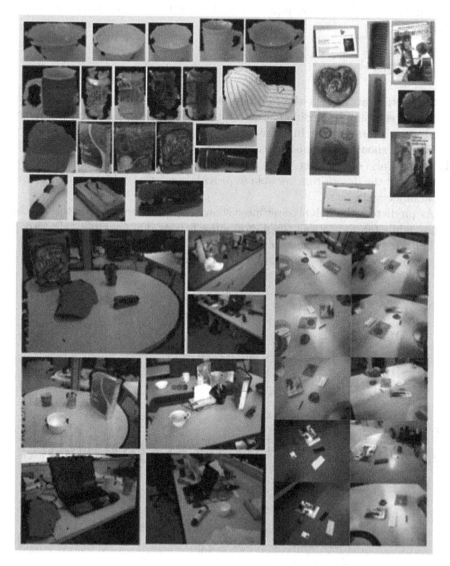

Fig. 3. All test scenes and object templates. The top left section represents object templates from the RGB-D dataset, and the templates from our dataset are in the top right. Bottom left and right are all test scenes from RGB-D and our dataset (Color figure online).

that, we manually found the ground truth poses of all object instances in each of the scenes.

The RGB-D dataset contains mostly objects with rich surface information. For our tests, we aimed at a higher variety of input data. Therefore we recorded another set of 10 scenes containing also flat objects (Fig. 3, bottom right), both with and without textures. All recordings were made with the *Primesense Carmine 1.09* RGB-D sensor. For each of the recorded scenes, we also found the ground truth pose. The used dataset is available at https://gitlab.com/caro-sdu/covis-data.

5   Results

In this section we present the results of each individual descriptor and for our method of combining the different descriptors. We have tested both the strength of the descriptors for matching, and for object detection.

Figure 4 shows the number of correct correspondences for each descriptor for the RGB-D and our dataset. From these results we can draw the first conclusion that none of the descriptors are able to provide consistently high matching rates for all objects classes.

As predicted, the SHOT descriptor shows high performance for the RGB-D scenes, while for our dataset the performance is poor. For example, this descriptor fails for the objects *magazine* and *visit card* (Fig. 3, top right). The ECSAD descriptor shows good performance on both datasets. It can be used to detect

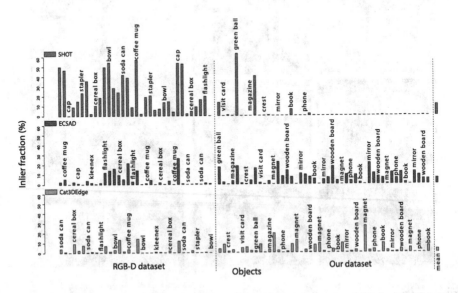

Fig. 4. Descriptor matching results. The part half of the graphs show results for the RGB-D dataset, the rightmost part for our dataset. The last, rightmost bar represents the mean value over all scenes from both datasets (Color figure online).

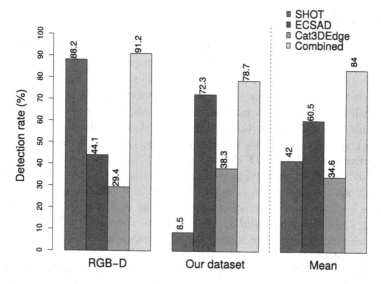

Fig. 5. Object detection rates on the RGB-D dataset (leftmost part), our dataset (middle) and all scenes (rightmost part) (Color figure online).

some of the objects in the RGB-D dataset, for example, *flashlight* and *cap* (Fig. 3, top left). Its performance for our dataset is better than for the RGB-D dataset. For our dataset it produces many correct correspondences for almost every object. Cat3DEdge shows the poorest performance for this data. On the other hand, this is the only descriptor that can be used to find flat objects such as *magnet*. The mean inlier fraction result for SHOT is 10.9 %, ECSAD 5.76 % and Cat3DEdge 3.34 %.

Figure 5 presents detection results, i.e. the number of correctly found object poses after applying a standard RANSAC pose estimation algorithm. The number of RANSAC iterations is set to 50000, and the Euclidean inlier threshold is set to 0.01 m. The result is split into three sections, where the first section represents the detection rate for the RGB-D dataset, the second section for our dataset and lastly the combined result over all scenes. As it can be seen from the figure, the performance of a combination of three feature descriptors is consistently higher than that of any individual feature. Note especially the high margin of the feature combination down to the individual features when considering all scenes, which represent high varieties in appearance and shape. The detection rate for SHOT is 79.7 % higher for the RGB-D dataset than for our dataset, while detection rates for ECSAD and Cat3DEdge are 28.2 % and 8.9 % higher for our dataset than RGB-D, as predicted from the descriptor matching results in Fig. 4. The mean value for all scenes for SHOT is 42 %, ECSAD 60.5 % and Cat3DEdge 34.6 %.

The presented results also show that the proposed multiple descriptor combination method will work even when some feature descriptors are showing poor performing for some objects, as long as at least one descriptor has a high matching rate.

6   Conclusion

In this paper we have presented a method that can be used for the detection of different objects. Instead of creating a new feature descriptor, we are proposing to focus on combining already available descriptors.

We tested our method on two different datasets: RGB-D, which contains objects with rich surface information, and our own dataset, which mostly contains flat objects with and without texture. First, we evaluated the number of correct correspondences during feature matching. The mean fraction of correct correspondences for the SHOT descriptor is 10.9 %, for ECSAD 5.76 % and for Cat3DEdge 3.34 %. The second part of our evaluations is on the object detection rate, which we tested using a standard RANSAC algorithm. Our results show an average improvement in terms of detection rate of 23.5 % relative to the best performing single descriptor and 49.4 % relative to the worst, indicating a potential for achieving significantly higher detection rates when combining multiple feature descriptors.

Additionally, in this paper we show that using edges as keypoints for state of the art descriptors such as SHOT and ECSAD produces high object detection rates. Using edge points for detection has the additional advantage that fewer points are considered (compared to using points on the surfaces), allowing for higher computational speed.

Future work will involve expanding the descriptor pool and the set of test objects with the aim of investigating different means of combining feature descriptors. In addition to this, we will compare our edge based detection algorithm with other keypoint based algorithms to validate the use of edges as keypoints for feature description and matching.

Acknowledgments. The research leading to these results has received funding from the European Communitys Seventh Framework Programme FP7/2007-2013 (Programme and Theme: ICT-2011.2.1, Cognitive Systems and Robotics) under grant agreement no. 600578, ACAT and by Danish Agency for Science, Technology and Innovation, project CARMEN.

References

1. Aldoma, A., Marton, Z.C., Tombari, F., Wohlkinger, W., Potthast, C., Zeisl, B., Rusu, R., Gedikli, S., Vincze, M.: Tutorial: point cloud library: three-dimensional object recognition and 6 dof pose estimation. IEEE Robot. Autom. Mag. **19**(3), 80–91 (2012)
2. Alexandre, L.A.: 3D descriptors for object and category recognition: a comparative evaluation. In: Workshop on Color-Depth Camera Fusion in Robotics at the IEEE/RSJ International Conference on Intelligent Robots and Systems (IROS) (2012)
3. Besl, P., McKay, N.D.: A method for registration of 3-d shapes. IEEE Trans. Pattern Anal. Mach. Intell. **14**(2), 239–256 (1992)
4. Canny, J.: A computational approach to edge detection. IEEE Trans. Pattern Anal. Mach. Intell. **8**(6), 679–698 (1986)

5. Choi, C., Trevor, A.J., Christensen, H.I.: RGB-D edge detection and edge-based registration. In: 2013 IEEE/RSJ International Conference on Intelligent Robots and Systems (IROS), pp. 1568–1575. IEEE (2013)
6. Hinterstoisser, S., Cagniart, C., Ilic, S., Sturm, P., Navab, N., Fua, P., Lepetit, V.: Gradient response maps for real-time detection of textureless objects. IEEE Trans. Pattern Anal. Mach. Intell. **34**(5), 876–888 (2012)
7. Jeong, W., Lee, S., Kim, Y.: Statistical feature selection model for robust 3D object recognition. In: 2011 15th International Conference on Advanced Robotics (ICAR), pp. 402–408, June 2011
8. Jørgensen, T.B., Buch, A.G., Kraft, D.: Geometric edge description and classification in point cloud data with application to 3D object recognition. In: International Conference on Computer Vision Theory and Applications (VISAPP) (2015)
9. Kiforenko, L., Buch, A.G., Bodenhagen, L., Kruger, N.: Object detection using categorised 3D edges. In: SPIE, vol. 9445 (2015)
10. Lai, K., Bo, L., Ren, X., Fox, D.: A large-scale hierarchical multi-view RGB-D object dataset. In: IEEE International Conference on Robotics and Automation (ICRA), pp. 1817–1824 (2011)
11. Lv, T., Liu, G., bin Huang, S., Wang, Z.X.: Selective feature combination and automatic shape categorization of 3D models. In: Sixth International Conference on Fuzzy Systems and Knowledge Discovery, 2009, FSKD 2009, vol. 5, pp. 447–451, August 2009
12. Ohbuchi, R., Furuya, T.: Distance metric learning and feature combination for shape-based 3D model retrieval. In: Proceedings of the ACM Workshop on 3D Object Retrieval, 3DOR 2010, pp. 63–68. ACM, New York (2010)
13. Rusu, R.B., Cousins, S.: 3D is here: point cloud library (pcl). In: IEEE International Conference on Robotics and Automation (ICRA), pp. 1–4 (2011)
14. Salti, S., Tombari, F., Di Stefano, L.: Shot: unique signatures of histograms for surface and texture description. Comput. Vis. Image Underst. **125**, 251–264 (2014)
15. Sotelo, M., Parra, I., Fernandez, D., Naranjo, E.: Pedestrian detection using svm and multi-feature combination. In: Intelligent Transportation Systems Conference, 2006, ITSC 2006, pp. 103–108. IEEE, September 2006
16. Tombari, F., Salti, S., Di Stefano, L.: A combined texture-shape descriptor for enhanced 3D feature matching. In: 2011 18th IEEE International Conference on Image Processing (ICIP), pp. 809–812, September 2011
17. Tombari, F., Franchi, A., Di Stefano, L.: Bold features to detect texture-less objects. In: The IEEE International Conference on Computer Vision (ICCV), December 2013

Differential Optical Flow Estimation Under Monocular Epipolar Line Constraint

Mahmoud A. Mohamed$^{(\boxtimes)}$, M. Hossein Mirabdollah,
and Bärbel Mertsching

GET Lab, University of Paderborn,
33098 Paderborn, Germany
{mahmoud,mirabdollah,mertsching}@get.upb.de
http://getwww.upb.de

Abstract. In this paper, a new method is presented to use the epipolar constraint for the estimations of optical flows. We derive the necessary formulation to add the epipolar constraint in terms of optical flow components and force the components to transform points from the first frame to the next consecutive frame such that the points lie on their correspondent epipolar lines. In this work, no smoothness term is utilized and the performance of the proposed method is evaluated based only on data terms. We conducted different evaluations using two different point matching methods (SIFT and Lucas-Kanade) and used them in two different fundamental matrix estimation methods required to calculate epipolar line coefficients. It is demonstrated that epipolar constraint yields noticeable improvements almost in all of the cases.

1 Introduction

Optical flow is defined as the apparent motion of pixels between two consecutive frames. Thus, a flow field describes the dynamics of a scene and involves two independent motions; the ego-motion of the camera and motions of objects. In literature, many differential optical flow methods, which are mainly dependent on the brightness constancy assumption have been proposed. In these methods, it is assumed that the intensities of correspondent pixels do not change if objects or cameras move. Unfortunately, not every object motion yields changes in gray values and not every changes in gray values are generated by body motion. Challenging outdoor scenes with poorly textured regions, illumination changes, shadows, reflections, glare, and the inherent noise of the camera image may yield gray value changes while the depicted object remains stationary. Especially in poor illumination conditions, the number of photons collected by a pixel, may vary over time.

Recently, many methods have presented different optical flow models to tackle with the problem of illumination changes. A robust energy is proposed in [1], which take into account multiplicative and additive illumination factors. Nevertheless, dealing with motion estimations and illumination variations in one energy function gives rise to a more complex optimization problem. Additionally, the accuracy

© Springer International Publishing Switzerland 2015
L. Nalpantidis et al. (Eds.): ICVS 2015, LNCS 9163, pp. 354–363, 2015.
DOI: 10.1007/978-3-319-20904-3_31

of the optical flow estimation is adversely affected, if the assumption of illumination factors is not accurate. Moreover, [2] proposed a photometric invariant of the dichromatic reflection model. This model is only applicable to color images with brightness variations. Furthermore, [3] proposed an illumination-invariant total variation with L1 norm (TV-L1) optical flow model by replacing the data term proposed in [4] with the Hamming distance of two census transform signatures. Census signatures encode local neighborhood intensity variations, which are very sensitive to non-monotonic illumination variation and random noise. In addition, the census transform discards most of the information casting from neighbors, and cannot distinguish between dark and bright regions in a neighborhood which called saturated center.

In addition, the normalized cross correlation was utilized in [5] as a data term and led to increasing the robustness of the estimated optical flow. In turn, [6] tackles the problem of poorly textured regions, occlusions and small scale image structures by incorporating a low level image segmentation process that has been used in a non-local total variational regularization term in a unified variational framework. In addition, an optical flow estimation method based on the zero-mean normalized cross-correlation transform was introduced in [7].

Dense descriptors such as census [3], histogram of oriented gradient (HOG) [8] and local directional pattern (LDP) [9] and [10] have been incorporated directly into the classical energy minimization framework in order to gain robustness for the estimated optical flow in real-world vision systems. Nevertheless, the algorithms fail in the case of poorly textured regions.

In case that optical flows are mostly induced by camera motion, i.e. the objects are stationary, the epipolar geometry can be used to obtain one more extra constraint for the flow of pixels. In this regard, the fundamental matrix related to the motion of the camera between two frames is firstly estimated; consequently, given each point in the first frame, the place of the correspondent point in the next frame will be constrained over a line known as the epipolar line. Fundamental matrices can be estimated using the 8-point [11] or the 7-point [12] methods. In [13], by searching over epipolar lines and using a semi-global block matching technique, the correspondent points are found. The method has two main shortcomings: block matching methods are slow and they use calibration information and also an approximation for the rotation matrix which is valid for rotation angles of less than $10°$. In this paper, we introduce a differential method which works with uncalibrated cameras and does not make any assumptions concerning rotation matrices. Our contribution in this paper is to utilize epipolar constraint in a differential multi resolution scheme to gain much more accurate optical flow estimations even for low textured scenes.

The paper is organized as follows: in Sect. 2, the sparse optical flow calculation based on brightness consistency is reviewed, while the optical flow model is discussed in Sect. 3. The inclusion of the epipolar constraint in the calculation of optical flow is discussed in Sect. 4. Evaluation of the proposed method is conducted in Sect. 5. Section 6 concludes this paper.

2 Brightness Constancy Assumption (BCA)

Most sub-pixel optical flow estimation are based on the (linearized) brightness constraint, which assumes that the intensity of a pixel stays constant if objects or cameras move. Given two gray level images such as $I(x, y)$ and $I'(x, y)$, we are interested to map each pixel, namely (x, y), in the image I to a pixel, namely (x', y'), in the image I' using a translation vector such as $[u \ v]^T$. The brightness constraint states that:

$$x'_i = x_i + u_i \tag{1}$$

$$y'_i = y_i + v_i \tag{2}$$

such that $I(x, y) = I'(x', y')$. In a differential optical flow calculation, the intensity consistency constraint can be approximated as follows:

$$I_x(x, y)u + I_y(x, y)v = -I_t(x, y) \tag{3}$$

where $I_x(x, y) = \frac{\partial I(x,y)}{\partial x}$, $I_y(x, y) = \frac{\partial I(x,y)}{\partial y}$ and $I_t(x, y) = I'(x, y) - I(x, y)$.

Nevertheless, the brightness constraint in Eq. 3 has one inherent problem: it yields only one constraint to solve for two variables. It is well known that such an under-determined equation system gives an infinite number of solutions. For every fixed u a valid v can be found fulfilling the constraint and vice versa.

3 Optical Flow Model

Lucas-Kanade method [14] assumed a constant (or affine) optical flow field in a small neighborhood of a pixel and calculate the flow based on the least square method. Such a neighborhood typically consists of $N = n \times n$ pixels with n smaller than 15. The brightness constraint is then evaluated with respect to all pixels within this neighborhood window N. The brightness constraint will usually not be perfectly fulfilled for all pixels as the assumption of equal flow vectors within the window might be violated.

Assuming that the optical flow changes smoothly in a neighborhood or remains constant in a small neighborhood, more equations in terms of u and v can be obtained. Nevertheless, it is also necessary that the intensities of pixels vary at least in two different directions, otherwise the equation system becomes singular and will have infinite solutions. The singularities occur in low textured images or for the pixels located at the edges (aperture problem). Typically, the equation system is formed with more than two equations and it should be solved using the least squared method. Consequently, weighting equations differently yields different solutions. Thus, given a set of neighbor pixels such as $\{(x_i, y_i)|i = 0...n\}$, the equation system will be:

$$
\begin{bmatrix} w_1 & 0 & \cdots & 0 \\ 0 & w_2 & & 0 \\ \vdots & \cdots & \ddots & 0 \\ 0 & & \cdots & w_N \end{bmatrix} \begin{bmatrix} I_x(x_1,y_1) & I_y(x_1,y_1) \\ I_x(x_2,y_2) & I_y(x_2,y_2) \\ \vdots & \\ I_x(x_N,y_N) & I_y(x_N,y_N) \end{bmatrix} \begin{bmatrix} u \\ v \end{bmatrix} = \begin{bmatrix} w_1 & 0 & \cdots & 0 \\ 0 & w_2 & & 0 \\ \vdots & & \ddots & 0 \\ 0 & & \cdots & w_N \end{bmatrix} \begin{bmatrix} I_t(x_1,y_1) \\ I_t(x_2,y_2) \\ \vdots \\ I_t(x_N,y_N) \end{bmatrix}
$$
$$(4)$$

where (x_0, y_0) is the center point for which the optical flow should be calculated and $(w_1, w_2, ..., w_N)$ are the weight of each equation. The weights are also assumed to be normalized: $\sum_{i=1}^{N} w_i = 1$.

The computed flow vector is sub-pixel accurate. But due to the Taylor approximation, the method is only valid for small displacement vectors. Larger displacements are found by embedding the method into a pyramid approach, solving for low frequency structures in low resolution images first and refining the search on higher resolved images. While the maximum track length depends on the image content, generally speaking, flow vectors with large displacements are less likely to be found than those within few pixel displacements.

4 Epipolar Constraint

As stated before, Eq. 4 can be singular in low textured scenes, i.e., all equations will be dependent. Nevertheless, if the optical flow field between two images is mostly induced by the camera motion, another constraint known as the epipolar constraint can be leveraged to calculate optical flow more robustly even for low textured images. Given two matched points: (x, y) and (x', y') between two images captured at two different camera positions, the following equation holds:

$$\mathbf{q}^T F \mathbf{p} = 0 \qquad (5)$$

where $\mathbf{p} = [x \ y \ 1]^T$, $\mathbf{q} = [x' \ y' \ 1]^T$ and F is a 3×3 matrix known as the fundamental matrix. The fundamental matrix can be determined using the 8-point method [11] or the 7-point method [12]. As a result, given a point in the image I the location of the correspondent point in the image I' is constrained with a line equation (epipolar line). In this regard, Eq. 5 can be rewritten as follows:

$$ax'_i + by'_i + c = 0 \qquad (6)$$

where $[a \ b \ c]^T = \frac{1}{\eta} F \mathbf{p}$, where η is a normalization factor such that $a^2 + b^2 = 1$. By substituting Eq. 2 in Eq. 6, an equation in terms of u and v is obtained:

$$au + bv = -ax - by - c \qquad (7)$$

Equation 7 gives one more linear equation of u and v which can be inserted in Eq. 4:

$$
\begin{bmatrix} w_1 I_x(x_0,y_0) & w_0 I_y(x_0,y_0) \\ \vdots & \vdots \\ w_n I_x(x_n,y_n) & w_n I_y(x_n,y_n) \\ w_{n+1} a & w_{n+1} b \end{bmatrix} \begin{bmatrix} u \\ v \end{bmatrix} = \begin{bmatrix} -w_1 I_t(x_0,y_0) \\ \vdots \\ -w_n I_t(x_n,y_n) \\ -w_{n+1}(ax_0 + by_0 + c) \end{bmatrix} \qquad (8)
$$

Since Eq. 2 is based on a linear approximation, usually the optical flow is calculated in an iterative context in which the optical flow is enhanced in each iteration. Therefore, the equation system should be reformed based on the enhanced variables, namely δu^k and δv^k. As a result, the optical flow components are iteratively modified as follows:

$$u^{k+1} = u^k + \delta u^k \tag{9}$$

$$v^{k+1} = v^k + \delta v^k \tag{10}$$

In this case, to guarantee that the matched point in the second image lies on the epipolar line, the following equation should hold in each iteration:

$$a(u^k + \delta u^k) + b(v^k + \delta v^k) = -ax_0 - by_0 - c \tag{11}$$

Thus

$$a\delta u^k + b\delta v^k = -a(x_0 + u^k) - b(y_0 + v^k) - c \tag{12}$$

Therefore, we obtain the following equation system in an iterative context:

$$\begin{bmatrix} w_1 I_x(x_0, y_0) & w_1 I_y(x_0, y_0) \\ \vdots & \vdots \\ w_n I_x(x_n, y_n) & w_n I_y(x_n, y_n) \\ w_{n+1}a & w_{n+1}b \end{bmatrix} \begin{bmatrix} \delta u^k \\ \delta v^k \end{bmatrix} = \begin{bmatrix} -w_1 I_t(x_0 + u^k, y_0 + v^k) \\ \vdots \\ -w_n I_t(x_n + u^k, y_n + v^k) \\ -w_{n+1}(a(x_0 + u^k) + b(y_0 + v^k) + c) \end{bmatrix} \tag{13}$$

So far we have focused on the calculation of small optical flow if the flows are about a few pixels. Obviously, in case of a large displacement optical flows, using the discussed method causes the iterations to get stuck in local minima. An efficient well-known solution to this problem is the pyramid analysis in which an optical flow is calculated step by step from coarse to fine levels. In this case, using the epipolar line is a bit tricky since the line equations should be changed depending on the level of the pyramid in which the optical flow is calculated. Assuming the level of the pyramid denoted as $l < 1$ and the scale factor of the pyramid to be s, it can be verified that in the epipolar line equation c will be changed as follows:

$$c_l = s^l c_0 \tag{14}$$

where $c_0 = c$.

The weight of the neighborhood pixels is chosen to follow a Gaussian distribution. The weight of the epipolar constraint determines the importance of the constraint. Experimentally, we found that the weight 1.5 gives the best results.

Figure 2 shows comparisons of the AEE and the AAE for each image from 194 training images and presents significant improvements of the accuracy for the new data term as shown in Fig. 3. However, in some scenarios such as sequence 150, the average errors based on epipolar constraint were larger for the epipolar constraint. In such scenarios such as Fig. 4, the camera had obviously side translations and relatively high rotations which typically gave rise to high errors in the estimation of the fundamental matrix for even a small amount of measurement noise.

5 Experimental Results

For a quantitative evaluation, we tested our method on the well-known KITTI dataset [15]. The dataset contained images with a resolution of (1240 × 376) pixels. The KITTI dataset provided a very challenging testbed for the evaluation of optical flow algorithms. Pixel displacements in the data set are generally large, exceeding 250 pixels. Furthermore, the images exhibit less texture regions, strongly varying lighting conditions, and many non-Lambertian surfaces, especially translucent windows and specular glass, and metal surfaces. Moreover, the

Table 1. Average end point and average angular error of the estimated optical flow for the 194 training sequences from KITTI data set.

Method		Average End Point Error AEE			Average Angluar Error AAE		
		(3×3)	(7×7)	(15×15)	(3×3)	(7×7)	(15×15)
Epipolar Line Constraint	LK 7 Points	**17.74**	**10.01**	**7.83**	**9.93**	**7.93**	**7.29**
	LK 8 Points	19.11	11.55	9.33	13.42	11.24	10.47
	SIFT 7 Points	17.87	10.25	8.19	10.35	8.12	7.92
	SIFT 8 Points	18.65	11.15	9.01	12.43	10.51	9.84
Brightness Constraint		127.85	29.69	14.56	36.88	17.23	11.07

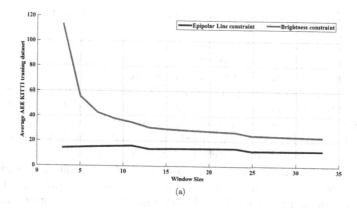

(a)

Fig. 1. The average error for each sequence of the 194 sequences of the KITTI training data set. (a) AEE. (b) AAE.

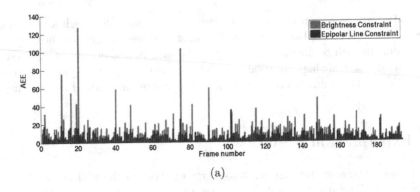

(a)

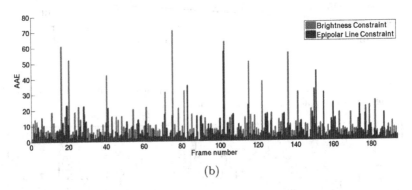

(b)

Fig. 2. The average error for each sequence of the 194 sequences of the KITTI training data set. (a) AEE. (b) AAE.

high speed of the forward motion creates large regions on the image boundaries that move out of the field of view between frames, such that no correspondence can be established.

For the estimation of optical flow, there are two concerns: which feature matching method should be applied and which method for the estimation of the fundamental matrix is more appropriate. Hence, we applied two different feature matching methods: SIFT [16] and the pyramid Lucas-Kanade optical flow [17] (both are implemented in openCV). Additionally, we applied 7-point and 8-point methods in the context of a RANSAC algorithm for the fundamental matrix estimation. For the 8-point method, we used 9 matched points and for the 7-point method we used 8 matched points. A problem concerning the 7-point method was that it might yield up to three distinct valid solutions, while only one solution was needed. As eight points were used in the 7-point method, we assumed that the solution should not deviate from the 8-point solution; therefore, we selected the solution which was generated based on the smallest root of the third order polynomial obtained in the 7-point method.

(a)

(b)

(c)

Fig. 3. Comparison between ground truth (red) and estimated optical flow (green) for sequence 24 of the KITTI training data set for some feature points. (a) Using epipolar constraint based on 7-points method. (b) Using brightness constrain. (c) Estimated epipolar lines (Color figure online).

In the first experiment, we calculated the average end-point error (AEE) and the average angular error (AAE) of the estimated optical flow using the data term based on the epipolar constraint and the data term of brightness constraint based on [14]. Table 1 shows the average errors using different window sizes and demonstrates that the epipolar constraint has lower average errors for 194 training images. As it can be seen, the best performance was achieved using the LK tracker and the 7-point method. The reason lies in the fact that SIFT works based on blob features and these features are not sub-pixel or even pixel accurate enough. The 7-point method also performs better than the 8-point method as it needs less points, which make it robust against outliers in the RANSAC algorithm. In Fig. 1, the effect of increasing the size of surrounding window is depicted. As can be seen, brightness constraint has very poor performance for the small window sizes, whereas using the epipolar constraint yielded good results even for the small windows.

Fig. 4. Comparison between ground truth (red) and estimated optical flow (green) for sequence 150 of the KITTI training data set for some feature points. (a) Using epipolar constraint based on 7-points method. (b) Using brightness constrain. (c) Estimated epipolar lines (Color figure online).

6   Conclusion

We derived the necessary formulation to augment epipolar constraint for an uncalibrated camera in a differential method for the calculation of the optical flow. The proposed algorithm was evaluated with different sequences of the KITTI datasets and provided more correct flow fields and increased the robustness. For future work, applying this method to dense flow estimations should be considered.

References

1. Kim, Y.H., Martinez, A.M., Kak, A.C.: Robust motion estimation under varying illumination. Image Vision Comput. **23**, 365–375 (2005)
2. Mileva, Y., Bruhn, A., Weickert, J.: Illumination-robust variational optical flow with photometric invariants. In: Hamprecht, F.A., Schnörr, C., Jähne, B. (eds.) DAGM 2007. LNCS, vol. 4713, pp. 152–162. Springer, Heidelberg (2007)

3. Mueller, T., Rabe, C., Rannacher, J., Franke, U., Mester, R.: Illumination-robust dense optical flow using census signatures. In: Mester, R., Felsberg, M. (eds.) DAGM 2011. LNCS, vol. 6835, pp. 236–245. Springer, Heidelberg (2011)
4. Zach, C., Pock, T., Bischof, H.: A duality based approach for realtime TV-$L1$ optical flow. In: Hamprecht, F.A., Schnörr, C., Jähne, B. (eds.) DAGM 2007. LNCS, vol. 4713, pp. 214–223. Springer, Heidelberg (2007)
5. Molnar, J., Chetverikov, D., Fazekas, S.: Illumination-robust variational optical flow using cross-correlation. Comput. Vis. Image Underst. **114**, 1104–1114 (2010)
6. Werlberger, M., Pock, T., Bischof, H.: Motion estimation with non-local total variation regularization. In: CVPR, pp. 2464–2471. IEEE (2010)
7. Drulea, M., Nedevschi, S.: Motion estimation using the correlation transform. IEEE Trans. Image Process. **22**, 3260–3270 (2013)
8. Rashwan, H.A., Mohamed, M.A., García, M.A., Mertsching, B., Puig, D.: Illumination robust optical flow model based on histogram of oriented gradients. In: Weickert, J., Hein, M., Schiele, B. (eds.) GCPR 2013. LNCS, vol. 8142, pp. 354–363. Springer, Heidelberg (2013)
9. Mohamed, M.A., Rashwan, H.A., Mertsching, B., Garcia, M.A., Puig, D.: Illumination-robust optical flow using local directional pattern. IEEE Trans. Circuits Syst. Video Technol. **24**, 1–9 (2014)
10. Mohamed, M.A., Rashwan, H.A., Mertsching, B., Garcia, M.A., Puig, D.: On improving the robustness of variational optical flow against illumination changes. In: Proceedings of the 4th ACM/IEEE International Workshop on Analysis and Retrieval of Tracked Events and Motion in Imagery Stream, pp. 1–8. ACM (2013)
11. Hartley, R.I.: In defense of the eight-point algorithm. IEEE Trans. Pattern Anal. Mach. Intell. **19**, 580–593 (1997)
12. Hartley, R.I., Zisserman, A.: Multiple View Geometry in Computer Vision. Cambridge University, Cambridge (2004)
13. Yamaguchi, K., McAllester, D.A., Urtasun, R.: Robust monocular epipolar flow estimation. In: CVPR, pp. 1862–1869. IEEE (2013)
14. Lukas, B., Kanade, T.: An iterative image registration technique with an application to stereo vision. In: Image Understanding Workshop (1981)
15. Geiger, A., Lenz, P., Stiller, C., Urtasun, R.: Vision meets robotics: the KITTI dataset. Int. J. Robot. Res. **32**(11), 1231–1237 (2013)
16. Lowe, D.G.: Distinctive image features from scale-invariant keypoints. Int. J. Comput. Vision **60**(2), 91–110 (2004)
17. Bouguet, J.Y.: Pyramidal implementation of the Lucas Kanade feature tracker. Intel Corporation, Microprocessor Research Labs (2000)

General Object Tip Detection and Pose Estimation for Robot Manipulation

Dadhichi Shukla$^{(\boxtimes)}$, Özgür Erkent, and Justus Piater

Intelligent and Interactive Systems, Institute of Computer Science,
University of Innsbruck, Technikerstr. 21a, 6020 Innsbruck, Austria
`dadhichi.shukla@uibk.ac.at`

Abstract. Robot manipulation tasks like inserting screws and pegs into a hole or automatic screwing require precise tip pose estimation. We propose a novel method to detect and estimate the tip of elongated objects. We demonstrate that our method can estimate tip pose to millimeter-level accuracy. We adopt a probabilistic, appearance-based object detection framework to detect pegs and bits for electric screw drivers. Screws are difficult to detect with feature- or appearance-based methods due to their reflective characteristics. To overcome this we propose a novel adaptation of RANSAC with a parallel-line model. Subsequently, we employ image moments to detect the tip and its pose. We show that the proposed method allows a robot to perform object insertion with only two pairs of orthogonal views, without visual servoing.

Keywords: Pose estimation · Tool tip detection · Peg-in-hole insertion

1 Introduction and Related Work

A fundamental challenge for robots operating in environments not designed for robots lies in generic, vision-guided manipulation skills. While factory settings can control the robot's environment to reduce variability, uncertainty and thus perceptual requirements to a minimum, in uncontrolled environments a robot must be able to interact in flexible, reactive perception-action loops.

One generic sensorimotor skill that arises in many different contexts is the insertion of elongated objects into their receptacle, such as screws or pegs into holes, drills onto pilot holes, or screwdriver bits onto the screw head. These operations require the pose of the insertable tip of the object to be estimated with sufficient precision.

Here we present a generic, robust and accurate method for detecting tips of generic, elongated objects for purposes such as robotic insertion. Examples of such objects are shown in Figs. 1a and 1b.

Many prominent strategies involve visual servoing methods [3,7,14] and rely on 3D models of the objects or on visual markers to solve peg-in-hole-style challenges. Song et al. [9] recently proposed an automated peg-in-hole method for complex-shaped parts. However, such methods critically depend on CAD models

© Springer International Publishing Switzerland 2015
L. Nalpantidis et al. (Eds.): ICVS 2015, LNCS 9163, pp. 364–374, 2015.
DOI: 10.1007/978-3-319-20904-3_33

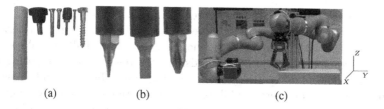

Fig. 1. (a)–(b) Elongated objects: peg, variety of screws, screwdriver bits. (c) Robot inserting a screw into a hole.

of the objects involved. An important aspect in image-based visual servoing is to determine the set of visual features to be used in the control scheme. Visual servoing methods proposed by Chaumette [2] and Liu et al. [8] employed image moments as image features which can efficiently increase the stability of the system. Since the objects in this work are very small in size compared to the robot hand, they are often strongly occluded, making their visual features difficult to track. Recent work by Hoffman et al. [5] can be related to this study of estimating tool tip location. The method localizes the tool tip by using 3D depth information to segment the tool from the background and performing contour segmentation based on level sets [1]. The method proposed by Stückler and Behnke [10] also falls in this category. It would be difficult to adapt these methods for the objects in this study since there will be no or negligible depth information due to the minuscule size of the objects.

In this study, therefore, we propose a novel strategy independent of CAD models, fiducial markers or depth information that applies to different types of screws or other elongated objects. After tip pose estimation, it relies on a calibrated camera/robot setup to insert the tip into its receptacle. We do not use visual servoing; instead, we introduce a discrete visual feedback system capable of inserting the object with only two pairs of orthogonal views of the object in hand. Details are discussed in Sect. 4. The experimental setup of this work is shown in Fig. 1c, where the left robot arm grasps the object, and the eye-in-hand system is mounted on the right robot arm.

The vision part of the system contains two steps: (1) Detection of the object held by the robot hand, and (2) Estimation of the tip of the object. The objects of interest in this work are textureless or reflective. Thus, conventional, appearance-based methods have trouble detecting the object. Therefore, we adopt a probabilistic object detection framework based on image gradients proposed by Teney and Piater [12], which naturally accommodates variability in scale, shape and appearance of the objects. A brief description of the approach is presented in Sect. 2.1.

However, screws are difficult to detect using this framework due to their reflective characteristics. At the high spatial resolution we require for precise tip estimation, these create spurious image features like edges and corners. We turn this problem to our advantage: Screw threadings exhibit conspicuous, linearly-aligned corner features which are conveniently detected using RANSAC [4]. We use a parallel-line model to detect parallel pairs of collinear points. We further discuss our RANSAC parallel-line (RPL) model in Sect. 2.2.

Precise pose estimation normally requires accurate object models. In this work, however, we seek a generic, object-independent method. Precisely estimating tool tips without tool-specific models is a serious challenge. We succeed thanks to a combination of three methods: First, screws are detected using *RPL*, and all other objects using *Teney et al.'s method*. Then, building on the assumption that the object of interest exhibits suitable rotational or reflective symmetry about its principal axis, we compute *image moments* proposed by Hu [6] on the objects segmented by either of the first two methods, which greatly increases the localization accuracy of the estimated tip poses. A brief description of image moments and their use in this study is given in Sect. 3.

After estimating the tip, we plan a trajectory for the insertion movement using the KOMO motion planner proposed by Toussaint [13]. This motion planner produces trajectories that avoid self-collisions and obstacles in the scene. We illustrate in Sect. 5 that the fully integrated system can achieve object insertion at millimeter-level accuracy.

2   In-Hand Object Detection

Partial occlusions are prevalent in in-hand object detection. The objects of interest like screws are highly occluded due to their tiny size relative to the hand. Features detected on the hand are confounded with the object features, which further adds to the detection problem. Note that peg-shaped objects can be detected by either of the strategies discussed in the two sections below.

2.1   Probabilistic Appearance-Based Model

Learning Object Models: Pose-Appearance Space. The probabilistic appearance-based model proposed by Teney and Piater [12] performs object detection, recognition and pose estimation in 2D images. The framework is trained on only three real images of the screw-driver bits as shown in Fig. 1b. Edge features of each image are defined on $\mathbb{R}^2 \times S_1^+$, accounting for the position and orientation defined as the appearance space A. Edge points x are then associated with the respective pose w to create *pose/appearance* pairs (x_i, w_i). These pairs from all training images are concatenated to form the training set $T = (x_i, w_i)_{i=1}^{M}$. The training set is then used to define a continuous probability distribution ψ on the *pose/appearance* space given by

$$\psi(w, x) = \frac{1}{M} \sum_{(w_i, x_i) \in T} K_1(w, w_i) K_2(x, x_i), \tag{1}$$

where $w \in SE(3)$ and $x \in A$. The use of kernels K_1 and K_2 can be seen here as a Gaussian smoothing over the available training edge points. In a similar fashion the edge features of a test image are stored as the *observations* $O = \{x\}_{i=1}^{N}$, where $x_i \in A$. These are then used to define a probability density ϕ on A as

$$\phi(x) = \frac{1}{N} \sum_{x_i \in O} K_2(x, x_i). \tag{2}$$

Pose Inference. The observation density ϕ is now matched to the learned model ψ in order to find the pose of the object in the test image. The pose w is modelled as random variable $W \in SE(3)$, and its distribution is given by

$$p(w) = \int_A \psi(w, x)\, \phi(x)\mathrm{d}x. \tag{3}$$

The above expression measures the compatibility of the training data at pose w with the distribution of features observed in the test image. It essentially computes the cross-correlation of the distribution ϕ of observations with the model distribution $\psi(w, \cdot)$ at a given pose. Estimating the pose w then involves maximizing $p(w)$ over w, which is done using an efficient scheme [11,12]. An advantage of this framework is that the method generates one flexible model of a generic bit that can be applied to detect a variety of distinct screw-driver bits. Illustrative bit detection results are shown in Fig. 2a.

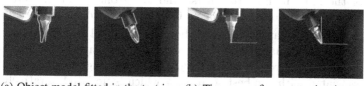

(a) Object model fitted in the test im- (b) Tip pose refinement using image
age (section 2.1).   moments (section 3).

Fig. 2. Tip detection comparison between appearance-based method [12] and image moments.

2.2 RANSAC Parallel-Line Model

The position of the screw can be detected by fitting a pair of parallel lines passing through a pair of collinear corner features. To understand the proposed RANSAC Parallel-Line (RPL) model let us take n input data points from a test image I. For screws, corner features from the threadings are given as the input data points to RPL, as shown in Fig. 4a. In the case of a peg, locations of the edge features are given as the input data. A pair of parallel lines can be represented by three points. The goal of RPL is to best fit the parallel lines l_1 and l_2 to the observed data. Importantly, the inlier sets $\mathcal{L}_1$ and $\mathcal{L}_2$ associated with the lines l_1 and l_2, respectively should not overlap, i.e., $\mathcal{L}_1 \cap \mathcal{L}_2 = \emptyset$.

To find the location of the screw, we propose a scoring scheme based on three objectives: (1) to maximize total number of inliers $|\mathcal{L}| = |\mathcal{L}_1| + |\mathcal{L}_2|$, (2) to maximize the orthogonal distance $d_{l_1 l_2}$ between the parallel lines, and (3) to minimize the longitudinal distance $d_{c_1 c_2}$ between the centroids of the two inlier sets, i.e. the distance between the centroid c_1 and the projection of the centroid c_2 onto the line l_1. These variables are normalized by scaling them to the unit interval as

$$\hat{L} = \frac{|\mathcal{L}|}{n}, \quad \hat{d}_{l_1 l_2} = \frac{d_{l_1 l_2}}{I_{diag}}, \quad \hat{d}_{c_1 c_2} = \frac{d_{c_1 c_2}}{I_{diag}},$$

where, I_{diag} is the length of the diagonal of the image.

For a given model l_1, l_2 which fits the observed data, the variables $\hat{L}$, $\hat{d}_{l_1 l_2}$ and $\hat{d}_{c_1 c_2}$ are independent. We would like to fit the model l_1, l_2 that maximizes score s based on the aforementioned objectives. We compute the score s of a hypothesis l_1, l_2 as the likelihood function given by

$$P(\hat{L}, \hat{d}_{l_1 l_2}, \hat{d}_{c_1 c_2} | l_1, l_2) = P(\hat{L} | l_1, l_2) P(\hat{d}_{l_1 l_2} | l_1, l_2) P(\hat{d}_{c_1 c_2} | l_1, l_2). \qquad (4)$$

The likelihoods $P(\hat{L} | l_1, l_2)$, $P(\hat{d}_{l_1 l_2} | l_1, l_2)$ and $P(\hat{d}_{c_1 c_2} | l_1, l_2)$ of the three individual observations are given by the normal distributions. Therefore, the score of the fitting model at each iteration is given by

$$s = \mathcal{N}(\hat{L}; \mu_{\hat{L}}, \sigma_{\hat{L}}^2) \mathcal{N}(\hat{d}_{l_1 l_2}; \mu_{\hat{d}_{l_1 l_2}}, \sigma_{\hat{d}_{l_1 l_2}}^2) \mathcal{N}(\hat{d}_{c_1 c_2}; \mu_{\hat{d}_{c_1 c_2}}, \sigma_{\hat{d}_{c_1 c_2}}^2). \qquad (5)$$

The mean values of these distributions are set as follows, $\mu_{\hat{L}}$ is set to 1 to advocate the inherent notion of RANSAC that the consensus set of the fitting model consists of the most number of inliers. And the geometry of the screw allows us to set $\mu_{\hat{d}_{l_1 l_2}} > 0$, in our experiments 0.5 and $\mu_{\hat{d}_{c_1 c_2}}$ to 0 which attributes to the width of the screw and symmetry about its principal axis, respectively. The variances of these normal distributions are easily set empirically; alternatively, they can be estimated from training data. The best fitting model to the observations is associated with the best score s_{best} which is updated iteratively within RANSAC. Our RANSAC parallel-line fitting method is described in Algorithm 1.

Algorithm 1. Proposed RANSAC Parallel-Line (RPL) model

---

1. Select three random points p_1, p_2 and p_3 from n data points.
2. Define parallel lines l_1 and l_2 passing through p_1, p_2 and p_3 respectively.
3. If $l_1 = l_2$ discard p_1, p_2, p_3 and goto step 1.
4. Find all the inliers $\mathcal{L}$ given a distance threshold t.
5. Compute score s as given by Eq. 5.
6. If $s_{\text{best}} < s$ discard p_1, p_2, p_3 and goto step 1, else update $s_{\text{best}} = s$.
7. Repeat these steps until a good model has been found with high confidence.

Some hypotheses are shown in Fig. 3. Evidently, the hypothesis with the highest score is the best fit to the observed data points, as shown in Fig. 3e. The location of the screw detected by our RPL model can be seen in Fig. 4c. It can be seen that despite the presence of spurious corner features the proposed method performs robustly in practice.

3   Tip Detection and Pose Estimation Using Image Moments

The outcome of both aforementioned object detection strategies are satisfying from an object-detection point of view. Given accurate, object-specific models,

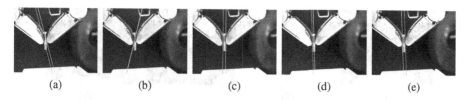

Fig. 3. RANSAC parallel-line (RPL) model: (a)–(e) some of the parallel-line hypotheses, (e) best fitting model with the highest score.

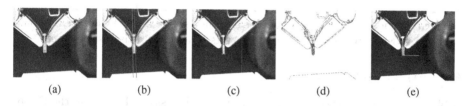

Fig. 4. (a)–(c) Screw detection using our RANSAC parallel-line (RPL) method. (d)–(e) Screw tip detection using image moments (Sect. 3); $\theta = 91.98°$.

these would be sufficient for accurate tip pose estimation. However, even a slight perturbation in the estimated object pose can lead to substantial errors in the estimated tip location. If we fit the learned model to the test images as shown in Fig. 2a, we can see that the estimated tip is off the actual tip. Though the probabilistic framework can detect the objects reliably, precise estimation of the tip location is a challenge. To overcome this problem, we adopt image moments as described by Hu [6]. A shape can be summarized by a function of few lower-order moments. We can characterize the image properties like area, centroid, orientation using these moments. For example, to detect object pose we can compute image orientation using second-order central moments.

Image moments have been extensively used to compute geometric features of a shape in a binary image. We adopt image moments to detect the tip of the object. Let us consider an example of the detection of the bit of the screw driver and the screw as shown in Figs. 4c and 5a, respectively. The location of the object is given by the bounding box (bb). First, the image features like edges (x_{bb}) within the bounding box I_{bb} are retained as shown in Fig. 5b. Then a binary mask is created from those edge points. In the case of screws, the extreme corner features are connected to create the binary mask as shown in Fig. 4c. Morphological operations are then carried out to eliminate islands or unwanted features. Finally, the major axis and orientation θ of the shape is computed using second-order central moments, which is equivalent to fitting an ellipse. It can be seen in Figs. 4d and 5c that one of the end points of the major axis is located closest to the tip. Now the problem is reduced to finding a nearest neighbour. Since we know the pose of the robot hand, we also know whether the tip is facing vertically *up or down*. Based on this the appropriate end point ep_j of the major axis, either ep_1 or ep_2, is selected. The estimated tip of the object is

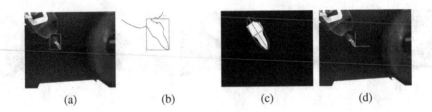

(a)   (b)   (c)   (d)

Fig. 5. (a) Screw driver bit detection using probabilistic method [12]. (b)–(d) Tip detection (Sect. 3); $\theta = 123.23°$.

the nearest edge point to ep_j. It can be seen in Figs. 4e and 5d that the outcome of the proposed tip detection method results in a very precise estimation.

4   Object Insertion

A block diagram of the overall object insertion process can be seen in the Fig. 6. At the start, the pose $\mathbf{p}_h$ of the hole is assumed to be known and the estimation for the pose $\hat{\mathbf{p}}_o$ of the object tip is unknown. All the poses in the diagram include the 6-DoF variables ($\mathbf{p} \in \mathbb{R}^3 \times S^3$). The difference between $\mathbf{p}_h$ and $\hat{\mathbf{p}}_o$ is given as the error $\mathbf{e}$ to the control system. The decision maker in Fig. 6 plans the motion of the robot such that the camera gathers maximum possible information to estimate the pose of the object tip. This is achieved by taking orthogonal views in this study. As mentioned earlier we integrate our system with the KOMO motion planner provided by Toussaint [13]. It should be noted that due to inaccuracies in the encoder readings of the robot ($\tilde{\mathbf{J}}_R$), there will be a steady-state error between the desired input $\mathbf{u}_R$ and the actual output pose of the robot. Since these errors are not systematic, in our evaluation we measure the final error between the desired and the actual object poses.

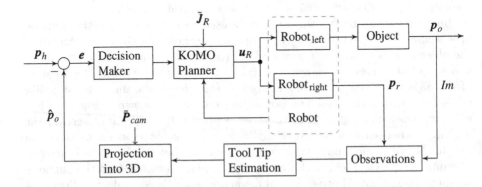

Fig. 6. Block diagram of the overall system.

The experimental setup is situated in a world frame (XYZ) as shown in Fig. 1c. It consists of an eye-in-hand camera setup for the right arm while a hand

Fig. 7. *L-R*: Tip pose estimation in two pairs of orthogonal views $(u, u')_1$, $(u, u')_2$. Views $(u, u')_1$ are chosen to align the axes of the object and the hole. Views $(u, u')_2$ are chosen to compute translation error of the object tip with respect to the hole in X and Y axes, respectively, in the world frame. $\theta_{u_1} = 91.69°$, $\theta_{u'_1} = 75.00°$, $\theta_{u_2} = 93.90°$, $\theta_{u'_2} = 90.38°$.

mounted on the the left arm grasps the object. The camera initially looks towards the left arm from a distance d. The robot first moves to a known 3D location in the world frame. To estimate the pose $\mathbf{p}_o$ of the object after robot motion, an observation is made by acquiring the image Im and estimating the current pose $\mathbf{p}_r$ of the camera from the encoder readings of the robot. Here, the first pair of orthogonal views u, u' of the object in hand is captured by rotating the end effector of the left arm. The tip pose estimation of the object aligns its axes with the hole. The tip detection results of the screw in the first pair of orthogonal views can be seen in Fig. 7. The tip location $(t_x, t_y)_u$, $(t_x, t_y)_{u'}$ and orientation θ_u, $\theta_{u'}$ is computed in both views. Then we can estimate the object tip in the world frame by using the camera projection matrix. We observe that mere alignment of the object tip is not enough for the insertion. There will be a small error in the projection due to inaccuracies in the calibration of the camera parameters ($\tilde{\mathbf{P}}_{cam}$), which is inevitable. These errors affect the position of the object tip mainly along the X and Y axes.

The tip estimation is mainly affected by the accumulation of different errors in the robot system due to transformation $\mathbf{e}_t$, calibration $\mathbf{e}_c$ and tolerances of the motion planner. To limit these errors we repeat the procedure to capture a second pair of the orthogonal views. We re-capture view u and estimate the tip location to achieve position correction along the X axis. Since the object is aligned with the hole, at this step, we move camera to an orthogonal location with respect to view u to capture view u'. The tip estimation in view u' reduces the error along the Y axis. Furthermore, this procedure can be repeated multiple times until position corrections along X and Y axes converge to zero. In practice we achieve tip insertion with only two iterations within admissible error values. In the evaluation we demonstrate that the combined position corrections along X and Y axes increase the number of successful insertions. Tip detection of the screw in the second pair of orthogonal views can be seen in Fig. 7.

5   Experiments and Results

The experiments were carried out with the wooden peg, different types of screws and screw-driver bits in the experimental setup as shown in Fig. 1c to verify the proposed tip detection and insertion method. The setup consists of two 6-DoF

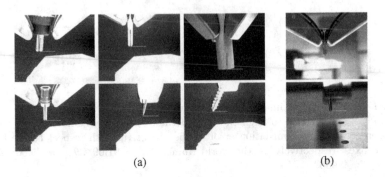

(a)   (b)

Fig. 8. (a) Tip detection results on a variety of screws and a peg; L-R: $\theta_1 = 83.79°$, $\theta_2 = 90.46°$, $\theta_3 = 94.79°$, $\theta_4 = 89.34°$, $\theta_5 = 76.29°$, $\theta_6 = 65.85°$. (b) Tip detection in distinct backgrounds; T-B: $\theta = 91.66°$, $\theta = 95.68°$

KUKA-LWR (Light-Weight Robots), a Schunk SDH hand, and a BlackFly camera (BFLY-PGE-13E4C-CS). The parameters of interest for the KOMO motion planner are position precision $P_p = 10^{-4}$ m, alignment precision $A_p = 10^{-6}$ m, position tolerance $P_t = 0.005$ m and angular tolerance $A_t = 0.1$ rad. These parameters were experimentally determined.

The effectiveness of the proposed tip detection algorithm was verified by several trials of insertion. We divide the objects in two groups based on the width of the tip: (1) *thick* objects with a tip of width ≥5 mm and (2) *thin* objects with a tip of width <5 mm as shown in the top and bottom rows of Fig. 8a, respectively. Six insertion trials are made with thick objects and five insertion trials are made with thin objects. The results in Fig. 8b show that the proposed method can work under different lighting conditions and background. On visual inspection it can be seen that the proposed method can successfully estimate the tip location in the image for a variety of objects.

We consider tip pose estimation to be successful if the object tip can be inserted into the hole. Quantitative results can be seen in Figs. 9a and 9b, where independent trials are coded with distinct colors. Trials that fall inside the dotted circles have errors less than 3.5 mm and 3 mm for thick and thin object tips, respectively. Three insertion attempts are made for each trial discussed as follows. The points marked ★ are the attempts after aligning the object tip with the hole as described in Sect. 4. It can be seen from the plot that the insertion attempts with mere object tip alignment are often quite far from the hole. As mentioned earlier, to overcome this the position corrections along X and Y axes are performed by capturing a second pair of orthogonal views $(u, u')_2$, respectively. The insertion attempts after position correction only along the X axis are marked with ✱, and the insertion attempts with position corrections along X and Y axes combined together are marked with ●. These position corrections bring the object tip on top of the hole.

We include these position corrections to overcome the inevitable accumulation of camera calibration and steady-state errors along with tolerances of the

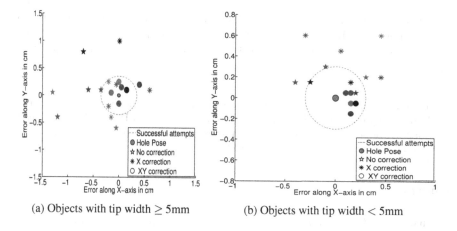

(a) Objects with tip width $\geq$ 5mm   (b) Objects with tip width $<$ 5mm

Fig. 9. Quantitative results of tip insertion. Trials that fall inside the dotted circle are successful attempts of insertion.

motion planner to some extent. Moreover, tip insertion significantly depends on estimation of the tip in the world frame. Despite accurate tip detection in the camera frame, the estimation in the world frame also depends on the width of the object tip. It was observed that the estimates were more accurate for the thin objects as compared to the thick objects, as expected. For six insertion trials of thick objects, the number of successful insertions are zero, three and five after no corrections, correction along the X axis and correction along the X and Y axes, respectively. For five insertion trials of thin objects, the number of successful insertions are two, one and five after no corrections, correction along the X axis and correction in X and Y axes, respectively. It can be seen that the errors are reduced dramatically after corrections along the X and Y axes.

6 Conclusion

In this work, we propose a novel object tip detection and pose estimation method for elongated objects. The proposed method was tested with two 6-DOF KUKA Light Weight Robots to perform peg-in-hole style tasks. The principal contribution is that this method is able to extract object tip poses with high accuracy, without using object-specific models. This allows our method to be used flexibly in a wide range of application settings. The only key assumption is that the tip to be estimated lies on the major axis of the elongated object.

The following conclusions were drawn from this study:

- We achieve object insertion task with only two pairs of orthogonal views.
- A success rate of 100 % can be achieved by the system for objects with a sharp tip. However, the errors increase as the width of the object tip increases.
- The proposed method can estimate the tip location even with high occlusion levels.

– Since this study focuses on visual object tip localization, we validated accuracy using stiff robot position control. Using impedance control instead, practical insertion performance can be significantly increased, especially for wider objects.

Acknowledgments. The research leading to these results has received funding from the European Communitys Seventh Framework Programme FP7/2007-2013 (Specific Programme Cooperation, Theme 3, Information and Communication Technologies) under grant agreement no. 610878, 3rd HAND.

References

1. Chan, T.F., Vese, L.A.: Active contours without edges. IEEE Trans. Image Process. **10**(2), 266–277 (2001)
2. Chaumette, F.: Image moments: a general and useful set of features for visual servoing. IEEE Trans. Rob. **20**(4), 713–723 (2004)
3. Dantam, N.T., Amor, H.B., Christensen, H.I., Stilman, M.: Online multi-camera registration for bimanual workspace trajectories. In: 14th IEEE-RAS International Conference on Humanoid Robots (Humanoids), pp. 588–593. IEEE (2014)
4. Fischler, M.A., Bolles, R.C.: Random sample consensus: a paradigm for model fitting with applications to image analysis and automated cartography. Commun. ACM **24**(6), 381–395 (1981)
5. Hoffmann, H., Chen, Z., Earl, D., Mitchell, D., Salemi, B., Sinapov, J.: Adaptive robotic tool use under variable grasps. Rob. Auton. Syst. **62**(6), 833–846 (2014)
6. Hu, M.K.: Visual pattern recognition by moment invariants. IRE Trans. Inf. Theory **8**(2), 179–187 (1962)
7. Huang, S., Yamakawa, Y., Senoo, T., Ishikawa, M.: Dynamic compensation by fusing a high-speed actuator and high-speed visual feedback with its application to fast peg-and-hole alignment. Adv. Rob. **28**(9), 613–624 (2014)
8. Liu, S., Xie, W.F., Su, C.Y.: Image-based visual servoing using improved image moments. In: International Conference on Information and Automation, 2009, ICIA 2009, pp. 577–582. IEEE (2009)
9. Song, H.C., Kim, Y.L., Song, J.B.: Automated guidance of peg-in-hole assembly tasks for complex-shaped parts. In: 2014 IEEE/RSJ International Conference on Intelligent Robots and Systems (IROS 2014), pp. 4517–4522. IEEE (2014)
10. Stückler, J., Behnke, S.: Adaptive tool-use strategies for anthropomorphic service robots. In: 14th IEEE-RAS International Conference on Humanoid Robots. IEEE (2014)
11. Teney, D., Piater, J.: Continuous pose estimation in 2D images at instance and category levels. In: Tenth Conference on Computer and Robot Vision, pp. 121–127. IEEE, May 2013. https://iis.uibk.ac.at/public/papers/Teney-2013-CRV.pdf
12. Teney, D., Piater, J.: Multiview feature distributions for object detection and continuous pose estimation. Comput. Vis. Image Underst. **125**, 265–282 (2014). https://iis.uibk.ac.at/public/papers/Teney-2014-CVIU.pdf
13. Toussaint, M.: Newton methods for k-order markov constrained motion problems. CoRR abs/1407.0414 (2014). http://arxiv.org/abs/1407.0414
14. Wang, J., Cho, H.: Micropeg and hole alignment using image moments based visual servoing method. IEEE Trans. Industr. Electron. **55**(3), 1286–1294 (2008)

Visual Estimation of Attentive Cues in HRI: The Case of Torso and Head Pose

Markos Sigalas[1,2]($\boxtimes$), Maria Pateraki[1], and Panos Trahanias[1,2]

[1] Institute of Computer Science, Foundation for Research
and Technology - Hellas, Heraklion, Greece
pateraki@ics.forth.gr

[2] Department of Computer Science, University of Crete, Rethymno, Greece
{msigalas,trahania}@ics.forth.gr

Abstract. Capturing visual human-centered information is a fundamental input source for effective and successful human-robot interaction (HRI) in dynamic multi-party social settings. Torso and head pose, as forms of nonverbal communication, support the derivation people's focus of attention, a key variable in the analysis of human behaviour in HRI paradigms encompassing social aspects. Towards this goal, we have developed a model-based approach for torso and head pose estimation to overcome key limitations in free-form interaction scenarios and issues of partial intra- and inter-person occlusions. The proposed approach builds up on the concept of *Top View Re-projection* (TVR) to uniformly treat the respective body parts, modelled as cylinders. For each body part a number of pose hypotheses is sampled from its configuration space. Each pose hypothesis is evaluated against the a scoring function and the hypothesis with the best score yields for the assumed pose and the location of the joints. A refinement step on head pose is applied based on tracking facial patch deformations to compute for the horizontal off-plane rotation. The overall approach forms one of the core component of a vision system integrated in a robotic platform that supports socially appropriate, multi-party, multimodal interaction in a bartending scenario. Results in the robot's environment during real HRI experiments with varying number of users attest for the effectiveness of our approach.

Keywords: Body pose estimation · Head pose · Model-based · Tracking · Particle filtering

1 Introduction

As robots become integrated into daily life, they must increasingly deal with two important aspects: robust navigation in cluttered environments [1,2], and effective human-robot interaction (HRI). The latter is addressed in this work, aiming at continuous, natural and socially appropriate HRI. In this framework, perception of humans, tracking and recognition of humans actions [3,4] can be realized by an appropriate vision system that is able to operate effectively in

© Springer International Publishing Switzerland 2015
L. Nalpantidis et al. (Eds.): ICVS 2015, LNCS 9163, pp. 375–388, 2015.
DOI: 10.1007/978-3-319-20904-3_34

dynamic scenes, capturing information from multiple users in the robot's vicinity. An important perceptual variable in the analysis of group behaviour is the focus of attention, which indicates the object or person one is attending to. It often happens that people turn toward their focus of attention, thereby physically expressing their attention by means of posture, gaze, and/or head orientation. Commonly, head orientation is intrinsically linked with visual gaze estimation, since the perceived gaze direction is dictated by the orientation of the head [5]. Therefore, reliable estimation of both torso and head pose, as forms of nonverbal communication, support the derivation of the focus of attention, a key variable in the analysis of human behaviour in human-robot interaction paradigms encompassing social aspects. The main challenge of visual pose estimation relates to the method's robustness and invariance in scene- and image-changing factors. Namely non-uniform illumination, background clutter, diversity in human appearance, shape and expression, as well as occlusions are some of the factors which set the problem as non-trivial and a large body of research deals with the problem of body and head pose extraction and tracking [6,7]. The emergence of low cost real-time depth cameras, such as the Kinect^{TM} sensor [8], led to numerous important approaches to the pose extraction and tracking problems for body [9,10] and face [11,12], significantly pushing forward the state of the art. Despite the fact that most of the contemporary approaches perform well in usual cases, when dealing with complex, realistic interaction scenarios involving multiple users, limiting factors appear, affecting the overall effectiveness. One such drawback is the inherent requirement for an initialization period, either explicitly, demanding a specific predefined pose(e.g. [13]) or implicitly, by registering and tracking the user over a time-window(e.g. [10]). Additionally, the anthropometric and kinematic inconsistencies encountered in many of the non-model-based approaches, results to erroneous pose extraction and, thus, may severely deteriorate performance. Even more importantly, a serious limitation of most of the state-of-the-art approaches, is the poor capability to cope with instances of severe occlusions, and hence the inferior performance in such cases. Although some works have attempted to address self-imposed occlusions [14], coping with inter-person occlusions remains problematic. With respect to face pose estimation, methods can be distinguished in appearance and feature-based using 2D images, depth data or combination of both. Appearance-based methods depend on a time-consuming training phase (e.g. [11]), and most feature-based methods are limited by the requirement to define pose-dependent features (e.g. [15]).

The objective of our work is to extract accurate pose-related information from body and face in realistic complex scenarios in the presence of occlusions. Towards this goal, we have developed a model-based approach to overcome key limitations in free-form interaction scenarios under the assumption that no initialization phase is possible and that the pose recovery and tracking should remain unaffected from partial intra- and inter-person occlusions. The proposed approach utilizes information from RGB-D sequences and it builds up on the concept of *Top View Re-projection* (TVR), initially introduced for the case of torso in [16], and further extended to uniformly treat the respective body parts, modelled as cylinders (Sect. 2). An appropriate metric (Sect. 2.2) is associated with

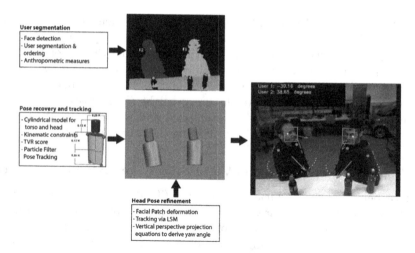

Fig. 1. Overview of the torso and head pose recovery methodology. The first step concerns the user segmentation and depth-based ordering, the second step the pose recovery and tracking and the third step the head pose refinement.

each assumed pose, and pose estimation for torso and head is derived through local minimization. For each body part a number of pose hypotheses is sampled from its configuration space. Each of the pose hypotheses is evaluated against the TVR scoring function and the hypothesis with the best score yields for the assumed pose and the location of the joints. The overall framework for torso and face pose recovery based on the aforementioned TVR scoring function and the sampling/update of pose hypotheses of each body part is discussed in Sect. 3 and illustrated in Fig. 1. Besides, a refinement step on head pose is applied based on tracking facial patch deformations via grey-level minimization (Sect. 3.1) to account for the horizontal off-plane rotation. The implemented method forms one of the core components of a vision system integrated in a robotic platform that supports socially appropriate, multi-party, multimodal interaction in a bartending scenario. Results in the laboratory as well as in the robot's environment during real human-robot interaction experiments with varying number of users (Sect. 4) attest for the effectiveness of our approach.

2 Cylindrical Modeling and Scoring

The torso and head parts of the human body are represented as cylinders with an underlying kinematic model (Fig. 1). The torso is modeled with an elliptic cylinder whereas the head with circular cylinder. The two cylindrical body parts are connected via the spherical joint of the neck featuring three Degrees of Freedom (DoF) and the remaining joints, namely the two shoulders and the two hips are derived from the elliptic cylinder of the torso.

The employed model is used to constrain the workspace of each body part via linear and angular limits and distinguish between valid and invalid poses.

Additionally, the cylindrical modeling of the body parts benefits from the TVR property, explained in Sect. 2.1, and greatly facilitates its application for torso and head pose recovery and tracking. To dynamically infer the size of each body part and the location of joints, we use established anthropometric measurements for the human body [17]. Assuming an adult human, individual body part sizes can be expressed proportionally to the user's height H, as illustrated in Fig. 1. The model has been experimentally established and is able to handle proportional variations among users without affecting the overall performance.

2.1   Top View Reprojection (TVR) Property for Cylindrical Objects

The idea behind the *Top View Re-projection* (TVR) stems from the natural observation that the visible area of any object, i.e. it's projection on an image plane, varies according to the point of view of the camera and becomes minimum at certain views, depending on the object's shape. This is quantitatively formulated by introducing the *reprojection ratio* f_{reproj} of an object, namely the ratio of the number of reprojected (visible) points N_{Pr} to the total number of 3D points of the object N_{3D}

$$f_{reproj} = \frac{N_{Pr}}{N_{3D}} \tag{1}$$

Interestingly, in the case of pure (simulated) cylindrical objects, the reprojection ratio has a single minimum when the view axis of the camera is aligned to the major axis of the object, namely the object's *Top View*, introduced in [16], to estimate the torso pose using as input the user's point cloud. The Top View minimum ratio property of cylindrical objects can therefore be exploited to derive the pose of individual human body parts, assuming cylinder-based modeling.

2.2   TVR Scoring Function

As explained above, in the case of simulated data, f_{reproj} has a single, well defined, minimum at the object's Top View. However, in reality the extraction of pose-related information from torso and head entails greater complexity due to the following reasons. Firstly, we seek the best out of a sampled set of hypothesized 3D cylinders, namely the one that is best aligned to the point cloud of the segmented body part and for which the reprojection ratio becomes minimum. In this aspect hypotheses with small number of points and therefore small values in the reprojection ratio may be favored although they do not align to the observation. Occlusions may also affect the overall performance, namely alter the ratio's behavior -by creating several local minima, valleys and plateaux or even by shifting the global minimum. Moreover, collisions across different users should also be taken into consideration, thus penalizing or exempting collided hypotheses. Consequently, the formulation of a generic scoring function, aiming to select the best hypothesis, must incorporate the above aspects in order to effectively cope with challenging cases of occlusions and frequent interactions among users. Towards this goal the scoring function f_{TVR} is formulated as:

$$f_{TVR} = f_{reproj} \times f_{align} \times f_{discr} \tag{2}$$

where f_{reproj} is the reprojection ratio, f_{align} represents an alignment term that penalizes misalignments between hypotheses and observation data, and f_{discr} represents a discrepancy term that compensates for erroneous minima caused by occlusions and/or collisions across body parts.

Reprojection Ratio f_{reproj}. Let a hypothesized cylinder for a specific body part, and let the 3D points from the segmented user point cloud. The reprojection ratio f_{reproj} is computed as the ratio of the number of reprojected points N_{Pr} lying inside the hypothesized cylinder to the total number of 3D points lying inside the hypothesized cylinder N_{3D} as in Fig. 2. In this way each hypothesis controls the segmentation of the respective body part via the minimum reprojection ratio property.

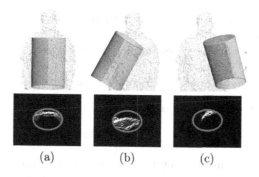

Fig. 2. Computation of f_{reproj} for three different torso pose hypotheses (top) and their corresponding top-views with the reprojected points (bottom). (a) hypothesis with the minimum score, (b) an erroneous hypothesis and (c) a misaligned hypothesis.

Alignment Term f_{align}. The alignment term coins its name to the alignment between hypothesis and actual observation. While the *reprojection ratio* remains a strong indicator for the Top View and respective body part pose, there are cases where f_{reproj} favors certain pose hypotheses due to the small number of 3D points lying inside the hypothesized 3D cylinder, although they do not align to the observation as in the example of Fig. 2 (c). The introduction of the f_{align} penalizes those hypotheses increasing low scores via the ratio of the number of 3D points visible from the physical camera viewport representing each hypothesized 3D cylinder N_{cyl} to the number of 3D points that intersect with the hypothesized cylinder N_{3D}. The former can be approximated by the cylinder's area giving rise to f_{align} being computed as:

$$f_{align} = \frac{N_{cyl}}{N_{3D}} \tag{3}$$

Discrepancy Term f_{discr}. The term f_{discr} integrates aspects of occlusions and collisions, aiming to:

    (a)   (b)   (c)   (d)   (e)

Fig. 3. Pixel characterization for a torso pose hypothesis. (a) RGB input. (b) The 3D point cloud of the scene and the hypothetical torso cylinder. (c) Side view of (b). (d) Side view, characterization of 3D points into D_{3D} (green points) and D_{all} (red points), based on the hypothesis. (e) Side view, pixels characterized as inlier pixels P_{in} (green pixels), outlier pixels P_{out} (red pixels) and occluded pixels P_{occl} (blue pixels)(Color figure online).

(a) compensate for minima caused by occlusions, by favoring occluded hypotheses which would have better score if they were not occluded.
(b) favor hypotheses with high overlapping areas between the segmented point cloud and the 3D cylinder.
(c) penalize invalid hypotheses which collide with other body parts.

f_{discr} is consequently formulated as:

$$f_{discr} = f_{occl} \times f_{coll} \times f_{ovl} \qquad (4)$$

where f_{occl} is the occlusion factor, f_{coll} is the collision factor and f_{ovl} is the overlap factor. Their computation is described below (Sect. 2.2) in detail. The estimation of f_{discr} assumes the rendering of cylinder hypotheses for which we use the ray tracing technique and the projective geometry of quadrics, described thoroughly in [16,18]. This technique is perfectly suitable for the task at hand, due to the cylindrical modeling of body parts.

Pixel Characterization and Computation of Scoring Factors. The 3D rendering generates the depth map of the hypothetical 3D cylinder D_{cyl} which, in turn, is compared against the depth map of the segmented 3D points D_{3D} of the body part hypothesis and the original acquired depth map D_{all}. The later, D_{all}, is used to detect potential occluded pixels. Depth maps are superimposed and pixels are characterized according to Fig. 3 as:

- *Inlier pixels* P_{in}. Pixels with valid depth in D_{cyl} and in D_{3D}, for which their absolute difference is below a certain threshold T, experimentally estimated.
- *Outlier pixels* P_{out}. Pixels with valid depth in D_{cyl} but not in D_{3D} and in D_{all}.
- *Occluded pixels* P_{occl}. Pixels with valid depth in D_{cyl} and in D_{all}, for which their difference is above the threshold T.

The normalization factor f_{ovl} is taken as the ratio of the number of outlier pixels to that of inliers. f_{coll} is the percentage of collided pixels -calculated in

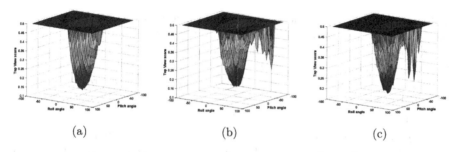

(a)   (b)   (c)

Fig. 4. Indicative graphs of f_{TVR} score under different percentages of occlusion compared to ground truth data: (a) no occlusion, (b) 30 % and (c) 60 % occlusion. The two *bottom* axes are the pitch and roll angles, namely the hypothesis configuration, and the vertical axis is the corresponding f_{TVR}.

the rendering process, as N_{coll}- and is used to penalize invalid hypotheses which collide with other body parts. Finally, the percentage of the estimated number of occluded pixels with respect to the number of 3D points of the hypothesized cylinder is used to calculate the occlusion factor f_{occl}. Accordingly, f_{occl}, f_{coll}, f_{ovl} are computed as:

$$f_{occl} = 2 - \frac{P_{occl}}{N_{D_{cyl}}}, \quad f_{coll} = 1 + \frac{N_{coll}}{N_{D_{cyl}}}, \quad f_{ovl} = 1 + \frac{P_{out}}{P_{in}} \tag{5}$$

where $N_{D_{cyl}}$ is the total number of 3D points of the hypothesized cylinder. Notice that f_{coll} and f_{ovl} are not allowed to assume zero values by the addition of the unity term, and f_{occl} assumes the $(2 - \frac{P_{occl}}{N_{D_{cyl}}})$ formula in order to favor larger values of the second term. The derived formulation of the TVR score guarantees high detection rates and accuracy, even in cases of occlusions. This is illustrated in Fig. 4, where the score of several torso pose configurations, namely different pitch and roll angles, is compared against ground truth data for different occlusion scenarios, namely 0 %, 30 % and 60 % of occlusion. *Bottom* axes represent the pitch and roll angles and the vertical axis is the corresponding TVR score for each pitch/roll configuration. More precisely, the pitch and roll axes indicate the angular distance from the ground truth which lies on the center of the bottom grid, namely at (0,0). As observed, f_{TVR} maintains the global minimum property and despite the fact that in the cases of occluded torso the function's behavior is altered with the appearance of local minima, indicating a torso configuration coinciding to the actual ground truth.

3   Torso and Face Pose Estimation Framework

Figure 1 depicted the three main steps of the pose recovery methodology, initiating from a user-segmentation and ordering step to the main pose recovery and tracking part. At the final stage the head pose is refined with respect to horizontal off-plane rotation. The *User segmentation* step is used to detect all users in the scene and segment their corresponding point clouds. This step is based

on the detection of human heads and is implemented as in [16]. As a byproduct it also encompasses the estimation of a set of anthropometric measures for
each segmented user, based on the height of each user. The *Pose recovery and
tracking* step utilizes the *TVR scoring function* for each body part examined in
a top-to-bottom order, starting from the head to recover their respective pose.
Individual poses are tracked by a separate Particle Filter (PF), consisting of
three steps:

- *Hypothesis sampling*. At each iteration, a set of valid pose hypotheses is generated for the corresponding body part from the kinematic model (Sect. 2),
  respecting at the same time established anthropometric constraints.
- *Hypothesis evaluation*. Generated hypotheses are evaluated based on the *TVR*
  scoring function.
- *Hypothesis update*. The N-best hypotheses with lowest f_{TVR} are used to
  extract the current part pose and are propagated to the next sampling step.

The *Head Pose refinement* step is further used to estimate the horizontal off-
plane rotation (yaw angle) via grey-level minimization of the facial mask and
incorporate it in the final head pose result.

3.1 Head Pose Refinement

The head is modeled with a circular cylinder instead of an elliptical, since the
depth variations exhibited by the facial features at distances from the camera
of 1 m and beyond are small. Therefore, within the model-based framework we
are able to estimate the 3D position of the head as well as the pitch and roll
angles. For the subsequent estimation of the yaw angle, namely the horizontal
off-plane rotation we utilize an additional step based on greyscale information
from Kinect sensor. Extracted facial blobs are fed to a Least-Squares Matching
(LSM) module which is used to derive differential rotations via facial patch
deformations across image frames as in [19,20]. Horizontal off-plane rotations
of the head mainly deform the facial patch in x-shift and x-scale and using
the transformation equations of the vertical perspective projection, described
thoroughly in [19,20] we are able to compute the respective rotation angle. In
Fig. 5, p_x denotes the "initial" patch width and p'_x is the "deformed" patch
width in two consecutive image frames (middle and right image of Fig. 5). At
the occurrence of an off-plane rotation around the y-axis, the facial patch shifts to
a new position and deforms to a patch of smaller x-scale with $p'_x < p_x$. x_1 and x'_1
are the minimum and maximum x image coordinates of "initial" patch, assuming
frontal view of the face with respect to the camera, such that $p_x = |x'_1 - x_1|$.
Similarly x_2 and x'_2 are the minimum and maximum x image coordinates of the
"deformed" patch, such that $p'_x = |x'_2 - x_2|$.

  To compute the rotation angle, we utilize a spherical coordinate system
(R, ϕ, λ) and the mapping equations of the vertical perspective projection given
by the transformation equations

$$x = k'\cos\phi \cdot \sin(\lambda - \lambda_0)$$
$$y = k'[\cos\phi_1 \cdot \sin\phi - \sin\phi_1 \cdot \cos\phi \cdot \cos(\lambda - \lambda_0)] \tag{6}$$

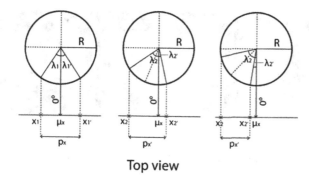

Top view

Fig. 5. Computation of head off-plane rotation around the y-axis.

where (ϕ_1, λ_0) are the coordinates of the projection center and origin and P is the distance of the point of perspective in units of sphere radii

$$k' = (P - 1)/(P - cosc) \tag{7}$$

and

$$cosc = sin\phi_1 \cdot sin\phi + cos\phi_1 \cdot cos\phi \cdot cos(\lambda - \lambda_0) \tag{8}$$

We compute the horizontal angle λ from $\lambda_0 = 0°$ with $\phi = 0°$ and $\phi_1 = 0°$. Accordingly (6) reduces to

$$x = k' sin(\lambda) \tag{9}$$

and the horizontal rotation λ_h from μ_x position is computed according to (10) and (11).

$$\lambda_2 = \arcsin(\frac{x_2 - \mu_x}{k'})$$
$$\lambda_2' = \arcsin(\frac{x_2' - \mu_x}{k'}) \tag{10}$$

$$\lambda_h = \frac{\lambda_2 + \lambda_2'}{2} \tag{11}$$

4   Experimental Results

4.1   Evaluation in Realistic Environments

To evaluate the performance of the proposed approach, we conducted a series of experiments of varying setup and difficulty level. The experiments were conducted in various areas of an indoor environment, involving single and multiple persons, acting and interacting arbitrarily in the scene. Illustrative instances from the named experiments are presented in Fig. 6. In all cases, the algorithm was able to process the camera's input stream at a rate exceeding 23 frames per second for a single user and 15 frames per second for two users in the scene on a standard personal computer with no GPU support.

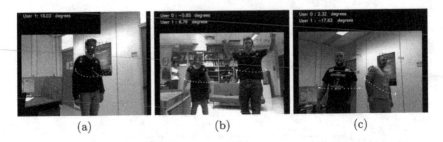

(a)   (b)   (c)

Fig. 6. Qualitative results of torso and head pose estimation in office environment.

Table 1. Confusion matrices for (a) the body and (b) the head orientation. Each matrix encodes the perceived orientations (rows) for each intended orientation (columns) in the range of (a) 0 ± 40 degrees with a step of 5 degrees and (b) 0 ± 90 degrees with a step of 10 degrees. The matrices contain data for both left and right directions.

Body Intended Orientation

Body Est. Orientation	5°	10°	15°	20°	25°	30°	35°	40°
5°	85	15	5	0	0	0	0	0
10°	10	77	8	0	0	0	0	0
15°	4	9	75	8	0	0	0	0
20°	0	0	11	80	0	0	0	0
25°	0	0	0	3	85	8	2	0
30°	0	0	0	3	9	70	9	4
35°	0	0	0	0	5	12	75	10
40°	0	0	0	0	0	8	10	90

(a)

Head Intended Orientation

Head Est. Orientation	10°	20°	30°	40°	50°	60°	70°	80°	90°
10°	100	3	0	0	0	0	0	0	0
20°	0	94	4	0	0	0	0	0	0
30°	0	3	87	2	0	0	0	0	0
40°	0	0	9	81	5	0	0	0	0
50°	0	0	0	9	78	6	5	0	0
60°	0	0	0	7	12	74	10	5	6
70°	0	0	0	0	5	17	71	10	0
80°	0	0	0	0	0	2	10	67	12
90°	0	0	0	0	0	0	5	10	65

(b)

Moreover, we performed quantitative evaluation by setting up a series of experiments, acquired in the lab. The experiments involved different users conducting several poses in various relative to the camera positions and orientations. Furthermore, to obtain ground truth information we have attached markers on the shoulders of the users (e.g. Fig. 6(a),(c)). We stored the quantitative evaluation results, derived from image sequences of 10'000 image frames in a confusion matrix (Table 1(a)) that encoded the estimated orientation around the y axis for each measured orientation in the range of 0 ± 40 degrees with a step of 5 degrees. Similarly, for the yaw angle of head orientation we quantitatively analyzed the estimated head orientations and intended head orientations in the range of 0 ± 90 degrees. For this analysis a setup was used with points of interest (POIs) placed around the user at equal angular distances of 10 degrees. The user was asked then to look and turn his head at specific POIs and the percentages were derived from image sequences of a total of 7000 image frames. The resulting confusion matrix (Table 1(b)) encoded the perceived orientation for each intended orientation. As can be easily seen, the algorithm achieves high success rates for small

Fig. 7. Illustrative frames of an actual interaction sequence in the robot bartending scenario with two users and estimation of torso and head pose results. The computed torso orientation around the y axis is shown on the upper left corner. The head yaw angle estimation via the LSM module is indicated near the deformed facial patch.

angles (user looks in directions close to the direction of the camera) which are decreased for larger angles (the user looks away from the camera). The algorithm is able to maintain significant success rates (more than 50 %) even for angles up to 90 degrees, where only a small part of the facial patch is visible.

4.2   Field Trials

The vision system has been evaluated individually as well as part of the overall robot's system during field trials and user evaluation studies. The robot hardware consists of two manipulator arms with humanoid hands mounted in a position to resemble human arms, along with an animatronic talking head. The robot is equipped with two Bumblebee stereo cameras and two Kinect sensors: one Kinect is used for the vision processing and the other for automatic speech recognition. The software architecture uses a standard three-layer structure: lowlevel components deal with modality-specific, highly detailed information such as spatial coordinates, speech-recognition hypotheses, and robot arm trajectories; the mid-level components deal with abstract, cross-modal representations of states and events; while the high-level components reason about the most abstract structures, such as knowledge and actions represented in a logical form. Interested readers may refer to [21,22] for more details on the different modules of the robot's system and on the user evaluation studies with respect to the robot's social behaviour during interaction with humans.

During field trials the users enacted variations on a drink-ordering scenario and were served by the robot. Both the torso and head pose estimation formed the basis for determining whether the user is seeking attention and wants to be served or turns its attention towards another user or object in the scene. Thus, of key importance are the orientations for both torso and head around the vertical y axis, namely the yaw angle estimation. Figure 7 shows different frames from an actual interaction sequence of 1800 frames in the robots environment (Kinect camera) with overlayed results from torso and head pose estimation. As it can be observed users feature typical bar postures, their torsos are directed towards

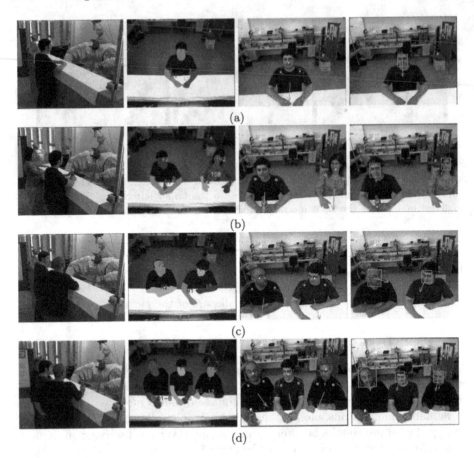

Fig. 8. Indicative frames from four different sequences (top to botttom) with varying number of users captured during evaluation of the complete system, enacting variations on the drink-ordering scenario. Images from left to right: (i) image from external camcorder, (ii) face and hand (and object in (d)) tracking results overlayed on the image, captured from a Bumblebee camera overlooking the robot's environment, (iii) torso pose and (iv) face pose estimation results both (iii) and (iv) overlayed on the RGB image of the Kinect camera.

the bar at an angle and their head orientations, exhibit more frequent motions and provide information as to whether each user looks at the other or towards the bar.

Figure 8 shows indicative results of the latest evaluation of the system, comprising of 18 enactments on the drink-ordering scenario with varying number of users. An external camcorder grabbed the complete interaction in the robot's environment with sound and image in real time and the vision output was grabbed simultaneously from the pc screen during on-line processing. Four different enactments are presented with results from the face and hand classification, the torso and the head pose respectively. Hand and face classification runs of the stereo Bumblebee due to superior performance of the image quality compared to the color image of the Kinect sensor. Blobs classified as faces are marked with an "F", left hands are marked with an "L", and right hands are marked with an "R". In Fig. 8(d) additionally object detection tracking (blue bottle) is invoked based on color as with the hand and face tracking technique. The 3D position of the face blobs is projected on the Kinect for the subsequent estimation of torso and head pose. Robust computation of torso and head pose initiated interaction without delays and the robot was able to respond to an attention bid in less than 1 ms.

5   Conclusions

We have presented a model-based approach for torso and head pose estimation to overcome key limitations in free-form interaction scenarios and issues of partial intra- and inter-person occlusions. This has been achieved by the introduction and formulation of the *Top View Reprojection* (TVR) concept, competent at treating the torso and head body parts in a unified manner. The overall approach forms one of the core component of a vision system integrated in a robotic platform that supports socially appropriate, multi-party, multimodal interaction in a bartending scenario. Results from field trials and user evaluation studies have confirmed its effectiveness and robustness in different drink-ordering scenarios; the presented results are also backed-up by long lasting videos featuring complex interaction scenes with multiple users.

Our planned future work addresses the study of more complex and involved interactions among users, including occlusions with longer durations, a case that challenges most contemporary approaches to pose-recovery.

Acknowledgments. This work was partially supported by the European Commission under contract number FP7-270435 (JAMES project).

References

1. Baltzakis, H., Trahanias, P.: Hybrid mobile robot localization using switching state-space models. In: Proceedings of IEEE International Conference on Robotics and Automation (ICRA), pp. 366–373 (2002)
2. Tsonis, V.S., Chandrinos, K.V., Trahanias, P.E.: Landmark-based navigation using projective invariants. In: Proceedings of IEEE/RSJ International Conference on Intelligent Robots and Systems (IROS), pp. 342–347 (1998)
3. Baltzakis, H., Argyros, A.A., Lourakis, M.I.A., Trahanias, P.: Tracking of human hands and faces through probabilistic fusion of multiple visual cues. In: Gasteratos, A., Vincze, M., Tsotsos, J.K. (eds.) ICVS 2008. LNCS, vol. 5008, pp. 33–42. Springer, Heidelberg (2008)
4. Sigalas, M., Baltzakis, H., Trahanias, P.: Gesture recognition based on arm tracking for human-robot interaction. In: Proceedings of IEEE/RSJ International Conference on Intelligent Robots and Systems (IROS), pp. 5424–5429 (2010)

5. Langton, S.R., Honeyman, H., Tessler, E.: The influence of head contour and nose angle on the perception of eye-gaze direction. Percept. Psychophysics **66**(5), 752–771 (2004)
6. Moeslund, T.B., Hilton, A., Kruger, V., Sigal, L. (eds.): Visual Analysis of Humans - Looking at People. Springer, London (2011)
7. Murphy-Chutorian, E., Trivedi, M.: Head pose estimation in computer vision: a survey. IEEE Trans. Pattern Anal. Mach. Intell. **31**, 607–626 (2009)
8. Microsoft kinect for xbox 360
9. Escalera, S.: Human behavior analysis from depth maps. In: Perales, F.J., Fisher, R.B., Moeslund, T.B. (eds.) AMDO 2012. LNCS, vol. 7378, pp. 282–292. Springer, Heidelberg (2012)
10. Shotton, J., et al.: Efficient human pose estimation from single depth images. IEEE Trans. Pattern Anal. Mach. Intell. **35**, 2821–2840 (2013)
11. Fanelli, G., Gall, J., Gool, L.V.: Real time head pose estimation with random regression forests. In: Proceedings on Computer Vision and Pattern Recognition (CVPR), pp. 617–624 (2011)
12. Cai, Q., Gallup, D., Zhang, C., Zhang, Z.: 3d deformable face tracking with a commodity depth camera. In: Proceedings of the 11th European Conference on Computer Vision: Part III. ECCV 2010, pp. 229–242. Springer-Verlag, Heidelberg (2010)
13. Zhu, Y., Fujimura, K.: Constrained optimization for human pose estimation from depth sequences. In: Yagi, Y., Kang, S.B., Kweon, I.S., Zha, H. (eds.) ACCV 2007, Part I. LNCS, vol. 4843, pp. 408–418. Springer, Heidelberg (2007)
14. Ye, M., Wang, X., Yang, R., Ren, L., Pollefeys, M.: Accurate 3d pose estimation from a single depth image. In: IEEE International Conference on Computer Vision (ICCV), pp. 731–738 (2011)
15. Yang, R., Zhang, Z.: Model-based head pose tracking with stereovision. In: Proceedings of IEEE International Conference on Automatic Face and Gesture Recognition, pp. 255–260 (2001)
16. Sigalas, M., Pateraki, M., Trahanias, P.: Robust articulated upper body pose tracking under severe occlusions. In: Proceedings of IEEE/RSJ International Conference on Intelligent Robots and Systems (IROS), pp. 4104–4111 (2014)
17. NASA: Man-systems integration standards - revision b (1995)
18. Stenger, B., Thayananthan, A., Torr, P.H., Cipolla, R.: Model-based hand tracking using a hierarchical bayesian filter. IEEE Trans. Pattern Anal. Mach. Intell. **28**, 1372–1384 (2006)
19. Pateraki, M., Baltzakis, H., Trahanias, P.: Visual estimation of pointed targets for robot guidance via fusion of face pose and hand orientation. Comput. Vision Image Underst. **120**, 1–13 (2014)
20. Pateraki, M., Baltzakis, H., Trahanias, P.: Using dempster's rule of combination to robustly estimate pointed targets. In: IEEE International Conference on Robotics and Automation (ICRA), pp. 1218–1225 (2012)
21. Giuliani, M., et al.: Comparing task-based and socially intelligent behaviour in a robot bartender. In: Proceedings of the 15th ACM on International Conference on Multimodal Interaction (ICMI), pp. 263–270, New York (2013)
22. Foster, M., et al.: Two people walk into a bar: dynamic multi-party social interaction with a robot agent. In: Proceedings of the 14th ACM International Conference on Multimodal Interaction (ICMI), pp. 3–10 (2012)

Vision Systems Applications

Efficient Media Retrieval
from Non-Cooperative Queries

Kevin Shih[1]([✉]), Wei Di[2], Vignesh Jagadeesh[2], and Robinson Piramuthu[2]

[1] Department of Computer Science, University of Illinois
at Urbana-Champaign, Urbana, IL, USA
kjshih2@illinois.edu
[2] EBay Research Labs, 2065 Hamilton Ave., San Jose, CA, USA
{wedi,vjagadeesh,rpiramuthu}@ebay.com

Abstract. Text is ubiquitous in the artificial world and easily attainable when it comes to book title and author names. Using the images from the book cover set from the Stanford Mobile Visual Search dataset and additional book covers and metadata from openlibrary.org, we construct a large scale book cover retrieval dataset, complete with 100 K distractor covers and title and author strings for each.

Because our query images are poorly conditioned for clean text extraction, we propose a method for extracting a matching noisy and erroneous OCR readings and matching it against clean author and book title strings in a standard document look-up problem setup. Finally, we demonstrate how to use this text-matching as a feature in conjunction with popular retrieval features such as VLAD using a simple learning setup to achieve significant improvements in retrieval accuracy over that of either VLAD or the text alone.

Keywords: Large scale · Media retrieval · Text

1 Introduction

Large-scale image-based product look-up is an increasingly sought after feature as more people begin to make financial transactions through their mobile devices. In order for such a feature to be practical, not only must it be accurate, but also able to return results within a matter of seconds for huge databases. The type of methods that best fit this bill are generally built around Bag-of-Words features as they are compatible with hash tables and approximate nearest neighbor approaches. In this work, we attempt to use text recognition techniques to treat image retrieval as an actual text document look-up problem.

In this work, we focus on the book cover based image retrieval. As is the case for many artificial products, there is a significant amount of informative textual information on almost every cover that would be extremely beneficial in the retrieval process. This idea has been applied successfully in book spine look-up [18], but there is no existing study to our knowledge that tests this on

© Springer International Publishing Switzerland 2015
L. Nalpantidis et al. (Eds.): ICVS 2015, LNCS 9163, pp. 391–403, 2015.
DOI: 10.1007/978-3-319-20904-3_35

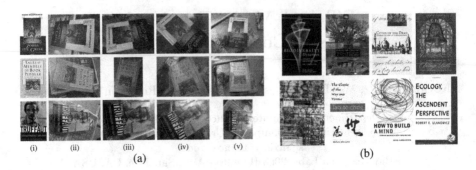

Fig. 1. (a) Samples from Stanford mobile visual search dataset [2]. Each column corresponds to pictures taken by a specific camera model: (i) Reference (ii) Canon G11 (iii) iPhone 4 (iv) Motorola Droid (v) Nokia N5800. Note the orientation, illumination, background variations. Some backgrounds include other books, which makes this a challenging task (b) Illustration of clean catalogue distractors from openlibrary.org. Using their database, we were able to extract over 100k book covers and their corresponding title and author information.

a large-scale setting. Further, unlike [18], we are interested in cases where the text is much harder to localize, such as mobile snapshots taken from suboptimal angles and lighting conditions.

Recognizing the dearth of large-scale book cover retrieval datasets with text annotations, we create our own for this work. Using an existing retrieval dataset [2] comprising mobile snapshots of book covers, we augment it with more than 100 K additional distractor book cover images to emulate a large-scale use case. We then provide textual book cover and author information for all book covers, including for the distractors, which is not only readily available but also extremely helpful in the retrieval task as we will demonstrate.

In addition to providing a large-scale text-augmented dataset, we look at how to robustly use text in cluttered and poorly oriented images to match against clean text annotations. While there is extensive work in detecting text in natural images, many have focused on performing well in popular datasets such as ICDAR '11 [15], which feature mostly horizontal images. In our particular case of mobile book cover images, we expect text to appear at random orientations and viewing angles, as well as to have occasional occlusions. Running off-the-shelf OCR software directly on the image will generally yield no useful output as software such as Tesseract generally assumes text to be horizontal and well aligned. Using OCR software in conjunction with state-of-the-art text localization methods, we still expect the results to be riddled with transcription errors due to the awkward viewing angles, thereby ruling out any matching technique that relies on full words. In our work, we demonstrate a method to robustly extract and use noisy and erroneous chunks of text from such images to match with clean text strings using methods based on approximate string matching.

Finally, we present a clean SVM-based formulation for combining multiple ranking signals such as text with popular retrieval features such as VLAD [7].

While the parameters for combining the signals can be easily determined with grid search, our use of rankSVM [8] performs just as well and is straightforward to extend to any additional set of features.

The beauty of our approach is the simplicity to tackle the useful and practical real-world problem of media retrieval. This is a big challenge in commerce applications for non-cooperative queries, especially when mobile devices like smartphones are used.

In summary, our contributions are

- creating a large dataset for book cover retrieval based on the existing SMVS dataset, adding an additional 100 K distractors complete with author and title text strings for each (distractors and queries).
- demonstrating a simple technique for applying text-based document lookup to any image containing text, as long as short word fragments can be retrieved with OCR.
- demonstrating the diversity in signal introduced by a text-based feature and argue that it should be used in conjunction with common visual features when possible for significant improvement.
- seamless integration of multiple techniques using rankSVM

2   Related Work

Popular datasets for image retrieval settings consist of a set of query images and their ground truth, however the set of query images are typically too small to emulate a large-scale setting. For large scale testing, millions of distractor images are usually added to the dataset. However, most of the current available datasets contain only natural scene images such as the INRIA holiday dataset [6], Oxford buildings [14], and Zurich Building [16].

One notable product-retrieval dataset which we use to build our own is the Stanford Mobile Visual Search dataset (SMVS) proposed by Chandrasekhar *et al.* [2]. This dataset contains smart-phone images of various products, CD covers, book covers and outdoor landmarks. For books, the reference images are clean catalogue images obtained from the product sites. The query images were taken indoors under varied lighting conditions with cluttered backgrounds. While the query images depict a realistic scenario of product queries taken by the average smart-phone wielding consumer, the dataset itself still lacks in both scale as well as relevant textual annotations that we will be exploiting in this work. In Sect. 3.1, we describe how we augment the book cover portion of this dataset to better emulate real-world product look-up scenarios.

On the whole, literature on large-scale product retrieval, especially book covers, has been quite limited. One of the few relevant works is Matsushita *et al.* [12] which introduces an interactive bookshelf system. The system includes cameras that can take pictures when a book is being stored or removed from the shelf, and uses the standard Speeded Up Robust Features (SURF) [1] feature to match the book to database, which obtain invariance to scale, illumination change, occlusion and rotation. However, the performance of such systems is not satisfactory as the exclusive use of such local image features as SURF, which are developed primarily for natural/wholistic images, does not leverage the rich text information [18] available in nearly every image instance. Other available studies on book products focus on recognizing books on shelves [3,18]. However, these approaches focus on book-spines which have easily localizable vertical text. Further, we are not aware of any large-scale extensions of these works.

3   Method

We describe a framework for book cover look-up given a potentially poorly angled, lit, and focused query image. Example queries can be seen in Fig. 1(a). The query image is a mobile photo of a book taken from various angles and orientations with significant background clutter. Given a query image, we wish to quickly retrieve the corresponding clean catalogue image from a database.

Our proposed algorithm has two main steps. We first rank our retrieval results using an ensemble of several BoW features (Sects. 3.2 and 3.3), as these can be matched quickly and are robust to various distortions. We learn the combining weights using a rankSVM [8] based formulation. Next, we select a cutoff point in the ranking with sufficiently high recall and perform more expensive linear-time template matching on the top results (Sect. 3.3).

3.1   Dataset

We apply our method on book cover queries provided by Stanford Mobile Visual Search dataset [2]. For book covers, this dataset provides up to 4 queries from different mobile devices for 101 book titles, resulting in a total of 404 queries. To demonstrate the benefit of text-based features in product look-up, we added additional annotations in the form of title and author names for each book cover. Further, we created a distractor set of 104,132 additional distractor images taken from openlibrary.org to emulate large databases, each with title and author information (when available). The distractor set was pruned for possible duplicates with the original 101 titles. To our knowledge, this is the first large-scale book cover retrieval dataset to contain author and title text annotation for every single image. The augmented text annotations and distractor images will be released to public for other researchers to test on.

3.2   Ranking Features

We discuss the BoW features we use to rank catalogue images in a database, given a query. As previously mentioned, we use BoW features as they can be quickly used to generate feature vectors and are compatible with many fast look-up algorithms such as approximate nearest-neighbors. In this work, we focus on the use of VLAD [7] and our proposed method of extracting textual N-grams from images. Because the two methods differ significantly in the types of mistakes they make, a hybrid ranking should be able to perform noticeably better than either alone.

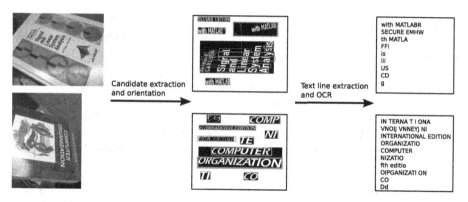

Fig. 2. Two examples of text being extracted from adversarial mobile queries. Given a query image, blocks of text are first identified and oriented using a radon-transform based heuristic. Then we identify roughly co-linear characters as lines and feed them through Tesseract OCR to obtain text output. The entire set of extracted text from the image will be treated as a text document in a standard document look-up problem to match against strings of author and book title annotations. The shown text and detection outputs are only a subset of the actual output on the presented images.

VLAD. To construct the Vector of Locally Aggregated Descriptors (VLAD) [7], we first densely extract SURF descriptors, and cluster them using k-means with $k = 256$ to generate the vocabulary. When distractors are used, we use a subset of 15 k distractor images to learn the dictionary, otherwise we use only the 101 ground truth catalogue images. The similarity metric is based on the L2 distance between normalized VLAD descriptors.

OCR Localizing Oriented Text. Performing OCR on non-cooperative queries is especially challenging – lines of text can be oriented any which way, appear in any location, and vary significantly in font size and style within the same image. Further, specularities and distortions can block out important characters and text appearing in the background can contribute significant noise. Here, we propose a robust pipeline for matching text information given such adversarial conditions.

We first use [4] to extract clusters of text in the form of binary masks. Unlike most available text localization methods, this extracts text in an orientation-agnostic manner rather than assuming horizontal alignment.

Next, we need to re-orient the text so that we can extract independent lines. We orient the text clusters to horizontal alignment via projection analysis. We compute a radon transform and select the angle of the line with the least projected area. The assumption behind this is that lines of text will be longer than they are tall. This also works for clusters with multiple lines, but occasionally fails for tall and slim blocks of text. One such failed case can be seen in Fig. 2.

To extract individual lines of text, we use simple clustering of proximal characters. Our goal is to achieve as high recall as possible, without regard to overalapping duplicates and false positives. Initially, we identify MSER [11] regions as potential characters within the segmented image. To group character candidates into lines, we attempt to combine regions of similar height if they are adjacent or if their bases have a close y value. We rule out unrealistic line candidates based on aspect ratio (length/width > 15).

Finally, we crop out the lines of text and feed them through Tesseract OCR [17] to extract text. Because the oriented text lines could be upside down, we also feed in the 180 degree rotated version of each cropped line to obtain a separate output. We find that Tesseract works best with pre-localized text lines as its internal text localization isn't robust enough to handle unoriented input.

Extracting Tokens. Because we expect the OCR output to be very noisy and corrupted, we propose to match character N-grams as opposed to entire words. Character N-grams are commonly used as a low-computation and low memory solution to approximate string-matching [13]. To do this, we run a sliding window of size N across each word with sufficient length and ignore non-alphabets. For a 3-gram example, the phrase, "I like turtles" would be broken down into "lik," "ike," "tur," "urt," "rtl," "tle," "les." The benefit of this method is that we can still achieve a match as long as OCR is able to correctly return a sequence of at least 3 characters in a row. For simplicity, we also ignore case by converting everything to lowercase.

Efficient Matching. In our dataset, we assume each book cover to be annotated with book title and author information. This information allows us to use a text-based document retrieval approach.

As is common in document retrieval, we retrieve our documents by taking the inner product of tf-idf [10] weighted normalized histogram of N-grams. This normalized inner product can be computed very efficiently using inverted file indexing, and can be trivially converted to a normalized euclidean distance.

Let f be the un-normalized histogram of N-grams for each document. We compute similarity score using normalized histograms of query and document, $N_2(N_1(f)^T \gamma)$ and $N_2(N_2(f)^T \gamma)$ respectively, where N_1 and N_2 are functions for computing L1 and L2 normalization respectively. The vector γ is the vector of idf-weights. For each unique N-gram g, we compute its corresponding idf weight as $\gamma(g) = \ln \frac{|D|}{|d \in D : g \in d|}$: the natural log of the number of documents in the database divided by the number containing the N-gram g. We found that the choice of pre-idf weighting normalization matters little, but that the final normalization should be L2 as we are using euclidean distances.

Robustness to False Positives. Due to the nature of our inner-product based matching mechanism, we are able to have our OCR pipeline focus more on recall and to disregard the existence of the false positives. As can be seen in some of the example output in Fig. 2, many false positives will appear as either single characters or improbable character sequences due to accidental recognition on background patches or our consideration of 180 degree rotated text lines.

The improbable sequences will have little effect on the matching as said sequences will rarely occur in the retrieval set. The single character false positives will be completely ignored by setting a sufficiently large N-gram length.

Runtime. While our code is not fully optimized for speed, the main components of our OCR pipeline are fairly efficient and very easily parallelizable. This aspect is important for commercial search systems where query times should not exceed a couple of seconds. Our main bottleneck is the extraction of multiple text candidates from each query image. While fairly clean images will finish in 2-3 s, images with many blob-like regions will trigger large amounts of false positives, each of which will need to be independently run through Tesseract and may take up to 30 s total in our unoptimized setup. Further, while it is clear that independent calls to Tesseract can be run in parallel, which we have implemented, the runtime will then be lower-bounded by that of a single call to Tesseract.

The matching component is implemented with an inverted file index and, when properly implemented with hash tables, will compute all inner products with all 101 book titles in less than a second per query.

3.3   Re-Ranking

We define the vector $\Phi(x,y) = [S_1(x,y)\ S_2(x,y)\ \cdots\ S_M(x,y)]^T$, where each $S(x,y)$ represents a similarity measure from any feature type such as VLAD or OCR between query image x and reference image y. We wish to learn an optimal weighting for $\Phi(x,y)$ for the purposes of ranking and retrieval.

While the weighting can be easily determined through trial-and-error for two or three distance measures, we formulate the problem as a more scalable learning problem. Specifically we optimize the following objective:

$$arg\,min_{\boldsymbol{w}}\frac{1}{2}\boldsymbol{w}^T\boldsymbol{w} + C\sum \xi_{i,j}$$
$$\text{s.t.}\,\boldsymbol{w}^T(\Phi(x_i,y_i) - \Phi(x_i,y_j)) > 1 - \xi_{i,j}\ \forall i,j \neq i, \xi_{i,j} \geq 0\ \forall i,j \tag{1}$$

Simply put, we wish to learn the optimal weighting $\boldsymbol{w}$ for our combined distance metric $\Phi(x,y)$ such that the similarity between a correct query/reference match $(i = j)$ is always greater than that of an incorrect one $(i \neq j)$. This is very similar to the objective for structured-SVMs and can be efficiently optimized using the SVMRANK package [8]. This model is referred to as the rankSVM model in later sections.

Because our dataset does not have a train/test split, we compute our final results using a simple two fold cross validation. The query set of mobile book images is split into two parts and we alternate their roles by training on one and evaluating on the other. This ensures that no query image was evaluated by a model trained on itself.

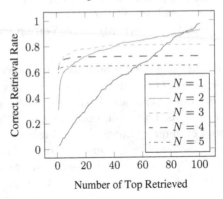

Fig. 3. Retrieval performance of N-gram character OCR at different N

RANSAC Rectification with HOG Matching. We finalize our pipeline with a brute-force RANSAC instance matching and HOG template matching based search on the top K results. If the pipeline thus far is sufficient to bring the correct result within the top K, then it may be worth it to incur a constant cost to refine the ranking using a more expensive method. To rectify matches with RANSAC, we first isolate the top K clean book cover results from the retrieval set. Then for each result, we use SURF and RANSAC to crop out and rectify the instance of the catalogue book cover in the image. Ideally this should only work if the catalogue book cover is actually contained within the image. We determine whether the extraction was a success by matching the catalogue cover image with its corresponding cropped and rectified patch from the query in HoG space. To match the HOG representation, we first resize the reference and rectified query to 256 by 256 pixels, and compute the inner product of normalized HOG representations with 8 orientations, 8 by 8 pixels per cell, and 2 by 2 cells per block.

4   Results

In the following section, we test performances of individual components of our method on our data, first without distractors, then with them in Subsect. 4.4. In our result figures, we look at how large a retrieval set needs to be grown to obtain the correct catalogue image corresponding to the mobile query image. To do this, we plot the fraction of queries that were correctly matched against the size of the retrieval set. In Table 1, we detail the exact retrieval rate of various methods at sizes 1, 5, 10, and 20. Example retrievals for select queries can be seen in Fig. 5.

4.1   OCR N-gram Size

We test the performance of OCR for the N-gram character representation using varying sizes of N in Fig. 3. We find $N = 3$ to perform best for our purposes

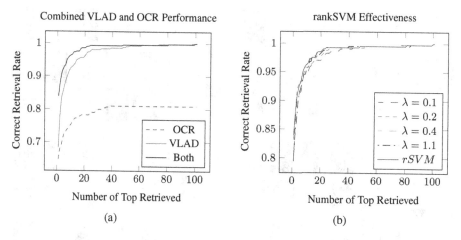

Fig. 4. Retrieval performance of combined OCR and VLAD rankings. (a) OCR and VLAD have complementary information (b) Comparison of learned rankSVM model against models with hard-coded λ values

on the annotated books dataset. Little to no additional gain in performance was observed at larger sizes N, while recall declined as expected. $N = 2$ performed reasonably with better recall than $N = 3$, but accuracy at top 1 retrievals dropped from .65 to .31. $N = 1$ was mostly noise as it had few means of dealing with the noise from our text-extraction process. However, it is worth noting that by not pruning out anything, $N = 1$ achieves near-perfect recall at the end. We use $N = 3$ (ocr-3) in all future experiments unless otherwise noted.

4.2   VLAD+OCR

First, we look at the results of combining OCR and VLAD scores with our learned weights in Fig. 4(b). Here, we compare our learned model with the model resulting from several values of a hard-coded λ. The final scores of the hard-coded

Table 1. Detailed retrieval rate values at specific points of curves as seen in other figures. ocr-N represents the OCR-only curves of gram size N. VLAD represents VLAD-only curves. rsvm refers to OCR+VLAD combined results with learned weighting. rr-K refers to the RANSAC-reranked curves based on the top K on top of rsvm results. Columns suffixed with a '-d' refer to retrieval rates with all distractor data included. The best performing values are bolded in each row (based on un-rounded value). The distractor set results are bolded separately from the rest.

retrieved	ocr-1	ocr-2	ocr-3	ocr-4	ocr-5	VLAD	rsvm	rr-5	rr-10	rr-15	rr-101	ocr-3-d	VLAD-d	rsvm-d	rr-15-d
1	0.03	0.31	0.65	0.62	0.59	0.68	0.84	0.9	0.93	**0.94**	0.92	0.31	0.18	0.6	**0.67**
5	0.09	0.6	0.73	0.7	0.65	0.87	0.93	0.93	0.96	**0.96**	0.96	0.41	0.26	0.69	**0.69**
10	0.17	0.65	0.75	0.71	0.65	0.93	0.96	0.93	0.96	**0.98**	0.96	0.46	0.31	**0.73**	0.7
20	0.31	0.72	0.78	0.72	0.65	0.96	0.99	0.93	0.96	**0.98**	0.97	0.5	0.33	**0.77**	0.71

Fig. 5. Top 5 queried results on from the dataset for each feature type in descending rank from left to right using the mobile image to the left of each 'V'. Rows starting with 'O' refer to top results ranked only with OCR-3, 'V' for only VLAD, and 'R' for rankSVM re-ranking. Note the different types of mistakes made by OCR and VLAD. The former makes mistakes based on similar words appearing in a book. The latter makes more visual pattern based mistakes.

models are $S_{VLAD} + \lambda S_{OCR}$. Our learned model results were generated with two-fold cross validation and no distractors were used in this experiment. Results show that the learned model performs comparably to the best-performing hard-coded models.

Next, we compare the performance of a combined OCR and VLAD rankSVM model to that of its individual features in Fig. 4(a). The combined model performs at least as well as the individual components, with a significant improvement in the top-1 retrieval result. In Table 1, we see that the combined model (rankSVM) has a retrieval rate of 0.84 using only the top retrieval, as compared to 0.65 and 0.68 for ocr-3 and VLAD respectively.

We visualize the top queries of each ranking feature individually in Fig. 5 to try to understand the improvement. As can be seen, OCR and VLAD make very different types of errors. Most OCR-based errors involve assigning high scores to other books with similar-sounding titles. VLAD on the other hand tends to assign higher scores to candidates with similar visual patterns. Often, the only candidate they agree on is the correct one, a pattern that is exploited by the rankSVM combined model.

4.3   Fine-Grained Reranking with RANSAC and HOG

We look at the effects of our previously described RANSAC+HOG reranking in Fig. 6(a). As this method is time consuming compared to BoW approaches, we use it to rerank the only the top K=5, 10, and 15 results. In most cases, if the

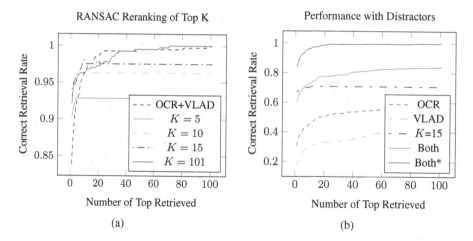

Fig. 6. (a) Retrieval performance with RANSAC reranking (b) Retrieval performance with distractors (see Fig. 1(b)). Here, Both refers to OCR+VLAD, K=15 is OCR+VLAD+ransac reranking on top 15. We include the non-distracted curve (Both*) for ease of comparison. Results were plotted up to 101 retrievals (number of non-distractor images).

ground truth falls within the top K retrievals, it will be re-ranked to the top if it isn't already assuming the RANSAC localization was successful. We also compute an expensive upper bound by re-ranking over all 101 catalogue images.

As can be seen in Fig. 6(a), the reranked result curves will flatten out due to the fixed max window size K. However, often it will flatten out even before reaching K retrievals. This is because the method does not have a 100 % success rate even when the ground truth is included in the top K. This can be easily seen in the curve for $K = 101$ in how it performs worse than that of the smaller K values.

The problem with this method can be explained by its two failure points. First, if RANSAC fails to localize, then it will be impossible for HOG to find a match. Next, because we are using raw unweighted HOG features instead of a set of trained HOG weights, the model will tend to assign high scores to highly textured candidates. While there is little that can be done about the shortcomings of RANSAC, it is likely that replacing the HOG filters with an exemplar detector such as with [9] or [5] could rectify the latter issue.

4.4 Performance with Distractors

Finally, we evaluate our methods with the presence of over 100 K distractors. We looked at how the additional distractor data affected individual feature performances, as well as with everything combined.

As with previous evaluations, we plot the retrieval rate against the size of the retrieval set in Fig. 6(b). While all aspects took a significant hit in performance, the combined performance is now significantly better than that of VLAD or

OCR alone as compared to the relatively tight gap between curves in Fig. 4(b). Finally, we once again demonstrate that with an inexpensive ransac reranking of just the top 15 retrieved candidates still yields up to 7 % improvement for the accuracy of the top 1 result as seen in the last two columns of Table 1.

Finally, we note that OCR was more robust to the effect of the added distractors than VLAD. At the top 1 retrieval, OCR dropped from 0.65 to 0.31, a difference of 0.34. VLAD on the other hand dropped from 0.68 to 0.18, a much greater drop of 0.5. This suggests that OCR can be more discriminative than VLAD overall on this specific data. Nevertheless, the fact that the combined performance is significantly better than either alone suggests that the types of mistakes they made were different enough such that combining was able to correct many of them.

5   Conclusion

We present a starting point for future research in large-scale book cover retrieval. As existing work in book cover retrieval is fairly limited and their datasets are lacking in realistically readily available author and title text annotatoions, we first augment an existing mobile-image based book cover dataset to make-up for these shortcomings. Building on the mobile book cover dataset provided by [2], we first expand it with over 100 K distractor cover images to emulate large scales, then include author and title information as a single string for each queryable cover (including the originally provided 101 covers).

Using our augmented dataset, we then demonstrated the general effectiveness of using text-based information in conjunction with other traditional BoW features such as VLAD. Because our query images are poorly conditioned and ill-suited for off-the-shelf OCR techniques, we demonstrate the use of character N-grams to robustly match against clean text annotations while using erroneous and noisy OCR output.

We recognize that many techniques we used can be easily improved upon and are far from comprehensive. However, our primary goal was to demonstrate the effectiveness of text-based information in realistic retrieval settings. Future work includes accelerating and improving the RANSAC/HOG re-ranking procedure, improving the robustness of our text-line extraction procedure, and trying new additional BoW features to further improve retrieval accuracy.

References

1. Bay, H., Tuytelaars, T., Van Gool, L.: SURF: speeded up robust features. In: Leonardis, A., Bischof, H., Pinz, A. (eds.) ECCV 2006, Part I. LNCS, vol. 3951, pp. 404–417. Springer, Heidelberg (2006)
2. Chandrasekhar, V.R., Chen, D.M., Tsai, S.S., Cheung, N.M., Chen, H., Takacs, G., Reznik, Y., Vedantham, R., Grzeszczuk, R., Bach, J., et al.: The stanford mobile visual search data set. In: Proceedings of the Second Annual ACM Conference on Multimedia Systems, pp. 117–122. ACM (2011)

3. Chen, D.M., Tsai, S.S., Girod, B., Hsu, C.H., Kim, K.H., Singh, J.P.: Building book inventories using smartphones. In: Proceedings of the International Conference on Multimedia, pp. 651–654. ACM (2010)
4. Gomez, L., Karatzas, D.: Multi-script text extraction from natural scenes. In: 2013 12th International Conference on Document Analysis and Recognition (ICDAR), pp. 467–471. IEEE (2013)
5. Hariharan, B., Malik, J., Ramanan, D.: Discriminative Decorrelation for Clustering and Classification. In: Fitzgibbon, A., Lazebnik, S., Perona, P., Sato, Y., Schmid, C. (eds.) ECCV 2012, Part IV. LNCS, vol. 7575, pp. 459–472. Springer, Heidelberg (2012)
6. Jegou, H., Douze, M., Schmid, C.: Hamming embedding and weak geometric consistency for large scale image search. In: Forsyth, D., Torr, P., Zisserman, A. (eds.) ECCV 2008, Part I. LNCS, vol. 5302, pp. 304–317. Springer, Heidelberg (2008)
7. Jégou, H., Douze, M., Schmid, C., Pérez, P.: Aggregating local descriptors into a compact image representation. In: 2010 IEEE Conference on Computer Vision and Pattern Recognition (CVPR), pp. 3304–3311. IEEE (2010)
8. Joachims, T.: Training linear svms in linear time. In: Proceedings of the 12th ACM SIGKDD International Conference on Knowledge Discovery and Data Mining, KDD 2006, pp. 217–226. ACM, New York (2006). http://doi.acm.org/10.1145/1150402.1150429
9. Malisiewicz, T., Gupta, A., Efros, A.A.: Ensemble of exemplar-svms for object detection and beyond. In: 2011 IEEE International Conference on Computer Vision (ICCV), pp. 89–96. IEEE (2011)
10. Manning, C.D., Raghavan, P., Schütze, H.: Introduction to Information Retrieval. Cambridge University Press, New York (2008)
11. Matas, J., Chum, O., Urban, M., Pajdla, T.: Robust wide baseline stereo from maximally stable extremal regions. In: British Machine Vision Conference, pp. 384–393 (2002)
12. Matsushita, K., Iwai, D., Sato, K.: Interactive bookshelf surface for in situ book searching and storing support. In: Proceedings of the 2nd Augmented Human International Conference, p. 2. ACM (2011)
13. Navarro, G., Baeza-yates, R., Sutinen, E., Tarhio, J.: Indexing methods for approximate string matching. IEEE Data Eng. Bull. **24**, 2001 (2000)
14. Philbin, J., Chum, O., Isard, M., Sivic, J., Zisserman, A.: Object retrieval with large vocabularies and fast spatial matching. In: 2007 IEEE Conference on Computer Vision and Pattern Recognition, CVPR 2007, pp. 1–8. IEEE (2007)
15. Shahab, A., Shafait, F., Dengel, A.: Icdar 2011 robust reading competition challenge 2: Reading text in scene images. In: 2011 International Conference on Document Analysis and Recognition (ICDAR), pp. 1491–1496. IEEE (2011)
16. Shao, H., Svoboda, T., Van Gool, L.: Zubud-zurich buildings database for image based recognition. Computer Vision Lab, Swiss Federal Institute of Technology, Switzerland, Technical report 260 (2003)
17. Smith, R.: An overview of the tesseract ocr engine. ICDAR. **7**, 629–633 (2007)
18. Tsai, S.S., Chen, D., Chen, H., Hsu, C.H., Kim, K.H., Singh, J.P., Girod, B.: Combining image and text features: a hybrid approach to mobile book spine recognition. In: Proceedings of the 19th ACM International Conference on Multimedia, MM 2011, pp. 1029–1032. ACM, New York (2011). http://doi.acm.org/10.1145/2072298.2071930

Quantifying the Effect of a Colored Glove in the 3D Tracking of a Human Hand

Konstantinos Roditakis[1] and Antonis A. Argyros[1,2]([⊠])

[1] Institute of Computer Science - FORTH, Heraklion, Greece
[2] Computer Science Department, University of Crete, Heraklion, Crete, Greece
{croditak,argyros}@ics.forth.gr

Abstract. Research in vision-based 3D hand tracking targets primarily the scenario in which a bare hand performs unconstrained motion in front of a camera system. Nevertheless, in several important application domains, augmenting the hand with color information so as to facilitate the tracking process constitutes an acceptable alternative. With this observation in mind, in this work we propose a modification of a state of the art method [12] for markerless 3D hand tracking, that takes advantage of the richer observations resulting from a colored glove. We do so by modifying the 3D hand model employed in the aforementioned hypothesize-and-test method as well as the objective function that is minimized in its optimization step. Quantitative and qualitative results obtained from a comparative evaluation of the baseline method to the proposed approach confirm that the latter achieves a remarkable increase in tracking accuracy and robustness and, at the same time, reduces drastically the associated computational costs.

1 Introduction

We are interested in the problem of tracking the 3D pose and full articulation of a human hand based on visual information acquired by an RGBD camera. The problem is interesting from a theoretical but also from a practical point of view, as its solution is valuable to a broad range of application domains. Given that human actions and intentions are manifested in the way hands move, a detailed and accurate estimation of this motion can support action interpretation and intention inference.

Clearly, the interest of the relevant research community is focused on the case of markerless tracking of the human hand(s). This is because markerless hand tracking is not invasive and poses far less restrictions to any application domain. Nevertheless, marker-based tracking is indeed useful and acceptable in many application domains. For example, in the domain of rehabilitation of patients suffering by stroke, hand motions are observed and quantified in a constrained laboratory setting. A scenario of a subject wearing a colored glove is not considered unacceptable, especially if in return, tracking accuracy and robustness is greatly improved. In other scenarios in the domain of wearable haptics research,

© Springer International Publishing Switzerland 2015
L. Nalpantidis et al. (Eds.): ICVS 2015, LNCS 9163, pp. 404–414, 2015.
DOI: 10.1007/978-3-319-20904-3_36

the hand to be tracked is anyway augmented with devices of known form and appearance that could facilitate the hand observation process.

Motivated by the above observations, in this work we are interested in quantifying the level at which a state of the art 3D hand tracking method like [12] can benefit from richer-than-markerless visual observations. To this end, we design a color glove and we modify the 3D hand model and objective function definition employed in [12] to enable the exploitation of the richer set of observations. Then, we perform extensive quantitative and qualitative experiments and a comparative evaluation of the proposed method with the baseline method of [12]. The obtained results demonstrate that the proposed approach achieves impressive performance/accuracy gains and justify fully our approach from a computer vision systems perspective. As an example, in a challenging sequence showing a normal-speed hand motion obtained at low (3 fps) frame rate, the proposed approach achieves half of the error compared to [12] by using only the 1/8th of the computational resources.

1.1 Related Work

Markerless hand articulation tracking methods can be classified [3,12] based on how candidate 3D hand poses are generated and tested against the observations. The appearance based approaches [1,9,15,16,21] generate a large set of hand configurations off-line. Visual features are extracted for each of the generated poses, resulting in a database where each pose is associated with image features. During online operation, comparable features are extracted from the acquired image(s) and searched for in the offline database. The reported solution is the stored pose that match the computed features. Model-based methods [2,3,6,12–14,18] generate hand poses, extract features and compare them to the observed ones at runtime. Typically, the 3D hand pose that best explains the available observations is estimated based on the solution of a high dimensional optimization problem.

Appearance-based methods are computationally more efficient compared to model-based ones, at the cost of having a fixed accuracy that depends on the density of sampling of the 3D hand pose space. Furthermore, they are more difficult to adapt to different problems, because changing the object to be tracked requires to generate the off-line database anew. In contrast, model-based methods can be adapted easily to different scenarios, since all that is required is a change of the model of the object to be tracked. Furthermore, accuracy improves as the computational budget increases. Despite the relatively high computational requirements of model-based methods, implementations that exploit GPGPUs have resulted in near real time performance [12]. Quite recently, a new approach to the problem has been proposed [10] based on quasi-random sampling of the parameter space.

While markerless tracking of bare hands is the more general formulation of the problem and, as such, the most interesting one, several works have dealt with the problem of marker-based tracking. In the case of some commercial systems, tracking relies on gloves augmented with sensors[1] or reflectors of infrared light[2].

---

[1] http://www.metamotion.com/hardware/motion-capture-hardware-gloves-Cyberglo ves.htm.

[2] http://www.metamotion.com/motion-capture/optical-motion-capture-1.htm.

Such systems provide accurate hand motion capture in real time, at the cost of expensive hardware that may obstruct the action of the hand. In order to alleviate these problems, researchers have tried to simplify the required hardware setup (both the glove design and the employed camera setup) by using color information. With the exception of [20], previous work in color-based hand tracking dealt with limited application domains [19] or short sequences [5]. Wang and Popovic [20] proposed an appearance-based/data-driven 3D hand pose estimation method. Their approach relies on a distinctive color pattern appearing on the glove that provides unambiguous information on the pose of the hand and, thus, turns the hand pose estimation problem into a database lookup problem. While their method is not as accurate as traditional optical motion capture methods, it requires a single camera and an inexpensive cloth glove. A similar approach has been proposed by [17] to track humanoid robotic hands.

The approach proposed in this paper shares the motivation of the method of Wang and Popovic [20]. However, instead of using color information to cast the 3D hand tracking problem as a nearest neighbour database search problem, color information is used to drive a model-based, hypothesize and test approach. Thus, the accuracy of the proposed method is not bounded by the inevitable sparse sampling of hand poses from which appearance based methods suffer and can easily be adapted to deal with different problem variants (e.g., tracking two hands as in [13]).

2   Method Description

To track the full articulation of a hand wearing a color glove, we built upon the method presented in [12], where 3D hand tracking is formulated as an optimization problem on the 26D space of hand 3D pose and articulation parameters. A hand model consists of 37 appropriately transformed geometric primitives that are connected in a kinematic structure that matches closely that of a human hand. The optimization problem seeks for the 27D hand configuration[3] that minimizes the discrepancy between hand hypotheses and hand observations in visual input acquired by an RGBD camera. The optimization minimizes an objective function that compares a hand hypothesis to hand observations. The method in [12] deals with markerless observations of the human hand. In our case, a purposefully designed colored glove provides richer and less ambiguous visual input and is expected to improve the obtained tracking results. To do so, the 3D hand model and the objective function of the optimization problem need to be designed carefully so that tracking takes advantage of the additional information.

2.1   Glove Design

The use of a color glove aims at facilitating the robust and accurate identification of specific parts of the hand. In this work, we aim to detect each finger and the palm

---

[3] The optimization space has one more dimension than the degrees of freedom of the hand model due to the quaternion representation of 3D hand orientation.

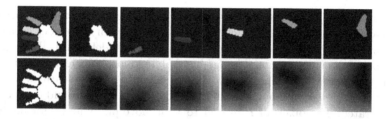

Fig. 1. Feature mapping of the segmented RGB glove image. 1st row: Segmented glove image and binary masks containing the individual hand parts. 2nd row: global foreground mask and distance transformed versions of the binary masks of the hand parts (Color figure online).

as separate parts. In this direction, the palm is assigned with white color and the pinky, ring, middle, index and thumb fingers are assigned with the easily identifiable and discriminative red, blue, yellow, green, and pink colors, respectively (see top left thumbnail in Fig. 1). By following a model-based, hypothesize-and-test tracking method, different glove colors or patterns can be used depending on the application, without requiring time-consuming learning and training processes. For example, new colors should be learned and the chromatic appearance of the 3D hand model needs to be specified. Still, this does not depend on the hand configuration, as happens with discriminative/appearance based methods that have to learn the appearance of hands in different poses anew.

2.2   Hand Model

We adopt the kinematic and geometric structure as well as the parametrization of the hand model defined in [12]. The kinematic structure of the hand is defined as a 26-DOF forward kinematics model. Six DOFs represent its global position and orientation and 20 DOFs model the articulation of the five fingers. These 26 DOFs define the parametric space S on which optimization is performed. More precisely, they translate to a total of 27 parameters due to the redundant quaternion representation of hand orientation.

As [12] considers a skin colored hand, geometric primitives are not assigned specific colors. What is important in that work is the 3D structure of the hand in its various configurations. In contrast, in the 3D hand model employed in this work we define a coloring of the relevant primitives to match the glove design.

2.3   Preprocessing

The raw input consists of an RGB image I and an accompanying depth map D, both in VGA resolution. To filter-out noise, I is first smoothed with a Gaussian kernel. To perform color classification, we employ a standard method employing a color-based Gaussian Mixture Model (GMM) [4]. Given a set of training images of the glove and their manual segmentation, we build a GMM representation of each of the glove colors. Each color is represented as a mixture of three Gaussians.

The parameters of the Gaussians and the mixture weights are estimated based on the EM algorithm. At run time, each pixel is assigned a color class label, depending on the probability that this color is drawn from each model GMM. We eliminate noisy labels from the segmented image by applying morphological filtering.

This segmentation is then employed to generate several features that are provided as observation input V to our method. First, a foreground binary mask F is generated. The pixels of F are set to 1 for glove pixels and 0 for non-glove pixels (see the bottom left image in Fig. 1). A distance map M is also generated by applying the distance transform to F. M has a value of 0 in all points that correspond to foreground points of F. All other points of M (background points of F) have a value that is equal to their distance from the closest foreground point in F. From D and F a new depth map S is computed, where only depth values of D that correspond to glove pixels in F are kept. Maps F_l, M_l and S_l are computed for each and every individual color class l belonging to the set of color/label classes L. The observation input V consists of $V = \{F, S, F_l, M_l, S_l\}$.

2.4   Hand Model Rendering

The evaluation of a hand hypothesis h requires its comparison to the observation input V. To achieve this, h needs to be transformed to features comparable with observations. This is achieved by decoding the 27D hypothesis h through graphics rendering. To shape the hand, we apply forward kinematics over the parameters of h. Given camera calibration information C, a simulated labels map and a simulated depth map D' is acquired. Theses maps correspond to the labels map and D map that result from the acquisition and preprocessing steps of the RGB-D information. Having those, it is straightforward to compute all other relevant maps. Thus, comparable features R, which result from the rendering of a hypothesis h, consist of the set $R = \{F', S', F_l', S_l'\}$.

2.5   Objective Function and its Optimization

During the optimization process, Particle Swarm Optimization (PSO) generates a set of candidate poses that need to be evaluated. An objective function E is defined that quantifies the discrepancy of a hypothesized hand pose h to the observed hand pose. Thus, the best-scoring hypothesis is the one that minimizes the objective function. The input to the objective function is the observation input features V (see Sect. 2.3) and a hand hypothesis h. As explained in Sect. 2.4, by assuming knowledge of the calibration parameters C of the employed RGBD sensor, we can transform the hand hypothesis h to features R that are comparable to observations V. The objective function $E(V, R)$ consists of the linear combination of three terms:

$$E(V, R) = w_1 K(V, R) + w_1 M(V, R) + w_2 DT(V, R). \qquad (1)$$

In the above equation, $w_1 = 0.02$ and $w_2 = 0.002$ are experimentally determined weighting factors. The term $K(V, R)$ is defined as

$$K(V, R) = \frac{\sum min(|S - S'|, T)}{\sum (F \vee F') + \epsilon} + \alpha \left(1 - \frac{2 \sum F \wedge F'}{\sum F \wedge F' + \sum F \vee F'}\right). \quad (2)$$

The term $K(V, R)$ serves two purposes, (a) penalizes depth discrepancies between the S and S' depth maps (left term) and (b) penalizes discrepancies between the F and the F' foreground masks (right term). In Eq. (2), $\alpha = 75$ is an experimentally determined normalization parameter, T is a clamp value set to $40\,mm$ and $\epsilon = 10^{-6}$ is added to avoid possible divisions by zero. In the first term of $K(V, R)$, the sum of depth differences is clamped with the predetermined threshold T, in order to prevent the influence of noisy observations. Differences are normalized over their effective areas. In the second term of $K(V, R)$, $F \vee F'$ and $F \wedge F'$ yield binary maps, which are the result of the pixel-wise disjunction and conjunction respectively, of the corresponding binary maps. Summations yield the number of foreground pixels in the resulting maps. Essentially, the second term of $K(V, R)$ represents the F1-score[4] between F and F'.

The term $M(V, R)$ is similar to $K(V, R)$, however, it considers all different hand parts (the palm and each of the five fingers) individually. For a particular label l, we define:

$$M(V, R, l) = \frac{\sum min(|S_l - S_l'|, T)}{\sum (F_l \vee F_l') + \epsilon} + \alpha \left(1 - \frac{2 \sum F_l \wedge F_l'}{\sum F_l \wedge F_l' + \sum F_l \vee F_l'}\right). \quad (3)$$

Given the above definition of $M(V, R, l)$, $M(V, R)$ is then defined as

$$M(V, R) = \frac{1}{|L|} \sum_{\forall l \in L} M(V, R, l), \quad (4)$$

where $|L|$ is the number of all labels.

The last term $DT(V, R)$ of the objective function is again dependent on each label and takes into account the distance transformed versions of the observations. We define $DT(V, R, l)$ as

$$DT(V, R, l) = \frac{1}{N_l'} \sum M_l F_l'. \quad (5)$$

The pixelwise multiplication of M_l with F_l' is zero when the space occupied by each color label in the hypothesis is exactly the same as the space it occupies in the observation. Thus, the perfect hypothesis for the location of a hand part does not introduce any penalty in this term and the objective function. The summation is normalized with the number N_l' of image points of the rendered label l. Finally, $DT(V, R)$ is defined as

$$DT(V, R) = \frac{1}{|L_o|} \sum_{\forall l \in L_o} DT(V, R, l), \quad (6)$$

where L_o is the set of observed labels.

---

[4] http://en.wikipedia.org/wiki/F1_score.

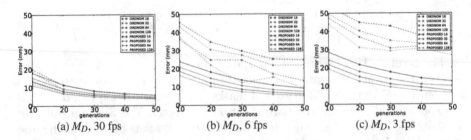

(a) M_D, 30 fps   (b) M_D, 6 fps   (c) M_D, 3 fps

Fig. 2. Median error M_D for hand pose estimation (in mm) for the proposed method (solid lines) is illustrated in comparison to that of [12] (dashed lines). In all plots the performance of different PSO budgets is shown. The synthetic sequence used represents the same hand motion sampled at(a) 30fps (b) 6 fps, (c) 3 fps.

The optimization of the resulting objective function is performed based on Particle Swarm Optimization (PSO) [7,8] as suggested in [12]. PSO is a population based stochastic optimization method that iteratively searches the optimal value of a defined objective function in a specified search space. The population (swarm) consists of particles each of which represents a candidate solution to the problem. The candidate solutions evolve in runs which are called generations, according to a policy which emulates social interaction. At the end, the candidate solution that achieved the best objective function score, through all generations, is selected as the estimated solution. The number of particles N and generations G determine the computational requirements of the optimization process, as their product defines the number of objective function evaluations. More details on the application of PSO to the problem of 3D hand tracking as well as information on the relevant tracking loop are reported in [12].

3   Experimental Evaluation

Synthetic as well as real-world sequences were used to evaluate experimentally the performance of the proposed method. In all performed experiments, we compare quantitatively and qualitatively the proposed method with the baseline [12]. To do so we utilize the same C++ code base for both methods, a fact that facilitates their fair comparison.

The quantitative evaluation of the proposed method has been performed using synthetic data. This approach for evaluation is often used in the relevant literature [6,11] because ground truth from real-world image sequences is hard to obtain. In order to synthesize realistic hand motions we first acquired a real-world sequence (30 fps, VGA resolution) with an Xtion sensor[5]. Then, we tracked this sequence using [12]. The resulting track was used to generate synthetic sequences through rendering.

To quantify the accuracy for a given optimization configuration, we adopt the metric used in [6]. For each processed frame, we compute the mean Euclidean 3D

---

[5] http://www.asus.com/Multimedia/Xtion_PRO/overview.

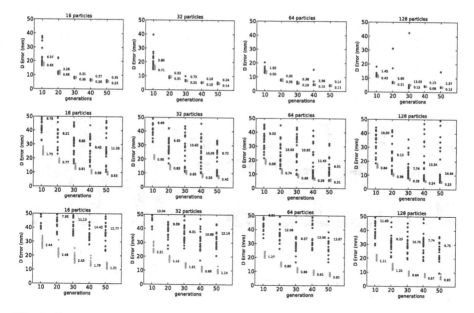

Fig. 3. Errors in hand tracking (in mm) for the proposed method (red points) in comparison to that of [12] (blue points). Each row corresponds to a different image acquisition fps. Figure columns correspond to different particle counts. Each point represents a single run. For a particular parameter set, 20 runs were performed. The number assigned to each group of points denotes the standard deviation of the error is these 20 runs (Color figure online).

distance between the estimated phalanx endpoints and their ground truth counterparts. The average of this measure for all frames constitutes the resulting error estimate D. Since the optimization is stochastic, each distinct configuration was conducted 20 times. The median M_D of the resulting $D_{i=1..20}$ errors quantifies the accuracy obtained for a particular set of particle and generations counts.

In a first experiment, we employed a synthetic dataset of 682 frames where a hand performs motions and gestures, such as finger counting, closed fist formation, palm rotations, etc. For this dataset, two variants were identified. In the first, all hand parts were assumed to be uniformly colored, so that the sequence can be fed to the method of [12]. In the second variant, hand parts were colored according to our colored glove design, so as to give rise to input that is appropriate for the proposed approach.

Figure 2(a) shows the median errors M_d for both methods, as a function of PSO parameters. Each distinct line represents a particle configuration. We observe that the proposed work marginally outperforms [12], except for results coming from low PSO budgets. Both approaches exhibit similar behaviour as the particle and generation counts increase. The increase of accuracy for configurations larger than 32 particles and 30 generations is very small compared to to the increase of the computational budget.

Individual errors D take values between $3.3\,mm$ and $18.7\,mm$ for the proposed method and between $2.9\,mm$ and $52.3\,mm$ for [12]. Moreover, as shown in the first row of plots of Fig. 3, the resulting standard deviation for low computational budgets ($N = 16$, $N = 32$ and $G = 10$), is an order of magnitude lower for the proposed method ($\sigma \simeq 0.7\,mm$) compared to that of [12] ($\sigma \simeq 6\,mm$).

Fig. 4. Snapshots from an experiment with real data. Cropped 320×240 regions from the original 640×480 images are shown. 1st row: proposed method, 2nd row: the performance of the method in [12] with the same computational budget (64 particles running for 50 generations). See text for details.

We use the same dataset but we only employ one out of each 5 frames. The resulting synthetic sequence is subject to a dual interpretation. It is either a dataset which contains a hand acting five times faster than the previous one, or a dataset with five times lower acquisition rate. Lower acquisition rates occurs either because of higher computational requirements, or when the framework is employed on weaker hardware. Moreover, in the new dataset a decrease in accuracy is expected due to larger displacement of the hands between consecutive frames.

Figure 2(b) shows the corresponding median errors obtained in the new dataset. It can be verified that the proposed method performs strikingly better compared to [12]. The performance of our method for 16 particles is better than the performance of [12] for 128 particles. This constitutes a more than 8-fold reduction of the computational time. Additionally, in the second row of Fig. 3, the obtained errors D are visualized for all 20 experiments and for different particle counts. As it can be verified, in our method errors are not only smaller in absolute terms, but the variability in performance in different runs is also very much decreased.

The third experiment is similar to experiment 2, with the difference that we temporally subsample the original dataset every 10 frames (3 fps). Figure 2(c) as well as the third row of Fig. 3 demonstrate that the difference in performance between the proposed and the baseline method is further widened, in favour of the proposed method.

Towards the qualitative evaluation of the proposed approach in real data, several long real-world image sequences were captured. Figure 4 illustrates indicative results obtained from one such sequence (690 frames) where the human hand wears the designed color glove. As it can be observed in the first row of snapshots, the estimated hand models are in very close agreement with the image data, despite the complex articulation of the performing hand and the low (3 fps) framerate. The color information was also processed to come up with a full hand segmentation so as to make the method in [12] applicable to this input. As shown in Fig. 4, 2nd row, [12] fails in this case. A video accompanying the paper[6] illustrates the obtained results.

4   Summary

The interest on markerless 3D hand tracking is unquestionable. Nevertheless, the interest in systems that perform mildly invasive, marker-based, 3D hand tracking is also undeniable. In this work we capitalized on a powerful 3D hand tracking approach and we enabled it to benefit from color information that disambiguates hand parts. We achieved this by purposefully designing a color glove and by appropriately modifying the hand model and the objective function of the baseline approach. Quantitative and qualitative experimental results demonstrate that our approach achieves dramatic accuracy improvement over the baseline (smaller errors and error variances in several runs) with a fraction of the computational resources. Future work includes the design and the evaluation of gloves tailored to specific applications, in order to minimize invasiveness and maximize accuracy, robustness and computational performance.

Acknowledgments. This work was partially supported by the EU FP7-ICT-2011-9 project WEARHAP.

References

1. Athitsos, V., Sclaroff, S.: Estimating 3D hand pose from a cluttered image. In: CVPR, pp. II-432–II-439. IEEE (2003)
2. Ballan, L., Taneja, A., Gall, J., Van Gool, L., Pollefeys, M.: Motion capture of hands in action using discriminative salient points. In: Fitzgibbon, A., Lazebnik, S., Perona, P., Sato, Y., Schmid, C. (eds.) ECCV 2012, Part VI. LNCS, vol. 7577, pp. 640–653. Springer, Heidelberg (2012)
3. de La Gorce, M., Fleet, D.J., Paragios, N.: Model-based 3D hand pose estimation from monocular video. IEEE Trans. PAMI **33**, 1–15 (2011)
4. Dempster, A.P., Laird, N.M., Rubin, D.B.: Maximum likelihood from incomplete data via the em algorithm. J. Roy. Stat. Soc. Ser. B (Methodol.) **39**(1), 1–38 (1977)
5. Dorner, B.: Chasing the colour glove: visual hand tracking. Ph.D. thesis, Simon Fraser University (1994)
6. Hamer, H., Schindler, K., Koller-Meier, E., Van Gool, L.: Tracking a hand manipulating an object. In: ICCV, pp. 1475–1482 (2009)
7. Kennedy, J., Eberhart, R.: Particle swarm optimization. In: International Conference on Neural Networks, vol. 4, pp. 1942–1948. IEEE, January 1995
8. Kennedy, J., Eberhart, R., Yuhui, S.: Swarm Intelligence. Morgan Kaufmann, San Francisco (2001)

---

[6] http://youtu.be/9nkHIgFYtzE.

9. Keskin, C., Kirac, F., Kara, Y., Akarun, L.: Real time hand pose estimation using depth sensors. In: ICCV Workshop, pp. 1228–1234 (2011)
10. Oikonomidis, I., Argyros, A.A.: Evolutionary quasi-random search for hand articulations tracking. In: IEEE CVPR, Columbus, Ohio, USA (2014)
11. Oikonomidis, I., Kyriazis, N., Argyros, A.A.: Markerless and efficient 26-DOF hand pose recovery. In: Kimmel, R., Klette, R., Sugimoto, A. (eds.) ACCV 2010, Part III. LNCS, vol. 6494, pp. 744–757. Springer, Heidelberg (2011)
12. Oikonomidis, I., Kyriazis, N., Argyros, A.A.: Efficient model-based 3d tracking of hand articulations using kinect. In: BMVC, Dundee, UK (2011)
13. Oikonomidis, I., Kyriazis, N., Argyros, A.A.: Tracking the articulated motion of two strongly interacting hands. In: CVPR, pp. 1862–1869. IEEE, June 2012
14. Rehg, J.M., Kanade, T.: Model-based tracking of self-occluding articulated objects. In: ICCV, p. 612, Los Alamitos, CA, USA. IEEE Computer Society (1995)
15. Romero, J., Kjellstrom, H., Kragic, D.: Monocular real-time 3D articulated hand pose estimation. In: IEEE-RAS International Conference on Humanoid Robots. IEEE, December 2009
16. Rosales, R., Athitsos, V., Sigal, L., Sclaroff, S.: 3D hand pose reconstruction using specialized mappings. In: ICCV (2001)
17. Schroder, M., Elbrechter, C., Maycock, J., Haschke, R., Botsch, M., Ritter, H.: Real-time hand tracking with a color glove for the actuation of anthropomorphic robot hands. In: 2012 12th IEEE-RAS International Conference on Humanoid Robots, pp. 262–269. IEEE (2012)
18. Sudderth, E.B., Mandel, M.I., Freeman, W.T., Willsky, A.S.: Visual hand tracking using nonparametric belief propagation. In: CVPR Workshop on Generative Model-based Vision (2004)
19. Theobalt, C., Albrecht, I., Haber, J., Magnor, M., Seidel, H.-P.: Pitching a baseball - tracking high-speed motion with multi-exposure images. In: Proceedings of the SIGGRAPH 2004, pp. 540–547. ACM SIGGRAPH (2004)
20. Wang, R.Y., Popović, J.: Real-time hand-tracking with a color glove. ACM Trans. Graph. **28**(3), 63:1–63:8 (2009)
21. Wu, Y., Huang, T.S.: View-independent recognition of hand postures. In: CVPR, vol. 2, pp. 88–94. IEEE (2000)

An Efficient Eye Tracking Using POMDP for Robust Human Computer Interaction

Ji Hye Rhee[1], Won Jun Sung[2], Mi Young Nam[3], Hyeran Byun[1],
and Phill Kyu Rhee[2(✉)]

[1] Department of Computer Science, Yonsei University, Seoul, South Korea
jhrhee@yonsei.com, hrbyun@cs.yonsei.ac.kr
[2] Department of Computer Science & Engineering, Inha University, Incheon,
South Korea
memorise8@gmail.com, pkrhee@inha.com
[3] YM-Naeultech, Incheon, South Korea
nammiyoung@gmail.com

Abstract. We propose an adaptive eye tracking system for robust human-computer interaction under dynamically changing environments based on the partially observable Markov Decision Process (*POMDP*). In our system, real-time eye tracking optimization is tackled using a flexible world-context model based *POMDP* approach that requires less data and time in adaptation than those of hard world-context model approaches. The challenge is to divide the huge belief space into world-context models, and to search for optimal control parameters in the current world-context model with real-time constraints. The offline learning determines multiple world-context models based on image-quality analysis over the joint space of transition, observation, reward distributions, and an approximate world-context model is balanced with the online learning over a localized horizon. The online learning is formulated as a dynamic parameter control with incomplete information under real-time constraints, and is solved by the real-time Q-learning approach. Extensive experiments conducted using realistic videos have provided us with very encouraging results.

Keywords: Eye tracking · POMDP · Real-time Q-learning · World-context model · Image-quality analysis

1 Introduction

Recently, much attention is devoted to eye tracking technology for use with Human Computer Interaction (HCI) applications. Automatic eye tracking allows unobtrusive and hands-free HCI for many potential applications, such as for smart spaces, smart TVs, mobile devices, Web usability, and advertising analyses. However, the performance requirement for most commercial applications cannot be satisfied due to cost limitations and/or technical immaturity. Therefore, low-cost eye tracking technology with easy or no initial setup is necessary for successful vision-based HCI systems. Only a small amount of research has been done with the aim of obtaining a more general eye tracking technology without complicated control situations [1]. Most eye tracking

© Springer International Publishing Switzerland 2015
L. Nalpantidis et al. (Eds.): ICVS 2015, LNCS 9163, pp. 415–423, 2015.
DOI: 10.1007/978-3-319-20904-3_37

techniques used in loosely-controlled and low-cost environments, however, are still not mature enough to be used in practical vision-based HCI applications. This is because of their intrinsic brittleness, such as varying types of illumination, viewing angle, scale, individual eye shape, and jittering [2].

Most eye tracking systems very often experience serious difficulties in guaranteeing robust performance due to the uncertainty caused by dynamically changing environments. However, if the system control parameters, such as threshold values and parameters for adjusting eye tracking are explored in accordance with dynamic changes, the performance can be optimized and guaranteed for practical use. The intuitive rationale of our eye tracking optimization framework based on POMDP [3, 4] is that it allows the agent to decide the state that represents the best system control parameters in order to optimize tracking performance while considering environmental changes. Since image-quality analysis of an input image frame cannot be perfect, the system control parameters are determined by trial and error based on past experience and domain knowledge. The agent must struggle with uncertainty from the varying environment when deciding the best system control parameters. By employing POMDP to help determine the system control parameters, the agent can decide which system control parameters are more acceptable in the current environment. Once a POMDP is formulated to solve real-world problems with large and complex search spaces, an approximation technique is employed that is either offline [10] or online [12]. POMDP applications can be found in many areas such as robot systems, human-robot interaction systems [5, 6], medical applications [7], people assisting systems [8], and dialog systems [9]. However, most POMDP algorithms exhibit intrinsic difficulties when used in real-time applications in which the search space is not sufficiently narrow.

In this paper, the optimization of an eye tracking system is formulated as a domain-specific POMDP, called the context-aware POMDP (CA-POMDP), which takes advantage of flexible world-context models by combining online and offline learning. In general, world-context models are learned from interaction history such as actions, observations, and rewards [13]. The approaches with the multiple world-context models play an important role in improving the scalability of the POMDPs. The CA-POMDP perceives the context of the current world-context model and adjusts the system control parameters in accordance with the current context, while keeping the real-time constraints. The offline learning of world-context models reduces the huge search space of a POMDP formulation, only the focused space is explored online, resulting in minimized computation overhead. The state belief space is not directly searched, but is approximated by real-time Q-learning to satisfy the real-time constraints. Image distortions are approximated using an image-quality analysis technique instead of direct analysis, and uncertainty in eye tracking is tackled using our proposed CA-POMDP framework. The proposed eye tracking system consists of the image-quality module, eye tracking algorithm, and CA-POMDP module (Fig. 1). The image-quality module perceives an image-quality label and is used to determine the system control parameters in CA-POMDP module. The agent learns world-context models offline using collected data, and processes online learning and adaptation using the real-time Q-learning approach. The eye tracking algorithm acquires the system control parameters decided by the CA-POMDP module and performs the eye tracking mission accordingly.

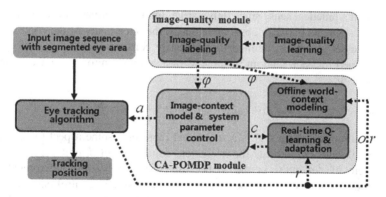

Fig. 1. Flow diagram of the proposed adaptive eye tracking system using the *CA-POMDP* framework: *a* denotes action; *o*, observation; *r*, reward; *c*, world-context model; and ϕ, image-quality label.

2 Context-Aware *POMDP*

The *CA-POMDP* is formulated as 8-tuples $\{S, A, O, T, \Omega, R, \gamma, \Phi\}$, where Φ indicates the context space. The context space is associated with factors that affect the appearance of eye image such as lighting direction, brightness, object viewing angle, and scale. The context space can be represented by image-quality measures that consider the image-capturing environment. For example, the context state can be represented by the variables, e.g., Φ_1 as lighting direction, Φ_2 as brightness, Φ_3 as object viewing angle, and Φ_4 as object scale. Assuming that these factors can be measured as discretized values, a context state φ can be represented by assigning a value to each variable Φ_j, i.e., $\varphi = \{\Phi_1 = \varphi_1, \ldots, \Phi_M = \varphi_M\}$. The state space S is defined as the system control parameter eye tracking space that is affected by varying environments. The exact estimation of the context is impossible, and thus state space S can be thought of and treated as being partially observable. Since the image-quality states are not measurable in a practical sense, they are approximated by the image-quality label ϕ'. The state space is a set of the system control space X relying on the context space Φ. That is, $S = (X|\Phi)$, where $X = \{X_1, \ldots, X_L\}$ and $\Phi = \{\Phi_1, \ldots, \Phi_M\}$, are the sets of random variables in the system control space relying on the context space. A random variable X_i indicates a threshold or an adjustment parameter in an eye tracking system. $x = \{X_1 = x_1, \ldots, X_L = x_L\}$ denotes the value of a system control parameter assigned to individual random variables. The state s in state space S is denoted by

$$s = \{(\{x_i\}_{i=1}^{L} | x_i \in D_i, \varphi \in \Phi\} \tag{1}$$

where each dimension of $s \in S$ is a scalar that represents some aspect of the agent's environment, and D_i is the discretized domain of a system control parameter X_i. Note that the agent can change the system control parameters in the eye tracking system, but it cannot change the image-quality in the context space. The image-quality is not fully measurable in a practical sense since only partial, limited information is available. Also note that the state s is partially observable due to the uncertainty of the context space.

The finite set of actions defined for each state constitutes an action space A. An action is defined for each random variable X_i in a system control space X relying on a context space Φ.

$$a = \{(\{a_i\}_{i=1}^{L} | a_i \in [-d_i, 0, +d_i], \varphi \in \Phi\} \tag{2}$$

where each dimension of $a \in A$ is a scalar that represents some aspect of the agent's action; $-d_i$, 0, and $+d_i$ indicate the decrement adjustment of d_i units, stationary, and the increment of $+d_i$ units in the X_i horizon, respectively. It is interpreted as an adjustment decision of the corresponding threshold or system control parameter.

The next state of the eye tracking algorithm is denoted by a transition probability function T that models the uncertainty. Given a current state s, context state $\varphi \in \Phi$, and action a, it indicates the probability of transit from s to a next state s'. The probability function of the state transition, $T : (S \times A \times S | \Phi) \mapsto [0, 1]$ defines a probability distribution over the next state s':

$$
\begin{aligned}
T(s, a, s' | \varphi) &= P(s_{t+1} = s' | s_t = s, a_t = a, \varphi_t \in \Phi) \\
&= P(x_{t+1} = x' | s_t = s, a_t = a, \varphi_t \in \Phi)
\end{aligned}
\tag{3}
$$

where $\sum_{s' \in S, \varphi \in \Phi} T(s, a, s' | \varphi) = 1$. The observation space O is the distribution space over the eye tracking performance and the image-quality, i.e., $O = \{\tau, \varphi\}$. Recall that τ and φ are the tracking accuracy and image-quality measures, respectively. An observation o is defined over the observation space using the observation probability function, $\Omega : S \times A \times O \mapsto [0, 1]$, as follows:

$$\Omega(s', a, o') = P(o'_\tau, o'_\varphi | o_\tau, o_\varphi, a_t = a) = P(o'_\tau | a) P(o'_\varphi | a) \tag{4}$$

where o_τ and o_φ are the observations of the tracking accuracy and image-quality measures, respectively. Reward, the immediate payoff by an action is defined as the function $R : S \times A \to \Re$ and is denoted by $r = R(s, a)$. Here, the reward function is measured based on the tracking performance, i.e., if the tracking confidence is greater than a threshold value, the high score is returned as the reward; otherwise, the low score is returned.

To the overcome huge computational requirements, CA-POMDP is approximated by taking advantage of flexible world-context models and online learning for each world-context model. The world-context models are pre-compiled over the joint space of transition, observation, and reward distributions in offline learning. The online learning is formulated as a dynamic adjustment of the system control parameters of the eye tracking algorithm under incomplete information and real-time constraints, and is solved by the real-time Q-learning approach [16]. CA-POMDP constructs the world-context models offline, and chooses the best one in accordance with the probability distributions T, Ω, and, R during execution. The online policy calculation can also be balanced by compromising between the system accuracy and the real-time constraints. CA-POMDP carries out both offline learning in the world-context space and online learning for the states relying on the current world-context model. Limiting the cardinalities of the sets S, A, O, and R, CA-POMDP allows sufficient constraints on the distributions on transition, observation, and reward. The offline learning pre-complies world-context models in the joint space defined by $CM = T \times \Omega \times R$. Similar approaches can be found in [17] but their models do not consider the context space represented by image-quality labels. Figure 2 illustrates the difference between the standard POMDP and our CA-POMDP.

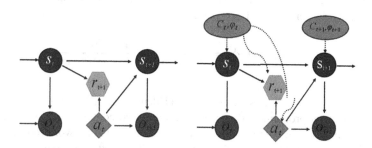

Fig. 2. (Left): Standard POMDP, (Right): CA-POMDP

While the actions are controlled by a single world-context model in a standard POMDP, the transition dynamics in CA-POMDP are affected by both the current state and the world-context model. CA-POMDP constructs multiple world-context models, each of which has a local belief space over underlying MDP. CA-POMDP assumes the Markovian property of partial observations of all the interactions with the environment.

Let random variables A, O, and R be associated with probability distributions T, Ω, and R. Let $O_1, O_2, \cdots, O_n$ be a random i.i.d. data set from Ω, $A_0, A_1, \cdots, A_{N-1}$ from T, and $R_1, R_2, \cdots, R_N$ from R. For actions $A_0 = a_0, A_1 = a_1, \cdots, A_{N-1} = a_{N-1}$, we have observations $O_1 = o_1, O_2 = o_2, \cdots, O_N = o_N$ and rewards $R_1 = r_1, R_2 = r_2, \cdots,$ $R_N = r_N$, respectively. Let the collected training data for world-context model c over CM space be denoted by $h = \{(a_0, o_1, r_1), (a_1, o_2, r_2), \ldots, (a_n, o_n, r_n)\}$. The entire training data for all world-context models are then denoted as $H = \bigcup_{c \in CM} \{h\}$. Both the world-context model and underlying states are partially observable, and the joint belief is factored as

$$b(s, c|h, \varphi) = b_c(s)b_{CM}(c|\varphi) \qquad (5)$$

where $b_c(s) = b(s|c, h)$ and is determined by the belief update. Actions are selected using some arbitrary belief $b_{CM}(c|\varphi)$ over a world-context model to maximize the expected discounted return over the local horizon. Let $b_{CM}(c)$ denote a belief over world-context model c; it can be approximated as follows [17]:

$$b_{CM}(c|\varphi) \approx w(c|\phi) = \sum w_i \delta(c_i, c, \phi) \qquad (6)$$

where $\delta(c_i, \cdot)$ is a delta function of world-context model c_i under image-quality label ϕ, and w_i indicates the weight associated with c_i. Note that context state φ is approximated by image-quality label ϕ [18] since φ is not a closed form. The belief over world-context models is determined with respect to the history of domain actions, observations, and rewards. Assuming that our transition, observation, and reward models are the case of discrete multinomials, we can use Dirichlet priors and well-known Bayesian methods to learn the distributions [19]. Given new random variables (a, o, r), the posterior is calculated over the current world-context models and the next world-context model is determined using MAP classification rule. A posterior is defined over world-context model c as follows:

$$P(c|(a,o,r), H, \phi) = \frac{p((a,o,r)|c,h,\phi)P(c|\phi)}{\sum_{c \in CM} p((a,o,r)|c,h,\phi)P(c|\phi)} \tag{7}$$

where $p((a,o,r)|c,h)$ indicates the conditional density of the current world-context model, and the prior probability $P(c)$ is the current world-context model belief $b_{CM}(c)$. Recall that h and H denote the training data set of an individual world-context model and the whole world-context models, respectively. The next world-context model for the new random variables is determined using MAP classification rule as follows:

$$\hat{c}_{MAP} = argmaxp((a,o,r)|c,h,\phi)P(c|_{c \in CM}\phi). \tag{8}$$

The consistency of the exploration strategy can be enhanced by keeping the same world-context model over some duration. The world-context model is changed based on sufficient coherence of actions, observations, and rewards over some duration of time-steps rather than an individual time-step. The current world-context model is voted using the past world-context models determined by Eq. 8, since the next coming actions cannot be observed at the time-step. That is, the world-context model at time-step t is voted using the world-context models observed at k previous time-steps.

3 Performance Measures

We adopted the real-time tracking mean [21] to evaluate online performance based on the real-time matching threshold. Here, we briefly review the real-time measure. Given image sequence $I = (I_1, \ldots, I_N)$, let x_t be the number of reference pixels on the boundary of the iris defined in frame I_i by the partial *Hough* transform in the frame I_i, and let y_t be the number of pixels detected on the iris boundary area. Let $X = (x_1, \ldots, x_N)$ and $Y = (y_1, \ldots, y_N)$. The *real time tracking mean* (RM) at time step t is defined as the local mean of successfully tracked adjacent frames between time-steps $t - u$ and $t + u$ as follows:

$$RM(X, Y, t, m) = \frac{\sum_{k=t+u}^{k=t+u} f(x_k, y_k, m)}{\sum_{k=t-u}^{k=t+u} \|x_k\|} \tag{9}$$

where u is a smoothing parameter used for visualization of the real-time tracking mean. The success of eye tracking at image frame I_t at time-step t is defined using the constraint of the real-time matching threshold m.

We created test videos of varying image qualities. Each video had approximately 1,200 image frames, and thus a total of 60 videos and approximately 48,000 image frames were used. Eight volunteers were involved in gathering video data sets, and three different types of videos; specifically, videos A, B, and C were recorded for each person.

The stability of the same world-context model over some duration provides the advantage of consistency and performance in the exploration strategy. We determined the world-context model using Eq. 8. When the look-backward parameter k is set to zero, the world-context model is determined by considering only the current world-context model. When k is to 10, the world-context model is determined by voting eleven previous world-context models, including the current one (Fig. 3).

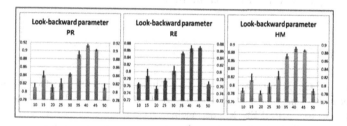

Fig. 3. Effects of different durations of looking backward (look-backward parameter) in deciding the current world-context model in terms of precision (PR), recall (RE), and harmonic mean (HM) for Q-learning parameters $\varepsilon = 0.15$, $\alpha = 0.19$, $\gamma = 0.93$, and $u = 40$

The offline eye tracking performances are shown for different world-context models in terms of precision, recall, and harmonic mean using the ground-truth tracking positions in Fig. 4. The best performances were obtained when world-context models approximately matched the properties and structure types of the various videos.

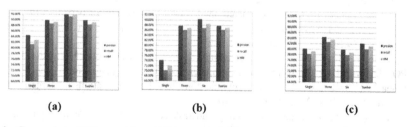

(a)   (b)   (c)

Fig. 4. Comparison of the tracking performance of different world-context models in terms of precision, recall, and harmonic mean for image sequences with various properties and structure types: (a) Video A, (b) Video B, and (c) Video C. Q-learning parameters were set to $\varepsilon = 0.15$, $\alpha = 0.19$, $\gamma = 0.93$, and $u = 40$.

Video A provides the best performance in the six world-context model. In video B, the best performance was obtained using the six world-context model. Video C has a much lower complexity than videos A and B, and gives the best performance using the three world-context model.

4 Conclusion

CA-POMDP, a novel augmented POMDP approach, CA-POMDP finds high-performing world-context models and value domains of the states under varying environments offline and optimizes the system parameters for eye tracking online by relying on the current world-context model. The offline learning of world-context models with global approximation and the online learning focused over a localized horizon balance the approximate offline value function and real-time performance. We showed empirically that our proposed method can improve eye tracking performance by searching the limited belief space and focusing on the right horizons.

References

1. Vazquez, L.J.G., Minor, M.A.: Low Cost Human Computer Interface Voluntary Eye Movement as Communication System for Disabled People with Limited Movements. In: PAHCE, pp. 165–170. IEEE, Rio de Janeiro (2011)
2. Corcoran, P.M., Nanu, F., Petrescu, S.: Real-time eye gaze tracking for gaming design and consumer electronics systems. IEEE Trans. Consum. Electron. 58(2), 347–355 (2012)
3. Barto, A.G.: Reinforcement Learning: An Introduction. MIT Press, Cambridge (1998)
4. Shani, G.: A survey of point-based POMDP solvers. Auton Agent Multi-Agent Syst 27(1), 1–51 (2012)
5. Broz, F., Nourbakhsh, I.: R., Simmons: Planning for Human-Robot Interaction in Socially Situated Tasks. International Journal of Social Robotics 5(2), 193–214 (2013)
6. Gianni, M., Kruijff, G.J.M., Pirri, F.: A stimulus-response framework for robot control. ACM Trans. Interact. Intell. Syst. 4(4), 1–41 (2015). Article 21
7. Bennett, C.C., Hauser, K.: Artificial intelligence framework for simulating clinical decision-making: a markov decision process approach. Artif. Intell. Med. 57(1), 9–19 (2013)
8. Hoey, J., Poupart, P., et al.: Automated hand washing assistance for persons with dementia using video and a partially observable Markov decision process. Comput. Vis. Image Underst. 114(5), 503–519 (2010)
9. Yoshino, K., Kawahara, T.: Conversational System for Information Navigation based on POMDP with User Focus Tracking. Computer Speech & Language 26(5), 349–370 (2015)
10. Pineau, J., Gordon, G., Thrun, S.: Anytime point-based approximations for large POMDPs. J. Artif. Intell. Res. 27, 335–380 (2006)
11. S., Paquet: Distributed decision-making and task coordination in dynamic, uncertain and real-time multiagent environments. Ph.D. thesis, Laval University (2006)
12. Ross, S., Pineau, J., Paquet, S., Chaib-Draa, B.: Online planning algorithms for POMDPs. J. Artif. Intell. Res. 32, 663–704 (2008)
13. Doshi, F., Pineau, J., Roy, N.: Reinforcement learning with limited reinforcement: using Bayes risk for active learning in POMDPs. In: ICML 2008 Proceedings of the 25th international conference on Machine learning, pp.256–263. New York (2008)

14. Doshi-Velez, F.: The infinite partially observable Markov decision process. Adv. Neural Inf. Process. Syst. **22**, 477–485 (2009)
15. Krause, A., Ihmig, M., et. al.: Trading off prediction accuracy and power consumption for context-aware wearable computing. In: Proceedings of the 9th IEEE International Symposium on Wearable Computers, pp. 20–26. IEEE (2005)
16. Au, L., Batalin, M.A., et. al.: Episodic sampling: Towards energy-efficient patient monitoring with wearable sensors. In: Proceedings of the IEEE Annu. International Conference Engineering in Medicine and Biology Society, pp. 6901–6905. IEEE, Minneapolis (2009)
17. Bhanu, B., Peng, J.: Adaptive integrated image segmentation and object recognition. IEEE Trans on Systems, Man, and Cybernetics-PART C: Appl. Rev. **30**(4), 427–441 (2000)
18. Sellahewa, H., Jassim, S.A.: Image-quality-based adaptive face recognition. IEEE Trans Instrum. Meas. **59**(4), 805–813 (2010)
19. Dearden, R., Friedman, N., Andre, D.: Model based Bayesian exploration. In: UAI 1999 Proceedings of the Fifteenth conference on Uncertainty in artificial intelligence, pp. 150–159. Morgan Kaufmann, San Francisco (1999)
20. Rhee, P.K., Nam, M.Y., Wang, L.: Pupil location and movement measurement for efficient emotional sensibility Analysis. In: 2010 IEEE International Symposium on ISSPIT, pp. 1–6 (2010)
21. Kadal, Z., Mikolajczyk, K., Matas, J.: Tracking-learning-detection. IEEE Trans. Pattern Anal. Mach. Intell. **34**(7), 1409–1422 (2012)
22. Shen, Y., Shin, H.C., Sung, W.J.: Evolutionary adaptive eye tracking for low-cost human computer interaction applications. J. Electron. Imaging **22**(1), 013031 (2013)

A Vision-Based System for Movement Analysis in Medical Applications: The Example of Parkinson Disease

Sofija Spasojević[1,2,3]($\boxtimes$), José Santos-Victor[3], Tihomir Ilić[4],
Slađan Milanović[5], Veljko Potkonjak[1], and Aleksandar Rodić[2]

[1] School of Electrical Engineering, University of Belgrade, Belgrade, Serbia
potkonjak@yahoo.com,
[2] Mihailo Pupin Institute, University of Belgrade, Belgrade, Serbia
{sofija.spasojevic,aleksandar.rodic}@pupin.rs
[3] Institute for Systems and Robotics, Instituto Superior Técnico,
Universidade de Lisboa, Lisbon, Portugal
jasv@isr.tecnico.ulisboa.pt,
[4] Department of Clinical Neurophysiology of Military Medical Academy,
Belgrade, Serbia
tihoilic@gmail.com
[5] Department of Neurophysiology of Institute for Medical Research,
Belgrade, Serbia
sladjan.milanovic@imi.bg.ac.rs

Abstract. We present a vision-based approach for analyzing a Parkinson patient's movements during rehabilitation treatments. We describe therapeutic movements using relevant quantitative measurements, which can be applied both for diagnosis and monitoring of the disease progress.

Since our long-term goal is to develop an affordable and portable system, suitable for home usage, we use the Kinect device for data acquisition. All recorded exercises are approved by neurologists and therapists and designed to examine the presence of characteristic symptoms caused by neurological disorders. In this study, we focus on Parkinson's patients in the early stages of the disease.

Our approach underlines relevant rehabilitation measurements and allows to determine which ones are more informative for separating healthy from non-healthy subjects. Finally, we propose the symmetry ratio, well known in motor control, as a novel feature that can be extracted from rehabilitation exercises and used in the decision-making (diagnosis support) and monitoring procedures.

Keywords: Movement analysis · Medical applications · Kinect

1 Introduction

Conventional diagnosis techniques in Parkinson's disease (PD) rely on the clinical assessment tools such as Unified Parkinson's Disease Rating Scale (UPDRS) [1]. However, these tools are based on the subjective evaluation of some disease factors and are not fully interpretable. Another shortcoming is that traditional rehabilitation treatment is often slow, monotonous, disempowering and a non-motivational process, from

L. Nalpantidis et al. (Eds.): ICVS 2015, LNCS 9163, pp. 424–434, 2015.
DOI: 10.1007/978-3-319-20904-3_38

which patients can easily give up. Due to all these facts, there is a clear need to introduce new techniques into the rehabilitation processes able to enhance both, the therapist evaluation procedure and the patient's motivation.

Our ultimate goal is to build a multifunctional, affordable and portable system, to be used as a support to the conventional rehabilitation practice as well as home rehabilitation. In this work, we present an important part of the future rehabilitation structure – the analysis of patient's movements along with the decision-making (diagnosis support) scheme.

The main limitation of our approach results from the relatively modest accuracy of the Kinect and its inability for tracking finger joint trajectories without additional equipment.

The remaining of the paper is structured as follows. Section 2 reviews the state of the art of rehabilitation techniques applied to neurological disorders with special emphasis on those used in Parkinson's disease. Section 3 explains the procedure of data acquisition using the Kinect. Section 4 describes the experimental group of subjects used in this study and the performed exercises/movements. Section 5 explains the algorithm we developed for extracting relevant measurements. Section 6 summarizes the results of classification between patients and controls and the analysis of the most informative features to support the decision-making (diagnosis support) process. In Sect. 7 we draw some conclusions and propose future extensions of this work.

2 Related Work

Recent approaches for rehabilitation treatment, combining the medical background and new sensing and data-analysis technologies, have a large potential to improve the diagnosis and rehabilitation therapy. However, they still face substantial challenges regarding the practical integration and application in a clinical setting. Some of the main challenges concern the inclusion of the technical systems into medical protocols, implying lengthy certification procedures, costly equipment and software and overall system complexity.

Marker-based motion capture (mocap) systems [2] are often used for movement acquisition during rehabilitation sessions, as they can be extremely accurate but also extremely costly. Other alternatives include the integration of different sensor types attached to the patient's body [3] or hand (data glove) and, more recently, low-cost marker-free mocap systems such as Kinect and Xtion [4]. The performance of lower-cost systems has been tested and shown to possess a satisfactory accuracy for the application in the rehabilitation therapy [5–7]. While some examples of Kinect-based rehabilitation systems are described in [8–11], little attention has been devoted to the specific case of Parkinson's disease [12, 13]. Recently, authors in [12] have studied the Kinect accuracy for measuring movements of Parkinson's patients, but they did not implement the movement analysis. They compared the Kinect to the VICON mocap system through a set of rehabilitation exercises. Their results suggest similar temporal accuracy between the two systems, when measuring the movement duration and spatial accuracy regarding to the upper body movements. Their general conclusion is that the Kinect has potential to be used for movement analysis in Parkinson's disease and promising application in the future for home rehabilitation.

To raise a patient's motivation during therapy, some studies have introduced virtual environments into data acquisition and processing procedures for Parkinson's disease [13, 14]. Main limitations with the use of virtual environments and rehabilitation games are the lack of official safety-evidence and proof of clinical effectiveness.

Rehabilitation studies for neurological disorders usually concentrate on the analysis of particular body functionalities such as postural control [13], gait [15], upper body movements [16] or even the observation of the behavior of a concrete joint [17]. Our work incorporates the analysis of such main human – gait and upper body – functionalities, based on the characteristic skeleton joint coordinates acquired with a Kinect during rehabilitation exercises. So far, most rehabilitation studies have been developed in order to monitor the treatment and observe a patient's progress [8–11, 13–17]. Our approach extends these aspects by including a comparison between patients and control subjects in order to determine benchmark ranges of relevant rehabilitation measurements (features) for assisting the diagnosis. We describe in detail how to define a set of measurements to characterize the movements of a subject. In addition, we propose the symmetry ratio, widely used as a validity criterion for models in biomechanics and motor control [18, 19], a new feature for rehabilitation. In fact, it has been shown that the symmetry of kinematic speed profiles results exclusively from neurological mechanisms [20, 21], without any interference from changes of conditions or variables of the performed task. In this paper, we introduce the full potential and the importance of this new proposed measurement together with standard rehabilitation features for diagnosis and monitoring in Parkinson's disease.

3 System Description and Data Acquisition

All data-acquisition techniques in the rehabilitation practice can be broadly categorized in two main approaches, depending on the adopted sensor technologies: (i) body-fixed or (ii) vision based sensing. Due to the complicated process of attaching the sensors or special markers to the body, as well as the discomfort felt by the subjects, patients often manifest the resistance according to the techniques based on the body-fixed sensors. On the other hand, visual systems composed by a large set of cameras can be quite complex in terms of system integration, costly and require a technician's presence. For those reasons, several recent research efforts in the rehabilitation field have explored the use of motion sensing devices, such as the Kinect and Xtion [4]. These low-cost devices may offer a suitable alternative to more expensive and complex vision-based mocap systems used today in rehabilitation practice.

The use of the Kinect has advantages, compared to the traditional rehabilitation techniques, in terms of the patient's motivation during the therapy and opening the possibility of home rehabilitation. The process of the data acquisition is based on the visual skeleton tracking and the possibility of storing 3D positions of characteristic joints for every frame using marker free based technique. The maximum frame rate for the Kinect is 30 frames per second (30 Hz), but in our case due to additional processing in order of data collection, frame rate drops down to 27 Hz. The acquired data consist of 3D positions (x, y and z coordinates) of characteristic skeleton joints, collected

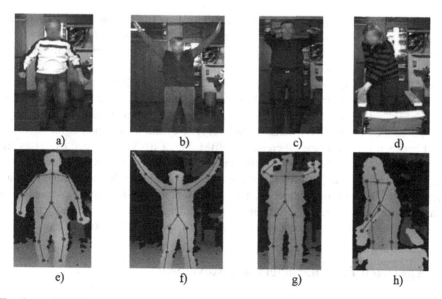

Fig. 1. (a-d) RGB stream and (e-h) depth stream from Kinect with detected skeleton and collected joints

during the movement performance, along with RGB and depth video sequences (Fig. 1).

A few papers have discussed the Kinect accuracy and justified its use in the rehabilitation practice [5–7]. Results suggest that the Kinect accuracy is sufficient for the rehabilitation treatment of the Parkinson's disease [12], but they also report the variations of the data accuracy depending on the distance to the subject, tracked body-part and the range of movement. Since the accuracy drops down significantly with the increase of distance to the Kinect [5], we have chosen the smallest possible distance that would still allow full body tracking, which was around 1.5 m.

4   Experimental Groups and Performed Exercises

Our experimental group consists of twelve patients with Parkinson's disease of the first, second and third stage [22]. In addition to commonly used rehabilitation features, we measure the symmetry ratio from specific upper body movements and it will be shown later in the paper that this measure contains significant information relevant for the movement analysis and to discriminate among healthy and non-healthy subjects.

Following the therapist's advice, all rehabilitation exercises are designed to recover or enhance one of the three main human functionalities – balance, mobility in the sense of normal gait and upper body movements [23]. Due to clinical protocol, the gait test is fairly present in the majority of rehabilitation procedures and it can have different forms depending on the equipment used and the measured gait features [23]. In our work, the gait test is carried out in accordance with the available Kinect range [6], with the starting and end points placed at 3.5 m and 1.5 m away from the Kinect, respectively. Under the gait test, patients have crossed the selected distance of 2 m six times with normal and natural gait rhythm (Fig. 1-a). The relevant measurements extracted from the gait are the gait speed and a measure of hand rigidity during walking. The procedure for extracting relevant measurements is explained in detail in the next section.

The rest of the tested exercises belong to a group of 3 upper body movements: adjusted shoulder abduction-adduction (SAA) (Fig. 1-b) until maximum possible range of motion, shoulder flexion-extension (SFE) (Fig. 1-c) and movements of the right-left hand between the boundaries (hereinafter HBM, Fig. 1-d). The first two exercises are well known in the rehabilitation practice and the third one is introduced in order to test the patient's movement performance when focusing on a target. Regarding the relevant measures of the first two exercises, range of motion, speed of the movement and symmetry ratio are measured. From the hand boundary movements, we chose only the speed as relevant performance measure, due to the specific nature of the test.

5 Approach for Characterizing Movements

We have used several measurements (features) that represent the motion of the different body parts of the subject. The choice of features was partly resulting from discussions with doctors, therapists and other domain experts. All together we have used 9 different features that result from the combination of four categories of measurements (speed, rigidity, range of motion and symmetry) applied to 4 categories of lower/upper body movements, as illustrated in Table 1.

Measurements extracted from gait movements are commonly used in the rehabilitation practice and treatment [23]. From our gait movements, we consider two measurements – speed of the gait and hand rigidity during walking. We have observed the mean gait speed V (1) during each two-meter sequence. Due to possible deviations of the starting and end point of the gait test, and in order to improve the accuracy, the path length (the numerator in (Eq. 1)) has been calculated as the total trajectory of the torso during each gait sequence, instead of setting the path length of 2 m. The total trajectory is obtained by summing up the Euclidean distances (d) between the torso joint coordinates X_i (x_i, y_i, z_i) and X_{i-1} (x_{i-1}, y_{i-1}, z_{i-1}) for each consecutive frames i and i-1 during the gait sequence. The time duration of the gait sequence (denominator in (Eq. 1)) is expressed in seconds and has been computed as the ratio between the total number of

Table 1. The features used result from a combination of 4 body movements and 4 different measurements (speed, rigidity, range and symmetry).

Movements /feature categories	Speed	Rigidity	Range of Motion (ROM)	Symmetry Ratio (SR)
Gait	• f_1	• f_2		
Shoulder abduction adduction (SAA)	• f_4		• f_3	• f_5
Shoulder flexion extension (SFE)	• f_7		• f_6	• f_8
Hand boundary movements (HBM)	• f_9			

frames (m and n denote respectively the starting and last frame of the sequence) and the frame rate, f = 27 Hz.

$$V = \frac{\sum_{i=m}^{n} d(X_i, X_{i-1})}{(n - m + 1)/f} \tag{1}$$

The position of the arms during walking can reveal rigidity, one of the main indicators of the Parkinson's disease [1]. In the case of healthy subjects, the arms usually swing in a certain rhythm during gait activity, in contrast to the Parkinson's patients. We compute a measure of rigidity, based on the hands position during the gait test. The rigidity symptom can be noticed in the variation of the distance between the hip and hand during the gait sequence. For healthy subjects, the temporal evolution of these distances is approximately periodic, due to normal arms swinging. In contrast, for patients with one rigid arm, the distance between the rigid hand and the closest hip does change significantly over time (Fig. 2-a). The measure of rigidity is calculated in two steps. First, we record the difference between the left/right hand-hip distances, during the gait movement.

In patients with rigid arm, the difference signal is larger, because the healthy arm performs a normal swing and the rigid arm remains more or less static. Instead, healthy subjects display a lower-amplitude signal, due to the normal swing of both hands. Finally, we take the highest value of the (absolute) difference signal as an indicator of rigidity.

Inspired by well-known and widely used rehabilitation measure for upper body movements, we have computed the range of motion [23] for the shoulder abduction-adduction and shoulder flexion-extension exercise. The range of motion represents an angle of the movement relative to a specific body axis, which can be measured at various joints such as elbow, shoulder, knee, etc. In our case, we measure the evolution of the shoulder angle during the movement in relation to the longitudinal

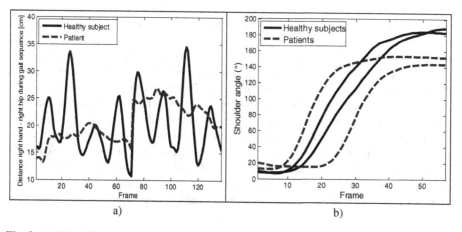

Fig. 2. (a) The difference between the left/right hand-hip distances shows the rigidity symptom. (b) evolution of the shoulder angle profiles during shoulder abduction movements.

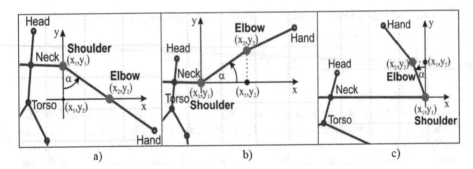

Fig. 3. Definition of the shoulder angle for different scenarios depending on the arm position

body axis (Fig. 3). Depending on the relative positions of the shoulder (x1, y1) and elbow (x2, y2) joints (z coordinate is not relevant), the shoulder angle may take the value of α (Fig. 3-a), $90° + \alpha$ (Fig. 3-b) and $180° + \alpha$ (Fig. 3-c) in the first, second and third quadrant, respectively.

As a specific movement descriptor we have used the range of motion (maximum achieved shoulder angle). Examples of the shoulder angle profiles of both normal subjects and patients for the shoulder abduction movement are shown in Fig. 2-b. The range of motion is higher for healthy subjects (more than 180°) than for patients (142°, 150°). In addition, the trajectory of shoulder angle is steeper for healthy subjects, indicating a higher speed of movement. We calculated the mean movement speed for all three tested upper body exercises. The applied procedure was the same for the gait speed (Eq. 1), setting the path length to the total length of hand trajectory during the movement.

The comparison between relevant left/right body-side movement descriptors can suggest which side or limb is more affected by the neurological disorder. For healthy subjects, these differences are usually negligible, while they can become quite large for Parkinson patients, depending on the disease stage. Important movement descriptors such as profiles of joint angles (Fig. 2-b) and angular velocity profiles (Fig. 4 - a) can reveal the symmetry of the movements. In order to quantitatively assess the movement symmetry, we have extracted symmetry ratio from the shoulder abduction-adduction and shoulder flexion-extension exercises. In motor control, the symmetry ratio (SR) [18–21] (Fig. 4-b) is defined as the ratio between acceleration (t_{ACC}) and deceleration (t_{DEC}) times, during one movement. Figure 4-a shows that the maximum angular velocity of the shoulder abduction movement is higher for healthy subjects than it is for Parkinson patients. In addition, healthy subjects reach the maximum angular velocities of the left/right arm movements approximately at the same time as opposed to non-healthy subjects, where a difference of about 20 frames is typical. The consequence is unbalance in symmetry ratios between left and right arm for the same movement. Thus, in our experiments we obtained larger left-right differences of the symmetry ratios for Parkinson patients than in healthy subjects.

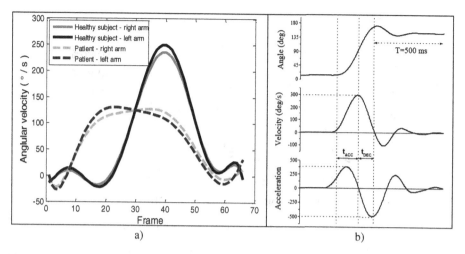

a)   b)

Fig. 4. (a) Evolution of the shoulder angular velocity profiles during shoulder abduction movements and (b) symmetry ratio calculation

6 Results

The normalized ranges of the relevant measurements extracted from patients and healthy subjects data are illustrated in the boxplot on the Fig. 5. Values of range of motion and gait/movement speed are lower in the patient group, while the left-right arm differences of the symmetry ratio, during shoulder movements, are much larger in patients, as expected. By adopting the proposed relevant measurements, we obtain 9-dimensional feature vectors (Fig. 5), which can be used in a classification system to assist diagnosis. We applied a process of dimensionality reduction to the 9-dimensional feature space, in order to improve the classifiers efficiency and accuracy, as well as to determine the most informative features for rehabilitation. Dimensionality reduction is

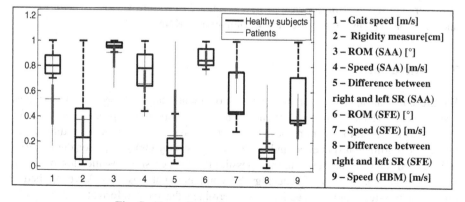

Fig. 5. Normalized relevant measurement ranges

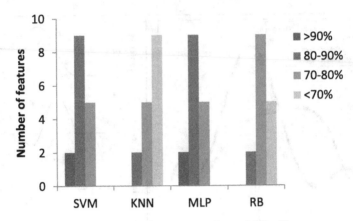

Fig. 6. Classification accuracy for each classifier

performed using Linear Discriminant Analysis (LDA) [24], that allowed us to transform our original 9-dimensional data set into a new 2-dimensional feature space.

As a side-result, the LDA method also ranks the original features in terms of their contribution to the reduced 2-dimensional feature space, and five features (1, 9, 5, 7 and 8 from the Fig. 5) have shown significantly higher impact compared to the other ones. This result suggests that, in addition to the speed of the gait and upper body movements, both symmetry ratio features are associated to a group of the most relevant features.

Classification between healthy and non-healthy subjects is performed based on the original feature set, the five most relevant features and the two new obtained features from LDA, using four different classifiers (Fig. 6): SVM – support vector machines with RBF kernel (bandwidth of the RBF kernel, σ and regularization parameter, C: $0.01 < \sigma < 1$, $0.01 < C < 10$), KNN (number of nearest neighbors, $k \in 1, 3, 5$) and two types of neural networks (various structures with different number of hidden layers and nodes): MLP – multilayer perceptron and RB – radial basis (bandwidth of the RBF kernel: $0.01 < \sigma < 2$). Parameters of classifiers are chosen from listed ranges in a validation procedure in order to achieve the highest accuracy rate. The best results for all classifiers are reported in the case of new created 2-D feature vectors, whereby SVM and MLP have shown higher accuracy compared to KNN and RB.

7   Conclusion

We presented an approach for therapeutic movement analysis based on the low-cost vision system (Kinect), to support the traditional rehabilitation procedures both for diagnosis and monitoring purposes. Our results have shown significant differences between experimental (patients) and control (healthy subjects) groups for the majority of proposed relevant measures and the possibility of successful classification based on the observed measures. For reducing the computational cost, we have applied a dimensionality-reduction procedure and determined the most informative features in terms of assisting the medical diagnosis process. This result underlines the significant role of new measurement we proposed – the symmetry ratio feature for classification procedure. For the future work we plan to extend this research and to introduce additional devices, such as data gloves in order to design a comprehensive movement analysis system.

Acknowledgment. This work was funded by the Ministry of Education, Science and Technology Development of the Republic of Serbia under the contracts TR-35003, III-44008 and III- 44004; the EU Project POETICON ++, the Portuguese FCT Project [UID/EEA/50009/2013] and the Alexander von Humboldt project "Emotionally Intelligent Robots - EIrobots", Contract no. 3.4-IP-DEU/112623.

References

1. Goetz, C., Tilley, B., Shaftman, S., et al.: Movement disorder society-sponsored revision of the unified parkinson's disease rating scale (mds-updrs): scale presentation and clini-metric testing results. Mov. Disord. **22**, 2129–2170 (2008)
2. Zhou, H., Hu, H.: Human motion tracking for rehabilitation – a survey. Biomed. Sign. Process. Control **3**, 1–18 (2008)
3. Patel, S., Park, H., Bonato, P., et al.: A review of wearable sensors and systems with application in rehabilitation. J. NeuroEngineering Rehabil. **9**, 21 (2012)
4. Gonzalez-Jorge, H., Riveiro, B., Vazquez-Fernandez, E., et al.: Metrological evaluation of microsoft kinect and asus xtion sensors. Measurement **46**, 1800–1806 (2013)
5. Khoshelham, K., Elberink, S.: Accuracy and resolution of kinect depth data for indoor mapping applications. Sensors **12**, 1437–1454 (2012)
6. Clark, R., Pu, Y., Fortina, K., et al.: Validity of the microsoft kinect for assessment of postural control. Gait Posture **36**, 372–377 (2012)
7. Chang, C., Lange, B., Zhang, M., et al.: Towards pervasive physical rehabilitation using microsoft kinect. In: Proceedings of PervasiveHealth, pp. 159–162 (2012)
8. Chang, Y., Han, W., Tsai, Y.: A kinect-based upper limb rehabilitation system to assist people with cerebral palsy. Res. D. Disabil. **34**, 3654–3659 (2013)
9. Chang, Y., Chen, S., Huang, J.: A kinect-based system for physical rehabilitation: a pilot study for young adults with motor disabilities. Res. Dev. Disabil. **32**, 2566–2570 (2011)
10. Gama, A., Chaves, T., Figueiredo, L., et al.: Guidance and movement correction based on therapeutics movements for motor rehabilitation support systems. In: 14th Symposium on Virtual and Augmented Reality (2012)
11. Calin, A., Cantea, A., Dascalu, A., et al.: Mira – upper limb rehabilitation system using microsoft kinect, studia univ. babes-bolyai. Informatica **56**(4), 63 (2011)
12. Galna, B., Barry, G., Jackson, D., et al.: Accuracy of the microsoft kinect sensor for measuring movement in people with parkinson's disease. Gait and Posture (2014). http://dx.doi.org/10.1016/j.gaitpost.2014.01.008
13. Galna, B., Jackson, D., Schofield, G., McNaney, R., et al.: Retraining function in people with parkinson's disease using the microsoft kinect: game design and pilot testing. J. Neuroengineering Rehabil. **11**, 11–60 (2014)
14. Albiol-Pérez, S., Lozano-Quilis, J., Gil-Gómez, H., et al.: Virtual rehabilitation system for people with Parkinson's disease. In: 9th International Conference on Disability, Virtual Reality and Associated Technologies (ICDVRAT), pp. 423–427 (2012)

15. Lange, B., Koenig, S., McConnell, E., et al.: Interactive game-based rehabilitation using the microsoft kinect. In: Virtual Reality Short Papers and Posters IEEE, pp. 171–172 (2012)
16. Lum, P., Burgar, C., Shor, P., et al.: Robot-assisted movement training compared with conventional therapy techniques for the rehabilitation of upper-limb motor function after stroke. Arch. Phys. Med. Rehabil. 83, 952–959 (2002)
17. Vaisman, L., Dipietro, L., Krebs, H.: A comparative analysis of speed profile models for wrist pointing movements. IEEE Transactions on Neural Systems and Rehabilitation Engineering 21(5), 756–766 (2013)
18. Plamondon, R.: A kinematic theory of rapid human movements. Part I. movement representation and generation. Biol. Cybern. 72, 295–307 (1995)
19. Gribble, P., Ostry, D.: Origins of the power law relations between movement velocity and curvature: modeling the effects of muscle mechanics and limb dynamics. J. Neurophysiol. 76, 53–59 (1996)
20. Bullock, D., Grossberg, S.: Adaptive neural networks for control of movement trajectories invariant under speed and force rescaling. HMS 10, 3–53 (1991)
21. Mirkov, D., Milanovic, S., Ilic, D., et al.: Symmetry of discrete and oscillatory elbow movements: does it depend on torque that the agonist and antagonist muscle can exert? Mot. Control 6, 271–281 (2002)
22. Hoehn, M., Yahr, M.: Parkinsonism: onset, progression and mortality. Neurology 17, 427–442 (1967)
23. Keus, S., Bloem, B., Hendriks, E., et al.: Evidence-based analysis of physical therapy in parkinson's disease with recommendations for practice and research. Mov. Disord. 22(4), 451–460 (2007)
24. Fisher, R.A.: The use of multiple measurements in taxonomic problems. Ann. Eugenics 7, 179–188 (1936)

Estimating the Number of Clusters with Database for Texture Segmentation Using Gabor Filter

Minkyu Kim[(✉)], Jeong-Mook Lim, Heesook Shin, Changmok Oh, and Hyun-Tae Jeong

Electronics and Telecommunications Research Institute, Daejeon, Korea
{thechaos16,jmlim21,hsshin8,chmooh,htjeong}@etri.re.kr

Abstract. This paper addresses a novel solution of the problem of image segmentation by its texture using Gabor filter. Texture segmentation has been worked well by using Gabor filter, but there still is a problem; the number of clusters. There are several studies about estimating number of clusters with statistical approaches such as gap statistic. However, there are some problems to apply those methods to texture segmentation in terms of accuracy and time complexity. To overcome these limits, this paper proposes novel method to estimate optimal number of clusters for texture segmentation by using training dataset and several assumptions which are appropriate for image segmentation. We evaluate the proposed method on dataset consists of texture image and limit possible number of clusters from 2 to 5. And we also evaluate the proposed method by real image contains various texture such as rock stratum.

Keywords: Texture segmentation · Number of clusters · Gabor filter · Weight optimization

1 Introduction

Image segmentation is one of the most fundamental problems in computer vision. Image segmentation has been applied in various areas such as face recognition, object recognition, and surveillance. The most popular way to divide an image into several segments is based on image feature, and the central question in image segmentation is how to define appropriate feature. Image features can be defined differently along the goal of algorithm. For example, clustering algorithms such as k-means clustering use color or intensity of each pixel or window as a feature, and the others such as object detection and recognition use edge and corner as a feature for segmentation.

We used edge of image as a feature in this paper because main goal of this paper is texture-based segmentation. Texture is defined as a descriptor of local brightness pattern in a small region in the image [14], and it is possible to recognize texture by analyzing number of edges in a small region. Gabor filter [5, 6] can convert edge in the image into intensity value. That is, texture with dense edge would be transformed to dark image while texture with sparse edge would be transformed to light region.

L. Nalpantidis et al. (Eds.): ICVS 2015, LNCS 9163, pp. 435–444, 2015.
DOI: 10.1007/978-3-319-20904-3_39

Otherwise, other methods can be used to recognize texture such as Grey-Level Co-occurrence Matrices (GLCM) [7] have introduced. We used Gabor filter to detect edge in image. Gabor filter is a linear filter using Gabor function which is thought to be similar with human visual system because the visual cortex of mammalian brain is modelled by Gabor wavelet [15].

After a step with Gabor filter, the next step of proposed method is to divide an image into several parts. Image segmentation can be achieved by k-means clustering or mean-shift clustering because the image is already converted into density map of edge at small region. However, it is challenging to decide how many segments the image contains. To solve this problem, we introduced two different criteria to measure accuracy of number of segments called continuity and equality. And we trained optimized weight of each criterion based on image database which contains texture from Brodatz texture images [13]. After that, we tested the proposed method by cross-validation method compared to other optimizing number of cluster algorithms.

Our contributions are as follow. First, we introduced novel criterion to optimize number of cluster for clustering algorithm which can be applied in various computer vision applications. We tested it with experiment with more than 50 texture patterns and real-world images such as rock type images. The other contribution is to propose a method to match between discrete and continuous data.

2 Background

2.1 Mean-Shift Clustering

Mean-shift clustering is one of the most popular algorithms to divide large dataset into k different clusters. Main goal of mean-shift algorithm is to find k maxima of density function driven by data. To construct density function, kernel density estimation [1], [16], multivariate kernel density estimator with kernel K and bandwidth matrix H computed in point x is represented by (1).

$$\hat{f}(x) = \frac{1}{n} \sum\nolimits_{i=1}^{n} K_H(x - x_i) \tag{1}$$

Kernel function is defined as a non-negative function like probability density function. Bandwidth is a positive parameter for smoothing. K_H in formula (1) represents scaled kernel which is scaled by bandwidth H.

Mean-shift procedure has iterative steps. (1) Randomly select initial points for k means. (2) Compute the weighted mean of the density in window determined by kernel function. (3) Update means until it converges. To approve stability of mean-shift algorithm, there are several researches about refining initial point for k means [2]. In the second step of mean-shift procedure, new weighted mean is estimated as Eq. (2).

$$m(\mathbf{x}) = \frac{\sum_{x_i \in N(x)} K(x_i - x)x_i}{\sum_{x_i \in N(x)} K(x_i - x)} \tag{2}$$

where m(x) represents weighted mean to be updated, N(x) represents to neighborhood of x, and K is kernel function. Gaussian kernel is normally used for it. Mean-shift procedure applied to clustering in computer vision called mean-shift clustering, and it is widely used for image segmentation [1].

2.2   Gabor Filter

There are several different ways to recognize texture of image. An algorithm using GLCM [7] which is defined as the matrix of the joint probability of occurrence of two grey level values, but we used Gabor filter to analyze texture because it is similar with human visual system [15]. Gabor filter is used to texture analysis [9, 10] by detecting visible edges that given image contains. Analyzing texture with Gabor filter has 2 steps: (1) Construct filter bank by varying direction and scale. (2) Compute response matrices by convolution input image and filter bank. For the first step, two-dimensional Gabor functions are used to construct filter bank. The basic format of Gabor function is given by (3).

$$g_{\lambda,\theta,\psi,\sigma,\gamma}(x,y) = \exp\left(-\frac{x'^2 + \gamma^2 y'^2}{2\sigma^2}\right)\exp\left(i\left(2\pi\frac{x'}{\lambda}+\psi\right)\right) \qquad (3)$$

where (x,y) is location, λ represents wave length of Gabor wavelet, θ is an orientation of Gabor function, ψ is phase offset in degree, σ represents standard deviation of Gaussian kernel, and γ means spatial aspect ratio. Filter bank contains various Gabor filters by changing its orientation in Eq. (3). In the second step, response matrices have been developed by convolution input image and every element in filter bank. After convolution, smoothing procedure is followed. As a result, a set of images representing density of visible edge of specific orientation is constructed.

Figure 1 shows texture image as an input and one result from set of filtered images. In (b), dark area in upper right side of image indicates that area contains a lot of visual edges of specific orientation while light side only contains a few. Because Gabor filter convert texture image into edge-density map, Gabor filter make the image to be easily

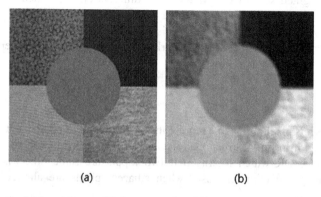

(a)   (b)

Fig. 1. (a) Input image, (b) One example of filtered image by Gabor filter

divided by its texture. After Gabor filter, popular intensity-based clustering algorithm such as mean-shift clustering can be used for image segmentation.

3 Algorithm

The proposed method consists of two steps. The first step is called texture segmentation, which divides given image into specific number of clusters iteratively by changing the number of clusters. In the second step, the proposed method estimates the most appropriate number of clusters for given image by estimating energy function for each number of clusters.

3.1 Texture Segmentation

Texture segmentation part has three steps; Constructing Gabor filter bank, Filtering, and Mean-shift clustering. The first step is filtering the image with bank of Gabor filters. Filter bank [5] requires $6log_2\left(N_c/2\right)$ filters for the case of orientation separation of 30 degree or it requires $4log_2\left(N_c/2\right)$ filters for the case of orientation separation of 45 degree. In both cases, N_c represents the number of pixel in a row of image. In the second step, input image is converted into edge-density map by convolution every elements in filter bank and input image and by smoothing the convolution result. After the second step, more than 40 results for given image are generated, and, in the third step, mean-shift clustering procedure is applied to every image made in the second step. As a result, many segmented images are generated, and each pixel is aligned to one of the clusters which occur most.

3.2 Estimating Number of Clusters with Database

In this step, we define the energy function which estimates propriety of each number of clusters, and choose the number that has the minimum energy. The energy function is defined by weighted sum of two values from different criteria called continuity and equality. The first criterion called continuity is based on an assumption that adjacent pixels tend to be in the same cluster. This assumption is widely used in computer vision, especially for algorithms using Markov Random Fields [17]. Energy function for continuity is defined as follow:

$$E_1 = \sum_i \sum_{j \in neighbour(i)} XOR(c_i, c_j) \tag{4}$$

where i represents pixel of image, j represents neighborhood of pixel i, and c_i represents cluster for pixel i. In Eq. (4), diagonal pixels are not included in neighborhood. XOR means exclusive OR which returns 0 if two inputs are same otherwise returns 1. Therefore, energy function increases when adjacent pixels are aligned to different clusters. However, because expected value of E_1 increases if number of clusters increases, energy function should be modified as follow:

$$E_{1,k} = \frac{k}{k-1} \sum_i \sum_{j \in neighbour(i)} XOR(c_i, c_j) \qquad (5)$$

where k is number of clusters. In Eq. (5), E_1 is modified to $E_{1,k}$ by multiplying only $\frac{k}{k-1}$ because expected value of E_1 given k is equal to $\frac{k-1}{k}C$ where C is value independent to k. Therefore, energy function for continuity robust to number of clusters is defined as Eq. (5).

The second criterion called equality is based on assumption that each cluster should contain approximately same number of pixels. This criterion indicates that texture should have reasonable size, so the proposed method can detect stripe pattern for one texture instead of two. To compute energy function for the second criterion, a set S should be defined as a set consist of pixels in same cluster. Then, E_2, the energy function for equality, has defined as standard deviation of the set. As contrast to E_1, because expected value of E_2 increases if number of clusters decreases, E_2 should be refined as well. $E_{2,k}$ is defined as E_2 times function proportional to k.

The optimized number of clusters by given image is defined as weighted sum of two energy functions.

$$k_{opt}(img) = argmin_k(w_1 \cdot E_{1,k} + w_2 \cdot E_{2,k}) \qquad (6)$$

where w_i represents weight for each energy, and $argmin_k$ means that value of argument which minimizes value inside.

The next step is optimizing weights of energy function with image set. Image set contains more than 30 images consist of from 2 to 5 different textures. Some textures are from Brodatz image, and the others are fabric textures. To optimize weights for each criterion, gradient descent rule [8, 11, 12] has been used. However, there is a problem to apply gradient descent in this case. Weights are in the continuous space while true number of clusters is in discrete space. To solve this problem, another step called rough optimization should be introduced before adapting gradient descent rule. In rough optimization, initial point for gradient descent is estimated by searching weight pair which minimizes difference between estimated k and ground truth. Then, optimal k for each image in database is estimated by choosing the number with the least energy. From roughly optimized result, gradient descent rule has been applied to optimize value of each weight. In this procedure, the direction of iteration is to maximize Euclidean distance between energy of optimal k and energy of others which is defined as Eq. (7).

$$GD(k_{opt}) = \sum_{i \neq k_{opt}} ||(w_1 \cdot E_{1,k_{opt}} + w_2 \cdot E_{2,k_{opt}}), (w_1 \cdot E_{1,i} + w_2 \cdot E_{2,i})||_2 \qquad (7)$$

where k_{opt} represents number of clusters estimated in rough optimization step. As we mentioned, initial value of w_1 and w_2 are estimated in rough optimization, and it would be updated iteratively by maximizing GD until it converges.

When the new image comes, the propose algorithm computes optimal k for given image with optimized weights and energy functions for two criterion.

4   Experiment

In experiment section, the proposed method is evaluated on image dataset containing various types of texture. The dataset consists of images with over 50 different types of texture. Types of texture are from Brodatz image which contains different textures and other fabric textures. We constructed database containing 40 images consist of different textures. To compare the proposed method, estimating number of clusters using gap statistics [3, 4] has been tested as well on same dataset. Two different methods share the first step of algorithm, and they estimate optimal number of cluster for each image respectively. Because the proposed method uses database while gap statistic does not, we estimate it with cross-validation method. In addition, we evaluate the proposed method with real images containing various textures such as rock layer, brick, and rock image containing a fossil of ancient animal inside.

4.1   Texture

Database for our experiment contains 40 texture images consist of Brodatz image and fabric texture. Database has been separated into 5 parts containing 8 texture images respectively, and we tested the proposed method with cross-validation which trains the algorithm with 32 images and tests it with the others. We also tested popular method in statistics to determine optimal number of clusters for clustering, called gap statistic [3, 4] to compare with the proposed one.

Figure 2 shows an example of experimental result. Original texture image is shown in (a), while (b) shows segmented results. In (b), segmented image with 4 clusters (red box) is selected by the algorithm.

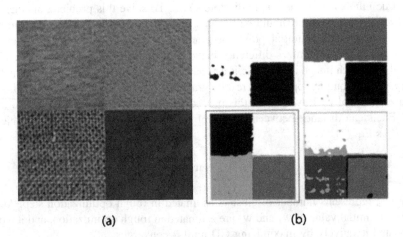

(a)   (b)

Fig. 2. (a) Original image, (b) Segmented image with 2, 3, 5, 4 clusters in counter clockwise order from top-left (Color figure online)

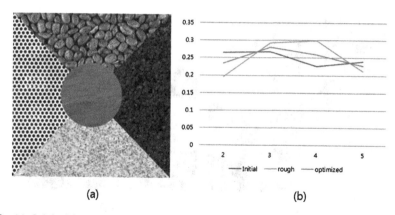

(a)   (b)

Fig. 3. (a) Original image, (b) Graph of initialized, roughly optimized, final energy functions respectively (Color figure online).

Table 1. Accuracy of our method and gap statistic. Each row represents result for subsets, and the last row shows the overall result.

	Match number	Total number	Accuracy	Gap statistic
Set 1	6	8	75.0 %	–
Set 2	8	8	100.0 %	–
Set 3	5	8	62.5 %	–
Set 4	5	8	62.5 %	–
Set 5	6	8	75.0 %	–
Overall	30	40	75.0 %	47.5 %

Figure 3 shows the impact of optimization step for clustering. With initialized weight (blue line), the optimal number of cluster for image is 4. After the first step of optimization, called rough optimization, the least energy function indicates there are two clusters (red line). However, we can check that energy function of 5 clusters is dropped as well. After the second step of optimization, the system can conclude 5 is the optimal number of cluster for this image based on green line.

Table 1 shows the comparison between result of the proposed method and gap statistic. Because gap statistic does not need database, the last column has only one result while the others have five. As shown in Table 1, accuracy of the proposed method is 75 % while accuracy of gap statistic is 47.5 %. 75 % is not enough to conclude the proposed method works well for optimizing number of clusters. However, there are a few images which have similar textures to make texture segmentation malfunction.

In Fig. 4(a), there are 5 different textures in the original image which makes ground truth of this image 5. However, in (b), it seems that the optimal number of clusters of this image is 4 because there are two different textures which have similar edge density. That is, the more acceptable number of clusters in given image by (a) is 4 based on

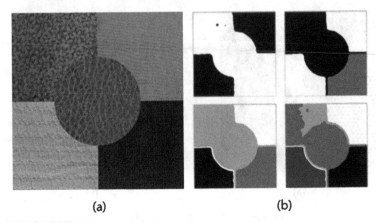

Fig. 4. (a) Original image (b) Segmented image with 2, 3, 5, 4 clusters in counter clockwise order from top-left

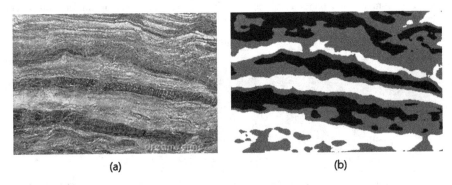

Fig. 5. (a) Original image (b) Most appropriate segmented result

segmentation result. Therefore, with modified ground truth by that means, accuracy of our method increases 87.5 % while gap statistic increases into 60 %.

4.2   Rock-Type Texture

In this part, we applied our method to images containing rock type texture. This result has no validity for accuracy, but it can show applicability our result to real images. In this experiment, 18 different images containing fossil, rock layer, and brick are used. Database is divided into 5 different subsets same as previous experiment.

Figure 5 shows an example of experimental result. (a) shows the original image which is rock layer, and (b) shows segmented image by proposed algorithm. In this case, the proposed algorithm chooses that there are 3 different texture types which seem appropriate.

Table 2 shows accuracy of our method applied to rock texture. Each row represents to accuracy of one subset of data, and the last row shows overall result. Ground truth of

Table 2. Accuracy of our method on images containing rock-type textures. Each row shows the result for subsets.

	Match number	Total number	Accuracy (%)
Set 1	3	4	75.0 %
Set 2	2	4	50.0 %
Set 3	2	4	50.0 %
Set 4	3	3	100.0 %
Set 5	3	3	100.0 %
Overall	13	18	72.2 %

rock-type texture images is determined by votes by more than 20 different people. We discarded images under with under 3-quarter votes for the best. Although the accuracy shown in Table 2 is lower than it in Table 1, over 70 % is enough to apply this algorithm into general image segmentation which contains different textures.

5   Conclusion

In this article, a novel method to optimize the number of clusters for mean-shift clustering to solve texture segmentation problem is introduced. The method is based on two criteria called continuity and equality. This method estimates energy functions of segmented image based on these criteria, and selects a number which makes minimum energy. To define energy function, database consist of various texture image has to be constructed. Energy function can be generated by weighted sum of energy for each criterion where these weights are optimized by a procedure using database. The method determines the optimal number of segments of given image by estimating defined energy function along limited cases.

Our main contributions are as follow. First, novel criteria to measure the most appropriate number of textures in given image is proposed. The second one is to introduce an approach to optimize continuous value with discrete ground truth. In near future, we plan to extend the method by modifying set of criteria. We plan to add few criteria including original image or filtered image to consider distance among mean clusters as a parameter. In addition, we have a plan to test our method to real-world images beyond the images containing rock-type textures.

References

1. Comaniciu, D., Meer, P.: Man shift: a robust approach toward feature space analysis. IEEE Trans. Pattern Anal. Mach. Intell. **24**, 603–619 (2002)
2. Bradley, P.S., Fayyad, U.M.: Refining initial points for K-Means clustering. In: International Conference on Machine Learning, pp. 91–99 (1998)
3. Zheng-Jun, Z., Zhu, Y.Q.: Estimating the image segmentation number via the entropy gap statistics. In: Second International Conference on Information and Computing Science, pp. 14–16 (2009)

4. Tibshirani, R., Guenther, W., Trevor, H.: Estimating the number of clusters in a data set via the gap statistics. J. Roy. Statist. Soc. **63**, 411–423 (2001)
5. Hammouda, K., Jernigan, E.: Texture segmentation using gabor filters. Cent. Intell. Mach. **2** (1), 64–71 (2000)
6. Roslan, R., Jamil, N.: Texture feature extraction using 2-D gabor filters. In: IEEE Symposium on Computer Applications and Industrial Electronics, pp. 173–178 (2012)
7. Rampun, A., Strange, H., Zwiggelaar, R.: Texture segmentation using different orientations of GLCM features. In: Proceedings of the 6th International Conference on Computer Vision/Computer Graphics Collaboration Techniques and Applications, 17 (2013)
8. Bach, F.: Adaptivity of averaged stochastic gradient descent to local strong voncexity for logistic regression. J. Mach. Learn. Res. **15**, 353–627 (2014)
9. Sivalingamaiah, M., Reddy, B.V.: Texture segmentation using multichannel gabor filtering. IOSR J. Electron. Commun. Eng. **2**, 22–26 (2012)
10. Wang, M., Han, G., Tu, Y., Chen, G., Gao, Y.: Unsupervised texture Image segmentation based on gabor wavelet and multi-PCNN. In: Second International Symposium on Intelligent Information Technology Application, pp. 376–381 (2008)
11. Juang, C.F., Chen, G.C.: A high-order fuzzy classifier learned through clustering and gradient descent algorithm for classification problems. In: 2014 IEEE 9th Conference on Industrial Electronics and Applications, pp. 226–230 (2014)
12. Wang, Y., Chen, L., Mei, J.P.: Stochastic gradient descent based fuzzy clustering for large data. In: 2014 IEEE International Conference on Fuzzy Systems, pp. 2511–2518 (2014)
13. Brodatz, P.: Texture: A Photographic Album for Artists and Designer. Dover Pubns, New York (1966)
14. Russ, J.C.: The Image Processing Handbook, 3rd edn. CRC Press, Boca Raton (1999)
15. Marcelja, S.: Mathematical description of the responses of simple cortical cells. JOSA **70** (11), 1297–1300 (1980)
16. Duda, R.O., Hart, P.E.: Pattern Classification and Scene Analysis, vol. 3. Wiley, Oxford (1973)
17. Liu, T., Yuan, Z., Sun, J., Wang, J., Zheng, N., Tang, X., Shum, H.Y.: Learning to detect a slient object. IEEE Trans. Pattern Anal. Mach. Intell. **33**(2), 353–367 (2011)

Robust Marker-Based Tracking for Measuring Crowd Dynamics

Wolfgang Mehner[1]([envelope]), Maik Boltes[2], Markus Mathias[1], and Bastian Leibe[1]

[1] Visual Computing Institute, Computer Vision Group,
RWTH Aachen University, Aachen, Germany
{mehner,mathias,leibe}@vision.rwth-aachen.de
[2] Forschungszentrum Jülich GmbH, Jülich, Germany
m.boltes@fz-juelich.de

Abstract. We present a system to conduct laboratory experiments with thousands of pedestrians. Each participant is equipped with an individual marker to enable us to perform precise tracking and identification. We propose a novel rotation invariant marker design which guarantees a minimal Hamming distance between all used codes. This increases the robustness of pedestrian identification. We present an algorithm to detect these markers, and to track them through a camera network. With our system we are able to capture the movement of the participants in great detail, resulting in precise trajectories for thousands of pedestrians. The acquired data is of great interest in the field of pedestrian dynamics. It can also potentially help to improve multi-target tracking approaches, by allowing better insights into the behaviour of crowds.

Keywords: Vision system application · Multi-target tracking · ID-markers

1 Introduction

The field of *pedestrian dynamics* deals with the analysis of collective behaviour of crowds of people, *e.g.*, investigating and modelling human behaviour during the evacuation of large public buildings. In order to assess basic properties of this behaviour, for example to determine the capacity of emergency exits, laboratory experiments are invaluable [16]. Only with such experiments one can do parameter studies, for example to investigate the influence of the width of an emergency exit on its throughput. A whole community [5,20] performs research on this subject and uses data from laboratory experiments for the estimation and validation of pedestrian models. They generate statistics of crowd motion, observe behavioural patterns, and collect empirical data for influencing norms and policy making.

When conducting such experiments with hundreds or thousands of participants not many technologies are available [3]. Motion capturing does not work for the targeted density and the number of participants. Other technologies, such

© Springer International Publishing Switzerland 2015
L. Nalpantidis et al. (Eds.): ICVS 2015, LNCS 9163, pp. 445–455, 2015.
DOI: 10.1007/978-3-319-20904-3_40

as RFID chips [17], do not offer sufficient precision, cannot track the required number of persons, or would be too cost intensive. Therefore, we propose a system based on video and use visual markers to detect and track participants. This system generates trajectories which can be analysed in great detail later on.

When conducting experiments, each participant wears a hat with a marker printed on it (Fig. 1). Using our proposed markers, each participant can be uniquely identified. We are then able to analyse motions of individuals across different runs of the experiments, and link it to other information, such as their gender and age.

In our application the main focus lies on precise measurements of the position and head orientation of all participants. To that end the frame rate during recording should at least be 16 fps, to enable the capturing of sudden motions. The tracking should not introduce any smoothing and not make assumptions about the underlying behaviour, as our application requires precise measurements. To achieve these goals, we create a special laboratory environment. This contrasts to classical tracking applications, where models have to be used to enable tracking and the reacquiring of targets after occlusions.

Our main contributions are: (1) We present a system to conduct measurements during laboratory experiments with thousands of pedestrians. (2) We propose a design for markers which guarantees a minimal Hamming distance between the used codes, even in the presence of rotated versions of the markers. (3) We present a pipeline to detect and precisely localize the resulting marker trajectories in 3D. We show the systems' applicability by using it on large scale experiments. It has been used to analyse about 200 experiments. Every experiment has been recorded by 12 to 24 cameras. Individual runs have been performed with up to 1000 participants. Trajectories produced by our system are already used to conduct research in pedestrian dynamics.

The remainder of the paper is organized as follows. After summarizing related work in Sect. 2, Sect. 3 explains the system set-up. Section 4 introduces the rotation invariant markers. In Sect. 5 we present the processing pipeline and evaluate it in Sect. 6.

2   Related Work

In the pedestrian dynamics community, various experiments have been evaluated using video processing methods. Boltes et al. used structured markers to track pedestrians during laboratory experiments [2], but without the possibility to identify individual persons. Colour is used by Daamen et al. to mark different classes of participants in their experiments [7]. Recently, ID-markers have been used by Stuart et al. [19] and Bukáček et al. [4]. However, their markers are larger than heads, making them unsuitable for high densities. Motion capturing is employed by Lemercier et al. [11,13] for experimenting with pedestrians walking in a line. In this case, motion capturing seem ideal. The view of the pedestrians' shoulder, which are also equipped with reflective markers, will not be obfuscated by pedestrians walking next to them.

Fig. 1. An experiment in progress. The cameras are fixed to the same metal frame as the spotlights, 7.5 m above the floor. (image credit: Marc Strunz)

ID-markers have been the subject of research in the field of augmented reality. The software ARToolkitPlus [8] provides markers similar in grid size to those we use, but with an additional border. Our markers are better optimized for the given use case, i.e. they are better suited for smaller resolutions. Also the well-known QR Codes [1] require a minimum size of 11 by 11 marker bits, and therefore suffer the same problem of being difficult to read in low-resolution images.

Multi-target tracking and the analysis of human crowds are an active topic in computer vision research. For a comprehensive summary see [21]. Even though our tracking problem is more restricted, we target a different application with a special focus on high precision.

3   System Set-Up

The intended use of the system for conducting laboratory experiments yields a special set of requirements. The focus is on precise measurements. All participants should be tracked continuously, so occlusions have to be avoided. Furthermore, we rather want to report no measurement than a wrong one, since this is easier to correct in an interactive fashion. In conclusion, we focus on high precision in terms of the detection rate, precise positioning, and correct identification.

In the proposed set-up we use overhead views for the cameras, both to avoid occlusions and to facilitate the marker read out. We like to keep the viewing angles small, such that larger pedestrians can not occlude smaller ones, even at the borders of the field of view. Furthermore, small opening angles reduce the

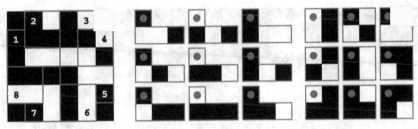

(a) Positions of the let-   (b) Encoding of the nine alpha- (c) Encoding as square
ters on the marker.   bet letters as L-shaped letters. letters.

Fig. 2. Marker Layout. (The red digits and the red dots mark the anchor points of each letter (Color figure online).)

image distortion. A large number of cameras increases the resolution to read out the markers for identification of the participants. We use a camera grid of six by four cameras (with a resolution of 1280 x 1024), mounted 7.5 m above the floor, which covers a little over 10 m by 10 m at ground level. The markers are of size 8.5 cm by 8.5 cm, resulting in an edge length of the marker bits of 1.4 cm.

Other than the grid cameras, one additional camera is placed in between two of the grid cameras to allow measuring the heights of the participants. Lastly, a fish-eye camera is placed in the middle of the grid, overlooking the entire experiment.

3.1   Camera Calibration

The internal calibration of each camera is computed beforehand [22]. The grid is calibrated using visual correspondences. A group of them is produced by laying out markers in the measurement area, which instantly gives identifiable feature points in the image spaces of the cameras. Additionally, out of plane correspondences are marked by hand. The calibration is then calculated via bundle adjustment [10] over the point correspondences.

4   Marker Design

The markers are designed to fulfil the constraints imposed by the experimental set-up (Sect. 3). Their maximum size is limited by several factors: the head size, the image resolution and the need for robust detection. A marker should not exceed the person's head, or have sharp edges, since that would be unsafe at the targeted density of up to six persons per square meter. Furthermore, the markers have to be readable from a distance of 6 m, given our camera resolution of 1280 x 1024.

The markers are encoded using an error-correcting code [6], which is able to detect errors caused by a wrong binarization of the markers. In coding theory, it is expected that unreliable channels distort the data, causing so-called transmission errors. Error-correcting codes encode messages (in our case the IDs of

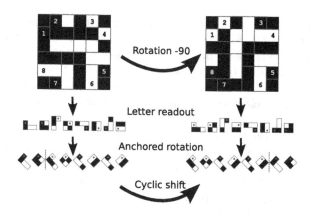

Fig. 3. Marker read out procedure and cyclic shifts. Each letter is indicated with a red rim, the number corresponds to the position of the letter in the codeword. After reading out each letters, the position of the number (now indicated with a red dot) corresponds to an anchor point. An anchored rotation aligns squares with a red dot. A rotation by 90 degrees corresponds to a cyclic shift of the codeword by two letters. (Color figure online).

the markers) with codewords. A minimal Hamming distance between each valid codeword guarantees the ability to detect or even correct transmission errors.

Rotation invariance can be resolved in various ways, *e.g.* by encoding rotation information into the marker design or by mapping different rotations of the marker to valid codewords.

We follow the second approach by ensuring that a rotation of the marker results in a valid codeword. To achieve this, we base our marker on a *cyclic* Reed-Solomon code [15]. Cyclic means that a cyclic shift of each valid codeword is still a valid codeword, e.g. if $(c_1, c_2, c_3, \ldots, c_8)$ is a valid codeword, so is $(c_2, c_3, \ldots, c_8, c_1)$.

Our marker layout is designed in a way that the readout of a rotated marker is just a cyclic shift of the readout of an unrotated marker. By design, all marker rotations are also valid codewords and fulfil the minimal Hamming distance.

Our Reed-Solomon code has messages of length $k = 5$ and codewords of length $n = 8$ over an alphabet with $q = 9$ letters. Figure 2a shows an example of a marker codeword consisting of 8 letters. Each letter is encoded with four bits (see Figs. 2b and 2c), the bits can be arranged L-shaped or squared. As can be seen, the letters may appear in different rotations. The positions of the numbers and red dots in Fig. 2 correspond to anchor points and define the rotation for each letter, *e.g.* in Fig. 2a letter 6 and letter 8 are the same.

By using only these 9 letters, we discard 7 $(= 2^4 - 9)$ combinations for potential letters. This helps us to impose additional structure on the marker, e.g. by not using letters which are completely white or black, and allowing only patterns with at least one black bit on the border of the marker.

With these parameters we are able to encode $q^k = 59049$ different messages. After identifying four different cyclic shifts of codewords, the number is reduced to $q^k/4 \approx 14762$. Some codewords are the same after a cyclic shift of 2 or 4 (or a rotation of 90° or 180°), which would not allow us to detect the full 360° rotation. After removing these markers, we can produce 14580 different markers.

The minimal distance of two codewords is $n - k + 1 = 4$, which allows us to detect two transmission errors and correct one. Here, a transmission error means that one of the eight letters which are encoded on the marker is binarized erroneously.

The encoding of the alphabet with the nine different bit patters, combined with the four black corner-bits, gives rise to desirable visual properties. At least twelve bits are always black, eight are always white, and equally distributed over the marker. Furthermore, at least four bits on each border are set to black. Therefore, our marker does not require an explicit border [8], as it has a sufficient amount of edge pixels along the border.

Figure 3 shows that reading out a marker and a rotated version of the same marker results in a cyclic shift of the codeword by two positions.

5   Marker Detection and Tracking

After recording the experiments, the analysis is done off-line. The markers are detected, read out (Sect. 5.1), and tracked (Sect. 5.2) in the images of the grid cameras. Then the generated trajectories are projected into the world coordinate system using pre-determined heights (Sect. 5.3). Afterwards the trajectories from the different cameras are combined, or stitched, which gives us the path of each participant through the whole set-up (Sect. 5.3).

5.1   Marker Detection

We first find regions-of-interest (ROI), image patches with potential markers. The goal of ROI detection is a hight recall, in order not to lose any markers in this stage.

To detect ROIs, we run Harris corner detection and look for parts of the image with many high-scoring corner points. Given the structure of the marker, we expect many corner point at their location. For each pixel we sum up all the corner responses in a window given by the marker size. This responses space is smoothed and non-maximum suppression is run to produce the ROIs.

The marker detection algorithm runs on these patches. We find lines using Hough transform. From the found lines, marker candidates are generated, which are then binarized and decoded to confirm that an actual marker has been found.

We first run Hough transform, where each pixels votes for a line, weighted by its gradient magnitude. The usual line parametrization (α, d) is used, with the angle $\alpha \in [0, 2\pi)$ and the distance to the origin $d \in [0, D_{max}]$. Then the voting space is collapsed and all votes for each angle accumulated. This allows us to compute the main orientation of the potential marker. We have to take into account that several angles belong to the same main orientation, separated by offsets $\Delta_{off} = \{0, \frac{\pi}{2}, \pi, \frac{3\pi}{2}\}$:

$$\alpha_{main} = \mathrm{argmax}_{\alpha} \sum_{d=0}^{D_{max}} \sum_{\delta \in \Delta_{off}} vote(\alpha + \delta, d) \qquad (1)$$

Using the main orientation we find lines by using non-maximum suppression on all the votes which have an angle α equal to the main orientation. For this step we fix the angles, and search for line candidates $C_{lines,i}$ along the main angles $\alpha_1 = \alpha_{main}$ and $\alpha_2 = \alpha_{main} + \frac{\pi}{2}$:

$$\begin{aligned}
C_{lines,1} &= \{(\alpha_1, d) \mid vote(\alpha_1, d - \epsilon) < vote(\alpha_1, d) > vote(\alpha_1, d + \epsilon)\} \\
C_{lines,2} &= \{(\alpha_2, d) \mid vote(\alpha_2, d - \epsilon) < vote(\alpha_2, d) > vote(\alpha_2, d + \epsilon)\}
\end{aligned} \qquad (2)$$

This gives us a set of lines from which to sample the 7 by 7 grid lines of the potential marker.

Each pair of lines from the candidate set $C_{lines,i}$ votes for the size of marker bits s_i along the directions given by α_i. All pairs of line candidates (α_i, d_a), $(\alpha_i, d_b) \in C_{lines,i}$ vote for marker bit sizes $|d_a - d_b|$. Using the lines and sizes, voting for the middle lines d_i of the marker can be performed next, using a similar idea as in the previous step.

We obtain the central point (m_x, m_y) by intersecting the lines given by (α_i, d_i). This yields candidate detections parametrized by $(m_x, m_y, \alpha_1, \alpha_2, s_1, s_2)$. These parameters describe an affine transformation, but the representation is better suited for our problem. We then rescore the candidates using the corner responses inside the area of the marker. Finally, the markers are binarized and read out.

5.2   Trajectory Generation

The tracking of the marker trajectories is in essence single-object tracking, since we can track one ID at a time. As we assume no severe measurement noise, we use the detections and IDs in every frame. Missing detections, which are located between frames with detections, are interpolated using optical flow, which is a procedure adapted from [18].

We use a variation of Lucas-Kanade image registration, which computes the rotation of the image patch as well. This is already outlined in their original paper [14]. We use a special instance of this problem, and register image patches F and G by minimizing:

$$E(t, \alpha) = \sum_{x \in R} \left(G\left(\begin{pmatrix} \cos(\alpha) & -\sin(\alpha) \\ \sin(\alpha) & \cos(\alpha) \end{pmatrix} x + t \right) - F(x) \right)^2 \qquad (3)$$

This way, we can interpolate over a gap (up to a maximum of 20 frames) in the trajectory in forward and backward direction, and compare the resulting tracks to improve the quality of the tracking.

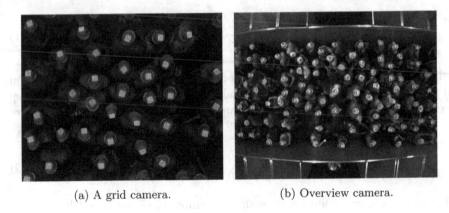

(a) A grid camera.   (b) Overview camera.

Fig. 4. Camera views with annotated markers.

5.3 3D Localization

To perform 3D localization, we also require the height of each participant. For this we use an additional camera in the grid. This camera shares its entire field of view with two other cameras, so we can cast rays and compute the heights of the pedestrians from the intersections of rays of corresponding marker detections. We use the middle of the 6 by 6 marker grid to define a precise image location.

After detecting and tracking the markers in the grid cameras, the desired 3D information in world coordinates has to be reconstructed. Since this is not directly possible from monocular cameras, we use the marker ID to obtain the height h of each participant. Then, for each tracked marker position, we cast rays and intersect them with a plane which is parallel to the ground plane at height h.

Only then we combine the different views of the grid cameras. All tracklets, the parts of the trajectories as seen in a single view, are stitched together in 3D space. This is done separately for each ID. If one person is seen and detected in the intersection area of two cameras, we take the detection which is closer to the centre of the image plane. Since all the cameras are of the same type, and mounted at the same height above ground, distances in the image plane are directly comparable.

6 Evaluation

In the following, the different steps of the processing pipeline are evaluated.

6.1 Marker Detection

The marker detection and tracking are evaluated in the view of a grid camera. We evaluate the different stages ROI generation, marker detection, and tracking

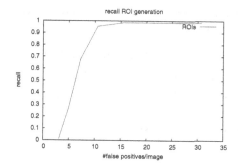

Fig. 5. Performance of the ROI generation.

Table 1. Performance of the marker detection and tracking, using different thresholds for the position.

Step	Recall	Precision	FP / image
ROI	0.99	0.60	15.56
Detection (5px)	0.78	0.93	1.27
Detection (10px)	0.78	0.94	1.24
Tracking (5px)	0.89	0.94	1.27
Tracking (10px)	0.95	0.95	1.12

in image space. As ground-truth data we use an annotated sequence of 600 frames, which contains both a completely empty scene and various densities of pedestrians (see Fig. 4a).

A region-of-interest is considered correct (true positive), if an actual marker falls inside its outline. Only one ROI is excepted per ground-truth detection. The score of a ROI is computed using the scores of the Harris corner points in its image patch. The recall of the ROI generation can be seen in Fig. 5. While the number of false positives per image is substantial, the precision is still satisfactory, reaching 0.60 at a recall of 0.99 (see Table 1), meaning that more than half of the ROIs correspond to actual markers.

Table 1 shows the performance of the different steps of the pipeline. The goal up to this stage is still a high recall, to lose as few actual trajectories as possible before stitching. A marker position, both detected and tracked, is considered correct if it is within 5 or 10 pixels of the actual position. This corresponds to a positioning error of approximately 1.5 cm or 3 cm in our set-up. The tracking is able to increase the recall while keeping the precision, by filling in gaps and rejecting isolated detections.

6.2 Tracking and Stitching

To evaluate the tracking trough the entire set-up, we use the multiple object tracking accuracy (MOTA) metric [12]. As ground-truth data, we use trajectories

454 W. Mehner et al.

Table 2. Performance after stitching. "Mostly Hit" are trajectories for which at least 80% of the positions have been found.

Experiment	MOTA	Traj	Mostly Hit	Mostly Tracked	Mostly Lost
Corridor	0.87	544	490	374	22
Crossing 90	0.86	599	569	534	8
Crossing 120a	0.87	710	639	587	16
Crossing 120b	0.89	783	688	604	22

which have been manually annotated in the view of the overview camera (see Fig. 4b). Several runs of experiments are used for this purpose, each with a different geometry. We evaluate using the IDs of the trajectories, so there can be no mismatches. Instead, all potential mismatches count as false positives. Furthermore, we report the number of mostly tracked and mostly lost trajectories. "Mostly tracked" means that more than 80% of the ground-truth trajectory are tracked in one continuous segment. We also report the number of "mostly hit" trajectories, which is the number of trajectories for which more than 80% of the positions of the ground-truth trajectory are found. The results are listed in Table 2. The "mostly hit" trajectories are fragmented, but are still useful in our case. Since all the data has to be cleaned up manually to be suitable for further research, fragments which can be stitched together still reduce the workload for that task.

7 Conclusion

In this paper, we introduced a new design for ID-markers, which guarantees a minimal distance in the presence of rotated versions of the marker. We presented a pipeline to detect and track these markers. We used them in a system to evaluate large-scale experiments with thousands of pedestrians. This system allows us to produce precisely localized marker trajectories in 3D. In the future, we plan to improve multi-target tracking systems by extracting insights of the behaviour of crowds from the generated data, which could yield better statistical models for tracking.

Acknowledgements. This study was performed within the project BaSiGo (Bausteine für die Sicherheit von Großveranstaltungen, Safety and Security Modules for Large Public Events) funded by the Federal Ministry of Education and Research (BMBF) Program on "Research for Civil Security – Protecting and Saving Human Life". Markus Mathias and Bastian Leibe are funded by the ERC Starting Grant Project CV-SUPER (ERC-2012-StG-307432).

References

1. Qr code - official website. www.qrcode.com
2. Boltes, M., Zhang, J., Seyfried, A., Steffen, B.: T-junction: experiments, trajectory collection, and analysis. In: ICCV Workshops, pp. 158–165 (2011)
3. Boltes, M.: Automatische Erfassung präziser Trajektorien in Personenströmen hoher Dichte. Ph.D. thesis, Forschungszentrum Jülich (2015)
4. Bukáček, M., Hrabák, P., Krbálek, M.: Experimental study of phase transition in pedestrian flow. Transp. Res. Procedia **2**, 105–113 (2014)
5. Chraibi, M., Boltes, M., Schadschneider, A., Seyfried, A. (eds.): Traffic and Granular Flow '13. Springer, Switzerland (2015)
6. Clark Jr., G.C., Cain, J.B.: Error-Correction Coding for Digital Communications. Springer, New York (1981)
7. Daamen, W., Hoogendoorn, S.: Capacity of doors during evacuation conditions. Procedia Eng. **3**, 53–66 (2010)
8. Daniel, W., Dieter, S.: Artoolkitplus for pose tracking on mobile devices. In: Proceedings of 12th Computer Vision Winter Workshop (2007)
9. Fiala, M.: ARTag, an improved marker system based on artoolkit. Technical report, Institute for Information Technology, National Research Council Canada (2004)
10. Hartley, R., Zisserman, A.: Multiple View Geometry in Computer Vision. Cambridge University Press, Cambridge (2003)
11. Jelić, A., Appert-Rolland, C., Lemercier, S., Pettré, J.: Properties of pedestrians walking in line: fundamental diagrams. Phys. Rev. E **85**(3), 036111 (2012)
12. Keni, B., Rainer, S.: Evaluating multiple object tracking performance: the CLEAR MOT metrics. EURASIP J. Image Video Process. **2008** (2008)
13. Lemercier, S., Moreau, M., Moussaïd, M., Theraulaz, G., Donikian, S., Pettré, J.: Reconstructing motion capture data for human crowd study. In: Allbeck, J.M., Faloutsos, P. (eds.) MIG 2011. LNCS, vol. 7060, pp. 365–376. Springer, Heidelberg (2011)
14. Lucas, B.D., Kanade, T.: An iterative image registration technique with an application to stereo vision. In: IJCAI, pp. 674–679 (1981)
15. Reed, I.S., Solomon, G.: Polynomial codes over certain finite fields. J. Soc. Ind. Appl. Math. **8**(2), 300–304 (1960)
16. Schadschneider, A., Klingsch, W., Klüpfel, H., Kretz, T., Rogsch, C., Seyfried, A.: Evacuation dynamics: empirical results, modeling and applications. In: Meyers, R.A. (ed.) Encyclopedia of Complexity and System Science, pp. 3142–3176. Springer, New York (2009)
17. Secoando, F., Plagemann, C., Jiménez, A.R., Burgard, W.: Improving rfid-based indoor positioning accuracy using gaussian processes. In: 2010 International Conference on Indoor Positioning and Indoor Navigation (IPIN) (2010)
18. Shi, J., Tomasi, C.: Good features to track. In: CVPR, pp. 593–600 (1994)
19. Stuart, D., Christensen, K., Chen, A., Kim, Y., Chen, Y.: Utilizing augmented reality technology for crowd pedestrian analysis involving individuals with disabilities. In: Proceedings of the ASME 2013 International Design Engineering Technical Conferences and Computers and Information in Engineering Conference (2013)
20. Weidmann, U., Kirsch, U., Schreckenberg, M. (eds.): Pedestrian and Evacuation Dynamics 2012. Springer, Switzerland (2014)
21. Zhan, B., Monekosso, D.N., Remagnino, P., Velastin, S.A., Xu, L.Q.: Crowd analysis: a survey. Mach. Vis. Appl. **19**(5–6), 345–357 (2008)
22. Zhang, Z.: A flexible new technique for camera calibration. PAMI **22**(11), 1330–1334 (2000)

Including 3D-textures in a Computer Vision System to Analyze Quality Traits of Loin

M. Mar Ávila[1], Daniel Caballero[2]([⊠]), M. Luisa Durán[1], Andrés Caro[1],
Trinidad Pérez-Palacios[2], and Teresa Antequera[2]

[1] Computer Science Department, Polytechnic School, University of Extremadura,
Av/Universidad S/n, 10071 Caceres, Spain
mmavila@unex.es
http://gim.unex.es/mmavila
[2] Food Technology, Research Institute of Meat and Meat Product (IproCar),
University of Extremadura, 10.003, Caceres, Spain
dcaballero@unex.es

Abstract. Texture analysis by co-occurrences on magnetic resonance imaging (MRI) involves a non-invasive nor destructive method for studying the distribution of several texture features inside meat products. Traditional methods are based on 2D image sequences, which limit the distribution of texture to a single plane. That implies a loss of information when texture features are studied from different orientations. In this paper a new 3D algorithm is proposed and included in a computer vision system to study the distribution of textures in 3D images of Iberian loin from different orientations. The semantic interpretation of textural composition in each orientation is also reached.

Keywords: Co-occurrence · 3D Textures · Iberian loin · MRI

1 Introduction

Computer vision systems are a subject of research and application for several industrial processes. These systems have been successfully applied in many engineering fields such as robotics, industrial image processing, food processing and other fields [1]. Quickness, possibilities for non-destructive evaluation, easy procedures for application, and quantum of output per unit time are some advantages that promote the application of computer vision systems to food engineering [2]. During the last years food industry have been among the top five industries in 3D computer vision applications. Researches into the development of appropriate techniques for evaluating 3D objects and scenes are being pursued [3].

The Iberian dry-cured meat products, mainly hams and loins, constitute an important industry in the South-western part of the Iberian Peninsula. These are usually targeted to the dry-cured product market, reaching a high sensory quality and first rate in consumer acceptance. Our research group has been using methods of texture analysis on images of meat products, especially from Iberian pigs [4].

L. Nalpantidis et al. (Eds.): ICVS 2015, LNCS 9163, pp. 456–465, 2015.
DOI: 10.1007/978-3-319-20904-3_41

Texture analysis methods have been applied to images obtained by means of MRI which allow seeing inside the product, without destroying the sample [5]. Relationships between computational texture features and physico-chemical characteristics such as fat, salt level, and moisture [6] have been established. And the prediction of sensory features such as acceptable color, tenderness on the palate, and acidity has been achieved [7].

MRI provides sequences of two-dimensional images showing transversal slices from the meat product. This enables us to make three-dimensional reconstructions of the bodies. The physical properties of the pieces are distributed inside the product, but not always in a uniform way. This idea leads to search for methods to analyse the distribution of different texture features inside the piece, exploring it as a volume, a three-dimensional space, instead of a sequence of images of slices.

The classical Gray-Level Co-Occurrence Matrix (GLCM) algorithm obtains texture features based on co-occurrence of gray levels found in each of the four orientations in the plane ($0°$, $45°$, $90°$, and $135°$), for 2D images. These co-occurrences are accumulated into a matrix, on which the texture features proposed by Haralick are calculated (energy, entropy, correlation, Haralick correlation,inverse difference moment, inertia, cluster prominence, cluster shade, contrast, and dissimilarity) [8]. The same method can be applied in all orientations in a three-dimensional space. This would be the natural evolution from 2D to 3D texture algorithm [9]. However, instead of accumulating all co-occurrences in a matrix, these can be analysed at different levels obtaining several points of view on feature textures inside the product. This is the key of the 3D texture algorithm proposed for our computer vision system.

The most recent advances in researches on three-dimensional images are focused on visual systems such as real scenes reconstruction and true textures recreation [10] even for face recognition applications [11]. There are other developed methods in the field of the to analyze internal tissues or tumor [12,13]. Only few attempts have been applied to analyse food products [9,14].

The objective of this work is to develop computer vision system to determine quality characteristics of loin, including a new 3D texture algorithm. The semantic content of the textures features is also aimed to be explained.

2   Material

Magnetic resonance images (MRI) from ten Iberian loins were generated at the Animal Source Foodstuffs Innovation Services (SiPA, Cáceres, Spain). A MRI scanner (ESAOTE VET-MR E-SCAN XQ 0.18 T) was used with nine different configurations differing in echo time (TE) and repetition time (TR). Sequences of Spin Echo (SE) T1 were applied with a field of view (FOV) of $150 \times 150\,\text{mm}^2$, slice thickness 4 mm, i.e., a voxel resolution $0.23 \times 0.23 \times 4\,\text{mm}^3$. Twenty nine slices per loin piece were obtained. The total number of 2D images is 2610 images (29 images $\times$ 10 loins $\times$ 9 configurations).

Physico-chemical analysis on loins were carried out in order to obtain values for moisture, color coordinates (L, a, b), salt content and lipid content. Those values

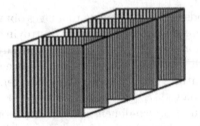

Fig. 1. 3D synthetic image

are related to the quality of the loin and were applied to correlate them with texture features calculated on 3D figures.

A set of 15 synthetic images ($512 \times 512 \times 5$) were used to evaluate the feasibility of the proposal. Figure 1 shows one of these images.

3   Methods

Figure 2 illustrates our computer vision system. This system obtains quality parameters of loins based on MRI and texture algorithms. Several texture algorithms have been tested to evaluate the performance of the system: two-dimensional texture algorithm (classical GLCM method) proposed by Haralick [8], three-dimensional texture algorithm (a readapted version of the 2D approach) [9], and our own 3D texture algorithm (called 3DTextFED).

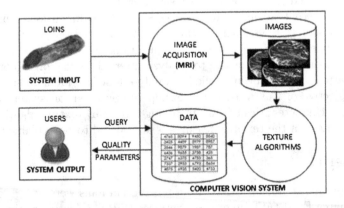

Fig. 2. Applied methodology

Figure 3 shows the flow chart explaining 3DTextFED, organized in three steps. First, in step (a) a 3D figure is constructed applying a linear interpolation function between each pair of slices. The linear interpolation function between two points a and b is calculated as:

$$f(p) = (1 - x) * f(a) + x * f(b)$$

where $f(a)$ and $f(b)$ are the values of the function for the a and b points, x is the distance between one of the points and p, the point where the value of f is interpolated.

The image acquisition process obtains sets of 2D images representing 3D spaces, by means of MRI. High resolution images are usually obtained (pixel resolution 0.23×0.23 in our case) nevertheless, the distance between consecutive images is not small enough (4 mm slice thickness in our case). However, it is better to have reasonable dimensions when trying to obtain textural information from volumetric structures. Otherwise, the voxel sizes would certainly be inconsistent in the Z dimension ($0.23 \times 0.23 \times 4\,\mathrm{mm}^3$). In 3DTextFED, this is achieved by interpolating four new images between each pair of consecutive MRI images, so that the voxel size becomes $0.23 \times 0.23 \times 0.8\,\mathrm{mm}^3$.

In step (b) textures are computed based on co-occurrences for each of the thirteen orientations. The classical GLCM algorithm [8] obtains texture features based on co-occurrence of gray levels found in each of the four orientations in the plane, for 2D images. These co-occurrences are accumulated into a single array, from which all the textural features are extracted. That implies a lack in the characterization of the objects from which textures are extracted, since an object can presents characteristics of high roughness in a plane (for example, in the XY plane), and characteristics of high uniformity in the perpendicular plane (for example, the YZ plane). If the calculations of all possible planes are accumulated in a single array from which the texture features are extracted, all this information would be lost. Classical 3D GLCM algorithms also compute all the co-ocurrences in the same matrix.

Our 3D texture algorithm (3DTextFED) solves this problem. It generates a independent co-occurrence matrix for each one of the thirteen orientations: $0°–180°$, $90°–270°$, $135°–315°$, $45°–225°$ in the XY plane, $0°–180°$, $135°–315°$, $45°–225°$ in YZ plane, $135°–315°$, $45°–225°$ in the XZ plane and $135°$, $315°$, $45°$, $225°$ in the XYZ plane (Fig. 3b). Thus, instead of accumulating all the co-occurrences of the thirteen orientations in just one array, a separate matrix for each of these orientations are obtained. This allows studying independently the behavior of the textures in each orientation.

Finally in step (c) seven texture features are computed in each of the thirteen matrices: energy, entropy, inverse difference moment (IDM), Haralick's correlation (HC), inertia, cluster shade (CS), and cluster prominence (CP), as Fig. 3(c) shows. Thus, considering the thirteen orientations and the seven textural features in each of the orientations, a total amount of 91 features are extracted for each of the Iberian loins (7×13).

Semantic content such as coarseness, homogeneity, symmetry, contrast are described based on the obtained values for calculated texture features. Therefore, different behaviors can be observed in different planes and orientations. For example, texture features could present a very rugged behavior in some of the planes, whereas in others the aspect could be completely uniform. This is illustrated in Figs. 4 and 5, showing different views from the synthetic image shown in Fig. 1.

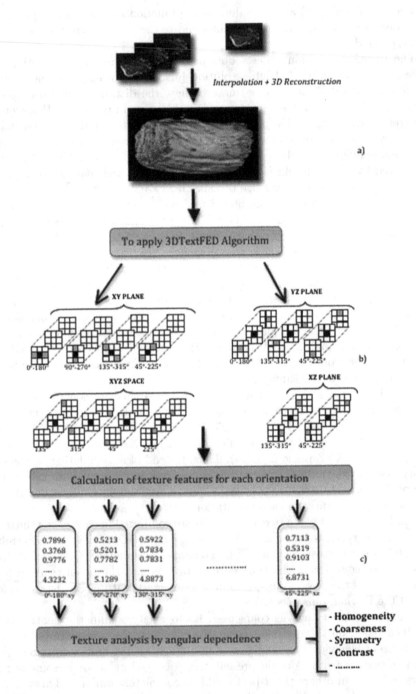

Fig. 3. The proposed 3D texture algorithm (3DTextFED).

Figure 4 shows an image from the viewpoint of the XY plane. The image is filled with vertical stripes. However, from the point of view of the YZ plane (Fig. 5) the image is formed by completely homogeneous planes, which clarifying the color according to the advance in the X coordinate. If all information will be stored in a single array, all that valuable knowledge would be lost.

Fig. 4. XY plane   **Fig. 5.** YZ plane of a 3D synthetic image
of a 3D synthetic
image

4   Results and Discussion

Table 1 shows the values of the texture features after applying the proposed methodology on the 3D synthetic image (Fig. 1).

The values of each feature are equal in the YZ planes, because they are completely homogenous planes. However, these values change in the other planes. Thus, it can be confirmed that this method can analyze 3D images from different angles, appreciating the different textures that they may present.

Table 1. Texture features obtained from a 3D synthetic image in each one of thirteen orientations

	Energy	Entropy	HC	IDM	Inertia	CS	CP
0°–180° xy	0.1586	0.7475	0.9513	0.0368	1.0000	1.0000	0.9515
90°–270° xy	1.0000	0.7475	1.0000	1.0000	0.0000	0.9141	1.0000
135°–315° xy	0.1586	1.0000	0.9513	0.0368	1.0000	1.0000	0.9515
45°–225° xy	0.1586	1.0000	0.9513	0.0368	1.0000	1.0000	0.9515
0°–180° yz	1.0000	0.7475	1.0000	1.0000	0.0000	0.9141	1.0000
135°–315° yz	1.0000	0.7475	1.0000	1.0000	0.0000	0.9141	1.0000
45°–225° yz	1.0000	0.7475	1.0000	1.0000	0.0000	0.9141	1.0000
135°–315° xz	0.1586	1.0000	0.9513	0.0368	1.0000	1.0000	0.9515
45°–225° xz	0.1586	1.0000	0.9513	0.0368	1.0000	1.0000	0.9515
135° xyz	0.1586	1.0000	0.9513	0.0368	1.0000	1.0000	0.9515
315° xyz	0.1586	1.0000	0.9513	0.0368	1.0000	1.0000	0.9515
135° xyz	0.1586	1.0000	0.9513	0.0368	1.0000	1.0000	0.9515
135° xyz	0.1586	1.0000	0.9513	0.0368	1.0000	1.0000	0.9515

Table 2. Texture features obtained from a fresh Iberian loin in each one of thirteen orientations

	Energy	Entropy	HC	IDM	Inertia	CS	CP
0°–180° xy	0.8439	0.0220	0.7696	0.9943	0.0003	0.2672	0.0001
90°–270° xy	0.6762	0.0426	0.7694	0.9980	0.0002	0.2943	0.0001
135°–315° xy	0.6205	0.0673	0.7701	1.0000	0.0010	0.2917	0.0001
45°–225° xy	0.8904	0.0191	0.7703	0.9858	0.0000	0.2997	0.0001
0°–180° yz	0.6358	0.0570	0.7696	0.9294	0.0004	0.2668	0.0001
135°–315° yz	0.7531	0.0380	0.7705	0.9534	0.0007	0.2717	0.0001
45°–225° yz	0.7720	0.0327	0.7703	0.9833	0.0001	0.2642	0.0001
135°–315° xz	0.6543	0.0372	0.7701	0.9718	0.0000	0.2946	0.0001
45°–225° xz	0.6684	0.0422	0.7702	0.9578	0.0002	0.2944	0.0001
135° xyz	0.6137	0.0635	0.7707	0.9991	0.0006	0.2860	0.0001
315° xyz	0.6220	0.0616	0.7710	0.9664	0.0008	0.2932	0.0001
135° xyz	0.8222	0.0281	0.7711	0.9528	0.0002	0.3046	0.0001
135° xyz	0.8817	0.0207	0.7709	0.9785	0.0001	0.2974	0.0001

Table 3. Texture features obtained from a dry-cured Iberian loin in each one of thirteen orientations

	Energy	Entropy	HC	IDM	Inertia	CS	CP
0°–180° xy	0.0280	0.7404	0.7159	0.2140	0.1237	0.4531	0.2516
90°–270° xy	0.0042	0.9050	0.7077	0.0180	0.4608	0.4804	0.2500
135°–315° xy	0.0079	0.8651	0.7119	0.0687	0.2768	0.4824	0.2599
45°-225° xy	0.0069	0.8811	0.7031	0.0286	0.4236	0.4783	0.2390
0°-180° yz	0.0112	0.8064	0.7147	0.1155	0.1527	0.4528	0.2605
135°–315° yz	0.0161	0.8054	0.7142	0.1239	0.1802	0.4595	0.2661
45°–225° yz	0.0171	0.7834	0.7140	0.1242	0.1519	0.4476	0.2536
135°–315° xz	0.0056	0.8834	0.7061	0.0272	0.3596	0.4798	0.2670
45°–225° xz	0.0057	0.8803	0.7066	0.0333	0.3808	0.4802	0.2617
135° xyz	0.0083	0.8607	0.7100	0.0556	0.2726	0.4733	0.2691
315° xyz	0.0086	0.8524	0.7107	0.0770	0.2513	0.4853	0.2686
135° xyz	0.0073	0.8809	0.7018	0.0314	0.4011	0.4865	0.2482
135° xyz	0.0078	0.8712	0.7022	0.0349	0.3583	0.4765	0.2465

The set of synthetic images were used to prove the feasibility of the algorithm and also to determine the semantic content of the texture features. The meaning of the texture features is a key aspect to understand them. Applying this methodology to each 3D Iberian loin piece, texture features in thirteen orientations are obtained. Below, two examples are shown, one of them referent to fresh loin (Table 2) and the other one referent to dry-cured loin (Table 3).

Table 4. Correlation coefficients R between physico-chemical parameters and texture features from GLCM.

	2D	3D	3DTextFED
Moisture	0.948	0.931	**0.956**
Water activity	0.950	0.956	**0.956**
Lipid	**0.791**	0.638	0.773
Salt	0.949	0.946	**0.963**
Color L	0.902	0.906	**0.913**
Color a	**0.851**	0.820	0.819
Color b	**0.786**	0.733	0.774

The homogeneity of the fresh Iberian loin can explain the low variation into the values in Table 2. Slight variations can be observed when obtained values for the fresh and cured loin are compared, because of the types of meat (fresh and cured meat, respectively).

Analyzing the meaning of the values of the texture features (Table 2), it can be determined that the fresh loin is uniform (high energy values, close to (1). Therefore, it does not have a messy texture (low entropy), being very homogeneous (very high IDM), with a quite low contrast, i.e. there is not large clusters of pixels with the same or similar gray level (low inertia, as fresh meat is very uniform), and it is not symmetrical in its structure (very low CS), nor gray levels (very low CP).

Regarding the values of features in the cured loin (Table 3), it can be seen that the energy decreases, so the cured loin is more rough than the fresh loin. And therefore, the entropy is high, presenting quite low IDM values, since it is not as homogeneous. The contrast increases and also the degree of symmetry, because the meat is cured.

Texture features are used as explanatory variables in a system of equations applying multiple linear regression (MLR). The free software WEKA (Waikato Environment for Knowledge Analysis) (http://www.cs.waikato.ac.nz/ml/weka/) was used for carrying out multiple linear regression [15]. The obtained equations provide values which have been correlated with real data obtained by physico-chemical analysis. Table 4 shows these correlations. Correlation of over 0.75 has been achieved in almost all cases, being in some of them of over 0.9.

Better correlations were obtained for 2D GLCM texture algorithm when compared to 3D GLCM texture algorithm. Five of the seven quality parameters (moisture, lipid, salt, color a, and color b) obtained better correlation for the 2D than for the 3D approach. That could imply that 3D textures, despite providing extra information, are not a satisfactory solution. However, our 3D algorithm provides the ability of considering multiple points of view (different angles), by computing the co-occurrences in different matrix. This allows better correlation ratios. The 3DTextFED algorithm obtained the best correlations for four of the seven quality parameters, and then was chosen as texture algorithm for the computer vision system.

Nevertheless, there is a high correlation between the parameters obtained by traditional destructive techniques and data obtained by means of textures analysis based on volumetric information. Quality parameters can be obtained in a non destructive nor invasive way, by using 3D textures. This is an important development for the meat industries, since it determines that it is not necessary to destroy any pieces to obtain parameters related to the quality of them.

5   Conclusion

A computer vision system to obtain quality parameters of loin based on MRI and texture algorithms has been tested and validated. The 3DTextFED algorithm is suitable for studying volumetric texture features from MRI loin, and the texture distribution has been analyzed in different orientations. Texture features in 3DTextFED reach high correlations with physico-chemical parameters of Iberian loin. Analyzing volumetric textures in different planes is a better option than applying simple adaptations of the classical 2D texture methods. The semantic content for the texture features of loins has been explained.

Acknowledgments. The authors wish to acknowledge the funding received for this research from Ministerio de Ciencia e Innovacion and FEDER-MICCIN-Infrastructure Research Project (UNEX10-1E-402), Gobierno de Extremadura - Consejeria de Empleo, Empresa e Innovacion and funds by FEDER (European Regional Development Funds). We also wish to thank Animal Source Foodstuffs Innovation Services (SiPA) from Faculty of Veterinary of University of Extremadura.

References

1. Mahendran, R., Jayashree, G.C., Alagusundaram, K.: Application of Computer Vision Technique on Sorting and Grading of Fruits and Vegetables, J. Food Process. Technol. S1–001 (2012)
2. Brosnan, T., Sun, D.-W.: Improving quality inspection of food products by computer vision - a review. J. Food Eng. **61**, 3–16 (2004)
3. Gunasekaran, S.: Computer vision technology for food quality assurance. Trends Food Sci. Technol. **7**, 245–256 (1996)
4. Cernadas, E., Durán, M.L., Antequera, T.: Recognizing marbling in dry-cured iberian ham by multiscale analysis. Pattern Recogn. Lett. **23**, 1311–1321 (2002)
5. Caro, A., Durán, M., Rodríguez, P.G., Antequera, T., Palacios, R.: Mathematical morphology on mri for the determination of iberian ham fat content. In: Sanfeliu, A., Ruiz-Shulcloper, J. (eds.) CIARP 2003. LNCS, vol. 2905, pp. 359–366. Springer, Heidelberg (2003)
6. Petrón, M.J., Durán, M.L., Ávila, M., Cernadas, E., Antequera, T.: A computer vision system to discriminate iberian pigs from ham images. Electron. J. Environ. Agric. Food Chem. **2**(5), 549–557 (2003)
7. Antequera, T., Muriel, E., Rodríguez, P.G., Cernadas, E., Ruiz, J.: Magnetic resonance imaging as a predictive tool for sensory characteristics and intramuscular fat content of dry-cured loin. J. Sci. Food Agric. **83**, 268–274 (2003)

8. Haralick, R.M., Shapiro, L.G.: Computer and Robot Vision. Addison-Wesley, Reading (1993)
9. Ávila, M.M., Durán, M.L., Antequera, T., Palacios, R., Luquero, M.: 3D reconstruction on MRI to analyse marbling and fat level in iberian loin. In: Martí, J., Benedí, J.M., Mendonça, A.M., Serrat, J. (eds.) IbPRIA 2007. LNCS, vol. 4477, pp. 145–152. Springer, Heidelberg (2007)
10. Lopez, A., Pla, F., Ribelles, J.: 3D modeling of structured scenes through binocular stereo vision. In: Scandinavian Conference on Image Analysis (2001)
11. Traver, V.J., Latorre-Carmona, P., Salvador-Balaguer, E., Pla, F., Javidi, B.: Human gesture recognition using three-dimensional integral imaging. J. Opt. Soc. Am. Opt. Image. Sci. Vis. 31(10), 2312–2320 (2014)
12. Mahmoud-Ghoneim, D., Toussaint, G., Constans, J.M., de Certaines, J.D.: Three dimensional texture analysis in MRI: a preliminary evaluation in gliomas. Magn. Resonnance Imaging 21(9), 983–987 (2003)
13. El-Baz, A., Casanova, M.F., Gimel'farb, G., Mott, M., Switala, A.E.: Autism diagnostics by 3D texture analysis of cerebral white matter gyrifications. Med. Image Comput. Assist. Interv. 10, 882–890 (2007)
14. Brosnan, T., Sun, D.-W.: Improving quality inspection of food products by computer vision, a review. Comput. Electron. Agric. 36, 193–213 (2002)
15. Perez-Palacios, T., Caballero, D., Caro, A., Rodrguez, P.G., Antequera, T.: Applying data mining and computer vision techniques to MRI to estimate quality traits in Iberian hams. J. Food Eng. 131, 82–88 (2014)

Adaptive Neuro-Fuzzy Controller
for Multi-object Tracker

Duc Phu Chau[1]([✉]), K. Subramanian[2], and François Brémond[1]

[1] STARS Team, INRIA Sophia Antipolis, Valbonne, France
{Duc-Phu.Chau,Francois.Bremond}@inria.fr
[2] School of Computer Engineering, Nanyang Technological University,
Singapore, Singapore
kartick1@e.ntu.edu.sg

Abstract. Sensitivity to scene such as contrast and illumination intensity, is one of the factors significantly affecting the performance of object
trackers. In order to overcome this issue, tracker parameters need to
be adapted based on changes in contextual information. In this paper,
we propose an intelligent mechanism to adapt the tracker parameters,
in a real-time and online fashion. When a frame is processed by the
tracker, a controller extracts the contextual information, based on which
it adapts the tracker parameters for successive frames. The proposed
controller relies on a learned neuro-fuzzy inference system to find satisfactory tracker parameter values. The proposed approach is trained on
nine publicly available benchmark video data sets and tested on three
unrelated video data sets. The performance comparison indicates clear
tracking performance improvement in comparison to tracker with static
parameter values, as well as other state-of-the art trackers.

1 Introduction

The research in field of object tracking [1,2,6,17] is seeing growing interest due to
its importance in the area such as video surveillance, motion-based recognition,
human computer interaction. These trackers aim to accurately associate multiple
objects across multiple frames. However, there are various challenges in this
field. One of the main challenges is real-time object association by trackers.
Moreover, the change in scene context might also affect the tracking performance
drastically. In order to overcome this issue, various real time trackers as well as
tracker parameter tuning mechanisms have been developed in literature.

An online learning scheme based on computationally expensive Adaboost is
proposed in [3], to calculate a discriminative appearance model for each mobile
object. Whereas, computationally expensive genetic algorithm based approach
is employed in [5] to search for best tracker parameters. Moreover, genetic algorithm suffers from the tendency to get stuck in local optimal solution space. In
literature, work employing multiple trackers to find the best parameters based
on contextual information has also been proposed [6]. In these works, there are
strong limitations on the online processing ability and self-adaptability to scene

© Springer International Publishing Switzerland 2015
L. Nalpantidis et al. (Eds.): ICVS 2015, LNCS 9163, pp. 466–476, 2015.
DOI: 10.1007/978-3-319-20904-3_42

variations. In [7], an online parameter tuning approach to adapt the tracking parameters of [4] to scene variations has been proposed, and code-books are utilized to store the learned parameters. The parameter tuning is however done using a nearest neighborhood search, which is not accurate when the training set is not large enough. To summarize, all these approaches have some limitations in genericity, efficiency or performance.

In literature of soft computing, various prediction/ forecasting techniques have been proposed, such as support vector regression [8] or artificial neural networks [11] which can learn efficiently even over small data sets. With the development of evolving/ online learning algorithms, the training data is learned when it appears without the need to be stored. This results in significantly reduced space and time complexity in learning. The above mentioned learning mechanisms can learn any given data efficiently. However, they fail to generalize the learned knowledge over unseen data. Recently, in [9], a Meta-Cognitive sequential learning algorithm for evolving Neuro-Fuzzy Inference System (McFIS) has been proposed which can self-regulate its learning to attain better training as well as generalization accuracy.

In this paper, we propose a generic, efficient et robust controller which relies on McFIS to adapt online tracker parameters for scene context variations. The proposed approach brings the following contributions:

- Evolving Learning
  - One-shot meta-cognitive learning for faster training.
  - Evolving/adaptive learning to estimate the functional relationship between tracking contextual features and tracking parameters.
- Online Control
  - A generic controller for tuning parameters of any tracker to cope with video content variation.
  - Accurate estimation of tracker parameters utilizing all rules.
  - Fast inference of tracker parameters.

The proposed controller is trained on nine publicly available video data sets and is tested on three unrelated video data sets. The results indicate a significant improvement in comparison to other recent state-of-the-art trackers.

The rest of the paper is organized as follows. In Sect. 2, we present the proposed object tracker controller mechanism. The performance of the proposed system is evaluated in Sect. 3. The paper is concluded and future work discussed in Sect. 4.

2 Tracker Control Mechanism

In this section, an overview of the proposed tracker control mechanism is described. The control mechanism consists of two phases, namely, a learning phase and an online control phase (as shown in Fig. 1). The aim of the learning phase is to find a functional relationship (F) between the contextual features of detected objects (**C**) and the best tracker parameters (**P**), for a given video chunk (v).

The online control phase determines the satisfactory tracker parameters ($\mathbf{P}$) for a given contextual feature set ($\mathbf{C}$) based on the learned functional relationship. Since the proposed mechanism is not dependent on video, but only on video meta-data (contextual information), it is applicable to unknown/unseen video sequences. The generalization ability of the controller to unseen video depends on how efficient the learned functional relationship $\mathbf{C} \to \mathbf{P}$. In this work, we employ a meta-cognitive neuro-fuzzy inference system [9] for learning the underlying functional relationship between $\mathbf{C}$ and $\mathbf{P}$.

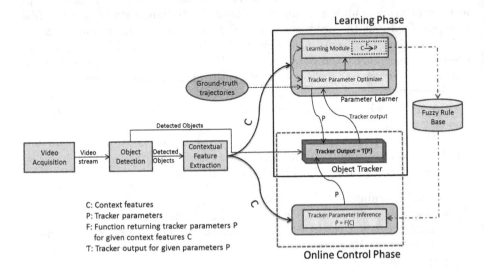

Fig. 1. Working of proposed tracker control mechanism

Two practical assumptions made in realizing this control mechanism:

- There is no drastic change in the observed scene over a short period of time (1–2 s).
- The controlled tracker has a set of important parameters which could be adjusted online to improve tracking performance.

Six scene contextual parameters are employed in this study, and they will be described in detail in the next section. The video chunk size (v) is decided based on tracking context variation. Fast variation requires a small chunk size and vice-versa. Also, the learning phase and the online control phase are mutually independent and hence they could be run in parallel.

Next, we describe the contextual features employed in this study. To control the parameters of the tracker, a fuzzy controller is employed. The control rules for this controller are learned in an adaptive fashion, employing a meta-cognitive learning algorithm. A detailed description on the fuzzy controller and its learning algorithm, together referred to as Meta-Cognitive Neuro-Fuzzy Inference System is detailed in Sect. 2.2.

2.1   Contextual Features

In this work, we use the six following features to define a context (or tracking context). These features are selected based on their effect on the tracker performance. The features employed are: density, occlusion, contrast, contrast variance, 2D area and 2D area variance. The calculation of each of these features and their effect on tracking is described next.

Density of Mobile Objects: Density of mobile objects affects the detection and tracking. More the mobile objects appear in scene, more the tracking issues can happen such as switch or lost of object identity. In this work, density of mobile objects at time t is defined as their 2D area occupancy over 2D camera view area.

Occlusion Level of Mobile Objects: Occlusion renders an object more difficult to detect and to track. Moreover, the variation of occlusion level results in loss of coherence of object appearance and causes the object tracking errors as consequence. The occlusion level of mobile objects at instant t is defined as the ratio between the 2D overlap area of objects and the object 2D areas.

Contrast of Mobile Objects: The contrast of an object is defined as the color intensity difference between this object and its surrounding background. Objects with low contrast imply a low discrimination between them, in particular for color descriptor-based trackers. In this work, contrast of an object at time t is calculated as the Earth Mover's Distance between the normalized intensity histograms of this object and its surroundings. The contrast value of mobile objects at frame t is defined as the mean value of all object contrasts at this frame.

Contrast Variance of Mobile Objects: In a video, when different contrast values exist, mean value cannot be representative of the multi-object contrast accurately. As a result, the variance of contexts across different objects in a scene is considered. The contrast variance at a frame is defined as the standard deviation of the contrast values computed at this frame.

2D Area of Mobile Objects: The 2D area characterizes the reliability of the object appearance for tracking. Greater the object area, higher object appearance reliability. The 2D area feature value at a frame is defined as the mean value of the 2D areas of mobile objects at the same frame.

2D Area Variance of Mobile Objects: Similar to contrast variance of mobile objects, 2D area variance of mobile objects is also defined as the standard deviation of the 2D areas of objects at the same frame.

McFIS based tracker controller infers the tracker parameters based on the above given scene contextual information and the knowledge stored in its knowledge base.

2.2   Meta-Cognitive Neuro-Fuzzy Inference System

In this section, we describe the employed fuzzy controller and its learning algorithm. The aim of the learning algorithm is to find the functional relationship between the contextual features $\mathbf{C}$ and tracker parameter values $\mathbf{P}$. The learned functional relationship is stored in form of Gaussian fuzzy rules. A fuzzy rule r is represented by three values: $[\boldsymbol{\mu}_r, \sigma_r, \boldsymbol{\alpha}_r]$ where $\boldsymbol{\mu}_r, \sigma_r$ denote the center and spread of the rule (representing information of the six above contextual features) and $\boldsymbol{\alpha}_r$ denotes its weightage (representing the tracker parameter values). For any given contextual input features set, McFIS calculates its similarity with existing fuzzy rules (membership). The tracker parameters are inferred as the weighted sum of these memberships. For example at any given time, let the controller consist of R fuzzy rules. The predicted tracker parameter values $\hat{\mathbf{P}}^t$ for a given scene contextual feature set $\mathbf{C}^t$ at time t, are then given as:

$$\hat{\mathbf{P}}^t = \frac{\sum_{r=1}^{R} \boldsymbol{\alpha}_r \phi_r}{\sum_{p=1}^{R} \phi_p} \tag{1}$$

where ϕ_r is a membership function and it represents the distance of context C to rule r and is defined in form of Gaussian function as follows:

$$\phi_r = \exp\left(-\frac{\|\mathbf{C}^t - \boldsymbol{\mu}_r\|^2}{2\sigma_r^2}\right) \tag{2}$$

During sequential learning, the aim of the meta-cognitive algorithm is to adapt/evolve the knowledge (fuzzy rules) such that the error $\mathbf{e}^t$ between the optimal tracker parameter values $\mathcal{P}^t$ (obtained using ground-truth data) and predicted tracker parameter values $\hat{\mathbf{P}}^t$ (computed by Eq. 1) is minimized.

Using this error value, the meta-cognitive learning algorithm employs a set of strategies, viz., sample deletion strategy, sample learning strategy and sample reserve strategy, to adapt/evolve the fuzzy control rules. The sample deletion strategy deletes the current input/output $(\mathbf{C}^t, \mathcal{P}^t)$ without being learned, if the prediction error $\mathbf{e}^t$ is significantly low $(\mathbf{e}^t < E_d)$. The sample learning strategy results in either a new rule being evolved or the parameters of the existing rules being adapted.

A new rule is added if prediction error is significantly high $(\mathbf{e}^t > E_a)$ and the existing rules do not sufficiently cover the current sample $(\psi^t < E_S)$. Here, ψ^t is a measure of rule coverage given by:

$$\psi^t = \frac{\sum_{r=1}^{R} \phi_r}{R} \tag{3}$$

During rule evolution, the $(R+1)^{th}$ rule is added as

$$\mu_{R+1} = \mathbf{C}^t \tag{4}$$

$$\sigma_{R+1} = \kappa \|\mathbf{C}^t - \boldsymbol{\mu}_{nr}\| \tag{5}$$

$$\alpha_{R+1} = \mathbf{P}^t - \frac{\sum_{r=1}^{R} \phi_r \alpha_r}{1 + \sum_{p=1}^{R} \phi_p} \tag{6}$$

where nr denotes the nearest rule to the context feature and κ is a predefined rule overlap factor (chosen in interval $[0.5, 0.9]$). The parameters of existing rules are updated using an extended Kalman filtering scheme if prediction error is higher $(\mathbf{e}^t > E_d)$.

3   Performance Evaluation

In the previous sections, we have presented McFIS based controller for object tracking. In this section, we evaluate the performance of the proposed controller. The parameters E_a, E_s and E_d of the proposed approach are fixed for all following experiments.

We select a baseline tracker using different object appearance descriptors [4] to experiment the proposed controller. We present the tracking results in three cases: baseline tracker (with fix parameters) [4], baseline tracker with a parameter tuner based on code-book [7], and baseline tracker with the controller proposed in this paper. The performance of the tracker with the proposed controller is compared against other state-of-the-art tracking algorithms. The performance comparison shows improved performance of a tracker with the proposed controller over state-of-the-art trackers.

3.1   Appearance Based Tracker

We employ the appearance-based tracker proposed in [4] to study the proposed control mechanism. The principle of this tracker is similar to many different appearance-based trackers in state of the art. This tracker relies on the computation of object similarity across different frames using different object appearance descriptors (e.g. 2D area, color histogram, color covariance). Since the object descriptor reliability is influenced by context, the descriptor weights w_k need to be set and tuned along changes in context. The approach [4] proposes a scheme to learn offline the values of these weights but cannot adjust them online.

In this work, we aim to predict the values of these weights all along the current video. We have selected the weights of the five following descriptors for tuning as they have a significant influence to tracker performance: 2D shape ratio, 2D area, color histogram, color covariance and dominant color. Therefore the set of parameters w_k corresponding to these descriptors represent the control parameters **P** in Sect. 2.

3.2   Training Phase

Initially, the proposed controller is trained on nine video sequences: six videos from CAVIAR dataset[1] and three from ETISEO dataset[2]. The videos are selected such that they represent a large of tracking contextual information (e.g.. low/high density of objects in the scene, strong/weak object contrast). The video chunk size v for controller (Sect. 2) is set to 50 frames. A training sample is the value set of six contextual features over a video chunk of 50 frames. The offline training phase requires the ground-truth of object tracking as input. The best descriptor weight values are found using grid-search technique, such that the F1-score is maximized.

---

[1] http://homepages.inf.ed.ac.uk/rbf/CAVIAR/.
[2] www-sop.inria.fr/orion/ETISEO.

At the end of the training phase, 91 rules are created after training 260 samples. This shows that the proposed learning scheme is convergent. Using these learned rules, we can define a mapping function to link the contextual features of the given 50 frames to the best tracking descriptor weights to maximize the tracking performance on the next video chunk.

3.3   Online Control Phase

The proposed controller is evaluated on two public datasets (PETS 2009 and TUD), and the third one from Vanaheim European project (recorded in a subway station). For all these videos, the observed scenes are different from the ones of training videos. As a new frame is presented to the controller, it extracts the six contextual values from HOG-based detector output. Upon concatenating the contextual features over 50 frames, the controller adapts the tracking descriptor weights to the change in contextual information using the mapping function.

PETS Dataset 2009. In this test, the sequence S2_L1, camera view 1, time 12:34 is selected for testing because this sequence is used for evaluation in several state of the art trackers. It consists of 794 frames with 21 mobile objects with different degrees of inter-person and person-object occlusion. The performance of the tracker is compared with respect to two metrics defined in [14]: Multi-object tracking precision (MOTP) and multi-object tracking accuracy (MOTA). Illustrations of tracking performance for frames 146, 149 and 158 are shown in Fig. 2.

The controller adapts the tracking parameters from frame 100 to frame 200 as follows: $w_1 = 0$ (2D shape ratio weight), $w_2 = 0.15$ (2D area weight), $w_3 = 0.3$ (color histogram weight), $w_4 = 0.4$ (color covariance weight) and $w_5 = 0.15$ (dominant color weight). This parameter tuning is reasonable. The color covariance descriptor can handle occlusion, so its weights is more important than the others. The color histogram performance is better than the dominant color when object resolution is small. The 2D shape ratio descriptor (defined as the ratio between the 2D width and 2D height) is not used as most of persons in the scene have quite similar shape ratio. Results show that all person trajectories are correct, in particular the person of ID 1104 (red trajectory) even when this person is heavily occluded in continuous frames.

| Frame 146 | Frame 149 | Frame 158 |

Fig. 2. Tracking results for persons in PETS data set. The tracking performance is correct even in the presence of high static and dynamic occlusion.

Table 1. Performance comparison for PETS 2009 video. The best values are printed in **red** (not taking into account the two offline approaches: [2] and [1]).

Approaches	#Ground truth	MOTA	MOTP
Amir et al., [2] (**offline tracker**)	21	*0.90*	*0.69*
Izadinia et al., [1] (**offline tracker**)	21	*0.90*	*0.76*
Berclaz et al., [15]	21	0.80	0.58
Shitrit et al., [12]	21	0.81	0.58
Chau et al., 2011 [4]	21	0.62	0.63
Chau et al., 2013 [7] ([4] with code-book based controller)	21	0.85	0.71
Proposed approach ([4] **with McFIS based controller**)	21	**0.86**	**0.73**

Table 1 gives the performance analysis on PETS video compared with other state-of-the-art trackers. The result of [12] is provided by [2]. In order to highlight the advantage of the proposed controller, the performance is also compared against the employed tracker [4] without the proposed controller and with a code-book controller [7]. It could be observed that the tracker performance of [4] is improved significantly thanks to the proposed McFIS controller. The MOTA value increases from 0.62 to 0.86, and the MOTP value increases from 0.63 to 0.73.

The obtained tracking performance also outperforms all the other considered trackers, except [1,2]. However, these two approaches are fully offline. In [2], the tracker requires the whole video for maximizing their results. In [1], the approach is optimized iteratively, rendering it offline. The proposed approach is fully online, wherein a frame is processed by the tracker one and only once. This makes the controller ideal for any real-time situations. Moreover, the controller achieves this precision based on training on other video sequences.

TUD-Stadtmitte. The second test is conducted with the the TUD-Stadtmitte sequence. This video is very challenging due to heavy and frequent object occlusions. Figure 3 shows a snapshot of the tracking performance of the proposed Tracker-Controller pair.

Fig. 3. Illustration of object tracking for the TUD-Stadtmitte video

Table 2 presents the tracking results of the proposed approach and three recent trackers from the state of the art. In this experiment, the following tracking evaluation metrics are used to easily compare with other approaches. Let GT be the number of trajectories in the ground-truth of the test video. The first metric MT (mostly tracked) computes the percentage of trajectories correctly tracked for more than 80 % of length. This metric represents the true positive value. The second metric PT (partially tracked) computes the percentage of trajectories correctly tracked between 20 % and 80 % length. The last metric ML (mostly lost) is the percentage of the remaining trajectories. The ML metric represents the false negative value.

Table 2. Tracking results for the TUD-Stadtmitte sequence. The best values are printed in **red**.

Methods	GT	$MT(\%)$	$PT(\%)$	$ML(\%)$
Kuo et al., [13]	10	60	30.0	10.0
Andriyenko et al., [16]	10	60.0	30.0	10.0
Chau et al., 2011 [4]	10	50.0	30.0	20.0
Chau et al., 2013 [7] ([4] with code-book based controller)	10	**70.0**	10.0	20.0
[4] **with McFIS based controller**	10	**70.0**	**30.0**	**0.0**

For this video, the proposed controller helps to increase the MT value from 50 % to 70 % and to decrease the ML value from 20 % to 0 %. Compared to [7], we obtain the same MT value (always 70 %), but much lower ML value (0 % compared to 20 %). We obtain the best MT and ML values compared to the other trackers.

Subway Video. The video of the third test belongs to an European project (anonymity). The test sequence contains 36006 frames and lasts 2 h. Figure 4 illustrates the correct tracking of three persons with low resolutions over time. In the second image, the contrast with respect to the surrounding background of the two persons with tracker ID 4 and 5 (corresponding to cyan and pink trajectories) are very low. They occlude each other at several frames but they are still correctly tracked (see the right image).

Fig. 4. Tracking of the motion of 3 persons in the subway video over time. The tracking is correct even with low person resolutions and low person contrast (in second image).

Table 3. Tracking results on the subway video. The proposed controller improves significantly the tracking performance. The best values are printed in **red**.

Approaches	GT	MT(%)	PT(%)	ML(%)
Souded et al., [10]	38	44.74	42.11	13.15
Chau et al., 2011 [4]	38	55.26	31.58	13.16
Chau et al., 2013 [7] ([4] with code-book based controller)	38	60.53	36.84	**2.63**
[4] with the McFIS based controller	**38**	**65.79**	**31.58**	**2.63**

Table 3 presents the performance of the proposed approach and three recent trackers from state of the art. For this sequence, the proposed controller improves the performance of the tracker [4]. The MT value increases from 55.26 % to 65.79 %. The ML value decreases significantly from 13.16 % to 2.63 %. The tracking result with the proposed controller gets the best quality among the trackers presented in table 3.

4 Conclusion

An online generic, efficient and robust controller, based on meta-cognitive neuro-fuzzy inference system, for an appearance-based tracker is proposed. It monitors the scene context over a chunk of frames to compute the satisfactory tracker parameter values for the next chunk of frames. The use of meta-cognitive learning strategies for the controller improves its generalization over unseen test data, in addition to reducing training time. The performance comparison on three untrained video sequences clearly highlights the tracking improvement with the proposed controller. In the future work, we will propose a method to determine automatically the most appropriate context scene features to characterize more accurately videos depending on the selected tracker.

Acknowledgments. This work is supported by The Panorama and Centaur European projects as well as The Movement French project.

References

1. Izadinia, H., Saleemi, I., Li, W., Shah, M.: (MP)^{2}T: multiple people multiple parts tracker. In: ECCV (2012)
2. Zamir, A.R., Dehghan, A., Shah, M.: GMCP-tracker: global multi-object tracking using generalized minimum clique graphs. In: ECCV (2012)
3. Kuo, C.H., Huang, C., Nevatia, R.: Multi-target tracking by online learned discriminative appearance models. In: CVPR (2010)
4. Chau, D.P., Bremond, F., Thonnat, M.: A multi-feature tracking algorithm enabling adaptation to context variations. In: ICDP (2011)
5. Hall, D.: Automatic parameter regulation of perceptual system. J. Image Vis. Comput. **24**, 870–881 (2006)

6. Yoon, J.H., Kim, D.Y., Yoon, K.J.: Visual tracking via adaptive tracker selection with multiple features. In: ECCV (2012)
7. Chau, D.P., Badie, J., Bremond, F., Thonnat, M.: Online tracking parameter adaptation based on evaluation. In: AVSS (2013)
8. Drucker, H., Durges, C.J., Kaufman, L., Smola, A., Vapnik, V.: Support vector regression machines. Adv. Neural Inf. Process. Syst. **9**, 155–161 (1997)
9. Subramanian, K., Suresh, S.: A meta-cognitive sequential learning algorithm for neuro-fuzzy inference system. J. Appl. Soft Comput. **12**, 3603–3614 (2012)
10. Souded, M., Giulieri, L., Bremond, F.: An Object tracking in particle filtering and data association framework, using SIFT features. In: ICDP (2011)
11. Psaltis, D., Sideris, A., Yamamura, A.: A multilayered neural network controller. IEEE Control Syst. Mag. **8**, 17–21 (1988)
12. Shitrit, J., Berclaz, J., Fleuret, F., Fua, P.: Tracking multiple people under global appearance constraints. In: ICCV (2011)
13. Kuo, C., Nevatia, R.: How does person identity recognition help multi-person tracking? In: CVPR (2011)
14. Kasturi, R., Soundararajan, P., Garofolo, J., Bowers, R., Korzhova, V.: How does person identity recognition help multi-person tracking? In: CVPR (2011)
15. Berclaz, J., Fleuret, F., Turetken, E., Fua, P.: Multiple object tracking using k-shortest paths optimization. IEEE Trans. Pattern Anal. Mach. Intell. (TPAMI) **33**, 1806–1819 (2011)
16. Andriyenko, A., Schindler, K.: Multi-target tracking by continuous energy minimization. In: CVPR (2011)
17. Chen, S., Fern, A., Todorovic, S.: Multi-object tracking via constrained sequential labeling. In: CVPR (2014)

Human Action Recognition Using Dominant Motion Pattern

Snehasis Mukherjee[1]([✉]), Apurbaa Mallik[2], and Dipti Prasad Mukherjee[3]

[1] IIIT Chittoor, Sricity, India
snehasis.mukherjee@iiits.in
[2] TCS Inovation Lab, Kolkata, India
apurbaa.mallik@tcs.com
[3] ISI, Kolkata, India
dipti@isical.ac.in

Abstract. The proposed method addresses human action recognition problem in a realistic video. The content of such videos are influenced by irregular background motion and camera shakes. We construct the human pose descriptors by using a modified version of optical flow (we call it as hybrid motion optical flow). We quantize the hybrid motion optical flow (HMOF) into different labels. The orientations of the HMOF vectors are corrected using probabilistic relaxation labelling, where the HMOF vectors with locally maximum magnitude are retained. A sequence of 2D points, called tracks, representing the motion of the person, are constructed. We select top dominant tracks of the sequence based on a cost function. The dominant tracks are further processed to represent the feature descriptor of a given action.

1 Introduction

Human action recognition is one of the most important topics of interest in computer vision [1]. The action recognition techniques consist of two broad steps – feature extraction and classification. We calculate improved motion vector at every pixel of the video eliminating noise due to background motion and camera. In order to reduce inconsistencies in motion vector direction at a pixel with respect to motion vectors of its neighbours, we use relaxation labeling approach. Correspondences between motion vectors along temporal scale are established minimizing a cost function. This results in finding motion tracks or paths of moving objects in video. Finally, dominant tracks out of the calculated motion paths are selected to characterize the motion.

The feature extraction methods found in the literature, can be classified into three broad categories. First, the *Space Time Volume (STV)* features are extracted by concatenating the consecutive silhouette of the person along time [2,3]. The change of silhouette along the consecutive frames can represent a human action. Second, the *critical points* on the human silhouette, have been used for action recognition [4,5]. Frequencies of the trajectories of the critical points on the human silhouette are used for recognizing action.

© Springer International Publishing Switzerland 2015
L. Nalpantidis et al. (Eds.): ICVS 2015, LNCS 9163, pp. 477–487, 2015.
DOI: 10.1007/978-3-319-20904-3_43

The STV and *critical point* based features are global features and are constrained by the changes in viewpoint. Third, low-level features, e.g., Scale Invariant Feature Transform (SIFT) [6], Histogram of Oriented Optical Flow (HOOF) [7], Histogram of Oriented Gradient (HOG) [8]. Some other features like gradient weighted optical flow (GWOF) have been proposed, combining global and local changes of human silhouette during action [9,10]. The optical flow matrix of each frame is point-wise multiplied with the magnitude of the gradient of the corresponding pixels of the corresponding frame. The result matrix is called GWOF, which is capable of minimizing the errors in the background pixels due to camera shaking during optical flow computation. A good effort has been made to tackle the problem due to camera motion using Warp Optical Flow feature [11]. The noise in optical flow due to camera motion is reduced by combining the HOOF and the Motion Boundary Histogram (MBH). In calculating MBH, the horizontal and vertical components of the optical flow measure are treated as separate images, the local gradients of the images are taken separately and then the corresponding gradient magnitude and directions are used as weighted votes into local orientation histograms [12]. In the proposed approach we have calculated the MBH over the GWOF [10], instead of the HOOF. We call the proposed combination of GWOF and MBH as hybrid optical flow (HMOF). The GWOF feature effectively reduces the small background motions due to camera shaking. With the help of MBH the background noise due to camera motion is further reduced to achieve better accuracy. We apply probabilistic relaxation labelling technique to update the orientation of the pixels in optical flow computation [13].

After feature extraction, next task is to classify the actions. Graph-based techniques perform good in action classification due to robustness under varying lighting conditions [9,10]. In [9], the poses related to the action are represented as nodes in a graph. The rank of the poses are determined by a graphical technique depending on the simultaneous occurrence of the poses during the action. In [10], separate graph-based classification methods have been proposed for recognizing actions depicting global changes in optical flow measure throughout the person's body and depicting local changes at some portion of the person's body. The main disadvantage of [9,10] is the lack of robustness of the classification systems for persons whose height vary across the frames.

The proposed technique constructs tracks for action classification. Each track is a sequence of 3D points depicting the dominant motion direction obtained by minimizing a cost function. This paper contributes by (i) proposing HMOF, (ii) applying probabilistic relaxation labelling technique to minimize the noise related to the direction of motion of the person and (iii) selecting dominant motion patterns related to the action. The proposed method produces good results compared to the state-of-the-art when applied to the LIRIS dataset [14]. The relaxation labelling technique is discussed in Sect. 3 followed by a description on the proposed classification technique in Sect. 4. The experimental results are shown in Sect. 5 followed by conclusions in Sect. 6. Before all these we discuss the proposed feature extraction process.

2   Feature Extraction

We use HMOF feature to perform the action recognition. This GWOF measure combines the benefit of motion information from optical flow field and pose information from the gradient field. The background pixels have almost zero magnitude of the gradient, and hence, after multiplying with the optical flow measure, the background pixels get almost zero value in the result matrix. The edge pixels of the person have high gradient value and hence, give an accumulated measurement after multiplying with the optical flow. As a result, the noises in optical flow measurement at the background pixels due to camera shaking is reduced. We construct the GWOF feature for each frame as,

$$G = |E| .* O, \tag{1}$$

where E and O are the gradient and the optical flow vectors.

We apply the Motion Boundary Histogram (MBH) technique to further reduce the noise due to camera shaking [12]. HMOF is obtained by taking derivatives of the GWOF measure (instead of using optical flow as in [11]). The intention of using MBH over GWOF measure is to prune out the camera motion and only keep trajectories from the body of the person. We treat the flow components of x and y directions as separate images. We take the local gradients of both x and y components of the GWOF measure separately and find the corresponding gradient magnitudes and orientations. We use these magnitude and orientation as weighted votes into local orientation histograms. We consider the orientation of the gradient at each direction to vote for the direction of the GWOF measure at each pixel. Since camera motion has a lower impact on the orientation of gradient, application of MBH is expected to prune out the camera motion from the GWOF measure. Figure 1 shows how the proposed feature improves the optical flow measurement by reducing the noise due to camera shaking.

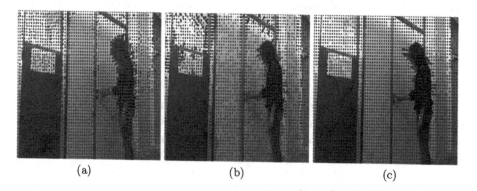

(a)   (b)   (c)

Fig. 1. (a) Optical flow, (b) GWOF and (c) The proposed HMOF over a frame taken from a video of the action, 'A person tries to enter an office unsuccessfully' of the LIRIS dataset [14]. The background noises in (a) are removed in (b). But (b) has some flow measure at the edges of the doors, due to camera motion, which is removed in (c).

We assign a label L to the HMOF vector obtained from GWOF and MBH of each pixel of the frame. Here, L can take any integer value from the closed interval $[1, l]$, where l is any integer greater than 1. We have taken the value of l as 8, as we quantize the orientation of the HMOF into 8 directions (octant) in every 45 degrees. Quantization in 8 directions are sufficient for pixel level accuracy avoiding sub-pixel definition. For any value of L in $\{1, 2, ..., 8\}$, each label L denotes a particular octant in the angular radian space. After quantization, each pixel is assigned with a label L according to the quantized value of the direction of the optical flow. Next we discuss the process of updating the HMOF at the edge (of the person) pixels using the probabilistic relaxation labelling technique.

3   Probabilistic Relaxation Labelling

In a relaxation labelling problem, we work with (i) a set of features (HMOF), (ii) a set of labels for each feature (the initial labels assigned to the pixels, as described in the previous section), (iii) a neighbour relation over the features and (iv) a constraint relation over labels of the neighbouring features. The output of the relaxation labelling technique is a label assigned to each feature in a manner which is consistent with respect to some given constraint relation. For HMOF to depict a dominant motion we realign the label (which is based on the direction of HMOF) using probabilistic relaxation labelling in each frame and along the flow of time.

The labelling process starts with an initial assignment of probabilities for each label. The algorithm updates the probabilities according to some relaxation schedule. This process of updating the probabilities is repeated until a little or no change in probability values occur between two successive iterations.

3.1   Initial Probability Assignments

We start with the HMOF measures and the assigned initial labels. If $P_{x,y}^{(0)}$ denotes the initial (at 0th step) probability of the $p_{x,y}$ pixel to have the assigned label, then $P_{x,y}^{(0)}$ is calculated as

$$P_{x,y}^{(0)} = \frac{m_{x,y}}{max_{x,y} m_{x,y}}, \tag{2}$$

where $max_{x,y} m_{x,y}$ defines the maximum of all the magnitude values $m_{x,y}$ of all the pixels $p_{x,y}$ of a frame and z is the total number of pixels in the frame. Next we discuss the process of measuring the compatibility of the probability values assigned to the pixels with respect to the neighbouring pixels.

3.2   Compatibility Coefficients

We perform the process of relaxation labelling assuming that the velocities of two neighbouring points constrain each other so that their magnitudes and directions can not be very different. This relation among the neighbouring pixels is further strengthened by the distance between the two neighbouring pixels. The compatibility between two neighbouring pixels can therefore be determined from the difference between the two velocities and the distance between the two neighbouring pixels (i.e., the pixel $p_{x,y}$ and the neighbour $p_{h,k}$ of $p_{x,y}$) of a frame.

We take the 8-neighbours of each pixel $p_{x,y}$ as the neighbourhood. Let the pixels $p_{h,k}$ are the neighbouring pixels of $p_{x,y}$, where $(h, k) \in Z^2$. We denote the probability of the pixel $p_{x,y}$ and its neighbouring pixels $p_{h,k}$ as $P_{x,y}$ and $P_{h,k}$ respectively. The labels for pixels $p_{x,y}$ and $p_{h,k}$ are denoted by $L_{x,y}$ and $L_{h,k}$. The label of a pixel can take any integer values ranging from 1 to 8. Our intention is to measure the consistency between the labels $L_{x,y}$ and $L_{h,k}$.

We define the compatibility coefficient $C_{h,k}$ to describe the relationship between $L_{x,y}$ and each neighbouring pixel label $L_{h,k}$. Here the compatibility coefficient depends on two parameters: (i) The difference between the labels of neighbouring pixels and (ii) The distance between the pixels. We define the difference between the labels of the current pixel and the neighbouring pixels as,

$$\alpha_{h,k} = \cos\theta_{h,k}\left(1 - \frac{|L_{x,y} - L_{h,k}|}{max_{h,k}\left(L_{x,y}, L_{h,k}\right)}\right), \tag{3}$$

where $\theta_{h,k} = \frac{\pi}{4}|L_{x,y} - L_{h,k}|$ and $max_{h,k}\left(L_{x,y}, L_{h,k}\right)$ is the maximum between the labels of $p_{x,y}$ and all the neighbouring pixels. The ratio $\left(1 - \frac{|L_{x,y} - L_{h,k}|}{max_{h,k}\left(L_{x,y}, L_{h,k}\right)}\right)$ is the relative difference between magnitudes of the two labels normalized in $[0,1]$.

Note that, when $L_{x,y}$ and $L_{h,k}$ are the same labels, the relative difference between their magnitudes (the ratio) is 1, hence, $\alpha_{h,k} = \cos\theta_{h,k}$. In this case, the two labels are most compatible, i.e., $\alpha_{h,k} = 1$, if $\theta_{h,k} = 0$. The labels are most incompatible, i.e., $\alpha_{h,k} = -1$, if $\theta_{h,k} = \Pi$.

In case the labels are in the same direction, from (3) we get, $\alpha_{h,k} = \left(1 - \frac{|L_{x,y} - L_{h,k}|}{max_{h,k}\left(L_{x,y}, L_{h,k}\right)}\right)$. So, the two labels are most compatible, i.e., $\alpha_{h,k} = 1$, if the relative difference between the labels is 0 and most incompatible, i.e., $\alpha_{h,k} = 0$ if the relative difference between the labels is 1. In general, the combined effect from label direction and magnitude differences is that, $\alpha_{h,k} \in [-1, 1]$. And, $\alpha_{h,k} = 0$ indicates that the two labels are independent of each other.

We define the distance between the pixels $p_{x,y}$ and $p_{h,k}$ as,

$$\beta_{h,k} = \exp\left(\frac{-d_{h,k}}{d_0}\right), \tag{4}$$

where the constant d_0 is the maximum possible Euclidian distance between any two neighbouring pixels and the distance $d_{h,k}$ is calculated as the Euclidean distance between the pixels $p_{x,y}$ and $p_{h,k}$. Here, $\beta_{h,k}$ is normalized in $[0,1]$. For every label L, the compatibility coefficient between $L_{x,y}$ and each of the neighbouring pixel labels $L_{h,k}$ is given by

$$C_{h,k} = \alpha_{h,k}.\beta_{h,k}. \tag{5}$$

We update the label $L_{x,y}$ with the maximum of all the corresponding $C_{h,k}$ values. Next we discuss the process of updating the probabilities in each iteration.

3.3   Updating Probabilities

We update $P_{x,y}^{(n)}$, the probability of $L_{x,y}$ in the nth iteration according to all the $C_{h,k}$ values. The $C_{h,k}$ value is weighted by the probability of the neighbouring pixel $P_{h,k}^{(n)}$. For example, for every label $L_{x,y}$, the total support for $L_{x,y}$ is

$$q_L^n = \sum_{h,k} C_{h,k}.P_{h,k}^{(n)}. \tag{6}$$

A support function is needed in each iteration to update the probability. This support function indicates the support for the pixel $p_{x,y}$ to have the label $L_{x,y}$. The support function for the nth iteration for label L is calculated as,

$$s_L^n = \frac{1}{T(max_L q_L^n)}.q_L^n, \tag{7}$$

where $|max_L q_L^n|$ corresponds to the largest value of the support found within the label $L_{x,y}$ of $p_{x,y}$. T is a constant which controls the speed of convergence of the probability values. The updated probability $P_{x,y}^{(n+1)}$ is calculated as,

$$P_{x,y}^{(n+1)} = \frac{P_{x,y}^{(n)}(1+s_L^n)}{\sum_{h,k} P_{h,k}^{(n)}(1+s_L^n)}. \tag{8}$$

We terminate the iteration when the change in the probability value in two consecutive iterations is less than 0.001. Next we discuss the process of action classification after finding the dominant tracks.

4   Proposed Classification Technique

We use the HMOF vectors of the video marked with the relaxed labels. These vectors are used for learning the motion patterns of the person. The motion field is a collection of independent optical flow vectors detected in each frame of the video. A motion pattern can be defined as a group of HMOF vectors that are part of the same physical process. We combine the relaxed HMOF vectors from all frames of the video to get the top N tracks (series of position of a pixel across frames) of the video representing its global motion field.

4.1   Estimation of Tracks

Each pixel $p_{x,y}$ of the fth frame contains a neighbourhood of pixels $p_{h,k}$ belonging to the $(f+1)$th frame, where $p_{h,k}$ are actually the 8 neighbourhood pixels of $p_{x,y}$. The position of one of these neighbouring pixels $p_{h,k}$, is added to the track based on some cost function. Considering there is no significant high inter-frame motion, we can establish connection between the HMOF measure of the pixel $p_{x,y}$ of the fth frame and the pixel $p_{h,k}$ of the $(f+1)$th frame. This correspondence is established by minimization of a cost function based on the following criteria:

(i) The two pixels $p_{x,y}$ and $p_{h,k}$ should be spatially close to each other, (ii) The absolute difference between the magnitudes $M_{x,y}$ and $M_{h,k}$ of the HMOF measure at pixels $p_{x,y}$ and $p_{h,k}$ respectively, should be minimized, (iii) The angle of the HMOF vector $\theta_{x,y}$ at $p_{x,y}$ and $\theta_{h,k}$ at $p_{h,k}$ should be close to each other. So we define the cost function $cost_{h,k}$ between the source pixel $p_{x,y}$ of frame f and its neighbouring pixels $p_{h,k}$ of frame $(f+1)$ as

$$cost_{h,k} = \frac{|M_{x,y} - M_{h,k}|}{max_{h,k}(|M_{x,y} - M_{h,k}|)} + a.\frac{1 - cos(\theta_{x,y} - \theta_{h,k})}{max_{h,k}(1 - cos(\theta_{x,y} - \theta_{h,k}))}, \quad (9)$$

where a is a constant between 0 and 1. Note that, both the ratios in (9) can have values between 0 and 1. Hence, the cost function is normalized as,

$$cost'_{h,k} = min_{h,k}(\frac{cost_{h,k}}{max_{h,k}(cost_{h,k})}). \quad (10)$$

The position of the pixel $p_{h,k}$ which has the minimum value of the cost function $cost'_{h,k}$ among all the neighbourhood pixels $p_{h,k}$ in frame $(f+1)$ (with respect to the pixel $p_{x,y}$ in the fth frame) is taken as the next position of the track. Here position of a pixel means the 2D coordinate of the pixel. If there is any conflict, we resolve the conflict by choosing the neighbouring pixel $p_{h,k}$ for which $|M_{x,y} - M_{h,k}|$ value is minimum. We get multiple number of options (taking different sizes of blocks) to find tracks for a video, each track representing a series of 2D coordinates. For experimentation, we choose the tracks represented by taking block size of 1×1, 4×4, 8×8, 16×16 and 32×32 pixels of the image and select the top dominant tracks.

4.2   Selecting Top Dominant Tracks

We have a set of tracks represented by the series of coordinates $(x_1, y_1), (x_2, y_2), \ldots, (x_F, y_F)$ where there are F number of frames in the video. We define the distance covered by a track as

$$dist = \sum_f \sqrt{(x_{f+1} - x_f)^2 + (y_{f+1} - y_f)^2}, \quad (11)$$

where (x_f, y_f) is the coordinate of the track in frame f. The $dist$ of all the tracks are sorted and the top N values are chosen and the corresponding tracks are considered. These chosen tracks form the N top dominant tracks of the video. These dominant tracks represent the global motion of the video depicting the action. We construct direction invariant action descriptors from the top dominant tracks.

For all the N dominant tracks of a video, we determine the vectors V between every two consecutive points of a track. Let V_f be the vector between consecutive points (the $(f-1)$th and fth pixels) of a track where $f = 2, 3, \ldots, F$. Then,

$$V_f = (x_f - x_{f-1})^i + (y_f - y_{f-1})^j, \quad (12)$$

where $(x_f - x_{f-1})^i$ and $(y_f - y_{f-1})^j$ are the components of V_f along the X and Y directions respectively. We calculate the angle between the vectors V_f and V_{f+1}, which is a direction invariant feature of an action, representing the change of direction made during the action, as follows:

$$\Theta_f = \arccos \left(\frac{V_f . V_{f+1}}{|V_f||V_{f+1}|} \right). \tag{13}$$

We form the proposed action descriptor corresponding to each action, using Θ_f. The action descriptor is a 8D vector, depicting the eight possible octant of Θ_f (quantized into 8 octant) and calculated as follows:

$$h_i = \sum_f M_{x,y} \; if \; \Theta \; is \; in \; ith \; bin$$

$$= 0 \; Otherwise \tag{14}$$

We learn the h_f values from the query videos using binary Support Vector Machine (SVM). We classify the query actions by matching the descriptor of the query video with the action descriptors for each action. Next we discuss the results of applying the proposed method on the LIRIS dataset.

5   Experiments and Results

We have used LIRIS human activities dataset [14] in our experiments. We have experimented with 9 actions with 7 videos for each action, where each video has 200–250 frames on an average. All frames are gray scale images having a size of 480×640. The actions we have considered in the dataset are: (1) A person gives an item to a second person, (2) An item is picked up or put down, (3) A person enters or leaves an office, (4) A person tries to enter an office unsuccessfully, (5) A person unlocks an office and then enters, (6) A person leaves baggage unattended, (7) Handshaking of two people, (8) A person types on a key-board, (9) A person talks on a telephone. The dataset contains background clutter, dynamic illumination changes and camera movements. Large variation between the classes introduced by various sources like the changes in camera viewpoint, shapes and sizes of different actors, different dressing styles, changes in execution rate of activity, individual styles of actors increases the level of difficulty in classification.

We use some parameters in our approach: (1) We have quantized the dense optical flow into 8 bin histogram so that it is resolved in eight directions in digital grid, i.e., in every 45 degrees, (2) In relaxation labelling, we keep the compatibility factor T as 1.05 for optimum speed of convergence. However, the value of T does not have any impact on the accuracy of the proposed approach. (3) A 4×4 neighbourhood was considered while updating the labels in each frame and a $3 \times 3 \times 3$ neighbourhood was considered while updating the labels along the temporal axis, (4) While constructing the tracks, we have considered blocks of 1×1 pixel, 4×4 pixels, 8×8 pixels, 16×16 pixels and 32×32 pixels. Then we have taken top N dominant tracks belonging to all of these levels. Here we have taken $N = 5$ on experimental basis, (5) For computing the cost function we have taken the value of a as 0.5 to establish the dominance of the effect of magnitude over angle of the HMOF vectors. Figure 2 shows the impact of the parameters N on the performance (in terms of $Fscore$) of the proposed approach.

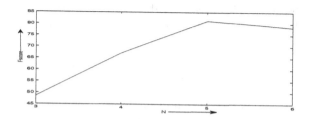

Fig. 2. Impact of the value of N on the accuracy of the proposed approach.

For classification of actions, we have used the binary Support Vector Machine (SVM) with leave-one-out cross validation scheme. We use *Recall*, *Precission* and *Fscore* as the metric for evaluation of the proposed approach. Table 1 shows the confusion matrix, where the rows and columns represent the predicted and actual actions respectively. Table 2 shows that the proposed method performs better compared to the state-of-the-art, in terms of *Recall*, *Precission* and *Fscore*.

Table 1. Confusion matrix.

	Action1	Action2	Action3	Action4	Action5	Action6	Action7	Action8	Action9
Action1	52	0	3	0	0	0	0	1	0
Action2	1	33	2	4	4	3	4	0	5
Action3	2	2	47	0	0	2	1	1	1
Action4	0	2	0	48	2	2	0	1	1
Action5	1	2	2	1	43	2	2	1	2
Action6	0	5	0	2	0	47	0	0	2
Action7	0	2	0	4	0	2	44	0	4
Action8	2	0	0	0	0	0	0	54	0
Action9	3	1	1	2	1	3	1	2	42

In the proposed approach we assumed that the person always have high degree of motion. If an action has very less motion, then the system may fail to estimate the tracks properly. In the videos where the person has very less motion, HMOF due to camera motion and illumination changes are dominant. Thus the computed track may not be always correct. So the top dominant tracks calculated in this situation may not portrait the motion of the person always. Application of graphical models may increase the efficiency in such videos.

Table 2. Performance of the proposed approach compared to the state-of-the-art.

Methods	Recall (%)	Precision (%)	Fscore (%)
Mukherjee et al. [10]	83.92	77.05	80.34
Wang et al. [11]	58.93	70.21	64.07
Proposed classification method with GWOF	75.01	73.68	74.33
Proposed classification method with HMOF	81.34	81.21	81.27

6   Conclusions and Future Scope

We apply a human action recognition technique proposing to use HMOF feature to avoid noise due to camera motion. We use probabilistic relaxation labelling technique to update the direction of the flow of the pixels across frames. The proposed mechanism for employing dominant motion pattern enhances the performance of the action recognition process. The future work may be to classify more complex human actions in real time videos having varying speed of the object, high camera motions and simultaneous occurrence of actions.

References

1. Ziaeefar, M., Bergevin, R.: Semantic human activity recognition: a literature review. Pattern Recognition (2015) doi:10.1016/j.patcog.2015.03.006
2. Shechtman, E., Irani, M.: Space-time behavior based correlation. In: Computer Vision and Pattern Recognition (CVPR), pp. 405–412. IEEE Press (2005)
3. Wang, J., Xu, Z.: STV-based video feature processing for action recognition. Sig. Process. **93**(8), 2151–2168 (2012)
4. Laptev, I., Marszaek, M., Schmid, C., Rozenfeld, B.: Learning realistic human actions from movies. In: Computer Vision and Pattern Recognition (CVPR), pp. 1–8 (2008)
5. Beaudry, C., Peteri, R., Mascarilla, L.: Action recognition in videos using frequency analysis of critical point trajectories. In: International Conference on Image Processing (ICIP), pp. 1445–1449. IEEE Press (2014)
6. Lowe, D.G.: Distinctive image features from scale-invariant keypoints. Int. J. Comput. Vis. **60**, 91–110 (2004)
7. Chaudhry, R., Ravichandran, A., Hager, G., Vidal, R.: Histograms of oriented optical flow and Binet-Cauchy kernels on nonlinear dynamical systems for the recognition of human actions. In: Computer Vision and Pattern Recognition (CVPR), pp. 1932–1939. IEEE Press (2009)
8. Dalal, N., Triggs, B.: Histograms of oriented gradients for human detection. In: Computer Vision and Pattern Recognition (CVPR), vol. 1, pp. 886–893. IEEE Press (2005)
9. Mukherjee, S., Biswas, S.K., Mukherjee, D.P.: Recognizing human action at a distance in video by key poses. IEEE Trans. Circ. Syst. Video Technol. **21**(9), 1228–1241 (2011)
10. Mukherjee, S., Biswas, S.K., Mukherjee, D.P.: Recognizing interactions between human performers at a distance by 'Dominating Pose Doublet'. Mach. Vis. Appl. **25**(4), 1033–1052 (2014)

11. Wang, H., Schmid, C.: Action recognition with improved trajectories. In: International Conference on Computer Vision (ICCV), pp. 3551–3558. IEEE Press (2013)
12. Dalal, N., Triggs, B., Schmid, C.: Human detection using oriented histograms of flow and appearance. In: Leonardis, A., Bischof, H., Pinz, A. (eds.) ECCV 2006. LNCS, vol. 3952, pp. 428–441. Springer, Heidelberg (2006)
13. Wu, Q.X.: A correlation-relaxation-labelling framework for computing optical flow-template matching from a new perspective. IEEE Trans. Pattern Anal. Mach. Intell. 17(9), 843–853 (1995)
14. Wolf, C., Mille, J., Lombardi, L.E., Celiktutan, O., Jiu, M., Baccouche, M., Dellandrea, E., Bichot, C., Garcia, C.-E., Sankur, B.: Evaluation of video activity localizations integrating quality and quantity measurements. Comput. Vis. Image Underst. 127, 14–30 (2014)

Human Action Recognition Using Dominant Pose Duplet

Snehasis Mukherjee$^{(\boxtimes)}$

Indian Institute of Information Technology Chittoor, Sricity, India
snehasis.mukherjee@iiits.in

Abstract. We propose a Bag-of-Words (BoW) based technique for human action recognition in videos containing challenges like illumination changes, background changes and camera shaking. We build the pose descriptors corresponding to the actions, based on the gradient-weighted optical flow (GWOF) measure, to minimize the noise related to camera shaking. The pose descriptors are clustered and stored in a dictionary of poses. We further generate a reduced dictionary, where words are termed as pose duplet. The pose duplets are constructed by a graphical approach, considering the probability of occurrence of two poses sequentially, during an action. Here, poses of the initial dictionary, are considered as the nodes of a weighted directed graph called the duplet graph. Weight of each edge of the duplet graph is calculated based on the probability of the destination node of the edge to appear after the source node of the edge. The concatenation of the source and destination pose vectors is called pose duplet. We rank the pose duplets according to the weight of the edge between them. We form the reduced dictionary with the pose duplets with high edge weights (called dominant pose duplet). We construct the action descriptors for each actions, using the dominant pose duplets and recognize the actions. The efficacy of the proposed approach is tested on standard datasets.

Keywords: Action recognition · Optical flow · Gradient · Pose duplet

1 Introduction

Recognizing human action in video is a challenging problem attracting computer vision scientists during the last couple of years. Automatic recognition of human action in video leads to several applications like elderly monitoring, detecting unusual behaviour, of human in video and several robotic applications. The growing demand of efficient video surveillance systems in smart cities, motivates the computer vision scientists to provide more sophisticated algorithms for human action recognition.

Several attempts have been made by the computer vision researchers, to recognize human actions in video [1]. A typical action recognition technique consists of two broad steps – feature extraction and classification of the actions. The processes for feature extraction, found in the literature, are of three categories.

© Springer International Publishing Switzerland 2015
L. Nalpantidis et al. (Eds.): ICVS 2015, LNCS 9163, pp. 488–497, 2015.
DOI: 10.1007/978-3-319-20904-3_44

First, the *Space Time Volume (STV)* features are obtained by concatenating the silhouette of the person in consecutive frames [2,3]. But the STV feature causes a memory overhead in case of actions with periodic occurrence of poses. Because in that case, temporal changes in the person's silhouette is less important compared to the similarity of the periodic poses of the person during action. Second, the *interest points* on the human silhouette, have been used for action recognition [4,5]. In this approach, frequencies of the trajectories of the interest points on the human silhouette are used for recognizing action. The STV and *interest point* based features are global features and are prone to give inconsistent measurements for viewpoint changes. Third, some low-level features like, Scale Invariant Feature Transform (SIFT) [6], Histogram Oriented Optical Flow (HOOF) [7], Histogram of Oriented Gradient (HOG) [8] and some other shape based and appearance based features are used for recognizing action. Low-level features work well for action recognition in challenging videos because of emphasizing the low-level motion details of the body parts of the person during action. But camera shaking creates problem in the recognition process with low-level features. Warp Optical Flow (WOF) feature is proposed by Wang et.al., to tackle the problem due to camera motion [11]. The noise in the optical flow computation due to camera motion, is reduced by combining the HOOF and the Motion Boundary Histogram (MBH). The optical flow is calculated for each frame in the horizontal and vertical directions separately and then the absolute displacement of a pixel across frames, is calculated from the measure of displacements in both the directions [12]. A good attempt has been made by obtaining a combination of global and local pose patterns together for action recognition [9,10]. This combination of global and local patterns of poses is called the gradient weighted optical flow (GWOF) feature. The optical flow matrix of each frame is pointwise multiplied with the magnitude of the gradient of the corresponding pixels of the frame. The result matrix is GWOF, which is capable of minimizing the errors in the background pixels, due to camera shaking. In the proposed approach we tested with both the GWOF feature and the WOF feature and made a comparison between the results of applying the two features. In this work, the WOF feature is found to perform slightly better than the GWOF feature for video captured by kinect camera (e.g., LIRIS dataset [13]). But in case of videos where the camera is kept at a distance from the camera, GWOF performed a little better (e.g., UT-Interaction dataset [14]).

For action classification, graph-based techniques are found to give good result due to robustness under varying lighting conditions of the video [9,10]. In [9], Bag of Words (BoW) based classification technique is used, where the size of the dictionary of poses is reduced by ranking the poses in the initial dictionary according to an ambiguity measure, which is calculated by representing the poses as nodes in a graph called pose graph. In [10], separate graph-based methods have been proposed for measuring ambiguity of poses depicting global changes in optical flow measure, throughout the person's body and depicting local changes at some portion of the person's body. The main disadvantage of [9,10] is that, these methods work good for actions which are periodic in nature, i.e., the same set of poses occur in a cycle, but in real-life videos the action of the persons may not be periodic, as we found in the LIRIS dataset [13]. The proposed method introduces a technique for measuring the ambiguity of the poses related to an action, by applying the novel concept of pose duplet.

The pose duplets refer to pair of poses from the initial dictionary of poses. For each action, we construct a weighted directed graph called duplet graph representing poses from the initial dictionary as nodes. Weight of an edge of a duplet graph depicts the probability of occurrence of the source node and destination node sequentially, during an action. The concatenation of the source and destination pose vectors is called pose duplet. The pose duplets are ranked according to the weight of the edge between them. The reduced dictionary is constructed with the pose duplets with high edge weights (called dominant pose duplet). The dominant pose duplets are stored in a dictionary and are used to construct the action descriptors for each action. Action descriptors are vectors representing the frequencies of each dominant pose duplet during an action. For a query video, the action of the person is recognized based on the minimum distance of the descriptor of the query video from all the action descriptors present in the final dictionary. We use leave one out cross validation scheme for classification using binary Support Vector Machine (SVM).

The construction of duplet graph for each action and the procedure for ranking of pose duplets to select the dominant pose duplet are described in Sect. 3. The experimental results and comparison with the state-of-the-art, are shown in Sect. 4, followed by a conclusion in Sect. 5. Before all these we discuss the proposed feature extraction process to build the initial dictionary, in the next section.

2   Feature Extraction and Building the Initial Dictionary

As discussed in the introduction, the proposed action classification method is tested by constructing the pose descriptors using two different forms of optical flow measurements: GWOF and WOF. We first discuss the procedure of obtaining the two forms of optical flow measures, sequentially. Finally we discuss the process of constructing the pose descriptors from either of GWOF or WOF measures.

Process of Obtaining GWOF Measure. The magnitude of the optical flow of each frame (except the first frame) of a video is pixel-wise multiplied with the magnitude of the gradient of the same frame to produce another matrix. We keep the direction of each pixel of the result matrix the same as the direction in the optical flow matrix. So the result matrix represents a scaled optical flow vector corresponding to each of its pixels. This result matrix is called the Gradient-weighted optical flow (GWOF) [10]. This GWOF measure of each frame grabs the benefit of motion information from optical flow field and pose information from the gradient field. The background pixels have almost zero value as the magnitude of the gradient. So after multiplying the gradient with the optical flow measure, the background pixels of the result matrix get almost zero value. The pixels on the silhouette of the person have high gradient value and hence, get an accumulated measurement in the GWOF matrix, after multiplying with the optical flow. As a result, the noises in optical flow computation, due to camera shaking, is reduced.

Process of Obtaining WOF Measure. The optical flow feature for each frame is combined with MBH, to reduce the unwanted optical flow measures due to camera shaking [11]. The optical flow is calculated for each pixel of the frame in the horizontal and vertical directions separately. The absolute displacement of each pixel across consecutive frames, is calculated from the measure of displacements in both the directions [12]. Two different forms of optical flow measurements: GWOF and WOF are calculated for each frame to test the proposed action classification technique with both the features separately and compare the results. Before going to the action classification, pose descriptors are necessary to be constructed, with either of the two forms of optical flow measurements. Next we discuss the process of constructing the pose descriptor.

Process of Constructing the Pose Descriptors. The directions of the optical flow (GWOF or WOF) vectors are quantized into some 8-bin histograms. For each pixel, we note the direction of the optical flow vector and the corresponding bin of the 8-bin vector is increased by the magnitude of the optical flow at that pixel. These 8-bin quantized histograms are constructed at three different levels, where the first level is the whole frame matrix, second level splits the whole frame into four equal blocks and the third level splits the whole frame into sixteen equal blocks, each producing an 8-bin vector. We concatenate all the 8-bin vectors of different levels and $L1$-normalize the concatenated vector to form a 168-dimensional pose descriptor [9].

Building the Initial Dictionary. We get pose descriptors corresponding to each frame of the videos related to an action. The initial dictionary is a collection of all "distinct"pose descriptors (called the poses) related to the action. The poses are treated as "words" in the Bag-of-Words (BoW) model and kept in the initial dictionary. We cluster all the pose descriptors to build the initial dictionary of poses, using Max-diff kd-tree (which is a special kind of binary tree), as according to [10], Max-diff kd-tree based data mining technique gives better result compared to any other clustering technique, for optical flow based pose descriptors. The process of clustering the pose descriptors and selecting the poses, is detailed in [10]. However, we give a brief overview of the procedure to make the paper self contained. All the poses are kept in the root directory at the first step. Based on some statistical measurements, the pose descriptors are classified into two subsets and sent to the two children. The same operation is performed for the two children as well, to further separate the pose descriptors into two children each. This process goes on until we reach the leaf nodes. Poses in the leaf nodes of the kd-tree form clusters. We choose one element from each cluster as the representative pose and store in the initial dictionary. For each cluster, the pose descriptor with minimum Euclidean distance from all other pose descriptors of the same cluster, is selected as the representative pose of that cluster and stored in the initial dictionary.

In [10], the depth T of the kd-tree is decided by intuition. Here we experimented on the value of T for each action. We do the action classification task for different values of T ranging from 2 to 5. We found that the accuracy (in terms of $Fscore$) of the proposed method initially increases over T, but for $T = 3$ and above, the accuracy almost remains the same. The result of this experiment is shown graphically in Fig. 2(b). The reason for this behaviour of the result is that, for lower value of T, we do not get sufficient number of different poses related to the action. As T increases, we get more number of poses, but if we take a sufficiently big value of T, then the number of poses increase, confusing the process of selecting pose duplet. So, the unnecessary poses are automatically deleted in the next step. So, we work with the optimal value of $T = 3$ (i.e., 2^3 poses per action). Next we discuss the proposed technique for action classification by constructing a reduced dictionary of dominant pose duplets.

3   Reduced Dictionary of Dominant Pose Duplets

We construct a reduced dictionary of dominant pose duplets from the initial dictionary of poses, by ranking the pose duplets using a duplet graph. We discuss the procedure of forming the duplet graph in Subsect. 3.1 and the procedure of selecting the dominant pose duplets from the duplet graph, to form the reduced dictionary and constructing the action descriptors in Subsect. 3.2.

3.1   Building the Duplet Graph

We construct the duplet graph by taking the poses of the initial dictionary as vertices. The weight of a directed edge e_{ij} from the vertex v_i to the vertex v_j represents the probability of occurrence of the pose v_j after the pose v_i during the action. If the vertex v_j never appears after the pose v_i during the action, then there will be no directed edge from v_i to v_j. Formally we define a duplet graph as follows:

Definition 1. A duplet graph $G(V, E)$ is a weighted directed graph with a non-empty vertex set $V = \{v_1, v_2, v_3, \ldots, v_n\}$ with n vertices and the edge set E that may or may not be non-empty, where any pair of vertices are called a duplet and the directed edge e_{ij} from the vertex v_i to the vertex v_j represents a probability value P_{ij} depending on a pre-defined relationship between the two vertices. If there is no pre-defined relationship between v_i and v_j, then $P_{ij} = 0$.

The proposed concept of duplet graph can be used in any application area, where the probability values P_{ij} will be defined by the knowledge from the application domain. For the problem of action classification, we calculate the empirical probability P_{ij} for the vertex v_j to occur after the vertex v_i and use P_{ij} as the weight of the edge e_{ij}.

For each action we construct a duplet graph. The probability value P_{ij} for the edge e_{ij} is calculated as follows:

$$P_{ij} = \frac{N_{ij}}{N_{in}}, \tag{1}$$

where N_{ij} is the number of occurrence of the vertex v_j after the vertex v_i and N_{in} is the number of occurrence of any pose other than v_j. For calculating N_{ij} and N_{in}, we first identify all the cycles starting with pose v_i among all the videos related to the action. In a repeating action like running, walking, etc., same set of poses repeats sequentially. A cycle of a repeating action starts with the vertex v_i and ends at the vertex v_k where v_k occurs just before the next occurrence of v_i. For the lth cycle starting with the pose v_i, we calculate N_{jl} as,

$$N_{jl} = \sum_{k_l} 1 \; if \; v_{k_l} \; and \; v_j \; are \; the \; same$$
$$= 0 \; Otherwise \tag{2}$$

where K_l are the vertices in the lth cycle, after v_i. Now, N_{ij} and N_{in} are calculated as follows:

$$N_{ij} = \sum_l N_{jl}, \quad N_{in} = \sum_l k_l. \tag{3}$$

We calculate P_{ij} for all $i, j \in \{1, 2, 3, \dots, n\}$ for the action. If $P_{ij} = 0$ for any i, j, then their is no directed line from v_i to v_j for the duplet graph G for the action. Next we construct the reduced dictionary of dominant pose duplets.

3.2   Selecting Dominant Pose Duplets for Reduced Dictionary

We construct duplet graph for each action separately and select the dominant pose duplets for each action from the duplet graph of the action. The dominant pose duplets are defined as follows:

Definition 2. Any vector V formed by concatenation of any two poses v_i and v_j (sequentially) of the duplet graph G for the action, is called a pose duplet. A pose duplet V formed by v_i and v_j, is called a dominant pose duplet for the action, if $P_{ij} \geq \delta$ for some $\delta \in (0, 1)$.

We rank the pose duplets according to the probability value, used as the edge weight between the two poses. We select the first m pose duplets as the dominant pose duplets for the action. The dominant pose duplets of all the actions are obtained in the same way and kept in the reduced dictionary. Figure 1 shows examples of some pose duplets as recognized by the proposed method.

For the training videos, we construct a vector of the same dimension as the total number of dominant pose duplets for all the actions, where we count the

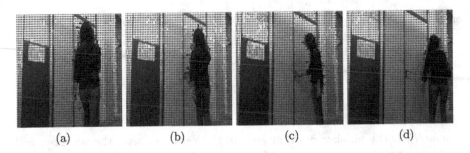

(a)   (b)   (c)   (d)

Fig. 1. Examples of two pose duplets as recognized by the proposed method. Frames with GWOF measures are shown in the pictures. (a), (b) and (c), (d) are chosen as pose duplets. The frames are taken from a video of 'A person tries to enter an office unsuccessfully action', from the LIRIS dataset [13].

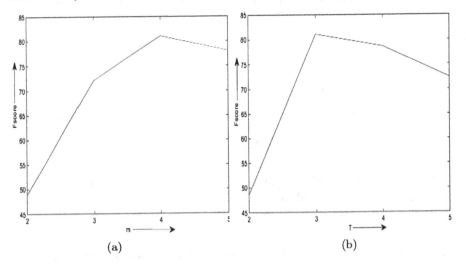

(a)   (b)

Fig. 2. Performance of the proposed method on LIRIS dataset [13], for different values of (a) m (for the optimal value of T) and (b) T.

frequency of each dominant pose duplet in the video. We find the cluster center of all such vectors related to an action. This cluster center vector is considered as the action descriptor of the action. We find the action descriptors for all the actions. For a test video, we find the Euclidean distances of the vector of the test video from all the action descriptors. The action descriptor with minimum distance from the vector of the test video, is considered as the action of the test video.

We use binary Support Vector Machine (SVM) for classification, with leave-one-out cross validation scheme. We experimented with different values of m ranging from 2 to 5, in the process of selecting the dominant pose duplets, for the optimal value of T. The proposed method gives best result for $m = 4$. The graph in Fig. 2(a) shows how the proposed method has performed (in terms of

Table 1. Confusion matrix for the proposed approach with WOF feature, applied on LIRIS dataset [13].

	Action1	Action2	Action3	Action4	Action5	Action6	Action7	Action8	Action9
Action1	49	0	4	0	0	1	0	2	0
Action2	1	33	2	4	4	3	4	0	5
Action3	2	2	47	0	0	2	1	1	1
Action4	0	2	0	48	2	2	0	1	1
Action5	1	2	2	1	43	2	2	1	2
Action6	0	5	0	2	0	47	0	0	2
Action7	0	2	0	4	0	2	44	0	4
Action8	2	0	0	0	1	0	0	53	0
Action9	3	1	1	2	1	3	1	2	42

$Fscore$ for different values of m. Next we discuss on the Experiments and results of the proposed approach.

4 Experiments and Results

We have experimented the proposed method for action recognition on LIRIS human activities dataset [13] and UT-Interaction dataset [14]. In LIRIS dataset we worked with 9 actions each having 7 gray-scale videos, each video containing 200–250 frames on an average, of size 480×640. The following actions are considered for experimentation: (1) A person gives an item to a second person, (2) An item is picked up or put down, (3) A person enters or leaves an office, (4) A person tries to enter an office unsuccessfully, (5) A person unlocks an office and then enters, (6) A person leaves baggage unattended, (7) Handshaking of two people, (8) A person types on a key-board, (9) A person talks on a telephone. The dataset contains challenges like background clutter, dynamic illumination changes, camera movements, changes in camera viewpoint, shapes and sizes of different actors and different dressing styles. We apply the binary Support Vector Machine (SVM) with leave-one-out cross validation scheme, for classification.

Two sets of video data are found in the UT-Interaction dataset [14], with at least two performers in each video. Each set of video data contains 10 videos of 6 different actions: 'Handshaking (Hs), 'Hugging(Hg), 'Kicking (Kc), 'Pointing (Pt), 'Punching (Pn) and 'Pushing (Ps). The videos in set 1 of the UT-Interaction dataset are with almost uniform background whereas in set 2 the videos are more challenging with non-uniform background and poor light. We tested the proposed method by leave-one-out cross validation scheme, on the combination of all videos in both the sets.

We use the standard metrics like *Recall, Precission* and *Fscore*, for evaluation. Tables 1 and 2 show the confusion matrices for the LIRIS and UT-Interaction datasets respectively. The rows and columns in Tables 1 and 2 represent the predicted and actual actions respectively. Table 3 shows the performance of the proposed method compared to the state-of-the-art.

Table 2. Confusion matrix for the proposed approach with GWOF feature, applied on UT-Interaction dataset [14].

	Hs	Hg	Kc	Pt	Pn	Ps
Hs	80	0	0	20	0	0
Hg	0	90	0	0	0	10
Kc	5	0	85	0	10	0
Pt	5	0	0	80	15	0
Pn	5	0	0	10	85	0
Ps	0	10	0	0	0	90

Table 3. Performance of the proposed approach compared to the state-of-the-art.

Methods	Dataset	Recall (%)	Precision (%)	Fscore (%)
Mukherjee et.al. [10]	LIRIS [13]	83.92	77.05	80.34
	UT-Interaction [14]	81.92	78.69	80.27
Wang et.al. [11]	LIRIS [13]	58.93	70.21	64.07
	UT-Interaction [14]	54.23	69.91	61.08
Proposed method with WOF feature	LIRIS [13]	83.27	78.34	80.73
	UT-Interaction [14]	80	85.16	82.5
Proposed method with GWOF feature	LIRIS [13]	83.12	78.24	80.61
	UT-Interaction [14]	82.5	87.66	85

The proposed pose duplet based method can recognize non-repeating actions, but for repeating actions like running or walking, the temporal occurrence of any two poses often alters, which may affect the performance. For example, the Handshaking action of the UT-Interaction dataset, is a repeating action and hence, the proposed method shows a less accuracy for handshaking action, which is depicted in Table 2. However, considering the sequential occurrence of poses in the proposed pose duplet based method may be useful for event detection (which is a possible application of the proposed method), where an event is a sequential occurrence of actions.

5   Conclusions and Future Scope

We apply a novel graph-based technique for human action recognition, capable of dealing with camera motion. We introduce the concept of dominant pose duplet related to each action to construct a compact dictionary, after ranking the pair of poses according to their probability of occurring sequentially, during the action. This graph-based technique can be applied to any area of video content analysis, where temporal occurrence of some pattern in the frames have a significance to some video-related applications. The GWOF and WOF features used in the proposed approach, can only remove the background noise in optical flow computation. But handling the error in computing the orientation of the optical flow at the pixels on the silhouette of the person, is still a challenge, which may be another potential future research direction.

References

1. Ziaeefar, M., Bergevin, R.: Semantic human activity recognition: a literature review. Pattern Recogn. **48**(8), 2329–2345 (2015). doi:10.1016/j.patcog.2015.03.006
2. Shechtman, E., Irani, M.: Space-time behavior based correlation. In: Computer Vision and Pattern Recognition (CVPR), pp. 405–412. IEEE Press (2005)
3. Wang, J., Xu, Z.: STV-based video feature processing for action recognition. Sig. Process. **93**(8), 2151–2168 (2012)
4. Laptev, I., Marszaek, M., Schmid, C., Rozenfeld, B.: Learning realistic human actions from movies, In: Computer Vision and Pattern Recognition (CVPR), pp. 1–8 (2008)
5. Beaudry, C., Peteri, R., Mascarilla, L.: Action recognition in videos using frequency analysis of critical point trajectories. In: International Conference on Image Processing (ICIP), pp. 1445–1449. IEEE Press (2014)
6. Lowe, D.G.: Distinctive image features from scale-invariant keypoints. Int. J. Comput. Vision **60**, 91–110 (2004)
7. Chaudhry, R., Ravichandran, A., Hager, G., Vidal, R.: Histograms of oriented optical flow and Binet-Cauchy kernels on nonlinear dynamical systems for the recognition of human actions. In: Computer Vision and Pattern Recognition (CVPR), pp. 1932–1939. IEEE Press (2009)
8. Dalal, N., Triggs, B.: Histograms of oriented gradients for human detection. In: Computer Vision and Pattern Recognition (CVPR), vol. 1, pp. 886–893. IEEE Press (2005)
9. Mukherjee, S., Biswas, S.K., Mukherjee, D.P.: Recognizing human action at a distance in video by key poses. IEEE Trans. Circuits Syst. Video Technol. **21**(9), 1228–1241 (2011)
10. Mukherjee, S., Biswas, S.K., Mukherjee, D.P.: Recognizing interactions between human performers at a distance by 'Dominating Pose Doublet'. Mach. Vis. Appl. **25**(4), 1033–1052 (2014)
11. Wang, H., Schmid, C.: Action recognition with improved trajectories. In: International Conference on Computer Vision (ICCV), pp. 3551–3558. IEEE Press (2013)
12. Dalal, N., Triggs, B., Schmid, C.: Human detection using oriented histograms of flow and appearance. In: Leonardis, A., Bischof, H., Pinz, A. (eds.) ECCV 2006. LNCS, vol. 3952, pp. 428–441. Springer, Heidelberg (2006)
13. Wolf, C., Mille, J., Lombardi, L.E., Celiktutan, O., Jiu, M., Baccouche, M., Dellandrea, E., Bichot, C., Garcia, C.-E., Sankur, B.: Evaluation of video activity localizations integrating quality and quantity measurements. Comput. Vis. Image Underst. **127**, 14–30 (2014)
14. Ryoo, M.S., Aggarwal, J.K.: UT-interaction dataset, ICPR contest on semantic description of human activities (SDHA) (2010). http://cvrc.ece.utexas.edu/SDHA2010/Human_Interaction.html

Online Re-calibration for Robust 3D Measurement Using Single Camera-PantoInspect Train Monitoring System

Deepak Dwarakanath[1,2]([✉]), Carsten Griwodz[1], Pål Halvorsen[1],
and Jacob Lildballe[2]

[1] Simula Research Laboratory, University of Oslo, Oslo, Norway
[2] ImageHouse PantoInspect A/S, Copenhagen, Denmark
deepakdw@ifi.uio.no

Abstract. Vision-based inspection systems measures defects accurately with the help of a checkerboard calibration (CBC) method. However, the 3D measurements of such systems are prone to errors, caused by physical misalignment of the object-of-interest and noisy image data. The *PantoInspect Train Monitoring System* (PTMS), is one such system that inspects defects on pantographs mounted on top of the electric trains. In PTMS, the measurement errors can compromise railway safety. Although this problem can be solved by re-calibrating the cameras, the process involves manual intervention leading to large servicing times.

Therefore, in this paper, we propose Feature Based Calibration (FBC) in place of CBC, to cater an obvious need for online re-calibration that enhances the usability of the system. FBC involves feature extraction, pose estimation, back-projection of defect points and estimation of 3D measurements. We explore four state-of-the-art pose estimation algorithms in FBC using very few feature points.

This paper evaluates and discusses the performance of FBC and its robustness against practical problems, in comparison to CBC. As a result, we identify the best FBC algorithm type and operational scheme for PTMS. In conclusion, we show that, by adopting FBC in PTMS and other related 3D systems, better performance and robustness can be achieved compared to CBC.

1   Introduction

Nowadays, industries make extensive use of 3D measurement systems to cater for inspection applications. The *PantoInspect Train Monitoring System* (PTMS) [1] adopted by Rail Net Denmark, Sydney Trains Australia and others, is a system that inspects defects occurring on pantographs of electric locomotives (their root-mounted carbon structures that are in-contact with electric wires). PTMS makes use of lasers and a camera to measure defects with a priori knowledge of camera calibration parameters, i.e. camera intrinsic (focal length, principal axes) and extrinsic (position, orientation). The quality of this calibration governs the accuracy of its 3D measurements.

© Springer International Publishing Switzerland 2015
L. Nalpantidis et al. (Eds.): ICVS 2015, LNCS 9163, pp. 498–510, 2015.
DOI: 10.1007/978-3-319-20904-3_45

Fig. 1. PTMS system to inspect defects on the pantographs (Color figure online)

In this application scenario, practically unavoidable situations such as camera/pantograph misalignment (change in position and orientation) can occur. Camera misalignment is caused by mishandling PTMS during transportation and servicing. Pantograph misalignment is caused by the movement of train and thrust of pantograph against the catenary wire. In such cases, the calibration data is not useful anymore and therefore leads to inaccurate defect measurements. Hence, practical misalignment degrades the performance of PTMS, unless the camera is re-calibrated. Currently, PTMS adopts traditional checkerboard calibration (CBC) [8]. The typical placement of PTMS (see Fig. 1) requires that it is unmounted before CBC, leading to huge maintenance and servicing times. Therefore, PTMS is in need of an automatic camera calibration process.

In this paper, we explore *Feature Based Calibration* (FBC) methods [3–6] to provide an alternative solution for PTMS. Since FBC can be performed without unmounting, PTMS and other related applications acquire robustness against camera/pantograph misalignment effects. FBC is a calibration process that consists of feature extraction and 3D-2D pose estimation to measure the defects.

Four state-of-art 3D-2D pose estimation algorithms [7–10] were selected for FBC. Although these algorithms can work independently on arbitrary points, the challenges in adopting these algorithms for PMTS are: (a) PMTS yield only few feature points, and (b) feature points are noisy due to misalignment errors and motion blur. Thus, evaluation of the algorithms becomes important to understand the practical implications of adopting FBC. We use CBC as the reference and compare the robustness of FBC-based methods against practical problems. The evaluation was carried out on a dataset from the PTMS testing facility, which offered a variety of sample data and noise-free reference measurements.

This paper is organized as follows: Functional overview of PTMS is explained in Sect. 2. Section 3 outlines the proposed FBC methodology for PTMS. The evaluation setup and their results are discussed in Sects. 4 and 5, respectively. In Sect. 6, we conclude the results and identify a suitable FBC algorithm that performs better than CBC and is more feasible for dynamic environments.

2   PTMS System

PTMS is a non-tactile fault detection system, which inspects pantographs and measures the defects in the carbon strips. Pantographs are mechanical structures with carbon strips, fixed on top of train wagons, which are raised to touch the overhead contact wire for electricity. In the course of time, due to constant contact of carbon strips with the wire, various types of defects (vertical crack, edge chip, abnormal wear and missing carbon) might occur. PTMS is meant to discover when these defects become severe, while allowing for expected wear.

PTMS is mounted over the train tracks (see Fig. 1). When the train passes right below the system, range sensors (red lines in Fig. 1) detect the pantograph and three laser lines are projected onto the carbon strips (green line in Fig. 1). The camera captures a near infrared image of the laser lines, termed as *profile image*. When defects are present, the laser lines are deformed and define the geometry of the defects. The system then detects the defects, measures their width & depth and raises an alarm if measurements are above certain thresholds.

3   Proposed Calibration Methodology

We propose a feature based calibration (FBC) as in Fig. 2(a), which involves a 2-step process consisting of (1) Feature Extraction and (2) Pose Estimation. This is done by extracting features from the same *profile images* that are taken to detect defects. These features allow the estimation of the camera pose, and subsequent 3D measurements of defects.

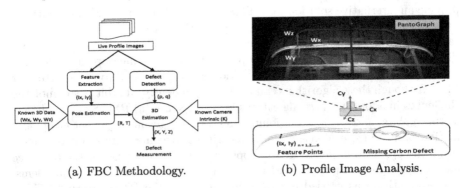

(a) FBC Methodology.   (b) Profile Image Analysis.

Fig. 2. Feature Based Calibration for PantoInspect

3.1   Feature Extraction

PTMS casts 3 parallel laser lines, each yielding 2 distinctive, well-known points that can be detected in each *profile image* as shown in Fig. 2(b), for a total of 6 feature points. Notice that the shape of the line traverses the shape of the pantograph and bends on both ends, where the carbon strip ends. These 6 end points are extracted from the profile image using known feature extraction techniques. These points serve as 2D feature points (I_x, I_y) for calibration. The corresponding 3D points always lie on an imaginary 3D plane parallel to the surface of the pantograph.

The 3D reference axis (world coordinate system) is assumed to be on the pantograph, as shown in Fig. 2(b). Pantographs have standard dimensions of length, by which real metric measurement of each points in 3D world coordinate system (W_x, W_y, W_z) can be obtained. Thus, both 2D feature points and 3D world points are determined and further used for camera pose estimation process.

3.2   Pose Estimation

Camera Pose Estimation refers to estimating rotation (R) and translation (T) parameters of the camera with respect to the world coordinate system. As the 2D and 3D points lie on a plane, a homography between camera and world coordinate system can be found. Estimating the projective mapping and thereby extracting the camera parameters $[R,T]$ is the goal of camera pose estimation. The parameter R is an orthonormal 3×3 matrix representing rotations in x,y,z axes. T is a 3×1 matrix representing camera translation along 3 axes.

There are several state-of-art algorithms [7–13] for estimating single camera pose. Out of those, we select few well-known good performing algorithms named, FBC-boug [8], FBC-zhang [9], FBC-gold [10] and FBC-epfl [7] as candidates for calibrating PTMS. All methods can operate with $n \geq 4$ point correspondences and they assume that the intrinsic camera parameters (K) are known.

FBC-boug method initially estimates planar homography using the Quasi-Linear algorithm and recovers $[R,T]$ parameters, which are further optimized to minimise reprojection error through Gradient Descent. **FBC-zhang** method estimates planar homography using the Direct Linear Transformation followed by a non-linear optimization (Levenberg Marquardt) based on Maximum Likelihood criterion. Then, $[R,T]$ are recovered using orthogonal enforcement. **FBC-gold** method estimates a projective geometric transformation using Gold Standard algorithm before recovering $[R,T]$. Unlike other methods, **FBC-epfl** is non-iterative approach to PnP problem. Under PnP problem, 3D points are expressed in camera coordinate system and then, the Euclidean motion that aligns both world and camera references is used to retrieve $[R,T]$. This method adopts the idea of expressing n 3D points as weighted sum of four virtual control points, which reduces complexity and noise sensitivity.

3.3   3D Estimation

Since the reference 3D points lie on an imaginary plane, the conversion from 2D (p,q) to 3D (X,Y,Z) points becomes merely a ray-plane intersection [10], as shown in Eq. 1, where the points are expressed in homogeneous coordinates.

$$\begin{bmatrix} p \\ q \\ 1 \end{bmatrix} = K[R|T] \begin{bmatrix} X \\ Y \\ Z \\ 1 \end{bmatrix} \qquad (1)$$

K, R and T are obtained by the FBC process. The Z-axis of 3D points are zero for points on a plane. Now, expanding the matrix R and vector T, we have Eq. 2, and 3D points (X,Y) of the defects on the plane can be estimated.

$$\begin{bmatrix} p \\ q \\ 1 \end{bmatrix} = K * \begin{bmatrix} r_{11} & r_{12} & r_{13} & t_1 \\ r_{21} & r_{22} & r_{23} & t_2 \\ r_{31} & r_{32} & r_{33} & t_3 \end{bmatrix} \begin{bmatrix} X \\ Y \\ 0 \\ 1 \end{bmatrix} = K * \underbrace{\begin{bmatrix} r_{11} & r_{12} & t_1 \\ r_{21} & r_{22} & t_2 \\ r_{31} & r_{32} & t_3 \end{bmatrix}}_{H} \begin{bmatrix} X \\ Y \\ 1 \end{bmatrix} \qquad (2)$$

3.4   Defect Measurement

Referring to Fig. 3(b), in each of the three lines, three major points (M_1, M_2, M_3) are determined for measurement purposes. These major points are back-projected to estimate their 3D coordinates ($\widehat{M_1}$, $\widehat{M_2}$, $\widehat{M_3}$) as in Eq. 2.

$$Width = \widehat{M_3} - \widehat{M_1} \qquad and \qquad Depth = AbsMax(H1, H2) \qquad (3)$$

$$where, \qquad H1 = \widehat{M_1} - \widehat{M_2} \qquad H2 = \widehat{M_3} - \widehat{M_2}$$

All defects are characterized by a width and depth, which are computed using Eq. 3. Thus, PTMS can estimate FBC parameters (Sects. 3.1 and 3.3), and use the parameters to measure the defects (Sects. 3.3 and 3.4).

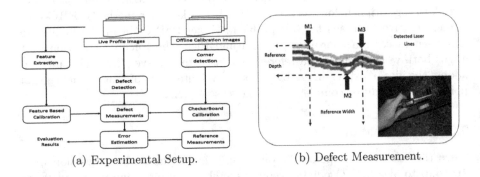

(a) Experimental Setup.   (b) Defect Measurement.

Fig. 3. Evaluation scenario

4   Evaluation

The evaluation determines the performance traits of PTMS in estimating defect width and depth measurements by adopting the four proposed FBC methods, in comparison with the currently used CBC method.

The evaluation methodology is illustrated in Fig. 3(a). CBC is carried out offline using around 20 images of a checkerboard pattern with the help of the Matlab Calibration Toolbox [2], whereas FBC is carried out online, with only 6 feature points that are extracted from the *profile image*.

Every *profile image* is used for defects detection. Whenever the lines in the profile image are not straight, there is potentially a defect (Fig. 3(b)). After defects are identified, their width and depth are measured based on the estimated calibration parameters of both CBC and FBC. Using reference measurements (Table 1), the error estimations are computed. These errors were compared to a ground truth and used for evaluating the performance of PTMS over various calibration methods.

4.1   Datasets

Defect measurements were carried out on Pantographs (BR and EG types) provided by BaneDanmark (Rail Net Denmark). The dataset was obtained from product testing conducted at the PTMS factory. The real width and depth of each of these defects were measured using a calibrated caliper to acquire the ground truth (Fig. 3(b) and Table 1). The experiments were conducted on 5 readings of 2 types of pantographs having 4 types of defects on them, for a total of 40 data samples. To avoid noisy features extracted and to focus on correct evaluation, every feature point was manually annotated. However, the performance with noisy data is analysed later in our study.

Table 1. Reference measurements of defects of two pantograph types

Measurement	Pantograph-type			
(in millimeters)	BR-type		EG-type	
Defects	Width	Depth	Width	Depth
Vertical crack	2.38	17	5.88	20
Missing carbon	77.98	17	39.04	20
Edge crack	24.21	6	21.18	5
Abnormal wear	19.36	6	14.78	5

4.2   Operational Schemes

FBC can be carried out on every *profile image* before conducting the measurement, but one cannot guarantee a noise-free image that is good enough to extract features. A noisy profile image will worsen the quality of re-calibration. Alternatively, calibration can be carried out only when the accuracy of the system deteriorates (one way of measuring this is by checking if the measured depth is larger than the pantograph thickness). Alternatively, calibration can be carried out at regular interval. However, a more stable scenario can be to calibrate during servicing and maintenance periods, where full control on measurements is possible. In this paper, we have considered two operational schemes for evaluation.

Scheme 1: FBC is carried out on every *profile image* and the defect is measured on those images using its respective calibration parameter.

Scheme 2: FBC is carried out on a random *profile image* and measurement is carried out on the rest of all profile images with the same calibration parameters.

4.3   Practical Implications

Feature point mis-detection introduces noise in the feature point locations. These are caused by poorly visible images, which can be due to laser misalignment, flash under/over exposure, motion blur or sunlight.

Since the pantographs are the moving elements that are in contact with the caternary wire, there might be linear and angular displacements of the structure. Linear displacements can occur due to vertically upward movement, called *Uplift*, which is deliberately made to provide more upward thrust to the wire. And angular displacements occur due to uneven forces being exerted on the pantograph over time, when the wire in contact is off-centered. Theses displacements are called *Yaw Angle*, *Roll Angle*, and *Pitch Angle*, referring to rotation around 3 axes. We have considered these practical implications in our study.

Table 2. Absolute angular difference in degrees between CBC and FBC - scheme1

FBC-type	R_x (Tilt)	R_y (Roll)	R_z (Pan)
epfl	7.17	3.50	9.46
boug	9.99	8.21	11.93
zhang	10.86	6.7	11.30
gold	11.51	5.96	10.99

5   Results and Discussion

The FBC was carried out for 4 candidate methods, namely FBC-epfl, FBC-boug, FBC-zhang and FBC-gold (explained in Sect. 3.2) and their rotational parameter difference from that of CBC was noted (Table 2). The camera rotational parameter plays an important role in the accuracy of FBC for measurements in PTMS. In the first experiment, width and depth error of defects (in millimeters) were computed for the 4 FBC methods in comparison to CBC, yielding a mean absolute error over several samples and defects for both schemes.

5.1 Width Measurement of Defects

Intuitively, the angular deviation (Table 2), in the estimated camera pan and camera roll parameters contribute to the errors in width measurements. The Figs. 4(a) and (b) show the result of width measurement for both schemes. For *edge crack* and *abnormal wear*, FBC-epfl, FBC-boug and FBC-gold introduced only around 1–2 mm mean error compared to CBC. All FBC types performed with accuracy very close to CBC for *missing carbon* defect, which had sufficiently large width reference (see Table 1). On the lower side, the width of *vertical crack* is about 2–6 mm and the profile image was captured from 3 m distance. Hence, profile detection of a narrow width structure introduced noise, which thereby resulted in width error as seen in the figures. In this case, the accuracy of FBC-zhang degraded, whereas other FBCs showed mean errors between 2–4 mm in both schemes. However, *scheme 1* is most suitable in this case. It is observed that all FBC types are more sensitive to narrow widths (<5 mm) in *scheme 2* than in *scheme 1*, because in *scheme 2*, once FBC is carried out, the pantograph position can be misaligned, which results in wrong measurements.

Overall, FBC-epfl and FBC-boug performed best for width measurement compared to CBC, with a maximum increase in the mean error of about 1 mm for *scheme 1* and 1.5 mm for *scheme 2*.

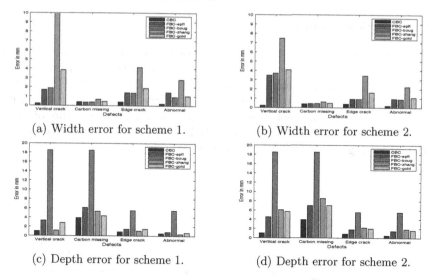

(a) Width error for scheme 1.   (b) Width error for scheme 2.

(c) Depth error for scheme 1.   (d) Depth error for scheme 2.

Fig. 4. Mean difference of width and depth measurements for both schemes

5.2 Depth Measurement of Defects

Depth measurement results for both schemes are shown in Figs. 4(c) and (d). Depth errors were introduced due to deviations, mainly in camera pitch rotational parameter. The figures show that all FBC types except FBC-boug performed very close to the CBC with mean errors between 1–3 mm in both schemes.

FBC-boug uses the same algorithm for pose estimation as in CBC, but there is a difference in the feature point locations. The feature points in CBC assume z axis = 0 (places the checkerboard in XZ plane of world coordinate system) and both depth & width are determined along the X and Z axes, respectively. In FBC, feature points lie on the XY plane and depth is measured along the Z axis. Here, the thinness of the pantograph itself restricts the feature plane for FBC on which the feature points were detected. Hence, estimation of mean depth error gave a higher value for FBC-boug. For *edge crack* and *abnormal wear*, FBC types performed with a mean error difference of about 1 mm compared to CBC. For both *vertical crack* and *missing carbon*, FBC introduced mean errors of about 2 mm for *scheme 1* and 3 mm for *scheme 2*. The errors were higher for these two defects because the long narrow depth in *vertical crack* was detected with noise and a large depth in *missing carbon* is strongly affected even by small deviations in the camera pitch angle. Table 2 shows the rotational parameter offsets that cause such depth errors. It is observed that scheme 1 is more suitable for depth measurements in terms of accuracies.

Overall, FBC-epfl, FBC-zhang and FBC-gold performed the best for depth measurement compared to CBC, with a maximum increase in mean error of about 1.5 mm for *scheme 1* and 3 mm for *scheme 2*.

5.3 Error Distribution

To accommodate the randomness of the error, we considered to observe and compare the error distributions. We assumed an ideal error distribution as a baseline for comparison. Computed Cumulative Density Function (CDF) for all (width and depth) errors, are shown in Fig. 5, where a tendency of divergence of FBC/CBC from ideal baseline can be seen. To quantify the measure of divergence, we used Kullback-Leibler distance (KLD) [14]. For discrete PDFs P and Q, the KL divergence of Q from P is defined as in Eq. 4.

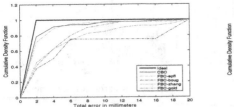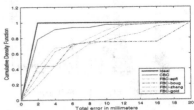

Fig. 5. Cumulative Density Function for scheme 1 and 2.

$$D_{KL}(P||Q) = \sum_i P(i) ln \frac{P(i)}{Q(i)} \tag{4}$$

The KLD values for FBC/CBC methods are given in Table 3. From the table, it is quite evident that for both *scheme 1* and *scheme 2*, FBC-boug performed the best reduction of width error, which was summarized in the Sect. 5.1. Similarly, FBC-epfl showed the best performance for depth and overall error in *scheme 1* as summarized in Sect. 5.2. Evidently, FBC-epfl performed better than CBC for depth measurement. Unlike in mean error estimates for *scheme 2* shown in Fig. 4(d)), FBC-boug showed performance closer to FBC-epfl in terms of error distribution, as in Fig. 5. FBC-zhang and FBC-gold performed alternatively better than each other in various configurations, but still not up to FBC-epfl and FBC-boug.

Eventually, we see that FBC methods have performed with better accuracy in *scheme 1* configuration than in *scheme 2*.

Table 3. Kullback-Leibler Divergence values for total (width + depth) error

Measurement	Ideal	CBC	FBC-epfl	FBC-boug	FBC-zhang	FBC-gold
Scheme-1						
Width	0	1.29	1.39	**0.92**	1.39	1.20
Depth	0	0.51	**0.39**	0.69	0.52	0.80
Total	0	0.24	**0.34**	0.98	0.80	0.88
Scheme-2						
Width	0	1.29	1.29	**0.80**	1.61	1.39
Depth	0	0.52	0.92	**0.70**	1.39	1.12
Total	0	0.24	0.88	**0.83**	1.61	1.16

5.4 Resilience

Next, both the FBC and CBC were evaluated for resilience to practical disturbances, which are feature detection error (*pixel noise*) and pantograph misalignment (*uplift, yaw, roll, pitch*), as explained in Sect. 4.3. Variations of these parameters were emulated within a practical range of values and a new set of observations and feature points were obtained. Using new sets of data, FBC was carried out for each perturbation of the parameter and the KLD was computed. Only *scheme 1* operation, which had shown better performance so far, was considered to evaluate resilience of FBC and CBC.

For pixel noise variation, gaussian noise with a variance between 10 and +10 was added to the signal. The uplift was emulated by varying the vertical axes from −0.5 m to +0.5 m. All rotations (yaw, roll and pitch) were allowed to vary between −10 and +10 degrees. All subfigures in the first column of Fig. 6 show resilience of width error estimation to all five practical implications. Similarly, resilience of depth error is shown in subfigures of the second column.

For pantograph misalignment disturbances, CBC errors are higher than one or more of the FBC-types. In CBC, the reference world coordinate axis is fixed in space based on the position of the checkerboard. For FBC, on the other hand, the reference world axis is located on the pantograph itself. Hence, misalignment

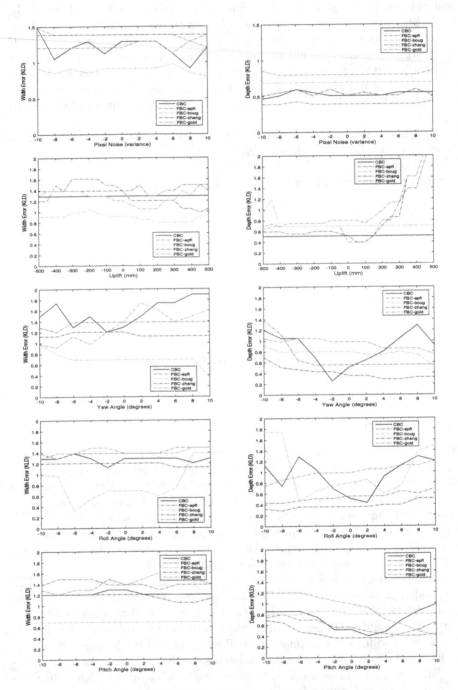

Fig. 6. Experimenting resilience over physical implications

of the pantograph does not affect the measurements using FBC, and several FBC methods are more robust to pantograph misalignment than CBC.

For feature detection errors, FBC-types will be obviously more sensitive than CBC, because FBC relies on noise-free feature points for high quality calibration. However, FBC-boug and FBC-epfl showed better resilience than CBC in terms of handling noisy feature points, because their optimization yielded better results with the localization of world coordinate system on the pantograph.

Width error of FBC-boug consistently showed the best resilience over CBC and other FBC types. Although FBC-boug is similar to CBC in terms of pose estimation procedure, FBC-boug used only 6 points compared to CBC, which used more than 200 points for bundle optimized solution for the pose.

In most of the pantograph rotational disturbances, the depth error for FBC-types showed a consistently flatter response compared to CBC, which was very sensitive to rotational disturbances. However, FBC-zhang and FBC-epfl showed the best resilience.

6   Conclusion

Considering the PantoInspect Train Monitoring System as a usecase, we have outlined the specific practical problem underlining the usage of vision based inspection systems. The paper is motivated with the need for online-recalibration and how CBC fails to fulfill the need.

We proposed FBC methods for PTMS, which uses very few points in an image. We have evaluated four state-of-art algorithms for camera pose estimation. The results have shown that FBC has outperformed CBC in many cases. The FBC-epfl and FBC-boug methods have shown best results in terms of accuracy and robustness for depth and width error, respectively. Carrying out FBC on every profile image before analysing the defect (scheme 1), is found to be more accurate. However, if the image is too noisy to extract features, recent FBC parameter needs to be re-used. All FBC methods can be executed in real-time, without relevant penalty to the system speed.

Hence, we conclude that online re-calibration for error-sensitive 3D measurement systems (such as PTMS), is possible using FBC methods that give effectively a better performance and robustness than CBC. This tremendously increases the usability of 3D vision inspection systems with greater flexibility of using online re-calibration without any manual intervention.

References

1. Imagehouse PantoInspect A/S, Denmark. http://www.pantoinspect.dk/
2. Bouguet, J.Y.: Camera calibration toolbox for Matlab (2008). http://www.vision. caltech.edu/bouguetj/calib_doc/
3. Li, C., Lu, P., Ma, L.: A camera on-line recalibration framework using SIFT. Vis. Comput. **26**(3), 227–240 (2010). Springer-Verlag

 4. Dwarakanath, D., Eichhorn, A., Griwodz, C., Halvorsen, P.: Faster and more accurate feature-based calibration for widely spaced camera pairs. In: Second International Conference on Digital Information and Communication Technology and it's Applications (DICTAP), pp. 87–92 (2012)
 5. Mavrinac, A., Xiang, C., Tepe, K.: Feature-based calibration of distributed smart stereo camera networks. In: Second ACM/IEEE International Conference on Distributed Smart Cameras, ICDSC 2008, pp. 1–10 (2008)
 6. Carr, P., Sheikh, Y., Matthews, I.: Point-less calibration: camera parameters from gradient-based alignment to edge images. In: IEEE Workshop on the Applications of Computer Vision (WACV) (2012)
 7. Lepetit, V., Moreno-Noguer, F., Fua, P.: EPnP: an accurate O(n) solution to the PnP problem. Int. J. Comput. Vis. 81(2), 155–166 (2009)
 8. Bouguet, J.Y.: Visual methods for three-dimensional modeling Ph.D. Thesis, California Institute of Technology (1999). http://www.vision.caltech.edu/bouguetj/thesis/thesis.html
 9. Zhengyou, Z.: A flexible new technique for camera calibration. IEEE Trans. Pattern Anal. Mach. Intell. 22, 1330–1334 (1998)
10. Hartley, R., Zisserman, A.: Multiple View Geometry in Computer Vision, 2nd edn. Cambridge University Press, New York (2003). ISBN: 0521540518
11. Faugeras, O.: Three-Dimensional Computer Vision: AGV. MIT Press, Cambridge (1993)
12. Tsai, R.Y.: A versatile camea calibration technique for high-accuracy 3D machine vision metrology using off-the-shelf TV camera and lenses. IEEE J. Robot. Autom. 3, 323–344 (1987)
13. Lu, C.-P., Hager, G.D., Mjolsness, E.: Fast and globally convergent pose estimation from video images. IEEE Trans. Pattern Anal. Mach. Intell. 22, 610–622 (2000)
14. Kullback, S., Leibler, R.A.: On information and sufficiency. J. Ann. Math. Stat. 22(1), 79–86 (1951)

Image Saliency Applied to Infrared Images for Unmanned Maritime Monitoring

Gonçalo Cruz[1](✉) and Alexandre Bernardino[2]

[1] Research Center, Portuguese Air Force Academy, Sintra, Portugal
gccruz@academiafa.edu.pt
[2] Computer and Robot Vision Laboratory, Instituto de Sistemas e Robótica,
Instituto Superior Técnico, Lisboa, Portugal
alexandre.bernardino@tecnico.ulisboa.pt

Abstract. This paper presents a method to detect boats and life rafts on long wave infrared (LWIR) images, captured by an aerial platform. The method applies the concept of image saliency to highlight distinct areas on the images. However saliency algorithms always highlight salient points in the image, even in the absence of targets. We propose a statistical method based on the saliency algorithm output to distinguish frames with or without targets. To evaluate the detection algorithm, we have equipped a fixed wing unmanned aerial vehicle with a LWIR camera and gathered a dataset with more than 44000 frames, containing several boats and a life raft. The proposed detection strategy demonstrates a good performance, specially, a low rate of false positives and low computational complexity.

Keywords: Image saliency · Detection · Infrared images · LWIR · UAV · Maritime surveillance

1 Introduction

In recent years, many maritime safety issues have challenged the international community. Since year 2000, more than 22400 emigrants have lost their lives on the Mediterranean Sea [1]. Countries in South-East Asia carried out large scale search and rescue operations over sea [2] and waters of the Somali coast and Malacca Straight have been populated with pirates that endanger vital navigation routes [9]. On one hand, assuring maritime safety is paramount to protect human lives and to the world economy, but on the other hand, it is very difficult to guarantee a proper surveillance or monitoring over a wide area.

Even though there has been a huge investment on technologies to perform surveillance and monitoring [11] namely coastal radars, manned aircraft and satellites, there is still a lot to be done on improving the coverage and persistence of these tasks. One of the rising trends, due to recent significant technological advances, is the use of unmanned aerial vehicle (UAV). Fixed wing UAVs are specially attractive because they have large endurance, when compared to its rotary wing counterparts or similar manned aircraft. They also offer a more

© Springer International Publishing Switzerland 2015
L. Nalpantidis et al. (Eds.): ICVS 2015, LNCS 9163, pp. 511–523, 2015.
DOI: 10.1007/978-3-319-20904-3_46

flexible deployment than coastal resources and satellites, as well as a smaller cost than other alternatives. Despite its advantages, the vast majority of UAVs have serious restrictions on the payload which limits the type of sensor they can carry, being the most commons electro-optical sensors - visible image and infrared (IR).

This paper focuses on the detection of boats and life rafts in the ocean using a UAV with cameras observing the ocean surface. We aim at a persistent surveillance of a large area, which requires the analysis of a huge amount of data gathered by the sensors. The data in most of the cases does not convey any useful information and even hampers the ability of the human operators to analyse the imagery [5]. Additionally, visible images have drawbacks as they highly depend on the illumination conditions and often contain distractors like waves and sun glare.

To circumvent the issues presented for images on the visible spectrum, we have instrumented a fixed wing UAV with an infrared camera able to detect radiation with wavelength between 8–14 μm. Radiation in this range, is often called Long Wavelength IR (LWIR) or thermal infrared. This designation is based on the fact that, in this range the intensity of radiation emitted by a given body depends largely on its temperature.

On an ocean monitoring flight most of the observed background is water with approximately the same temperature, at each time of the day. Objects like vessels and life-rafts are expected to present areas with different temperature and therefore emit LWIR radiation with higher intensity. Sun shades and waves have a much lower influence at this radiation spectrum that in the visible range. Nonetheless, the analysis of infrared imagery still presents some challenges. Temperature difference may be very small in some objects. Moreover, an object may be visible only for a short period of time due to low flying altitude of a small UAV and consequent small observed area at each given instant.

This work addresses these issues by proposing the application of saliency algorithms to IR images to detect vessels. Saliency algorithms are inspired in the ability of humans to easily segment image regions that are distinct from their neighbourhood, independently of their absolute intensity levels and contrast [8]. Thus they have the advantage of detecting regions on the sea that have only slight temperature differences to the background. Furthermore, they operate in single frames, which allow detections of boats that only persist for a few frames. However, classical saliency algorithms are designed to always detect the most salient points in an image. This is a problem for our application because in most of the time the observed images have only background. The most salient objects detected in these images have no relevance to the application and will produce false alarms. To tackle this problem, we propose a statistical analysis of the maps produced by the saliency algorithms. This allows to determine whether we have a relevant signal or simply background noise, thus reducing the rate of false alarms.

The paper is organized as follows. In Sect. 2, we will discuss the related work. In Sect. 3 our problem is detailed and our approach presented. In Sect. 4, we evaluate the performance of the proposed algorithm with real data. Finally, in Sect. 5, we present our conclusions and some directions for future work.

2   Related Work

Aircraft have been used as a privileged observation platform since its appearance. As new sensing technologies emerge, they are readily integrated in aerial platforms for possible applications [21]. One of the most successfully applied technologies has been infrared imaging. These images can provide information that is not present on the visible spectrum (like temperature of a given object), and therefore may overcome limitations of human vision or complement it [23].

A lot of work has been developed on automatic detection using infrared sensors for military aircraft. Most works focus on the detection of airborne targets like missiles or other combat aircraft, which typically have high temperature engines and exhaust [20]. The detection of high temperature objects in IR images was also exploited to detect fires [10,12].

Other scenarios have also been considered for the detection based on infrared images gathered by aircraft. For instance, in [15], a UAV detects and follows a river based on Near-IR images; in [18,24] is also reported the detection and tracking of ground targets. Detection of people also had the attention of several works, on both visible [22] and IR images [16].

The detection of objects on the ocean has not yet been thoroughly explored. There are some works which deal with images gathered by surface platforms [17,19] which impose constraints on the appearance of the objects to be detected. There are also some works that use airborne visible images [3] that extract features and successively select objects of interest. Particularly, in [3] the authors use five features that depend directly on the three RGB channels. That approach, while successful on visible spectrum images, is not suitable for LWIR images, once no color is available.

Another important aspect is that, when observed from an airborne platform, vessels may have a multitude of appearances, depending on several factors like the type of vessel, its size, the height of observing aircraft, etc. Facing this restriction, we would like to detect a given object, without knowing its appearance beforehand. Itti *et al.* [8] have introduced a saliency model that mimics the visual search process of humans. That saliency model indicates areas of a given image that would be examined on a second stage with more detail. More recently, works like [6,7] have explored the spectral characteristics of an image to create similar saliency maps. Compared to Itti's approach, those techniques show a better detection performance and much faster computation time. With such advantages, these approaches became very attractive for the application at hand. There is still one major limitation for this technique in our scenario: the algorithm is designed to highlight salient areas of the image and therefore will produce detections, regardless if there is a foreground or not.

3   Detection on LWIR Images

The rationale behind the usage of a camera sensitive to infrared light with wavelengths comprised between 8 and 14 μm is that the water in the ocean has an approximately uniform temperature and objects of interest have different temperatures. With this assumption in mind, it is expectable that, while observing the ocean, the thermal image has approximately uniform intensity for the water background and brighter or darker areas corresponding to objects of interest.

Typically, LWIR cameras have smaller resolution than common RGB cameras, so we expect to observe less details of the vessels. Additionally, in the case of small boats, we expect their temperature to be approximately the same as the ocean. In the case of bigger vessels some parts (like the engines or the exhausts) have higher temperatures and therefore are more noticeable.

As visible in Fig. 1(a), when acquired, the image exhibits an almost uniform background and a foreground with very small contrast. The image presented in Fig. 1(b) shows a more perceivable foreground and was enhanced by histogram equalization. Histogram equalisation highlights high contrast areas that, despite improving the vessel appearance, also increase the image noise level. Therefore, a simple thresholding technique is prone to numerous false positive detections. Saliency methods can reduce this effect because they analyse image neighborhoods instead of single points. However, as we will describe next, they still present problems when no targets are present in the image.

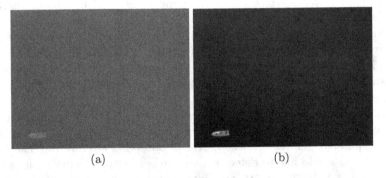

(a)   (b)

Fig. 1. Sample LWIR image: (a) acquired image; (b) image with contrast improved by off-line processing.

3.1 Image Signature

An image with characteristics like exhibited in Fig. 1 is prone to the application of saliency detection algorithms. They do not require a full characterization of the object of interest but rather highlight areas that are different from the background. As stated before, algorithms that explore the spectrum of the image, like [6,7], have shown good performance and low computational cost. Therefore, these algorithms are specially interesting for our application. We have tested and compared both approaches, hereafter designated as Spectral Residual [7] and Image Signature [6]. To perform this evaluation, we have implemented both algorithms. The mean computation time to create a saliency map of 64 by 48 pixels was 6.5 and 5 ms for Spectral Residual and for Image Signature, respectively. Even though the detection of saliency in LWIR images was similar, the improvement in computation time lead us to the selection of Image Signature algorithm.

3.2   Description of the Method

In [6] the authors show that, for an image x expressed as

$$x = f + b, \quad x, f, b \in \mathbb{R}^N \tag{1}$$

where N is the number of pixels, f represents the foreground and b represents the background, the separation of f and b can be performed given only x. The assumption followed is that the foreground is sparsely supported in image space and the background is sparsely supported in the Discrete Cosine Transform (DCT) basis. The method consists of isolating the spatial support of f, which is accomplished by computing the sign of x in the DCT domain and then transform back to the spatial domain. This operation is written as

$$\bar{x} = \text{IDCT}\,[\,sign(\,\text{DCT}(x)\,)\,], \tag{2}$$

where $\bar{x}$ is the saliency map and IDCT is the Inverse Discrete Cosine Transform. The intuition behind Eq. 2 is that the sign of $\text{DCT}(x)$ is more strongly correlated with the sign of $\text{DCT}(f)$ than with the sign of $\text{DCT}(b)$. In one hand, because $\text{DCT}(b)$ is sparse, most of its coefficients are zero or very close to zero outside its support Ω_b. Thus:

$$sign(\text{DCT}(x)) = sign(\text{DCT}(f) + \text{DCT}(b)) \approx sign(\text{DCT}(f)). \tag{3}$$

On the other hand, inside Ω_b, because f and b are independent, there is still a positive correlation between the signs of $\text{DCT}(f)$ and $\text{DCT}(x)$. As shown in [6]:

$$\text{Prob}(sign(\text{DCT}(x) = sign(\text{DCT}(f))) \geq 0.5. \tag{4}$$

In practice, we resize x to an image of 48 by 64 pixels, which results in four-fold decrease in computation time and still highlights the areas of interest. The final saliency map (examples in Fig. 2) is obtained by convolving the result with a Gaussian kernel, to reduce noise.

With a saliency map already computed, we would like to isolate the objects of interest in the image. However, the separation between different areas must be done carefully. According to the authors' premise that a foreground is present and has a sparse spacial representation, the saliency map will always highlight the most conspicuous areas of the image. In cases where no foreground is present, slight variations on the intensity of radiation emitted by the ocean's surface as shown in Fig. 2(b), will be amplified. This fact precludes the direct application of a thresholding technique, as it will produce numerous false positives.

In [7], the authors suggest an empirical method to isolate foreground from background. Their method consists on setting a threshold to three times the

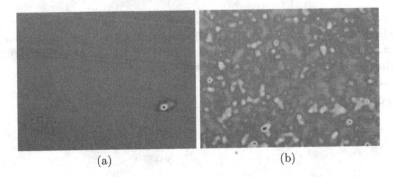

Fig. 2. Saliency maps overlayed on the LWIR images: (a) image with boat present; (b) image without boat present. Areas in red are more salient and areas where grey is visible are considered less salient (Color figure online).

average of the saliency map and then segment this map. We think that this approach is highly dependent on the adjustment of the threshold by an user, otherwise the results may be poor. We extend this idea by multiplying different scalars (α) and we will designate it as Saliency Threshold (ST) algorithm.

However, a Saliency Threshold method lacks the ability to associate a confidence level to the obtained detections. Confidence levels are important for a number of applications, such as giving feedback to a human operator or feeding probabilistic time filtering methods like HMMs [14]. To address this issue, we analyse the statistical distribution of the saliency values in the saliency maps with two different options, that we will designate as histogram ratio saliency confidence (HRSC) and entropy saliency confidence (ESC). By assigning a score to each detection based on the statistical properties, instead of setting a fixed threshold, we are able to easily set the operating point of the algorithm (trade-off between precision and recall rates) according to the task at hand. The first strategy considers the properties of the histogram of saliency values. In cases where a boat is visible, most of the pixels are contained in the lower saliency range, as shown by Fig. 3(a). In the cases where only ocean is visible, then, there are more pixels with other intensities (Fig. 3(b)). Based on this fact, we compute a confidence score (HRSC) for each image as

$$\rho = 1 - \frac{\text{bin}_{\#2} \text{ count}}{\text{bin}_{\#1} \text{ count}} \tag{5}$$

where $\text{bin}_{\#1}$ count and $\text{bin}_{\#2}$ count are the number of pixels in the lower intensity bin and in the second lowest bin. If the ratio between the histogram bins is small, then it is more likely to have a boat in sight and therefore a higher score is assigned. In case the ratio is bigger, then the confidence will be closer to zero and is less likely to have a boat in the image.

The second option to perform the statistical analysis, is the use of saliency map entropy. As we have shown in Fig. 2, images with no boats produce apparently random saliency maps, while images with boats produce more structured

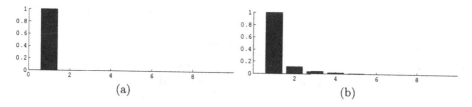

Fig. 3. Normalized intensity histogram of the saliency map (a) for a image with a boat present and (b) for a image without boat present.

maps. Image entropy is a measure of the randomness of the information contained in a given image and is computed as

$$\eta = -\sum_{i}^{n}(p_i \log_2(p_i))$$
(6)

where p_i is the normalized value of bin i, of the saliency map histogram. As before, we define a confidence score varying from zero to one, which results from normalizing the image entropy (that in this case, we will designate as Entropy Saliency Score - ESC). If η has a high value, then is less likely to have a boat in the image and therefore, the score is low. If the entropy of the map is low, then the confidence score will be higher.

In the final step of the proposed method, we isolate the areas of the saliency map with higher values. We use Otsu's method [13] to compute the threshold value. This method does not need an adjustment, as it minimizes the variance in each of the classes (in the resulting binary image). After thresholding the map, a connected components algorithm clusters the pixels into detections. At last, a bounding box for each detection is created and scaled back to the original image size, as shown in Fig. 5(b). The algorithms are summarized in Table 1.

4   Experimental Results

The dataset used to test the algorithms consisted of a sequence with 44677 frames, with a resolution of 384 by 288 pixels. This sequence corresponds to 24 min and 49 s of images captured by a LWIR camera on-board a UAV (represented in Fig. 4(a)). The camera is a GOBI-384 (Fig. 4(b)), equipped with a 18 mm lens and a relative aperture of $f/1$. The camera has an Ethernet connection to the UAV's computational board, which allows us to store the images directly on a digital format. The UAV flew over two small boats (with a length of 16 and 12 m) and a life-raft.

The sequence was annotated manually with the position of the boats and life raft in each frame. The annotation consisted of a bounding box that encompassed each vessel and that we use as Ground Truth (GT). The GT is represented in Fig. 5(b) as a red rectangle.

To evaluate the performance of the algorithm and compare it against other approaches, we have followed a method similar to what is proposed in [4].

Table 1. Saliency Confidence (HRSC and ESC) and Saliency Threshold algorithm.

Algorithm 1. Saliency Confidence	**Algorithm 2.** Saliency Threshold
Input: LWIR image	Input: LWIR image
Parameters: detection threshold	Parameters: multiplying factor α
Resize LWIR image	Resize LWIR image
Compute **saliency** with Eq. 2	Compute **saliency** with Eq. 2
Compute **confidence** with Eq. 5 or Eq. 6	Compute **average** of saliency map
If confidence < detection threshold	Segment pixels with intensity $> \alpha \times$ **average**
Apply Otsu segmentation	Apply connected components
Apply connected components	Compute bounding box
Compute bounding boxes	Output: Bounding boxes
Else	
Discard image	
End	
Output: Bounding boxes	

The evaluation pipeline that we have followed has a slight difference to the original method. The difference consists in considering a detection as a true positive as long as its center is included on the GT Bounding Box. The results are presented as a ratio between Precision and Recall.

On our trials, we have tested histogram ratio saliency confidence, entropy saliency confidence, saliency threshold and some other simple methods as benchmark. These methods were naive approaches and consisted on direct segmentation without analysing any properties of the image or the saliency map. The benchmark methods are described in Table 2.

The evaluation method assumes that each detection has a confidence score associated. In the proposed methods, HRSC and ESC, these scores are intrinsic to the method, but the other tested approaches do not have a confidence level

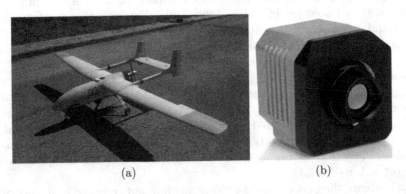

(a)   (b)

Fig. 4. (a) UAV and (b) LWIR camera used to obtain the set.

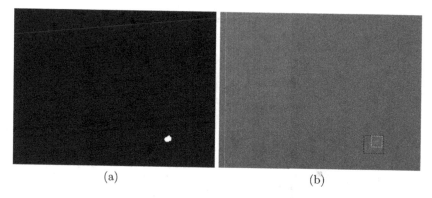

Fig. 5. (a) Binary image with a boat present; (b) Original LWIR image with bounding boxes visible. Ground Truth annotation represented in red and the output of the algorithm represented in green (Color figure online).

associated. To overcome this hindrance, for evaluation purposes, we superimpose a unitary confidence value to each detection. In practice, this means that these different approaches will have only one working condition.

Figure 6 present the scores of HRSC and ESC. These results, were compared against Saliency Threshold with different multiplying scalars and also the six combinations of direct segmentation. In the case of LWIR THRSH, LWIR THRSH CE and SM THRSH, we searched the optimal value by testing a sufficiently large range of values, and chose the one that, for each case achieved better precision-recall values.

The results of the six benchmark methods were poor, with numerous false positives, even when an optimal threshold value was used. These results indicate the need for a better detection strategy. We would like to mention that SM Otsu (which happens to be overlapped by ST with $\alpha = 3$) is a particular case of HRSC and ESC, when no criteria is applied to validate or discard images. Saliency Threshold with $\alpha = 3$ had poor results. However, when higher α were used, it attained a good performance, with its scores near the plots of HRSC and ESC.

Table 2. Benchmark algorithms.

Benchmark algorithms	Description
SM Otsu	Apply Otsu method on a saliency image
SM THRSH	Use an optimal value to segment the saliency map
LWIR THRSH CE	Use an optimal value to segment the LWIR image with contrast enhancement
LWIR Otsu CE	Apply directly Otsu method on a LWIR image with contrast enhancement
LWIR Otsu	Apply directly Otsu method on a LWIR image
LWIR THRSH	Use an optimal value to segment the LWIR image

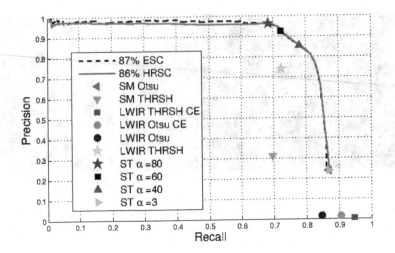

Fig. 6. Precision-Recall results obtained in the LWIR image sequence. Scores presented for ESC and HRSC represent the area under the curve.

HRSC and ESC demonstrated a performance similar to Saliency Threshold but provided a confidence parameter that may be incorporated on another detection layer. For instance, it could be used on a temporal filter and therefore improve the overall performance of the system even further.

When analysing the absolute performance of the proposed methods, one of the results that we would like to focus on is the relatively low rate of false positives. This is an indicator that the strategies to compute the confidence score were adequate. After considering the different results between the histogram ratio approach and the entropy approach, we believe that the best option is to use the Entropy Saliency Confidence. Not only is a more tangible concept but on a system performing a search task, is usually preferable to have lower rate of false positives (higher precision) than a low rate of missed detections (high recall). As visible in Fig. 6, the option based on entropy may be set to an operating point with slightly higher precision, while maintaining a considerable recall. With the system running at a high frame rate, there is a considerable probability that the object may be detected in at least one frame.

We consider the results particularly encouraging, because most of the missed detections consisted of demanding conditions even for a human operator. In Fig. 7, we present some of the typical situations where the algorithm fails. The left and center images represent situations where boats are visible but at least one is near the border of the image. The right image represents a missed detection of a life raft. The life raft was the object that was mostly present from frame 36000 to 42500, which corresponds to the big areas highlighted in red. The detection of the life raft, however, is very challenging as can be seen in the image that already has its contrast enhanced for visualization purposes. One of the reasons for this difficulty was the fact that it was unmanned and had no heat source. Due to its small size and mass, the temperature converged rapidly to the ocean's temperature.

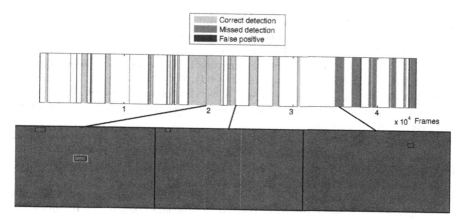

Fig. 7. Typical distribution along the image set of the occurrence of correct detections, missed detections and false positives. Area in white represents frames without boats. Three images bellow represent common cases of missed detections.

5   Conclusion and Future Work

This papers presents the use of a saliency algorithm to detect vessels in thermal images, captured by a UAV. This saliency algorithm is designed to separate foreground from background and therefore two strategies were proposed to deal with the cases where only ocean is visible. The tests on real data showed a good performance of the algorithm, more so because no temporal information is being considered. For future work we consider adding temporal information and incorporate the confidence parameter in a temporal filter. Now, we considered the entropy of the entire saliency map but the computation of entropy of subsets of the map may be useful to deal with images with regions of different characteristics. These challenges, that span from sun glare, to wave crests, to bright sky, have hindered the application of saliency-based methods to visible spectrum images in maritime context.

Acknowledgments. This work was partially supported by project SEAGULL (QREN SI IDT 34063) and by FCT project [UID/EEA/50009/2013]. The authors would like to thank the team involved in obtaining these images and annotating the ground truth.

References

1. Brian, T., Laczko, F.: Fatal Journeys Tracking Lives Lost during Migration, 1st edn. International Organization for Migration, Geneva (2014)
2. Joint Agency Coordination Center: Search for MH370 Facts and statistics. Technical report, Australian Government, April 2014
3. Dawkins, M., et al.: Tracking nautical objects in real-time via layered saliency detection. In: SPIE Defense + Security. International Society for Optics and Photonics, p. 908903 (2014)

4. Dollar, P., et al.: Pedestrian detection: an evaluation of the state of the art. IEEE Trans. Pattern Anal. Mach. Intell. **34**(4), 743–761 (2012)
5. Donaldson, P.: Cloudy skies. Unmanned Veh. **18**(5), 32–34 (2013)
6. Hou, X., Harel, J., Koch, C.: Image signature: highlighting sparse salient regions. IEEE Trans. Pattern Anal. Mach. Intell. **34**(1), 194–201 (2011)
7. Hou, X., Zhang, L.: Saliency detection: a spectral residual approach. In: Proceedings of the IEEE Computer Society Conference on Computer Vision and Pattern Recognition 800 (2007)
8. Itti, L., Koch, C., Niebur, E.: A model of saliency-based visual attention for rapid scene analysis. IEEE Pattern Anal. Mach. Intell. **20**(11), 1254–1259 (1998)
9. Kang, H.K.: Gulf of Aden vs Malacca Strait: Piracy and Counter-piracy efforts. Institute of Peace and Conflict Studies (2009)
10. Kontitsis, M., Valavanis, K.P., Tsourveloudis, N.: A UAV vision system for airborne surveillance. In: Proceedings of the IEEE International Conference on Robotics and Automation, ICRA 2004, vol. 1 (2004)
11. Maritime Security and Surveillance - Case Study. Technical report. Centre for Strategy and Evaluation Services, January 2011
12. Merino, L., et al.: An unmanned aircraft system for automatic forest fire monitoring and measurement. J. Intell. Robot. Syst. Theory Appl. **65**, 533–548 (2012)
13. Otsu, N.: A threshold selection method from gray-level histograms. Automatica **11**(285–296), 23–27 (1975)
14. Rabiner, L.: A tutorial on hidden Markov models and selected applications in speech recognition. Proc. IEEE **77**(2), 257–286 (1989)
15. Rathinam, S., et al.: Autonomous searching and tracking of a river using an UAV. In: Proceedings of the American Control Conference, pp. 359–364 (2007)
16. Rudol, P., Doherty, P.: Human body detection and geolocalization for UAV search and rescue missions using color and thermal imagery. In: IEEE Aerospace Conference Proceedings (2008)
17. Teutsch, M., Kruger, W.: Classification of small boats in infrared images for maritime surveillance. In: 2010 International WaterSide Security Conference, pp. 1–7, November 2010
18. Teutsch, M., Kruger, W.: Detection, segmentation, and tracking of moving objects in UAV videos. In: 2012 IEEE Ninth International Conference on Advanced Video and Signal-Based Surveillance, pp. 313–318 (2012)
19. Toet, A.: Detection of dim point targets in cluttered maritime backgrounds through multisensor image fusion. In: AeroSense 2002, vol. 4718, pp. 118–129 (2002)
20. Venkateswarlu, R., et al.: Design considerations of IRST system. In: AeroSense 1997. International Society for Optics and Photonics, pp. 591–602 (1997)
21. Wadsworth, A., et al.: Aircraft experiments with visible and infrared sensors. Int. J. Remote Sens. **13**(6–7), 1175–1199 (1992)
22. Westall, P., et al.: Improved maritime target tracker using colour fusion. In: International Conference on High Performance Computing & Simulation, HPCS 2009, pp. 230–236 (2009)
23. Xiang, T., Yan, L., Gao, R.: A fusion algorithm for infrared and visible images based on adaptive dual-channel unit-linking PCNN in NSCT domain. Infrared Phys. Technol. **69**, 53–61 (2015)
24. Zhang, S.: Object tracking in unmanned aerial vehicle (UAV) videos using a combined approach. In: Proceedings of the IEEE International Conference on Acoustics, Speech, and Signal Processing, (ICASSP 2005), vol. 2, pp. 681–684 (2005)

CBIR Service for Object Identification

Josef Hák[1], Martin Klíma[1], Mikuláš Krupička[2($\boxtimes$)], and Václav Čadek[2]

[1] ProTyS, a.s., Václavská 12/316, 120 00 Praha 2, Czech Republic
{josef.hak,martin.klima}@protys.cz
http://www.protys.cz/
[2] CertiCon a.s., Evropská 11, 160 00 Praha 6, Czech Republic
{mikulas.krupicka,vaclav.cadek}@certicon.cz
http://www.certicon.cz/

Abstract. This paper proposes an architecture for an exact object detection system. The implementation as well as the communication between individual system components is detailed in the paper. Well known methods for feature detection and extraction were used. Fast and precise method for feature comparison is presented.

The proposed system was evaluated by training the dataset and querying the dataset. With 12 Workers, the response time of querying the dataset consisting of 100 000 images were just below 20 seconds. Also system trained dataset of this size with same amount of workers in about an hour.

Keywords: CBIR · QBIC · Image retrieval · Hamming exact search · Message broker · Image processing · Computer vision · Sift · Freak

1 Introduction

The Content Based Image Retrieval (*CBIR*) is a problem that attracted attention of many researchers since the first articles about this topic appeared. One of the first papers was published by Niblack *et al.* [2]. The authors introduced a system for storing images and information about them and were the first ones who described images with multiple features such as color, texture and shape. The articles about *CBIR* from the early years up to 2000 were nicely wrapped by Smeulders *et al.* [7] followed by Datta *et al.* [14] up to year 2004.

In the first survey, authors categorize problem to three classes:

- *search by association* – User has no specific aim other than find interesting things. Often implies iterative refinement of the search.
- *search for object* – User aims at specific object. Often done by *search by example* which means that user supplies image with the object he wants to find.
- *search for category* – The third class aims at retrieving an representative image of a specific class. Class is also often specified by an example image.

Authors then covered different approaches of how to describe content of image. Specifically color description, shape description and texture description. They thendiscussed interpretation and similarity of information captured from images.

© Springer International Publishing Switzerland 2015
L. Nalpantidis et al. (Eds.): ICVS 2015, LNCS 9163, pp. 523–532, 2015.
DOI: 10.1007/978-3-319-20904-3_47

The latter survey sumarizes articles published from 1995 to 2004. It builds on the prior article and describes progress in each field. Also the prior work is extended by surveying the available articles about pre-classification of input images to style classes (paint, photograph, synthethic image) for better selection of following further steps.

Our application falls under the second category (*search for object*). We want to find particular object described by the query image in preprocessed database. And we specifically aim at paintings.

One of the few methods describing *search for object* can be seen in paper published by Wangming *et al.* [15]. The authors used well known SIFT algorithm [4] for detecting and extracting object features from an image.

Very few papers about precise searching for paintings were published so far. One of the first articles about art querying were published by Hatano [3]. Authors however focused mainly on storing and describing images rather than querying. Probably also due to technical restrictions in the time of creation. Survey about *CBIR* in art can be found in Chen *et al.* [12]. Majority of published articles however focus on automatic classification of painting style [8,10,11,16] rather than searching for same work of art.

A description of a similar application we present can be found in Tabernik *et al.* [19]. Their authors however focused also on classical categorization of similar objects rather than searching for specific ones. They used Apache Storm framework[1]. But their implementation is due to long response times inappropriate for real-time use. Also the training time of the dataset is not given.

The rest of the paper is organized as follows: In Sect. 2 we present description of the proposed *CBIR* system. The database training step and the query step. In Sect. 3 the application is described. It's implementation, used tools and communication between processes is detailed. Performance of the whole system is covered in Sect. 4. And lastly, the conclusion is given in Sect. 5.

2   Method Description

Our method consists of several parts.

- **Image Transform** – This step transforms an image to a vector of keypoints and their descriptors (further called "Image Features").
- **Compare Image Features** – Compare two Features which results in one Score.
- **Build Database** – In this step, the set of images is transformed to Image Features and stored in database.
- **Query Database** – It is basically comparing Image Features in database with query image for set of best Scores.

---

[1] http://storm.apache.org/.

2.1   Image Transform

In this step, we transform input image to set of image features called Image Features (see Fig. 1). Firstly, we find the keypoints using SIFT [4] algorithm from which we have their position, size and angle. Each keypoint is then described using FREAK descriptor [18]. So for each keypoint we have it's position, size, angle and 512 bit vector. This is called "Image Feature".

The last part of this step is optimization of keypoint descriptors. The population count (Hamming weight) for each keypoint descriptor is computed. Thus Hamming weight can vary values from 0 to 512. All Image Features are then sorted according to the Hamming weight and lookup table of length 513 (values from 0 to 512) is computed. Each item in this table is assigned with the closest Image Feature according to Hamming Distance. This lookup table is then used in *Compare Image Features* step to achieve better performance (see Fig. 6 for comparison with brute force matching).

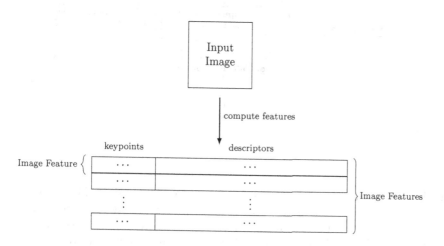

Fig. 1. Scheme of computing Image Features.

2.2   Compare Image Features

We start this step with two sets of Image Features. Firstly the potential matching descriptors are computed with our fast algorithm described in the following section. For each of the resulting pair, the Angle Consistency Score, Size Consistency Score and Homography Consistency Score are computed. As can be seen in Fig. 2, the final Score is then calculated from the preceding steps.

The final matching score is obtained as

$$S = a \cdot S_{hamming} + b \cdot S_{size} + c \cdot S_{angle} + d \cdot S_{homography}. \tag{1}$$

where $S_{hamming}$ is "hamming features matches", S_{size} is "size consistency score", S_{angle} "angle consistency score" and $S_{homography}$ is "homography consistency score". All are described in the sections below. The a, b, c and d are weights of each individual score which can be tuned for specific application. For our task, the $a = 1$, $b = 10$, $c = 100$ and $d = 1000$ showed as best. This is done for each image in the database. The images with the highest score are then considered more similar to query image than those with lower score.

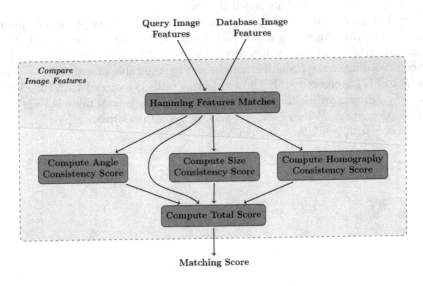

Fig. 2. Scheme for comparing Image Features.

Calculate Hamming Features Matches for Hamming Threshold H. For each keypoint descriptor in query image, we calculate the nearest neighbor descriptor from the test image (according to Hamming distance) using the previously calculated lookup table. For maximum Hamming distance H, the algorithm have to compare only subset of descriptors (from index $i1 = P - H$ to index $i2 = P + H$). Where P is Hamming weight of query feature descriptor. It ensures higher performance without any accuracy loss. If Hamming distance between query feature descriptor and the nearest test descriptor is less than H, we append this image feature couple (query image feature and test image feature) as Hamming match and store it in matches list. This is done for each query image descriptor.

Calculate Angle Consistency Score. For each feature match from the previous section, we calculate difference of keypoints angles. All computed differences are then transformed to histogram with 18 bins (each bin with 20 degree size). The bin with maximal value is then selected and all corresponding feature matches have set their angle flag. The count of these matches is angle consistency score.

Calculate Size Consistency Score. For each hamming feature match, we calculate ratio of keypoint sizes. All computed ratios are then transformed to histogram with 40 bins. The bin with maximal value is then selected and all corresponding feature matches have set their size flag. The count of these matches is size consistency score.

Calculate Homography Consistency Score. Again, each feature match from the *Hamming matches* section is included in calculation of homography consistency score. We use RANSAC algorithm [1]. Then each keypoint satisfying found transformation is marked with homography flag. Count of these matches is homography consistency score.

2.3 Build Database

Database consists of records from transformed images (see Sect. 2.1, thus each record is set of image features). These records are sequentially stored for each dataset in one table. And because each record is independent from others, our solution is highly parallelizable when querying and training the database.

2.4 Query Database

When querying database, first what we have to do is to transform query image to Image Features. This is then subsequently compared with each record from our database. The diagram for comparing these sets of Features can be seen in Fig. 3. For each comparison we obtain a score and these comparisons are then sorted and returned as results.

3 Distributed Approach

This section will describe our approach from application design perspective. Each component can reside on different computer or they can be all together on single machine. Our application is thus horizontally scalable while also keeping ability to run on single machine.

3.1 Application Components

Our application is divided to several modules which communicate to each other. The communication scheme can be seen in Fig. 4. The main (controlling) module is named Dispatcher. It receives tasks from the User Interface and assigns jobs to Workers. It is the central point of all communication. It also handles storing and withdrawing image data from database server. All components are asynchronous and can operate independently to the state of others.

The User Interface receives requests from clients and informs them about current states of the tasks and about the results of already finished tasks. This is why it comunicates also with database server.

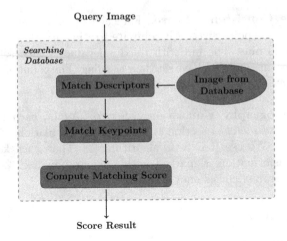

Fig. 3. Scheme of database search.

The Worker main role is to transform images to sets of Image Features and to compare pairs of these sets. Workers communicate solely with Dispatcher so they are independent from how the data are stored or how the client request was received.

The database module serves as a place for storing datasets, task results and also for intermediate results so the client can see the state of the task.

3.2 Thread Communication

Within Dispatcher and Workers we run several threads to manage communication between them and to deal with prioritizing work. For this communication we use queues provided by message broker. We have one master queue and two queues for each task (request and response). It allows us to compute multiple tasks at once. So if there is a one demanding high resources, it doesn't block the less demanding tasks. It's an effective load balancing on Worker side.

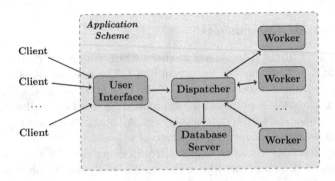

Fig. 4. Overview of application components.

Whenever Dispatcher receives a new task, it launches new thread and two new queues are created (one for distributing data from Dispatcher to Workers and second for Workers to send results back to Dispatcher). The task is then splitted to several parts and distributed to Workers through the request queue. After Worker finishes his part of work, it then sends the results back through the response queue. The results are received by Dispatcher and further collected and written to database.

3.3   Used Software

The User Interface is implemented as an REST service [6] in Python language which serves us as a thin client towards user requests. For database server we used MongoDB[2] because of its scalability. Workers are written in C++ and for computer vision tasks we use OpenCV library [5]. This gave us an ability to use highly optimalized code for image processing algorithms which are provided by this library. Dispatcher is also written in C++ as a single point in our architecture which we currently can not scale effectively. For communication between User Interface, Dispatcher and Workers we used message broker RabbitMQ[3] which is an implementation of AMQP [13].

4   Performance

The proposed architecture was evaluated on three machines, 12 × Intel Core i7-3930K CPU 3.2 GHz, 16 GB RAM and two machines with 8×Intel Core i7-4770 CPU 3.4 GHz, 8 GB RAM.

Evaluation was done on the MIRFLICKR-1M dataset[4] [17]. We used subsets of these images to show the application scalability. The selected datasets were:

- 1 000 images – MIRFLICKR-1M/images0/1/10*
- 10 000 images – MIRFLICKR-1M/images0/1/*
- 100 000 images – MIRFLICKR-1M/images0/*

In the Table 1 and Fig. 5 can be seen, that in the dataset processing phase (see Sect. 2.3), the computation time of our architecture scales almost perfectly linearly (with respect to Worker counts). With $100k$ images in dataset and 12 Worker instances, the training phase took about one hour. While with 3 Workers it took more than 8 hours. Also, ten times smaller dataset took an order of magnitude less time. Which means that work is distributed equally to all Workers and that no Worker is unnecessarily idle.

The second evaluation was done for querying the dataset (see Sect. 2.4). We also used selected number of workers (1, 3, 6, 12) and evaluated on the same datasets ($1k$, $10k$, $100k$). As can be seen in Table 2 and Fig. 6, the response

---

[2] https://www.mongodb.org/.
[3] http://www.rabbitmq.com/.
[4] http://press.liacs.nl/mirflickr/.

Table 1. Dataset processing time [s].

Dataset size	Worker count			
	1	3	6	12
1k	306	98	55	37
10k	2903	980	555	372
100k	30041	10864	5559	3705

Table 2. Average query time [s].

	Dataset size	Worker count			
		1	3	6	12
	1k	1.4	0.9	0.9	0.8
	10k	9.5	3.8	3.6	2.3
	100k	95.3	40.9	25.2	18.2
brute force matching	10k	21.3	7.5	6.9	4.3

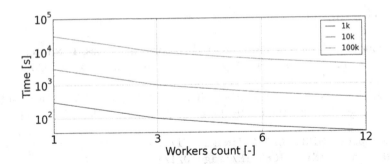

Fig. 5. Graph for processing datset.

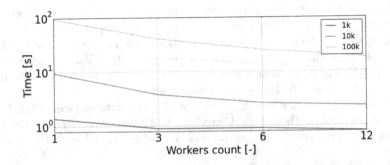

Fig. 6. Graph for querying dataset.

times scaled a bit worse than in training phase (but for larger datasets it is still significant gain). For $100k$ image dataset and 12 workers, average time for one query was $18.2s$. In the smaller datasets the benefit of more workers is not exactly apparent while in bigger ones there is definitely one. We assume that the reason is, that when response times are lower than few seconds, the system is limited by network bandwith.

In the last row of Table 2 can be seen comparison with brute force matching which is approximately two times slower. All other measurements are taking advantage of our Hamming Weight optimalization (described in Sect. 2.1).

Success rate of our system was evaluated on Zubud database [9] with F1 score 0.889, Recall 0.953 and Precision 0.833.

5   Conclusion

In this paper we presented the implementation of distributed painting detection system. We implemented a high-performance application with focus on effective load balancing in task distribution (Table 1 and Fig. 5). We also used well known algorithms for keypoint detection in image [4] and for keypoint description [18]. We then presented the optimized method for precise comparison of binary image features (Fig. 6 for comparison). Our application was evaluated on up to 12 Worker instances with dataset processing time about one hour (Table 1 and Fig. 5) and query time below $20s$ (Table 2 and Fig. 6).

Acknowledgments. This research has been supported by the grant MV0 VF20132015030.

References

1. Fischler, M.A., Bolles, R.C.: Random sample consensus: a paradigm for model fitting with applications to image analysis and automated cartography. Commun. ACM. **24**, 381–395 (1981)
2. Niblack, C.W., Barber, R., Equitz, W., Flickner, M.D., Glasman, E.H., Petkovic, D., Yanker, P., Faloutsos, C., Taubin, G.: QBIC project: querying images by content, using color, texture, and shape. In: IS&T/SPIE's Symposium on Electronic Imaging: Science and Technology, pp. 173–187 (1993)
3. Hatano, H.: Image processing and database system in the national museum of western art; an integrated system for art research. INSPEL **30**, 259–267 (1996)
4. Lowe, D.G.: Object recognition from local scale-invariant features. In: The Proceedings of the Seventh IEEE International Conference on Computer Vision, pp. 1150–1157 (1999)
5. Bradski, G.: The OpenCV Library. Dr. Dobb's Journal of Software Tools (2000). http://code.opencv.org/projects/opencv/wiki/CiteOpenCV
6. Fielding, R.T., Taylor, R.N.: Principled design of the modern web architecture. In: Proceedings of the 22nd International Conference on Software Engineering, pp. 407–416 (2000)

7. Smeulders, A.W.M., Worring, M., Santini, S., Gupta, A., Jain, R.: Content-based image retrieval at the end of the early years. IEEE Trans. Pattern Anal. Mach. Intell. **22**, 1349–1380 (2000)
8. Wang, J.Z., Li, J., Chen, C.C.: Interdisciplinary research to advance digital imagery indexing and retrieval technologies for asian art and cultural heritage. In: Proceedings of ACM Multimedia, Workshop on Multimedia Information Retrieval (2002)
9. Shao, H., Svoboda, T., Gool, L.V.: ZuBuD-Zurich Buildings Database for Image Based Recognition. Technical report 260, Computer Vision Lab, Swiss Federal Institute of Technology, Switzerland (2003)
10. Jiang, S., Gao, W., Wang, W.: Classifying traditional Chinese painting images. In: 2003 Joint Conference of the Fourth International Conference on Information, Communications and Signal Processing, 2003 and Fourth Pacific Rim Conference on Multimedia, pp. 1816–1820 (2003)
11. Jiang, S., Huang, Q., Ye, Q., Gao, W.: An effective method to detect and categorize digitized traditional Chinese paintings. Pattern Recogn. Lett. **27**(7), 734–746 (2006)
12. Chen, C.C., Wactlar, H.D., Wang, J.Z., Kiernan, K.: Digital imagery for significant cultural and historical materials. Int. J. Digit. Libr. **5**, 275–286 (2005)
13. Vinoski, S.: Advanced message queuing protocol. IEEE Internet Comput. **10**(6), 87–89 (2006)
14. Datta, R., Joshi, D., Li, J., Wang, J.Z.: Image retrieval: ideas, influences, and trends of the new age. ACM Comput. Surv. **40**, 5:1–5:60 (2008)
15. Wangming, X., Jin, W., Xinhai, L., Lei, Z., Gang, S.: Application of image SIFT features to the context of CBIR. In: 2008 International Conference on Computer Science and Software Engineering, pp. 552–555 (2008)
16. Shen, J.: Stochastic modeling western paintings for effective classification. Pattern Recognit. **42**(2), 293–301 (2009)
17. Huiskes, M.J., Thomee, B., Lew, M.S.: New trends and ideas in visual concept detection: the MIR flickr retrieval evaluation initiative. In: MIR '10: Proceedings of the 2010 ACM International Conference on Multimedia Information Retrieval, pp. 527–536 (2010)
18. Alahi, A., Ortiz, R., Vandergheynst, P.: FREAK: fast retina keypoint. In: 2012 IEEE Conference on Computer Vision and Pattern Recognition, pp. 510–517 (2012)
19. Tabernik, Domen, Čehovin, Luka, Kristan, Matej, Boben, Marko, Leonardis, Aleš: A web-service for object detection using hierarchical models. In: Chen, Mei, Leibe, Bastian, Neumann, Bernd (eds.) ICVS 2013. LNCS, vol. 7963, pp. 93–102. Springer, Heidelberg (2013)

Soil Surface Roughness Using Cumulated Gaussian Curvature

Thomas Jensen[1,3](✉), Lars J. Munkholm[2], Ole Green[3],
and Henrik Karstoft[1]

[1] Department of Engineering, Aarhus University,
Finlandsgade 22, 8200 Aarhus, Denmark
thje@eng.au.dk
[2] Department of Agroecology, Aarhus University,
Blichers Allé 20, 8830 Tjele, Denmark
[3] Kongskilde Industries A/S,
Skælskørvej 64, 4180 Sorø, Denmark

Abstract. Optimal use of farming machinery is important for efficiency and sustainability. Continuous automated control of the machine settings throughout the tillage operation requires sensory feedback estimating the seedbed quality. In this paper we use a laser range scanner to capture high resolution maps of soil aggregates in a laboratory setting as well as full soil surface maps in a field test. Gaussian curvature is used to estimate the size of single aggregates under controlled circumstances. Additionally, a method is proposed, which cumulates the Gaussian curvature of full soil surface maps to estimate the degree of tillage.

Keywords: Soil surface · Laser scan · Rugosity · Gaussian curvature

1 Introduction

In modern farming efficiency and sustainability are important factors. This calls for optimal use of the farming machinery. However, in the majority of fields the soil texture, moisture, and other factors, having an impact on the outcome of the tillage operation, are highly variable [12]. Hence, current soil treatment machinery does not ensure an optimal tillage as they lack the necessary sensory feedback for automatic control. Automatic sensing of soil surface properties provides extensive information relevant for soil treatment, creating a knowledge base for future automated cultivation systems capable of establishing homogeneous high quality seedbeds under heterogeneous soil conditions.

A number of aspects influence the seedbed quality and thus plant germination. Among these aspects are soil surface roughness and the aggregate size distribution of the soil (cloddiness of the soil) [1,2]. Large clods results in a too airy seedbed, with the risk of drying out the seeds. On the other hand, a too processed seedbed has the risk of sealing the soil surface after heavy rain and thus resulting in bad germination [6]. In order to optimize and control the tillage performance, it is important to be able to estimate quality parameters of the

© Springer International Publishing Switzerland 2015
L. Nalpantidis et al. (Eds.): ICVS 2015, LNCS 9163, pp. 533–541, 2015.
DOI: 10.1007/978-3-319-20904-3_48

seedbed. The soil surface roughness is a classical seedbed quality parameter [3, 7] that can be estimated with several methods. In the field, a simple method for a quick estimate of the surface roughness is to lay a chain across the surface [9]. The ratio between the true length of the chain and the projected length estimates the surface roughness. The chain method and other similar manual methods of detecting the soil surface roughness are, however, not practical when assessing an entire field. Using modern sensor equipment to record maps of the soil surface can speed up process and improve both the precision and resolution of the measurements. When a 2D surface map is available others methods can also be applied. Rugosity is the equivalent to roughness for a full 2D surface, since it is the ratio of the surface area to the orthogonal projection of the surface [4].

Multiple methods have previously been used to acquire a map of the soil surface, e.g. stereo vision [10, 13], structured light [11] and laser measurement systems [8, 9].

In the following paper we propose a sensor based method for measuring the degree of tillage, for a seedbed cultivator moving in the field. We characterize the seedbed using the cumulated Gaussian curvature [5, p.373–380] and compare this measure with the rugosity of the surface.

2   Materials and Methods

2.1   Study Area and the Soil Surface Scanner

The experimental data and soil samples used in this paper was recorded and gathered October 3rd 2012 near Herlufmagle, Denmark (+55 18 26.62, +11 41 32.39) on a sandy loam soil. The soil contained no crop residues in the tillaged top layer (10 cm). The weather was cloudy and there had been little to no rain in the three days prior to the experiment and the soil was drained to normal tillage condition. 12 plots, with a size of 0.5×1 meter each, were recorded both before and after soil tillage with a Kongskilde Germinator seedbed cultivator.

To record the soil surfaces we used a setup of two tripods with an aluminum bar spanning between. A toothed rack was mounted on the bar allowing a train carrying the sensor equipment to ride along the bar. The sensor used was a SICK LMS111 Laser Measurement System mounted on the train facing down towards the soil surface. The laser measurement system is a line scanner recording the distance from sensor to surface along this line. The laser was mounted roughly 1 m above the soil surface and an angular resolution of $0.25\,°$ was used. The laser range scanner was configured not to use any internal digital filtering. Combining the data from the laser scanner with the position of the train as it rides along the bar results in a point cloud mapping the soil surface. The polar data from the laser scanner is converted to cartesian coordinates and interpolated creating a depth image of the soil surface. An image of the setup is shown in Fig. 1.

2.2   Rugosity

Soil surface roughness is a measure of how rough the soil surface is. This parameter has for many years been used in soil studies and is based on the soil surface

Fig. 1. A drawing (top) and photo (bottom) of the setup used to record the soil surface maps.

profile [3,7]. It can be estimated with several methods, but in the field, a simple method for a quick estimate of the surface roughness has been to lay a metal chain across the surface [9]. The ratio between the true length of the chain and the projected length estimates the surface roughness. Rugosity is the equivalent to roughness for a full 2D surface [4]. Similar to roughness, it is a ratio of the surface area to the orthogonal projection of the surface.

$$r = \frac{A_r}{A_p} \tag{1}$$

where A_r is the true surface area of the soil and A_p is the area of the orthogonal projection of the surface.

2.3 Gaussian Curvature

The Gaussian curvature measures the 2D curvature of a surface in a point, and is analog to 1D curvature of a curve. The Gaussian curvature describes how a surface bends and is in this paper used as an alternative to rugosity. A point with a positive Gaussian curvature is an elliptic point (the surface bends the same way creating a dome- or bowl-like shape), and a point with a negative Gaussian curvature is a hyperbolic point (the surface bends in different directions creating a saddle shape). It can be calculated as the ratio between the determinants of the second and first fundamental form [5, p.373–380]

$$K = \frac{\det(\mathrm{II})}{\det(\mathrm{I})} = \frac{eg - f^2}{EG - F^2} \tag{2}$$

where E, F, and G are coefficients of the first fundamental form and e, f, and g are coefficients of the second fundamental form. For a surface image with the pixel value $x(u, v)$, in the pixel with coordinates (u, v), the coefficients of the first fundamental form are given by first order partial derivatives

$$E = \left| \frac{\partial x}{\partial u} \right|^2 \tag{3}$$

$$F = \frac{\partial x}{\partial u} \cdot \frac{\partial x}{\partial v} \tag{4}$$

$$G = \left| \frac{\partial x}{\partial v} \right|^2 \tag{5}$$

The coefficients of the second fundamental form are given by the second order partial derivatives and the unit normal vector, n

$$n = \frac{\frac{\partial x}{\partial u} \times \frac{\partial x}{\partial v}}{\left| \frac{\partial x}{\partial u} \times \frac{\partial x}{\partial v} \right|} \tag{6}$$

$$e = n \cdot \frac{\partial^2 x}{\partial u^2} \tag{7}$$

$$f = n \cdot \frac{\partial^2 x}{\partial u \partial v} \tag{8}$$

$$g = n \cdot \frac{\partial^2 x}{\partial v^2} \tag{9}$$

3   Results

3.1   Gaussian Curvature of a Surface of Ideal Aggregates

With the assumption that a soil aggregate is perfectly round, e.g. a sphere, it is possible to determine its radius of the sphere from the Gaussian curvature in a single point. This is a property of a sphere, since it has the same curvature in every point, and the curvature is equal to $Radius^{-2}$.

For testing this method an image was created containing 10 larger spheres and 20 smaller spheres, with a radius of 20 and 10 pixels respectively. These spheres were placed without overlap. The spheres are viewed top-down creating an image where the upper hemispheres are visible, see Fig. 2.

When nearing the edge of a sphere and especially right on the edge, the curvature calculation will be wrong due to quantization and the singularities along the curves where the sphere intersects the ground plane. The surface is not smooth along these curves, hence the Gaussian curvature is not well defined.

Finding the radius of a sphere is done by calculating the square root of the reciprocal of the curvature in a pixel. In the radius image shown in Fig. 2, the area between the spheres has been set to 0 as the curvature of a flat surface

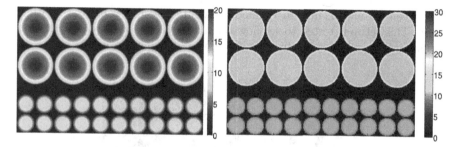

Fig. 2. The top-down image of the spheres (left) and the radius calculated in each pixel using Gaussian curvature (right)

is 0 which results in an infinite radius (a product of dividing by zero). As the image shows, the radius found from the Gaussian curvature closely match the real radius of the created spheres. As predicted, right at the edge of the spheres the radius calculation breaks down.

This is, however, in an ideal situation without noise. Adding noise (normal distributed) has been found to impact the curvature calculation significantly. The noise gets exaggerated in the first and second order derivatives. Even after smoothing the image with a Gaussian filter, the noise has impact on the calculated curvature and therefore radius. Figure 3 shows the radius image where normal distributed noise with a standard deviation of 1 has been added to the sphere image. The flat area outside the spheres have been zeroed for better illustrating the effect on the spheres. Even with this relatively small amount of noise the radius image gets very affected.

Fig. 3. Radius image of a noisy sphere image

3.2   Gaussian Curvature on Real Aggregates

When trying this method on real scanned images of soil surfaces the methods has to cope with noise from the sensor, non-spherical aggregates and aggregates fused together and overlapping. Figure 4 shows a photo and corresponding scanned depth image of real aggregates laid out on a flat surface in the lab. The aggregates are between 16 and 32 mm in diameter and are laid out separately with no overlap. This setup is tested to see how the method copes with sensor noise and non-spherical aggregates. In this test setup we do not have overlap.

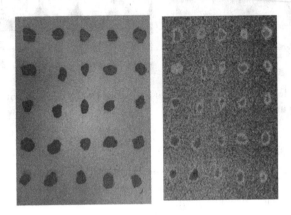

Fig. 4. Images of the 16–32 mm soil aggregates. Photo of the aggregates (left) and raw depth image (right)

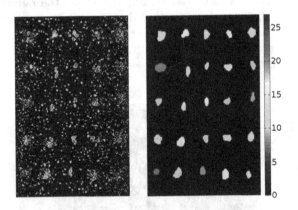

Fig. 5. Radius images of 16–32 mm soil aggregates without (left) and with (right) smoothing and segmentation

We smooth the depth image using a Gaussian filter. We then segment the depth image and fill each segment with the median value of all pixels from the radius image corresponding to the segment. This creates a radius image where each blob has a homogenic value. The median value is chosen since it is resistant to outliers, whereas the mean could be affected by a single extreme outlier. Figure 5 shows the resulting radius images with and without smoothing and segmentation. The radius image is improved by the smoothing and segmentation, but the resulting radius estimate is slightly low. The estimates lie around 10–25 mm where it was expected to be 16–32 mm. The scanned aggregates are, however, very irregular and not sphere shaped as the method assumes.

3.3   Gaussian Curvature and Rugosity on Field Data

The sensor system was also used to scan 12 plots during a field test of a cultivator. The 12 plots were scanned both before and after the cultivation process. Figure 6 shows the resulting depth images after a slight smoothing to remove noise. Note that the color scales are different before and after cultivation. Since the soil surface is much smoother after cultivation, these different color scales were chosen to better visualize the surface. The surface is noticeably more smooth and even after cultivation. The periodic pattern visible in the depth images after cultivation is left by the rolls on the cultivator.

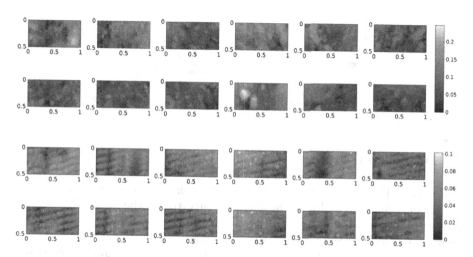

Fig. 6. Depth images of the soil surface before and after cultivation. Note the different color scales. All dimensions in the images are in meters.

In a real soil surface the aggregates are both fused and overlapping. This means that a good segmentation of all aggregates is difficult, hence we choose not to use the Gaussian curvature on a point basis. Instead we sum up the absolute values of the Gaussian curvature of the entire surface in each plot and use this as a roughness measure. The sum of curvature is normalized by dividing it with the number of pixels used in the summation. We call this measure the Cumulated Gaussian Curvature. The Cumulated Gaussian Curvatures are graphed and compared with the rugosity of the surfaces in Fig. 7.

As seen in the figure, both rugosity and Cumulated Gaussian Curvature separates the cultivated surface from the untreated soil. There is some correlation between the two measures, which is to be expected as they both describe the surface curvature (although in different ways). The variance of the two measures is smaller after cultivation as seen by a closer gathered cloud of points in the figure. This is also expected since one of the goals of the cultivator is to make a more homogeneous seedbed.

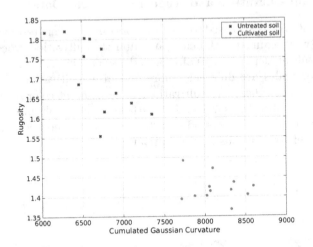

Fig. 7. Rugosity and Cumulated Gaussian Curvature of the field data.

4   Discussion

The initial idea was to estimate the aggregate size distribution from the histogram of radii calculated with the Gaussian curvature of the surface. The study, however, indicates that a full estimate of the aggregate size distribution may be difficult to achieve based on the Gaussian curvature alone.

For a quick assessment of the seedbed quality a single measure, based on the aggregate sizes in the topsoil, can be useful. The Cumulated Gaussian Curvature discloses a sort of mean value instead of a full aggregate size distribution which can be harder to interpret.

A system for on-line measurement of the seedbed quality will be useful in future automation of tillage machinery. Automated, on-line setup of the tillage machinery can help the farmer increase yield since the tillage machinery, throughout the field, evaluates the soil and corrects the settings of the machinery accordingly. Additionally it saves time and may possibly reduce fuel consumption of the tillage operation since the farmer may be performing a too intense tillage. Field tests with a laser range scanner system mounted on a seedbed cultivator are currently being done. Initial results show that it is possible to use the laser range scanner to map the soil surface, however with a limited resolution compared to the stationary setup due to the speed of the machinery.

5   Conclusion

The sensor setup using a SICK LMS111 laser range scanner successfully captures high resolution depth maps of the soil surface. Soil surface maps were recorded both before and after tillage with a seedbed cultivator.

Gaussian curvature has been used to characterize both single aggregates in a laboratory setting and complete depth maps of soil surfaces recorded in the field. Under controlled circumstances it is possible to estimate the size of aggregates, however, in real seedbeds the aggregates are fused and overlap. Here the Cumulated Gaussian Curvature was used to measure the degree of tillage.

References

1. Braunack, M., Dexter, A.: Soil aggregation in the seedbed: a review i. effect of aggregate sizes on plant growth. Soil Tillage Res. **14**(3), 259–279 (1989)
2. Braunack, M., Dexter, A.: Soil aggregation in the seedbed: a review ii. effect of aggregate sizes on plant growth. Soil Tillage Res. **14**(3), 281–298 (1989)
3. Frede, H.G., Gäth, S.: Soil surface roughness as the result of aggregate size distribution 1. report: measuring and evaluation method. Zeitschrift für Pflanzenernährung und Bodenkunde **158**(1), 31–35 (1995)
4. Friedman, A., Pizarro, O., Williams, S.B., Johnson-Roberson, M.: Multi-scale measures of rugosity, slope and aspect from benthic stereo image reconstructions. PLoS ONE **7**(12), e50440 (2012)
5. Gray, A.: Modern Differential Geometry of Curves and Surfaces with Mathematica, 2nd edn. CRC Press, Boca Raton (1997)
6. Håkansson, I., Myrbeck, Å., Etana, A.: A review of research on seedbed preparation for small grains in Sweden. Soil Tillage Res. **64**(1), 23–40 (2002)
7. Helming, K., Roth, C.H., Wolf, R., Diestel, H.: Characterization of rainfall-microrelief interactions with runoff using parameters derived from digital elevation models (dems). Soil Technol. **6**(3), 273–286 (1993)
8. Jensen, T., Munkholm, L.J., Green, O., Karstoft, H.: A mobile surface scanner for soil studies. In: Second International Conference on Robotics and associated High-technologies and Equipment for Agriculture and Forestry, pp. 187–194 (2014)
9. Jester, W., Klik, A.: Soil surface roughness measurement - methods, applicability, and surface representation. Catena **64**(2), 174–192 (2005)
10. McDonald, A., Crossley, S., Bennet, J., Brown, S., Cookmartin, G., Morrison, K., Quegan, S.: Stereo vision measurements of soil surface characteristics and their use in model validation. In: SAR workshop: CEOS Committee on Earth Observation Satellites. vol. 450, p. 575 (2000)
11. Scharstein, D., Szeliski, R.: High-accuracy stereo depth maps using structured light. In: 2003 IEEE Computer Society Conference on Computer Vision and Pattern Recognition 2003, vol. 1, pp. I–195. IEEE (2003)
12. Stafford, J.V.: Implementing precision agriculture in the 21st century. J. Agric. Eng. Res. **76**(3), 267–275 (2000)
13. Zribi, M., Ciarletti, V., Taconet, O., Boissard, P., Chapron, M., Rabin, B.: Backscattering on soil structure described by plane facets. Int. J. Remote Sens. **21**(1), 137–153 (2000)

Author Index

544   Author Index

Printed in the United States
By Bookmasters